MW01093832

Foreign Intervention in Africa

after the Cold War

Ohio University Research in International Studies

This series of publications on Africa, Latin America, Southeast Asia, and Global and Comparative Studies is designed to present significant research, translation, and opinion to area specialists and to a wide community of persons interested in world affairs. The series is distributed worldwide. For more information, consult the Ohio University Press website, ohioswallow.com.

Books in the Ohio University Research in International Studies series are published by Ohio University Press in association with the Center for International Studies. The views expressed in individual volumes are those of the authors and should not be considered to represent the policies or beliefs of the Center for International Studies, Ohio University Press, or Ohio University.

Executive Editor: Gillian Berchowitz

Foreign Intervention in Africa after the Cold War

SOVEREIGNTY, RESPONSIBILITY, AND THE WAR ON TERROR

Elizabeth Schmidt

Foreword by William Minter

Ohio University Research in International Studies
Global and Comparative Studies Series No. 19
Athens, Ohio

Ohio University Press, Athens, Ohio 45701
ohioswallow.com
© 2018 by Ohio University Press
All rights reserved

To obtain permission to quote, reprint, or otherwise reproduce or distribute material from Ohio University Press publications, please contact our rights and permissions department at (740) 593-1154 or (740) 593-4536 (fax).

Printed in the United States of America
The books in the Ohio University Research in International Studies Series are printed on acid-free paper ∞ ™

Cover image: Young boy in Beni, North Kivu Province, Democratic Republic of Congo, playing near a MONUSCO vehicle, December 5, 2014. Photo by Abel Kavanagh/MONUSCO.

28 27 26 25 24 23 22 21 20 19 18   5 4 3 2 1

Library of Congress Cataloging-in-Publication Data
Names: Schmidt, Elizabeth, 1955- author.
Title: Foreign intervention in Africa after the Cold War : sovereignty, responsibility, and the war on terror / Elizabeth Schmidt ; foreword by William Minter.
Other titles: Research in international studies. Global and comparative studies series ; no. 19.
Description: Athens, Ohio : Ohio University Press, 2018. | Series: Ohio University research in international studies. Global and comparative studies series ; no. 19 | Includes bibliographical references and index.
Identifiers: LCCN 2018031702| ISBN 9780896803206 (hc : alk. paper) | ISBN 9780896803213 (pb : alk. paper) | ISBN 9780896805040 (pdf)
Subjects: LCSH: Africa--Foreign relations--1960- | Africa--Politics and government--1960- | Africa--Foreign economic relations. | Terrorism--Africa--Prevention--History. | Political stability--Africa--History.
Classification: LCC DT31 .S295 2018 | DDC 327.6009049--dc23
LC record available at https://lccn.loc.gov/2018031702

Contents

CHAPTER 13

Epilogue

Trump and Africa (2017–)

368

CONCLUSION

Assessing the Impact of Foreign Intervention

389

Notes

393

Glossary

425

Index

435

Suggested Readings follow chapters 2–12

Illustrations

Maps

Photographs

Foreword

Elizabeth Schmidt's earlier work, *Foreign Intervention in Africa* (2013), focused on the period 1945–91, with a brief concluding chapter on 1991–2010. This companion volume focuses on 1991–2017, with a final chapter highlighting the potential impact of the Trump presidency. Schmidt's approach in the two volumes is similar. Her aim is not to provide a comprehensive narrative or advance an explanatory theory, but to introduce a series of case studies, taking into account global narratives and common factors as well as the particularity and nuances of each case.

Intended for undergraduate and graduate students as well as policymakers, humanitarian and human rights workers, activists, and other concerned citizens, both books provide succinct and readable narratives, without detailed footnotes but with abundant recommended readings for those who wish to dig more deeply into particular cases.[1] As such, they are unique resources that provide an overview and introduction to the complex realities they portray, complementing but not duplicating more detailed scholarly or journalistic accounts of specific cases.

As this foreword is written in early 2018, the Trump presidency in the United States has been the catalyst for a level of uncertainty about the shape of the international political order not matched since World War II. Any predictions would be perilous, except to affirm that African countries will continue to be gravely affected by global political developments as well as by the distinct internal dynamics of specific countries and regions.

As Schmidt explains, global narratives are both essential and misleading in explaining the course and outcomes of intervention in specific conflicts. Thus the grand narrative of the "Cold War" between the United States and the Soviet Union, from 1945 to 1991, was decisive for interventions in African conflicts insofar as it motivated perceptions and policy in Washington, Moscow, and other capitals. Cold War perceptions conflating radical African nationalism and communism affected policymakers, the media, and public opinion, not only in countries such as the United States and South Africa, but also in transnational networks and multilateral organizations.

Even in this period, however, the Cold War paradigm was not fully hegemonic. The alternative framework of a united stand against Nazism, racism, and colonialism, linked to the common experience of World War II, was shared by Southern African liberation movements and by governments and movements around the world, including many in Western Europe and North America. An exclusive focus on the superpowers, moreover, ignores the distinct interests and roles of other external actors, including the European colonial powers and other communist states, most prominently Cuba and China. And finally, the interests of the African actors involved in conflicts, and the colonial and precolonial histories of specific countries, also shaped the outcomes. In some cases, African parties to conflict sought out foreign interventions—for their own reasons.

Unraveling the course of any specific intervention thus requires a high degree of granularity, at the risk of asking the reader to assimilate a potentially bewildering range of names and places. Political actors such as states, parties, and agencies are not unitary: each is made up of subgroups and individuals with distinct interests, ideologies, and analyses. Schmidt's clear writing style balances brevity with nuance. Readers who take their time and pay attention will be rewarded—not with definitive answers, which the author does not promise, but with a solid basis for asking more questions and pursuing further research.

In the post–Cold War period examined in this book, Schmidt identifies two distinct paradigms applied by policymakers. A specific intervention might fall primarily under the paradigm of a "response to instability," some cases of which might also fit under the newly defined multilateral rubric of the "responsibility to protect." Alternatively, an intervention might fit within the framework of the "war on terror." Or, as in the case of Somalia, both paradigms might be at work simultaneously. Characteristically, war on terror interventions were often counterproductive, increasing rather than decreasing the impact of movements defined as terrorist threats. Globally, these interventions were driven particularly by the United States, with accelerated militarization in Africa as well as around the world in the period following the 2001 terrorist attacks on the World Trade Center and the Pentagon.

Interventions in response to instability, including those justified by the responsibility to protect, on the other hand, featured a far wider range of subregional, regional, and global actors. There was vacillation between indifference, leading to failure to respond in a timely way, and complex multiyear efforts in diplomacy and peacekeeping. The actors most consistently involved, for their own reasons, were neighbors of the countries beset by conflict, as well as African multilateral organizations such as the African Union and its subregional counterparts. And, as the cases considered in this book illustrate, the results, as well as the motives of outside actors, were decidedly mixed. The outcomes were difficult to evaluate, as were the possible alternative courses of action that might have produced different results (counterfactuals). While the United States was often a partner in multilateral efforts, consistent policy and commitment to multilateral engagement was in short supply.

Despite the end of the Cold War in 1991 and the shift of paradigms justifying foreign intervention in Africa, there were many institutional continuities in the international order in the period that followed. The "Western alliance" continued, with prominent roles for NATO and the United Nations. The UN Security Council, with its five permanent members, continued to dominate international peacekeeping policy. Africa remained at the margins of foreign policymaking for the United States and other powers outside the African continent, with the exception of the North African region, given its proximity to Europe and close links with the Middle East.

The marginal position of Africa in global politics is almost certain to continue for the foreseeable future. But the election of Donald Trump has brought unprecedented questioning about the continuity of multilateral institutions and alliances, and challenges to the frameworks for understanding them. The incoherence of policymaking under Trump, rapid staff turnover in his immediate entourage, lack of staffing in government agencies, and the ongoing investigations into his administration make even the immediate future highly uncertain. But there can be little doubt that new elements have been introduced into the international arena, including high-level advocacy of Islamophobia and white nationalism, as well as a Hobbesian disregard for any values other than narrow political and economic self-interest. It is clear both that the United States retains enormous power for destructive action on the world stage and that its capacity for constructive engagement and leadership is plummeting. And whatever remains to be revealed about the ties between the Trump campaign and Putin's Russia, there is abundant confirmation of the ideological convergence between the two in legitimizing kleptocracy and autocracy and in heralding "traditional" values of hierarchy and exclusionary identity in contrast to "cosmopolitan" values such as peace, development, and human rights.

What does this mean for ongoing conflicts in Africa in which multi-lateral institutions or outside powers are engaged, or for future conflicts that are highly likely to emerge? The case studies in this book make clear that no easy generalizations can be applied. But one can perhaps suggest a few questions that will need to be posed.

1. *To what extent will US policy toward Africa under the Trump administration be distinctively new or a continuation of previous trends? Will there be "no policy" on Africa, or "bad policy?"*[2]

At the most general level, both globally and by extension in Africa, one can say that there will be a continuation of the so-called war on terror that has driven US policy since 2001. But both global debates and responses to specific African cases may vary enormously, depending on the level of attention from the White House and on the outcome of debates between zealots and the few more sober-minded members of the administration. As for responses to humanitarian crises, these will undoubtedly be affected by the general climate of increased US disrespect for multilateral institutions and by the "America First" ideology. The extent of the damage will also depend on reactions not only from within executive branch agencies but also from the US Congress and public.

2. *If, as expected, the Trump presidency leads to a loss of US influence on the world stage, what regional or global powers will gain influence on policies related to intervention in Africa?*

Most analyses of global economic or geostrategic changes anticipate rising influence on the part of China and other regional or midlevel powers, as well as reduced international capacity for a Europe facing its own internal divisions. But it is not at all clear what these macro-level power balances imply for multilateral or bilateral interventions in Africa. A scenario in which a rival alternative power or coalition replaces the United States as the most prominent party in defining global agendas, including intervention in Africa, seems improbable. Instead, there will likely be even more uncertainty about which outside actors will be involved and the extent to which there will be coordination or conflict among them.

3. *Finally, what will be the effects of structural factors such as climate change, global inequality, economic stresses, gross human rights violations by states, ethnic and national stereotypes, and others? To what extent, and how, will they increase the risks of conflict and subsequent intervention?*

Such structural issues go far beyond the scope of this book. But whether the issue is climate change, economic policy, or the fate of global human rights norms, Africa cannot escape the fallout from worsening global trends or the failure to find global solutions. The impact of these structural issues on conflict in Africa will surely be as great as, or greater than, the impact of policy decisions on intervention in specific crises.

In her concluding chapter, Schmidt notes that her book offers no solutions. Rather, "its goal is to question faulty assumptions, to expose superficial understandings and simplistic analyses, and to offer deeper knowledge to those hoping to glean lessons from the past that will enhance future prospects for positive social change." Her key point is that durable solutions cannot come from formulas, from leaders of states, or from multilateral agencies, but instead must build on inclusion of voices from African civil society.

In previous generations, African movements fighting against colonialism and racism inspired worldwide mobilizations that changed Africa and the world. Now, as Africa and the world are struggling to confront new challenges and address the unfinished agendas of struggles for freedom, the Trump administration epitomizes the impulse to return to a past explicitly based on hatred, division, and inequality.

Both national states and multilateral agencies have a role to play in setting a different course. But these efforts will fall short unless they are driven by mobilization on the part of social movements and committed individuals working within those structures. We need a vision as encompassing as that evoked by Nelson Mandela, speaking to a rally in London's Trafalgar Square in 2005:

"As long as poverty, injustice and gross inequality persist in our world, none of us can truly rest. . . . Like slavery and apartheid, poverty is not natural. It is man-made and it can be overcome and eradicated by the actions of human beings. . . . Overcoming poverty is not a gesture of charity, it is an act of justice. . . . Sometimes it falls on a generation to be great. You can be that great generation. Let your greatness blossom."[3]

William Minter
Washington, DC, April 15, 2018

Acknowledgments

This book would not have seen the light of day had it not been for the insightful critique and encouragement of William Minter, my friend, colleague, and collaborator for nearly four decades. An invaluable partner as I wrote *Foreign Intervention in Africa: From the Cold War to the War on Terror* (Cambridge University Press, 2013), Bill kindly agreed to serve as my developmental editor for this volume as well. Without his keen social scientist's eye, the proverbial trees of the historical narrative would surely have overwhelmed the forest. His deep understanding of the continent and its complexities helped me produce a far better manuscript, and his grasp of recent scholarship kept me abreast of rapidly changing events.

Others to whom I owe a great debt include Allen Isaacman, Regents Professor of History at the University of Minnesota, for his diligent and perceptive reading of the entire manuscript; David Newbury, Gwendolen Carter Chair in African Studies and Professor Emeritus of History at Smith College, for his astute reading and commentary on the Rwanda chapter; and Steve Howard, professor in the School of Media Arts and Studies at Ohio University, who commented on the Sudan chapter. All of these scholars saved me from many errors and oversimplifications; those that remain are solely my own. I also thank the anonymous external readers for Ohio University Press, from whom I received much valuable advice. Finally, I am grateful to a multitude of activist academics, friends, and colleagues who have modeled the integration of scholarship and solidarity.

At Ohio University Press, Gillian Berchowitz, director and editor in chief, believed in the project's potential and accommodated its long delay. Managing editor Nancy Basmajian and production manager Beth Pratt guided the manuscript through the production process, and Sebastian Biot tracked down the perfect cover image. I am also grateful to other staff members at the Press who applied their skills to bring the project to fruition.

Other individuals and institutions supported the project in important ways. In particular, I thank the staff of Loyola Notre Dame Library for their ever-prompt responses to my requests for materials and advice. Loyola University Maryland contributed significant financial support. The Research and Sabbatical Committee, the Center for the Humanities, the deans of the College of Arts and Sciences, and the vice president for Academic Affairs provided sabbatical funding and paid for maps, photographs, and developmental editing. Cartographer Philip Schwartzberg at Meridian Mapping produced the maps to precise specification and patiently dealt with multiple changes. Many photographers endured difficult conditions to take powerful pictures, which they kindly allowed me to use. Catherine Sunshine provided superb professional copyediting and stylistic advice.

Last but certainly not least, I thank my inestimable network of friends and family. For their love, support, and encouragement, I am grateful to my parents, Albert and Kathryn Schmidt; to my son Jann Grovogui; and to countless friends and colleagues—all of whom provided joy and perspective and tolerated the mood swings that book writing always entails.

Abbreviations

ACOTA	Africa Contingency Operations Training and Assistance program (United States)
ACRI	African Crisis Response Initiative (United States)
AFDL	Alliance of Democratic Forces for the Liberation of Congo-Zaire (Alliance des Forces Démocratiques pour la Libération du Congo)
AFISMA	African-led International Support Mission in Mali
AFRICOM	United States Africa Command
AGOA	African Growth and Opportunity Act of 2000 (United States)
AMIS	African Union Mission in Sudan
AMISOM	African Union Mission in Somalia
AQAP	al-Qaeda in the Arabian Peninsula (Saudi Arabia and Yemen)
AQI	al-Qaeda in Iraq
AQIM	al-Qaeda in the Islamic Maghreb
ARPCT	Alliance for the Restoration of Peace and Counter-Terrorism (Somalia)
ARS	Alliance for the Re-liberation of Somalia
AU	African Union
BRICS	Brazil, Russia, India, China, and South Africa
CDR	Coalition for the Defense of the Republic (Coalition pour la Défense de la République) (Rwanda)
CENTCOM	United States Central Command
CFA	African Financial Community (Communauté Financière en Afrique)

CIA	Central Intelligence Agency
CJTF-HOA	Combined Joint Task Force–Horn of Africa
CMA	Coordination of the Movements of Azawad (Coordination des Mouvements de l'Azawad) (Mali)
CNDP	National Congress for the Defense of the People (Congrès National pour la Défense du Peuple) (Democratic Republic of Congo)
CPA	Comprehensive Peace Agreement (Sudan)
DDPD	Doha Document for Peace in Darfur (Sudan)
DPA	Darfur Peace Agreement (Sudan)
DPKO	United Nations Department of Peacekeeping Operations
DRC	Democratic Republic of Congo (République Démocratique du Congo)
EACTI	East Africa Counterterrorism Initiative
EARSI	East Africa Regional Strategic Initiative
ECCAS	Economic Community of Central African States
ECOMICI	Economic Community of West African States Mission in Côte d'Ivoire
ECOMOG	Economic Community of West African States Monitoring Group (Liberia and Sierra Leone)
ECOWAS	Economic Community of West African States
EEC	European Economic Community
EO	Executive Outcomes
EU	European Union
EUCOM	United States European Command
FBI	Federal Bureau of Investigation (United States)
FDLR	Democratic Forces for the Liberation of Rwanda (Forces Démocratiques de Libération du Rwanda)
FESCI	Student Federation of Côte d'Ivoire (Fédération Estudiantine et Scolaire de Côte d'Ivoire)
FIS	Islamic Salvation Front (Front Islamique du Salut) (Algeria)
FLC	Front for the Liberation of Congo (Front de Libération du Congo) (Democratic Republic of Congo)
FLN	National Liberation Front (Front de Libération Nationale) (Algeria)

FPI	Ivoirian Popular Front (Front Populaire Ivoirien)
FRCI	Republican Forces of Côte d'Ivoire (Forces Républicaines de Côte d'Ivoire)
G7	Group of Seven
G8	Group of Eight
G20	Group of Twenty
GHI	Global Health Initiative (United States)
GIA	Armed Islamic Group (Groupe Islamique Armé) (Algeria)
GPOI	Global Peace Operations Initiative (United States)
GSPC	Salafist Group for Preaching and Combat (Groupe Salafiste pour la Prédication et le Combat) (Algeria)
ICC	International Criminal Court
ICGLR	International Conference on the Great Lakes Region
ICJ	International Commission of Jurists
ICU	Islamic Courts Union (Somalia)
IGAD	Intergovernmental Authority on Development (East Africa)
IMF	International Monetary Fund
ISIL	Islamic State in Iraq and the Levant
ISIS	Islamic State in Iraq and Syria
JEM	Justice and Equality Movement (Darfur, Sudan)
JSOC	Joint Special Operations Command (United States)
LIFG	Libyan Islamic Fighting Group
LJM	Liberation and Justice Movement (Darfur, Sudan)
LURD	Liberians United for Reconciliation and Democracy
M23	March 23 Movement (Mouvement du 23 Mars) (Democratic Republic of Congo)
MCC	Millennium Challenge Corporation (United States)
MINUCI	United Nations Mission in Côte d'Ivoire (Mission des Nations Unies en Côte d'Ivoire)
MINUSMA	United Nations Multidimensional Integrated Stabilization Mission in Mali (Mission Multidimensionnelle Intégrée des Nations Unies pour la Stabilisation au Mali)

MJP	Movement for Justice and Peace (Mouvement pour la Justice et la Paix) (Côte d'Ivoire)
MLC	Movement for the Liberation of Congo (Mouvement de Libération du Congo) (Democratic Republic of Congo)
MNJTF	Multinational Joint Task Force (Nigeria)
MNLA	National Movement for the Liberation of Azawad (Mouvement National pour la Libération de l'Azawad) (Mali)
MODEL	Movement for Democracy in Liberia
MONUC	United Nations Organization Mission in the Democratic Republic of the Congo (Mission de l'Organisation des Nations Unies en République Démocratique du Congo)
MONUSCO	United Nations Organization Stabilization Mission in the Democratic Republic of the Congo (Mission de l'Organisation des Nations Unies pour la Stabilisation en République Démocratique du Congo)
MPCI	Patriotic Movement of Côte d'Ivoire (Mouvement Patriotique de Côte d'Ivoire)
MPIGO	Ivoirian Patriotic Movement of the Far West (Mouvement Populaire Ivoirien du Grand Ouest) (Côte d'Ivoire)
MRNDD	National Republican Movement for Democracy and Development (Mouvement Républicain National pour la Démocratie et le Développement) (Rwanda)
MUJWA	Movement for Unity and Jihad in West Africa (Mouvement pour l'Unicité et le Jihad en Afrique de l'Ouest/ MUJAO) (Mali)
NAACP	National Association for the Advancement of Colored People (United States)
NASOC	Nigerian Army Special Operations Command
NATO	North Atlantic Treaty Organization
NCP	National Congress Party (Sudan)
NEPAD	New Partnership for Africa's Development
NGO	nongovernmental organization
NPFL	National Patriotic Front of Liberia
OAU	Organization of African Unity

OEF-TS	Operation Enduring Freedom–Trans Sahara
OFDA	Office of US Foreign Disaster Assistance, USAID (United States)
OPA	Ouagadougou Political Agreement (Côte d'Ivoire)
PACOM	United States Pacific Command
PARMEHUTU	Party for Hutu Emancipation (Parti du Mouvement de l'Émancipation Hutu) (Rwanda)
PDCI	Democratic Party of Côte d'Ivoire (Parti Démocratique de Côte d'Ivoire)
PEPFAR	President's Emergency Plan for AIDS Relief (United States)
PNAC	Project for the New American Century (United States)
PREACT	Partnership for Regional East Africa Counterterrorism
PSI	Pan-Sahel Initiative
R2P	responsibility to protect
RCD	Congolese Rally for Democracy (Rassemblement Congolais pour la Démocratie) (Democratic Republic of Congo)
RDR	Rally of Republicans (Rassemblement des Républicains) (Côte d'Ivoire)
RPF	Rwandan Patriotic Front (Front Patriotique Rwandais)
RUF	Revolutionary United Front (Sierra Leone)
SADC	Southern African Development Community
SADCC	Southern African Development Coordination Conference
SADF	South African Defence Force
SLA	Sudan Liberation Army (Darfur, Sudan)
SLA-AW	Sudan Liberation Army–Abdel Wahid (Darfur, Sudan)
SLA-MM	Sudan Liberation Army–Minni Minawi (Darfur, Sudan)
SOCAFRICA	Special Operations Command Africa (United States)
SOCOM	United States Special Operations Command
SPLA	Sudan People's Liberation Army
SPLM	Sudan People's Liberation Movement
SRF	Sudan Revolutionary Front
SRRC	Somali Reconciliation and Restoration Council

TFG	Transitional Federal Government (Somalia)
TSCTI	Trans-Sahara Counterterrorism Initiative
TSCTP	Trans-Sahara Counterterrorism Partnership
UK	United Kingdom of Great Britain and Northern Ireland
ULIMO	United Liberation Movement of Liberia for Democracy
ULIMO-J	ULIMO led by Roosevelt Johnson (Liberia)
ULIMO-K	ULIMO led by Alhaji Kromah (Liberia)
UN	United Nations
UNAMID	African Union–United Nations Mission in Darfur (Sudan)
UNAMIR	United Nations Assistance Mission for Rwanda
UNAMSIL	United Nations Mission in Sierra Leone
UNCTAD	United Nations Conference on Trade and Development
UNDP	United Nations Development Programme
UNICEF	United Nations Children's Fund
UNITA	National Union for the Total Independence of Angola (União Nacional para a Independência Total de Angola)
UNITAF	Unified Task Force (Somalia)
UNMIL	United Nations Mission in Liberia
UNMIS	United Nations Mission in Sudan
UNMISS	United Nations Mission in South Sudan
UNOCI	United Nations Operation in Côte d'Ivoire
UNOMSIL	United Nations Observer Mission in Sierra Leone
UNOSOM	United Nations Operation in Somalia
USAID	United States Agency for International Development
USC	United Somali Congress

Map 0.1. Africa, 2018. (Map by Philip Schwartzberg, Meridian Mapping, Minneapolis.)

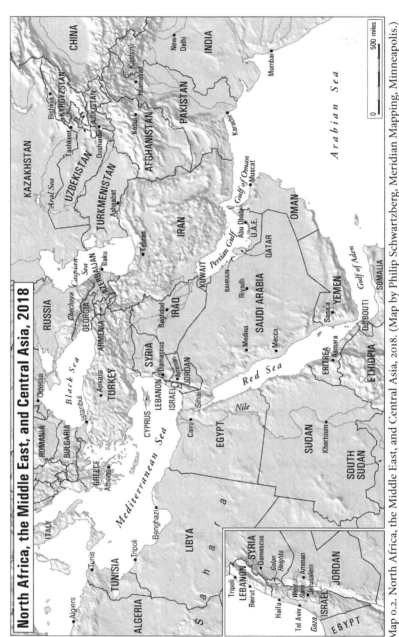

Map o.2. North Africa, the Middle East, and Central Asia, 2018. (Map by Philip Schwartzberg, Meridian Mapping, Minneapolis.)

1

Outsiders and Africa

Political and Military Engagement
on the Continent (1991–2017)

AFRICA IS A continent that is often misunderstood. Misleading stereotypes smooth over differences among the continent's fifty-four countries,
resulting in oversimplifications and distortions. During the periods of
decolonization (1956–75) and the Cold War (1945–91), discussions of
Africa evoked images of poverty, corruption, and communist subversion. African nationalists, who were viewed as threatening to Western
interests, were dismissed by many as communists controlled by external
powers. During the first post–Cold War decade (1991–2001), images of
brutal civil wars, and their expansion into regional conflagrations, dominated media portrayals of the continent. In the wake of the September 11,
2001, terrorist attacks on the United States, the presence of terrorists in
Africa—real and imagined—became the new bogeyman.[1]

As is the case with many stereotypes, there is a grain of truth in these
simplistic understandings. Poverty, corruption, and violent conflicts
have devastated many African countries. Less well known is the fact that
many of the challenges facing the continent today are rooted in colonial
political and economic practices, in Cold War alliances, and in attempts
by outsiders to influence African political and economic systems during
the decolonization and postindependence periods. Although conflicts in
Africa emerged from local issues, external political and military interventions altered their dynamics and rendered them more lethal.

This book provides a new framework for thinking about foreign
intervention in Africa, its purposes, and its consequences. It is not intended for specialists. It does not advance new theories, present the

results of recent primary research, or provide a detailed survey of current literature. Its target audience includes policymakers, humanitarian and human rights workers, students, and the general reading public. Its purpose is pedagogical, and the main points are illustrated with case studies synthesized from previously published work. The book's format minimizes footnoting in favor of Suggested Reading sections at the conclusion of each chapter. This approach allows readers to follow the outlines of the argument without the distraction of footnotes and yet benefit from the direction of bibliographic essays. The recommended readings are limited to sources in English; most of the articles, reports, and documents are readily available online.

This book is the companion to an earlier work, *Foreign Intervention in Africa: From the Cold War to the War on Terror* (Cambridge University Press, 2013). Both volumes elucidate the role of outside powers in the political and economic crises that plague Africa today. The earlier volume focuses on foreign political and military intervention in Africa during the periods of decolonization and the Cold War, when the most significant intervention came from outside the continent. Intervention during those periods involved the former colonial powers (France, the United Kingdom, Belgium, and Portugal), as well as the Cold War powers (the United States, the Soviet Union, the People's Republic of China, and Cuba).[2] External support for repressive regimes that served internal elites and outside interests and stole the people's patrimony laid the foundations for numerous post–Cold War conflicts, which in turn attracted further foreign intervention. The present volume investigates external political and military intervention in Africa during the quarter century following the Cold War (1991–2017), when neighboring states and subregional, regional, and global organizations and networks joined extracontinental powers in support of diverse forces in the war-making and peace-building processes.[3] During this period, the Cold War paradigm as justification for intervention was replaced by two new ones: response to instability, with the corollary of responsibility to protect, and the war on terror. These paradigms are developed more fully in chapter 2.

Historical Background: Decolonization and the Cold War

The following assessment of decolonization and the Cold War in Africa establishes the basis for understanding the conflicts that troubled the continent in their aftermath. During these overlapping periods, which spanned the years 1956 to 1991, European imperial powers and Cold War superpowers struggled to control African decolonization. As popular forces challenged the existing order, external powers intervened to impose or support African regimes that catered to their political and economic interests. Former colonial powers and the United States tended to support regimes that opposed communism and left colonial economic relationships intact. They often confused radical nationalism with communism, imagining Soviet manipulation where none existed. Western patronage was often based on the willingness of local actors to serve as Cold War allies and regional policemen, providing military bases for Western use and thwarting radical movements among their neighbors. With fewer means at its disposal and less intrinsic interest in the continent, the Soviet Union tended to increase its presence in response to escalated Western and, to a lesser extent, Chinese involvement. It supported movements and regimes that declared themselves in favor of scientific socialism and a Soviet-style model of development—regardless of their internal practices—as well as radical nationalist regimes that were shunned by the West. Although perceived by the United Sates to be following the Soviet lead, Cuba often took an independent route that was not always to the liking of its Soviet ally. China favored African political parties, movements, and regimes that opposed Soviet influence and ideology, which sometimes resulted in unofficial collaboration with the United States.

Serving outside interests and internal elites rather than popular majorities, many postcolonial African leaders were autocrats who used state resources to bind loyalists to them in a system called neopatrimonialism.[4] Weakened by corruption and mismanagement, their governments clung to power through repression, co-optation, and fraud. Since colonial times, African countries had exported cheap primary commodities and imported expensive manufactured goods. Following the worldwide economic crises of the 1970s and 1980s, they faced crushing debts. They turned to international financial institutions and foreign banks and governments for relief. Embracing a market-oriented economic model known as neoliberalism, these Western-dominated entities required African countries to reduce state involvement in the economy as a condition for loans.[5] Such policies imposed the greatest burdens on the poor, provoking food and fuel shortages, inflation, and unemployment. Economic hardship, political repression, and widespread corruption, which exacerbated growing income gaps, led to a continentwide surge of pro-democracy movements in the early 1990s. Popular forces increasingly challenged repressive regimes, demanding fundamental political and economic reforms.

As their economies went into a tailspin, neopatrimonial states could no longer perform their basic functions: monopolizing the means of coercion, safeguarding their territories, and providing protection and so-cial services to their citizens. Weakened leaders lost the means to appease their loyalists with power and resources. Dictators once bolstered by out-side powers were swept away as internal prodemocracy forces struggled with warlords and other strongmen to control the political process.[6] The ensuing chaos provided fertile ground for a new wave of foreign in-tervention, both internal and external to the continent. Resource-rich countries were particularly vulnerable as outsiders fought to control the production and flow of oil, natural gas, and strategic minerals.

During the 1990s and the early twenty-first century, extracontinen-tal powers, neighboring states, and subregional, regional, and global organizations became entangled in numerous African conflicts, sup-porting governments and rebel movements as well as war-making and peace-building processes. Although countries outside the continent con-tinued to involve themselves in African affairs, the most consequential foreign intervention during this period was intracontinental. A number of African states, sometimes assisted by extracontinental powers, supported warlords, dictators, and dissident movements in neighboring countries and fought for control of their neighbors' resources. The United Nations (UN), the African Union (AU), and various subregional organizations regularly intervened to broker, monitor, and enforce peace agreements.[7] However, conflicting interests, corrupt practices, and human rights abuses by some member states at times worsened the strife.

The launch of the war on terror following the 2001 terrorist attacks on the United States brought new forms of intervention to Africa. Wash-ington cultivated alliances with African governments and trained and equipped their militaries to assist in the US counterterrorism agenda. Some of these governments, like their Cold War predecessors, used US training and equipment to quash internal opposition. The United States also intensified unconventional military actions on the continent, deploy-ing Special Operations Forces and utilizing unmanned drones outside of established war zones. US support for repressive regimes, warlords, and foreign occupiers sometimes intensified local support for antigovernment insurgencies. International terrorist networks often seized the opportunity to harness local grievances and expand into territories they previously had not penetrated.

The Arab Spring (2011–13) generated another wave of external involvement as prodemocracy demonstrators and rebel movements ousted repressive rulers across North Africa and the Middle East. Extracontinental organizations, political powers, and networks responded to the instability with both unilateral and multilateral actions, allying themselves with forces they hoped would protect their long-term interests. International terrorist networks led by al-Qaeda and its Iraqi offshoot, the Islamic State, took advantage of local grievances to support a wide range of violent extremists, including drug smugglers, human traffickers, and petty criminals, as well as indigenous groups fighting secular or supposedly impious Muslim governments.

The societal breakdown that characterized the late Cold War and early post–Cold War periods resulted in the emergence of two new rationales for foreign intervention: response to instability—with its corollary, responsibility to protect—and the war on terror. Military intervention in a number of African countries was justified on the grounds that their domestic instability threatened international peace and security. In some cases, where large numbers of civilians were at risk and population displacement exacerbated regional tensions, the response to instability was reinforced by claims of the responsibility to protect. A relatively new international legal norm, this standard holds nation-states accountable for securing their citizens against "genocide, war crimes, ethnic cleansing and crimes against humanity" and grants the international community the right to intervene if governments fail to fulfill their "responsibility to protect."[8] Emerging from the post–World War II expansion of democratic values and concern for human rights, the principle gained support after the Cold War, when internal breakdown in Eastern Europe, Central Asia, and Africa forced the international community to rethink its allegiance to the seventeenth-century principle of state sovereignty. In 2005, UN member states concluded that a state's failure to protect its citizens could warrant foreign intervention.

The war on terror, which is generally associated with the George W. Bush administration and the 9/11 attacks, had roots in the late Cold War period. During the Cold War, the United States often deployed religion in the struggle against communism. The US Central Intelligence Agency (CIA) backed conservative Christian parties in Europe after World War II, hoping to undermine the appeal of communism to populations devastated by the war. In the Middle East, the CIA countered radical nationalism—which it erroneously conflated with communism—by supporting autocratic Muslim regimes that shared Western interests in opposing communism and in controlling the region's enormous oil wealth. Where radical nationalists came to power, their secular regimes were frequently challenged by local Islamists, who believed that Islamic religious principles should serve as the basis of the social, political, and legal order.[9] The secular regimes frequently responded with repression, arresting and imprisoning Islamists and forcing others to flee into exile. When the Soviet Union invaded Afghanistan in 1979 to shore up its regional interests, the United States seized the opportunity to rally support from a Muslim minority who had turned to violence to achieve their ends. In collaboration with Saudi Arabia, Pakistan, and other allies, the United States mobilized a multinational coalition that recruited, trained, armed, and financed Muslim militants from around the world to fight the 1979–89 Soviet occupation of Afghanistan. After Soviet withdrawal, the militants dispersed, taking their weapons and terror tactics to new battlegrounds around the globe. Osama bin Laden, founder and patron of al-Qaeda, was among the most prominent of the Soviet-Afghan War veterans who spearheaded the emerging terrorist networks. In the 1990s, his organization was responsible for a number of attacks on US citizens and property, culminating in the September 11, 2001, strikes on the World Trade Center and the Pentagon.

The 9/11 attacks opened a new chapter in the war on terror and marked the beginning of another era of US military intervention, first in Central Asia and the Middle East, and subsequently in Africa. Cold War experiences had left a deep imprint on US attitudes and actions. Having mobilized violent extremists who claimed the mantle of Islam to counter the communist menace during the Cold War, the United States contributed to the globalization of terror in its aftermath. Following the demise of the Soviet Union, Soviet-Afghan War veterans and their acolytes turned their attention to the United States as the last remaining superpower and patron of what they perceived as impious Muslim regimes. During the Cold War, the United States had confounded radical African and Arab nationalism with communism and intervened in

local conflicts, with disastrous results. After the Cold War, ma
US government viewed a wide range of Muslims with suspici
to distinguish between nonviolent Muslims with conservative rel₁ₕ
beliefs and a small minority with questionable religious credentials who
used violence to achieve their ends. Officials in Washington often glossed
over differences between those who targeted local regimes due to longstanding grievances and a much smaller segment who attacked Western
countries that, in their view, supported impious rulers, oppressed Muslims, and defiled Muslim holy lands. As a result, the US war on terror,
like the war on communism, had unintended consequences that sometimes intensified local support for violent opposition groups.

Central Propositions

The impact of foreign political and military intervention in Africa after
the Cold War is illuminated by a series of subregional case studies, described at the end of this chapter. They provide evidence to support the
book's four central propositions.

First, free market austerity policies, imposed by international financial institutions acting through weak postcolonial states during decolonization and the Cold War, contributed to deadly struggles over power
and resources in the post–Cold War period. As dictators were driven
from power, indigenous strongmen, and in some cases neighboring
states, intervened to further their own interests. Other international
actors interceded in an attempt to restore regional stability or protect
civilian lives. However, they tended to engage selectively, choosing conflict zones that impinged on their own political, economic, and strategic
interests, while ignoring other conflicts and casualties. Although some
interventions benefited civilian populations, others harmed them. The
failure to intervene when strategic interests were not at stake also had
dire consequences.

Second, the war on terror, like its Cold War antecedent, increased
foreign military presence on the African continent and generated new
external support for repressive governments. Expanded US involvement
was particularly noteworthy. Concerned about US energy and physical
security, Washington focused on countries rich in energy resources and
those considered vulnerable to terrorist infiltration. US military aid,
combined with commercial military sales and arms left over from the

Cold War, contributed to an escalation of violence in many parts of Africa. Rather than promoting security, US military and covert operations often intensified strife and undermined prospects for peace.

Third, although US counterterrorism initiatives cast a long shadow, they were not the only foreign interventions in Africa during this period. After the Cold War, the UN, the AU, and African subregional organizations played a growing role in diplomacy and peacekeeping initiatives, sometimes leading to multilateral military action. France, a former colonial power, maintained a strong military presence on the continent and intervened in numerous conflicts. Emerging powers such as China, India, Brazil, Turkey, and the Gulf states, which were heavily invested in African oil, minerals, and agricultural land, exerted new political influence.[10] While these countries often reinforced the powers of repressive regimes, in some instances they used their authority to promote peace and security efforts. The success of externally brokered agreements was largely determined by the degree to which all parties to the conflict and representative civil society organizations were engaged in the process. Accords imposed from above or outside, with little buy-in from relevant groups on the ground, were least likely to succeed. Public pressure for humanitarian intervention in response to African crises also contributed to new waves of foreign involvement. Activist groups in Western countries put the spotlight on mass atrocities and mobilized support for action to protect African civilians. However, they often oversimplified complex issues and sometimes proposed the kinds of military solutions that historically have harmed civilian populations.

The fourth proposition suggests that during the period under consideration, foreign political and military intervention in Africa often did more harm than good. External involvement motivated by the war on terror tended to intensify conflicts, and foreign response to instability often rendered local conflagrations more lethal. In addition, the emphasis on quick military action diverted attention from the political, economic, and social grievances that lay at the root of the conflicts. Even humanitarian missions, which were premised on the responsibility to protect, sometimes hurt the people they were intended to help. They were often weakened by inadequate mandates and funding and undermined by conflicting interests.

In the second decade of the twenty-first century, the merits and demerits of foreign intervention remained hotly contested, while the impact of failures to intervene was also the subject of much debate. The voices of African civil societies were not yet central to the discussions, nor were the concerns of affected populations foremost on the agenda. The prioritization of these constituencies is critical to the long-term success of any peace initiative.

Scope and Limitations

For the purposes of this study, foreign political and military intervention refers to the involvement of external powers or organizations in the internal affairs of an African country. These entities may be based on other continents, or they may be neighboring African states or subregional or regional organizations. The term "intervention" implies an unequal power relationship. It occurs when a dominant country or organization uses force or pressure to exert power over a weaker sovereign entity or when a weaker entity requests external assistance to restore order, monitor a peace accord, or end a humanitarian crisis. Intervention can be viewed in a positive light, such as when powerful nations intervene to halt a genocide or enforce peace agreements. However, when outsiders have intervened to enslave, conquer, colonize, overthrow or install governments, or plunder resources, intervention has had extremely negative ramifications.

Although this book focuses on political and military intervention, the enormous problems that afflict Africa today cannot properly be understood without taking into account the impact of foreign intrusion into African economies, externally induced climate change, and environmental destruction and plunder of resources by outside forces. These factors, which have contributed to many African conflicts, are beyond the purview of this book, as is the growing presence of China. However, their significance should not be underestimated, as noted briefly below.

Foreign Intrusion into African Economies

Although outside powers had attempted to control the lucrative African trades in gold, ivory, and slaves for centuries before the Industrial Revolution, it was rapid industrialization in nineteenth-century Europe that sparked the continentwide scramble for African resources, labor, and markets. The Berlin Conference of 1884–85 devised rules to legitimate European claims, and imperial powers rushed to establish "effective occupation" that would entitle them to a share of what Belgian King Leopold II termed "this magnificent African cake."[11] The ensuing "scramble for Africa" unleashed a wave of foreign intervention that brought most of the continent under European authority within a few decades. France, the UK, Belgium, Portugal, Germany, Italy, and Spain established regimes to extract African wealth—especially rubber, minerals, cotton, and plant oils—and to force African people to provide the labor and taxes necessary to keep the system afloat.

Political independence, beginning in the 1950s, did little to alter the unequal economic relationships established during the colonial era. Former imperial powers sustained governments that perpetuated the status quo. Resource extraction, primarily for the benefit of outsiders and small groups of indigenous elites, continued, along with political repression to guarantee access. The Cold War exacerbated tensions in new African states as rival powers, seeking to protect their own economic and strategic interests, supported repressive regimes.

The colonial legacy of unequal exchange between African commodity producers and industrialized countries has contributed to the deep impoverishment of African populations. When African colonies achieved political independence in the mid- to late twentieth century, the inequality inherent in these economic relationships persisted in a system dubbed neocolonialism. In the words of pan-African leader Kwame Nkrumah, neocolonial states had "all the outward trappings of international sovereignty," but their economies and political programs were "directed from outside."[12] Deeply rooted economic inequalities were exacerbated by the steep rise in oil prices in the early 1970s and the worldwide collapse in commodity prices at the end of that decade. African political economies, which had been structured to export primary products and import manufactured goods, suffered severe balance of trade deficits. The economic crisis stemming from structural inequalities was aggravated by inflated military budgets, corruption, and economic mismanagement. With their economies crumbling, many African countries turned to the International Monetary Fund (IMF), the World Bank, and Western commercial banks and governments for help.

Foreign assistance came with strings attached. Embracing free market ideologies that promote global capitalism, the Western-dominated international financial institutions required governments to implement draconian stabilization and structural adjustment programs as a condition for foreign loans. Private banks usually required the IMF's seal of approval before granting commercial loans. Western development agencies and nongovernmental organizations (NGOs) refused assistance to projects that did not conform to neoliberal free market norms. The result was the imposition of economic development models in which African populations had no voice. The Washington Consensus, named for the power hub of the IMF, the World Bank, and the US government, limited government involvement in the economy, requiring an end to subsidies, price controls, and protective tariffs. The mandated government cutbacks undermined health and education systems and destroyed social safety nets. Obligatory currency devaluations brought about soaring inflation and import shortages. Enforced privatization resulted in widespread retrenchment, higher unemployment, and an upsurge in crony capitalism as state-owned assets were transferred to government loyalists. These measures were particularly damaging to women, children, the elderly, and the poor. Imposed from above, the structural adjustment programs were inherently undemocratic. In many countries, the new balance of power favored governments with the means to impose unpopular measures. Foreign intervention in African economies thus resulted in widespread economic hardship and increased political repression, constituting a fundamental denial of African sovereignty.

Massive foreign debts incurred by African governments in the 1970s and 1980s continued to take their toll in the decades that followed. In many cases the borrowed money was spent on extravagant showcase projects, or on military rather than economic development; or it was lost to corruption. Successor governments were forced to service the debts with scarce foreign currency, which exhausted export earnings and resulted in further borrowing. Debt service to foreign governments, banks, and international financial institutions consumed a large percentage of government revenues that might otherwise have been allocated to essential services and economic development. Externally imposed economic policies thus laid the foundations for the political crises of the 1980s and 1990s.

When the Cold War ended, Western powers cut ties to repressive regimes they had once cultivated as Cold War allies and regional policemen. Aid pipelines were shut down, and bank loans were no longer forthcoming. Neoliberal reforms, which promoted the privatization of assets previously controlled by the state, failed to strengthen state institutions as intended. Instead, they laid the groundwork for new kinds of patronage networks that enriched loyal political and military officials, who benefited from the privatization schemes, and marginalized others, who were laid off. Some of those who were sidelined, along with others who sought a greater share of the spoils, abandoned established political and economic structures and began to operate as warlords. The warlords mobilized loyalists from the ranks of downsized functionaries and established militias of unpaid former soldiers, unemployed youth, and press-ganged children. The economic crises and externally imposed reforms thus sparked new political turmoil, which in turn stimulated further waves of political and military intervention.

After the Cold War, countries with emerging economies in the Global South joined former colonial and Cold War powers in taking a new interest in Africa. Foreign powers and corporations focused their attention on countries that were rich in crude oil, natural gas, and strategic minerals.[13] They also paid attention to those that offered access to arable land, markets for manufactured goods, and lucrative infrastructure contracts. However, economic interests were rarely the primary motives for military intervention, and the relationship between the two was varied and complex. Three points should be borne in mind. First, the interests of foreign governments and corporations were not always in sync, although critics frequently conflate them. Governments sometimes protected private interests with military might; however, they also compromised those interests for broader political gains. Second, external actors made deals with African governments and local strongmen that gave them direct access to desired commodities, and they acquired rule-making powers that tipped the system in their favor. They generally prized stability, and only when political mechanisms failed did they consider military means. Third, although competition for strategic minerals figured in many conflicts, control over those resources was not always the source of the conflict. Rather, disputes with diverse origins sometimes expanded to include struggles for control over resources that in turn fueled the war efforts.

Externally Induced Climate Change

Like foreign intrusion into African economies, climate change, caused primarily by greenhouse gases generated by industrialized countries, has contributed to a growing number of the continent's conflicts.[14] As the gases trap heat in the earth's atmosphere, glaciers have melted and oceans have warmed, causing sea levels to rise, water to evaporate, and ocean storms to intensify. These factors have resulted in increased rainfall over the oceans and less over adjacent land, provoking both severe flooding and extreme drought in many parts of the African continent. The warming of the Indian Ocean has contributed to the intensification of droughts from the Horn of Africa to the Cape and across the Eastern Sahel, while the warming of the Atlantic Ocean and Gulf of Guinea have exacerbated droughts in the Western Sahel. Climate change has dried up lakes and rivers and destroyed crops, herds, fish, and game. It has threatened food production, drinking water, and hydroelectric capabilities. Residents in drought-ravaged areas, in search of fuel, have denuded hills of trees; when rains finally come, they wash away the topsoil. Malnutrition and tropical diseases associated with high temperatures and humidity have grown more severe. The rapidly expanding desert has encroached on arable land. All of these factors have led to human migration on an unprecedented scale.[15] Massive population displacements caused by climate change have resulted in competition for increasingly scarce arable land and water, which in turn has generated conflict between farmers and herders and between members of different ethnic groups, clans, and lineages.[16] The confluence of these factors has provided fertile ground for extremist ideologies that have harnessed local discontent and mobilized populations with few alternatives for channeling their grievances.

Environmental Destruction and Plunder of Resources by Outsiders

Environmental destruction resulting from climate change has contributed to several of the regional conflicts investigated in this study. Foreign interest in African resources to mitigate the effects of climate change and population growth on other continents may be an important factor in future conflicts. The global food crisis and the search for new sources of fuel have led to substantial African land grabs by emerging economic powers, which are producing food and biofuels in Africa for consumption elsewhere. Former imperial powers that continue to hold land in their old colonies have been joined by China, India, Qatar, Saudi Arabia, the United Arab Emirates, Singapore, and Malaysia, which have taken over major land assets in Cameroon, the Democratic Republic of Congo, Ethiopia, Madagascar, Morocco, the Republic of Congo, Sudan, Tanzania, and elsewhere. Foreign investors, primarily from Singapore and

Malaysia, control virtually all of Liberia's arable land, while 86 percent of Gabon's arable land is under foreign contract, most of it held by Singapore. African citizens have had little if any say in these arrangements, which include no provisions for African food security or for environmental controls to protect the land, water, and air from pollution. Competition for arable land and clean water, already a factor in contemporary conflicts, is likely to contribute to future conflicts as well.

Environmental destruction as a by-product of foreign ventures is also the source of considerable conflict in Africa. Pollution of land, water, and air by foreign oil and gas companies, deforestation by foreign timber interests, and the destruction of wildlife habitats and toxic waste dumping by other external interests have jeopardized lives and livelihoods across the continent. Pollution by foreign oil companies has destroyed the fishing and agricultural industries of the Niger Delta and led to civil unrest, military crackdowns, and the emergence of criminal gangs that engage in illegal oil tapping, piracy, and kidnapping for ransom as alternative sources of subsistence. Similarly, unauthorized fishing and toxic waste dumping by foreign concerns have devastated the local fishing industry in northeastern Somalia, while climate change–induced droughts have decimated food crops and pastureland. Unemployed men have turned to piracy, first demanding fees from South Korean, Indian, and Taiwanese fishing fleets, then attacking oil tankers and container ships and holding their crews for ransom. Individual ventures have been transformed into sophisticated criminal rackets led by warlords who at times have controlled thousands of gunmen.

Economic growth and technological development outside of Africa have sparked a new scramble for African resources, which has fueled repressive governments, separatist movements, and broader regional conflicts. Corrupt politicians, military personnel, and warlords have contracted with foreign interests to extract and export valuable resources for enormous profits. "Conflict diamonds" were the object of wars in Angola, Liberia, Sierra Leone, and the Democratic Republic of Congo (DRC), and also helped fund those wars. In the DRC, control over coltan, tin, tungsten, gold, and cobalt was also at stake, while the Liberian war was financed by timber as well as diamonds, and cocoa bankrolled the war in Côte d'Ivoire. Competition for Africa's vast and largely unexploited oil and natural gas reserves is likely to be at the root of future conflicts involving both internal and external interests.

China's Growing Presence

The expanding role of China on the African continent has been the focus of considerable attention, both in Africa and in the West. The United States and Western Europe have seen their African trade and investments eclipsed by those of the Asian giant. Their leaders have warned that Beijing is exploiting African resources, taking African jobs, supporting African dictators, and demonstrating disregard for human rights, good governance, and sound environmental practices on the continent. African civil society organizations have frequently leveled the same criticisms—although many note the irony in the concerns of former imperial and Cold War powers, which historically have engaged in similar practices. Chinese involvement is primarily economic, rather than political or military, and thus falls outside the scope of this study. However, because Beijing's practices may be laying the groundwork for future conflicts, a brief description of China's impact on the continent is warranted.

The People's Republic of China developed an interest in Africa during the Cold War, when it supported African liberation movements and governments that strove to build socialist societies—as well as others that opposed Beijing's Cold War rivals. Seeking allies in the global arena, China was motivated principally by politics rather than economics. Its attitude shifted in the mid-1990s, after a massive program of industrialization and economic development transformed the Chinese economy into one of the world's most powerful. Africa was no longer viewed as an ideological proving ground, but rather as a source of raw materials and a market for Chinese manufactured goods. By the first decade of the twenty-first century, China had surpassed the United States as Africa's largest trading partner, and it had become the third-largest source of the continent's direct foreign investment. In exchange for guaranteed access to energy resources, agricultural land, and other strategic materials, China spent billions of dollars on African infrastructure—developing and rehabilitating roads, railroads, dams, bridges, ports, oil pipelines and refineries, power plants, water systems, and telecommunications networks. Chinese concerns also constructed hospitals and schools and invested in clothing and food processing industries, agriculture, fisheries, commercial real estate, retail, and tourism.

Unlike the Western powers and the international financial institutions they dominated, Beijing did not impose political and economic prescriptions as conditions for its loans, investments, aid, and trade.

Although it mandated that infrastructure contracts be awarded to Chinese companies and that Chinese supplies be used, the agreements did not require economic restructuring, adherence to democratic principles, respect for human rights, or the implementation of labor and environmental protections. While Beijing's noninterference policies were often popular in ruling circles, civil society organizations frequently criticized them. African labor, business, civic, and human rights organizations noted that Chinese firms drove African-owned enterprises out of business and often employed Chinese workers rather than providing local populations with jobs. When they hired African labor, Chinese concerns paid poverty-level wages and engaged in practices that endangered worker health and safety. Most importantly, Beijing backed corrupt African elites in exchange for unfettered access to resources and markets, strengthening regimes that stole the people's patrimony, engaged in domestic repression, and waged wars of aggression against neighboring states. Like the Western-backed autocrats who preceded them, China's clients are likely to face popular discontent in the future.

Although China's involvement in Africa is principally economic, the country's economic clout has been accompanied by growing political and military influence. Beijing's decades-long policy of noninterference in host country affairs has shifted noticeably in recent years, motivated by its desire to protect Chinese economic interests and citizens living abroad. In the early 2000s, Beijing joined multinational mediation efforts and UN peacekeeping operations for the first time, focusing on countries and regions where it had valuable investments and export markets. In 2006, for instance, China pressed Sudan, an important oil partner, to accept an AU-UN peacekeeping force in Darfur, and in 2015 it worked with an East African subregional organization and Western powers to mediate peace in South Sudan. Initially, China refrained from military involvement, preferring to contribute medical workers and engineers. It provided a 315-member engineering unit to the peacekeeping mission in Darfur, but no troops. However, as Beijing's global stature and interests grew, so too did its military engagement. In 2013, Beijing supplied some 400 engineers, medical personnel, police, and combat troops to the UN peacekeeping mission in Mali, marking the first time Chinese combat forces had joined a UN operation. Similarly, in 2015, Beijing assigned 350 engineers, medical personnel, and other noncombatants to the UN peacekeeping mission in South Sudan. However, it also contributed an infantry battalion composed of 700 armed peacekeepers—the first Chinese infantry battalion ever deployed in a UN peacekeeping mission. Chinese military presence was also notable in UN peacekeeping missions in Burundi (2004–6) and the Central African Republic (2014–).

The trend toward heightened Chinese political and military engagement in Africa culminated in a 2016 agreement that permitted China to construct a military base in Djibouti—its first permanent military facility overseas. Strategically located on the Gulf of Aden near the mouth of the Red Sea, the base will allow Beijing to resupply Chinese vessels involved in UN antipiracy operations and to protect Chinese nationals living in the region. It will also enable China to monitor commercial traffic along its evolving 21st Century Maritime Silk Road, which will link maritime countries from Oceania to the Mediterranean in a vast production and trading network.[17] It will allow China to safeguard its supply of oil, half of which originates in the Middle East and transits through the Red Sea and Djibouti's Bab al-Mandeb Strait to the Gulf of Aden. Most of China's exports to Europe follow the same route. Because China's growing economic interests in Africa have led to greater concern about the continent's political stability, the projection of Chinese military power in Africa is likely to intensify in the future. Such developments will have significant implications in Africa. However, they are a topic for another book.

The Book's Architecture and Case Studies

This book explores foreign political and military intervention in Africa after the Cold War through the lens of case studies from East, Central, West, and North Africa. Southern Africa is not a primary focus. Although that subregion was the site of significant foreign intervention during the Cold War, it was largely exempt from external political and military interference during the first two and a half decades that followed.[18] However, South Africa, the subregion's leading power, wielded continental and global influence and played an important role in international peace initiatives on the continent. Its efforts are discussed in case studies focusing on the other subregions.

Chapters 1 through 3 establish the book's framework. This first chapter introduces the book's purpose, historical and chronological context, and central propositions, and explains the book's scope and limitations. Chapter 2 begins with a portrait of Africa at the end of the Cold War, when political and economic crises attracted a new wave of outside engagement. It develops the two paradigms that were used to justify foreign intervention after the Cold War—response to instability and the war on terror—and examines common Western misconceptions about Islam and its history, which have influenced the trajectory of the war on terror. Chapter 3 introduces the key international actors that intervened in Africa after the Cold War and explores their motivations and rationales for intervention.

At the heart of the book, chapters 4–11 present a series of subregional case studies, illustrating the two paradigms that were used to justify foreign intervention. Some cases exemplify foreign intervention as a response to instability and its corollary, responsibility to protect. Others typify external action as a component of the war on terror, a justification that was especially prevalent after the September 2001 attacks on the United States. Some cases are characterized by a single paradigm, while others bridge the two. Together the case studies offer evidence that supports the book's four central propositions. Although the political, economic, and social components of each conflict are described, the case studies emphasize the impact of foreign intervention rather than the internal dynamics of the struggles. They offer overviews of each conflict and do not attempt to evaluate the relative importance of internal and external factors. For readers interested in other aspects of the conflicts, Suggested Reading sections are appended to each chapter.

Chapters 12 and 13 look more closely at the role of the United States. Chapter 12 investigates US involvement in Africa after the Cold War, from the Clinton through Obama administrations. Concerns about political and economic instability and international terrorism shaped US policies and had a significant impact on outcomes in Africa. Chapter 13 offers a window on US Africa policy during the first year of the Trump administration, exploring continuities and discontinuities with previous administrations. The Conclusion summarizes the pitfalls of foreign political and military intervention in Africa during the first quarter century after the Cold War and suggests some requirements for the establishment of lasting peace.

The sections below briefly summarize the case studies featured in chapters 4–11, grouped by subregion, and the elements of US Africa policy discussed in chapters 12–13, noting how they illustrate the paradigms used to justify foreign intervention after the Cold War.

East Africa: Somalia, Sudan, and South Sudan

Chapter 4 focuses on foreign intervention in Somalia from
2017. After the central state collapsed in 1991, warlords and
for control. The UN, the United States, the AU, and neighboring cu.
tries interceded, initially motivated by the response to instability and the
responsibility to protect, but increasingly galvanized by the war on terror
as a jihadist insurgency emerged in response to outside intervention. The
response to instability/responsibility to protect paradigm is applicable to
Somalia for the entire period. The war on terror paradigm is relevant to
the period before September 2001, but it took on greater urgency in the
aftermath of the 9/11 attacks.

Chapter 5 examines foreign intervention in Sudan (1991–2017) and
South Sudan (2011–17). In Sudan, civil war, local insurgencies, ethnic
cleansing, and terrorist networks generated enormous instability inside
the country and across its borders. Neighboring states supported rival
factions in the north-south civil war (1983–2005), while the UN, the
United States, European countries, and African subregional organizations mediated problematic peace accords that ended the war but laid the
groundwork for future conflicts. The AU and the UN staged inventions
to prevent ethnic cleansing in the Darfur region of western Sudan from
2003, but they failed to sustain the operations until peace was restored.
The response to instability/responsibility to protect paradigm is applicable to Sudan for the entire period. The war on terror paradigm is relevant
to much of the 1990s; however, by the end of the decade Khartoum had
begun to collaborate in the US-led war on terror in the hope that its cooperation would lead to the lifting of sanctions.

Central Africa: Rwanda and the Democratic Republic of Congo

Chapter 6 investigates foreign involvement in Rwanda before and during
the 1994 genocide, and chapter 7 examines foreign intervention in neighboring Zaire/Democratic Republic of Congo from 1994 to 2017.[19] In both
cases, France exercised its presumed right as the world's dominant francophone power, intervening unilaterally or pushing the UN Security Council
to act. Neighboring states also promoted their own interests, sometimes
backing existing governments and at other times supporting rebel movements. UN peacekeeping missions, weakened by conflicts inside the Security Council, were ineffectual and marred by controversy. In Rwanda,
France sustained the genocidal regime, while Uganda supported the rebel

movement that ousted it. As the genocide unfolded, powerful members of the Security Council terminated a peacekeeping operation and refused to authorize an intervention to halt the killing. When Rwandan refugees streamed into Zaire, that country became a new battleground. Regional powers took sides, with some supporting the ruling regime and others backing rebel proxies. All parties fought over Zaire's riches, while the UN made futile efforts to reestablish peace. The response to instability/responsibility to protect paradigm applies to both Rwanda and the DRC during the period under consideration. The war on terror did not play a role in international response to the crisis in either country.

West Africa, Part 1: Liberia, Sierra Leone, and Côte d'Ivoire

Chapter 8 explores foreign intervention in the West African countries of Liberia (1990–2003) and Sierra Leone (1991–2002), while chapter 9 considers external involvement in Côte d'Ivoire (2002–11). In each case, war and plunder took an enormous toll after the Cold War. A West African subregional body interceded in all three conflicts, purportedly to reestablish peace and security, but sometimes to further member states' political and economic interests. Liberia promoted a proxy war in Sierra Leone, and this in turn stimulated intervention by the UN, foreign mercenaries, and the UK, which asserted its prerogative as the former colonial power. France claimed a similar prerogative in Côte d'Ivoire. Neighboring states meanwhile pursued their own interests, either through the subregional body or unilaterally. The AU provided mediators, and the UN sent a peacekeeping mission. In all three cases, the response to instability/responsibility to protect paradigm was paramount; the war on terror was not a factor.

North Africa: Tunisia, Egypt, and Libya

Chapter 10 considers the role of foreign intervention in North Africa from 2011 to 2017. This period encompasses the Arab Spring (2011–13), a series of popular uprisings that challenged authoritarian regimes and transformed the political landscape in North Africa and the Middle East. It also considers the uprisings' aftermath (2013–17), when old regime remnants and other armed groups vied with prodemocracy forces for control. The chapter gives special consideration to Tunisia, Egypt, and Libya—the three African countries involved in the movement for social and political change. France, the United States, the European Union (EU), the North Atlantic Treaty Organization (NATO), Saudi Arabia,

Qatar, and the United Arab Emirates were the most consequential foreign actors. They intervened first in response to instability and, in the case of Libya, to protect civilian lives. In Libya, regime change was also the goal of several external powers. After the old regimes fell and international terrorist networks joined the fight, the war on terror paradigm was used to justify further foreign involvement.

West Africa, Part 2: Mali, Nigeria, and the Western Sahel

Chapter 11 examines foreign intervention in the Western Sahel states of Mali and Nigeria during the period 2009 to 2017.[20] Regime change in Libya provoked an influx of fighters and weapons into the Western Sahel, where they destabilized weak governments. In Mali, these developments bolstered a secessionist movement and stimulated a military coup, an insurgency linked to al-Qaeda, and another round of foreign intervention that had ripple effects across the region. The most significant external actors included the UN, the AU, the EU, a West African subregional body, France, and the United States. In Nigeria, militants who had trained in Mali's al-Qaeda-linked camps returned home with weapons from Libyan arsenals, which they used to strengthen a growing insurgency in the northeast. The Nigerian conflict spilled into neighboring Niger and Cameroon and attracted fighters from Mali, Mauritania, and Algeria. It also garnered support from the Islamic State and sparked another wave of intervention by foreign governments and institutions. Neighboring states joined forces with the Nigerian military to respond to regional instability, while Western nations, worried by the presence of al-Qaeda and the Islamic State and motivated by the war on terror, provided military training, technical, and financial support.

The United States and Africa

Chapter 12 investigates the evolution of US Africa policy from 1991 through 2017, focusing especially on the Bill Clinton, George W. Bush, and Barack Obama administrations. As the dominant world actor after the Cold War, the United States used its political, economic, and military clout to sway international bodies and influence world events. In Africa, the United States supported initiatives that improved health and promoted economic development—prerequisites for social stability. It also strengthened the military capabilities of African states and intervened with force when its perceived interests were deemed threatened. During the 1990s, US actions were most often justified by the response to insta-bility/responsibility to protect paradigm. However, after the September 2001 attacks, the US counterterrorism agenda took increasing prece-dence. Washington provided money, training, hardware, and equipment to dozens of countries that were considered vulnerable to terrorist activ-ity. It provided air support in conventional military actions and engaged in a growing number of covert military operations. The increasing secu-ritization of US Africa policy shifted attention and resources from health and development to counterterrorism and favored countries that were rich in resources or strategically located over other countries that may have had more pressing needs.

Chapter 13, focusing on 2017, surveys the first year of Donald Trump's presidency and suggests how his administration's policies and perspectives are likely to affect Africa. Based on statements made during the presiden-tial campaign and evidence from Trump's first year in office, the chapter explores continuities and discontinuities with policies of past administra-tions. It foresees the continued militarization of US Africa policy and a diminished emphasis on public health, economic development, good gov-ernance, and human rights. Although the counterterrorism agenda gained precedence in the Bush and Obama administrations, officials in those administrations regarded physical well-being, economic prosperity, and accountable governance as critical components of the counterterrorism toolkit. Trump, in contrast, sees little value in diplomacy and foreign aid. He opposes US support for UN peacekeeping efforts and for postconflict nation building. Although early renditions of Trump's "America First" for-eign policy hinted at a rollback of US intervention, his subsequent actions in Yemen, Syria, Iraq, Afghanistan, and Somalia suggest an intensification of US military involvement in global trouble spots. In Africa, such inter-ventions are likely to be justified by the war on terror paradigm.

THE NEXT CHAPTER advances the book's agenda in three ways. First, it offers an overview of Africa in the 1990s, when political and economic crises opened the door to a new round of external involvement. Second, it develops more fully the paradigms used to justify foreign invention, providing historical context for the constituent ideas and examining their evolution. Finally, the chapter discusses common misunderstand-ings about Islam that have influenced the execution of the Western war on terror and that continue to influence government actions.

2

The Post–Cold War Context

Shifting Paradigms and Misconceptions

THIS CHAPTER PROVIDES historical context for foreign intervention in Africa after the Cold War, performing three important tasks. First, it describes how the political and economic crises of the 1970s and 1980s, which were rooted in colonial and Cold War policies, ushered in a new wave of external involvement in the 1990s. Second, it shows how the outside powers that responded to this instability had additional tools at their disposal. Post–World War II institutions and legal frameworks threw into question longstanding views concerning state sovereignty and international law. Postwar conventions and interpretations advanced new rationales for foreign intrusion into the affairs of nation-states that threatened regional stability and civilians' lives. The paradigms of response to instability/responsibility to protect and the war on terror—put to use after the Cold War—emerged from this intellectual ferment. Third, the chapter investigates Western misconceptions about Islam that underpinned the war on terror and had devastating effects on millions of Muslims worldwide.

Africa after the Cold War

The roots of many problems afflicting Africa today lie in its colonial and Cold War past. Distinctions in power and privilege and conflicts over natural resources have long been a part of human history; in Africa, these phenomena predated the colonial period. However, the plundering of riches through unequal exchange was embedded in colonial economic practices, and colonial-era ethnic and regional hierarchies—sometimes built on preexisting distinctions—often assumed new potency after independence. Internal corruption, economic mismanagement, and pyramids of privilege resulted in unstable societies marked by huge disparities in wealth and power. Money and weapons distributed by Cold War patrons entrenched power differentials and rendered local conflicts deadlier than those of previous eras. The end of the Cold War introduced a new set of problems with roots in this troubled past.

The Cold War drew to a close in the late 1980s and early 1990s, when the Soviet Union collapsed economically and politically. African conflict zones that were once Cold War battlegrounds were increasingly ignored, and dictators who were no longer useful to their Cold War patrons were rapidly abandoned. Across the continent, nations suffered the consequences of depleted resources, enormous debts, dysfunctional states, and regional wars over the spoils. Weapons left over from the Cold War poured into volatile regions and fueled new competition for riches and power. Countries already weakened by economic and political crises descended into violent conflicts that often transcended international borders. In some cases, popular movements or armed insurrections ousted dictators who had lost the support of outside powers. However, because war and repression had stymied organized political opposition in many countries, warlords and other opportunists often moved into the power vacuums. Unscrupulous leaders manipulated ethnicity to strengthen their drive for power and privilege, sometimes unleashing ethnically based terror.

During the first post–Cold War decade, foreign intervention assumed a new character. Many Western nations that had been implicated in African conflicts during the Cold War turned their attention elsewhere. The United States, as the self-proclaimed Cold War victor, showed little interest in direct military intervention and severely reduced its economic assistance as well. However, in keeping with its call for African solutions for African problems, Washington initiated new programs to bolster African military capabilities and others that focused on free market economic development and trade. Recognizing that Africa's enormous external debts, often incurred by Cold War clients, and the HIV/AIDS pandemic contributed to political and economic instability, the United States also introduced programs to address these problems. The policy shift meant that most military interventions during the 1990s were conducted by African countries—sometimes to reestablish regional peace and security, but in other cases to support proxy forces that granted access to their neighbors' resources.

Although extracontinental powers were less likely to inter
laterally during the 1990s, multilateral intervention by both Af
non-African powers intensified and took shape under new aus
UN, the Organization of African Unity (OAU), and various suɔ.ᴄg.ᴄ.
bodies intervened in response to instability—to broker, monitor, and enforce peace accords and to facilitate humanitarian relief operations. Peacekeeping and humanitarian interventions were viewed positively by many
African constituencies, although disparities in power meant that African
agents had little authority over external forces once implanted on African
soil. In a striking deviation from Cold War trends, critics castigated the international community for not acting quickly or boldly enough—as in the
case of the Rwandan genocide in 1994, the Liberian civil war that ended in
2003, and the Darfur conflict in Sudan that began in 2003. The UN Security
Council, in particular, was criticized for its refusal to thwart the Rwandan genocide and to act more forcefully in Darfur. Under pressure from
human rights and humanitarian lobbies and from African civil societies,
the UN General Assembly passed a resolution in 2005 that held countries
responsible for protecting their citizens from "genocide, war crimes, ethnic
cleansing and crimes against humanity." Sometimes called the R2P resolution, the General Assembly action granted the international community
the right to intervene through UN Security Council–sanctioned operations if governments failed to fulfill their "responsibility to protect" (R2P).[1]

Appeals for humanitarian intervention in African affairs increased
during the first decade of the twenty-first century; military intervention
for other ends also intensified. The ongoing struggle to secure energy
and other strategic resources and the onset of the war on terror brought
renewed attention to the continent. Heightened foreign military presence, external support for repressive regimes, and disreputable alliances
purportedly intended to root out terror resulted in new forms of foreign
intervention in Africa. The continent, its people, and its resources again
became the object of internal and external struggles in which local concerns were frequently subordinated to foreign interests.

Paradigm 1: Response to Instability and the Responsibility to Protect

The political, economic, and social upheavals that characterized the
late Cold War and early post–Cold War periods resulted in severe instability in numerous African states and regions. Foreign powers and

multilateral institutions took note when domestic turmoil was perceived to jeopardize international peace and security. In most instances, their involvement entailed brokering, monitoring, and enforcing peace agreements. Diplomatic and military interventions were often justified on the grounds that outside actors had both the right and the responsibility to guarantee international peace and security if individual states failed to do so. In such cases, intervention was authorized under Chapters VI, VII, or VIII of the United Nations Charter, adopted in 1945.[2] In instances where large civilian populations were at risk and refugee flows heightened regional tensions, the response to instability was bolstered by newer claims that the international community had a responsibility to protect civilian lives. In such cases, intervention was justified by the 2005 UN General Assembly resolution, mentioned above, that bestowed on the international community the responsibility to protect civilians when their governments were unable or unwilling to do so.

Post–Cold War intervention in African affairs saw increased involvement by multinational bodies that drew on changing notions concerning the right to intervene. Since the mid-1990s, when the international community largely ignored appeals to thwart the Rwandan genocide, growing constituencies in Africa and the West have called for humanitarian interventions to end human rights abuses and protect civilians, with or without the consent of the states in question. Such interventions might include military force, sanctions, or the forcible delivery of humanitarian aid. Although the notion of humanitarian intervention has gained support, it remains controversial. External interference in a state's domestic affairs challenges a premise of international law, national sovereignty, that has held sway for more than three and a half centuries.

The contemporary system of international law emerged from the 1648 Peace of Westphalia, a series of treaties that concluded the Thirty Years' War in Europe and laid the foundations for the modern nation-state. Enshrined in the treaties is the principle of national sovereignty, which granted monarchs control over feudal princes and inhabitants of their territories, as well as absolute power to maintain order within their realms and to protect the state from external forces. Deemed above the law, sovereigns were exempt from moral scrutiny. From 1648 until the end of World War II, the sovereignty of the nation-state was defined in such a way that internal conflicts and their consequences were considered domestic matters outside the purview of the international community. However, another seventeenth-century principle of international law eventually established a framework for a more expansive understanding of national sovereignty. The notion that a state and its citizenry are bound by a social contract that carries reciprocal rights and responsibilities gradually superseded the view that sovereigns are beyond moral scrutiny. If the social contract requires citizens to relinquish some of their liberties in exchange for state protection, then the state bears a responsibility to ensure its citizens' welfare by protecting their rights and liberties and maintaining peace and security within state borders.

The mass exterminations of European Jews and other populations during World War II challenged the principles of international law that had allowed such crimes to occur, and the impunity of national leaders was called into question. The Nuremberg trials (1945–49), which held key individuals in Nazi Germany's political, economic, and military establishment accountable for war crimes and crimes against humanity, led to increased scrutiny of national leaders. The postwar order witnessed an expansion of democratic values and institutions. Universal principles of human rights were enshrined in the International Bill of Human Rights, comprising the Universal Declaration of Human Rights (1948), the International Covenant on Civil and Political Rights (1966), and the International Covenant on Economic, Social and Cultural Rights (1966). In 1948, the UN General Assembly adopted the Convention on the Prevention and Punishment of the Crime of Genocide (the Genocide Convention), which required member nations "to prevent and to punish" genocide wherever and whenever it is found.[3] Emergent human rights and humanitarian movements gave primacy to individual over states' rights and emphasized the protection of minorities and other vulnerable members of society. National laws were no longer off limits to international investigation. Subject peoples in Europe's African and Asian empires embraced universal human rights claims and demanded equal treatment under the law and national self-determination. In the 1950s and 1960s, their efforts culminated in widespread decolonization.

The establishment of the United Nations in 1945 further undermined the seventeenth-century notion that state sovereignty is absolute. Like the post–World War I League of Nations, the UN was founded to promote international peace and security. However, the UN's mission, which was uniquely premised on respect for universal human rights and freedoms, led to a supplementary mandate. The UN was also charged with promoting "the economic and social advancement of all peoples."[4] Aware that conflicts were frequently rooted in material deprivation and in unequal distribution of power and resources, political and human rights leaders argued that the maintenance of international peace and security required governments to use their capacities to benefit all their citizens and that states should be held accountable for the protection of basic human rights within their borders.

The end of the Cold War brought additional challenges to the state sovereignty principle. The Soviet Union had disintegrated, and the United States and other Western powers no longer felt the same need for strongmen to protect their interests. Newly critical of their clients' corrupt practices and human rights abuses, they withdrew their support from longstanding dictators and called for accountability in governance. These momentous political shifts provided opportunities for new ways of thinking, and a cadre of public intellectuals in the Global North and South began to argue for a fundamental reconceptualization of the premises of state sovereignty, one that harkened back to the social contract that sometimes had confounded sovereigns' ability to wield their power with impunity. These thinkers charged that to legitimately claim sovereignty, a state must provide basic conditions for the well-being of its citizenry, including not only peace, security, and order, but also adequate food, clean water, clothing, shelter, health care, education, and employment. In some polities, dominant groups target populations who differ in race, ethnicity, or religion from those in power. In some cases, the state not only fails to protect vulnerable populations from gross human rights violations, ethnic cleansing, or genocide, but is also complicit in perpetrating those crimes. According to the new paradigm, a state that is unable or unwilling to fulfill its foundational responsibilities forfeits the right to sovereignty over its territory and people—and its exemption from outside interference.

It was in this new context that the UN moved toward a broader definition of international responsibility for the protection of human rights. In June 1993, governmental and nongovernmental representatives from 171 nations met in Vienna at the UN-sponsored World Conference on Human Rights, where they endorsed the claim that "All human rights are universal, indivisible and interdependent and interrelated. . . . While the significance of national and regional particularities and various historical, cultural and religious backgrounds must be borne in mind, it is the duty of

States, regardless of their political, economic and cultural systems, to promote and protect all human rights and fundamental freedoms."[5] In theory, a state's failure to protect its citizens could warrant UN intervention.

After the Cold War, the disintegration of the Soviet Union, the splintering of states in Eastern Europe and Central Asia, and challenges to other states elsewhere produced millions of refugees and spawned untold numbers of armed insurgents who crossed borders and fomented instability. Because the UN's purpose is to "maintain international peace and security," and because massive human rights violations have ripple effects that affect entire regions, rectifying such wrongs increasingly was understood to be within the UN's purview.[6] However, UN actions did not keep pace with the expanded understanding of the organization's jurisdiction. Prioritizing their own domestic and foreign policy agendas, permanent members of the Security Council opposed measures that might have thwarted the genocide in Rwanda in 1994 and ethnic cleansing in Sudan's Darfur region in 2003–4. Continued pressure from nongovernmental organizations and human rights activists pushed the UN General Assembly to pass the 2005 R2P resolution, which allowed the international community to intervene if governments did not protect their citizens from gross human rights violations.[7] Supported by 150 countries, the R2P resolution upended an understanding of state sovereignty that had been one of the fundamental tenets of international law since the seventeenth century. In theory, deference to "state sovereignty" no longer could be used as an expedient to allow ethnic cleansing, genocide, or other crimes against humanity to proceed unhindered.

Once again, the reality was far more complicated. New principles of international intervention had been endorsed, but enforcement remained problematic. Governments were reluctant to set precedents that might be used against them in the future, and powerful members of the Security Council rarely committed the resources or personnel necessary to implement the R2P resolution. If a culpable state opposed external involvement, outside powers ordinarily persisted only if their own interests were at stake. Action was likely solely in the case of weak states or those without powerful allies on the Security Council—that is, in states that could not effectively challenge foreign intervention.

As calls for multilateral diplomacy evolved into appeals for military intervention under the mantle of responsibility to protect, there was sharp disagreement over the motives of those intervening, the means they employed, and the nature of the outcomes, that is, whether intervention provided protection for civilians or only increased their insecurity. Some governments reacted to international scrutiny by invoking the old principle of national sovereignty. Others charged that international human rights laws were based on Western capitalist norms that give primacy to the rights of individuals over those of society and thus were not applicable to their cultures or conditions. They argued that Western claims regarding the universality of their human rights definitions were yet another example of cultural imperialism and neocolonialism. Still others claimed that humanitarian intervention was simply a guise for Western powers' pursuit of their own economic or strategic objectives, and they warned that Western countries were attempting to recolonize the Global South. In countries and regions affected by conflict, governments and citizens were divided on the merits of outside intervention, whether by international organizations, neighboring states, or extracontinental powers. Many remained skeptical of outsiders' motives and their capacity to bring peace, even when their actions were part of an approved multilateral initiative.

Similar problems have plagued the International Criminal Court (ICC), which was established in 2002 to investigate and prosecute individuals believed to have engaged in war crimes, crimes against humanity, or genocide. Just as the UN Security Council may not intervene without a host country's consent unless the government has failed to protect its citizens from gross human rights violations, the ICC is authorized to act against alleged human rights abusers only if their national governments and courts are unable or unwilling to do so. However, the ICC's jurisdiction is far from universal. The international court may investigate alleged crimes in countries that have ratified the ICC treaty, in cases referred to it by the UN Security Council, or when the ICC prosecutor opens a case of his or her own volition. Although 123 UN member states had ratified the ICC treaty by 2017, 70 others had not. Among the holdouts were three permanent members of the UN Security Council that have veto-wielding powers: the United States, China, and Russia. These countries refused to recognize the ICC's jurisdiction over their own citizens, and they also shielded their allies from the court's authority. ICC member states have also undermined ICC operations. Although they are technically obliged to comply with the court's decisions, the ICC has no police or military to enforce summonses or arrest warrants. As a result, alleged perpetrators with powerful allies avoid prosecution, while those without connections are more likely to be held accountable.

Like advocates of R2P, the ICC has been accused of bias against African countries and norms. The court is authorized to investigate human rights abuses worldwide, but nine of the ten investigations it conducted between 2002 and 2017 and all of its indictments, prosecutions, and convictions involved African political and military figures. As a result, some critics have charged that the ICC is simply another neocolonial institution. Criticism from the African Union has been especially sharp, with some African leaders urging AU member states to withdraw from the international court—a step that Burundi took in 2017. However, other African leaders and many civil society organizations have voiced strong support for the court and urged it to expand its protection of African civilians rather than to reduce it. The degree to which the ICC can promote equal justice in an unequal international order remains an open question.

Paradigm 2: The War on Terror

If the roots of the first paradigm can be traced to post–World War II understandings of the need for peace, justice, and human rights to ensure a stable international order, the seeds of the second paradigm can be found in the Cold War struggle between capitalism and communism. From the outset, the United States recognized the power of religion as a weapon against its atheistic opponents, and it mobilized conservative religious groups to fight the communist menace. In Europe, it supported Christian parties and organizations that opposed the Italian, Greek, and French communist parties that had gained strength during World War II and its aftermath. In the Middle East, it backed conservative Muslim organizations and regimes that sought to suppress both communism and radical nationalism. When the pro-Western Shah of Iran was overthrown in January 1979 and replaced by militants who embraced the Shi'a branch of Islam, Washington rallied extremists in the rival Sunni branch to counter Iran's growing prominence.[8] Saudi Arabia, a staunch US ally, promoter of fundamentalist Sunni teachings, and competitor with Iran for regional dominance, joined the United States in its patronage of Sunni militants.

Most relevant for this study is the CIA-led multinational coalition that recruited, trained, armed, and financed Sunni militants from all corners of the globe to challenge the decade-long Soviet occupation of Afghanistan (1979–89). After ousting the Soviets from Afghanistan, the fighters dispersed to their home countries, where they founded new organizations and spearheaded insurgencies, primarily against Muslim states they deemed impious. These Soviet-Afghan War veterans played prominent roles in most of the extremist groups that emerged in Africa and the Middle East in the decades that followed. A brief summary of that history provides the context for the war on terror.

In 1978, a military coup in Afghanistan installed a communist government that was sympathetic to Moscow. It was also brutal, internally divided, and challenged by popular opposition, including an Islamist-backed Sunni insurgency. Faced with instability on its borders, the Soviet Union had two fundamental concerns: first, that the Afghan government would fall and that a new regime would ally with US interests; and second, that the Islamist-backed insurgency in Afghanistan might stimulate similar uprisings in the Soviet republics of Central Asia, which included large Muslim populations. To bolster the Kabul regime, Moscow invaded Afghanistan in December 1979, beginning an occupation that would result in a decade-long war. Determined to secure US dominance over Indian Ocean communication lines and the oil-rich countries of the Persian Gulf, the United States mobilized an international coalition to challenge the Soviet Union in Afghanistan and undermine its authority in adjacent Soviet republics.

For the duration of the ten-year war, the United States and its allies recruited tens of thousands of Muslim fighters from Africa, Asia, Europe, and North America to combat the Soviet occupation. The anti-Soviet recruits, many of whom were inspired by Saudi Arabia's fundamentalist teachings, referred to themselves as *mujahideen*—those who struggle to defend the Islamic faith. Spearheaded by the CIA, the endeavor was largely funded by the United States and Saudi Arabia. The CIA provided the militants with sophisticated weapons, including shoulder-fired, heat-seeking Stinger antiaircraft missiles that easily circumvented Soviet decoy flares.[9] The CIA and the US Army, Navy, and Air Force Special Operations Forces, along with the UK's Special Air Service, trained and instructed Pakistani officers and mujahideen leaders in guerrilla and terrorist tactics. Pakistan's intelligence services trained the bulk of the mujahideen forces on the ground and provided critical logistical, intelligence, and military support, while France, Israel, Egypt, and Morocco also helped train and arm the anti-Soviet forces. Iran played a significant but independent role, training both Shi'ite and Sunni militias.

The CIA and Pakistani intelligence countered Iran's support for Shi'ite militants in Afghanistan by bolstering Sunni organizations such as that of Osama bin Laden, a wealthy Saudi of Yemeni descent whose family had close ties to the ruling Saudi dynasty and had made its fortune in business and finance. Bin Laden's organization raised funds, recruited, and provided services for the mujahideen, including a hostel for Algerian, Egyptian, Saudi, and other fighters in Pakistan and a camp in Afghanistan. After the Soviet withdrawal from Afghanistan in 1989, some Afghan militants—primarily religious students and mujahideen fighters—reconstituted themselves as the Taliban (Seekers of the Truth) and fought regional warlords and other mujahideen factions for political control. By 1996, the Taliban had seized most of the country, imposing law and order in areas rife with corruption, banditry, and the drug trade. Turning to opium and heroin to finance their operations, the Taliban employed brutal methods to impose their own interpretation of Islamic law.

After the Soviet departure, the foreign fighters carried their terror tactics and sophisticated weapons to new battlegrounds around the globe. Soviet-Afghan War veterans were at the forefront of guerrilla insurgencies in Algeria, Bosnia and Herzegovina, Egypt, Gaza, Kashmir, the Philippines, the West Bank, and Yemen. They engaged in terrorist activities in Kenya, Sudan, Tanzania, France, and the United States. CIA-backed drug lords and allies, including Osama bin Laden, funded the new networks, joined by Muslim banks and charities.

One of the most significant terrorist networks was al-Qaeda (The Base), which was established from the core of fighters and other volunteers who had passed through Osama bin Laden's camps. Founded in 1989 with bin Laden as its primary organizer and patron, al-Qaeda advocated jihad against apostate Muslim regimes and their supporters worldwide.[10] Although bin Laden considered Saddam Hussein's secular Arab nationalist regime in Iraq to be apostate, he opposed military intervention by the US-led coalition during the First Gulf War (1990–91); he also denounced the Saudi government's decision to allow hundreds of thousands of US and allied troops to be stationed in Saudi Arabia, which was home to the holy cities of Mecca and Medina. The Saudi government responded by expelling bin Laden from the country and, eventually, revoking his citizenship. When the Gulf War ended, the United States retained its military bases and thousands of troops on the Arabian Peninsula. The removal of US military forces from the holy land was one of al-Qaeda's primary objectives. As a result, the United States—bin Laden's onetime ally—would become an important al-Qaeda target.

The First Gulf War also precipitated the 1991 transfer of al-Qaeda's headquarters and training camps to Sudan. From there the organization launched a network of cells and allied organizations that radiated into the Greater Horn of Africa, a geographic region that included Burundi, Djibouti, Eritrea, Ethiopia, Kenya, Rwanda, Somalia, Sudan, Tanzania, and Uganda. In May 1996, under pressure from the United States, Saudi Arabia, and the UN Security Council, the Sudanese government asked bin Laden to leave. He moved al-Qaeda's headquarters back to Afghanistan, where the organization allied with the Taliban. Blaming the United States for his ejection from Sudan, bin Laden focused new attention on this distant enemy. In August 1996 he issued a declaration of jihad against US military forces in Saudi Arabia and called on all Muslims to expel Americans and Israelis from Muslim lands.

Al-Qaeda's September 2001 attacks on the World Trade Center in New York City and the Pentagon in Washington, DC, were preceded by a number of other assaults against US citizens and infrastructure. These included the 1993 World Trade Center bombing as well as thwarted attacks on New York City bridges and tunnels, the UN headquarters, and the local office of the Federal Bureau of Investigation (FBI); the 1998 bombings of US embassies in Kenya and Tanzania; a failed attempt in 1999 to blow up Los Angeles International Airport; and in 2000, a successful attack on the US Navy destroyer *USS Cole*, which was docked in Yemen. Although al-Qaeda's September 2001 attacks opened a new chapter in the war on terror, the United States had been fighting the terrorist organizations it had helped to create since the mid-1990s.

Misconceptions about Islam

If the role of the United States and its allies in fomenting extremist violence is frequently overlooked, the role of Islam in abetting terrorism is often misunderstood. The US-led war on terror has inspired or reinforced many misconceptions about Islam, a religion that originated on the Arabian Peninsula in the seventh century and has spread around the world since then. The emergence of modern political movements operating under Islam's banner has led to considerable debate over appropriate ways to distinguish these movements and the terminology used to describe them. The lack of authoritative consensus has resulted in much confusion. Islamism, a twentieth-century ideology and movement pertaining to social, political, and religious life, has been confounded with Islamic fundamentalism, which pertains to religious doctrine. Similarly, political Islam—one aspect of Islamism—is often conflated with political terrorism, actions that are embraced by only a small minority of Muslims and whose legitimacy is widely challenged in the world Muslim community. Finally, the Arabic word *jihad* is frequently translated as "holy war" and associated with death by the sword. In Islam, however, there are three meanings of jihad, two of them nonviolent. Although experts continue to debate the precise meaning of these terms, this study has adopted the following definitions as the most appropriate.[11]

Islam is the name of a world religion, derived from the Arabic word *salema*, which means peace, purity, submission, and obedience. The name implies submission to Allah's will and obedience to his law. The two main branches of Islam, Sunni and Shi'a, agree on its five pillars: (1) faith in a monotheistic deity, Allah, whose messenger is Muhammad; (2) engaging in prayers five times daily; (3) giving alms to the poor; (4) fasting during the holy month of Ramadan; and (5) making a pilgrimage to Mecca at least once, if physically and financially able.

Islamic fundamentalism refers to Islamic beliefs that reject religious innovation or adaptation in response to new circumstances. Practitioners of fundamentalism, more generally, advocate a return to basic religious principles and the strict application of religious law. Fundamentalism often emerges as a reaction to liberalizing trends within a religion or to secularization in the broader society. It represents a struggle between tendencies within a given religion, rather than a clash between religions. The descriptor "religious fundamentalism" was first associated with late nineteenth-century Protestant Christians in the United States who embraced a literal interpretation of the Bible. Like their Christian counterparts, Islamic fundamentalists promote strict observance of their religion's basic tenets and laws. Their movements have gained strength in the face of the religious innovation, Westernization, and secularization that followed the establishment of European colonialism in the twentieth century and globalization in the twenty-first. The vast majority of Islamic fundamentalists are law-abiding and oppose violent jihad, focusing instead on the ethical, moral, and personal aspects of jihad (see below). They believe that an Islamic state will emerge from a Muslim community that has been purified from within through preaching and proselytizing and that such a state cannot be established through political or armed struggle.

Islamism refers to a social, political, and religious ideology and movement that emerged in response to European colonialism and the social instability wrought by encounters with the West. Its adherents hold that Islamic principles should serve as the basis of the social, political, and legal order and guide the personal lives of individual Muslims. Often led by intellectuals rather than clergy members, Islamist movements focus on social and political change rather than on religious doctrine. Moderate Islamists work within established institutions and political processes to pursue social and political reforms that, they hope, will result in states that are premised on Islamic law and built from the bottom up. Radical Islamists strive to monopolize political power so that they can construct Islamic states from the top down. Islamists do not reject all aspects of Western culture, and they may even embrace Western education and technology as useful tools for the construction of Islamic states. Islamists, in contrast to jihadis (defined below), reject the use of violence to achieve their objectives.

Political Islam is sometimes used synonymously with Islamism, even though it constitutes only one aspect of the social, political, and religious ideology and movement. Although political Islam employs the language of religion, it represents a political rather than a religious response to Westernization. Its adherents do not reject modernity, but they repudiate a particular brand of modernity. They refute the claim that the Western definition of modernity is a universal one and embrace an Islamist variant in its place.

Jihad means effort or struggle. A person who engages in jihad is a *mujahid* (plural, *mujahideen*). Jihad has three interrelated meanings: first, the inner spiritual struggle to live righteously, as a good Muslim; second, the struggle to build and purify the Muslim community; and third, the struggle to defend the Islamic faith from outsiders, with force if necessary. The first meaning, which refers to a personal spiritual struggle, constitutes the greater jihad. The second and third meanings, which focus on the outside world, comprise the lesser jihad. Historically, jihad has been understood first and foremost as an inner struggle that begins with the self and extends outward to the broader society. Those who undertake such struggle believe that social and political reforms are best achieved through preaching, proselytizing, and mobilizing the masses to effect change from the bottom up. Engaging in the lesser jihad is held to be a collective duty of the Muslim community, as determined situationally by religious and legal authorities, rather than a permanent personal duty as determined by individuals or self-appointed preachers.

Since the onset of the war on terror, Western observers have frequently collapsed all forms of jihad into one, erroneously defined as a "holy war" against nonbelievers. The concept of holy war originated among Christians in medieval Europe to justify crusades against Muslims; it has no direct counterpart in mainstream Islamic thought. Jihad is not one of the five pillars of Islam and thus is not a practice that is essential to Muslim identity.

Jihadism refers to a minority insurgent movement that broke from Islamism and employs violence in the name of religion. Jihadism emerged in the context of severe social, political, and economic inequalities, and in many cases, political persecution. The movement has primarily attracted young men who feel alienated from mainstream society. Its adherents reject the traditional interpretation of the lesser jihad as a collective struggle of the Muslim community, determined by officially recognized religious and legal authorities, and define it instead as a personal one, to be determined by each individual as he or she sees fit or by self-described clerics. From the early 1970s until the mid-1990s, jihadis generally targeted local secular and Muslim regimes that they deemed impure (the "near enemy"), with the goal of overthrowing them and Islamizing state and society from the top down. However, from the mid-1990s, a small minority began to focus on distant impious or non-Muslim regimes (the "far enemy"), heralding the emergence of global jihad.

Western commentators often overlook these distinctions, failing to differentiate between jihadist factions and frequently merging Islamism and jihadism under the misleading rubric of "Islamic terrorism." Some erroneously deem both movements a threat to Western societies and argue that both must be opposed in an open-ended war on terror and an effort to restructure the Muslim world. Policies based on this misunderstanding have tended to result in increased hostility and an even greater threat to the West.

A *jihadi* is a militant Muslim activist who opposes the secular sociopolitical order at home, and Westernization and globalization more broadly, and who engages in armed struggle to establish an Islamic state. The term is not synonymous with *mujahid,* which refers to a person engaged in any of the three forms of jihad. The term jihadi (*jihadist*, adjective) was coined in the early twenty-first century by militants who self-identified as such. Jihadis who focus on local struggles against purportedly impious Muslim or secular regimes constitute the majority of this minority faction, while those who focus on distant or non-Muslim regimes—the so-called global jihadis—are a tiny minority of the minority movement.

Islamic terrorism is a commonly used but misleading term that associates religious doctrine with terrorist activity. Islamic fundamentalism, radical Islamism, and political Islam are not equivalent to Islamic terrorism. Muslims who engage in terrorism and claim religious justification for these activities constitute a minuscule minority of Muslims worldwide, and their actions are strongly condemned by the majority. Although these violent extremists deploy the language and symbols of religion to justify their actions, their turn to terrorism was often inspired by social, political, and economic grievances rather than by religious beliefs. This study rejects the use of the term Islamic terrorism as both inaccurate and dangerous. Violence that targets civilians for political reasons is described as "violent extremism" or simply "terrorism." In some instances, "Muslim extremist" is used to distinguish violent actors who claim to be operating on behalf of their Islamic faith from other violent actors.

Conclusion

Political, economic, and social instability in the late twentieth and early twenty-first centuries brought renewed attention to the African continent. Employing new justifications for their actions, foreign powers and multilateral institutions challenged the centuries-old principle of national sovereignty and claimed the right to intervene to restore stability, protect civilian lives, and combat terrorism. Although some of these interventions reestablished law and order and saved civilian lives, others left conflicts unresolved and laid the groundwork for future strife. Misinterpretations and distortions of Islam, which influenced external actions in the war on terror, often had devastating consequences for civilians. Chapter 3 introduces the major foreign actors involved in African conflicts after the Cold War, including extracontinental powers, neighboring states, multilateral state-based organizations, and nonstate actors associated with international terrorist networks.

Suggested Reading

Suggested readings relevant to specific countries follow chapters 4–11. The works listed below provide general overviews or are pertinent to multiple African countries.

African economic crises that began in the 1970s sparked many of the continent's political crises. The following works provide contrasting views of the origins of these crises and their solutions. For an insider's critique of the role of the IMF, the World Bank, and the World Trade Organization in promoting global inequality, see Joseph E. Stiglitz, *Globalization and Its Discontents* (New York: W. W. Norton, 2002). Nicolas van de Walle, *African Economies and the Politics of Permanent Crisis, 1979–1999* (New York: Cambridge University Press, 2001), argues that the internal dynamics of neopatrimonial African states rather than external impositions were primarily responsible for the postcolonial economic crises. David Sahn and colleagues contend that the policies mandated by international financial institutions did not harm the African poor, but neither were they sufficient to reduce poverty. See David E. Sahn, ed., *Economic Reform and the Poor in Africa* (New York: Oxford University Press, 1996); and David E. Sahn, Paul A. Dorosh, and Stephen D. Younger, *Structural Adjustment Reconsidered: Economic Policy and Poverty in Africa* (New York: Cambridge University Press, 1997). Léonce Ndikumana and James K. Boyce, *Africa's Odious Debts: How Foreign Loans and Capital Flight Bled a Continent* (London: Zed, 2011), focuses on capital flight from Africa and the role of foreign debt in the current crises.

Post–Cold War political crises in African states are considered from diverse perspectives. Books on the failure of state institutions written from Western political science perspectives include I. William Zartman, ed., *Collapsed States: The Disintegration and Restoration of Legitimate Authority* (Boulder, CO: Lynne Rienner, 1995); Robert I. Rotberg, *When States Fail: Causes and Consequences* (Princeton, NJ: Princeton University Press, 2004); and Robert H. Bates, *When Things Fell Apart: State Failure in Late-Century Africa* (New York: Cambridge University Press, 2008). A critique of Western theories of weak, fragile, troubled, failed, and collapsed African states and the ways in which Western powers have responded can be found in Charles T. Call, "The Fallacy of the 'Failed State,'" *Third World Quarterly* 29, no. 8 (2008): 1491–1507. Diverse views are offered in the collection edited by Leonardo A. Villalón and Phillip A.

Huxtable, *The African State at a Critical Juncture: Between Disintegration and Reconfiguration* (Boulder, CO: Lynne Rienner, 1998).

Jean-François Bayart, Stephen Ellis, and Béatrice Hibou, *The Criminalization of the State in Africa* (Bloomington: Indiana University Press, 1999), examines the role of the state in the plunder of resources, privatization of armies and state institutions, and involvement in global criminal networks. Patrick Chabal and Jean-Pascal Daloz, *Africa Works: Disorder as Political Instrument* (Bloomington: Indiana University Press, 1999), shows how African political actors have manipulated ethnic and regional tensions and used the ensuing disorder to obtain and maintain power. William Reno, *Warlord Politics and African States* (Boulder, CO: Lynne Rienner, 1998), considers the destruction of bureaucratic state structures of revenue collection, policing, and provision of social services in post–Cold War Africa and their replacement by warlords whose goal is to plunder economic resources rather than to mobilize citizens. Pierre Englebert, *Africa: Unity, Sovereignty, and Sorrow* (Boulder, CO: Lynne Rienner, 2009), argues that states have failed to protect their citizens yet continue to endure because they offer benefits to regional and national elites.

A number of works provide a deeper understanding of post–Cold War conflicts in Africa. Mary Kaldor, *New and Old Wars: Organized Violence in a Global Era* (Stanford, CA: Stanford University Press, 1999), explores the causes of increased ethnic violence in the 1990s and the reasons the international community failed to stop it. William Reno, *Warfare in Independent Africa* (New York: Cambridge University Press, 2011), focuses on African internal conflicts, including anticolonial movements, reformist rebellions, and warlord-led insurgencies. David Kilcullen, *The Accidental Guerrilla: Fighting Small Wars in the Midst of a Big One* (New York: Oxford University Press, 2009), offers an overview of the interactions of local insurgencies, international movements, and the global war on terror. Several edited collections examine diverse insurgencies and civil wars. Paul D. Williams, *War and Conflict in Africa*, 2nd ed. (Malden, MA: Polity, 2016), assesses the causes and consequences of more than 600 armed conflicts in Africa from 1990 to 2015, including the impact of outside intervention. See also Christopher Clapham, ed., *African Guerrillas* (Bloomington: Indiana University Press, 1998); Morten Bøås and Kevin C. Dunn, eds., *African Guerrillas: Raging against the Machine* (Boulder, CO: Lynne Rienner, 2007); Morten Bøås and Kevin C. Dunn, eds., *Africa's Insurgents: Navigating an Evolving Landscape* (Boulder, CO:

Lynne Rienner, 2017); Paul Richards, ed., *No Peace, No War: An Anthropology of Contemporary Armed Conflicts* (Athens: Ohio University Press, 2005); and Preben Kaarsholm, ed., *Violence, Political Culture and Development in Africa* (Athens: Ohio University Press, 2006).

Several works examine African conflicts and peace agreements. Two companion volumes edited by Alfred Nhema and Paul Tiyambe Zeleza examine the causes of and possible solutions to African conflicts from African perspectives: *The Roots of African Conflicts* and *The Resolution of African Conflicts* (Athens: Ohio University Press, 2008). Adebayo Oyebade and Abiodun Alao, eds., *Africa after the Cold War: The Changing Perspectives on Security* (Trenton, NJ: Africa World Press, 1998), assesses civil conflicts, economic crises, and environmental degradation as the primary threats to post–Cold War African security. Grace Maina and Erik Melander, eds., *Peace Agreements and Durable Peace in Africa* (Scottsville, South Africa: University of KwaZulu-Natal Press, 2016), offers a framework for evaluating prospects for a successful accord. Case studies for Côte d'Ivoire, the DRC, Somalia, and Sudan are especially relevant. Séverine Autesserre, *Peaceland: Conflict Resolution and the Everyday Politics of International Intervention* (New York: Cambridge University Press, 2014), explains why international peace interventions often fail, scrutinizing the modes of thought and action that prevent foreign interveners from thinking outside the box. A sharp assessment of past failures and future prospects for democracy can be found in Nic Cheeseman, *Democracy in Africa: Successes, Failures, and the Struggle for Political Reform* (New York: Cambridge University Press, 2015).

The post–World War II emphasis on human rights and humanitarian intervention is the focus of several works. Samantha Power, *A Problem from Hell: America and the Age of Genocide* (New York: Basic Books, 2002), analyzes six twentieth-century genocides and the US government's failure to stop them. This study has been pivotal to recent debates on international law and human rights policies and had an important political impact on the Obama administration. Samuel Moyn, *The Last Utopia: Human Rights in History* (Cambridge, MA: Harvard University Press, 2010), contends that post-1960s discontent with regimes established on the basis of utopian and anticolonial ideologies paved the way for human rights as a justification for international actions that challenged state sovereignty. Timothy Nunan, *Humanitarian Invasion: Global Development in Cold War Afghanistan* (New York: Cambridge University

Press, 2016), argues that foreign intervention in Afghanistan during the Cold War and its aftermath became the model for future humanitarian interventions that destabilized societies and undermined national sovereignty in the Global South. Alex de Waal, "Writing Human Rights and Getting It Wrong," *Boston Review*, June 6, 2016, casts a critical eye on humanitarian intervention lobbies, particularly those that focused on Somalia, Sudan, and Rwanda. He argues that their judgments were often ill-informed and reduced complex situations to straightforward narratives of heroes and villains; as a result, the military interventions they promoted sometimes did more harm than good. Carrie Booth Walling and Susan Waltz's website, Human Rights Advocacy and the History of International Human Rights Standards (http://humanrightshistory. umich.edu/). It is especially useful for teachers, students, researchers, and advocates.

A number of works examine the reshaping of international legal principles and the struggle for global accountability. Two are central to discussions of the responsibility to protect: Francis M. Deng, Sadikiel Kimaro, Terrence Lyons, Donald Rothchild, and I. William Zartman, *Sovereignty as Responsibility: Conflict Management in Africa* (Washington, DC: Brookings Institution, 1996); and Francis M. Deng, "From 'Sovereignty as Responsibility' to the Responsibility to Protect," *Global Responsibility to Protect* 2, no. 4 (2010): 353–70. Elizabeth Borgwardt, *A New Deal for the World: America's Vision for Human Rights* (Cambridge, MA: Harvard University Press, 2005), examines the role of New Deal visionaries in constructing the postwar international order that eroded the primacy of national sovereignty and strengthened the position of human rights.

Other works critique the new human rights/R2P discourse and international actions based on its principles. Robert Meister, *After Evil: A Politics of Human Rights* (New York: Columbia University Press, 2011), argues that the democratic capitalist world has monopolized the concept of "human rights," producing a version that does not challenge the structural inequalities that underlie poverty and oppression, and has used the responsibility to protect paradigm to justify militaristic ventures. Alex J. Bellamy and Paul D. Williams, "The New Politics of Protection? Côte d'Ivoire, Libya and the Responsibility to Protect," *International Affairs* 87, no. 4 (July 2011): 825–50, explores the role of external powers and stakeholders in determining which civilians are to be protected. A critical assessment of the International Criminal Court and its uneven record in advancing global accountability can be found in David Bosco, *Rough Justice: The International Criminal Court in a World of Power Politics* (New York: Oxford University Press, 2014).

Two important works focus on the UN's role in humanitarian intervention: Norrie MacQueen, *Humanitarian Intervention and the United Nations* (Edinburgh: Edinburgh University Press, 2011), provides an overview of UN interventions in various world regions, including sub-Saharan Africa, and assesses their impact and moral implications. Carrie Booth Walling, *All Necessary Measures: The United Nations and Humanitarian Intervention* (Philadelphia: University of Pennsylvania Press, 2013), investigates the ways in which human rights concerns have altered Security Council attitudes toward state sovereignty and explains the variation in UN response to violations.

The Cold War roots of international terrorist movements associated with Islam are explored in several texts. Three works investigate the CIA's role in recruiting, training, and financing Muslim fighters to wage war against Soviet forces in Afghanistan; they also explore how Soviet-Afghan War veterans subsequently established worldwide terrorist networks, including al-Qaeda and its spinoff, the Islamic State. See John K. Cooley, *Unholy Wars: Afghanistan, America and International Terrorism*, 3rd ed. (Sterling, VA: Pluto Press, 2002); Steve Coll, *Ghost Wars: The Secret History of the CIA, Afghanistan, and Bin Laden, from the Soviet Invasion to September 10, 2001* (New York: Penguin, 2004); and Mahmood Mamdani, *Good Muslim, Bad Muslim: America, the Cold War and the Roots of Terror* (New York: Pantheon, 2004). Jean-Pierre Filiu, *From Deep State to Islamic State: The Arab Counter-Revolution and Its Jihadi Legacy* (New York: Oxford University Press, 2015), exposes the ways in which Arab autocracies quashed the Arab Spring uprisings by unleashing internal security, intelligence, and military forces, as well as street gangs and violent extremists. He argues that these actions opened the door to the Islamic State. The origins of the Islamic State are also examined in Joby Warrick, *Black Flags: The Rise of ISIS* (New York: Doubleday, 2015), which contends that the policies of the George W. Bush and Barack Obama administrations aided in the organization's emergence and expansion.

Conceptions and misconceptions about Islamic fundamentalism, Islamism, and jihad are examined in a number of works. They include International Crisis Group, *Understanding Islamism*, Middle East/

North Africa Report 37 (Cairo/Brussels: International Crisis Group, 2005); Mamdani, *Good Muslim, Bad Muslim* (mentioned previously); and Martin Kramer, "Coming to Terms: Fundamentalists or Islamists?" *Middle East Quarterly* 10, no. 2 (Spring 2003): 65–77. Richard C. Martin and Abbas Barzegar, eds., *Islamism: Contested Perspectives on Political Islam* (Stanford, CA: Stanford University Press, 2009), presents diverse interpretations of Islamism by Muslim and non-Muslim intellectuals. Juan Cole, *Engaging the Muslim World* (New York: Palgrave Macmillan, 2009), dispels misconceptions about various movements within Islam, distinguishing between extremists and Islamic fundamentalists who reject violence. John L. Esposito, *Unholy War: Terror in the Name of Islam* (New York: Oxford University Press, 2002), contrasts the teachings of the Qur'an with their manipulation by a violent minority and examines the political roots of anti-Americanism in the Muslim world. Contributors to Roel Meijer's edited collection, *Global Salafism: Islam's New Religious Movement* (London: Hurst, 2009), explore commonalities and differences among various strands of Salafism and examine tensions between local and global goals. Fawaz A. Gerges, *The Far Enemy: Why Jihad Went Global*, 2nd ed. (New York: Cambridge University Press, 2009), argues that the majority of jihadis strive to transform or overthrow local regimes in the Muslim world and that only a small minority target the West. He also examines the reasons that global jihadism emerged in the late 1990s and analyzes the split in the jihadist movement that ensued. The United Nations Development Programme, *Journey to Extremism in Africa: Drivers, Incentives and the Tipping Point for Recruitment* (New York: UNDP, 2017), considers economic marginalization, low levels of education, absence of good governance, and security sector abuse as factors driving extremism, with religious knowledge often serving as a deterrent.

Two French scholars, Gilles Kepel and Olivier Roy, have engaged in a heated public debate about the origins of the violent extremism associated with contemporary jihadist movements. Gilles Kepel, *Jihad: The Trail of Political Islam* (Cambridge, MA: Harvard University Press, 2002), provides an overview of Islamist movements in the twentieth century, focusing especially on Iran, Saudi Arabia, Algeria, Egypt, and Afghanistan. Kepel argues that in the late 1990s, Islamist movements split into a majority faction that favored Muslim democracy and a small minority that engaged in terrorist attacks to promote their goals. Gilles Kepel, *The War for Muslim Minds: Islam and the West* (Cambridge, MA: Harvard

University Press, 2004), tracks the origins of global jihad to the Soviet-Afghan War and argues that al-Qaeda's ideology emerged both from Islam's strict Salafist and Wahhabi traditions, which advocate abstention from worldly affairs, and from the more political Muslim Brotherhood, whose goal is to establish an Islamic state. Gilles Kepel, with Antoine Jardin, *Terror in France: The Rise of Jihad in the West* (Princeton, NJ: Princeton University Press, 2017), examines Muslim youth who were radicalized in the West and targeted Western populations. Olivier Roy, *Globalized Islam: The Search for a New Ummah* (New York: Columbia University Press, 2004), disputes the significance of conservative Islamic traditions and instead explains violent jihad as a response to social, political, and economic changes, one that is politically rather than religiously inspired. Roy argues that Islam has not been radicalized, but rather that radicalism has been Islamized. Alienated youth who had not previously been religious turned to a distorted variant of Islam for meaning, identity, and respect, just as earlier generations had embraced other radical ideologies; the result is the nihilistic rejection of a society that has rejected them. In the West, these youths have been radicalized not by established religious scholars and mosques, but in prisons—where they often serve time for petty crime—and by self-proclaimed authorities on the internet. Roy's widely quoted challenge to Kepel's thesis appears in Olivier Roy, "Le djihadisme est une révolte générationnelle et nihiliste," *Le Monde*, November 24, 2015.

3

Identifying the Actors

Who Intervened and Why

POLITICAL, ECONOMIC, AND social instability in Africa after the Cold War resulted in new waves of foreign intervention. Global, regional, and subregional state-based organizations were central to war-making and peace-building processes, and nonstate actors associated with international terrorist networks played key roles in some conflicts. During the periods of decolonization and the Cold War, foreign states intervened in African affairs unilaterally or in collaboration with other states. Former imperial powers and new Cold War powers were the most significant sources of external intervention. After the Cold War, unilateral engagement continued. Onetime imperial and Cold War powers continued to intercede in their historical spheres of interest; Middle Eastern states and organizations took a special interest in North Africa; and African countries intervened in their neighbors' affairs. However, multilateral intervention by organized groups of states (intergovernmental organizations) and transnational networks of nonstate actors grew increasingly important.

This chapter introduces the major foreign actors involved in African conflicts after the Cold War, including nation-states on other continents, neighboring African countries, multilateral state-based organizations, and nonstate actors associated with international terrorist networks. It distinguishes the outside contestants in decolonization and Cold War conflicts from those involved in their aftermath, and it establishes a framework for understanding the interests and motivations of the foreign actors featured in the regional case studies.

During the post–Cold War period, Western nations continued to implicate themselves in African affairs. France and the United Kingdom intervened in their former colonies, while the United States focused on its former Cold War allies and on countries deemed strategic in the war on terror. In some instances, Western powers and their allies interceded under the auspices of intergovernmental organizations such as the UN, NATO, or the EU.[1] In other cases, they took unilateral action. Middle powers like the Nordic states also played significant roles in multilateral peace negotiations and peacekeeping operations, and they often engaged in independent diplomatic initiatives.[2]

The other former Cold War powers, China and Russia, ordinarily opposed political and military intervention in the internal affairs of other nations—their immediate neighbors excepted. As permanent members of the UN Security Council, they frequently challenged Western-sponsored initiatives focusing on human rights and governance issues. Like other industrial states, China was particularly interested in regions that were rich in strategic natural resources. In exchange for guaranteed access to such resources, China invested heavily in African industries and infrastructure and turned a blind eye to human rights abuses, political repression, and corruption. However, China, like the West, recognized that its economic interests would be best served by peace and stability. In consequence, Beijing expanded its involvement in multilateral disaster relief, antipiracy, and counterterrorism operations. In 2016, it contributed more military personnel to UN peacekeeping operations than any other permanent member of the Security Council. It engaged in mediation and peacekeeping efforts in Sudan and South Sudan, where it had significant investments in oil production and infrastructure, and also in Mali, where its primary interests lay in the oil and uranium of neighboring countries. China also joined France, the United States, Italy, and Japan in establishing a military facility in Djibouti, which overlooks one of the world's most lucrative shipping lanes.

Russia, like China, viewed post–Cold War Africa as a new frontier of political and economic opportunity. Itself the target of Western economic sanctions, Moscow had no interest in critiquing its partners' domestic human rights abuses or international transgressions. It offered goods and services to countries sidelined by Western restrictions and used its power on the Security Council to oppose robust military interventions that would encroach on national sovereignty and promote Western interests. Critical of Western influence over peacekeeping structures and initiatives, Moscow also recognized that its participation provided it with an avenue toward increased global prominence. Although its personnel contributions to African peacekeeping missions have been relatively small, Russia has trained African peacekeepers for both UN and AU missions, and it has sought leadership roles in the UN peacekeeping headquarters in New York and in missions on the ground. In Africa, Moscow's military imprint is more evident in its substantive weapons trade: a major military supplier to African governments during the Cold War, Moscow has continued to expand its arms trade on the continent. It has also used its military connections to extend its influence in other arenas. Although Russia's commerce with Africa is still small relative to that of China, Europe, and the United States, it has increased dramatically since 2000. Like China, Russia has focused its investments on the energy and mining sectors and on infrastructure development.

Middle Eastern powers also intervened in Africa after the Cold War. Historically, Middle Eastern countries maintained strong political and cultural ties with North Africa, which was commonly considered part of the Arab World. During the post–Cold War period, a number of Middle Eastern nations intervened in North Africa and the Horn of Africa, acting unilaterally or through the intergovernmental Arab League. Most significant for this study, the Gulf states and Turkey provided important political, economic, and military support to established governments and their opponents during the Arab Spring uprisings and their aftermath.[3]

African states also implicated themselves in their neighbors' affairs through the UN, the AU, and subregional organizations, as well as unilaterally. Like other outside powers, they often had mixed motives: they sought to engender peace and stability but also to further their own aims and interests. In some cases, they backed the governments in power. In others, they supported warlords or rebel movements.[4] Somalia (chapter 4) was the subject of interference from Djibouti, Egypt, Eritrea, Ethiopia, Kenya, Libya, and Uganda, while the conflict in Sudan (chapter 5) sparked intervention by Chad, Eritrea, Ethiopia, Libya, and Uganda. Uganda and Zaire implicated themselves in Rwandan affairs before and after the 1994 genocide (chapter 6), while wars in Zaire's successor state, the Democratic Republic of Congo (chapter 7), engaged Angola, Burundi, Chad, Namibia, Rwanda, Sudan, Uganda, and Zimbabwe. In West Africa's Mano River region (chapters 8 and 9), the civil war in Liberia involved intervention by Burkina Faso, Côte d'Ivoire, Guinea, and Libya;

the related civil war in Sierra Leone implicated Liberia and Libya; and the ensuing civil war in Côte d'Ivoire involved Liberia and Burkina Faso. The Egyptian military intervened in Libya after the Arab Spring revolt (chapter 10). In Mali, the French-led intervention to counter a secessionist movement and jihadist insurgency was joined by Burkina Faso, Chad, Mauritania, and Niger, while the Boko Haram insurgency in Nigeria was challenged by armies from Benin, Cameroon, Chad, and Niger (chapter 11).

Some individual states played outsized roles in their own subregions and, in a few cases, wielded considerable influence continentwide. In particular, Nigeria in West Africa and South Africa in Southern Africa were notable for both their subregional and continental influence. In North, East, and Central Africa, no single nation could claim subregional dominance. However, Algeria and Egypt possessed considerable clout in North Africa. Kenya and Ethiopia carried significant weight in East African affairs, while Egypt also aspired to wider influence in the Greater Horn.[5] In Central Africa, the DRC was large in size and rich in minerals, but internal conflicts prevented it from assuming a leadership role.

Several intergovernmental organizations and nonstate actors played key roles in shaping the post–Cold War order in Africa. The most consequential included one global organization, the United Nations; four regional bodies, the Organization of African Unity, the African Union, the European Union, and the Arab League; and five subregional organizations, the Economic Community of West African States (ECOWAS), the Economic Community of Central African States (ECCAS), the International Conference on the Great Lakes Region (ICGLR), the Intergovernmental Authority on Development (IGAD), and the Southern African Development Community (SADC). The most significant nonstate actors were the international jihadist networks, al-Qaeda and the Islamic State, along with their African branches and affiliates. The composition, purpose, and interests of these organizations are described below.

Global Organization: The United Nations

Established in 1945 to promote international peace, security, and social progress, the United Nations is dominated by the nations that won World War II. The UN General Assembly includes representatives of all member states. However, its resolutions are not legally binding, and it possesses no enforcement powers. The UN Security Council comprises five veto-bearing permanent members (the United States, the United Kingdom, France, Russia, and China) and ten rotating members that serve two-year terms and have no veto power. The Security Council can impose sanctions and authorize military intervention. The United States, which pays the largest share of the organization's operating expenses, dominated UN structures throughout the Cold War, when the US agenda generally prevailed. Since the end of the Cold War, the Security Council has continued to promote a Western agenda, although its powers have been limited by Russia and China, which historically have opposed UN intervention in the internal affairs of member nations.

Two chapters of the UN Charter spell out the organization's role in the peaceful settlement of disputes and in peacekeeping and peace enforcement. Chapter VI permits the Security Council to investigate disputes that threaten international peace and security, to issue recommendations, and to monitor peace accords. The main parties to the dispute must consent to UN involvement. Under a Chapter VI mandate, a neutral UN force composed of troops from member states is stationed between warring parties that have endorsed a peace accord and empowered the UN to monitor it and maintain the peace. UN troops may use their weapons only if attacked or threatened with attack. They are not authorized to use force to protect civilians or to disarm parties to the dispute. They may not impose peace in the context of war. If war resumes, peacekeeping forces authorized under Chapter VI are generally withdrawn or their mandate is transformed into a Chapter VII peace enforcement mandate. Chapter VII of the UN Charter provides for UN intervention to maintain or restore peace, even in cases in which the main parties to the conflict have not acceded to UN involvement. Under this more robust mandate, UN troops are permitted to use force to counter threats to international peace and security even when peacekeepers are not directly threatened. They also may be authorized to protect civilians, humanitarian aid workers, and relief convoys, and to disarm and demobilize warring parties.

Because the UN Security Council determines which peacekeeping operations will be authorized and funded, the five permanent members wield enormous power. They generally choose to fund only those operations that support their interests and to end operations that oppose or no longer serve their interests. The three Western members fund nearly half the peacekeeping budget.[6] Therefore they exercise disproportionate control over the operations, using their financial clout to determine where UN missions are sent and for how long.

Because East and West often failed to agree, there were few UN peacekeeping missions during the Cold War. In its immediate aftermath, Western powers were more concerned about maintaining the peace in Europe—specifically in the Balkans—than in Africa, where Cold War dictators were left to fail and rival forces jockeyed for position in the resulting power vacuums. During the 1990s, the Security Council withdrew UN peacekeepers from Somalia in the face of a deepening crisis and from Rwanda in the midst of a genocide, while the growing conflict in Liberia was ignored. By the decade's end, however, the Security Council had begun to work with African regional and subregional organizations to secure peace in Sudan, the DRC, Liberia, Sierra Leone, and Côte d'Ivoire—all countries of considerable interest to the West, and in the case of Sudan, also to China. The UN provided significant funds for these operations, which in turn enabled it to influence the substance of the peace agreements and, to a lesser extent, their implementation.

A third chapter of the UN Charter provides for subregional and regional involvement in dispute settlement. Chapter VIII stipulates that if strife within or between countries threatens international peace and security, subregional and regional bodies are the most appropriate first responders. If one or more states cannot resolve a conflict or are not deemed neutral arbiters, the appropriate subregional organization is expected to respond. If those efforts fail, the continentwide regional organization is called upon. If the subregional or regional body lacks material resources or political will, the UN may intervene, often in collaboration with those organizations. No enforcement actions may be taken by subregional or regional bodies without UN Security Council authorization.

Regional Organizations

Organization of African Unity

During the first post–Cold War decade, the most important regional organization in Africa was the Organization of African Unity. Established in May 1963 by thirty-two independent African states, the OAU promoted national liberation in territories still under colonial or white minority rule and provided liberation movements with military, economic, and diplomatic support. For nearly four decades the organization served as an important voice for African emancipation. Many African states argued that the OAU should assume responsibility for conflict prevention and resolution on the continent, countering the great-power bias on the UN Security Council. However, the OAU Charter was the product of compromise, drafted under the conservative influence of Ethiopian emperor Haile Selassie and sensitive to the political realities of a divided continent. It prohibited the organization's interference in the internal affairs of member states. Moreover, unity among African states was both fragile and superficial. The OAU was marked by political, economic, religious, and personal rivalries, and the organization represented the interests of autocratic rulers more often than those of grassroots citizens. Because the organization did not possess enforcement powers, its resolutions had little effect beyond their moral appeal.

African Union

In July 2002 the OAU was succeeded by the African Union, an amalgam of the OAU and the African Economic Community, which was established in 1991 to promote African economic integration. Addressing deficiencies in the OAU mandate, the AU's mission is to integrate Africa politically and economically and to promote peace, security, stability, and sustainable development on the continent. In contrast to the OAU Charter, which supported the principle of noninterference in the internal affairs of member states, the AU's Constitutive Act permits the organization to take punitive action against member states that violate principles of democracy, good governance, and the rule of law. It may authorize military intervention in a member state if it determines that "war crimes, genocide and crimes against humanity" are being committed or if the state's actions threaten regional stability.[7] However, even the AU's strengthened mandate provides insufficient protection to victims of human rights abuses. The actions of corrupt or authoritarian regimes may fall outside the categories stipulated in the Constitutive Act, and governments that engage in human rights abuses are unlikely to support intervention in states with similar practices. The Constitutive Act authorizes the establishment of an African standby force composed of military, police, and civilian brigades from each of Africa's five subregions, which would be capable of rapid deployment to crisis areas. However, such a force was still in the formative stages in 2017. Other factors that weaken AU effectiveness include rivalry between Nigeria and South Africa and AU dependence on outside sources for funding. Many of the organization's peacekeeping missions are financed by extracontinental entities—most importantly, the UN, the EU, the United States, and France. Their financial clout gives these external powers undue control over AU missions and actions.

European Union

Established in 1958 to promote economic cooperation between European countries, the European Economic Community (EEC) was renamed the European Union in 1993, reflecting an expanded mission that embraced foreign policy and security, climate change and environment, and international development and migration. In 2017, the EU had twenty-eight members.[8] Strong historical and geographic links and rich natural resources have made Africa central to European concerns. The Joint Africa-EU Strategy, endorsed in 2007 by eighty African and European heads of state, highlighted areas of common interest, including peace and security, international development and migration, and democracy, good governance, and human rights. The EU has provided substantial funds to strengthen African conflict resolution, security, and counterterrorism capacities and for African-led peacekeeping operations, such as the AU mission in Somalia. Its financial role gives the European organization significant influence over African affairs and establishes yet another kind of Northern dominance. The EU has also contributed considerable sums to develop African capacities to impede the flow of refugees and other migrants to Europe, an effort that serves European, rather than African, interests.

Arab League

Established in 1945 by Egypt, Iraq, Lebanon, Saudi Arabia, Syria, Transjordan, and Yemen, the League of Arab States, or Arab League, was a product of the pan-Arab nationalist movement that rose in response to Ottoman and European rule in the nineteenth and twentieth centuries. The League's vision also harkened back to the Islamic caliphates established by Muhammad and his successors, which, during the seventh and eighth centuries, united all Muslims in a single political entity. The organization aspired to promote collaboration between its member states, to protect their independence and sovereignty, and to advance Arab interests more generally. It opposed the violent settlement of disputes between members and often mediated in regional conflicts. However, it had no mechanism to enforce compliance with its resolutions, and only member states that approved the resolutions were bound to adhere to them. As a result, actions taken in the name of the Arab League were often motivated by the interests of particular member states, which financed and spearheaded the operations. In fact, Arab unity was more a hope than a reality. The Arab world, like other invented communities, was torn by rivalries—political, economic, religious, and personal. Member states' divergent interests often resulted in paralysis in the face of regional conflicts. Like the OAU, the Arab League has generally represented the interests of powerful autocratic regimes rather than those of its members' citizens.[9]

By 1958, the League included four newly independent North African nations: Libya, Sudan, Morocco, and Tunisia. In 2017 it comprised twenty-two member states, ten of which were African.[10] Although it remained on the sidelines in many African conflicts, the Arab League or its members played significant roles in some. Acting unilaterally or through the League, Egypt, Iran, Libya, Saudi Arabia, Syria, the United Arab Emirates, and Yemen intervened in Somalia's affairs after the Cold War. The Council of the Arab League endorsed the UN-imposed no-fly zone in Libya in 2011, and member states Qatar and the United Arab Emirates participated in the NATO-led military operation that paved the way for regime change in that country. During the Arab Spring and its aftermath, Qatar and the United Arab Emirates supported opposing sides in Libya's civil war and in Egypt, where an elected Islamist-led government was ousted in a military coup.

Subregional Organizations

A number of African subregional organizations were established in the 1970s and 1980s to deal with common economic, environmental, and political problems. Several of these organizations assumed important roles in conflict mediation, peace negotiations, and peacekeeping processes after the Cold War. Especially significant for their diplomatic and military efforts were the Economic Community of West African States (ECOWAS), the Economic Community of Central African

States (ECCAS), the International Conference on the Great Lakes Region (ICGLR), and the Intergovernmental Authority on Development (IGAD). The Southern African Development Community (SADC), which had been central to struggles against white minority rule during the periods of decolonization and the Cold War, was a less significant political and economic actor in later decades. Like the global and regional organizations described earlier, the subregional organizations also suffered from internal conflicts that reduced their effectiveness.

Economic Community of West African States

ECOWAS was established in 1975 by sixteen West African states whose leaders hoped to promote subregional economic cooperation and development.[11] Some members imagined ECOWAS as an instrument for undermining French influence in a subregion where the former imperial power maintained close political, economic, and military ties to its onetime colonies and intervened frequently in their affairs. Nigeria, the anglophone subregional powerhouse, hoped to use the organization as a launching pad for its own political and economic ambitions, which included weakening the francophone powers and establishing a common market with Nigeria as the linchpin.

Although ECOWAS was not conceived as a security organization, it increasingly assumed that role, especially after the Cold War, when external interest in Africa diminished. A 1981 protocol provided for mutual assistance against external aggression and for the establishment of an ECOWAS military force to protect member states from such aggression. The ECOWAS force was permitted to intervene in an internal conflict in a member state at the request of that state's government if the conflict was promoted by external forces and if it jeopardized subregional peace and stability. The 1999 "Protocol Relating to the Mechanism for Conflict Prevention, Management, Resolution, Peacekeeping and Security" elaborated on the force's function. It could assist in conflict prevention, humanitarian intervention to thwart subregional instability, sanctions enforcement, peacekeeping, disarmament, demobilization, and peace building, and in the policing of gun running, drug smuggling, and other transterritorial crimes. The protocol was to be applied in cases of threatened or actual external aggression or conflict in a member state, conflict between two or more member states, internal conflict that could provoke humanitarian disaster or threaten subregional peace and security, serious and massive violations of human rights and the rule of law, the overthrow or attempted overthrow of a democratically elected government, and other situations as determined by the ECOWAS Mediation and Security Council.

Although ECOWAS members agreed to cooperate on subregional security issues, francophone and anglophone states often maintained uneasy relationships. Even when the organization was charged with the purportedly neutral task of peacekeeping, its constituent members sometimes supported opposing sides of a conflict—as was the case in Liberia, Sierra Leone, and Côte d'Ivoire. Moreover, larger, wealthier states often wielded undue influence over the organization's actions. As the largest financial contributor to ECOWAS, for instance, Nigeria ensured that its own interests were protected and promoted. Because the AU funds many ECOWAS operations, powerful AU members states have had disproportionate influence over West African affairs.

Economic Community of Central African States

ECCAS was established in October 1983 by member states of the Central African Customs and Economic Union and of the Economic Community of the Great Lakes States. In 2017, ECCAS included eleven member states.[12] The organization's goal was to establish a wider economic community and to promote peaceful resolution of political disputes. Notably, in July 2015, the UN Security Council asked ECCAS to work with ECOWAS and the AU to develop a comprehensive strategy to combat the Boko Haram insurgency in Nigeria, Niger, and Cameroon—the latter an ECCAS member state. Like other multinational bodies, ECCAS was sometimes weakened by internal disagreements. Conflicts in the DRC, the geographic linchpin of the subregion, split the organization, with Angola and Chad supporting the DRC government and Burundi opposing it.

International Conference on the Great Lakes Region

ICGLR was established in 2000 by eleven African states to promote subregional cooperation for international peace and security, political stability, and sustainable development in the Great Lakes subregion.[13] The organization aspired to address the structural causes of enduring conflicts and underdevelopment. Like other subregional bodies, ICGLR was sometimes compromised by internal rivalries. Conflicts in the DRC pitted ICGLR member states Burundi, Rwanda, and Uganda against the DRC government, which was supported by Angola as well as by several non-ICGLR states. ICGLR mediation efforts were occasionally led by interested parties. Some questioned the organization's ability to engage impartially in the South Sudan conflict, noting Uganda's military support for the government, which along with rebel forces had been accused of massive human rights violations.

Intergovernmental Authority on Development

The Intergovernmental Authority on Drought and Development was established in 1986 by six East African countries to cooperate on problems resulting from the severe drought, environmental degradation, and economic crises of the 1970s and 1980s. In 1996 the organization was superseded by the Intergovernmental Authority on Development (IGAD), which expanded the areas of subregional cooperation to include the promotion of subregional peace and stability and the creation of mechanisms to prevent, manage, and resolve intra- and interstate conflicts through dialogue.[14] As was the case for other subregional organizations, IGAD was weakened by internal rivalries, and member states sometimes pursued parochial interests rather than promoting broader regional benefits. Ethiopia and Kenya struggled to assert subregional dominance, while Sudan and Uganda also jockeyed for influence. Operating within these constraints, IGAD helped broker an accord that established a transitional federal government in Somalia; it also provided a military force to protect that government and train its security forces. However, the foreign-backed regime, beholden to powerful warlords and their external patrons, had scant support inside Somalia. IGAD also played a key role in mediating an end to Sudan's civil war in 2005 and in attempting to resolve subsequent conflicts in South Sudan in 2014–17. However, the competing interests of IGAD member states and the continued support of some states for rival factions seriously undermined the resulting agreements.

Southern African Development Community

The Southern African Development Coordination Conference (SADCC) was established in 1980 by nine Southern African states to build new networks of trade, transportation, communications, and energy and to promote agricultural and industrial alternatives that would break apartheid South Africa's economic stranglehold on the subregion. In 1992, SADCC was reformulated as the Southern African Development Community, or SADC, which aimed to promote subregional integration, economic growth, development, peace, and security in the aftermath of white minority rule. SADC eventually broadened its membership to include fifteen African countries.[15]

Although SADCC had played a pivotal role in the struggles for majority rule in Zimbabwe, Namibia, and South Africa in the 1980s, its successor organization was less significant in the 1990s and 2000s. Member states sometimes promoted opposing strategies. In the DRC, for instance, Angola, Namibia, and Zimbabwe supported the Congolese government militarily, while South Africa attempted to mediate a negotiated solution to the conflict. In 2013, SADC as an entity became more directly involved in the DRC when it joined ICGLR in promoting a regional peace and security framework and contributed soldiers to the UN intervention brigade that was intended to enforce the agreement. South Africa also played an independent role outside SADC and the subregion, helping to broker peace agreements in Burundi, the Central African Republic, Côte d'Ivoire, the Democratic Republic of Congo, South Sudan, and Sudan.

Although the political, economic, and military destabilization associated with apartheid ended in 1994, South Africa continued to dominate the subregion and played a growing role on the continent and in the global arena. South African mining, construction, retail, and media and telecommunications companies invested heavily in the Southern African subregion and across the continent. Pretoria's economic clout was accompanied by growing political influence. After apartheid's demise, South Africa became the unofficial African voice in key international organizations. It played a prominent role in organizations that promote alternative visions in the Global South, including the AU, in which it was a prime mover, the Non-Aligned Movement, the United Nations Conference on Trade and Development (UNCTAD), and BRICS, an association that champions the interests of the major emerging economies of Brazil, Russia, India, China, and South Africa.

An advocate for populations in the southern hemisphere, South Africa also supported initiatives that strengthened the position of the

Global North. It encouraged participation in the AU-led New Partnership for Africa's Development (NEPAD), which embraces the neoliberal economic policies of international financial institutions and the Northern industrialized countries—particularly those of the powerful Group of Seven (G7), an organization that aims to build consensus on economics, energy, security, and terrorism.[16] In 2017, South Africa was the only African member of the Northern-dominated Group of 20 (G20), which included nineteen of the world's largest industrialized and emerging economies, plus the EU.[17] South Africa's prominence was also evident in its designation as one of the EU's strategic partners and its election to two terms on the UN Security Council (2007–8 and 2011–12), where it had a voice, if not a veto, on matters relating to foreign intervention in Africa. As a nonpermanent member of the Security Council, South Africa was susceptible to external pressure. It sometimes broke with AU positions to support those of the Western powers, as it did when it voted to establish a no-fly zone in Libya in 2011. However, it endorsed the AU's call for UN reforms that would grant African countries two permanent and five rotating seats on the Security Council. South Africa, like Nigeria, aspired to assume a veto-wielding position.

Pretoria's increasingly forceful presence in Africa and on the world stage was embraced by some on the continent as an example of Africans finding solutions for African problems. However, others charged that South Africa subordinated subregional and regional interests to its own interests—or to those of global capital. While Northern powers looked to Pretoria to protect their interests, Nigeria resisted South Africa's heightened continental profile, and neighboring states remained wary of the subregional giant, which, no longer fettered by international sanctions, aggressively expanded its economic reach. Egypt, Ethiopia, and Kenya—with their growing economies and strong ties to the West— joined Nigeria in challenging South Africa's presumed right to represent the continent in global bodies.

International Jihadist Organizations and Their African Branches and Affiliates

Nonstate actors also intervened in Africa after the Cold War. The most significant of these were the international jihadist networks, al-Qaeda and the Islamic State, along with their African branches and affiliates.

Al-Qaeda

Al-Qaeda's origins can be traced to the Cold War and to the intervention of outside powers in Afghanistan (see chapter 2). In December 1979, the Soviet Union invaded Afghanistan to assert control over a weak Afghan government that had failed to quash a Sunni insurgency that challenged Moscow's hegemony in Central Asia. During the ensuing Soviet-Afghan War (1979–89), the United States, Saudi Arabia, Pakistan, and their allies recruited, trained, and financed tens of thousands of Sunni militants from Africa, Asia, Europe, and North America to topple the Soviet-backed Afghan regime. After the Soviet withdrawal in 1989, the militants dispersed, fortified by sophisticated weaponry and new training in terror tactics. In the decades that followed, they established terrorist organizations and networks on several continents. Among the most significant was al-Qaeda, a Salafi jihadist organization that had established training camps in Afghanistan and Pakistan during the war.[18] In 1991 al-Qaeda moved its headquarters to Sudan, where it initiated a network of cells and allied organizations that operated in the Greater Horn.

AL-QAEDA'S AFRICAN AFFILIATES

In 2017, al-Qaeda had two important African branches: al-Shabaab (The Youth), which was based in Somalia and launched attacks in Somalia, Kenya, and Uganda; and al-Qaeda in the Islamic Maghreb (AQIM), which operated in North Africa and the Western Sahel.[19] Al-Qaeda also claimed a number of local affiliates and associated organizations. Some of these had splintered from AQIM because of internal disputes; others were the result of mergers between AQIM and groups that were indigenous to the region. Most of the African entities emerged from local conditions and turned to al-Qaeda for political, material, and propaganda aid after they were established. The following list, organized by country, is based on data collected in 2017. It is subject to change as allegiances fluctuate, existing organizations dissolve, and new ones form.

Algeria: Al-Mulathameen (Masked Brigade)—also known as al-Mua'qi'oon Biddam (Those Who Sign with Blood Brigade)—was founded by Mokhtar Belmokhtar, an Algerian veteran of the Soviet-Afghan and Algerian wars and a former AQIM leader. The organization cut ties to AQIM in December 2012 and reported directly to the al-Qaeda leadership.

Egypt: Ansar Beit al-Maqdis (Supporters of the Holy House) was established in the Sinai Peninsula after the 2011 ouster of the Mubarak regime. Although the organization's ideology was influenced by al-Qaeda, Ansar Beit al-Maqdis's focus was primarily local, and it was not a formal al-Qaeda affiliate. The group's activities intensified following the 2013 military coup that removed a democratically elected Islamist president and led to a brutal crackdown on Islamists and other opponents of the new regime. In 2014, the organization split when numerous members in the Nile Valley retained links to al-Qaeda, while many in Sinai pledged allegiance to the leader of the Islamic State. Another al-Qaeda associate, Jund al-Islam (Army of Islam), was established in Sinai in 2013. After initial activity and a four-year hiatus, it reemerged in 2017. The same year, Ansar al-Islam (Followers of Islam), a new al-Qaeda-linked organization, began operating in the desert southwest of Cairo.[20]

Libya: The Libyan Islamic Fighting Group (LIFG) was founded in 1995 by Libyan veterans of the Soviet-Afghan War. Al-Qaeda members have held prominent leadership positions in the organization. Al-Qaeda-linked groups that emerged in Libya after the 2011 overthrow of Muammar Qaddafi include Ansar al-Shari'a (Followers of Islamic Law) in Benghazi, Ansar al-Shari'a in Derna, Ansar al-Shari'a in Sirte, and the Abu Salim Martyrs' Brigade. The Derna Mujahideen Shura Council was formed in 2015 by Ansar al-Shari'a in Derna and the Abu Salim Martyrs' Brigade to counter the Islamic Youth Shura Council in Derna, which supported the Islamic State.

Mali: Ansar Dine (Defenders of the Faith) was established in 2011 and gained AQIM support after its founding. Movement for Unity and Jihad in West Africa (MUJWA) splintered from AQIM in 2011 but continued to collaborate with it. Al-Mourabitoun (The Sentinels), which reported directly to the al-Qaeda leadership, was formed in August 2013 as a merger of the Algerian-based al-Mulathameen and a MUJWA faction. Al-Mourabitoun fractured in 2015, with some members maintaining their ties to al-Qaeda and others pledging allegiance to the leader of the Islamic State. In late 2015, al-Mourabitoun's al-Qaeda faction affiliated with AQIM. The Macina Liberation Front, which aspires to reinstate the nineteenth-century Macina Empire in modern Mali, originated among Fulanis in central Mali in 2015. Although it was led by a fundamentalist cleric and collaborated with AQIM, MUJWA, and Ansar Dine, the organization presented itself as a liberation movement rather than a jihadist organization. In March 2017, Ansar Dine, al-Mourabitoun, and the Macina Liberation Front merged to form Jama'at Nusrat al-Islam wal-Muslimin (Group for the Support of Islam and Muslims).

Nigeria: Jama'atu Ahlis-Sunna Lidda'awati Wal-Jihad (People Committed to the Propagation of the Prophet's Teachings and Jihad), established in 2002, is commonly known as Boko Haram (Western Education Is Forbidden). In 2014, the UN Security Council listed the organization as an associate of AQIM. However, in 2015 Boko Haram pledged allegiance to the leader of the Islamic State and began to refer to itself as the Islamic State in West Africa Province. Jama'atu Ansarul Muslimina Fi Biladis-Sudan (Vanguards for the Protection of Muslims in Black Africa), commonly known as Ansaru, splintered from Boko Haram in 2012. In 2014, the UN Security Council listed Ansaru as an associate of AQIM.

Somalia: Al-Shabaab (The Youth), inspired by Somali veterans of the Soviet-Afghan War, originated as a youth militia linked to the Islamic Courts Union. It established ties to al-Qaeda following a US-backed Ethiopian invasion in 2006 and became an official branch of al-Qaeda in 2012. Its focus was primarily local. However, it also attacked Ethiopia and countries that contributed to an AU peacekeeping mission in Somalia.

Tunisia: Ansar al-Shari'a in Tunisia, established in 2011, had strong links to al-Qaeda. The Okba Ibn Nafaa Brigade, which drew much of its membership from Ansar al-Shari'a, described itself as an AQIM battalion. In 2014 some members of both groups switched their allegiance to the leader of the Islamic State.

<u>The Islamic State</u>

The Islamic State is also known as the <u>Islamic State in Iraq and Syria (ISIS)</u> or the Islamic State in Iraq and the Levant (ISIL).[21] In contrast to local Salafi jihadist groups that focus on establishing or purifying a Muslim state in a single country, the Islamic State aims to establish a caliphate that would unite Muslims worldwide in one political entity—a phenomenon last achieved in the eighth century. The origins of the modern Islamic State can be traced to the US-led military intervention in Iraq in 2003, which precipitated the Second Gulf War (2003–11). The invasion and occupation sparked a Sunni insurgency led by the Jordanian-Palestinian militant Abu Musab al-Zarqawi, who transformed his organization, Jama'at al-Tawhid wa'al-Jihad (Organization of Monotheism and Jihad), into al-Qaeda in Iraq (AQI), which targeted US military and international coalition forces as well as local collaborators. After Zarqawi was killed in a US airstrike in 2006, his successors began to refer to the al-Qaeda branch and associated organizations as the Islamic State in Iraq. When civil war broke out in Syria in 2011, the Islamic State expanded its reach into that country, and by 2013 it was calling itself the Islamic State in Iraq and Syria. Under the leadership of Abu Bakr al-Baghdadi, who honed his ideas and mobilizing skills in an US internment camp, the Islamic State recruited followers from among the Sunni minority that had been favored under Saddam Hussein but was marginalized politically after his ouster by US and coalition forces. In February 2014, al-Qaeda severed its ties to the Islamic State, criticizing its persistent aggression against Jabhat al-Nusra, al-Qaeda's Syrian affiliate, as well as its brutal treatment and indiscriminate killing of Muslim civilians, particularly Shi'as.[22] Noted for its ruthless methods, the Islamic State attracted international jihadis who felt that al-Qaeda was too moderate. However, both Muslims and non-Muslims widely condemned the organization for its harsh practices and attacks on civilians.

A number of African entities have pledged allegiance to the Islamic State leader. Like those that developed links to al-Qaeda, these groups emerged from local conditions and only later established ties to the international jihadist organization.

AFRICAN ORGANIZATIONS ASSOCIATED WITH THE ISLAMIC STATE

Algeria: Jund al-Khilafah (Soldiers of the Caliphate) in Algeria split from AQIM in 2014 and pledged allegiance to the leader of the Islamic State.

Egypt: Ansar Beit al-Maqdis, established in 2011, was influenced by al-Qaeda ideology but was not a formal affiliate. The organization fractured in 2014 when many Nile Valley members retained links to al-Qaeda, while others in Sinai pledged allegiance to the leader of the Islamic State and named their faction Wilayat Sinai (Province of Sinai) or Islamic State–Sinai Province.

Libya: A brigade of fighters from eastern Libya, who had fought on behalf of the Islamic State in Iraq and Syria, returned home in 2014 and reconstituted themselves as the Islamic Youth Shura Council in Derna. They declared eastern Libya to be a province of the Islamic State, which they called Cyrenaica Province. Two other Islamic State provinces were established in Libya in 2015: Tripolitania Province in the west and Fezzan Province in the south. In early 2015, Ansar al-Shari'a in Sirte split into two factions, with some members retaining ties to al-Qaeda and others pledging allegiance to the leader of the Islamic State.

Mali: Although most Malian jihadist organizations retained their ties to al-Qaeda, some al-Mourabitoun members left the organization in 2015 to form the Islamic State in Mali, subsequently renamed the Islamic State in the Greater Sahara (sometimes translated as the Islamic State in the Sahel).

Nigeria: Jama'atu Ahlis-Sunna Lidda'awati Wal-Jihad, commonly known as Boko Haram, switched its allegiance from AQIM to the Islamic State in 2015 and adopted the name Islamic State in West Africa Province.

Somalia: Abnaa ul-Calipha (Islamic State in Somalia), based in Puntland, broke from al-Qaeda-linked al-Shabaab in 2015. Another al-Shabaab splinter, Islamic State in Somalia, Kenya, Tanzania, and Uganda (also known as Jahba East Africa or the East African Front) emerged in early 2016.

Tunisia: Following a government crackdown, some remnants of Ansar al-Shari'a in Tunisia, previously associated with al-Qaeda, pledged allegiance to the Islamic State leader in 2014. Some members of the AQIM-linked Okba Ibn Nafaa Brigade also switched allegiances in 2014 and established a new organization, Jund al-Khilafah in Tunisia, which aligned with the Islamic State. The Tunisian jihadist group Mujahidin of Kairouan pledged allegiance to the Islamic State leader in 2015.

Conclusion

Sustaining a pattern established during decolonization and the Cold War, foreign governments and other entities intervened in African affairs in the decades that followed. Although individual states continued to inter-cede unilaterally, multilateral intervention by organized groups of states and by nonstate actors became more frequent than previously. In some cases, the presence of nonstate actors associated with international ter-rorist networks provoked intervention by foreign states or institutions. In other cases, intrusion by foreign entities stimulated local insurgencies that in turn attracted international terrorist support. State-based actors justified their involvement as a response to instability, an effort to pro-tect civilian lives, and a necessity for advancing the war on terror. How-ever, they also promoted their own more parochial interests. Conflicting agendas often weakened multilateral efforts, and the priorities of the most powerful countries generally took precedence. While African political and military leaders participated in war-making and peace-building pro-cesses, African civil society representatives remained in the background. These deficiencies undermined the prospects for a lasting peace, as the following case studies demonstrate.

Chapter 4, which focuses on Somalia, is the first of two chapters that explore post–Cold War intervention in East Africa. When foreign powers withdrew their support for the Somali government after the Cold War, insurgent forces overthrew the authoritarian regime. Concerned about the humanitarian crisis inside the country as well as the potential for regional destabilization, multilateral organizations, extracontinental powers, and neighboring countries intervened. Their motivations were varied, often at odds, and subject to change over time. Although some of the initial outcomes were positive, the long-term effects were largely negative, contributing to increased human suffering and instability.

Suggested Reading

African international relations are explored in a number of recent works. Two recommended volumes investigate the role of extracontinental powers in Africa after the Cold War, including the major Western powers along with Russia, China, Japan, India, the UN, the EU, and international financial institutions. See Ian Taylor and Paul Williams, eds., *Africa in*

International Politics: External Involvement on the Continent (New York: Routledge, 2004); and Ian Taylor, *The International Relations of Sub-Saharan Africa* (New York: Continuum, 2010). John W. Harbeson and Donald Rothchild, eds., *Africa in World Politics: Engaging a Changing World Order*, 5th ed. (Boulder, CO: Westview Press, 2013), explores interstate conflict, the impact of outside investment and externally induced political reforms, and the role of international peacekeeping forces. Errol A. Henderson, *African Realism? International Relations Theory and Africa's Wars in the Postcolonial Era* (Lanham, MD: Rowman and Littlefield, 2015), challenges the applicability of Eurocentric international relations theories to African cases and explores the relationship between Africa's domestic and international conflicts.

Several books examine the role of the UN in the post–World War II international order. Mark Mazower, *No Enchanted Palace: The End of Empire and the Ideological Origins of the United Nations* (Princeton, NJ: Princeton University Press, 2013), argues that the UN was created to protect the interests of empire but was reshaped by formerly colonized states and transformed into an instrument for ending the old imperial order. David L. Bosco, *Five to Rule Them All: The UN Security Council and the Making of the Modern World* (New York: Oxford University Press, 2009), explores the role of the five permanent members of the UN Security Council in shaping the post–Cold War world. A number of works investigate UN humanitarian and peacekeeping missions in Africa, elucidating the reasons for their success or failure. See Andrzej Sitkowski, *UN Peacekeeping: Myth and Reality* (Westport, CT: Praeger, 2006); Norrie MacQueen, *Humanitarian Intervention and the United Nations* (Edinburgh: Edinburgh University Press, 2011); Norrie MacQueen, *United Nations Peacekeeping in Africa since 1960* (London: Pearson Education, 2002); Adekeye Adebajo, *UN Peacekeeping in Africa: From the Suez Crisis to the Sudan Conflicts* (Boulder, CO: Lynne Rienner, 2011); and Adekeye Adebajo, *The Curse of Berlin: Africa after the Cold War* (New York: Columbia University Press, 2010).

Other books examine international peacekeeping in Africa. Two wide-ranging studies are particularly useful: Adebajo, *UN Peacekeeping in Africa* (mentioned previously); and Marco Wyss and Thierry Tardy, eds., *Peacekeeping in Africa: The Evolving Security Structure* (New York: Routledge, 2014), which considers UN, AU, EU, and ECOWAS operations, as well as unilateral actions by outside powers. For the role of African regional organizations and peacekeeping forces, see David J. Francis, *Uniting Africa: Building Regional Peace and Security Systems* (Burlington, VT: Ashgate, 2006); and Abou Jeng, *Peacebuilding in the African Union: Law, Philosophy and Practice* (New York: Cambridge University Press, 2012).

A number of recommended works consider the role of subregional peacekeeping forces. The strengths and weaknesses of ECOWAS peacekeeping missions in West Africa are investigated in Adekeye Abebajo, ed., *Building Peace in West Africa: Liberia, Sierra Leone, and Guinea-Bissau* (Boulder, CO: Lynne Rienner, 2002); Adekeye Adebajo and Ismail Rashid, eds., *West Africa's Security Challenges: Building Peace in a Troubled Region* (Boulder, CO: Lynne Rienner, 2004); Adekeye Adebajo, *Liberia's Civil War: Nigeria, ECOMOG, and Regional Security in West Africa* (Boulder, CO: Lynne Rienner, 2002); and Karl Magyar and Earl Conteh-Morgan, eds., *Peacekeeping in Africa: ECOMOG in Liberia* (New York: St. Martin's, 1998). SADC's efforts in Southern Africa are considered in Laurie Nathan, *Community of Insecurity: SADC's Struggle for Peace and Security in Southern Africa* (Burlington, VT: Ashgate, 2012).

Other studies examine the hegemonic influence of particular countries on the African continent. Adebajo, *The Curse of Berlin* (mentioned previously), considers South Africa, Nigeria, China, France, and the United States. Dane F. Smith Jr., *U.S. Peacefare: Organizing American Peace-Building Operations* (Santa Barbara, CA: Praeger, 2010), written by a diplomatic insider, focuses on the role of the United States in postconflict peace building. Bruno Charbonneau, *France and the New Imperialism: Security Policy in Sub-Saharan Africa* (Burlington, VT: Ashgate, 2008), investigates the impact of French security and cooperation policies in postindependence Africa and argues that French intervention denied Africans political freedom and sustained their political, economic, and social domination by outsiders. The growing role of China in Africa is considered in Deborah Bräutigam, *The Dragon's Gift: The Real Story of China in Africa* (New York: Oxford University Press, 2009); Ian Taylor, *China's New Role in Africa* (Boulder, CO: Lynne Rienner, 2008); David H. Shinn and Joshua Eisenman, *China and Africa: A Century of Engagement* (Philadelphia: University of Pennsylvania Press, 2012); and Howard W. French, *China's Second Continent: How a Million Migrants Are Building a New Empire in Africa* (New York: Knopf, 2014). Ian Taylor, *Africa Rising? BRICS—Diversifying Dependency* (Martlesham, UK: James Currey,

2014), provides a critical examination of the roles of Brazil, Russia, India, China, and South Africa in post–Cold War Africa, arguing that the emerging economics of the Global South, like the Western powers before them, have an interest in perpetuating an unequal system that consigns Africa to the bottom rung.

The emergence of South Africa as both a regional and continental player is considered in several works. Chris Alden and Maxi Schoeman explore South Africa's growing economic involvement in Africa and its expanding political role on the continent and the global stage. See Chris Alden and Maxi Schoeman, "South Africa in the Company of Giants: The Search for Leadership in a Transforming Global Order," *International Affairs* 89, no. 1 (January 2013): 111–29; and Chris Alden and Maxi Schoeman, "South Africa's Symbolic Hegemony in Africa," *International Politics* 52, no. 2 (2015): 239–54. William G. Martin, *South Africa and the World Economy* (Rochester, NY: University of Rochester Press, 2013), examines the transformation of South African political and economic power from the era of colonialism and white minority rule to the present, marked by its recent alliances with Northern industrialized powers and new challenges from Asia. Chris Alden and Miles Soko, "South Africa's Economic Relations with Africa: Hegemony and Its Discontents," *Journal of Modern African Studies* 43, no. 3 (September 2005): 367–92, differentiates between the roles played by the regional bodies, SADC and the Southern African Customs Union, on the one hand, and by South Africa's private and parastatal corporations, on the other. Fred Ahwireng-Obeng and Patrick J. McGowan examine the impact of South African trade, investment, and infrastructure and telecommunications developments in Africa in a two-part article: Fred Ahwireng-Obeng and Patrick J. McGowan, "Partner or Hegemon: South Africa in Africa, Part I," *Journal of Contemporary African Studies* 16, no. 1 (January 1998): 5–38; and Patrick J. McGowan and Fred Ahwireng-Obeng, "Partner or Hegemon: South Africa in Africa, Part II," *Journal of Contemporary African Studies* 16, no. 2 (July 1998): 165–95. Recent developments in South African foreign policy are explored in Chris Alden and Garth le Pere, *South Africa's Post-Apartheid Foreign Policy: From Reconciliation to Renewal?* Adelphi Paper 362 (London: International Institute for Strategic Studies, 2003); and Laurie Nathan, "Consistencies and Inconsistencies in South Africa Foreign Policy," *International Affairs* 81, no. 2 (March 2005): 361–72. Pretoria's role in conflict mediation in Burundi, Côte d'Ivoire, the DRC, and Sudan are assessed in Kurt Shillinger, *Africa's Peacemaker? Lessons from South African Conflict Mediation* (Johannesburg: Jacana Media, 2009).

For the role of warlords in post–Cold War African conflicts, see two important books by William Reno: *Warlord Politics and African States* (Boulder, CO: Lynne Rienner, 1998), and *Warfare in Independent Africa* (New York: Cambridge University Press, 2011).

For the role of al-Qaeda and the Islamic State in Africa, see the Suggested Reading for chapter 2.

Map 4.1. Horn of Africa, 2018. (Map by Philip Schwartzberg, Meridian Mapping, Minneapolis.)

4

Somalia

Conflicting Missions and Mixed Results (1991–2017)

FOCUSING ON SOMALIA from 1991 through 2017, this chapter explores how the collapse of the central state, conflict between warlords and Islamists, and a devastating humanitarian crisis stimulated intervention by the United Nations, the United States, the African Union, and neighboring countries. Foreign military involvement was initially justified as a response to instability and the responsibility to protect civilian lives. However, it was subsequently absorbed into the wider war on terror when a jihadist insurgency emerged in response to foreign intrusion. The response to instability/responsibility to protect paradigm is applicable for the duration of the intervention. The war on terror paradigm is relevant to the period before September 2001, but it assumed greater importance after the 9/11 terrorist attacks on the United States. The results of external involvement were mixed. Although the initial intervention thwarted some conflict-related starvation, subsequent actions jeopardized civilian lives and increased regional instability. Somalia's post–Cold War experience illuminates the ways in which foreign intervention can be counterproductive—not only failing to promote peace and security, but even provoking a terrorist insurgency. Rather than strengthening Somalia's internal peace-building and nation-building efforts, foreign powers and multilateral agencies often played roles that prolonged or exacerbated local tensions.

The post–Cold War conflicts in Somalia have deep historical roots, embracing the precolonial, colonial, and independence periods. The promises of political independence were undermined by the enduring effects of colonial policies, by corruption, and, eventually, by a military coup that installed a dictator who manipulated social divisions to maintain power. During the Cold War, Somalia allied first with the Soviet Union and then with the United States. As the East-West conflict waned, Washington abandoned the Somali dictatorship, and warlords and their clan-based militias overthrew the regime. The central government disintegrated in 1991, and Somalia fell into chaos. State institutions broke down, and basic services, if they were provided at all, were supplied by nongovernmental actors. Islamist organizations, especially, played critical roles in restoring order and reestablishing social services. External powers intervened, both to provide security for the Somali people and to advance their own interests.

(1)   The first post–Cold War intervention began in 1992 with a UN mandate to monitor a ceasefire and to provide protection for famine relief operations. It fell apart in 1993 with the downing of two US helicopters and the deaths of eighteen US soldiers and approximately one thousand Somalis, mostly civilians. The second intervention began in 2006 with
(2)   CIA support for anti-Islamist warlords and culminated in a US-backed Ethiopian invasion of Somalia the same year. External involvement accelerated the growth of a jihadist movement that quickly dominated the antiforeign insurgency. The UN, the AU, and IGAD were the most significant multilateral actors, lending their support to a new transitional government, while the EU joined in brokering peace talks and funding peacekeeping operations. The United States, Ethiopia, and Kenya played crucial roles, acting unilaterally or in conjunction with other entities, while neighboring Uganda and Djibouti also intervened in Somali affairs, mostly under AU and IGAD auspices. Turkey and the United Arab Emirates joined the UN, the EU, the UK, and the United States as the Somali government's primary security partners.[1] Eritrea, a regional outlier, supplied weapons to the jihadist insurgency, primarily to counter Ethiopian influence, while the al-Qaeda network also provided critical support.

The interests of external bodies and powers were not always in accord with those of the Somali people. The UN and US interventions that favored one warlord over another (1992–95), followed by Ethiopian incursions and support for diverse warlords (1996–2000), generated enormous hostility among the Somali population. The imposition of a corrupt transitional government by outside powers (2004), CIA backing of a new warlord coalition (February–June 2006), and a US-endorsed Ethiopian invasion and occupation (July 2006–January 2009) resulted in a backlash that intensified popular support for al-Shabaab (The Youth). This Islamist youth militia, inspired by Somali veterans of the Soviet-Afghan War, found recruits among the country's unemployed young men. The Ethiopian invasion sparked an antiforeign insurgency, with al-Shabaab at its helm. While the organization maintained a local focus, targeting primarily Somali military and government officials, it also established ties with al-Qaeda and expanded its attacks to Westerners working in Somalia and to neighboring states that were associated with the intervention.[2]

By early 2007, al-Shabaab insurgents had gained control of much of southern Somalia, provoking another round of foreign military interventions. In February the UN Security Council used Chapter VIII powers to authorize the African Union Mission in Somalia, which eventually sent some 22,000 peacekeepers to restore order. The conflict continued, and the election of yet another foreign-backed government in 2012 did little to resolve it. The government had limited authority outside the capital and relied on AU forces for defense. Its operations were characterized by widespread corruption and monopolization of power. Al-Shabaab continued to exploit legitimate local grievances for its own ends.

Setting the Stage: Somalia during the Cold War (1960–91)

A brief description of Somalia during the last decades of the Cold War provides a framework for understanding the conflicts that followed in its wake. A union of British and Italian colonies that had been joined at independence in 1960, Somalia was the object of US-Soviet competition.[3] With the Gulf of Aden to the north and the Indian Ocean to the east, Somalia was strategically placed to control access to the Red Sea and to Middle Eastern oil routes. The country was plagued by both internal and external problems that provided outsiders with opportunities for influence. Colonial boundary treaties had left millions of ethnic Somalis in Ethiopia, Kenya, and Djibouti. After independence, successive campaigns to unite all ethnic Somalis in a Greater Somalia led to numerous border conflicts and devastating regional wars. Inside Somalia, ethnic Somalis shared a common language, culture, and religion. However, genealogical groupings, reified by colonial policies as distinctive clan identities, were manipulated by political leaders to mobilize constituents and consolidate power.[4] Ethnic minorities, set apart by race, class, region, language, and occupation, suffered harsh discrimination. Among the most vulnerable were the Somali Bantu, a recently coined umbrella term for people with Bantu-speaking ancestors who settled along the Shabelle River centuries before the arrival of Somali speakers, as well as those in the Jubba River valley whose ancestors were brought to Somalia as slaves in the nineteenth century.

The first democratically elected postindependence governments were challenged by sectarian and patronage interests, corruption, and disputes over the country's expansionist goals. Relations with the United States were uneasy. Fearing Somali designs on its primary regional allies, Ethiopia and Kenya, Washington balked when Somalia requested military aid shortly after independence. The Soviet Union stepped into the gap. In October 1969, General Mohamed Siad Barre, commander in chief of the Somali army, seized power in a military coup. The following year, after Somalia expelled a number of US diplomats, military attachés, and the Peace Corps, Washington terminated all economic aid. Moscow intensified its military and economic assistance programs, and Siad Barre soon proclaimed that Somalia would follow the tenets of scientific socialism. During the early years of his regime, the country made important strides in mass literacy, primary education, public health, and economic development, particularly in the rural areas, while new laws on marriage, divorce, and inheritance expanded women's rights. However, the military strongman also abolished local authority structures, suspended the constitution, banned political parties, and imprisoned or killed dissenters.

Somalia's political, economic, and social tensions were exacerbated by the Somali-Ethiopian War of 1977–78. As one of sub-Saharan Africa's most heavily armed nations, Somalia possessed a 22,000-man army that had been trained and equipped by the Soviet Union and its allies. Ethiopia maintained an even stronger military apparatus, a 40,000-man army that had been trained and outfitted by the United States. A 1974 military coup had ousted the US-backed emperor of Ethiopia, and the new rulers had embraced Marxism-Leninism. Yet the alliance with Washington endured. Then, in July 1977, Somalia invaded Ethiopia in an attempt to annex Somali-inhabited land. The Kremlin, which was courting the Marxist regime, was furious. Aided by some 18,000 Cuban soldiers, advisors, and technicians, the Soviet Union threw its full weight to Ethiopia. The OAU, which viewed Ethiopia as the victim of Somali aggression, ignored Siad Barre's appeals for assistance. Although it officially distanced itself from Somali aggression in 1977, the United States covertly supported Mogadishu's war effort through third parties, mobilizing military aid through a consortium of allies led by Saudi Arabia, Iran, Egypt, and France. Unable to sustain the war without more substantial external support, Somalia was forced to withdraw from Ethiopia in 1978. Washington became a mainstay of the Siad Barre regime after its retreat. Between 1979 and 1986, the United States provided Somalia with $500 million in military aid, making it one of the largest recipients of US military assistance in sub-Saharan Africa.[5] Somalia had effectively switched sides in the Cold War.

US aid notwithstanding, Somalia was in dire straits by the mid-1980s. The Ethiopian war, corruption, and mismanagement had run the economy into the ground, dissipating the development achievements of the previous decade. Onerous taxes stimulated rural unrest, which was brutally repressed. Determined to crush all political opposition, Siad Barre imprisoned or killed his critics or drafted them into the Somali army while collectively punishing their clan members. Encouraging clan rivalry to disrupt his opponents and strengthen his hold on power, his regime was increasingly dominated by his Darod clan family members and their allies.[6]

By 1989, clans that had suffered from harassment or discrimination, and Islamists, who had been repressed by the dictatorship, were united in their hatred of the Siad Barre regime. In the north, where a large number of war refugees had been resettled on Isaaq clan land and government policies threatened Isaaq economic interests, the Ethiopian-backed Somali National Movement instigated an insurgency. Somali military planes, piloted by white South African and former Rhodesian mercenaries, bombed the northern city of Hargeisa, and government forces killed tens of thousands of Isaaq clan members. In the south, Islamist opposition was spearheaded by a Salafist study group, al-Itihaad al-Islamiya (Islamic Union). Many of the group's leaders had worked or studied in Saudi Arabia, Pakistan, or Kuwait, where they had been exposed to fundamentalist teachings. Most of the members were students or faculty from Somali secondary schools and colleges, or from the Somali National University. The massacre of 450 Islamist protesters in the capital city of Mogadishu in July 1989 prompted the transformation of al-Itihaad from a nonviolent association calling people to the faith into a jihadist organization whose goal was to establish an Islamic state in Greater Somalia. The new agenda attracted Somali veterans of the Soviet-Afghan War, who played a major role in al-Itihaad's metamorphosis. With their knowledge of military strategy and their training in guerrilla and terror tactics, the war veterans recast al-Itihaad as Somalia's most powerful military force following the breakdown of the central government in 1991.

Collapse of the Dictatorship, Rise of Warlords, and Foreign Intervention (1991–95)

While Somalia faltered, the Cold War also took a new turn. In the late 1980s the Soviet Union faced a severe political and economic crisis, and the alliance with Somalia was no longer critical to the United States. After the 1989 Mogadishu massacre, the George H. W. Bush administration expressed newfound concern about Siad Barre's human rights abuses, and Congress suspended military and economic aid. Without US support, the Siad Barre government was an easy target. In January 1991, the United Somali Congress (USC), led by General Mohammed Farah Aidid and dominated by the Hawiye clan family, overthrew the regime, and the USC's Ali Mahdi Mohamed was elected interim president. After the central government failed, personal, clan, and other rivalries split the opposition.[7] A war between the Aidid and Ali Mahdi factions destroyed much of Mogadishu in 1991–92. The formal economy ceased to function, and southern Somalia disintegrated into fiefdoms ruled by rival warlords and their militias. Followers were mobilized and opponents objectified through clan-based hate narratives. Clan cleansing, although instigated by Siad Barre, became a defining instrument of warlord control.[8]

As the fighting intensified in 1991, war-induced famine, compounded by drought, threatened the lives of 60 percent of the population, primarily in the southern and central regions.[9] Massive population displacement, the theft of food and livestock by marauding soldiers and militia members, and crop failure put 4.5 million people at risk of starvation. Mogadishu's port and airport were controlled by warlords who confiscated food aid and manipulated food supplies to reward their supporters, punish their opponents, and finance the purchase of weapons. By late 1992, some 300,000 Somalis had died from starvation and war-related disease and violence, and 2 million people had fled their homes.

The failure of the UN to respond to the crisis was criticized by many Somalis and international NGOs. Largely absent in 1991, the UN took a more active role in 1992 under the leadership of the new secretary-general,

Egyptian diplomat Boutros Boutros-Ghali, a onetime supporter of Siad Barre who was deeply hostile to Aidid and determined to undermine his power. The Security Council imposed an arms embargo in January 1992, which prohibited the delivery of any weapons or military equipment to Somalia. In April, the United Nations Operation in Somalia (UNOSOM I) was established with a Chapter VI mandate to monitor a ceasefire signed in March and to escort and protect aid convoys. It was authorized to include 50 unarmed observers and 500 armed guards. Boutros-Ghali appointed Algerian diplomat Mohamed Sahnoun both as his special representative in Somalia and as the head of UNOSOM. Intent on procuring a lasting political solution, Sahnoun mediated a series of negotiations that included warlords, patrilineage leaders, and community elders, as well as intellectuals, merchants, women, and youth. In July, the UN secretary-general brought attention to the humanitarian crisis when he charged that the Security Council was "fighting a rich man's war in Yugoslavia while not lifting a finger to save Somalia from disintegration."[10]

If the UN was slow to act, divisions within the US government also hindered a rapid American response. In December 1991, Andrew Natsios, a high-level official in the United States Agency for International Development (USAID), called Somalia "the worst humanitarian crisis today" and advocated American action.[11] In the State Department, Assistant Secretary of State for African Affairs Herman Cohen, the East Africa Desk, and the Bureau of Human Rights and Humanitarian Affairs also called for a strong US response. The chairman of the Joint Chiefs of Staff, General Colin Powell, who was under mounting pressure to demonstrate US leadership in response to humanitarian crises in Bosnia and Somalia, believed that a limited military operation in Somalia, although not desirable, would be more manageable than one in the Balkans. Those opposed to US military engagement included Assistant Secretary of State for International Organization Affairs John Bolton, who argued that Somalia was not strategic to US interests and thus did not warrant US help, and National Security Advisor Brent Scowcroft, who worried about the lack of an exit strategy. Leading officials in the Defense Department and in the US Central Command (CENTCOM), along with experienced ambassadors in the region, also warned against hasty military involvement without a clear plan or objective.[12]

These concerns notwithstanding, a major humanitarian disaster so close to the US presidential elections could not be ignored. In July 1992, the United States agreed to fund and transport 500 Pakistani troops to guard humanitarian shipments as part of the UNOSOM I mission. In August, while awaiting the Somali principals' acceptance of the UN force, President Bush announced the launch of a unilateral US military airlift. Operation Provide Relief supplied the equivalent of 12 million meals to Somalia between August and November. By October, the rains had begun and death rates were declining. Although highly effective in the short run, the operation also had drawbacks. Insecurity had not abated, and in some places it had grown more dire than previously. The massive increase in food supplies provided new opportunities for warlords and bandits to weaponize food, and in some ways it contributed to a widening of the conflict. Similarly, the introduction of foreign military forces generated hostility in some quarters and rendered a political solution more difficult.

Among the strongest critics of the use of military force was UN Special Representative Sahnoun. Although he credited the US airlift with saving lives, he opposed further militarization of the UN operation. Political negotiations were making progress, even if they were slowed by painstaking attention to local sensitivities. Faction leaders and community elders from all regions had endorsed the idea of a national conference to discuss national reconciliation. Aidid, Ali Mahdi, and other powerful faction leaders had agreed to permit 500 UN peacekeepers to deploy in Mogadishu; the port had been reopened, and food distribution had commenced. Alternatives to military intervention, including mediation by subregional bodies and the application of sanctions, had not been fully explored, and military intervention would undermine these delicate processes. Sahnoun publicly criticized the provision of military supplies and money to Ali Mahdi's forces in a UN plane, which contributed to Aidid's mounting distrust of the UN; Sahnoun also opposed the increase of the UNOSOM I force to 3,500 troops, authorized in August without warning to Sahnoun or consultation with Somali leaders. Irked by Sahnoun's public criticisms and his willingness to work with Aidid, Boutros-Ghali dismissed his special representative in late October. Sahnoun's successors failed to garner the same degree of trust among Somalis, and efforts to thwart the rising tensions between the Ali Mahdi and Aidid factions fell apart, as did agreements that allowed the safe passage of relief shipments.

Although Sahnoun's removal undermined the prospects for a political solution, the matter was not yet settled. The Western NGO community debated whether enhanced UN military involvement would exacerbate or ameliorate the situation. Some opposed foreign military presence of any kind; others resisted the use of troops beyond those needed to protect relief agencies and their supplies; still others called for a full-blown military intervention. Within the US government, leading officials continued to urge caution. By late November, increased media attention along with urging from bipartisan forces in Congress, president-elect Bill Clinton, and a growing chorus of NGOs tipped the balance toward action. Those who stressed the need to "do something"—with an eye to political and publicity concerns—held sway over those who endorsed prudence. Boutros-Ghali outlined several possible courses of action, including one that would allow a member state to undertake a military enforcement operation with UN Security Council authorization. The Bush administration informed the UN secretary-general that the United States was willing to lead such an intervention.

In December 1992, the Security Council authorized the establishment of a US-led multinational military task force, officially called Unified Task Force (UNITAF) and unofficially dubbed Operation Restore Hope. The military force would include nearly 26,000 US troops plus 11,000 more from two dozen other countries. UNITAF was granted a Chapter VII mandate to work with UNOSOM I to secure ports, airports, warehouses, feeding centers, and roads so that humanitarian relief could be delivered. It was not authorized to disarm or demobilize warring parties, confiscate heavy weapons, or intervene to stop fighting between rival groups. Its mandate was solely to ensure the delivery of humanitarian relief to the civilian population. The original charge continued to be the public face of the mission even after the US role had changed substantially.

The authorizations for UNITAF and UNOSOM I expired in May 1993, when UNOSOM II, also led by the United States, took over. Composed of 18,000 peacekeepers, including 4,200 Americans, UNOSOM II operated under a broader mandate than its predecessor, and one that was far removed from UNOSOM I's original peacekeeping role. Arguing that mass starvation could be averted only if local militias were neutralized, the UN Security Council prescribed a Chapter VII mandate and a course of action that included the forcible disarmament of Somali militias, particularly that of Mohammed Farah Aidid, whom the UN leadership was now determined to exclude from power.

Photo 4.1. US Marines participate in UNITAF search for General Mohammed Farah Aidid's weapons, Mogadishu, January 7, 1993. Photo by PHCM Terry C. Mitchell.

Tension between the UN and Aidid broke to the surface on June 5, when Aidid's militia ambushed and killed two dozen Pakistani peacekeepers who were attempting to inspect his radio station and weapons depots. The Security Council quickly expanded UNOSOM II's mandate, authorizing UN forces to arrest, detain, try, and punish those responsible for the killings. Having moved from the original mission of protecting aid convoys and relief workers to capturing, disarming, and punishing one faction in the fighting, the UN crossed the line from humanitarian intervention to choosing sides in a deadly conflict. As the mission's chief advocate and leader, the United States was now deeply embroiled in Somalia's civil war. Because US support had been key to Siad Barre's survival, many Somalis were already hostile to the United States and distrustful of its motives. In their view, the United States and its UN partner had declared war; their soldiers were now perceived as an occupation force.

On June 11–17, 1993, US military forces in AC-130 Spectre gunships and Cobra and Black Hawk helicopters attacked Aidid's radio station and a number of Mogadishu compounds believed to hold weapons caches. UN troops fired on the angry civilians who poured into the streets, killing and maiming a large number. In July, a similar airborne assault on

Photo 4.2. Children walk past graffiti criticizing Jonathan Howe, the UN special envoy sent to Somalia to oppose Aidid, Mogadishu, June 30, 1993. Photo by Eric Cabanis/AFP/Getty Images.

elders, clan and religious leaders, intellectuals, and businessmen, who were meeting to consider a UN peace initiative, killed sixteen prominent members of Aidid's party and dozens of others. The massacre intensified anti-UN and anti-American sentiment among the civilian population. Violent retaliation was directed at all foreigners, causing numerous relief organizations to withdraw from Somalia. US troops, in turn, regarded Somali civilians with growing disdain.

Although the delivery of food aid was the priority of the US military in early 1993, it was not the objective eight months later. From late August to early October, the US armed forces were bent on capturing or killing Aidid and his top lieutenants. The final raid took place on October 3, 1993, when 120 elite US Army Rangers and Delta Force troops attempted to capture key leaders of Aidid's militia in one of Mogadishu's most dangerous neighborhoods. By this time, al-Itihaad had formed an alliance of convenience with Aidid's militia. Both groups included members who had been trained and armed by al-Qaeda operatives who had fought in the Soviet-Afghan War and who were charged with expelling US and UN forces from Somalia. During the October 3 operation, Aidid's forces, assisted by al-Itihaad, shot down two Black Hawk helicopters, which crashed into children in the streets below.[13] Angry crowds attacked the surviving soldiers and those who came to rescue them. In the fighting that ensued, eighteen US soldiers and some one thousand Somali men, women, and children were killed. Eighty percent of the dead were civilians.

Within days of the debacle, President Bill Clinton announced that all US troops would be withdrawn from Somalia by the end of March 1994. Without US backing, the UN could not impose a political settlement that excluded Aidid. Although the crisis had not been resolved, the UN pulled out of Somalia in early 1995, declaring that UNOSOM II was over.

Islamism, Jihad, and Insurgency (1994–2017)

While the UN and the United States were preoccupied with the secular warlords, Somali Islamists were also building their base. Like many of its secular predecessors, al-Itihaad promoted irredentist claims with the goal of uniting ethnic Somalis from Ethiopia, Kenya, Djibouti, and Somalia in a single nation. However, in contrast to secular leaders, those in al-Itihaad envisioned Greater Somalia as an Islamic state. Perceiving opportunity in the chaos, al-Qaeda determined that Somalia was ripe for a jihadist insurgency that could serve as a launching pad for similar uprisings in Eritrea, Yemen, and the Muslim holy land of Saudi Arabia. By late 1993, Sudan, Iran, and al-Qaeda were supplying al-Itihaad with money, weapons, military training, and personnel to counter US influence in the region.

As the security situation deteriorated and Western aid organizations withdrew, Muslim charities supported by wealthy patrons in Saudi Arabia, the United Arab Emirates, and Kuwait filled the void. In a country with virtually no functioning infrastructure or social services, al-Itihaad provided assistance to the poor and established Qur'anic schools, Islamic courts, and militias to perform police duties. It invested in banking, telecommunications, export-import, and transportation, using business proceeds to finance social services and religious and political endeavors. Through the application of shari'a (Islamic law), the Islamic courts provided a justice system in a society buffeted by lawlessness and violence, where warlords and their gunmen raped, robbed, kidnapped, and killed at will. Desperate for law and order, a working economy, and basic social services, the Somali public generally supported al-Itihaad's efforts, while Somali business owners endorsed the courts and financed their law enforcement activities.

Instability in Somalia precipitated a new crisis with Ethiopia. In 1994, al-Itihaad established a military presence near the borders with Kenya and Ethiopia and launched numerous attacks inside Ethiopia, especially in the Somali-inhabited regions. By 1996, Ethiopia was making regular incursions into Somalia to challenge al-Itihaad and build alliances with Somali warlords. In 2000, a group of Ethiopian-backed warlords formed the Somali Reconciliation and Restoration Council (SRRC), led by Abdullahi Yusuf Ahmed, who would become president of Somalia in 2004 as a member of the foreign-backed Transitional Federal Government (TFG), and by Hussein Mohammed Aidid, who had succeeded his father, Mohammed Farah Aidid, as head of the powerful USC militia.

Instability in Somalia also inspired new US concerns. US counterterrorism experts warned that Somalia had become a haven for al-Qaeda—including operatives responsible for bombing the US Embassies in Kenya and Tanzania in 1998. These fears escalated after the September 2001 terrorist attacks on New York and Washington, DC. In October 2001, the UN included al-Itihaad on a list of organizations associated with al-Qaeda, and in December the United States placed al-Itihaad on the 2001 USA Patriot Act's "Terrorist Exclusion List." Businesses with purported ties to al-Itihaad were also targeted. Among these was Somalia's largest employer, al-Barakat, a money transfer company with telecommunications, internet, and other holdings that had assumed significant banking functions after the collapse of the country's banking system in the early 1990s. Al-Barakat had operations in forty countries, transferred some $140 million annually, and served as a lifeline for many Somalis, who depended on remittances from family members abroad to sustain them. In November 2001, the George W. Bush administration, claiming that al-Barakat served as a conduit for funds to al-Qaeda, closed its offices, froze its US assets, and pressured the UN Security Council to impose sanctions.[14] These actions effectively terminated al-Barakat's operations, jeopardizing the well-being of Somali citizens and generating increased animosity toward the United States.[15] Washington also sought common cause with Ethiopia, Somalia's regional rival, which for centuries had been dominated by Christian elites. In 2006, the US government referred to Ethiopia as "the linchpin to stability in the Horn of Africa and the Global War on Terrorism."[16]

Instability in Somalia also worried other external powers. The UN, the AU, the EU, the Arab League, and IGAD intensified their diplomatic involvement. In 2004, they helped broker an agreement to establish a central government in Somalia—the fourteenth attempt since Siad Barre was ousted in 1991. The resulting Transitional Federal Government was backed by these external entities, and by the United States and Ethiopia. However, the TFG had very little support inside Somalia. The negotiations had been deeply influenced by SRRC warlords who aspired to establish a clan-based federal system that would consolidate their own power. Although presented as a government of national unity, the TFG was dominated by the Mijerteen clan/Darod clan family of its president, SRRC warlord Abdullahi Yusuf Ahmed. It marginalized many of the Hawiye clans that had long controlled Mogadishu, and it purged the parliament of opposition members. Unable to enter Mogadishu's hostile environs, the TFG established its capital in Baidoa, 150 miles away, where it was protected by Ethiopian troops. It controlled little territory outside that city. Rife with nepotism and cronyism, the TFG was incompetent and corrupt. The salaries of senior army, police, and intelligence officers, as well as government ministers and parliamentarians, were paid by foreign donors, and government officials were not accountable to the Somali people. President Yusuf, the SRRC men he appointed to top positions, and his prime minister, Ali Mohamed Ghedi, were all closely linked to Ethiopia. As a result, many Somalis considered the TFG to be an Ethiopian puppet regime.

Supported by the United States, President Yusuf opposed all forms of political Islam and resisted the inclusion of Islamists in his government. As a result, the powerful Islamic courts and their proponents refused to support the TFG. President Yusuf's reliance on Ethiopian troops and his anti-Islamist actions helped rally support for the Islamic Courts Union (ICU), which had formed in 2000 to consolidate the power of the Islamic courts and improve their effectiveness. Courts affiliated with al-Itihaad promoted a strict, Salafist interpretation of Islamic law, while others interpreted the law according to the more tolerant Sufi traditions that most Somalis embraced.[17]

Disregarding popular support for the ICU, external powers were determined to undermine it. In early 2006, the CIA encouraged a group of clan militia leaders, businessmen, and warlords—including four TFG cabinet ministers—to join forces against the growing Islamist movement. The result was the Alliance for the Restoration of Peace and Counter-Terrorism (ARPCT). Violating the 1992 UN arms embargo, the CIA provided the

Photo 4.3. Ethiopian troops participate in AMISOM patrol in Baidoa, Somalia, March 27, 2014. Photo by Abdi Dagane/AU UN IST.

ARPCT with weapons and financed its militias. In return, the alliance became an accessory to the US war on terror—capturing and rendering to the United States suspected al-Qaeda operatives, specifically those believed to be involved in the 1998 US Embassy bombings in Kenya and Tanzania and the 2002 attacks on an Israeli-owned hotel and airliner in Kenya. Fighting between the ARPCT and the ICU broke out in February 2006. In May, warlord attacks on ICU militias in Mogadishu instigated some of the worst street fighting in the capital since Siad Barre's government fell apart in 1991. The TFG appealed for foreign military assistance and the United States, Ethiopia, Italy, and Yemen complied, again violating the UN arms embargo. Eritrea, in turn, provided weapons to the ICU militias to counter the influence of Ethiopia, its regional nemesis. In early June, ICU militias seized control of Mogadishu and ousted the warlords who had controlled the capital for fifteen years.

By July 2006, ICU militias had gained ascendancy over most of southern and central Somalia, including the key ports and airfields. In Mogadishu, the courts began to rebuild basic government services, establishing committees on sanitation, reconstruction, education, and justice. They cracked down on criminals, armed youth, and warlord militias, bringing a semblance of security to the capital city. Mogadishu's port and international airport, which had been closed for more than a decade, reopened. The ICU garnered immense popular support, even from secular Somalis who welcomed the implementation of Islamic law as way to stem crime and violence. François Lonseny Fall, at that time the UN special representative to Somalia, acknowledged that the ICU had "achieved great things in Mogadishu," while other human rights groups claimed that with Islam as a unifying factor, the ICU had been more successful than any previous government in uniting and disarming Somali clans.[18]

The ICU victory was precisely the opposite of what the CIA had hoped for when it backed the warlord alliance. In fact, foreign meddling had triggered a backlash that strengthened radical factions. In June 2006, Sheikh Hassan Dahir Aweys, a Salafi and former al-Itihaad leader, was appointed chair of the ICU consultative council, challenging the leadership of the executive council chair, Sheikh Sharif Sheikh Ahmed, a moderate Sufi cleric. A Somali national army colonel under Siad Barre and onetime member of Aidid's militia, Aweys had joined the al-Itihaad militia in the early 1990s and helped establish Islamic courts in Mogadishu at the end of that decade. Although Aweys hoped to implement Islamic law throughout Somalia, some analysts considered him to be a mitigating influence vis-à-vis extremists in al-Shabaab, the ICU's youth militia, which aspired to establish an Islamic state beyond Somalia's borders.

External support for the warlords and the TFG strengthened the position of radicals in the ICU. In early July 2006, Osama bin Laden called on Muslims worldwide to wage jihad in Somalia and warned that Muslim fighters would challenge all foreign troops, including UN and AU peacekeepers, if they intervened to support the TFG. Three weeks later, when ICU forces threatened the transitional government's headquarters in Baidoa, hundreds of Ethiopian soldiers, supported by tanks and helicopters, arrived to protect the government's position. In the weeks that followed, some 5,000 Ethiopian troops invaded Somalia, while more amassed on the border. ICU hardliners began to mobilize for confrontation with Ethiopia, appealing both to Somali irredentist claims and to religious sentiment against the predominantly Christian regime that sustained the warlords and propped up the TFG.

Although most Somalis did not support the jihadist agenda of the hardliners, and few wanted another war with Ethiopia—which still claimed one of the largest, most sophisticated armies in sub-Saharan Africa—the presence of Ethiopian troops in Baidoa and persistent Ethiopian incursions across Somalia's borders rallied the population behind the radicals. Moderates in the ICU, who previously had discussed elections and power sharing, also began talking war. Departing from his earlier position, Sheikh Hassan Dahir Aweys urged Somalis to prepare for jihad against Ethiopia. In late July and early August 2006, some forty senior government officials, including a number of cabinet ministers, abandoned the TFG. Some defected to the ICU, taking their own militias with them.

The fallout from foreign intervention rapidly transformed the Somali conflict into a regional conflagration. In October, the UN reported that ten nations were supplying arms to various Somali factions in violation of the UN embargo. Djibouti, Egypt, Eritrea, Iran, Libya, Saudi Arabia, and Syria were supporting the ICU, while Ethiopia, Uganda, and Yemen were furnishing weapons to the TFG. In November, as ICU militias routed TFG forces in the north, President Yusuf appealed for further external assistance. The United States responded, pushing through a UN Security Council resolution on December 6, 2006, that described the Somali situation as "a threat to international peace and security in the region" and authorized the AU and IGAD to establish a military force to protect the TFG and to train its security forces.[19] The resolution also created a loophole in the UN arms embargo that allowed the African peacekeeping forces—and implicitly, Ethiopian soldiers protecting the TFG—to be supplied with weapons, while continuing to deny arms to the ICU.

On December 14, US Assistant Secretary of State for African Affairs Jendayi Frazer referred to ICU leaders as "extremists to the core" who were "controlled by al-Qaeda."[20] Ethiopia took this high-level US condemnation as a green light for a full-scale invasion. Six days later, as ICU militias attempted to capture Baidoa, Ethiopian warplanes buttressed by thousands of Ethiopian and TFG soldiers struck back, decimating the poorly armed ICU militias. On December 24, 2006, after months of military buildup, some 8,000 Ethiopian troops, supported by tanks and attack helicopters, advanced on Mogadishu, bombing Somalia's two main airports along the way. The UN Security Council was silent. Its failure to condemn the Ethiopian invasion confirmed Somali views that the international body was not a neutral broker of peace, but a partisan force that had sanctioned foreign intervention to bolster a client regime that had virtually no internal support.

While the UN tacitly condoned the Ethiopian offensive, the United States actively supported it. The State Department referred to the invasion as a legitimate response to aggression by Somali Muslim extremists. Convinced that the al-Qaeda militants who had planned the 1998 and 2002 attacks in Kenya and Tanzania were hiding in southern Somalia under ICU protection, US intelligence officials were determined to root them out. The Combined Joint Task Force–Horn of Africa (CJTF-HOA), a Djibouti-based counterterrorism entity comprising nearly 2,000 US military and civilian personnel, provided satellite photos and other intelligence to the Ethiopian army to help it locate ICU fighters. Planes piloted by US Special Operations Forces took off from bases in Djibouti, Ethiopia, and Kenya and joined Ethiopian aircraft in bombing ICU strongholds. As the invasion progressed, US Special Operations Forces, functioning from a secret airfield in Ethiopia, entered Somalia alongside the Ethiopian army, purportedly to track down the al-Qaeda suspects.[21] US ground troops helped Ethiopian soldiers gather evidence, while the US Navy patrolled the Somali coast and intercepted ships to search for al-Qaeda operatives. Fearing massive bloodshed and the destruction of Mogadishu, business and clan leaders urged the ICU to disband and to abandon the capital without resistance. The ICU militias complied and retreated toward the Kenyan border, pursued by intelligence and security forces from Ethiopia, Kenya, Somalia, and the United States. In a rendition program run by Ethiopia, the United States, and the TFG, militants were rounded up and deported to secret detention facilities in Ethiopia. On January 8, 2007, TFG President Yusuf entered the capital for the first time since taking office in 2004.

The joint Ethiopian-US operation resulted in an increase, rather than a decrease, in chaos and violence. Within weeks of the foreign invasion, a homegrown insurgency had begun, rallying al-Shabaab and other ICU militias, clans that had been marginalized by the TFG, and a wide range of groups that benefited from anarchy, including warlord militias, hired gunmen, arms and drug traffickers, smugglers, and profiteers. The Somali insurgents were joined by fighters from Afghanistan, Pakistan, and the Arabian Peninsula who responded to the call to wage jihad against Ethiopia. Warlord and clan militias set up roadblocks and shook down residents. Banditry and extortion, which had been suppressed by the ICU, returned with a vengeance. Using weapons left over from the Cold War, including AK-47 assault rifles, mortars, and rocket-propelled grenades, insurgents attacked TFG and Ethiopian troops, government buildings, and infrastructure. Employing techniques developed by Iraqi resisters after the 2003 US invasion, they discharged landmines, suicide bombs, and improvised explosive devices, and they targeted TFG officials for assassination. In mid-January 2007, the TFG parliament declared a state of emergency and granted the president broad powers to enforce security.

Foreign involvement assumed a new dimension in February, when the UN Security Council authorized the establishment of the African Union Mission in Somalia (AMISOM), which was slated to deploy 8,000 African peacekeepers of diverse nationalities to replace the Ethiopian soldiers shoring up the TFG. Funded by the UN and the EU, the AU force appeared to many Somalis as yet another case of unwanted foreign intrusion. The fact that most of the troops came from the predominantly Christian countries of Uganda and Burundi augmented public hostility. Moreover, the AU force was slow to arrive—only 2,600 soldiers were in place by August 2008. As a result, Ethiopian soldiers would remain on Somali soil until early 2009.

In March 2007, the Ethiopian military launched an offensive on Mogadishu to capture key locations from insurgents who had held parts of the capital since the ICU's departure in January. Assisted by TFG police, Ethiopian soldiers cracked down on Hawiye neighborhoods and closed ports and airfields belonging to Hawiye businessmen, charging that the clan was supporting the insurgency. Widespread arrests, assaults, looting, and rape—perpetrated both by Ethiopian soldiers and by TFG police who were trained and paid by the UN Development Programme—intensified popular support for the insurgency.

The ensuing two-month-long battle for Mogadishu precipitated the most destructive fighting in a decade and a half. By the end of April, some 1,300 Mogadishu residents had been killed, and more than 400,000 had fled their homes. Human rights organizations accused participants on all sides of war crimes. They charged that Ethiopian forces had engaged in widespread and indiscriminate bombing of densely populated areas as well as the collective punishment of civilians, including mass arrests and summary executions. They also claimed that the Ethiopian military had intentionally shelled hospitals, pillaged medical equipment, and blocked the flow of humanitarian assistance, and that Ethiopian and TFG soldiers had raped, plundered, and killed with impunity. Human rights groups asserted that insurgents had also engaged in assassinations and summary executions and that they had demonstrated disregard for civilian lives by mounting attacks from densely populated neighborhoods, which then bore the brunt of Ethiopian and TFG retaliation.

Violence continued to escalate throughout 2007. Badly weakened by infighting and defections, the TFG was on the verge of collapse. By January 2008, al-Shabaab, other ICU militias, and their allies had recovered much of the territory they had lost a year earlier. Al-Shabaab garnered some civilian support, especially in southern Somalia, where it established a semblance of law and order and a justice system that followed years of abuse by warlord militias and government police. In March 2008, the US State Department designated al-Shabaab a "foreign terrorist organization."[22] Critics warned that the label could enhance al-Shabaab's popularity and at the same time render negotiations with the organization nearly impossible. Matters were further complicated in May, when a targeted US missile strike killed Aden Hashi Farah Ayro, al-Shabaab top's leader, who had fought in the Soviet-Afghan War. Prior to Ayro's killing, al-Shabaab had focused its attacks on Ethiopian and TFG soldiers. However, US actions redirected al-Shabaab's attention to the West. Declaring war on all foreigners, al-Shabaab began to target Western aid workers, journalists, and Somalis working with foreign organizations. As a result, a number of externally based organizations withdrew their personnel, and humanitarian operations were dramatically curtailed.

By mid-2008, insurgent forces controlled most of southern and central Somalia as well as most of Mogadishu. The TFG-Ethiopian alliance held only a few blocks of the capital, including the port, airport, and presidential palace. The support base for extremists was much larger and more radical than it had been before the Ethiopian invasion, and terrorist threats were far more serious. Even Western diplomats recognized that Islamists had to be included in negotiations for any future government that had a chance of success. In June, moderates in the TFG and the Alliance for the Re-liberation of Somalia (ARS), an opposition coalition composed of both Islamist and secular groups, met in Djibouti to negotiate terms for peace. Al-Shabaab, which controlled much of southern Somalia, opposed collaboration with the secular parties and refused to participate.

The ensuing Djibouti Agreement, backed by the UN, the AU, the EU, and the United States, resulted in a number of changes on the ground. In January 2009, the Somali parliament was enlarged to include moderate Islamists, representatives of citizens' groups, and Somalis from the diaspora. The parliament elected a new president, selecting Sheikh Sharif Sheikh Ahmed, an ARS leader and Sufi moderate who had led the ICU executive council before the foreign invasion. By the end of the month, Ethiopia had withdrawn its troops from Somalia. In April the new parliament voted to make Islamic law the basis of the Somali legal system. The insurgents' rallying points were severely weakened. The foreign occupier had withdrawn, an Islamist had been elected president, and Islamic law was being implemented throughout the country. A number of Muslim factions that had opposed the TFG agreed to lay down arms. Ahlu Sunnah Wal Jama'a (Followers of the Prophetic Way and Consensus), an alliance of Sufi militias backed by local clans, agreed to resist al-Shabaab and to back the Sheikh Sharif government. However, other factions persisted. In February 2009, an alliance of Muslim insurgent organizations that had rejected the Djibouti Agreement established Hizbul Islam (Islamic Party) under the leadership of Sheikh Hassan Dahir Aweys, erstwhile ICU consultative council leader, onetime Sheikh Sharif ally, and subsequent ally of al-Shabaab. In May, Hizbul Islam and al-Shabaab conducted a joint operation against TFG forces in Mogadishu, where AMISOM forces saved the government from destruction.

Despite the reforms mandated by the Djibouti Agreement, the TFG remained weak and unpopular. It was corrupt, unrepresentative of the popular majority, and beholden to outsiders. Determined to retain a monopoly on power and resources, it refused to engage with local political and military forces that might threaten its position. It failed to build state institutions and relied on foreign backers to uphold its power. In the northwest (Somaliland) and the northeast (Puntland), autonomous regional governments exercised de facto authority without Mogadishu's approval or support. Some TFG-allied militias, including Ahlu Sunnah Wal Jama'a, joined Ethiopian soldiers in targeting civilians and were roundly condemned by human rights organizations.

Although the departure of Ethiopian troops was widely applauded inside Somalia, the AMISOM force also generated intense hostility, even among those who opposed al-Shabaab. AMISOM's heavy shelling of urban neighborhoods, like the Ethiopian attacks, had resulted in large numbers of civilian deaths. Many Somalis also chafed at the presence of thousands of troops from neighboring countries where the regimes in power were dominated by Christians and where Muslims faced repression and discrimination. Al-Shabaab played on these sentiments and characterized AMISOM as a Christian invading force. Nor was AMISOM particularly effective. Al-Shabaab retained a strong presence in Somalia, and on AMISOM's watch it expanded its operations into neighboring countries. In July 2010, al-Shabaab engaged in its first cross-border operation, setting off coordinated bombs in Kampala, Uganda, that killed seventy-six people in retaliation for Uganda's central role in AMISOM. Although AMISOM expelled al-Shabaab from Mogadishu in August 2011, the insurgent organization continued to control most of the country's southern and central regions.

Al-Shabaab's tenacity sparked a new episode of foreign military intervention in 2011. In October, some 2,000 Kenyan troops, followed by hundreds of Ethiopian troops in November, crossed Somalia's southern border to attack al-Shabaab and establish a buffer between the two countries. The civilian death toll provoked animosity toward the Kenyan government, and al-Shabaab vowed to retaliate. Although Kenya claimed to be acting at the invitation of the TFG, the UN Security Council had tasked AMISOM with peacekeeping in Somalia. No other foreign entity was authorized to intervene militarily in Somali affairs. Nonetheless, the UN Security Council condoned Nairobi's unilateral action, and in July 2012 AMISOM formally assumed authority over the Kenyan occupation force, giving it a veneer of legitimacy. Responding to the escalated international response and hoping to boost its image and fighting capacity, al-Shabaab formally merged with al-Qaeda in February 2012.

The year 2012 marked the end of the eight-year transitional government, but not an end to the Somali crisis. The new political dispensation—complete with constitution, parliament, and president—was once again the product of outside forces. It was mediated by the UN, backed by the international community, and disavowed by large segments of Somali civil society, which had had little input into the process. The new president, Hassan Sheikh Mohamud, was a moderate Islamist with links to the Islamic Courts Union and Somalia's Muslim Brotherhood. He was also an educator and longtime civil society activist who had worked with the UN in various capacities. However, his ability to effect change was limited, and foreign troops continued to battle al-Shabaab on Somali soil.

In late September, Kenyan AMISOM soldiers, assisted by Somali government troops and militias, weakened al-Shabaab's economic base when they gained control of the strategic southern port of Kismayo. A key transit point for foreign fighters, weapons, and supplies entering Somalia, and for the export of sugar, livestock, charcoal, and khat, the port hosted an illegal trade that generated hundreds of millions of dollars a year for al-Shabaab and its collaborators in the local Somali administration, as well as for the Kenya Defence Forces and Kenyan government. Although Somalia and Kenya officially sought an end to the turmoil, the enormous profits engendered by a lawless society served as an incentive for many to continue the conflict.

By 2012 al-Shabaab was diminished, but not defeated. As it lost territory and revenues, the organization changed tactics, focusing increasingly on unprotected soft targets, including government offices, schools, hotels, and restaurants. As it was ousted from towns and cities and pushed to Somalia's southern border, al-Shabaab targeted rural populations in Kenya's North Eastern Province. Distrusted and neglected by the Nairobi government, the predominantly Somali population of this area was especially vulnerable. While these killings provoked little international response, world attention was captured by al-Shabaab's September 2013 attack on an exclusive Nairobi shopping mall that claimed the lives of sixty-seven people, including many foreign nationals. AMISOM forces, led by Kenyan soldiers, responded with an aerial offensive that killed some 300 al-Shabaab militants. In 2014, AMISOM forces were bolstered with more than 4,000 Ethiopian troops. Critics warned that the reengagement of the Ethiopian military would serve as a rallying cry for al-Shabaab.

Meanwhile, the United States escalated its low-intensity war against al-Shabaab operatives, deploying both private contractors and US Special Operations Forces, who trained and advised African partners, participated in raids, and interrogated prisoners. During 2014–16, US attacks killed Ahmed Abdi Godane, al-Shabaab's leader since Ayro's death in 2008; the organization's intelligence chief; the official who purportedly planned the 2013 Nairobi mall attack; and some 150 militants in an al-Shabaab training camp. However, middle-level commanders quickly replaced assassinated leaders, and the insurgents continued to attack AMISOM and Somali troops, government officials, and civilians. The defection of a high-level al-Shabaab commander to the Islamic State in

October 2015 and the formation of two new organizations, the Islamic State in Somalia and the Islamic State in Somalia, Kenya, Tanzania, and Uganda, resulted in even more brutality on the ground. Meanwhile, AMISOM forces were weakened. In 2016, the EU reduced its funding. The AU announced that AMISOM would begin to withdraw in 2018 after transferring authority to the Somali national army, which remained corrupt and ineffective. US covert operations in Somalia escalated in 2017, and the number of Special Operations troops on the ground peaked at nearly 500. At the year's end it was clear that the external response to instability had transformed the conflict, but it had not brought peace.

Conclusion

Recent conflicts in Somalia have deep historical roots. Their causes are complex, including both internal and external factors. Justifications for intervention have been equally complicated: they have varied from actor to actor and changed over time. Spurred initially by regional instability and the responsibility to protect, foreign powers were increasingly galvanized by the war on terror. The results were mixed. Although the immediate humanitarian crisis—widespread starvation—was to some extent averted, the long-term effects were largely negative. Foreign intervention provoked a terrorist insurgency that consumed civilian lives and increased regional instability. Externally brokered peace initiatives failed to end the conflict. Large segments of Somali civil society were not invited to the bargaining table, grassroots peace-building and nation-building efforts were ignored, and the interests of outsiders and Somali elites prevailed over those of ordinary Somali citizens. As a result, the ensuing agreements garnered little internal support, and a succession of weak Somali governments failed to provide services and security to citizens. Similar practices marked the course of foreign intervention in Sudan and South Sudan, to the west of Somalia, which is the subject of chapter 5.

Suggested Reading

For overviews of Somali history and society, three surveys are especially recommended. Lee V. Cassanelli's pathbreaking work, *The Shaping of Somali Society: Reconstructing the History of a Pastoral People, 1600–1900* (Philadelphia: University of Pennsylvania Press, 1982), explores the precolonial foundations of modern Somali society. I. M. Lewis, *A Modern History of the Somali: Nation and State in the Horn of Africa*, 4th ed. (Athens: Ohio University Press, 2002), is regarded as a seminal study of Somali politics and society from ancient times through the early 1990s. However, Lewis's characterization of Somali political identity as one largely based on clans and their segments—rather than one that embraces a fluid assortment of genealogical, language, religious, cultural, and economic factors—has been challenged by more recent scholarship. See, for instance, Abdi I. Samatar, "Debating Somali Identity in a British Tribunal: The Case of the BBC Somali Service," *Bildhaan: An International Journal of Somali Studies* 10 (2010), article 8. Finally, David D. Laitin and Said S. Samatar, *Somalia: Nation in Search of a State* (Boulder, CO: Westview Press, 1987), considers the precolonial and colonial periods and focuses especially on events since independence.

The early independence period is examined in two significant studies. Abdi I. Samatar, *Africa's First Democrats: Somalia's Aden A. Osman and Abdirazak H. Hussen* (Bloomington: Indiana University Press, 2016), focuses on the democratic political organizations that led the struggle for independence, the leaders who shaped the first democratically elected governments, and their opponents who were engaged in sectarian and patronage networks. Hannah Whittaker, *Insurgency and Counterinsurgency in Kenya: A Social History of the Shifta Conflict, c. 1963–1968* (Leiden: Brill, 2015), explores the dynamics of a secessionist war in northern Kenya, a region heavily populated by ethnic Somalis, where government counterinsurgency tactics alienated the Somali minority and exacerbated tensions between the Kenyan and Somali states.

Other historical studies explore the emergence of social and economic hierarchies in Somali society. Abdi I. Samatar, *The State and Rural Transformation in Northern Somalia, 1884–1986* (Madison: University of Wisconsin Press, 1989), investigates class formation and economic history in modern Somalia. Catherine Lowe Besteman, *Unraveling Somalia: Race, Violence, and the Legacy of Slavery* (Philadelphia: University of Pennsylvania Press, 1999), examines the historical development of hierarchies based on race, class, status, region, language, and occupation and the implications of these hierarchies after the breakdown of Somalia's central government. Three recommended works provide insight into the origins of the Somali Bantu as an ethnic group and the violence perpetrated against its members after the central government failed: Mohamed

Eno, *The Bantu-Jareer Somalis: Unearthing Apartheid in the Horn of Africa* (London: Adonis and Abbey, 2008); Catherine Besteman, *Making Refuge: Somali Bantu Refugees and Lewiston, Maine* (Durham, NC: Duke University Press, 2016); and Ken Menkhaus, "The Question of Ethnicity in Somali Studies: The Case of Somali Bantu Identity," in *Milk and Peace, Drought and War: Somali Culture, Society and Politics,* ed. Markus V. Hoehne and Virginia Luling (London: Hurst, 2010), 87–104.

A number of studies focus on Somalia during the Cold War. Laitin and Samatar, *Somalia: Nation in Search of a State* (mentioned previously), and Ahmed I. Samatar, *Socialist Somalia: Rhetoric and Reality* (London: Zed Books, 1988), examine Somalia under the Siad Barre regime. Jeffrey A. Lefebvre, *Arms for the Horn: U.S. Security Policy in Ethiopia and Somalia, 1953–1991* (Pittsburgh: University of Pittsburgh Press, 1991), uses declassified government documents and interviews to examine US relations with Somalia and Ethiopia over four decades, focusing especially on the massive influx of weaponry and its societal impact. Marina Ottaway, *Soviet and American Influence in the Horn of Africa* (New York: Praeger, 1982), focuses on the role of the Soviet Union and the United States in both countries. Louise Woodroofe, *"Buried in the Sands of the Ogaden": The United States, the Horn of Africa, and the Demise of Détente* (Kent, OH: Kent State University Press, 2013), and Nancy Mitchell, *Jimmy Carter in Africa: Race and the Cold War* (Stanford, CA: Stanford University Press, 2016), provide important new insights into Cold War dynamics in the Horn and US and Soviet involvement in the Ogaden war. For a brief overview of foreign intervention in the Horn during the Cold War, see Elizabeth Schmidt, *Foreign Intervention in Africa: From the Cold War to the War on Terror* (New York: Cambridge University Press, 2013), chap. 6.

Several works that examine Somalia since the dissolution of the Siad Barre regime focus on the origins of conflict and difference in Somali society. Grounded in sources that reveal grassroots perspectives, Lidwien Kapteijns, *Clan Cleansing in Somalia: The Ruinous Legacy of 1991* (Philadelphia: University of Pennsylvania Press, 2013), shows how Siad Barre promoted conflict and competition among clans in order to establish and protect his neopatrimonial state, and how the political elites, warlords, and rebels who succeeded him used similar strategies of clan mobilization and clan cleansing to obtain and maintain power. Afyare Abdi Elmi, *Understanding the Somalia Conflagration: Identity, Islam and*

Peacebuilding (London: Pluto Press, 2010), takes a different view, arguing that clan identity is deeply rooted, rather than a tool manipulated by elites, and that it must be considered if a political settlement is to endure. Contributors to Catherine Besteman and Lee V. Cassanelli, eds., *The Struggle for Land in Southern Somalia: The War Behind the War* (Boulder, CO: Westview Press, 1996), investigate contests over land and resources as stimuli for violent conflict. Besteman, *Unraveling Somalia* (mentioned previously), examines the ways in which war and violence have disproportionately affected rural southerners. M. J. Fox, *The Roots of Somali Political Culture* (Boulder, CO: Lynne Rienner, 2015), analyzes the source of divergent political cultures in Somalia, Somaliland, and Puntland. Mark Bradbury, *Becoming Somaliland* (Bloomington: Indiana University Press, 2008), explores political developments in the autonomous northern region that declared itself an independent state in 1991.

US and UN interventions in Somalia in the 1990s are the subject of several studies. John G. Sommer, *Hope Restored? Humanitarian Aid in Somalia, 1990–1994* (Geneva: Refugee Policy Group, 1994), investigates the dynamics of the humanitarian crisis that led to foreign military intervention, as well as debates within NGO and governmental circles about the merits of such actions. Rakiya Omaar, Alexander de Waal, and African Rights, *Somalia: Human Rights Abuses by the United Nations Forces* (London: African Rights, 1993), documents human rights violations by UN forces in Somalia in the months before the October 1993 US encounter with Somali militias and civilians. UN Special Representative Mohamed Sahnoun's account, *Somalia: The Missed Opportunities* (Washington, DC: United States Institute of Peace, 1994), provides an insider's view that is critical of the UN mission. John L. Hirsch and Robert B. Oakley, *Somalia and Operation Restore Hope: Reflections on Peacemaking and Peacekeeping* (Washington, DC: United States Institute of Peace, 1995), offers other insider perspectives. As US special envoy, Oakley led the humanitarian phase of the mission and was sharply critical of the military venture that followed. Hirsch served as political advisor to the relief effort. Written by a humanitarian aid worker in Somalia during the US-UN intervention, Kenneth R. Rutherford, *Humanitarianism Under Fire: The US and UN Intervention in Somalia* (Sterling, VA: Kumarian Press, 2008), examines the motivations for and legacy of that operation. Mark Bowden, *Black Hawk Down: A Story of Modern War* (New York: Atlantic Monthly Press, 1999), provides an account of the US Army Ranger–Delta Force intervention in Mogadishu from the perspective of an investigative journalist.

The influence of Islamism in Somali society is explored in a number of works. The history of the Islamic courts movement is examined in Cedric Barnes and Harun Hassan, "The Rise and Fall of Mogadishu's Islamic Courts," *Journal of Eastern African Studies* 1, no. 2 (July 2007): 151–60. Ken Menkhaus, *Somalia: State Collapse and the Threat of Terrorism* (New York: Oxford University Press, 2004), explores how Islamic courts, regional authorities, and municipalities governed in the absence of a central government and considers the relationship of Somali jihadist organizations to international terrorism. Contributors to Alex de Waal, ed., *Islamism and Its Enemies in the Horn of Africa* (Bloomington: Indiana University Press, 2004), focus on Islamist organizations that provided health and education services in the region and the impact on local struggles of the US-led war on terror.

The Horn as a battleground in the war on terror is the focus of several works. Robert I. Rotberg's collection, *Battling Terrorism in the Horn of Africa* (Washington, DC: Brookings Institution Press/World Peace Foundation, 2005), considers the Horn as a frontline in the US war on terror and explores the ways in which regional powers have been used to promote US interests. Peter Woodward, *US Foreign Policy and the Horn of Africa* (Burlington, VT: Ashgate, 2006), investigates US relations with Islamism in the Horn of Africa, using Somalia as a case study. Gregory A. Pirio, *African Jihad: Bin Laden's Quest for the Horn of Africa* (Trenton, NJ: Red Sea Press, 2007), offers a detailed narrative of the evolving relationship between some Somali jihadist organizations and al-Qaeda. Stig Jarle Hansen, *Al-Shabaab in Somalia: The History and Ideology of a Militant Islamist Group, 2005–2012* (New York: Oxford University Press, 2013), traces al-Shabaab's origins, evolution, and resilience and explores the impact of AU and US military actions on the organization's tactics and strategies, including its newer focus on East African countries that contribute to AU forces. Anneli Botha and Mahdi Abdile, *Radicalisation and al-Shabaab Recruitment in Somalia*, ISS Paper 266 (Institute for Security Studies, 2014), is based on interviews with former al-Shabaab fighters. It explores the reasons recruits were attracted to the organization, focusing on religion, politics, education, employment, and the search for collective identity and belonging.

The perspectives of ordinary Somalis are highlighted in several studies. Mary Harper, *Getting Somalia Wrong? Faith, War, and Hope in a Shattered State* (London: Zed Books, 2012), argues that viewing post-1991 Somalia through the lens of al-Qaeda and the war on terror distorts a more complex reality. In the face of state failure, Somalis developed new forms of local politics, justice, business, and education that contributed to a thriving society. Highlighting Somali voices and perspectives, the book is especially useful for its insights into state collapse, Islamism, piracy, and foreign intervention. Similarly, Peter Little, *Somalia: The Stateless Economy* (Bloomington: Indiana University Press, 2004), focuses on the ways in which Somalis developed a functioning economy in the absence of a central state. Jonny Steinberg explores the experiences of Somali displacement and exile in *A Man of Good Hope: A Refugee's Tale* (New York: Vintage, 2015), the biography of a Somali immigrant in a Cape Town slum. The book's protagonist escaped poverty and violence in Somalia only to face similar traumas in South Africa, where xenophobic hatred has had deadly consequences for Africans of other nationalities.

The novels of Somali author Nuruddin Farah offer critical insights into Somali experiences and perspectives after the failure of the central government in 1991. *Links* (New York: Riverhead Books, 2004) details the journey of a longtime exile who returns home after the departure of US troops in 1994 to find a devastated capital city controlled by warlords and youth gangs. *Knots* (New York: Riverhead Books, 2007) follows the path of a woman who escapes a failed marriage in the United States to pursue a new life in the fractured country where she was born. *Crossbones* (New York: Riverhead Books, 2011) focuses on another return by the *Links* protagonist, who faces Islamist governance and an Ethiopian invasion as he attempts to locate a relative who was recruited into the jihadist insurgency. *Hiding in Plain Sight* (New York: Penguin, 2015) continues the theme of exile and displacement, focusing on the lives of a Nairobi-based Somali UN worker, who was killed in an al-Shabaab attack on UN offices in Mogadishu, and his sister who lived in Rome.

Map 5.1. Sudan and South Sudan, 2018. (Map by Philip Schwartzberg, Meridian Mapping, Minneapolis.)

5

Sudan and South Sudan

Conflicting Interests and Inadequate Solutions (1991–2017)

THIS CHAPTER DEVELOPS four case studies to illuminate the impact of foreign political and military intervention in Sudan from 1991 through 2017, and in South Sudan after its establishment in 2011. Civil war, ethnic cleansing, and terrorist networks caused instability in both countries and also in neighboring states. Outside intervention was mobilized at various times in response to instability, to protect civilians, and to counter a terrorist threat. In contrast to neighboring Somalia, foreign troops in Sudan did not become key players in internal conflicts. External interests did not threaten the central government or attempt to establish a new one, but instead negotiated with the regime in power. The results of intervention were decidedly mixed. Some critics charged that more aggressive measures would have produced more desirable outcomes. Others contended that using greater force to address complex political, economic, and social problems would likely have sparked further violence and instability.

The first case study focuses on the period 1991 to 1996, when Osama bin Laden and his al-Qaeda network were headquartered in Sudan and the war on terror paradigm framed US policy. Washington, with the help of Saudi Arabia and the UN Security Council, successfully pressured Khartoum to expel bin Laden and his organization and to cooperate with the CIA in counterterrorism efforts. However, Sudan's north-south civil war (1983–2005), which was viewed as pitting Muslims against Christians, inhibited a close relationship between the two countries.

The second case study examines the north-south civil war and international response from 1991 to 2017. Although some of Sudan's neighbors supported rival factions and promoted their own interests in the war, the response to instability/responsibility to protect paradigm shaped broader international policy toward Sudan during this period. The UN, the United States, European countries, and the East African subregional organization IGAD mediated a peace accord that officially ended the war and was deemed a success by the international community. However, the settlement left key issues unresolved, and the flawed agreement laid the foundations for future strife that again implicated neighboring countries. A separate UN force with a narrow mandate was sent to the fledgling state of South Sudan in 2011, but it was unable to establish a lasting peace, and IGAD's efforts were hampered by its members' support for opposing camps.

The third case study investigates the internal and regional roots of the Darfur conflict in western Sudan from 2003 to 2006, and the fourth case study considers the international community's response to that conflict from 2003 to 2017. Once again, the response to instability/responsibility to protect paradigm was used to justify political and military intervention, and once more foreign intervention had mixed results. The AU and the UN staged limited peacekeeping inventions to prevent ethnic cleansing, but they failed to sustain the operations until peace was restored.

Setting the Stage: The Colonial and Cold War Context (1820–1991)

Until July 2011, Sudan and South Sudan were a single country, Sudan, which straddled the continent's north-south divide. The northern region of Sudan was largely covered by the Sahara Desert and semi-arid land, with population concentrated in the Nile River Valley, especially in the capital of Khartoum. The more fertile southern region was geographically part of sub-Saharan Africa. Both regions were multiethnic, but the north was predominantly Muslim and Arab while the south was inhabited primarily by practitioners of Christianity and indigenous religions.

Fragmented by race, religion, and language, Sudan was torn by violent conflict in the decades after independence, including two civil wars between the northern and southern regions. The first of these wars, sparked by a mutiny in 1955, lasted until 1972. The second took place from 1983 to 2005, culminating in an externally brokered peace agreement that led to the independence of South Sudan in 2011. However, South Sudan was also fractured by debilitating rivalries, which provoked renewed warfare in December 2013. Parts of northern Sudan were similarly torn by strife and rebellion. The most serious of these conflicts, in Darfur, began in 2003 and was ongoing in 2017. Rich oil resources were a complicating factor. They financed Sudan's multiple wars and stimulated new conflict between Sudan and South Sudan, as well as fighting within South Sudan. The desire for access to the region's oil reserves also motivated outside powers like China and the United States to search for a lasting peace.

Conflict in contemporary Sudan is rooted in unequal power relations, which both predated and outlasted colonialism. The dominant political and scholarly narrative characterizes the disparity as one that pitted an Arabized Muslim north against a non-Muslim African south.[1] Critics have charged, however, that the north-south/Arab-African paradigm fails to account for other internal conflicts and that it collapses into a single Arab identity qualities that pertain only to the ruling elite. An alternative, more nuanced hypothesis posits that the fundamental problems in Sudan are the dominance of the center—the ruling elites of Khartoum and the Nile Valley—over the rest of the country and the instability of ruling factions, which engage in a permanent competition for power and resources. Insecure political elites, in ever-changing configurations, do not possess the capacity to make peace or to sustain political and economic structures that serve the needs of the country's diverse populations. They have maintained power by constructing patronage networks to dispense largess to supporters and by mobilizing ethnically based militias that terrorize and subdue civilians and plunder their resources, including land, livestock, and oil. Often, their interest in perpetuating war is greater than their desire to promote peace. External powers, by supporting rival factions both inside and outside the government, have helped sustain this dynamic.

Foreign intervention in Sudan has a long history. Throughout most of the nineteenth century, the territory, composed of northern sultanates and the southern periphery, was under Ottoman-Egyptian rule. In 1820 Egyptian forces invaded Sudan and incorporated it into Egypt, then a semi-autonomous region of the Ottoman Empire. In 1885, under the leadership of the Sufi sheikh Muhammad Ahmad ibn Abd Allah—commonly known as al-Mahdi, or the Messiah—Sudanese nationalists and Islamic reformers based in Darfur drove the Ottomans and their British advisors from Khartoum. A decade later, the British toppled the Mahdist state and established the Anglo-Egyptian Condominium, which lasted from 1899 until independence in 1956. During the Cold War, Sudan, like Somalia, was first a Soviet and then a US ally. However, Sudan was never a Western proxy. Although Washington used Khartoum to counter Moscow's influence in Ethiopia, Khartoum also courted conservative Arab governments, Muammar al-Qaddafi's Libya, and, after the Cold War, al-Qaeda.

Proponents of the north-south paradigm often trace its origins to the period of Ottoman-Egyptian rule, when the Arabized Muslim north—in reality an amalgam of Arab and African cultures—plundered the non-Muslim south for ivory and slaves. Although the UK had outlawed slavery throughout its empire in 1833, its Southern Policy in Sudan continued the exploitative relationship between the territory's northern center and southern periphery. To inhibit both the slave trade and the spread of Islam, the colonial administration regulated the flow of northerners to the south and prohibited marriages between northerners and southerners. Economic and educational resources were concentrated in the north, particularly in Khartoum and its environs. The lower ranks of the colonial civil service were staffed by educated northerners, while southerners were forcibly conscripted into the colonial army. Although purportedly established to protect the south from northern domination, the Southern Policy in fact stunted the southern region's development and produced a population with little in the way of education, resources, or power.

After Sudan's independence in 1956, northern Muslims, particularly Arabs from the Nile Valley region around Khartoum, dominated the nation's public spheres. The unequal development of the colonial era continued, causing serious conflicts between the center and the periphery. In the south, northerners replaced the British in the civil service, army, and police. Following a military coup in November 1958, the government expelled foreign Christian missionaries from the south, took over missionary schools, introduced Arabic as a medium of instruction, and pressed nonbelievers to convert to Islam. A southern secessionist movement engaged in armed struggle from 1963 to 1972, when a peace accord granted some autonomy to the southern region. In 1969, after a brief return to civilian rule, the Sudanese military again seized power, this time under the leadership of Colonel Jaafar Nimeiri. A proponent of pan-Arab nationalism, socialism, and secularism, President Nimeiri opposed Sudanese Islamists, allied himself with the Sudanese Communist Party, and maintained close ties with the Soviet Union.[2] In 1972, Sudan's Muslim Brotherhood, an outgrowth of the Egyptian organization, and the Darfur-based Ansar (Followers of the Mahdi) began an armed uprising to establish an Islamic state. The Ansar insurgents were trained by the Islamic Pan-African Legion,

Photo 5.1. Armed children in southern Sudan during the civil war, March 8, 1971. Photo by John Downing/Getty Images.

a paramilitary force organized by Libyan ruler Muammar al-Qaddafi, whose goal was to build a vast Islamic empire in Africa that incorporated Libya, Chad, and the Darfur region of western Sudan.[3]

After the installation of a Marxist government in Ethiopia in 1974, the United States sought a regional ally to serve as a counterweight to Soviet influence in the east and Libyan influence in the west. US interests aligned with those of President Nimeiri, who worried about Moscow's aims in the Horn and Qaddafi's designs on Sudan amid a growing economic crisis and mounting external debt. In 1976, Nimeiri shifted his allegiance to the United States and expelled his Soviet advisors. To reinforce his domestic base, he reconciled with the Muslim Brotherhood, filled the Sudanese military with Islamists, and sought alliances with conservative Arab governments in Egypt and Saudi Arabia. During the Carter and Reagan administrations, Sudan was the largest beneficiary of US aid in sub-Saharan Africa. The Reagan administration made Sudan an important base for the CIA's covert campaign against Qaddafi and a regional center of operations during the Cold War.

Having reconciled with conservative Muslim interests, Nimeiri imposed his own version of Islamic law throughout Sudan in 1983. His actions violated the 1972 peace agreement, which had granted regional autonomy to the south. The implementation of Islamic law in the south, which was home to some 4 million Christians and practitioners of indigenous religions, ignited the second civil war. Spearheaded by the Sudan People's Liberation Movement (SPLM) and its army, the Sudan People's Liberation Army (SPLA), the southern resistance called for an end to northern Muslim dominance. It also demanded greater control over the wealth produced in south, which possessed most of the country's gold, arable land, and oil resources. Appealing to oppressed minorities throughout the country, the SPLA, under the leadership of John Garang, found support in all regions for a more equitable Sudan.[4] The Soviet Union, Cuba, and Ethiopia supported the rebel cause, hoping to weaken the Khartoum regime.

Military pressures exacerbated Sudan's ongoing economic crisis. In 1985, the country was devastated by a regional drought and famine that led to rising food and fuel prices. The effects of an IMF austerity program and a related series of currency devaluations compounded the crisis. The government's paralysis and mounting civil unrest led to Nimeiri's ouster in a military coup in April of that year. A return to civilian rule in 1986 and the election of Sadiq al-Mahdi, leader of the Sufi Umma Party, as prime minister increased the influence of Islamists in the political arena.[5] The Mahdi government sought rapprochement with Libya and embarked on a new southern strategy. Employing Arab and other ethnic militias to fight alongside army regulars, Khartoum waged a scorched earth campaign against the southern populations. Khalil Ibrahim, who organized some of the militias, would later spearhead the Justice and Equality Movement (JEM), an Islamist rebel movement in Darfur, where a different Khartoum government would use similar tactics against civilians in 2003.

Foreign Intervention after the Cold War (1991–2017)

Political and military intervention in Sudan after the Cold War assumed diverse forms and served a variety of interests. The complexities can best be understood if the narrative is broken into four case studies. The first, "Al-Qaeda and the United States," focuses on the period 1991 to 1996, with reflections on the period following the 2001 attacks on the United States. The second, "The North, the South, and the International Community," concentrates on the years 1991 to 2017. The third, "Internal and

Regional Roots of the Darfur Conflict," examines the struggle in Sudan's western region from 2003 to 2006. The fourth, "Darfur and the International Community," considers the same conflict from 2003 to 2017.

Some generalizations can be made about all four case studies. In the 1990s, foreign intervention in Sudan was limited. Concerns about terror and pressure from domestic constituencies framed Western policies. The north-south civil war and the establishment of al-Qaeda's headquarters in Sudan led to increased external involvement, but scant attention was paid to the growing conflict in Darfur, which was exacerbated by population movements driven by climate change and war in neighboring Chad. External interest grew after the turn of the millennium, motivated in large part by the responsibility to protect. Foreign powers helped broker peace agreements that officially ended the war between north and south and also the Darfur conflict. However, fundamental weaknesses in both agreements, which failed to redistribute power and resources from center to periphery, ensured that violence and destabilization would continue. Multilateral peacekeeping forces were sent to both regions, but government and rebel forces were considerably stronger, and they continued to promote disorder to protect their interests. The presence of petroleum resources complicated the issue, as oil became both an object of struggle and a means of perpetuating the violence.

Case Study 1: Al-Qaeda and the United States (1991–96)

In June 1989, when the prospect of a peace accord with the south threatened the nationwide status of Islamic law, Colonel Omar al-Bashir staged a coup that toppled the civilian government. Although Bashir was the titular ruler, the power behind the throne was Hassan al-Turabi, a leading Islamist politician who had helped establish Sudan's Muslim Brotherhood, spearheaded the institution of Islamic law throughout the country, and advocated the establishment of an Islamic state. Turabi's influence was immediately apparent. When Iraq invaded Kuwait in August 1990, Bashir announced that Sudan would join Egypt and Saudi Arabia in supporting Kuwaiti sovereignty. However, Turabi perceived an opportunity to undermine the anti-Islamist Gulf monarchies that had lined up behind Kuwait, and his position ultimately held sway. In the Gulf War that ensued, Sudan threw its support to Iraq and opened its doors to militants from across the Muslim world. Among them was Osama bin Laden and his al-Qaeda organization. With Soviet-Afghan War veterans from North and East Africa, the Middle East, Bosnia and Herzegovina, and Chechnya as his base, bin Laden established al-Qaeda training camps in Sudan and a network of cells and allied organizations in the Greater Horn.

US relations with Sudan deteriorated rapidly as the war on terror paradigm shaped its political and economic response. In August 1993, the State Department designated Sudan a "state sponsor of terrorism," resulting in an arms embargo and the suspension of nonhumanitarian aid.[6] Khartoum turned to Muslim banks, charities, and businesses to fill the funding gap. These organizations augmented the influence of fundamentalist strains of Islam, which challenged the more tolerant Sufi traditions practiced in much of the country. The perceived threat to US interests and allies deepened. In 1996, after the attempted assassination of Egyptian President Hosni Mubarak by Sudan-based militants, Washington withdrew its diplomatic mission from Sudan and supported a series of UN sanctions.

Terrorism, like communism, provoked disputes within the US State Department. During the Cold War, some officials argued that the confusion of radical nationalism with communism, and the consequent isolation of radical regimes, actually pushed some independent actors and governments into the communist camp. In the 1990s, another cohort contended that Washington's alliances with corrupt, secular regimes in the Middle East, which tended to categorize all Islamists as terrorists, stimulated rather than discouraged radicalism. These officials advocated negotiation, rather than isolation, as a mechanism for ending Khartoum's support for terrorism. A series of inconsistent US actions followed, their nature determined by which factions held sway at the time. When the United States vacated its embassy in Sudan in early 1996, for instance, departing Ambassador Timothy Carney urged Washington to accept an olive branch—Khartoum's offer to provide information about bin Laden's finances, contacts, and support for terrorism in Africa.[7] Khartoum hoped for the lifting of sanctions in return. Hardliners in the Clinton administration, however, opposed a quid pro quo and showed no interest in Khartoum's offer. Madeleine Albright, who became secretary of state in 1997, and Susan Rice, who served as senior director for African affairs in the National Security Council, joined other officials from the State Department and CIA in rejecting Khartoum's advances. Their position, that Sudan should expel bin Laden without a concomitant US promise to revoke sanctions, prevailed. In May 1996, under pressure from the

United States, Saudi Arabia, and the UN Security Council, Sudan expelled bin Laden and his al-Qaeda network. Any hope that bin Laden's ejection would lead to the end of economic restrictions was quashed by CIA reports that Sudan continued to support international terrorism—an assessment that was contested by the State Department's Bureau of Intelligence and Research. Instead, the Clinton administration intensified Sudan's isolation, imposing a comprehensive trade embargo in 1997 and freezing all Sudanese government assets in the United States.

US relations with Khartoum deteriorated further in 1998. In August, al-Qaeda operatives bombed the US Embassies in Kenya and Tanzania. Some 224 people were killed and thousands more were injured. Most of the victims were Kenyans and Tanzanians. In response, the Clinton administration ordered a cruise missile attack on a factory outside Khartoum, which, it alleged, manufactured chemical weapons components and was linked to Osama bin Laden. Independent investigators found no credible evidence to support either charge. Instead, they found that the factory made pharmaceuticals and had produced approximately half of Sudan's medications. The factory's destruction, combined with obstacles posed by economic sanctions, may have resulted in thousands of Sudanese deaths from otherwise treatable diseases.

Increasingly isolated at home and abroad, Bashir was desperate for allies and foreign investors to develop Sudan's oil industry and to alleviate the country's $22 billion debt. Toward this end, he sidelined a number of Islamist associates in late 1999 and early 2000, including Hassan al-Turabi, whom Bashir perceived as a threat to his own power. In late 2000, Washington and Khartoum began to cooperate on counterterrorism matters, and after the al-Qaeda attacks in September 2001, their collaboration deepened. During the George W. Bush administration, the CIA reopened its station in Khartoum and began to work with Sudanese intelligence. At Washington's request, the Bashir regime arrested foreign militants who were transiting through Sudan and delivered them to the United States. The rapprochement allowed US Special Operations Forces to hunt down presumed Saudi terrorists on Sudanese soil and helped Washington locate alleged al-Qaeda operatives in Somalia. Still, Washington refused to remove Sudan from its list of state sponsors of terrorism or to lift sanctions. Khartoum's ongoing atrocities against civilians in southern Sudan, and from 2003 in Darfur, impeded closer political and economic ties.

If the war on terror shaped US policy during al-Qaeda's Sudan years, Sudan's brutal civil war and its aftermath framed international actions more broadly from 1991 to 2017, when the response to instability/responsibility to protect paradigm prevailed. By the 1990s, the ongoing drought and war-induced famine threatened the health and well-being of up to 3 million Sudanese civilians. Both government and rebel forces used food as a weapon, destroying crops, blocking humanitarian relief efforts, and stealing food to feed fighters rather than civilians. The UN and other international relief agencies became reluctant collaborators: they paid off warlords to allow food to reach civilians in need and exchanged hard currency at half the commercial rate, knowing that the profits would be used to finance the war. Neighboring states also got involved. Threatened by Khartoum's support for radical Muslims and terrorist organizations, Egypt, Eritrea, Ethiopia, Kenya, and Uganda provided weapons to the SPLA. However, the four East African countries, worried about regional instability, also initiated peace talks under IGAD auspices. This initiative led to the 1994 Declaration of Principles, which identified underlying problems that needed to be resolved to ensure a lasting peace. Among the central issues were the distribution of the country's wealth and power, the right of the south to self-determination, and the relationship between religion and the state. Khartoum signed the declaration in 1997 following significant military losses to the SPLA, and the principles were incorporated into the Comprehensive Peace Agreement of 2005 (CPA).

The civil war had begun with disputes over central versus regional power and over religious and cultural domination. However, by the late 1990s, economic interests had become the dominant driver. After 1999, when crude oil was first exported from Sudan, control of the south's significant oil supplies became a primary objective of the war, as well as the main means of financing it. In 2001, the Sudanese government generated $580 million in oil revenues, 60 percent of which went to the military. With the oil proceeds, Khartoum acquired sophisticated weapons that it used to expel hundreds of thousands of southern farmers and herders from their oil-rich lands.

The United States found itself in an awkward position. Khartoum had become a US ally in the war on terror, and US companies were heavily invested in Sudanese oil. Yet from the American perspective, northern Muslims were enslaving and killing southern Christians in a devastating war that had cost 2.5 million lives and displaced 85 percent of the southern population. Driven by political and economic interests and in response to pressure from its conservative Christian base, the George W. Bush administration joined IGAD, the UK, Norway, and Italy to push for a negotiated settlement.[8] All parties justified their intervention as a response to instability that was costing civilian lives.

In 2002, Khartoum and the SPLM/SPLA signed the Machakos Protocol, which embraced the north-south paradigm and recognized the south's right to self-determination. In January 2005, the CPA ended the civil war and provided for democratic elections, power sharing between north and south, and equitable distribution between regions of the nation's wealth. The accord stipulated that the south, represented by the SPLM, would join the ruling National Congress Party (NCP) in a Khartoum-based coalition government for six years. It would also have its own autonomous government based in the southern city of Juba. A referendum in 2011 would determine whether the south would remain a part of Sudan or secede to form an independent nation-state. However, many in the international community hoped that the efforts of the transitional government would make continued unity appealing. The agreement would be monitored by the United Nations Mission in Sudan (UNMIS), a force of some 10,000 military and 715 civilian personnel who were authorized to observe and verify the implementation of the ceasefire agreement, help establish disarmament, demobilization, and reintegration programs, and assist in related nation-building and peace-building tasks.

The CPA was problematic from the outset. The product of a top-down process pushed through by foreign governments and institutions, it was essentially an agreement between two military organizations that excluded everyone but the ruling NCP and the SPLM. Civil society, the democratic opposition, and parties to the Darfur conflict were not part of the process. Nor were other aggrieved parties, such as those in South Kordofan and Blue Nile States, whose identities did not conform to the north-south paradigm. The agreement did little to shift power and resources from the center to the marginalized populations in Sudan's multiple peripheries. It failed to address local issues, such as disputes over land, which were at the root of many tensions. For leaders such as John Garang, who had envisioned a democratic, secular, and unitary country with a more equitable distribution of power and resources, the CPA was an imperfect compromise imposed under duress. Because it catered to the interests of the central power elites rather than the marginalized populations of the periphery, it risked perpetuating rather than resolving regional conflicts and instability.

The CPA faced major obstacles to implementation. Important provisions were ignored as the UN and the four Western nations pushed IGAD to the side. With key issues unresolved, continued conflicts were inevitable. Although 80 percent of Sudan's oil reserves were located in the south, most of the country's economic development and heavy infrastructure—including oil refineries, pipelines, and the major port—were in the north. The two sides rapidly reached an impasse over the determination of the north-south border, with the north demanding more oil-rich territory in its domain, and over division of the country's enormous oil revenues. Neither side disarmed, and both strengthened their militaries in the disputed areas, particularly in the Abyei region, which contained most of Sudan's oil wealth. In 2008, violence broke out and thousands of civilians were again caught in the crossfire. The April 2010 national elections, stipulated by the CPA, were boycotted by opposition parties that protested widespread fraud, bribery, and violence in the lead-up to the elections.

A power shift in the south also weakened the prospects for peace. Following the death of John Garang in July 2005, his vision of a more equitable but unitary country was replaced by the agenda of Salva Kiir, who replaced Garang as the south's vice president in the coalition government. Kiir was a committed secessionist. During the transitional period, he mobilized a vast patronage network funded by oil resources to achieve his goal. In January 2011, the population of southern Sudan voted to secede. On July 9, 2011, the independent state of South Sudan was established before agreements had been reached on boundaries in contested regions and on the apportionment of oil wealth. In one stroke, Sudan lost three-quarters of its oil production and half of its revenues.

With the dispute over profit sharing unresolved, South Sudan shut down its oil fields from January 2012 to September 2013. The closure had a devastating impact on both countries' economies.

Once again, violence flared, not only in contested regions such as Abyei, but in the Sudanese states of South Kordofan and Blue Nile, where issues unaddressed by the CPA continued to fester. Diverse populations in these areas, many of which had supported the south in the civil war, resisted Khartoum's continued control of their natural resources and the imposition of Islam as the state religion, shari'a as the source of law, and Arabic as the official language. In November 2011, former SPLA fighters from these regions regrouped under the banner of SPLM-North and joined the major Darfur rebel organizations to form the Sudan Revolutionary Front (SRF), which was supported by South Sudan.[9] The SRF argued that each region's concerns were part of a larger national problem that could be resolved only through regime change in Khartoum, the decentralization of political authority, an equitable distribution of resources, and an inclusive national identity. None of these issues had been adequately addressed by the externally brokered CPA.

Meanwhile, in South Sudan, Salva Kiir's Juba government was beset by corruption and mismanagement as Kiir governed through patronage networks rather than strong institutions. Loyalties were cemented by the distribution of oil wealth, which constituted 98 percent of government revenue, and the regime repressed political dissent. The security system expanded rapidly, growing from 40,000 employees in 2005 to more than 300,000 in 2011. Military, police, and militia commanders mobilized their families and ethnic groups to make claims on the central state and to target other communities. At the same time, the general population suffered from a severe absence of government services and infrastructure, increased food insecurity, and mounting violence. As the oil wealth disappeared and the government deficit grew, the patronage system began to collapse. No longer able to buy the loyalty of political rivals, Kiir began to oust them from government.

A power struggle within the ruling SPLM came to a head in July 2013 when President Salva Kiir fired his longtime political rival, Vice President Riek Machar, who had announced his plan to run for president. Kiir also dissolved the cabinet. Tensions between Kiir and Machar dated to an earlier struggle during the north-south civil war, when Machar, after failing to oust John Garang as head of the SPLM, split from the movement and mobilized his largely Nuer splinter group against the Dinka, an ethnic group whose members included both Garang and Kiir. In the Bor Massacre of November 1991, Machar's Nuer militias slaughtered some 2,000 Dinka civilians, leading to a seven-year conflict during which both sides committed atrocities, thousands of Dinka and Nuer civilians were killed, and tens of thousands starved to death as a result of war-related famine. Political struggles within the SPLM were not halted by the end of the north-south war, nor by the independence of South Sudan. After independence, continued economic marginalization and climate change–induced drought also exacerbated longstanding competition for grazing land and water.

In December 2013, a cluster of former cabinet ministers who had been fired in July accused President Kiir of abusing his power. The president in turn charged Machar, the dismissed vice president, with spearheading a coup attempt. The national army, cobbled together from the SPLA and undisciplined ethnic militias, broke down. As Dinka soldiers loyal to Kiir slaughtered Nuer civilians in the capital, Nuer soldiers defected to Machar's side. Machar's SPLA in Opposition, which also included non-Nuer dissidents, led mutinies in the oil-rich Jonglei, Unity, and Upper Nile States, where it took control of the oil fields and retaliated against Dinka civilians and others seen as sympathetic to the Juba government. Uganda, an ally of the SPLM during the north-south civil war, and JEM rebels from Darfur sent soldiers to fight alongside the national army and protect the oil fields. Weapons from China, Russia, and Israel also strengthened the government side. Meanwhile, Khartoum supplied weapons to the rebels who challenged the Juba government. The United Nations Mission in South Sudan (UNMISS), authorized the day before South Sudan's independence to safeguard regional peace and security, failed to protect the civilian population from either government or rebel forces.

Although the dispute between Kiir and Machar was primarily personal and political—aimed at consolidating wealth and position—both men mobilized ethnic communities to achieve these ends. The impact was devastating. Between December 2013 and December 2017, more than 50,000 civilians were killed, 2.4 million were displaced internally, and 2 million more fled to neighboring countries. By 2017, food insecurity was widespread and 5.5 million people were threatened by famine. UN investigators found that all parties to the conflict had engaged in mass killings and rape and had deliberately targeted civilians, and more than 16,000 children had been conscripted to fight.

Once again, IGAD intervened, motivated primarily by the threat to regional stability. In May 2014, Kiir and Machar signed an IGAD-mediated peace accord that called for a ceasefire, the formation of a transitional government, and the drafting of a new constitution followed by elections. Like the CPA of 2005, the 2014 agreement was based on unrealistic hopes rather than the reality on the ground. The only commonality between

Kiir and Machar was mutual distrust and a determination to retain the power that enabled them to control the country's resources. The violence continued as both sides fought to take charge of important towns and oil installations in order to shore up their bargaining positions. Like the CPA, the 2014 agreement was also the result of a top-down process that ignored key players. Independent ethnic militias and other armed groups, including those fighting on both sides of the Sudan–South Sudan border, were excluded from the IGAD process and continued to wreak havoc.

Not only was the 2014 agreement deficient, but IGAD had no means to enforce it or to hold warring parties accountable for their atrocities. The organization's efforts were weakened by internal divisions, including longstanding tensions between Uganda and Sudan, and by competition between Uganda and Ethiopia for dominance on matters relating to regional security. IGAD's members were also interested parties to the conflict. Uganda had provided military support to the Kiir regime. Sudan had supported Kiir by keeping the oil pipelines open, while simultaneously supplying Machar's rebel insurgency. Finally, Uganda and Kenya possessed substantial economic interests in South Sudan.

While IGAD's response was inadequate, other multinational bodies either resisted involvement or acted with little effect. The AU ignored the regional rivalries that undermined IGAD's efforts, and the UN Security Council refused to impose an arms embargo or economic sanctions that would prevent the country's oil wealth from financing the war. The International Conference on the Great Lakes Region weighed in to support the IGAD endeavor, but critics contested the neutrality of both organizations, noting the questionable involvement of member states Uganda and Sudan.

The expanded IGAD-Plus mediated another peace agreement in August 2015.[10] President Kiir reluctantly signed the new deal under intense pressure from IGAD, the UN, and the United States, which weighed in as South Sudan's largest foreign donor. Both Kiir and Machar repeatedly undermined the agreement and stalled on its implementation, while Kiir also proved adept at exploiting his benefactors' rivalries. Shifting alliances and the splintering of rebel groups not included in the accord further diminished its prospects for success.

Despite the distance that divided them, the government and rebel forces were united in their desire to preclude political dissidents and civil society representatives from the negotiation framework. Civil society organizations led by women, youth, religious practitioners, and other community members criticized the August 2015 agreement as yet another accord that focused on power sharing at the top rather than on the grievances at the root of the conflict. They charged that the latest peace pact did nothing to promote justice for the conflicts' victims or accountability for the perpetrators of violence. It simply turned back the clock to the precarious status quo of December 2013 when the conflict erupted. Critics argued that a lasting peace could only be achieved in a more inclusive South Sudan that empowered civil society groups whose rights and interests were recognized in a new constitution.

Case Study 3: Internal and Regional Roots of the Darfur Conflict (2003–6)

If foreign engagement in Sudan and South Sudan was justified as a response to instability and the desire to protect civilian lives, external reaction to strife in Darfur was rooted in similar concerns. This case study explores the internal and regional sources of the conflict. It also considers the impact of intervention by Sudan's neighbors—Libya, Chad, and Eritrea—which supported various rebel factions in order to promote their own interests.

Typically characterized as a struggle between Arabs and Africans, the Darfur conflict, like those in northern and southern Sudan, emerged from unequal power relations that pitted a dominant center against multiple peripheries. In Darfur, as elsewhere in Sudan, the term "Arab," commonly associated with the political and economic elites at the nation's center, obscures the enormous diversity of populations marked by historical, regional, socioeconomic, and ethnic differences. The Arab-African paradigm, like the north-south paradigm, smooths over shifting identities and alliances and ignores important political and economic factors.

The onset of the Darfur conflict in 2003 coincided with the denouement of the north-south civil war. Khartoum had been under enormous pressure from the UN, the United States, and other external powers to end the war with the south. Never enthusiastic about the elements of the 2005 peace accord, Bashir nonetheless believed that if he bent to international demands, the UN and Washington would normalize relations, facilitate IMF and World Bank loans, encourage investments, and put an end to Sudan's international isolation. These hopes were dashed by the conflict in Darfur. Located in western Sudan on the fringes of the Sahara Desert, Darfur had been the seat of the Fur sultanate (1596–1916), a powerful state that embraced Islam as the official religion and Arabic as the language of faith and government. For hundreds of years, camel caravans passed through the region en route to and from the Atlantic coast, thousands of miles away. Darfur became a rich melting pot dominated by a Fur-speaking elite and inhabited by scores of ethnic groups and clans who converted to Islam, conducted business with one another, and intermarried. Ethnic identities were fluid, and categorizations were largely based on livelihood and self-identification.

Following the sultan's defeat by British forces in 1916, Darfur was absorbed into Sudan under the authority of the Anglo-Egyptian Condominium. As was frequently the case elsewhere, ethnic identities became more rigid under colonialism and new hierarchies were established. Under Anglo-Egyptian rule, the diverse populations of Darfur were generally categorized as either Arab or African—classifications that most Darfuris reject today, but that continue to dominate political and media analyses. The ancestors of contemporary Darfuri Arabs hailed from such disparate places as West Africa and southern Sudan and intermarried with local lineages. Although sub-Saharan in origin, they speak Arabic as their mother tongue. Historically, Darfuri Arabs have tended to be nomadic herders. They include the Baggara, cattle herders who live primarily in the southern savanna and who have access to land, and the Abbala, landless camel herders who largely inhabit the Sahel and who are among Darfur's poorest, most marginalized people. Populations characterized as African, such as the Fur and the Masalit, have generally engaged in sedentary agriculture, while some, like the Zaghawa, have combined farming and semi-nomadic herding.

Competition for land and water was at the root of the conflict that began in 2003. Neither the competition nor the violence was new. However, the extent of the killing and the pivotal involvement of the central government were unique. For thousands of years, periodic droughts have ravaged Sudan and other countries in the Greater Horn. The devastating effects of cyclical droughts have been exacerbated in recent decades by desertification associated with climate change. In the past, camel-herding nomads from the drier northern reaches of Darfur brought their herds to the wetter southern region during the dry season, returning to the north when the rains began. During the 1970s and 1980s, however, horrific droughts and famines afflicted large sections of northern and eastern Africa. Water holes and seasonal rivers dried up. The encroaching desert, as well as land degradation resulting from the government's intensive agricultural policies, left many Darfuri Arabs impoverished. They began to establish permanent villages in the south, where farmers controlled much of the land. To protect their crops and pastures—and to reassert their claim to the land—farmers built a network of fences, closing migration routes and grazing lands to nomadic herders. The drought also pushed Zaghawa farmer-herders southward from the Chad-Sudan frontier onto land long occupied by Baggara cattle herders. Abbala Arabs who lost their camels sought work as farm laborers. When those jobs dried up, desperate former nomads joined militias and gangs that engaged in banditry. Peoples who previously had traded now fought one another for the resources necessary to survive. Local communities formed vigilante groups to protect themselves and to raid their foes.

The environmental crisis in Darfur coincided with the introduction of new ideas that stoked hostilities between Arabs and Africans. During the 1970s, Libya had emerged as the center of Arab nationalism in the Sahel, and Libyan strongman Muammar al-Qaddafi embarked on a campaign to build a transnational Arab Islamic state. In Darfur, he helped establish the Arab Gathering, an organization of militants closely associated with Qaddafi's paramilitary Islamic Pan-African Legion, which promoted an ideology of Arab supremacy that defined "Arab" broadly but made sharp distinctions between "Arab" and "African" Muslims. While the notion of Muslim Arab superiority vis-à-vis Christians/practitioners of indigenous religions/Africans had long been present in the conflicts between north and south, the new ideology in Darfur was not linked to Arab elites in Khartoum, but rather to Qaddafi's Libya across the Sahara.

The combined impact of the environmental crisis and the potent new racist ideology was compounded by the effects of a decades-long civil war in Chad (1966–87) that had involved several external powers. Military intervention in Chad by Libya, France, and the United States, and the consequent profusion of modern weaponry, had destabilized the entire region. As the war intensified, hundreds of thousands of Chadian refugees poured into Darfur, putting new pressures on land and water supplies. Semi-automatic weapons also filtered into Darfur, where they increasingly were used to commit acts of banditry and to settle local disputes. Along with the refugees came Chadian rebels who displaced Fur villagers and set up armed camps. The Fur, in turn, sought weapons and support from the Chadian government. They built fences, obstructed livestock routes, and burned pastures, threatening the Arab population's livelihood. Growing enclaves of Chadian Arabs swung the regional demographic balance in favor of the Arabs. With their survival at stake, they sought common cause with Darfuri Arabs, promoting the notion of a common Arab identity and the need to defend their interests against those of non-Arabs.

These tensions escalated into the Arab-Fur War of 1987–89, which destroyed hundreds of villages and killed thousands of people. The war was, at root, a conflict between those with land and those without. Fur farmers and Baggara Arab cattle herders possessed officially recognized homelands (*dar*), established during British rule, while Abbala camel herders and Chadian refugees did not. Following the 1989 military coup, which increased Islamist influence in Khartoum, the Abbala appealed to central government officials as fellow Arabs, offering political support in exchange for a homeland. When Khartoum granted land to Abbala nomads in Fur areas, it took sides in a deadly local conflict.

By February 2003, the strife in Darfur had been transformed into a rebellion against the central government. Initially, the rebellion was led by two distinct movements. The Sudan Liberation Army (SLA) emerged from Fur self-defense militias that had fought Libya's Islamic Pan-African Legion and Darfur Arab militias during the Arab-Fur War. Some of the organization's top leaders, however, were Zaghawa. The SLA manifesto focused on the region's political and economic marginalization, demanded the decentralization of power and a secular government, and insisted that Darfur and its concerns be included in the north-south peace negotiations then under way. The ideas presented in the SLA manifesto resonated with those of southern Sudan's SPLA, which provided the Darfur movement with weapons and military training.

The Justice and Equality Movement, in contrast, was Islamist in orientation. Its origins lay in Bashir's purge of Islamists from the central government in 1999 and 2000. After sidelining Hassan al-Turabi, Bashir had expelled Turabi's most vociferous supporters from the ruling party—including many Zaghawas from Darfur. In the wake of the ousters, Darfuri Islamists living in Khartoum produced a document that criticized the ruling elites who privileged the center and neglected the regions in the periphery. JEM emerged from this group. Controlled by members of the Kobe Zaghawa subgroup, who lived in Chad in greater number than in Darfur, JEM was led by Khalil Ibrahim, who previously had held

Photo 5.2. JEM rebels in Darfur, Sudan, 2007. Photo by Kalou Kaka.

high-level positions in Sudan's regional and central governments. As minister of health in North Darfur in 1993–94, Ibrahim had organized ethnic militias that were used against civilians in southern Sudan, burning villages, killing civilians, and enslaving children. Like Qaddafi, Ibrahim had expansionist aspirations. He hoped to unite Chad, Egypt, Libya, and Sudan in a single Islamic state, and he was prepared to mobilize the Muslim Africans of Darfur to realize his goal. Already under immense international pressure to make concessions to the south and to end the civil war, President Bashir perceived JEM and its expansionist agenda as a political threat.

Although JEM and the SLA promoted opposing sides in the north-south civil war, in Darfur they were united in their opposition to the Khartoum regime. The Darfur rebels also benefited from external support. The military dictatorship in Chad, threatened by a Sudan-backed insurgency, funneled weapons to JEM and the SLA in the hope of rallying Zaghawas on both sides of the border. Aspiring to a greater regional profile, Eritrea also armed both rebel movements.

Khartoum raised local militias to counter the rebels, initially arming Arab, Fur, and Tunjur men. However, after Fur and Tunjur recruits defected to the SLA with their weapons, the regime armed only Arabs, promising schools, clinics, water pumps, and animal vaccines in return for their services. Most Arab militiamen were enlisted from among the landless Abbala camel herders, rather than from the Baggara cattle herders who had been given homelands under the old colonial dispensation. The militias included unemployed young men, demobilized Sudanese soldiers, followers of the racist Arab Gathering, bandits, and some 20,000 displaced Chadians. Their victims referred to the militiamen as Janjaweed or "devils on horseback"—an insulting Arabic term for bandits who roam the desert robbing Arabs and non-Arabs, herders and farmers alike.[11] Although Khartoum recruited and unleashed the militias, it did not control them. Paid only a nominal amount by the government, the Janjaweed were expected to live off the land; in effect, they were given license to loot livestock and provisions in order to survive. Laying waste to vast areas, the Janjaweed terrorized the civilian population, raping, killing, plundering, and burning.

If the Janjaweed became the face of destruction in Darfur, they were not solely responsible for the devastation. The World Health Organization found that during 2003 and 2004, thousands of Darfuri civilians were killed by the Sudanese army and rebel fighters, as well by the Arab militias. By September 2004, some 1.8 million people had been driven from their homes and were dying at the rate of 10,000 per month from war-related hunger, malnutrition, and disease. By 2006, when the death toll reached 200,000, disease, rather than violence, was deemed the major cause.

 Case Study 4: Darfur and the International Community (2003–17)

The atrocities committed in Darfur in 2003–4 generated widespread support for an international response, motivated by the threat to regional stability and the destruction of human life. In the West, proponents of military intervention, in both governmental and nongovernmental sectors, declared that the killings in Darfur constituted genocide and thus warranted immediate international action. Opponents of military intervention disputed that characterization and warned of unforeseen consequences, pointing to the negative fallout that had followed military intervention in other parts of the continent.

The United States was among the countries that hesitated. Torn by internal disagreements and wary of its predecessors' mistakes, the George W. Bush administration dithered. The October 1993 fiasco in Somalia, where eighteen US soldiers were killed, had had serious domestic repercussions. When the mass slaughter of civilians began in Rwanda just six months later, the Clinton administration had refused to describe the situation as a genocide and pushed the UN Security Council to follow suit. Other nations had also failed to act, and the international community had stood by as an estimated 800,000 Rwandans were killed. Some Bush administration insiders warned of a similar catastrophe in Darfur and argued that, under the terms of the 1948 Genocide Convention, the international community had both a moral obligation and a legal right to intervene. Opponents of intervention offered a range of objections. Some cautioned against involvement in a complex situation with deep domestic and regional roots and no easy solutions. Others noted that US armed forces were already overextended in Afghanistan and Iraq and that intervention in Darfur might jeopardize Sudan's north-south negotiations that were critical to a broader regional peace. Still others observed that Khartoum was cooperating with the United States on counterterrorism measures and had become an important, if controversial, regional ally. Finally, there was the question of Sudanese oil. As war and instability consumed the Middle East, Washington was averse to alienating a country that was a major alternative source of petroleum. In the final analysis, the dominant voices in the George W. Bush administration were prepared to use strong words but unwilling to engage in strong actions.

Beyond the Bush administration, a growing US constituency called for a concerted response. In 2004, an election year for Congress and the presidency, both branches of government were under pressure. In Congress, an eclectic group of evangelical Christians, liberals, and members of the Congressional Black Caucus—all of whom supported the south in Sudan's north-south war—pressed the Bush administration to act against the Bashir regime. Outside the government, the Save Darfur Coalition, a broad-based grassroots network modeled on the antiapartheid movement of the 1980s, pushed the administration to label the Darfur crisis a genocide and to support international intervention to stop it. When Democratic presidential candidate John Kerry addressed the NAACP national convention in July 2004, he referred to the situation in Darfur as a genocide.[12] One week later, a resolution decrying genocide in Darfur unanimously passed both houses of Congress.

By September, the Bush administration felt compelled to respond. In testimony before the Senate Foreign Relations Committee, Secretary of State Colin Powell referred to the Darfur killings as a genocide, and the

Bush administration urged the UN Security Council to establish a commission of inquiry. While the commission's report, released in January 2005, found that Khartoum was not pursuing a "genocidal policy"—the intentional extermination of an entire group of people—it stated that the crimes carried out in Darfur "may be no less serious and heinous than genocide."[13] The commission found evidence that the Sudanese government and allied militias had perpetrated war crimes and crimes against humanity and that rebel forces had also engaged in war crimes. The Security Council subsequently referred the Darfur case to the International Criminal Court in The Hague, recommending criminal investigation and possible prosecution.

Although the Darfur solidarity movement, strengthened by the support of high-profile celebrities, continued to argue that the atrocities in Darfur constituted genocide, the situation on the ground had changed. Whereas the vast majority of war-related deaths in 2003–4 were the result of Sudanese army, air force, and Janjaweed attacks on civilians, a few years later diarrhea and malaria were the largest killers, and most violent deaths stemmed from fighting between rebel groups, contests between Arab militias for pasture land, and banditry. Moreover, the eclectic rebel movement had fractured. By 2005, the SLA and JEM had splintered into more than twenty factions, each largely identified with a particular ethnic group, clan, or village. All sides attacked humanitarian aid workers and AU peacekeepers and engaged in banditry. Two years into the conflict, Darfur increasingly resembled Somalia during the same period, with warlords vying for territorial dominance and bandit gangs raping, robbing, and killing civilians. In both cases, instability had opened the door to outside involvement. In Darfur, neighboring Chad, Eritrea, and Libya supported various factions to promote their own political agendas. Many advocates for foreign intervention refused to address these complexities, fearing that they would weaken the case for concerted international action.

Meanwhile, Sudan's north-south negotiations had reached a critical stage. The UN, the AU, and the United States pushed for an end to the Darfur conflict, which they feared would undermine a north-south peace accord, which had even greater regional implications. International mediators resisted dealing with Sudan's problems holistically, refusing to address underlying political and economic grievances in northern regions in the same peace agreement. The simplistic north-south bifurcation virtually ensured the continuation of conflicts in Darfur, South Kordofan, Blue Nile, and other northern areas.

Under strong external pressure, Khartoum and the Darfur rebel organizations signed a humanitarian ceasefire agreement in April 2004 that would allow relief workers and supplies into the conflict area. The AU agreed to send observers to monitor the ceasefire and soldiers to protect them. The resultant African Union Mission in Sudan (AMIS), launched in July 2004, would eventually number 7,200 people. Staffed by troops from African countries and financed by the United States and the EU, the AU force was mandated to protect unarmed military observers and civilian police who were monitoring the ceasefire, but it had no authority to enforce the ceasefire or to protect civilians. The ceasefire broke down almost immediately. Western countries, which had pledged to fund the operation, failed to fulfill their promises, leaving AMIS soldiers stranded in war zones without pay or equipment. Understaffed, underequipped, and underfunded, the peacekeeping force was ineffective and was deeply resented by the civilians it failed to protect.

As the AU force foundered, the UN was urged to intervene. Under pressure from diverse constituencies, the international body made an unprecedented move. In September 2005, the General Assembly adopted the R2P resolution that held states responsible for protecting their citizens from "genocide, war crimes, ethnic cleansing and crimes against humanity" and granted the international community the right to intervene militarily if states failed to meet their "responsibility to protect."[14] The AU was among those entities that urged the UN to take forceful action in Darfur. In January 2006, frustrated by its limited mandate and broken promises for external assistance, the AU asked the UN to assume responsibility for the peacekeeping mission. The United States and the EU, which had failed to fulfill their pledges, criticized AMIS's poor performance and joined the call for the UN to exert control. In February, the Security Council unanimously approved an US motion to deploy UN peacekeepers to Darfur to "protect civilians and enforce the cease-fire."[15] Characterizing UN intervention as an attempt by the West to recolonize the country, the government of Sudan vowed that UN forces would be perceived as enemy invaders and treated accordingly. The Sudanese government's opposition brought the situation to a stalemate. Without the government's consent or a "peace to keep," the UN was unwilling to deploy troops, despite the passage of the R2P resolution.

In May 2006, sixteen months after the adoption of the north-south peace accord, Khartoum and several Darfur rebel organizations signed the AU-mediated Darfur Peace Agreement (DPA). Written largely by outsiders, the pact was dysfunctional from the outset. Darfuri Arabs were not represented at the talks, on the premise that they were simply doing the government's bidding. Fearing that their interests would be subordinated to those of Khartoum, Darfuri Arab groups repudiated the accord. The largest rebel groups, including JEM and Abdel Wahid al-Nur's SLA faction (SLA-AW), refused to sign the document because it failed to meet their basic demands—which included, first and foremost, autonomy for Darfur. Darfuri civil society organizations, which had been excluded from the negotiations, also rejected it. The United States publicly backed Minni Minawi's SLA splinter group (SLA-MM) and was instrumental in obtaining his signature.[16] However, by the time the DPA was signed, Minawi had lost most of his popular support, which had never extended beyond a few Zaghawa clans. Bolstered by his new authority as the only rebel signatory to the accord, Minawi eliminated rivals who contested the agreement and collectively punished civilians in the territories under his control. Notorious for looting, raping, and killing Arabs and Africans alike, the Minawi faction was referred to locally as "Janjaweed 2."[17] AU forces further undermined their own legitimacy by colluding with Minawi, providing technical and logistical assistance to his faction because it had signed the DPA. Having positioned themselves on one side of an ongoing war, AU troops, like government soldiers, became targets of rebel attacks.

It was on the basis of the DPA—a peace agreement in name only—that Washington justified its push for a UN peacekeeping force in Darfur. In August 2006, claiming that there was now a peace to keep, the Security Council risked Bashir's wrath and expanded UNMIS's mandate to include Darfur. Operating under a Chapter VII mandate, the strengthened UN mission was slated to include some 17,300 soldiers, 3,300 civilian police personnel, and 16 Formed Police Units. The UN operation would replace or subsume the 7,200-person AU force by the end of the year. Fearing a ploy by Western powers to effect regime change, Bashir rejected the UN mission as a violation of Sudanese sovereignty.

External powers continued to apply pressure. In 2006, the Bush administration imposed sanctions that prevented the Sudanese government and rebel forces from owning property in the United States and banned US citizens from doing business with Sudan's oil industry. The next year

Washington imposed financial restrictions on two senior government officials and on JEM leader Khalil Ibrahim, who had refused to sign the DPA. However, the Bush administration rejected the imposition of an oil embargo, which would have threatened Sudan's main source of income but also hurt the United States and its allies. China, a major oil investor, weapons supplier, and ally of the Khartoum government, departed from its usual practice of noninterference in host country affairs to encourage the president to accept the international peacekeeping force.

Pressed by friends and foes alike, Bashir reluctantly agreed to a hybrid AU-UN peacekeeping mission, provided that the majority of soldiers were African. Khartoum's acquiescence opened the door to the establishment of the African Union–United Nations Mission in Darfur (UNAMID) in July 2007, which would deploy up to 25,987 peacekeepers—including 19,555 military personnel—in what would become the world's largest peacekeeping force to date. Unlike the AU peacekeepers, the hybrid group was authorized to use force to protect civilians, humanitarian relief workers, and UN personnel, facilities, and equipment, as well as to monitor and enforce the DPA. In reality, there was still no peace to keep. Only a minority of the warring parties had signed the peace agreement, and even they were not prepared to accept the unilateral imposition of a ceasefire by an external power. Bashir considered the AU-UN operation to be a lightly camouflaged US operation designed to oust him from power. Al-Qaeda denounced the enterprise as another United States intervention in Muslim lands, and Osama bin Laden called for jihad against UN "crusader invaders" in Darfur.[18]

Meanwhile, the Darfur lobby continued to exert pressure. A growing number of celebrities added their voices to the chorus of those urging outside military intervention—frustrating humanitarian relief workers who argued that an external military presence would inflame passions, turn NGO workers into targets, and obstruct their ability to deliver relief to those in need. Although the solidarity movement focused world attention on crimes committed in a remote region without oil or strategic interest, many members also reduced the conflict to a clear-cut struggle between good and evil and refused to recognize Arab grievances or rebel atrocities. The movement's promotion of a military fix for complex political and economic problems distracted attention from sustainable long-term solutions.

The controversy over foreign intervention escalated in March 2009, when the ICC ordered President Bashir's arrest on charges of perpetrating war crimes and crimes against humanity in Darfur.[19] The backlash in Sudan was immediate. Bashir responded to the initial indictment by shutting down thirteen Western humanitarian aid organizations, accusing them of collaborating with the ICC. JEM, which had signed a preliminary peace accord with Khartoum the preceding month, announced that it would negotiate no further with an alleged war criminal. While many in the West applauded the ICC action as past due, critics, including the AU, the Arab League, the Organisation of the Islamic Conference, and the Non-Aligned Movement, argued that the arrest warrant could provoke further violence, jeopardize peace negotiations, and seriously undermine humanitarian and peacekeeping operations. Other critics worried about the implications for African sovereignty, noting that since its establishment in 2002, the ICC had indicted and prosecuted only African political and military figures.

As international actors debated the proper approach to Sudan, controversy also erupted within the US foreign policy establishment. The Barack Obama administration, which took office in January 2009, was deeply divided over Sudan and had failed to establish a consensus about the nature of the violence in Darfur. The new UN ambassador, Susan Rice, referred to the killings in Darfur as ongoing genocide, while retired Air Force Major General J. Scott Gration, the president's special envoy to Sudan, characterized the situation as the "remnants of genocide" and argued that Sudan should be removed from the list of state sponsors of terrorism.[20] In October, the Obama administration shifted its policy focus from the responsibility to protect to regional stability and the war on terror, announcing that henceforth it would emphasize dialogue with Khartoum rather than isolation. The new policy was premised on the belief that if the CPA failed, a major regional crisis could ensue and Sudan could again become a haven for international terrorists. As a result, Washington prioritized the implementation of the north-south peace agreement rather than seeking a holistic resolution to the Sudan crisis that would include Darfur and other marginalized regions. President Obama hinted that there would be incentives for progress on the implementation of the CPA, for headway toward peace in Darfur, and for cooperation in fighting international terrorism. Alternatively, there would be "tough sanctions" and increased pressure if Khartoum fell short. However, he did not remove Sudan from the State Department's list of state sponsors of terrorism, and he referred to "gross human rights abuses and genocide in Darfur" as ongoing practices.[21]

While the Obama administration struggled over its Sudan policy, the peace process in Darfur foundered. The ill-conceived DPA had had little positive effect. In June 2008, the AU and the UN had convened a new round of negotiations in Doha, Qatar, under UNAMID auspices. As the negotiations dragged on, UNAMID pressed a number of fragmented rebel groups to form a single organization, which resulted in the establishment of the Liberation and Justice Movement (LJM) in February 2010. From that time on, only rebel movements belonging to the LJM or JEM were permitted to participate in the Doha discussions. Although the LJM included several SLA factions as well as other rebel groups, it had failed to attract Abdel Wahid al-Nur's SLA-AW, which had refused to participate in any negotiations after its rejection of the DPA. The absence of the SLA-AW meant that the interests of the Fur—Darfur's largest ethnic group, which had also suffered the greatest population displacement—were not represented at Doha by a strong rebel movement.[22]

The new round of negotiations culminated in the Doha Document for Peace in Darfur (DDPD), signed by Khartoum and the LJM on July 14, 2011—five days after South Sudan's independence. The DDPD, like its predecessor, was highly problematic. It had failed to gain the support of the most significant rebel movements. JEM, the strongest rebel organization in terms of military capacity, refused to endorse the accord. Although many Western power brokers favored the LJM for its non-Islamist orientation, it was by far the weakest of the rebel movements. Moreover, even as the DDPD was signed, the eclectic coalition had begun to disintegrate, with some Zaghawa and Masalit groups severing ties. Like its predecessor, the 2011 agreement was weakened by the lack of input from civil society organizations. Treating the LJM as a stand-in for Darfuri civilians, the mediators had refused to grant civil society groups negotiating status. Although civil society members were invited to participate in the final round of discussions, they constituted only 250 of the 600 participants, and internally displaced Fur and Abbala Arabs—two groups whose support was critical to an enduring peace—were not represented at all. Civil society delegates did not review or endorse the final document. Yet UNAMID mediators expected them to embrace the accord and to mobilize their constituents to do likewise. Although many Darfuris considered the DDPD to be no more than a draft agreement, UNAMID and Khartoum viewed it as a conclusive pact and threatened sanctions against parties that failed to implement it.

The defective agreement did not bring peace, and in some instances its terms exacerbated existing problems. For instance, the Doha Document opened the door to Darfur's reconfiguration as a series of ethnically divided states, which could contain the seeds of future conflict.[23] Some LJM leaders were appointed to official positions, a Special Court for Darfur was established to prosecute gross violations of human rights and international humanitarian law, and a general amnesty (excluding war crimes) was promulgated. However, neither the government of Sudan nor foreign governments and institutions provided the resources necessary to fund these complex undertakings. LJM soldiers, who had not been integrated into the national army as promised, were restless. Arab militias, initially armed by Khartoum to fight the rebels, were no longer under government control, and fighting between militias continued to displace large numbers of civilians. Meanwhile, in November 2011, Darfur's main rebel organizations—JEM, SLA-AW, and SLA-MM—joined the Sudan Revolutionary Front, uniting with insurgents in other parts of Sudan to promote a national agenda.

UN mediators continued to treat Sudan's regional conflicts in isolation, even as the internal opposition rallied to the view that the country's problems could be resolved only with an end to the center's dominance and a more equitable distribution of power and resources. Determined to safeguard the 2005 agreement between north and south, UNAMID had pushed to finalize the DDPD before South Sudan's independence in July 2011, despite its failings. Although the mission was a joint AU-UN endeavor, the UN had dominated the process, sidelining other AU initiatives that judged the crises in Darfur, South Kordofan, and Blue Nile to be part of a larger problem that required a democratic transition and the reallocation of resources throughout Sudan. In 2017, the Darfur crisis, which had cost some 300,000 lives and displaced more than 2 million people, was far from resolved. The externally mediated peace accord had failed to incorporate key constituencies and to address underlying problems. The violence and insecurity continued.

Conclusion

Foreign political and military intervention in Sudan after the Cold War, characterized by conflicting interests and inadequate solutions, met few of its stated objectives. The expulsion of Osama bin Laden and his al-Qaeda network in 1996 did not thwart the spread of terror; nor did it end Sudan's isolation in the international community. The externally imposed peace agreements that were intended to terminate the north-south civil war in 2005 and the Darfur conflict in 2011 left many issues unresolved. As a result, in 2017, Sudan was still beset by violence in the western region of Darfur, in the southern states of South Kordofan and Blue Nile, and in the contested region of Abyei on the Sudan–South Sudan border. Hostility toward the central government in Khartoum and a determination to bring about a more equitable distribution of the country's power and resources united diverse rebel movements against a common enemy, but with devastating consequences for the civilian population. Meanwhile, in the new nation-state of South Sudan, civilians were caught in the crossfire as rival leaders mobilized ethnically based constituencies to strengthen their hold on power and resources. Foreign countries and international bodies intervened in Sudan in response to instability, to protect civilian lives, and to counter a terrorist threat. However, they failed to address serious underlying grievances; they sidelined representatives of Sudanese civil society; and they did not sustain their political initiatives until viable peace agreements were achieved. Chapter 6 examines a contrasting case, the 1994 genocide in Rwanda, where the international community refused to intervene to protect civilian lives. In that case, the failure to respond produced a multinational crisis that exacerbated regional instability.

Suggested Reading

Several recommended studies investigate the roots of violent conflict in Sudan. Authored by Sudanese anthropologist and historian Jok Madut Jok, *War and Slavery in Sudan* (Philadelphia: University of Pennsylvania Press, 2001) examines the history of the enslavement of Sudan's southern peoples. Douglas H. Johnson, *The Root Causes of Sudan's Civil Wars: Peace or Truce* (Woodbridge, Suffolk, UK: James Currey, 2011), offers a historical overview of diverse conflicts in Sudan, focusing on the differential distribution of power and resources, the manipulation of ethnicity and religion, and the role of foreign governments, institutions, and aid organizations. Peter Woodward, *Sudan, 1898–1989: The Unstable State* (Boulder, CO: Lynne Rienner, 1990), investigates competition between ruling elites in Sudan. Philip Roessler, *Ethnic Politics and State Power in Africa: The Logic of the Coup–Civil War Trap* (New York: Cambridge University Press, 2016), examines the tempestuous balance between political factions and ethnic alliances in the Darfur conflict. Alex de Waal, "Sudan: The Turbulent State," in *War in Darfur and the Search for Peace*, ed. Alex de Waal (Cambridge, MA: Harvard University Press, 2007), critiques the dominant north-south analysis of Sudanese conflicts. He argues that the extreme concentration of power at the center and the perpetual competition among ruling elites are at the core of ongoing conflicts in the periphery. Ruth Iyob and Gilbert M. Khadiagala, *Sudan: The Elusive Quest for Peace* (Boulder, CO: Lynne Rienner, 2006), explores the failure of regional and international actors to resolve the problems at the base of the north-south conflict. Sudanese and other contributors to Gunnar M. Sørbø and Abdel Ghaffar M. Ahmed, eds., *Sudan Divided: Continuing Conflict in a Contested State* (New York: Palgrave Macmillan, 2013), examine conflicts in Sudan after the south's secession.

A number of works focus on history and conflict in Darfur. M. W. Daly, *Darfur's Sorrow: A History of Destruction and Genocide* (New York: Cambridge University Press, 2007), provides background to the current crisis, examining the region from the time of the Fur sultanate in the seventeenth century through Anglo-Egyptian rule in the twentieth century to the modern conflict in the twenty-first century. Gérard Prunier, *Darfur: A 21st Century Genocide*, 3rd ed. (Ithaca, NY: Cornell University Press, 2008), provides a comprehensive, accessible account of the Darfur conflict, its historical underpinnings, and the key players. Julie Flint and Alex de Waal, *Darfur: A New History of a Long War*, revised and updated (London: Zed Books, 2008), introduces the history of the conflict, the main participants, and the response of the AU and the broader international community. J. Millard Burr and Robert O. Collins, *Africa's Thirty Years War: Libya, Chad, and the Sudan, 1963–1993* (Boulder, CO: Westview Press, 1999), investigates the ways in which complex regional dynamics served as a prelude to the Darfur crisis.

Other studies emphasize local dynamics in Darfur and the thorny search for solutions. Mahmood Mamdani, *Saviors and Survivors: Darfur, Politics, and the War on Terror* (New York: Pantheon, 2009), explores the political, economic, and environmental roots of the crisis, including colonial policies that favored some groups over others and Cold War conflicts that involved both regional and extracontinental powers. Johan Brosché and Daniel Rothbart, *Violent Conflict and Peacebuilding: The*

Continuing Crisis in Darfur (New York: Routledge, 2012), identifies several interlocking conflicts, including those between farmers and herders, rebel factions, traditional and aspiring local leaders, marginalized groups in the periphery and the national government in the center, and Sudan and Chad. Contributors to de Waal, *War in Darfur and the Search for Peace* (mentioned previously), examine the players in the conflict, the role of ethnic and religious identities, and the prolonged search for peace by domestic and international actors. Jérôme Tubiana's chapter, "Darfur after Doha," in Sørbø and Ahmed, *Sudan Divided* (mentioned previously), offers a detailed assessment of the Doha peace process and the flawed nature of the final agreement.

Several studies investigate the role of international nonstate actors in focusing world attention on Darfur. Don Cheadle and John Prendergast, *Not on Our Watch: The Mission to End Genocide in Darfur and Beyond* (New York: Hyperion, 2007), a call-to-action publication of the Save Darfur Coalition, offers a window into the campaign's objectives and perspectives. Rebecca Hamilton, *Fighting for Darfur: Public Action and the Struggle to Stop Genocide* (New York: Palgrave Macmillan, 2011), provides an informed and highly readable insider's account of the Save Darfur Coalition, examining its strengths, weaknesses, and impact. Richard Cockett, *Sudan: The Failure and Division of an African State*, 2nd ed. (New Haven, CT: Yale University Press, 2016), explores the role of human rights activists, antislavery campaigners, and right-wing Christians in focusing international scrutiny on the Darfur crisis.

A number of studies focus on South Sudan, both before and after independence. Sørbø and Ahmed, *Sudan Divided* (mentioned previously), is again recommended. Øystein H. Rolandsen and M. W. Daly, *A History of South Sudan: From Slavery to Independence* (New York: Cambridge University Press, 2016), offers a historical overview of the country from the period of Ottoman-Egyptian rule in the nineteenth century through the postindependence struggles that began in 2013. Francis Deng, *Sudan at the Brink: Self-Determination and National Unity* (New York: Fordham University Press, 2010), written by a Sudanese scholar and diplomat who became South Sudan's first ambassador to the UN, explores Sudan's choices and dilemmas at the time of the January 2011 referendum. Matthew LeRiche and Matthew Arnold, *South Sudan: From Revolution to Independence* (New York: Columbia University Press, 2012), argues that the vote for secession and the continued violence in the region are a by-product of the failed 2005 peace agreement. In *A Poisonous Thorn in Our Hearts: Sudan and South Sudan's Bitter and Incomplete Divorce* (New York: Hurst, 2014), BBC Sudan correspondent James Copnall offers diverse Sudanese perspectives and argues that the two countries remain interdependent, despite the unresolved differences that threaten their futures. Alex de Waal, "The Price of South Sudan's Independence," *Current History* 114, no. 772 (May 2015): 194–96, examines the ways in which South Sudanese political elites mirrored Khartoum in militarizing ethnic groups as tools of control and buying their loyalties with oil wealth. De Waal contends that parties to the 2013 conflict were motivated by the desire to control the lucrative patronage system, rather than by ethnic animosity.

The evolution of US Sudan policy is considered in several works. Peter Woodward, *US Foreign Policy and the Horn of Africa* (Burlington, VT: Ashgate, 2006), includes a case study on Sudan. Donald Petterson, *Inside Sudan: Political Islam, Conflict, and Catastrophe*, rev. ed. (Boulder, CO: Westview Press, 2003), offers an insider account by a US ambassador to Sudan during the Clinton administration. Andrew S. Natsios, *Sudan, South Sudan, and Darfur: What Everyone Needs to Know* (New York: Oxford University Press, 2012), provides an insider perspective by the administrator of USAID and special envoy for Sudan during the George W. Bush administration.

Three recommended studies investigate the role of political Islam and jihadism in Sudan. Woodward, *US Foreign Policy and the Horn of Africa* (mentioned previously); Alex de Waal, ed., *Islamism and Its Enemies in the Horn of Africa* (Bloomington: Indiana University Press, 2004); and Gregory A. Pirio, *African Jihad: Bin Laden's Quest for the Horn of Africa* (Trenton, NJ: Red Sea Press, 2007), include insightful case studies on Sudan.

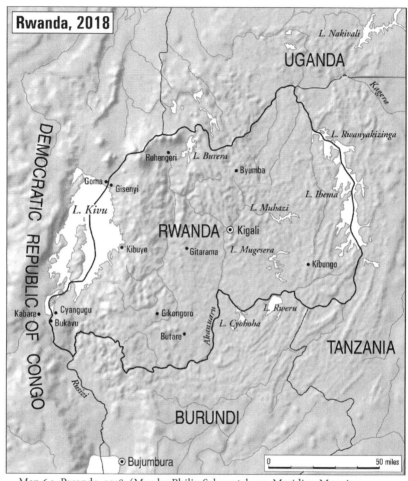

Map 6.1. Rwanda, 2018. (Map by Philip Schwartzberg, Meridian Mapping, Minneapolis.)

6

Rwanda

Genocide and the Failure to Respond (1991–94)

IN THE EARLY 1990s, as the Somali state collapsed and Sudan was torn by civil war, Rwanda moved from ethnic and political violence to genocide. During three and a half months in 1994, some 800,000 Rwandans were slaughtered. The victims included Hutu and Tutsi opponents of the Rwandan regime and three-quarters of the Tutsi minority population. Tens of thousands of women were raped, and hundreds of thousands of Rwandans fled into exile. Major players in the international community stood by—ignoring the threat to regional stability and failing to protect civilian lives. France, the United States, and the United Kingdom took the lead in opposing United Nations action to stop the violence, and France supported the extremist regime that perpetrated the carnage. The UN's belated response proved to be too little, too late. After a Tutsi rebel force backed by neighboring Uganda halted the genocide and ousted the government, more than a million Rwandans poured into neighboring Zaire, and another million refugees fled to Burundi, Uganda, and Tanzania.[1] Although the vast majority of refugees were Hutu civilians who were not implicated in the killings, genocide perpetrators also sought refuge in neighboring countries and prepared for a return to power. The failure of the international community to stop the genocide, the violent retribution against Hutu civilians, and the extremist aggression from adjacent states contributed to the destabilization of the Great Lakes region in the ensuing decades. The failure to act had especially devastating consequences for Zaire, the subject of chapter 7.

This chapter investigates the intervention of foreign entities and powers in the Rwandan genocide, as well as their failure to intervene. France, which continued to play a central role in postcolonial francophone Africa, supported the regime that directed the genocide.[2] Neighboring

Uganda backed the rebel movement that overthrew that regime. In the UN, powerful members of the Security Council terminated a peacekeeping operation that might have saved lives, and they approved an intervention force led by France—a party to the conflict—only after most of the killing was done. External actors that favored intervention generally emphasized the need for regional security, although some claimed that it was the obligation of the international community to protect civilians whose government was complicit in destroying them. The responsibility to protect paradigm emerged after the Rwandan genocide, stimulated in part by the international community's failure to stop the killings and the regret expressed by world leaders for their inaction. In the decades that followed, the new regime in Kigali became a strong US ally in a critical but unstable region. Having gained widespread international sympathy for halting the genocide, it was permitted to act with impunity in neighboring countries, especially Zaire, where it sowed the seeds of further conflict.

Setting the Stage:
The Precolonial to Postcolonial Context (1860–1989)

The 1994 Rwandan genocide was preceded by centuries of political, economic, and social interaction among people of varied backgrounds, a period of intense political violence and consolidation of state power by the Rwandan kingdom (1860–95), six decades of colonial rule (1898–1962), and three decades of independence punctuated by waves of interethnic violence and massive population displacement. The categorization of people according to socially constructed ethnic groups is a relatively recent phenomenon in Rwanda. Until the late nineteenth century, Rwandans tended to identify themselves by patrilineage or clan. Diverse peoples spoke the same language, engaged in commercial activities, and intermarried. Herding, farming, and hunting and gathering were the primary means of subsistence, and most populations engaged in various combinations of the three.

After the consolidation of state power during the second half of the nineteenth century, wealthy cattle holders associated with the Rwandan central court and monarchy increasingly became known as Tutsis—a referent that was later extended to pastoralists more generally. Sedentary agriculturalists without political connections or substantial cattle herds came to be known as Hutus. Hutus served as clients to Tutsi elites, laboring on their land, providing them with crops, and caring for their cattle. The small population of hunter-gatherers were referred to as Twa. Although hierarchical, Rwandan society was not static. Hutu families that established political connections—often through marriage to Tutsi women—and obtained substantial herds of cattle could, over the course of generations, come to be regarded as Tutsis. The reverse was also possible: Tutsis who lost power, status, and cattle could, over time, come to be viewed as Hutus. However, because Hutus alone performed unpaid manual labor for Tutsi chiefs, distinctions between Hutu and Tutsi identities became increasingly rigid and hierarchical. On the eve of colonial conquest, exploited Hutus revolted against their Tutsi overlords on numerous occasions. The European colonizers thus adapted and intensified a preexisting social, economic, and political system—which they erroneously attributed to racial differences.

Colonized in 1898 as a component of German East Africa, Rwanda was transferred to Belgium after World War I and administered as part of the League of Nations mandate of Ruanda-Urundi. By 1930, people identified as Hutus composed approximately 84 percent of the population, Tutsis constituted 15 percent, and Twas made up the remaining 1 percent. European administrators took advantage of the stratified society and implemented a system of indirect rule in which the Tutsi monarch, chiefs, and deputies extracted labor, collected taxes, and oversaw local justice on behalf of the imperial power. Tutsi chiefs benefited from increased control over land, labor, and cattle. The prerogatives of the Tutsi aristocracy as a whole were enhanced through an expanded system of patron-client relationships. The status system, which had been somewhat malleable until the late nineteenth century, hardened into an entrenched ethnic divide. In the census of 1933–34, Belgian administrators used perceived physical traits to define ethnic identities, which were then inscribed on identity cards. It was no longer possible for families to transition over time from one identity to another.

Although status differences predated colonialism, it was Belgian colonial rulers who introduced the myth of superior and inferior races, using similarity to European phenotypes as the measure of superiority. They endorsed the "Hamitic myth," popularized by the nineteenth-century British explorer John Hanning Speke, who hypothesized that the descendants of Noah's son, Ham, brought civilization from Ethiopia to central Africa, which at that time was purportedly inhabited by less intelligent, more primitive races. The Belgians defined taller, thinner, lighter-skinned people with aquiline noses as Tutsis, who were deemed superior, and shorter, stockier, darker-skinned people with broader noses as Hutus, who were considered inferior. Pseudo-scientific theories aside, centuries of intermarriage had undermined the validity of any categorization by phenotype. However, it was on the basis of these crude stereotypes that a minority of the population was granted access to privilege and resources and the majority of the population was denied them. Belgian Catholic missionaries welcomed Tutsi children into their schools, and Tutsis staffed the lower echelons of the colonial military and civil service, while Hutus were subjected to the most grueling forms of forced labor. According to the 1956 census, conducted six years before independence, Tutsis owned nearly all of Rwanda's cattle—historically, the main store of wealth—and controlled virtually all positions of power and prestige.

The corporate identity of Hutus was strengthened by their sense of shared oppression under both Tutsi and European rule. Hutu political consciousness began to emerge after World War II, influenced not only by their double oppression under Tutsi and Belgian authority, but also by the actions of Flemish priests who had migrated to the territory after the war. Because Belgium's Dutch-speaking Flemish majority had been dominated politically by the French-speaking Walloon minority, many priests identified with the Hutus' plight. They recruited Hutu children into mission schools, and by the late 1950s a new generation of Hutu intellectuals, supported by the Catholic Church that had spurned their ancestors, demanded majority rule and mobilized Hutu followers to overthrow the Tutsi aristocracy.

Under pressure to implement reforms in the territory, which became a UN trust in 1946, the Belgian colonial administration began to favor the Hutu majority. In the name of democracy, Belgian officials backed the Party for Hutu Emancipation (PARMEHUTU), which embraced the Hamitic myth that characterized Tutsis as foreign invaders, and advocated a transfer of power to the Hutu majority.[3] With the colonial administration and the Catholic Church in their camp, Hutu extremists began to employ ethnic violence to attain political power. During the Hutu Revolution of 1959–61, targeted killings focused on Tutsi power holders, primarily chiefs and subchiefs. The Tutsi monarchy was abolished, and some 10,000 Tutsis fled into exile. Over the next decade, armed invasions by Tutsi exiles provoked retaliatory massacres and new waves of refugees that drove hundreds of thousands of Rwandan Tutsis into Burundi, Uganda, Tanzania, and Zaire.

When Rwanda obtained independence in July 1962, PARMEHUTU's Grégoire Kayibanda, a southern Hutu, became president. The domination of one group by another continued, this time with the Hutus on top. A rigid system of ethnic quotas allotted Tutsis only a tiny percentage of the positions in schools and government and excluded them from the military. Exiled Tutsi insurgents organized armed attacks on Rwanda, and Hutu "self-defense" units retaliated against Tutsi civilians, killing more than 10,000 people in December 1963 alone. In July 1973, Major General Juvénal Habyarimana, a northern Hutu, seized power in a military coup. Manipulating both ethnicity and regionalism in his bid for power, Habyarimana brutally oppressed Tutsis and southern and central Hutus. He presided over a patronage system that staffed the government and military bureaucracies with loyalists from top to bottom. Political opponents—primarily Hutus—and civil society critics were imprisoned and killed.

By the late 1980s, political and economic crises threatened Habyarimana's hold on power. As the Cold War wound down, Western powers no longer needed loyal strongmen and regional policemen. Instead, they pressured African clients to open their countries to multiparty democracy and to improve human rights practices. In June 1990, French President François Mitterrand outlined a new Africa policy that linked French development aid to progress in these areas. To protect their relationships with France, Habyarimana and other African dictators made superficial reforms that suggested movement toward multiparty democracy, but which catered to the interests of political elites. The modifications failed to address the urgent needs of ordinary citizens, who suffered from growing poverty, landlessness, unemployment, and food insecurity—a serious shortcoming that later would be exploited by Hutu extremists. Nonetheless, the reforms opened the door to restive civil society organizations that increasingly agitated for fundamental structural change.

Rwanda's political tensions were compounded by an economic crisis that had roots both in the colonial past and in the neoliberal reforms of the late twentieth century. Like many former colonies, Rwanda was an overwhelmingly agrarian society that depended on agriculture for local sustenance and government revenue. Established to serve the needs of the metropole, Rwanda exported primary products and imported manufactured goods. As a result, its economy was deeply affected by the worldwide depression in commodity prices that began in the late 1970s, by concurrent droughts and famines, and by the impact of IMF and World Bank structural adjustment mandates that followed in their wake.

When coffee and tea prices plummeted in the mid-1980s and tin production was halted because of declining profits, Rwanda turned to international financial institutions for assistance. In November 1990, the IMF directed Rwanda to devalue its currency by 50 percent in order to strengthen its export market. The result was a dramatic increase in the cost of imported food, fuel, and other essential goods. A shortage of imported medicines led to the collapse of the health system, accompanied by a dramatic rise in malnutrition and preventable diseases. Reduced purchasing power led to business failures and escalating unemployment. Other externally imposed free market practices led to the removal of gasoline subsidies and to the imposition of new fees for health care, schooling, and even water.

Rising economic inequality widened the gulf between the haves and have-nots. Tens of thousands of young Rwandan men were landless, uneducated, unemployed, and without hope for marriage and social adulthood. Power elites faced growing insecurity as economic and political crises threatened the patronage system. In this context, Hutu extremists found fertile ground for their proselytizing. Tutsis were maligned as wealthy foreigners who had invaded Rwanda to take what rightfully belonged to the indigenous Hutu population. As such, they became convenient scapegoats for the country's problems.

Invasion and Civil War (1990–93)

By 1990, an estimated 400,000 to 600,000 Rwandan Tutsis were living in exile in neighboring countries, about half of them in Uganda, where they had been persecuted by successive dictatorial regimes. During the 1978–79 Uganda-Tanzania War, Rwandan Tutsis had joined Ugandan rebel leader Yoweri Museveni, whose units had fought alongside the Tanzanian army when it invaded Uganda and overthrew the Idi Amin regime. Tutsis had joined Museveni again during the 1981–86 Ugandan Bush War, when his National Resistance Army challenged the dictatorship of Milton Obote. When Museveni took power in January 1986, many of his top officers and 20 to 30 percent of his 14,000-man fighting force were Tutsis whose parents had fled Rwanda two and a half decades earlier. While some officers had come to Uganda as children, many of the rank and file had been born in Uganda. In 1990, the Ugandan national army included some 8,000 Rwandan Tutsis and their descendants; some 200,000 Rwandan Tutsis and their offspring were domiciled in Uganda, and most considered Uganda their permanent home. During the economically troubled times of the late 1980s, a growing number of Ugandans resented Rwandan Tutsis' proximity to power and began to complain about foreigners occupying influential and lucrative positions.

Under pressure to leave Uganda, Rwandan Tutsis also felt the pull of their parents' homeland. In December 1987, the descendants of earlier waves of refugees established the Rwandan Patriotic Front (RPF), a political and military organization whose goal was to repatriate Rwandan Tutsis and to share in political power. Two thousand RPF fighters crossed the border into Rwanda on October 1, 1990. Led by some of Museveni's key military commanders, the RPF force was composed mainly of Rwandan Tutsis who had absconded from the Ugandan army with their weapons. Most of the fighters had been born in Uganda and spoke English rather than French. Few had had any experience in contemporary Rwanda, but they nonetheless assumed that they would be welcomed as liberators. In actuality, Tutsi civilians feared the reprisals that invariably followed in the wake of cross-border operations, and the RPF found little local support. Tutsi and Hutu civilians fled the conflict zones, and uprooted populations were weakened by hunger and starvation. By 1993, the number of internally displaced persons approached 1 million. Thousands of young Hutu men sought refuge in the capital city of Kigali, where they joined the ranks of homeless, unemployed, and alienated youth who would be ready recruits for extremist militias.

External powers were embroiled in the new Rwandan conflict from the outset. Hoping that RPF success would lead to an exodus of Rwandan Tutsis, Ugandan President Museveni backed the RPF invasion to alleviate domestic tensions, and the Ugandan army covertly supplied its former members. The French government, which had trained, equipped, and financed Habyarimana's army, presidential guard, and allied militias, characterized the RPF operation as external aggression. Paris considered the RPF and its Ugandan backers to be part of an anglophone conspiracy to oust France from its longstanding sphere of influence in Central Africa. Zaire, a French ally and beneficiary, sent troops to support the Rwandan regime. France also intervened militarily. Three days after the RPF invasion, 600 French paratroopers landed in Rwanda in a venture called Operation

Noroît. Although the mission was publicly presented as an effort to protect French lives and evacuate French citizens, Paris was determined to thwart an RPF victory. French helicopter gunships inhibited the RPF advance, French soldiers directed artillery and assisted with communications, and a French officer served as the effective head of the Rwandan army.

Just as Rwandan civilians had feared, the RPF invasion provoked massive reprisals against the Tutsi population—which, until then, had not been specifically targeted by the Habyarimana regime. Regime propagandists portrayed resident Tutsis as a traitorous fifth column and stoked fears that Tutsi "foreigners" would usurp the land of Hutu farmers, who already suffered from acute land shortages and food insecurity. Between 1990 and 1993, Rwandan security forces and their civilian accomplices killed some 2,000 Tutsi civilians.

The invasion also halted the government's gestures toward reform and stimulated a crackdown on domestic opponents. The nascent prodemocracy movement came under fire. Using the invasion as a pretext, security forces arrested an estimated 10,000 people during October and November 1990—including both Tutsis and Hutus who opposed Habyarimana's abusive practices. With French assistance, the Rwandan army grew from 5,000 in October 1990 to 40,000 a few years later, finding ready recruits among unemployed Hutu youth. Meanwhile, weapons left over from the Cold War flooded into Rwanda and were absorbed by the security forces, militias, and civilian population. The elements for a violent confrontation between state and society were now in place.

The Arusha Accords (1993)

Concerned that violence in Rwanda might destabilize the region, neighboring countries, France, the United States, and the OAU sponsored a series of peace talks in 1992 and 1993 that were intended to find common ground between the government and the RPF. Habyarimana came under enormous pressure at home and abroad. Domestically, he was besieged by Hutu moderates, who called for an inclusive multiparty democracy that would entail power sharing with the RPF, and by Hutu extremists, who were determined to retain a monopoly on power and privilege. While the extremists rejected any accommodation, France asserted that compromise was a precondition for further bilateral assistance. The World Bank, Belgium, the United States, and other important donors concurred: if a peace agreement were not signed, there would be no further funds. Under duress, the Rwandan government joined the RPF in signing the Arusha Accords in August 1993.

The accords called for the establishment of a broad-based transitional government, followed by multiparty elections. Bargaining from a position of strength, the RPF successfully excluded the Hutu extremist Coalition for the Defense of the Republic (CDR) from the power-sharing arrangement and obtained for the Tutsi minority a disproportionate share of government and military positions. The ruling National Republican Movement for Democracy and Development (MRNDD) and the RPF would each fill five seats in the council of ministers and eleven seats in the Transitional National Assembly. RPF soldiers would be integrated into the Rwandan national army, which would include equal numbers of Hutu and Tutsi troops and officers. This arrangement meant that more than two-thirds of the Hutu soldiers and a large number of Hutu officers then serving faced demobilization and unemployment. Reference to ethnic groups would be eliminated from official documents, and Tutsi refugees and their descendants would be permitted to return to Rwanda. Their claims to ancestral land, although limited by the accords, nonetheless provoked anxiety in the densely populated rural areas, where inhabitants were already menaced by land shortages. Hutu extremists rejected the accords and claimed that Habyarimana had sold out. A virulent anti-Tutsi propaganda campaign ensued.

Aware of the agreement's fragility, the Arusha signatories called for a UN force to monitor and implement it and to provide security, assist with demilitarization, and aid in the integration of the armed forces. The RPF insisted that French troops, who were partial to the Habyarimana government, be removed and replaced by a neutral body. On October 3, as the UN Security Council deliberated about Rwanda, eighteen US soldiers were killed in Somalia during the ill-conceived mission that had begun as a UN effort to avert mass starvation. As the soldiers' bodies were dragged through the streets of Mogadishu, the United States balked at the prospect of another fiasco and opposed a substantial commitment in Rwanda. France, in contrast, pushed for a UN force that could protect the Habyarimana government from RPF advances. The result was a compromise: a peacekeeping mission with a weak mandate and insufficient personnel.

On October 5, the Security Council established the United Nations Assistance Mission for Rwanda (UNAMIR), a multinational peacekeeping force that would replace the French Operation Noroît. Canadian Brigadier General Roméo Dallaire was named commander. UNAMIR, which operated under Chapter VI of the UN Charter, was empowered to monitor and assist in implementing the peace agreement, but not to impose peace in the context of war. Peacekeepers could use their weapons only if attacked or directly threatened with attack. They were not authorized to protect civilians. If war resumed, the UN mission would be terminated—unless the mandate were changed. The Security Council had refused to authorize action under Chapter VII, which would have permitted UN troops to use force to counter threats to the peace and to act without the consent of all parties involved. It disregarded the Arusha Accords, which called for a force that could confiscate illegal weapons and guarantee security throughout Rwanda. Instead, it declined to let the peacekeepers seize arms and confined them to Kigali and its environs. Only 2,548 peacekeepers were authorized, although the UNAMIR commander had lobbied for three times as many.[4] The mission did not have an intelligence unit, possessed only a small civilian police force, and did not include a human rights cell.

Although the Arusha Accords had established a veneer of peace, the conflict was far from over. The weak UN force arrived in a country still in the throes of civil war. The transitional government had not been established, Rwandan soldiers and rebels had not been demobilized, and illegal arms were flooding into the capital. Hutu extremists, whose party had been excluded from the power-sharing agreement, were determined to seize power by other means.

Hutu Extremism: Prelude to Genocide

The institutionalization of Hutu extremism through exclusive sociopolitical organizations, political parties, militias, and media laid the groundwork for the 1994 genocide. In the late 1980s, First Lady Agathe Kanziga Habyarimana established Akazu (Little House or Inner Circle), an organization composed of her close relatives and high-level government, military, and police officials. By the early 1990s, Akazu's hold on wealth and power was threatened both by the internal prodemocracy movement and by the externally backed Arusha Accords. Akazu responded by organizing death squads that targeted government opponents and by obstructing the settlement's implementation. During the interlude between the RPF invasion in 1990 and the signing of the Arusha Accords in 1993, thousands of Tutsis and moderate Hutus were killed in attacks planned by Akazu and executed by the French-trained presidential guard and army, as well as by youth militias linked to extremist parties. The most notorious of these militias were the MRNDD-associated Interahamwe (Those Who Stay Together) and the CDR-associated Impuzamugambi (Those Who Share the Same Aim). Although organized by Hutu elites, the militias were made up of impoverished, unemployed Hutu youth with little schooling, who were trained by the national army and who killed on command. Radio stations run by Akazu or by the state became the leading propagandists for "Hutu Power," playing on economic grievances, spreading ethnic hatred, and rallying the Hutu populace against Tutsis, government opponents, and the Arusha Accords.

Events in neighboring Burundi also stoked the flames. Burundi, like Rwanda, had been a component of German East Africa; together they formed the western region of Ruanda-Urundi. After Germany's defeat in World War I, the territory was administered by Belgium as a League of Nations mandate and later as a UN trust territory. Rwanda and Burundi separated at independence in 1962. Burundi's population also comprised a Hutu majority and a Tutsi minority. However, in Burundi, the Tutsi elite retained power after independence. Tutsi dominance was challenged by a series of Hutu revolts that led to massacres and reprisals that claimed some 250,000 lives between 1965 and 1993. The vast majority of those killed were Hutus. In the early 1990s, Burundi, like other African countries, came under pressure from both domestic and international forces to democratize. A new constitution, followed by multiparty elections in June 1993, resulted in a parliament dominated by the largely Hutu Front for Democracy in Burundi and the first Hutu president, Melchior Ndadaye. In October 1993, extremists in the Tutsi-dominated army assassinated the president along with seven government ministers, sparking a Hutu uprising. The rebellion was violently suppressed by the army, and a cascade of interethnic revenge killings ensued, leaving some 100,000 civilians dead. More than 400,000 refugees poured into Rwanda, while almost as many sought safety in Zaire and Tanzania. The mass killing of Hutus in Burundi and the influence of Hutu refugees in Rwanda led to intensified propaganda against Rwandan Tutsis. Hutu refugees from Burundi, trained by Hutu extremists in Rwanda, would become active participants in the 1994 Rwandan genocide.

Within a month of the assassinations in Burundi, plans for mass killings in Rwanda were under way. In November 1993, hundreds of thousands of imported Chinese machetes appeared in Kigali, and diplomats and human rights workers warned that Hutu civilians and militias were arming themselves. In January 1994, UNAMIR commander Roméo Dallaire cabled the UN Department of Peacekeeping Operations (DPKO) in New York, alerting headquarters to reported plans to exterminate all Tutsis in Kigali, along with the Hutu political opposition. Tutsis were being registered, hit lists compiled, and death squads assembled. The DPKO replied that UNAMIR must adhere to its mandate, maintaining strict neutrality and operating with all parties' consent. Fearing a repeat of the Somalia debacle, the DPKO ordered Dallaire to abandon plans to raid the militias' weapons caches. Instead, he was instructed to report his findings to the Rwandan government and to the French, US, and Belgian embassies in Kigali—despite the fact that the Rwandan regime was complicit in the militias' activities. The DPKO did not transmit Dallaire's dire warnings nor his appeals for more troops to the Security Council. The UN's failure to respond convinced Hutu extremists that they could proceed without fear of UN intervention.

Meanwhile, the implementation of the Arusha Accords had stalled. The United States blamed the Habyarimana regime for failing to establish a transitional government and argued that the Security Council should consider terminating the peacekeeping mission. As the Security Council deliberated on April 5, 1994, Habyarimana flew to a summit of regional leaders in Arusha, where he was roundly criticized for his government's intransigence and for the flood of refugees that threatened to destabilize the region. Menaced with sanctions, Habyarimana agreed to form the long-delayed transitional government. In New York, the Security Council extended the UNAMIR mandate until July 29.

The Genocide (April–July 1994)

On April 6, 1994, Habyarimana's plane was shot down as it returned from the Arusha summit. The French-piloted aircraft also carried Burundi's new Hutu president, Cyprien Ntaryamira, and several high-level Rwandan officials. Kigali and Paris immediately blamed the RPF for the attack, while Belgian military intelligence officials, the US State Department's Bureau of Intelligence and Research, and the CIA concluded that the plane had been shot down by the presidential guard or other elements in the Rwandan military who felt that Habyarimana had sold out.[5]

Targeted killings by Hutu extremists began immediately. In less than an hour, the presidential guard and the Interahamwe erected road blocks. Hutu Power militants seized control of the government, and Akazu death squads began killing from preexisting lists. They turned first to moderate Hutu politicians who opposed the government's extremist policies and supported the Arusha Accords, and then proceeded to human rights activists, journalists, and other citizens who were educated or prosperous. Over the next few days, the targets were extended to include Tutsis of all backgrounds. The Akazu- and state-owned radio stations rallied the population against anyone who opposed the extremist agenda. The killings were directed by the army and militias and urged on by local government officials and power brokers, including teachers, doctors, and Catholic priests and nuns. Hutus who would not join in killing their Tutsi neighbors or family members were themselves killed. Between April 6 and July 18, some 800,000 Tutsis and moderate Hutus were murdered. Seventy-five percent of Rwanda's Tutsi population was slaughtered, and tens of thousands of Tutsi women were raped in a systematic attempt to further terrorize and destroy the Tutsi community. Hundreds of thousands of refugees poured across the borders into Burundi and Tanzania.

When the killings began, the UNAMIR force included 2,548 poorly equipped peacekeepers whose sole mandate was to monitor and assist in implementing the Arusha agreement. The peacekeepers were immediately ordered to protect moderate Hutu politicians who supported the Arusha Accords. However, they were not permitted to fire their weapons unless directly targeted. On April 7, ten Belgian peacekeepers attempted to escort Prime Minister Agathe Uwilingiyimana, a moderate Hutu, to the state-run radio station to appeal for calm. The group was confronted by the presidential guard, who disarmed and killed the peacekeepers before assassinating the prime minister. The next day, Belgium warned that it would withdraw its soldiers unless the UNAMIR mandate were expanded and the multinational force bolstered with troops from other countries. The Belgian peacekeepers, tasked with security in the capital, constituted the backbone of the UN force. The Security Council refused both requests, and Belgium withdrew from UNAMIR. Bangladesh followed suit, leaving troops from Ghana and Tunisia to take up the slack.

As the Security Council dithered, RPF soldiers poured across the Uganda-Rwanda border, and the civil war resumed. Although there was no longer a ceasefire to monitor or a peace to keep, the Security Council could have strengthened the UNAMIR mandate, transforming its mission from peacekeeping (Chapter VI) to peace enforcement (Chapter VII). A Chapter VII mandate would have permitted UNAMIR soldiers to protect civilians, to operate without the consent of the Hutu Power government, and to use force where warranted. Instead, the Security Council focused its energy and resources on the evacuation of foreign nationals. France took the lead, mounting a paramilitary action—code-named Operation Amaryllis—to evacuate 1,238 foreigners, high-level members of the Habyarimana regime, other Hutu extremists, and their families. Italy and Belgium also flew foreign nationals to safety, while a US convoy transported US citizens across the border into Burundi. UNAMIR personnel helped coordinate these evacuations, but they were not permitted to assist Rwandan civilians. Tutsi employees of foreign embassies, offices, and homes were abandoned as their employers fled. By the time the evacuations ended, most of Rwanda's political opposition had been eliminated.

Powerful interests in the UN thwarted a more forceful UN intervention that might have stopped the slaughter. UN Secretary-General Boutros Boutros-Ghali, an Egyptian diplomat, Sorbonne-trained lawyer, and close ally of France and the Habyarimana regime, embraced the French position that the killings were the result of longstanding ethnic hatreds and the product of spontaneous violence in an ongoing civil war. He contended that the problem was a weak state that had failed to implement the peace accords—rather than ethnic cleansing or a genocide orchestrated by the state itself. In the face of mounting evidence of genocide, Boutros-Ghali continued to deny its existence until early May. In the meantime, he refused to transmit to the Security Council information provided by Dallaire and others that might have bolstered the case for intervention.

The Security Council was divided in its assessment of the Rwandan situation and split over how to resolve it. The five permanent members, who wield veto power over any proposal or resolution, were unanimous in their opposition to stronger UN action. Both France and the United States characterized the violence as a civil war between armed opponents rather than the victimization of unarmed civilians by the government and its allies. France argued that the Rwandan government and military should be strengthened, which would enable them to restore order, and insisted that the government, now dominated by Hutu Power elements, be allowed to participate in any future negotiations. The United States, fresh from its humiliation in Somalia, had no desire to intervene in a country where it had no immediate strategic or economic interests. The Clinton administration argued that the situation in Rwanda was not a threat to international peace and security, and since there was no longer a ceasefire to monitor or a peace to keep, the UNAMIR operation should be terminated. Lawyers in the US State Department cautioned administration officials against using the term "genocide," which might compel the United States to act under the 1948 Genocide Convention.[6] The United Kingdom joined the other Western members in supporting UN withdrawal, as did Russia and China—the latter because it opposed intervening in other countries' domestic affairs.

The ten nonpermanent members of the Security Council, elected by the General Assembly to two-year terms, showed no such consensus. Rwanda had joined the Security Council in January 1994. During the genocide, Rwanda's UN ambassador, Jean Damascène Bizimana, represented the Hutu Power government. He participated in all Security Council deliberations and communicated sensitive information to Kigali. From his influential position, he discouraged concerted UN action to stop the massacres and assured his superiors in Kigali that the UN would not interfere. Other nonpermanent members, notably New Zealand, the Czech Republic, Spain, and Argentina, urged the Security Council to strengthen the UNAMIR mandate so that peacekeepers could protect Rwandan civilians. These measures were also supported by many African UN member states that were not represented on the council.

The noninterventionists carried the day. On April 21, the Security Council voted to withdraw all but a few hundred peacekeepers.[7] The new resolution authorized the remaining peacekeepers to negotiate a ceasefire, assist in the provision of humanitarian assistance, and monitor the safety and security of civilians who sought UNAMIR protection. However, it did not permit the peacekeepers to protect those civilians. When New Zealand attempted to include reference to genocide in a UN document on April 29, the United States successfully opposed it.

By early May, the RPF had reached the outskirts of the capital. On May 4, UN Secretary-General Boutros-Ghali, who remained hopeful that an RPF takeover could be thwarted, called the mass killings a genocide for the first time. On May 13 he recommended an expansion of the UNAMIR mandate, arguing that Rwanda was in the midst of a "major humanitarian crisis," with nearly 2 million people displaced internally and another 400,000 living as refugees in neighboring states.[8] On May 17, the Security Council increased the number of UNAMIR troops to 5,500 and adjusted the mission's mandate. Although France had pushed for a Chapter VII mandate to enable the UN force to halt the RPF advance, the council determined that UNAMIR II would continue to operate under Chapter VI as a deterrent rather than an enforcement body. However, the expanded UN operation would be authorized to protect vulnerable civilians, to establish secure humanitarian areas, and to provide security for relief operations. The resolution also imposed an arms embargo on both the Kigali government and the RPF. Successful implementation required a ceasefire, a sufficient body of troops, and adequate equipment, none of which was forthcoming. The Security Council's delayed action was quickly overtaken by events. Poised for military victory and distrustful of the UN, the RPF ignored appeals for a ceasefire. On May 21, rebel forces took the Kigali airport.

On June 8, two months after the mass killings began, the Security Council finally concluded that the situation in Rwanda was indeed a genocide. However, its members disagreed about what should be done and by whom. With the UNAMIR II deployment still months away, France requested permission to lead a multilateral intervention force with a Chapter VII mandate to protect Rwandan civilians in the interim. France would stand down once the UNAMIR force was fully operational. On June 22, the Security Council authorized Operation Turquoise, a French-led military action that was to last no longer than sixty days. The United States and the UK were happy to let France carry the burden. Brazil, China, New Zealand, Nigeria, and Pakistan demonstrated their ambivalence by abstaining. Outside the Security Council, critics accused France of using the UN for its own ends, which included saving the Hutu regime and stopping the RPF advance. The OAU and a number of international NGOs publicly opposed Operation Turquoise, while the UNAMIR commander, General Dallaire, argued that French intervention would endanger UNAMIR forces. The RPF had vowed to fight any military operation that included French soldiers.

Having readied its troops in advance, France launched Operation Turquoise on June 23. The 2,362-man force, financed primarily by France, was composed almost exclusively of French troops, with thirty-two Senegalese soldiers representing the only multinational component. Zaire, an important French ally and a staunch supporter of the Habyarimana

Photo 6.1. French soldiers in Operation Turquoise pass Hutu Rwandan army troops near Gisenyi, Rwanda, June 27, 1994. Photo by Pascal Guyot/AFP/Getty Images.

regime, served as the main base of operations, and soldiers, support staff, and equipment transited through that country. The mission included re-connaissance and ground attack aircraft, fighter-bombers, helicopters, and more than one hundred armored vehicles. However, no trucks were provided to transport displaced civilians. The operation seemed pre-pared for a military rather than a humanitarian mission.

Despite French efforts, the RPF ousted the Hutu extremist regime from Kigali on July 4. Five days later, the UN established a safe humani-tarian zone under French control in southwestern Rwanda. As the RPF advanced, hundreds of thousands of Hutu civilians fled toward the safe zone. High-level government officials, military and militia commanders, and other perpetrators of the genocide also found shelter in the protected area. Focused on thwarting the RPF and its anglophone backers, France did not disarm or arrest suspected war criminals or turn them over to UNAMIR forces. Instead, Operation Turquoise personnel helped per-petrators escape with their weapons into Zaire and the Central African Republic, where many trained for a return to power in Rwanda. Some Hutu Power officials eventually established residence in France and other European countries, where they lived covertly in order to evade prosecu-tion for war crimes.

On July 18, the victorious RPF declared a unilateral ceasefire. The genocide, which had claimed the lives of some 800,000 people, was over. However, the devastating aftermath had only begun. Nearly 40 percent of Rwanda's 7.6 million people had been driven into exile or killed. Three million people were internally displaced, and another 2 million were stranded in squalid refugee camps in neighboring Burundi, Tanzania, Uganda, and Zaire, where tens of thousands of refugees succumbed to cholera, dysentery, and other diseases. Although widely praised for halting the genocide, the RPF was also responsible for egregious human rights abuses. The UN High Commissioner for Refugees documented widespread and systematic killings of Hutu civilians by RPF forces, estimating that 25,000 to 45,000 Hutus were slaughtered between April and August 1994.[9]

On July 19, 1994, the RPF established a national unity government that included members from five political parties but excluded representatives from the MRNDD and the CDR. Pasteur Bizimungu, a Hutu moderate, was sworn in as president. However, the real power lay with the RPF commander Paul Kagame, who was named vice president and minister of defense. Hutus and Tutsis filled other cabinet positions.

Photo 6.2. Children orphaned or displaced during the Rwandan genocide search for food near Goma, Zaire (now the DRC), July 15, 1994. Photo by Dario Mitidieri/ Getty Images.

Within days, the new government was recognized by the United States, the United Kingdom, and Belgium. France, however, refused to send an ambassador and determined that Rwanda, with so many English speakers in high-profile positions, was no longer part of *la francophonie*.

Conclusion

The failure of the international community to halt the genocide in Rwanda, and its refusal to hold the perpetrators to account, contributed to the destabilization of the Great Lakes region. After the genocide, more than a million Rwandan civilians, 30,000 former soldiers, and tens of thousands of Hutu militia members flooded into Zaire. Hutu Power leaders, including former government officials, military officers, and militia leaders, asserted control over the UN-administered refugee camps and used them as a base for recruitment, training, and, they hoped, an eventual return to power in Rwanda. Their attacks on both sides of the border, and the failure of UN member states to thwart them, sparked two new wars that devastated eastern Zaire and ultimately involved most countries in the Great Lakes region. These wars and the international community's response are the subject of chapter 7.

Suggested Reading

The mass killings in Rwanda in 1994 and their violent aftermath continue to affect the lives of millions of people in the region. Scholarly debates concerning causes, consequences, and responsibility remain contentious. Two opposing groups compose the extremes: those who deny that a genocide occurred and conflate Tutsi civilians with the RPF elites, and those who demonize Hutus as a group and dispute claims that they, too, were victims. In the middle are scholars who produce complex, nuanced, empirically based assessments—and who are often criticized by those at both ends of the spectrum. Most of the sources mentioned below represent the middle group, although some of the more partisan works are also noted.

Succinct but nuanced summaries of the genocide and its political, economic, social, and historical context include Catharine Newbury, "Background to Genocide: Rwanda," *Issue: A Journal of Opinion* 23, no. 2 (1995): 12–17; and David Newbury, "Understanding Genocide," *African Studies Review* 41, no. 1 (April 1998): 73–97.

Among the empirically based scholarly works, several explore Rwanda's precolonial and colonial past and provide a foundation for understanding recent historical events. Four of these studies trace the roots of Rwandan social hierarchies and political violence to the precolonial period, examine the evolution of ethnic politics during the colonial period, and establish a historical framework for understanding mass killings and genocide perpetrated after independence. See Catharine Newbury, *The Cohesion of Oppression: Clientship and Ethnicity in Rwanda, 1860–1960* (New York: Columbia University Press, 1988); Catharine Newbury, "Ethnicity in Rwanda: The Case of Kinyaga," *Africa: Journal of the International African Institute* 48, no. 1 (1978): 17–29; Jan Vansina, *Antecedents to Modern Rwanda: The Nyiginya Kingdom* (Madison: University of Wisconsin Press, 2005); and Alison Des Forges, *Defeat Is the Only Bad News: Rwanda under Musinga, 1896–1931,* edited and with an introduction and epilogue by David Newbury (Madison: University of Wisconsin Press, 2011). René Lemarchand, *Rwanda and Burundi* (New York: Praeger, 1970), explores similar dynamics in Rwanda and Burundi, highlighting parallels, differences, and the influence of events in one country on the other. David Newbury, "Canonical Conventions in Rwanda: Four Myths of Recent Historiography in Central Africa," *History in Africa* 39 (2012): 41–76, challenges several common myths about Rwanda's past that hinder a proper understanding of recent historical events.

Other empirically based studies provide insight into the motivations behind and the organization of the genocide. They argue that the genocide was not rooted in ethnic hatred, but rather was motivated by a political agenda and was organized and implemented by political elites. See, especially, Alison Des Forges, *"Leave None to Tell the Story": Genocide in Rwanda* (New York: Human Rights Watch, 1999), a highly accessible, authoritative study that explores the historical background and events leading to the genocide, its organization and unfolding, the key players and their motivations, and the role of the international community. Scott Straus, *The Order of Genocide: Race, Power, and War in Rwanda* (Ithaca, NY: Cornell University Press, 2006), examines the extremist regime that orchestrated the killings, the indifference of the international community, and recent constructions of difference that cast all Tutsis as a threat to be extinguished. Lee Ann Fujii, *Killing Neighbors: Webs of Violence in Rwanda* (Ithaca, NY: Cornell University Press, 2009), also offers a nuanced assessment of the complex group dynamics and social ties that led neighbors to kill neighbors. Jennie Burnet, *Genocide Lives in Us: Women, Memory and Silence in Rwanda* (Madison: University of Wisconsin Press, 2012), focuses on Tutsi and Hutu women's experiences during the genocide, their agency in postgenocide reconstruction and peace building, the politicization of survivorship, and the impact of official policies that consider only Tutsis to be victims.

A number of works focus on the political, economic, and environmental factors that laid the groundwork for the genocide. Johan Pottier, *Re-Imagining Rwanda: Conflict, Survival and Disinformation in the Late Twentieth Century* (New York: Cambridge University Press, 2002), considers the impact of the collapse of world coffee prices and of the IMF-mandated structural adjustment program, externally imposed political reforms, elite manipulation of ethnicity to gain and maintain access to power, the RPF invasion, and events in neighboring countries. André Guichaoua, *From War to Genocide: Criminal Politics in Rwanda, 1990–1994*, trans. Don E. Webster (Madison: University of Wisconsin Press, 2015), and David Newbury, "Ecology and the Politics of Genocide: Rwanda 1994," *Cultural Survival* 22, no. 4 (Winter 1999): 32–35, examine background to the genocide, including economic and social inequalities, environmental degradation, famine, corruption, internal regional rivalries, the 1990–94 civil war, and events in neighboring Uganda and Burundi. Isaac A. Kamola, "The Global Coffee Economy and the Production of Genocide in Rwanda," *Third World Quarterly* 28, no. 3 (2007): 571–92, investigates coffee production and export as a source of growing landlessness, inequality, and food insecurity that had regional and ethnic components. The article also shows how the economic crisis led to mounting political unrest that divided ruling elites, threatened the regime, and led to mobilization for mass violence.

Other studies provide insight into particular aspects of the genocide. Gérard Prunier, *The Rwanda Crisis: History of a Genocide* (New York: Columbia University Press, 1997), is especially useful for its examination of the RPF's origins and evolution in Museveni's Uganda, the role of the 1990 invasion in creating a class of alienated Hutu youth who were recruited into extremist militias, and the ways in which France bolstered the Hutu extremist regime. Prunier also considers how the genocide and the international community's failure to respond laid the foundations for a new state that was permitted to act with impunity both inside Rwanda and in neighboring Zaire. Criticized for downplaying the RPF's responsibility for civilian deaths in the original 1995 version, Prunier included an additional chapter in the 1997 edition that permits a more balanced assessment of all the players. Mahmood Mamdani, *When Victims Become Killers: Colonialism, Nativism, and the Genocide in Rwanda* (Princeton, NJ: Princeton University Press, 2001), exposes the precarious situation of Rwandan Tutsis in Uganda that led to the formation of the RPF and the decision to return to Rwanda as a rebel force. More contentious are his claims that the colonial-era ideology describing Tutsis as racially superior alien settlers and Hutus as racially inferior natives was the cornerstone of the 1994 genocide. Jean-Paul Kimonyo, *Rwanda's Popular Genocide: Perfect Storm* (Boulder, CO: Lynne Rienner, 2016), explores the ways in which local political, social, and economic factors contributed to grassroots alienation and facilitated mobilization for genocide. The author, a senior advisor in the Kagame government, challenges the official position that precolonial Rwanda was characterized by peaceful coexistence and that ethnicity was solely a construct of colonial rule. Timothy Longman, *Christianity and Genocide in Rwanda* (New York: Cambridge University Press, 2009), investigates the history of Christianity in Rwanda and explores the power struggles that led to Christian participation in the genocide.

Journalists have provided highly readable investigative accounts. Linda Melvern, *Conspiracy to Murder: The Rwandan Genocide* (New York: Verso, 2006), provides a compelling document- and interview-based narrative that focuses on the elites who planned and instigated the genocide. Philip Gourevitch, *We Wish to Inform You that Tomorrow We Will Be Killed with Our Families: Stories from Rwanda* (New York: Farrar, Straus and Giroux, 1998), offers a powerful collection of personal stories that highlight Rwandan voices and the moral failure of the international community. Gourevitch's work, which influenced the Clinton administration's postgenocide Rwandan policies, has been criticized for focusing primarily on ethnic considerations, for minimizing political and economic factors, and for presenting the RPF and its leader, Paul Kagame, relatively uncritically.

Powerful firsthand accounts include Paul Rusesabagina with Tom Zoellner, *An Ordinary Man: An Autobiography* (New York: Viking, 2006), which explores how Rusesabagina, a hotel manager, protected more than 1,000 Rwandans from slaughter. In *Guns Over Kigali* (Accra: Woeli, 1997), a Ghanaian military officer and UNAMIR deputy force commander,

Henry Kwami Anyidoho, examines victimization and atrocities on both sides and provides insights into the RPF's concerns about the French-operated safe humanitarian zone. The United States Holocaust Memorial Museum website includes links to important primary source material on the Rwandan genocide, including official documents, eyewitness accounts, photographs, and other resources compiled in partnership with the National Security Archive at George Washington University (https://www.ushmm.org/confront-genocide/cases/rwanda).

The responsibility of outsiders for the magnitude of the killings is the subject of several studies, including two firsthand accounts. Roméo Dallaire, *Shake Hands with the Devil: The Failure of Humanity in Rwanda* (New York: Carroll & Graf, 2005), an insider account by the UNAMIR commander, exposes the UN's failure to respond to warnings about the impending genocide. Michael Barnett, *Eyewitness to a Genocide: The United Nations and Rwanda* (Ithaca, NY: Cornell University Press, 2002), by a staff member of the US Mission to the UN, explains the reasons the organization failed to act. Linda Melvern, *A People Betrayed: The Role of the West in Rwanda's Genocide* (London: Zed Books, 2000), criticizes the UN Security Council for its failure to respond and considers France especially culpable. (See also Melvern, *Conspiracy to Murder,* mentioned previously.) An OAU investigation resulted in *Rwanda: The Preventable Genocide,* report of the Organization of African Unity International Panel of Eminent Personalities to Investigate the 1994 Genocide in Rwanda and the Surrounding Events, July 7, 2000. The report, which included Canadian scholar Gerald Caplan among its lead authors, faults the UN Security Council, France, Belgium, and the United States for failing to prevent the genocide—and for failing to hold the RPF, as well as Hutu extremists, accountable for widespread slaughter.

Other critiques of the French role can be found in Prunier, *The Rwanda Crisis* (mentioned previously); Daniela Kroslak, *The French Betrayal of Rwanda* (Bloomington: Indiana University Press, 2008); and Andrew Wallis, *Silent Accomplice: The Untold Story of France's Role in the Rwandan Genocide* (New York: I. B. Tauris, 2006). Paris's controversial relationship with the Habyarimana regime is further revealed in French government documents available in Arnaud Siad, ed., *The Rwandan Crisis Seen through the Eyes of France,* part 1, "Leadup to the Genocide," trans. Christina Graubert, National Security Archive Electronic Briefing Book no. 461, March 20, 2014.

The role of the Rwandan genocide in generating wider conflicts in the Great Lakes region is explored in a number of important works. See, especially, Howard Adelman and Astri Suhrke, eds., *The Path of a Genocide: The Rwanda Crisis from Uganda to Zaire* (New Brunswick, NJ: Transaction, 1999); Christian P. Scherrer, *Genocide and Crisis in Central Africa: Conflict Roots, Mass Violence, and Regional War* (Westport, CT: Praeger, 2002); Thomas Turner, *The Congo Wars: Conflict, Myth and Reality* (London: Zed Books, 2007); René Lemarchand, *The Dynamics of Violence in Central Africa* (Philadelphia: University of Pennsylvania Press, 2009); Gérard Prunier, *Africa's World War: Congo, the Rwandan Genocide, and the Making of a Continental Catastrophe* (New York: Oxford University Press, 2009); Filip Reyntjens, *The Great African War: Congo and Regional Geopolitics, 1996–2006* (New York: Cambridge University Press, 2010); Jason Stearns, *Dancing in the Glory of Monsters: The Collapse of the Congo and the Great War of Africa* (New York: Public Affairs, 2011); and Scott Straus and Lars Waldorf, eds., *Remaking Rwanda: State Building and Human Rights after Mass Violence* (Madison: University of Wisconsin Press, 2011). Marie Béatrice Umutesi, *Surviving the Slaughter: The Ordeal of a Rwandan Refugee in Zaire,* trans. Julie Emerson (Madison: University of Wisconsin Press, 2004), is a firsthand account by a Rwandan Hutu who survived retaliatory killings by the RPF and its supporters in Rwanda and the mass slaughter of Hutu refugees in Zaire/DRC by Rwandan, Ugandan, Burundian, and Zairian/DRC forces.

A number of studies are critical of the RPF regime in postgenocide Rwanda. Pottier, *Re-Imagining Rwanda* (mentioned previously), argues that the exile-dominated RPF government had little concern for those who had remained in Rwanda. It explores the ways in which RPF power holders shaped Western media, government, and NGO understanding of Rwanda and of the postgenocide conflict in Zaire/DRC—masking the RPF's role in mass killings in both countries and rewriting precolonial history and practices to justify policies that served the interests of the new power elites. Lars Waldorf, "Instrumentalizing Genocide: The RPF's Campaign against 'Genocide Ideology,'" in Straus and Waldorf, *Remaking Rwanda* (mentioned previously), 48–66, examines postgenocide Rwandan laws that outlaw "genocide ideology" and implicitly cast only Tutsis as genocide victims and all Hutus as complicit. Waldorf argues that the laws are used to repress political dissent and civil society voices and to strengthen the RPF's hold on power. Guichaoua, *From War to Genocide* (mentioned previously), challenges the RPF's official story concerning the causes, developments, and ramifications of the genocide and argues that the underlying issues that culminated in genocide continue to influence political, judicial, and diplomatic actions in contemporary Rwanda. Judy Rever, *In Praise of Blood: The Crimes of the Rwandan Patriotic Front* (Toronto: Random House Canada, 2018), uses interviews and official documents to expose RPF abuses during and after the genocide, as well as the US coverup. Two articles fault a human rights NGO, African Rights, for uncritically accepting the RPF narrative and promoting an international response that failed to hold the RPF accountable for human rights abuses. See, especially, the self-critical assessment by African Rights co-founder Alex de Waal, "Writing Human Rights and Getting It Wrong," *Boston Review,* June 6, 2016. See also Luc Reydoms, "NGO Justice: African Rights as Pseudo-Prosecutor of the Rwandan Genocide," *Human Rights Quarterly* 38, no. 3 (August 2016): 547–88.

Some sources argue that a genocide did not occur or, alternatively, that it involved conspiracies with foreign actors. These works have generated significant controversy, and several have been challenged by longtime scholars of Rwanda. Edward S. Herman and David Peterson, *The Politics of Genocide* (New York: Monthly Review Press, 2010), charges that there was no genocide against Rwandan Tutsis, but rather, that the victims were Hutus killed by invading RPF forces intent on seizing state power. Claims of genocide, the authors argue, were the rationale for a US plan to gain a foothold in the region and direct access to mineral-rich Zaire. Peter Erlinder, *The Accidental . . . Genocide* (St. Paul, MN: International Humanitarian Law Institute, 2013), written by the lead defense counsel for the UN International Criminal Tribunal for Rwanda, claims that the RPF was a creation of the US Defense Department. Christian Davenport and Allan C. Stam, "What Really Happened in Rwanda?," *Miller-McCune* 2, no. 6 (November/December 2009): 60–69, significantly reduces the estimated number of Tutsi inhabitants of Rwanda prior to the killings, as well as the number of Tutsi victims, and argues that the majority of victims were Hutu. Critics have found fault with the authors' research methodology and the accuracy of their statistics. See, for instance, Marijke Verpoorten, "Rwanda: Why Claim that 200,000 Tutsi Died in the Genocide Is Wrong," *African Arguments,* October 27, 2014.

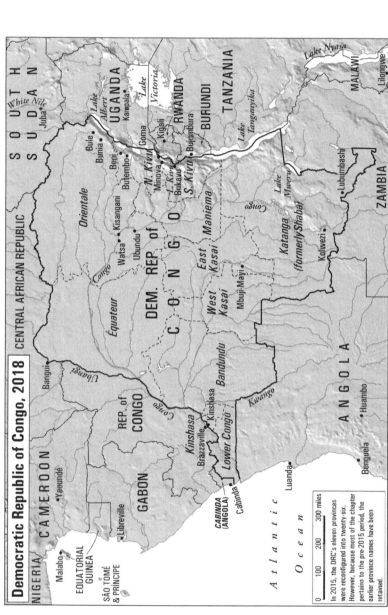

Democratic Republic of Congo, 2018

CENTRAL AFRICAN REPUBLIC

SOUTH SUDAN

White Nile

Juba

UGANDA

Lake Albert

Lake Victoria

Kampala

RWANDA

Kigali

Goma

N. Kivu

Minova

L. Kivu

Bukavu

S. Kivu

Bujumbura

BURUNDI

TANZANIA

Lake Nyasa

Lilongwe

MALAWI

Lake Tanganyika

Lubumbashi

ZAMBIA

Lake Mweru

Kolwezi

Katanga (formerly Shaba)

Congo

Bule

Bunia

Beni

Butembo

Orientale

Kisangani

Watsa

Ubundu

Maniema

Congo

DEM. REP. of CONGO

East Kasai

Mbuji-Mayi

West Kasai

Équateur

Bandundu

Kwango

ANGOLA

Huambo

Bangui

Ubangi

REP. of CONGO

Congo

Kinshasa

Brazzaville

Kinshasa

Lower Congo

Cabinda

CABINDA (ANGOLA)

Luanda

Benguela

GABON

Libreville

CAMEROON

Yaoundé

NIGERIA

Malabo

EQUATORIAL GUINEA

SÃO TOMÉ & PRÍNCIPE

Atlantic Ocean

0   100   200   300 miles

In 2015, the DRC's eleven provinces were reconfigured into twenty-six. However, because most of the chapter pertains to the pre-2015 period, the earlier province names have been retained.

Map 7.1. Democratic Republic of Congo, 2018. (Map by Philip Schwartzberg, Meridian Mapping, Minneapolis.)

7

The Democratic Republic of Congo

Outside Interests and Africa's World War (1994–2017)

FALLOUT FROM THE Rwandan genocide spilled into neighboring Zaire (later, the Democratic Republic of Congo), where more than a million Rwandans sought refuge and Hutu extremists prepared for a return to power.[1] Cross-border attacks by Hutu Power elements and the response of neighboring countries triggered a lengthy multinational conflict that some observers called "Africa's world war."[2] Often conceived as the First Congo War (1996–97) and the Second Congo War (1998–2002), the strife attracted foreign armies and their local proxies, who continued to fight over the nation's political future and mineral wealth after peace accords were signed. Strategic minerals in Zaire/DRC, like oil in Sudan and South Sudan, were both an object of struggle and the means of perpetuating the violence. Attempts by the UN, the AU, and African subregional bodies to establish stability and a framework for a new political order were fraught with weaknesses and failures. ICGLR and SADC, the subregional organizations charged with brokering peace agreements, included members who were parties to the conflict. Rwanda played a particularly problematic role, waging war in Zaire/DRC with its national army and through local proxies, committing atrocities against civilian populations, and plundering the country's mineral wealth. Having ignored the Rwandan genocide until it was too late, the Security Council was reluctant to hold the new Rwandan regime accountable.

This chapter explores political and military intervention in Zaire/DRC by neighboring countries to promote their own political and economic agendas; it also examines UN intervention in response to instability and to protect civilian lives, and efforts by the UN, the AU, and subregional bodies to broker peace. The multilateral peacekeeping efforts

resulted in a diminution of violence, but regional stability was not restored, civilians were not protected, and interested parties persisted in
promoting their own interests rather than those of the Congolese people.
Externally imposed peace accords, designed by political and economic
elites, failed to address Zaire/DRC's deep structural inequalities, and foreign interests continued to exploit local divisions for their own ends.

Setting the Stage:
The Postcolonial and Cold War Context (1960–97)

Bordering nine countries in a mineral-rich, strategic region, Zaire, a
former Belgian colony, was the largest and most populous country in
francophone Africa. The immediate impetus for external intervention
in the 1990s was the presence of Hutu extremists who had perpetrated
genocide in Rwanda and who continued to threaten that country. However, Zaire's vulnerability was rooted in inequalities and practices that
dated to the precolonial, colonial, and postcolonial periods. During the
Cold War, Zaire had served as a regional policeman for both the United
States and France, which along with Belgium were Zaire's primary pillars
of financial support. For more than three decades, Zaire was subjected
to the authoritarian rule of Mobutu Sésé Seko (originally, Joseph-Désiré
Mobutu), who assumed political power through military coups staged in
September 1960 and November 1965.[3] An important CIA protégé, Mobutu
allowed the United States to train and supply anticommunist Angolan
rebels on Zairian territory and helped keep a lid on radical movements
throughout the region. In return, Washington provided Zaire with more
than $1 billion in military and economic aid between 1961 and 1990 and
pressured the IMF and World Bank to favor the country with loans, rescheduled debts, and relaxed lending conditions. Hoping to expand its
influence in francophone Africa, France also supplied Zaire with gener-
ous loans, weapons, and military training.

During his thirty-two-year reign, Mobutu presided over a corrupt
patronage system. He treated Zaire's vast mineral resources, parastatal
companies, central bank, and tax offices as his own, plundering them
at will for the benefit of family members and loyalists. He amassed a
personal fortune worth billions of dollars, while Zaire's economy was
ravaged by plummeting copper prices, food shortages, inflation, and an
external debt that had reached $14 billion in 1997. Mobutu's regime was

notorious for its human rights abuses and the repression of political dissent. Nonetheless, it received strong military and economic support from Belgium, the United States, France, and Israel, which feared a communist takeover of the mineral-rich region without a strongman at the helm. The "Mobutu or chaos" argument guaranteed their backing until the end of the Cold War.[4]

As the Cold War waned in the late 1980s, Zaire, like many other African countries, was faced with a devastating economic crisis and mounting political unrest. Mobutu's strategic value had diminished, and by the early 1990s the Zairian dictator had been abandoned by key foreign sponsors. Belgium ceased all military and economic assistance in 1990, and France unveiled a new Africa policy that linked French development aid to human rights and democratic practices. Mobutu and other francophone autocrats implemented superficial reforms that would protect their relationships with France but preserve their power. During the same period, internal prodemocracy forces exerted enormous domestic pressure. In August 1991, Mobutu was forced to consider fundamental political change, convening a national conference where political opponents and civil society activists pushed for new governing institutions and multiparty democracy. In September, erratically paid soldiers rioted, civil unrest ensued, and 1,500 French and Belgian paratroopers arrived to evacuate 20,000 foreign nationals. In October, Mobutu appointed a transitional administration headed by opposition leader Étienne Tshisekedi, who was dismissed a week later for refusing to follow orders. By the end of the year, France and the United States had suspended their aid programs, the IMF had barred Zaire from further loans, and the World Bank had ended support for development projects. The following year was punctuated by demonstrations, violent crackdowns, and periodic closures of the national conference, as Mobutu obstructed any attempt at real reform.

Although domestic forces continued to mobilize for democracy, it was an externally backed insurgency and regional war that finally drove Mobutu from power. The insurrection and its aftermath were intimately linked to the 1994 Rwandan genocide. A longtime supporter of the Habyarimana regime, Mobutu had opened Zaire's borders to more than 1 million Rwandan Hutu refugees, as well as former government soldiers and militia members who had fled the advancing RPF. When genocide perpetrators asserted their dominance over the refugee camps, controlling the distribution of food, medicine, and other humanitarian aid, Mobutu turned a blind eye. Camp leaders trafficked in arms, conscripted and trained military cadres, conducted raids into RPF-governed Rwanda with impunity, and obtained millions of dollars in weapons from the UK, China, and South Africa. Zairian soldiers joined Rwandan Hutu extremists in ethnically cleansing eastern Zaire, displacing tens of thousands of indigenous Tutsis and killing thousands more. Some Tutsis, known as the Banyamulenge, had local roots that extended to the eighteenth and nineteenth centuries, when their ancestors had settled there. Others had been brought to the region by Belgian colonizers to serve as cheap labor on settler ranches and plantations. Still others had fled from ethnic violence in Rwanda during the early independence period. After the 1994 genocide in Rwanda, the citizenship of Zairian Tutsis was called into question. Tutsis became convenient scapegoats for the problems plaguing Zairian civilians, who found common cause with Rwandan Hutu extremists. Concerned by the extremist activities and angered by the treatment of Zairian Tutsis, Rwanda warned that it would invade Zaire if the militants were not restrained. Mobutu declined to sanction his allies, the United States resisted military engagement where it had no interests, and France refused to support Rwanda's RPF regime. Inhibited by powerful members, the UN Security Council did nothing.

The UN's failure to respond ultimately led to two wars that would embroil most countries in the surrounding area. In 1997, a rebel army backed by Rwanda and Uganda drove Mobutu from power. As indigenous and external forces rushed to fill the power vacuum, Zaire was propelled into more than two decades of chaos, violent conflict, and civil war. Between 1998 and 2007 alone, war claimed some 5.4 million lives—primarily from hunger, disease, and malnutrition resulting from massive displacement and economic collapse. UNICEF estimated that during this period, tens of thousands of children were abducted by government soldiers, local militias, and rebels and forced to work as fighters, miners, cooks, porters, and sex slaves.[5] In addition, Human Rights Watch found that more than 200,000 women and girls were raped or otherwise sexually brutalized in a country where sexual violence had become a primary weapon of war.

The decades-long turmoil involved, at various times, countries from three of Africa's five subregions. Rwanda and Uganda were deeply involved in the First Congo War, while the Second Congo War drew in most of the Great Lakes countries and others from East, Central, and Southern Africa.[6] A problematic peace agreement signed in December 2002 led to an elected government that continued many of the abusive practices of the past. Meanwhile, the conflict continued in the east, as neighboring states and local militias plundered the country's mineral wealth. A UN peacekeeping force, first deployed in 2000, did little to protect the civilian population and indeed was often party to the abuses. Peace remained elusive, and in March 2017 the Security Council renewed the peacekeeping mandate for another year.

The First Congo War (1996–97)

Foreign intervention in Zaire after the Cold War sparked the First Congo War. On its face an indigenous rebel insurgency, the war was in reality a continuation of the Rwandan civil war that had begun in 1990 and culminated in the 1994 genocide and the seizure of power by the RPF. In October 1996, after the international community ignored RPF appeals to halt extremist attacks, the Rwandan army launched a raid into Zaire to destroy Hutu refugee camps and to encourage Zairian Tutsis to rebel. A rebel army called the Alliance of Democratic Forces for the Liberation of Congo-Zaire (AFDL) was established a few weeks later. A creation of the Rwandan government, the AFDL operated under the authority of Colonel James Kabarebe, commander of Rwanda's presidential guard. It was staffed with Zairian exiles, including Zairian Tutsis who had joined the RPF in their struggle against the Habyarimana regime and who were anxious to avenge the deaths of family members in Zaire. Rebel soldiers—including some 10,000 unemployed youths and street children—were trained, equipped, and led by the Rwandan army. The organization's spokesman, Zairian warlord Laurent-Désiré Kabila, was handpicked by the Kigali regime.

A rebel leader during antigovernment insurrections in the 1960s, Kabila had established a personal fiefdom in Zaire's eastern region, which served as a base for extensive smuggling operations. In the decades after independence, Kabila grew rich from trafficking in gold, diamonds, ivory, and leopard skins and divided his time between luxury homes in Tanzania and Uganda. Entering Zaire with the Rwandan army in October 1996, he focused his operation on three geographic areas: the food- and gold-producing provinces of eastern Zaire; the copper- and cobalt-rich Shaba Province; and the diamond-rich East Kasai Province.[7] Along with their enormous wealth, these regions had a long history of rebellion against the central government.

By November, the AFDL and its Rwandan backers controlled the Zairian borderlands from Uganda to Burundi. Killing thousands of civilians in the east, where Tutsis had been persecuted, the rebel soldiers plundered everywhere they went. They quickly defeated Zaire's undisciplined army, which raped, looted, and killed as it retreated, and they emptied the refugee camps, forcing as many as 700,000 Hutus back into Rwanda. Another 300,000 to 600,000 Hutus and tens of thousands of Zairians fled westward into the rainforest, pursued by the AFDL and Rwandan forces. The rebels and their Rwandan backers slaughtered men, women, and children, making no distinction between former Hutu Power soldiers, government officials, and militia members, on the one hand, and innocent Hutu civilians on the other. Tens of thousands of people were killed outright, while tens of thousands more died of dysentery, cholera, malaria, and starvation. The response from the international community was muted. While aid organizations tried to cope with the humanitarian disaster, the UN Security Council remained on the sidelines. France called for humanitarian and military intervention, but its claim to humanitarian concern was weakened by its support for the Hutu Power regime during the genocide and its preoccupation with the dominance of anglophone countries. The United States and the United Kingdom, embarrassed by their failure to act in 1994, refused to countenance criticism of the RPF.

The Zairian war quickly became a regional one. As Kabila's rebel forces pushed north and west, the Ugandan army moved in to assist them. As they approached Angola, antigovernment rebels from the National Union for the Total Independence of Angola (UNITA), who were longtime Mobutu allies, joined Zairian soldiers in the fight. UNITA's involvement brought the Angolan government into the war on the side of the AFDL. The Luanda government permitted Kabila's soldiers to enter Zaire from Angolan territory and provided Angolan army auxiliaries to supplement their ranks. Zaire's third-largest city, Kisangani, which was poorly defended by Zairian soldiers and French and Serbian mercenaries, fell to the rebels in March 1997. A few days later, the rebels took Mbuji-Mayi, the capital of East Kasai. During the second week of April, the AFDL arrived in Lubumbashi, Zaire's second-largest city and

Photo 7.1. Rwandan Hutu refugees on the jungle track from Kisangani to Ubundu, DRC, June 8, 1997. Photo by Derek Hudson/Getty Images.

the capital of Shaba Province. Foreign mining interests—including South Africa's De Beers and Anglo American and Canada's America Mineral Fields—initiated contacts with the AFDL and began to discuss future investments. Zambia allowed the AFDL to attack the mining town of Kolwezi from Zambian territory, while Zimbabwe provided the rebels with military equipment. By the middle of April 1997, Kabila, his army, and his foreign backers controlled all of Zaire's major sources of revenue and foreign exchange.

As the rebels and their external supporters swept one thousand miles across Zaire toward the nation's capital, Mobutu's Western allies abandoned him; only France supported the regime to the bitter end. US officials established contact with Kabila's top political and military aides even before the AFDL took Kinshasa. In the Security Council, Washington blocked French initiatives for humanitarian intervention, which might have stopped the rebellion's progress, and in the final weeks the Clinton administration urged Mobutu to step down. Having "lost" Rwanda to anglophone interests, France was desperate to save Zaire for *la francophonie*. Determined to thwart Kabila, whom it viewed as a Ugandan proxy and promoter of US interests in the region, Paris initiated a covert operation shortly after the RPF invasion that provided Mobutu with combat aircraft, pilots, mechanics, and hundreds of French, Belgian, Serbian, Ukrainian, and South African mercenaries.

As Zaire's neighbors teamed up on opposing sides, South Africa assumed the role of mediator. In early May 1997, President Nelson Mandela hosted talks between Kabila and Mobutu. In a last-ditch attempt to cling to power, Mobutu proposed a transitional government followed by elections. Kabila, however, was not interested in democracy. He demanded instead that Mobutu hand over the reins of government or face the consequences. On May 17, Mobutu fled into exile. To avoid a bloodbath in the capital, the Zairian national army stood down, and the AFDL took Kinshasa without a fight. Kabila immediately declared himself president and renamed the country the Democratic Republic of Congo. Refusing to work with the internal democratic opposition that had mobilized against the Mobutu regime, he rejected the notion of a broad-based coalition government. Like Mobutu, Kabila outlawed opposition parties, imprisoned political opponents and human rights activists, and ruled by decree. Opposition leader Étienne Tshisekedi was imprisoned and then sent into internal exile, while Mobutu loyalists were rehabilitated and incorporated into the government. Kabila, like his predecessor, administered the country through relatives and cronies, dividing the spoils among them. Accepting Kabila as the lesser evil, Washington blocked Security Council condemnation of his regime.

The Second Congo War (1998–2002)

Kabila rose to power as Rwanda's and Uganda's proxy, but the honeymoon did not last. Kabila pursued his own agenda. Instead of destroying the remnants of the Hutu Power army, he used them to build his own fighting force, and his patrons quickly turned against him. The Second Congo War began in August 1998 when Rwanda, Uganda, and Burundi teamed up to oust the Kabila regime. Most Great Lakes countries entered the fray, along with some from East, Central, and Southern Africa. On Kabila's side were Angola and Zimbabwe, which had supported the AFDL during the First Congo War, along with Namibia, Chad, and Sudan—as well as 15,000 to 25,000 Hutu fighters from Rwanda and Burundi.

The movement toward war began in February 1998, when Rwandans in the AFDL leadership began to plot Kabila's removal. In July, suspecting disloyalty in the Congolese army, Kabila dismissed several high-level Rwandan commanders, including James Kabarebe, former head of Rwanda's presidential guard who served as the Congolese army's chief of staff. Kabila also launched an anti-Tutsi campaign in Kinshasa, where civilians had been humiliated and abused by Rwandan soldiers. The government's actions triggered new unrest in the capital and in the east, where Rwandan officers in the Congolese army instigated a rebellion. Blaming Rwanda for the strife, Kabila ordered all Rwandan and Ugandan troops to leave the DRC. Without its external backers, the Congolese army quickly disintegrated. When the Second Congo War erupted in August, James Kabarebe led the Rwandan operation.

Once again, Rwanda and Uganda enlisted indigenous proxies to promote their agendas. The disparate rebel factions, which had little popular support, included Congolese Tutsis linked to the Rwandan government, Mobutu cronies who hoped to return to power, disappointed office seekers denied positions in Kabila's government, and leftist intellectuals disenchanted with Kabila's corrupt personal rule. The largest rebel organization was the Congolese Rally for Democracy (RCD). Like the AFDL, the RCD was an instrument of the Kigali government. Rwandan army officers commanded the RCD military organization; its ineffectual political organization comprised an eclectic group of Mobutu loyalists and military officers, corrupt opportunists, and disillusioned intellectuals. Rife with internal rivalries, in 1999 the RCD broke into two. Rwanda threw its support to RCD-Goma, which was dominated by young Congolese Tutsis who sought land, citizenship, and opportunity in a country where they had suffered violence and discrimination. Uganda favored RCD-Kisangani, which was led by leftist intellectuals. Uganda also sponsored the Movement for the Liberation of Congo (MLC), led by multimillionaire Jean-Pierre Bemba—one of the DRC's wealthiest men and son of a close Mobutu associate. The MLC's military leadership included numerous veterans of Mobutu's army, many of whom had been trained in the United States, the United Kingdom, China, or Morocco. Uganda eventually forced a merger of the two organizations, establishing the Front for the Liberation of Congo (FLC) under Bemba's leadership.

The war shredded the country's social fabric. In the eastern DRC, Rwanda replaced indigenous chiefs with local administrations staffed by Congolese Tutsis and established militias and police forces to further its interests. Hoping to protect themselves from the depredations of Rwandan soldiers and their proxies, eastern communities formed self-defense forces known as Mai-Mai.[8] However, these armed groups also wreaked havoc in the countryside. Alienated, unemployed youths saw opportunities for enrichment through pillaging and bribes. Personal quarrels, land disputes, and clan and ethnic rivalries grew increasingly politicized and violent. Killings spurred retaliatory bloodshed, instigating spirals of violence. All sides systematically employed rape as a weapon of war to humiliate and terrorize the Congolese population.

As Rwanda, Uganda, and Burundi undermined Kabila, other countries came to his rescue. Zimbabwe, Angola, and Namibia cited the SADC security pact as the basis for their intervention, while Chad sent troops to bolster French and francophone influence, and Sudan sought to undermine Uganda in retaliation for its support for the SPLA insurgency. Zimbabwe's involvement was the most significant. Harare sent 12,000 soldiers to Kabila's aid, funding its war effort with the DRC's own resources. Although Zimbabwe had no legitimate security claims in the DRC, it did have economic interests. Kabila owed Zimbabwe for military equipment and supplies delivered during the 1996–97 war, and Zimbabwe was anxious for repayment. Moreover, Robert Mugabe's regime hoped that unfettered access to the DRC's riches would appease powerful domestic constituencies in Zimbabwe that might otherwise protest their own government's failed policies. Mugabe therefore gave Zimbabwean political, economic, and military elites free rein to plunder Katanga's copper and cobalt and to loot diamonds from East Kasai.

If Zimbabwe did not have legitimate security concerns in the DRC, Angola did. The Luanda government was anxious to protect Angola's oil and diamond regions, especially the oil-rich Cabinda Enclave, which was separated from the bulk of Angola by a wedge of Congolese territory. It was troubled by the presence of UNITA supply routes in the western DRC, the threat of renewed attacks from Congolese soil, and UNITA's illegal mining of Congolese diamonds to finance its war against the Angolan government. Beyond these immediate considerations, Luanda was disturbed by the growing power of Uganda and Rwanda in the Central African region and their support for rebel forces that included Mobutu stalwarts. Angola entered the war in the hope of shoring up the weak Kabila regime.

Namibia's concerns dovetailed with those of both Angola and Zimbabwe. Like Angola, Namibia was anxious to weaken UNITA, which supported a secessionist movement in the Caprivi Strip, while Namibian elites, like those in Zimbabwe, had developed extensive mining interests in the DRC.

Like Western powers in the twentieth century, the DRC's African neighbors bled the country dry. A 2001 UN Security Council report charged Rwanda, Uganda, and Burundi with the systematic looting of the DRC and also implicated Zimbabwe. These countries stole Congolese diamonds, gold, coltan, cobalt, copper, tin, timber, and cash crops worth billions of dollars, which they used to finance their own development. Other sources indicate that from 1996 to 2009, Rwanda dominated the mineral-rich provinces of North and South Kivu and effectively integrated them into its domestic economy. Rwanda's internationally acclaimed economic growth, achieved since the 1994 genocide, was actualized with the DRC's stolen wealth. Meanwhile, Ugandan soldiers took control of gold-bearing regions in North Kivu and Orientale Provinces, where they forced locals to extract the gold for Ugandan interests. After peace accords were signed in 2002, Rwanda and Uganda continued to support rebel proxies who plundered on their behalf.

Peace Accords and Continuing Crisis (2000–2008)

While neighboring states fought over the DRC's resources, other entities, led by South Africa and the OAU, attempted to mediate a lasting peace. A series of talks held in Zambia in 1999 resulted in a ceasefire and the establishment of the Inter-Congolese Dialogue, which included representatives of the Congolese government, rebel forces, the internal political opposition, and civil society organizations. In February 2000, the UN Security Council authorized the establishment of the United Nations Organization Mission in the Democratic Republic of the Congo (MONUC) with a Chapter VII mandate that allowed it to monitor the ceasefire and to protect UN personnel and facilities as well as Congolese civilians. However, the conflict continued as all parties violated the ceasefire agreement. After a devastating battlefield defeat in December 2000 and signals from Zimbabwe and Angola that they could no longer support his failing war, Kabila was forced to consider concessions. A new chapter began in January 2001, when Laurent Kabila was assassinated by a disgruntled bodyguard, and Joseph Kabila, a major-general in the Congolese army and onetime protégé of James Kabarebe, succeeded his father as president.

The younger Kabila initiated abrupt changes to many of his father's policies and reopened the stalled peace negotiations. A series of accords signed in 2002 were intended to conclude the Second Congo War. They provided the framework for multiparty elections, a transitional government, and the withdrawal of all 30,000 Rwandan and Ugandan troops from Congolese territory. A new national army was to be constituted, composed of government and rebel soldiers and former militia members. The entities that had devastated the DRC would henceforth be entrusted with protecting it.

The peace accords notwithstanding, violence in the DRC persisted. In May 2003, following the departure of Ugandan troops from Orientale Province, ethnic militias fighting for control of the region slaughtered hundreds of civilians. In response, the Security Council authorized the Interim Emergency Multinational Force, a peace enforcement mission with a Chapter VII mandate to protect civilians, infrastructure, and UN personnel and facilities in the region. Codenamed Operation Artemis, the enterprise was led by France and staffed primarily by French soldiers, and it promoted France's agenda of maintaining a strong presence in francophone Africa. In July, the Security Council strengthened MONUC's mandate, allowing it to use greater force in Orientale and North and South Kivu Provinces; it also imposed an arms embargo on rebel groups and militias.

In July 2003, while violence continued in the east, the transitional government took office in Kinshasa. Joseph Kabila remained at the helm, where he supervised four vice presidents representing various regions and constituencies. Members of the internal political opposition, prodemocracy movement, and other civil society bodies were notably absent. Two of the vice presidents were former rebel leaders. MLC/FLC leader Jean-Pierre Bemba was vice president in charge of the Economic and Finance Commission. Under his leadership, the FLC had stolen millions of dollars' worth of gold, timber, and customs revenues from territories under its control. Bemba's new position allowed him to oversee the continued plunder of Congolese riches. Azarias Ruberwa Manywa, secretary-general of RCD-Goma, assumed the vice presidency in charge of the Politics, Defence and Security Commission, which gave him authority over former rebels, militias,

Photo 7.2. Young soldiers of the Rwandan-backed Union of Congolese Patriots militia in Bule, DRC, 2003. Photo by Marcus Bleasdale/Human Rights Watch.

and the national army. Outside the government, Kabila loyalists, one-time rebel leaders, and local militiamen continued to control their respective fiefdoms.

The transitional period officially concluded in 2006 with the adoption of a new constitution, followed by presidential and parliamentary elections. The July 2006 elections were fraught with controversy. Several key opposition parties boycotted the vote, charging that Kabila, former warlords, and other contenders were using militias to intimidate the civilian population. Election Day was marred by violence and allegations of fraud. None of the presidential candidates won a majority. A runoff election was held in October, and Joseph Kabila was declared the winner. While international observers claimed that the October election was basically free and fair, runner-up Jean-Pierre Bemba disputed the results and refused to disband his militia. Fighting between the presidential guard and Bemba's militia in March 2007 resulted in 300 deaths and a warrant for Bemba's arrest on charges of high treason. Bemba fled into exile.[9]

Meanwhile, war in the eastern DRC continued. The Kigali regime, frequently working through Congolese Tutsis, was deeply implicated. Some collaborators had served in the Rwandan army, led Rwanda-backed rebel forces, and passed through the revolving door of Congolese rebel and army regulars in the wake of the peace accords. Many were engaged in minerals trafficking or other illicit activities. General Laurent Nkunda was emblematic of this trend. As a Congolese Tutsi living in Uganda, Nkunda had joined the RPF and served as an intelligence officer during the 1994 Rwandan genocide. He returned to Zaire with the AFDL forces that ousted Mobutu. During the Second Congo War, Nkunda led the Rwanda-backed RCD-Goma and was implicated in the mass slaughter of Hutu civilians. Following the 2002 peace accords, he joined the Congolese army. Two years later, he returned to the bush to fight for control of the eastern DRC, where his criminal network terrorized the local population and taxed the gold, coltan, tin ore, and agricultural products that passed through the region.

By 2007, Nkunda's movement, which he called the National Congress for the Defense of the People (CNDP), had some 4,000 members.

Photo 7.3. Child gold miner in Watsa, northeastern DRC, 2004. Photo by Marcus Bleasdale/Human Rights Watch.

Trained, equipped, and financed by the Rwandan army, the CNDP included former rebels and militia members who had been slated for integration into the new national army, but instead had languished in filthy, overcrowded camps. Others were child soldiers, many of whom had been recruited by force. Still others had been seconded from the Rwandan army—with the complicity of the Kigali regime. Outgunned and outmaneuvered, the poorly trained, ill-equipped Congolese national army allied with the Democratic Forces for the Liberation of Rwanda (FDLR), a Rwandan Hutu militia with links to the 1994 genocide.

In January 2008, following mediation by the AU, the EU, and the United States, the Kabila government, the CNDP, and twenty-one other rebel groups and militias signed a ceasefire and peace agreement. Like the 2002 accord, the 2008 agreement stipulated that thousands of rebels and militia members would be integrated into the national army. In August, however, the agreement collapsed. Nkunda charged the government with violating the terms of the ceasefire and, once again, returned to the bush to fight. At the end of October, Nkunda's forces, led by Jean Bosco Ntaganda, routed the Congolese army near Goma, the capital of North Kivu Province, where they burned homes, raped women and girls, executed men and boys, and press-ganged children. Neither the UN peacekeepers nor the retreating Congolese army intervened to protect the civilians.

Peace Accords and Continuing Crisis (2009–17)

Concerned that a third Congo war might be imminent, the international community pushed for further negotiations. In January 2009, the Kinshasa and Kigali governments signed a secret deal that was intended to end the conflict and strengthen the position of both presidents in their respective countries. Kabila agreed to allow 4,000 Rwandan soldiers to return to the DRC to disarm thousands of FDLR members, while Rwandan President Paul Kagame forced Nkunda out of the CNDP and arrested him when he fled to Rwanda. The CNDP's new leader was Jean Bosco Ntaganda, a Rwandan-Congolese Tutsi whom the ICC had charged with war crimes and crimes against humanity.[10] Ntaganda announced that he would give up the rebellion, integrate his forces into the Congolese national army, where he would assume the rank of general, and help the army destroy the Hutu militias.

The CNDP was officially brought into the process through an agreement signed on March 23 that was deeply flawed. The new accord met the rebels' central demands. CNDP political prisoners would be released, and amnesty would be granted in accordance with international law. Former rebels would be integrated into the DRC's military and police structures, and their organization would be transformed into a political party that would be permitted to participate in DRC political life. However, the accord also returned to Kigali some of the ground it had conceded in the secret January deal. Since 1996, Rwanda had sponsored numerous rebellions in the eastern DRC, and its desire to harness the region's mineral wealth to its own development had not diminished. The incorporation of CNDP cadres into the DRC's security forces provided Kigali with a proxy force inside the Congolese national army—one that had a veneer of legitimacy. In addition, the March 23 agreement failed to address other critical issues. Like its predecessors, the new accord ignored the internal causes of the Congolese conflict: competition for land and resources, the impunity of armed groups and their external backers, and the absence of responsive government, rule of law, and a security sector that could protect the civilian population. In short, the chances for a lasting peace remained slim.

The continued impunity of human rights abusers was immediately apparent. In January and February 2009, the DRC and Rwanda conducted a joint action against FDLR militias, followed by a DRC-MONUC operation that lasted through December. The DRC-Rwanda venture was marred by serious abuses against Congolese civilians. When MONUC replaced Rwanda as the DRC's partner, it did not impose preconditions or require the removal of human rights abusers from positions of authority. Jean Bosco Ntaganda served as deputy commander of the new enterprise, which included 60,000 Congolese army soldiers. MONUC helped plan the operation and supplied logistical and operations support, including trucks, attack helicopters, and weapons, as well as $1 million per month in daily rations, fuel, and other services. The United States, which provided one-quarter of the MONUC budget, assisted the Congolese army with intelligence gathering. In April, the UN Office of Legal Affairs warned that UN peacekeepers could not legally participate in operations that included Ntaganda, who was had been accused of serious human rights violations. The UN Policy Committee, which includes the heads of all UN agencies, asserted in June that MONUC could not engage in joint combat operations with Congolese forces if there were risks of human rights abuses. Despite these cautions, the joint mission proceeded as planned.

The ten-month-long DRC-MONUC operation took a horrific toll on the civilian population. More than 1,000 civilians were killed, and 1 million were displaced. Thousands of men, women, and children were press-ganged as porters for army or militia forces. The military campaign also worsened the DRC's rape epidemic. Between January and September 2009, the number of reported rapes tripled; the vast majority were committed by government soldiers. UN military commanders admitted that many of the 13,500 former rebels and militia members who recently had been integrated into the Congolese national army were looting, raping, and killing civilians. Yet it was not until November that MONUC suspended aid to Congolese army units that had been implicated in the abuses. The UN forces not only had failed to protect the civilians they were mandated to protect, but they had partnered with the army that actively abused them.

Anxious to shift the focus, Kabila charged the UN with violating Congolese sovereignty and insisted that MONUC forces begin to withdraw by June 2010, the fiftieth anniversary of Congolese independence. In May 2010, the Security Council authorized a reduction of military personnel in more secure areas but refused to sanction a complete withdrawal. To appease Kabila, it changed the name of the UN operation to the United Nations Organization Stabilization Mission in the Democratic Republic of the Congo (MONUSCO), suggesting that the UN peacekeepers were supporting the Congolese government rather than usurping its authority.

Assured of continued international backing, Kabila refused to address the DRC's deep structural problems and continued to consolidate his own power. Using bribery and coercion to thwart challenges to his authority, he curtailed the powers of parliament and the judiciary. An electoral commission staffed by Kabila loyalists declared him the winner of presidential elections in 2011 that were widely viewed as corrupt. Neither MONUSCO, which provided technical and logistical support for the elections, nor the EU and the UK, both of which helped to finance them, thwarted Kabila's attempts to assert control.

It was in this context that Kabila decided to sideline Ntaganda, who was wanted by the ICC on charges of war crimes. Ntaganda's removal would serve three purposes. First, it would appease international donors who were concerned about Ntaganda's involvement in human rights abuses. Second, it would weaken the CNDP's parallel structures within the national army, which threatened Kabila's authority. Third, it would offer the president an opportunity to rally the Congolese population against an external enemy (Rwanda), while diverting attention from his own deficiencies.

Kabila's move against Ntaganda was the last straw for former CNDP members who had joined the national army after the March 23, 2009, peace agreement. In April 2012, Congolese Tutsi soldiers, led by Ntaganda, defected from the national army, charging that the government had failed to fulfill the obligations delineated in the accords.[11] The March 23 Movement (M23) made common cause with local militias that were hostile to the central government and quickly asserted control over key parts of the eastern region. Once again, Rwanda and Uganda provided seasoned troops, weapons, logistical support, and tactical advice—in violation of a 2003 UN arms embargo. Routed in battle after battle, humiliated government soldiers raped, killed, and looted as they fled. As M23 gained strength, the DRC army teamed up with criminals and rejuvenated its alliance with Hutu extremists in the FDLR.

The international community was under pressure to respond. The United States and several EU member states reduced or temporarily suspended aid to Rwanda. However, they refused to impose sanctions and continued to ignore links between Rwanda's rapid economic development and its looting of Congolese resources. The question of Rwanda divided the US State Department. Two senior officials, Assistant Secretary of State for African Affairs Johnnie Carson as well as R. Barrie Walkley, special advisor for the Great Lakes and the Democratic Republic of Congo, insisted that Rwanda must cease its support for M23. In contrast, UN Ambassador Susan Rice claimed that there was no conclusive evidence linking Rwanda to the rebel organization, and she used her influence to shield Rwanda and Uganda from criticism in the UN Security Council.[12]

While the EU and the United States stood by, the UN, AU, ICGLR, and SADC initiated another round of peace negotiations. In February 2013, eleven ICGLR and SADC member states, including Rwanda, Uganda, and the DRC, signed a regional peace and security framework in which they agreed not to support armed groups against their neighbors or otherwise interfere in their affairs. The DRC also promised, once again, to reform its army and government, establish its authority in the eastern region, and promote reconciliation and democratization throughout the country. The UN, AU, ICGLR, and SADC were authorized to oversee implementation of the accord, while the EU, France, Belgium, the United Kingdom, and the United States were assigned supporting roles.

The 2013 agreement, like its predecessors, was a top-down affair conceptualized by outsiders that failed to address key underlying problems. Instability in the eastern DRC grew from local conflicts over land, minerals, power, and identity. None of the international efforts—including billions of dollars spent on UN peacekeepers—had addressed these issues. The 2013 framework was vaguely worded, and the mechanisms for enforcement were unclear. Two of the signatories, Rwanda and Uganda, had supported Congolese rebel insurgencies since 1996 and had profited enormously from the illicit minerals trade. They had little incentive to comply with the most recent endeavor. Rwanda was a mainstay of the AU-UN peacekeeping force in Darfur, and Uganda had taken the lead in the AU effort against al-Shabaab in Somalia. As significant players in African peacekeeping efforts and in the war on terror, both countries were confident of continued Western support, no matter what they did in the DRC. As long as instability prevailed across their borders, they were unlikely to refrain from intervention.

The regional peace initiative was followed by a UN effort to exert greater force against the Congolese rebels. In March 2013, the Security Council authorized the Force Intervention Brigade—the UN's first offensive combat formation—which would be permitted to disarm and neutralize rebel soldiers, monitor the UN arms embargo, and report on the flow of military personnel, arms, and equipment across international boundaries. The UN combat force, which included 3,069 soldiers from SADC member states South Africa, Malawi, and Tanzania, tipped the balance in favor of the DRC government. Following a string of defeats and significant loss of territory, M23 ended its insurgency in November and signed a peace accord in December. With M23 neutralized, the UN brigade was tasked with confronting other armed groups in the east, in particular the FDLR. In 2014 and 2015, it

Photo 7.4. Congolese army and MONUSCO reinforce their presence in and around Goma, DRC, after clashes with M23 rebels, May 21, 2013. Photo by Clara Padovan/MONUSCO.

successfully disarmed fighters from other organizations but did little to weaken the Hutu extremist force at the heart of Rwanda's concern. By 2017, the UN intervention brigade was widely deemed to have been ineffective. It had failed to hold the ground taken or to protect civilians under its care.

Once again, external military intervention brought short-term success, but no long-term solution. The prospects for peace in the DRC remained bleak. In 2016 Kabila completed his second and final term as president, but he refused to hold elections for a successor. Scores of people were killed and hundreds arrested when they protested the constitutional violation. New violence flared in Kasai and Kasai Central Provinces, where more than 5,000 people were killed and 1.5 million displaced between August 2016 and December 2017. Civilians in the eastern region continued to be preyed upon by armed groups and DRC security forces, which were incapable of neutralizing armed opponents and uninterested in protecting civilians.

Conclusion

Instability in the DRC was the product of both internal and external factors. Longstanding political, economic, and social inequalities, the legacies of colonial and Cold War practices, and the determination of political and economic elites to protect their power and wealth led to numerous domestic conflicts that foreign interests were able to exploit. Although the presence of Rwandan genocide perpetrators served as the immediate justification for intervention in the 1990s, this rationale masked many others. The DRC's mineral riches attracted the attention of outsiders, who pillaged the country's wealth to build their own. Plunder became both the object of war and the means of fueling it. Although the UN, the AU, and African subregional bodies sponsored plans to establish stability and a framework for a new political order, their efforts were hindered by the competing interests of their members and the failure to address underlying causes of local conflicts.

Local conflicts and resources exploited by outsiders, deficient agreements negotiated by political elites, and peacekeeping forces that failed to protect civilian lives also plagued the West African countries of Liberia and Sierra Leone. Civil war and foreign intervention in those countries ultimately brought the UN, African subregional bodies, and former colonial powers to the scene. These conflicts are the subject of chapter 8.

Suggested Reading

A number of studies establish a historical framework for the post–Cold War crisis in Zaire/DRC. Adam Hochschild, *King Leopold's Ghost: A Story of Greed, Terror, and Heroism in Colonial Africa* (New York: Houghton Mifflin, 1998), offers a compelling overview of colonial conquest, exploitation, and contemporary human rights protests that altered the course of the country's history. Elizabeth Schmidt, *Foreign Intervention in Africa: From the Cold War to the War on Terror* (New York: Cambridge University Press, 2013), provides an overview of foreign intervention in the Congo/Zaire during the Cold War. Surveys by two Congolese scholars offer important insights into the colonial, Cold War, and post–Cold War periods. Georges Nzongola-Ntalaja, *The Congo from Leopold to Kabila* (London: Zed Books, 2002), presents a highly accessible historical analysis, including a detailed account of the post–Cold War prodemocracy movement. Emizet François Kisangani, *Civil Wars in the Democratic Republic of Congo, 1960–2010* (Boulder, CO: Lynne Rienner, 2012), views five decades of Congolese conflicts through the lens of the politics of exclusion.

Several works explore the Congo crisis of 1960–65, which laid the groundwork for the three-decade-long Mobutu dictatorship. Stephen R. Weissman, *American Foreign Policy in the Congo, 1960–1964* (Ithaca, NY: Cornell University Press, 1974), and Madeleine G. Kalb, *The Congo Cables: The Cold War in Africa—From Eisenhower to Kennedy* (New York: Macmillan, 1982), use declassified government documents and interviews to illuminate US government involvement. David N. Gibbs, *The Political Economy of Third World Intervention: Mines, Money, and U.S. Policy in the Congo Crisis* (Chicago: University of Chicago Press, 1991), assesses the influence of American businesses in the making of US Congo policy. Piero Gleijeses, *Conflicting Missions: Havana, Washington, and Africa, 1959–1976* (Chapel Hill: University of North Carolina Press, 2002), examines the role of the UN, Western powers, and Cuba in the 1964–65 rebellion in eastern Congo and its aftermath. Two studies draw on recently opened archives to investigate Soviet involvement in the first postindependence Congo crisis. See Lise Namikas, *Battleground Africa: Cold War in the Congo, 1960–1965* (Washington, DC: Woodrow Wilson Center Press, 2013); and Sergey Mazov, *A Distant Front in the Cold War: The USSR in West Africa and the Congo, 1956–1964* (Washington, DC: Woodrow Wilson Center Press, 2010).

A number of works examine US and Belgian plots to assassinate the Congo's first prime minister, Patrice Lumumba. The results of a US congressional investigation are included in a report by the United States Senate, *Alleged Assassination Plots Involving Foreign Leaders: An Interim Report of the Select Committee to Study Governmental Operations with Respect to Intelligence Activities* (Washington, DC: US Government Printing Office, 1976). Lawrence Devlin, CIA station chief in the Congo in the early 1960s, provides insights into the US covert operations in his memoir, *Chief of Station, Congo: Fighting the Cold War in a Hot Zone* (New York: Public Affairs, 2007). Stephen R. Weissman, "An Extraordinary Rendition," *Intelligence and National Security* 25, no. 2 (April 2010): 198–222, uses declassified US government documents, memoirs of Belgian and US covert operatives, and interviews to provide a new interpretation of the US role in Lumumba's death. Ludo De Witte, *The Assassination of Lumumba,* trans. Ann Wright and Renée Fenby (New York: Verso, 2001), uses declassified Belgian government documents and interviews to expose the Belgian government role in Lumumba's death. Emmanuel Gerard and Bruce Kuklick, *Death in the Congo: Murdering Patrice Lumumba* (Cambridge, MA: Harvard University Press, 2015), includes new findings based on the 2000–2 Belgian parliamentary commission of inquiry into Lumumba's murder.

Several recommended books focus on Mobutu's Zaire. Crawford Young and Thomas Turner, *The Rise and Decline of the Zairian State* (Madison: University of Wisconsin Press, 1985), examines the transformation of the Belgian colonial bureaucracy into a corrupt, personalized, neopatrimonial state. Two books by Michael G. Schatzberg are also recommended. *The Dialectics of Oppression in Zaire* (Bloomington: Indiana University Press, 1988) demonstrates the ways in which scarcity and insecurity generated coercion, corruption, and economic exploitation in Zaire, while *Mobutu or Chaos: The United States and Zaire, 1960–1990* (Lanham, MD: University Press of America, 1991) focuses on US policy toward Zaire from independence to the end of the Cold War. Journalist Michela Wrong's *In the Footsteps of Mr. Kurtz: Living on the Brink of Disaster in the Congo* (New York: HarperCollins, 2001) provides a nuanced and highly readable account of the making of the Mobutu dictatorship and its support by Western powers.

The regional dynamics of the First and Second Congo Wars are explored in several volumes that emphasize the causes, internal dynamics, and effects of the conflicts, as well as the political and economic interests of outsiders. See, especially, Howard Adelman and Astri Suhrke, eds., *The Path of a Genocide: The Rwanda Crisis from Uganda to Zaire* (New Brunswick, NJ: Transaction, 1999); Christian P. Scherrer, *Genocide and Crisis in Central Africa: Conflict Roots, Mass Violence, and Regional War* (Westport, CT: Praeger, 2002); Thomas Turner, *The Congo Wars: Conflict, Myth and Reality* (London: Zed, 2007); René Lemarchand, *The Dynamics of Violence in Central Africa* (Philadelphia: University of Pennsylvania Press, 2008); Gérard Prunier, *Africa's World War: Congo, the Rwandan Genocide, and the Making of a Continental Catastrophe* (New York: Oxford University Press, 2009); Filip Reyntjens, *The Great African War: Congo and Regional Geopolitics, 1996–2006* (New York: Cambridge University Press, 2010); Jason K. Stearns, *Dancing in the Glory of Monsters:*

The Collapse of the Congo and the Great War of Africa (New York: Public Affairs, 2011); and Filip Reyntjens and René Lemarchand, "Mass Murder in Eastern Congo, 1996–1997," in *Forgotten Genocides: Oblivion, Denial, and Memory,* ed. René Lemarchand (Philadelphia: University of Pennsylvania Press, 2011), 20–36. Séverine Autesserre, *The Trouble with the Congo: Local Violence and the Failure of International Peacebuilding* (New York: Cambridge University Press, 2010), examines the international intervention in 2003–6 that neglected to address local grievances and thus failed to end the conflict. Philip Roessler, *Ethnic Politics and State Power in Africa: The Logic of the Coup–Civil War Trap* (New York: Cambridge University Press, 2016), examines the tempestuous balance between political factions, ethnic alliances, and external powers in the DRC conflict. Philip Roessler and Harry Verhoeven, *Why Comrades Go to War: Liberation Politics and the Outbreak of Africa's Deadliest Conflict* (New York: Oxford University Press, 2016), explains the regional war as an outgrowth of the failure to prioritize institution and nation building after Mobutu's ouster.

Several works focus on Rwandan actions in Zaire/DRC and the refusal of the international community to hold the RPF government accountable. Beyond the works mentioned in the previous paragraph, see, especially, two essays in Scott Straus and Lars Waldorf, eds., *Remaking Rwanda: State Building and Human Rights after Mass Violence* (Madison: University of Wisconsin Press, 2011): Filip Reyntjens, "Waging (Civil) War Abroad: Rwanda and the DRC," 132–51, and Jason Stearns and Federico Borello, "Bad Karma: Accountability for Rwandan Crimes in the Congo," 152–69. Marie Béatrice Umutesi, *Surviving the Slaughter: The Ordeal of a Rwandan Refugee in Zaire,* trans. Julie Emerson (Madison: University of Wisconsin Press, 2004), is a valuable account by a Rwandan Hutu who survived the mass slaughter of Hutu refugees in Zaire/DRC by Rwandan, Ugandan, Burundian, and Zairian/DRC forces. Johan Pottier, *Re-Imagining Rwanda: Conflict, Survival and Disinformation in the Late Twentieth Century* (New York: Cambridge University Press, 2002), described in Suggested Reading for chapter 6, explores the ways in which RPF power holders manipulated Western media, government, and NGO understandings of Rwanda and of the conflict in Zaire/DRC. In contrast, Philip Gourevitch sometimes blurs the distinction between Hutu civilian refugees from violence and genocide perpetrators. Critics have accused him of portraying RPF actions against Rwandan Hutu and Congolese civilians in Zaire/DRC as justified. See, especially, Philip Gourevitch, "Forsaken," *New Yorker* 76, no. 28 (September 25, 2000): 52–67. Gourevitch is taken to task by Howard French in *A Continent for the Taking: The Tragedy and Hope of Africa* (New York: Alfred A. Knopf, 2004).

Map 8.1. Liberia and Sierra Leone, 2018. (Map by Philip Schwartzberg, Meridian Mapping, Minneapolis.)

8

Liberia and Sierra Leone

Regional War and License to Plunder (1990–2003)

IN WEST AFRICA, as in the Democratic Republic of Congo, post–Cold War conflicts pitted neighbor against neighbor and attracted the attention of international bodies and extracontinental powers. By the turn of the twenty-first century, war had engulfed West Africa's Mano River region, including full-scale hostilities in Liberia, Sierra Leone, and Côte d'Ivoire. The fighting also impinged on Guinea, which was overwhelmed by hundreds of thousands of refugees and subjected to relentless attacks on its own population.[1] These wars consumed more than 250,000 lives between 1990 and 2003 and scattered millions of refugees to half a dozen neighboring countries. Weaponry flooded the region, with new stocks augmenting those left over from the Cold War. African countries orchestrated the most significant interventions—sometimes unilaterally, sometimes under the auspices of ECOWAS with UN or other extracontinental backing. Former colonial powers also played notable roles: the United Kingdom in the case of Sierra Leone, and France in the case of Côte d'Ivoire. The failure of the United States to take action in Liberia, which in many ways had been a quasi-colony, was an exception to the general practice. The predominant rationale for intervention was the desire to reestablish stability and to protect civilian lives. Although terrorist organizations had financial interests in the region and supported rebel factions that promoted their concerns, the war on terror was not a factor in foreign intervention during this period.

Although the response to instability/responsibility to protect paradigm encapsulates the prevailing justifications for intervention, once again, the reality was more complicated. The African subregional body ECOWAS interceded in all three conflicts—officially, to reestablish peace and security. Some member states played important mediation and peacekeeping roles. However, some states took advantage of the turmoil to further their own political and economic interests. Several ECOWAS members backed rebel groups and strongmen in their attempts to overthrow neighboring states; others supported the governments in power but allowed their soldiers to plunder with impunity. Mercenaries, private military companies, and international arms merchants, in search of new opportunities at the end of the Cold War, scoured the region for new outlets for their wares and services. Terrorist organizations, anxious to launder their finances, were eager to invest in the region's diamonds and offered rebel movements sophisticated weapons in return. In Liberia and Sierra Leone, diamonds, like strategic minerals in the DRC and oil in Sudan and South Sudan, became both an object of struggle and a means of perpetuating the violence.

This chapter examines foreign intervention in wars that engulfed Liberia (1990–2003) and Sierra Leone (1991–2002) and affected neighboring countries. Chapter 9 examines external involvement in the war in Côte d'Ivoire (2002–11), which was influenced by regional strife and began as the other wars were winding down. All three cases illustrate the complexities and mixed consequences of external involvement. In Liberia and Sierra Leone, unilateral intervention by neighboring countries exacerbated tensions and intensified violence. The engagement of multinational entities, although problematic, ultimately helped end the violence and establish new political orders. However, inadequate means for rebuilding the nations, aggravated by externally imposed structural adjustment programs, ensured that poverty, social tensions, and competition for power and resources would continue. The unresolved structural problems that lay at the root of the earlier wars thus remained a threat to regional peace and security.

Setting the Stage in Liberia: US Colony and Cold War Ally (1817–1985)

Liberia was the first of the Mano River countries to descend into war in the post–Cold War era. Founded by freed American slaves in the early nineteenth century, Liberia, like Mobutu's Zaire, was a vital US ally. For 133 years, Americo-Liberian settlers and their descendants, who constituted some 5 percent of the population, monopolized wealth and power in a system that oppressed the indigenous population. The United States provided a succession of Americo-Liberian dictators with substantial military and economic support in exchange for access to strategic resources and services as regional policemen. The Liberia-US alliance reached its apogee during the Cold War. As East-West tensions waned, Liberian strongmen provoked ethnic violence to maintain their hold on power, and the country was beset by a series of conflicts that ultimately engulfed the entire Mano River region.

The Liberian civil war of 1990–2003 was preceded by a century and a half of corrupt and repressive rule. The saga began with the trans-Atlantic slave trade, which removed millions of men, women, and children from West Africa over the course of more than 300 years. Although human trade across the Atlantic was effectively outlawed in 1807, it continued illegally throughout much of the nineteenth century.[2] Slavery itself was not banned in the United States until 1865. During the intervening years, many in the American power elite worried that the growing number of free people of African descent might encourage a large-scale slave revolt. Slave holders and their sympathizers therefore advocated the return of free blacks to Africa. At the same time, many free blacks and white abolitionists believed that resettlement in Africa might lead to happier, more productive lives for people of color. In 1817, the American Colonization Society was established to facilitate the back-to-Africa movement. The society purchased a strip of land on the West African coast and named its colony Liberia—the "land of freedom." In 1847 the colony became an independent state under the authority of Americo-Liberian settlers who, like their Euro-American contemporaries, considered Africans unfit to govern themselves.

During much of the twentieth century, Liberia was an American colony in all but name. The US government and American businesses had enormous influence over the country's affairs. In the early 1920s, US overseas investments in critical raw materials expanded rapidly, and rubber-rich Liberia was the focus of considerable interest. Tire tycoon Harvey Firestone obtained a 1 million acre concession in Liberia to develop what would become the world's largest rubber plantation. To guarantee the Firestone investment, a commission that included a US government advisor took charge of Liberia's finances. For the next three decades, Firestone Tire and Rubber Company virtually controlled the Liberian economy and retained Liberian government officials on the company payroll.

Liberian governmental corruption and repression peaked during the regime of President William Tubman, an Americo-Liberian who ruled the country from 1944 to 1971. Tubman built a powerful network of secret police and regarded the public treasury as his private bank. During the Cold War, he was a staunch US ally, and his regime was rewarded with massive military and economic support. During Tubman's reign, the United States built or enhanced a number of important facilities in Liberia: a Voice of America relay station, which broadcast US propaganda throughout Africa, the Middle East, and Southeast Asia; the Omega navigation station, which facilitated shipping along the West African coast; a critical CIA listening post; and Roberts Field, where US military planes landed and refueled on twenty-four hours' notice.

During the presidency of William R. Tolbert Jr. (1971–80), the global economic crisis, plummeting prices for iron ore and rubber exports, and deteriorating conditions in Liberia culminated in the rice riots of 1979. Following a major increase in the price of the dietary staple, unarmed protesters took to the streets. Police opened fire, killing at least forty people and injuring hundreds more. Under duress, Tolbert legalized opposition parties, but within months he again resorted to repression and arrested political rivals. In April 1980, dissidents in the Liberian army overthrew the Tolbert regime, killing the president and ending nearly a century and a half of Americo-Liberian rule.

The Liberian army was a US creation that was led by Americo-Liberian officers. However, the army's lower echelons were staffed by enlisted men drawn from the poorest strata of Liberian society— impoverished farmers, school dropouts, and hardened urban toughs, most of whom were members of the indigenous population. Their meager wages, if paid at all, were supplemented by an unofficial license to plunder. The 1980 coup leader was Master Sergeant Samuel Doe, a member of the Krahn ethnic group who had been trained by US Army Special Forces.[3] Doe's second-in-command, Thomas Quiwonkpa, was a member of the Gio ethnic group. The mutinous soldiers captured, tortured, and killed President Tolbert. Thirteen members of Tolbert's cabinet were executed by firing squad, and hundreds of other government officials and supporters were also slaughtered. Described as a strike against repressive Americo-Liberian rule, the coup d'état was initially applauded by many in Liberia and elsewhere. The new president promised to redistribute the nation's wealth and return the country to civilian rule. However, in short order, President Doe suspended the constitution, declared martial law, banned political activities, and imprisoned or executed his rivals. Burdened by a foreign debt totaling nearly three times the annual budget, he imposed an austerity program that ended rice subsidies and increased taxes in exchange for US aid and IMF loans. During his decade in power, Doe continued his predecessors' corrupt practices as he and his associates stole some $300 million from public coffers.

Under Doe, Liberia remained one of Washington's most important African allies. Although President Jimmy Carter, like earlier US presidents, had given significant support to an Americo-Liberian regime, his administration quickly embraced the new military government. During the Reagan administration, Liberia served as a staging ground for a CIA task force that targeted Qaddafi's Libya, which in 1979 had been included on Washington's state sponsors of terrorism list. The United States upgraded Roberts Field, which, along with air bases in Zaire, served as a key transit point for covert US aid to the rebel movement UNITA, which opposed Angola's Marxist government. In return, the Doe regime received significant financial support. In 1982, Liberia was the largest per capita recipient of US aid in sub-Saharan Africa. It garnered $500 million in military and economic aid from 1980 to 1989, a sum equivalent to one-third of the regime's operating budget.

When Doe assumed power, he promised that Liberia would return to civilian rule by 1985. Elections were duly held in October of that year; however, they were marred by intimidation and corruption. During the pre-election period, Doe banned opposition parties, outlawed criticism of his regime, and beat and imprisoned his opponents. During the vote, government operatives burned ballots and stuffed ballot boxes. The electoral commission that supervised the elections was stacked with Doe supporters. While international human rights groups condemned the electoral fraud, the United States accepted the elections as free and fair and endorsed the outcome.

Less than a month after the elections, Thomas Quiwonkpa, who had fallen out with Doe and lost his position as head of the Liberian armed forces, attempted to overthrow the Doe regime. Doe and his Krahn supporters responded with a brutal crackdown on members of the Gio ethnic group and on related Mano populations. Gio soldiers were purged from the Liberian armed forces, and reprisals were carried out in heavily Gio-populated Nimba County near the Côte d'Ivoire border. When the killing was over, Quiwonkpa and 3,000 others were dead. As these events unfolded, US Assistant Secretary of State for African Affairs Chester Crocker testified to Congress that democracy was dawning in Liberia.

The Liberian Civil War (1990–2003)

With Washington standing behind Doe and all moderate opposition quashed, warlords seized on popular anger. The most notorious strongman was Charles Taylor, a US-educated member of the Americo-Liberian elite. Although his father was a prominent Americo-Liberian, Taylor had ties to indigenous ethnic groups through his mother, a Gola woman, and his wife, who was both Gio and Thomas Quiwonkpa's niece. When Doe came to power, Taylor had obtained a coveted position as director of the General Services Agency. Tasked with procuring and distributing government property, Taylor was able to amass a sizable, but illicit, personal fortune. Perceiving Taylor as a threat to his own position, Doe accused him of embezzlement, and Taylor fled to the United States. Arrested in 1984 at the request of the Doe regime, Taylor escaped from jail in Massachusetts while awaiting extradition—under circumstances that have not been fully explained.

By early 1987, Taylor had established residency in Burkina Faso, where a cluster of Liberian exiles solicited support for military action against the Doe regime. In October, they helped Blaise Compaoré, a former army officer who served as a minister in the Burkinabe government, seize power in a coup that killed President Thomas Sankara. With Compaoré's assistance, Taylor made contact with Muammar Qaddafi, whose country had become an important hub for militants from Africa and other parts of the world. At Qaddafi's World Revolutionary Headquarters near Benghazi, Taylor received military training and developed important connections with other rebel leaders. From his Libyan base, he organized the National Patriotic Front of Liberia (NPFL), which included Liberian army deserters, Nigerian and Ghanaian dissidents, Gambians who had been involved in a 1981 coup attempt, and Chadians loyal to Idriss Déby, onetime head of the Chadian armed forces who had fled to Libya and would topple the Hissène Habré regime in 1990. Equipped with Libyan-supplied weapons, Taylor sought regional allies who would permit him to launch invasions from their territories. When President Joseph Momoh of Sierra Leone refused to back him, Taylor teamed up with Foday Sankoh, a former corporal in the Sierra Leonean army whom he had met in Libya. Together they organized the Revolutionary United Front (RUF), a rebel organization that would wreak havoc in Sierra Leone in the 1990s.

If President Momoh rejected Taylor's appeals, other heads of state were willing to help. President Compaoré of Burkina Faso provided political, economic, and military support, and Côte d'Ivoire's President Félix Houphouët-Boigny quickly emerged as Taylor's most important foreign backer. In December 1989, the NPFL launched an attack from Côte d'Ivoire into Nimba County, Liberia. Exploiting the rage of brutalized Gio and Mano civilians, Taylor distributed weapons to alienated, unemployed young men and to hundreds of boys whose parents had been killed in government raids. The latter formed the first Small Boy Units—child soldiers, emboldened by drugs, who were urged to seek revenge against the Krahn and Mandingo populations.[4] While Krahn soldiers had been responsible for many of the anti-Gio and Mano atrocities, Mandingos—who were primarily traders and small-scale entrepreneurs—were targeted for having prospered under the Doe regime. Taylor stoked religious as well as ethnic hatred. Although the majority of Liberians were Christian, 20 percent were Muslim, and most Muslims were Mandingo. A scripture-quoting Baptist lay preacher, Taylor encouraged Christians to attack Muslims, and by extension, all Mandingos. His crusade attracted high-profile support from leaders of the US religious right, including the Reverend Pat Robertson, founder of the Christian Broadcasting Network and host of the network's cardinal television program *The 700 Club.*

Samuel Doe's US-trained army responded to the NPFL invasion with a brutal counterinsurgency campaign against Gio and Mano civilians in both Nimba County and Monrovia, the capital. US ships staffed with more than 2,000 Marines evacuated US citizens and other foreigners but refused to intervene to stop the slaughter, describing the killings as an internal Liberian affair. Six months into the rebellion, the NPFL began to splinter, broken apart by warlords determined to consolidate their personal wealth and power. Prince Johnson, a former Liberian soldier who had served as Quiwonkpa's aide-de-camp, led a breakaway faction that beat Taylor's forces to Monrovia. However, Taylor gained control of Roberts Field, enabling him to import military supplies from Burkina Faso, and on July 27, 1990, a triumphant Taylor declared himself president of Liberia.

While the US armed forces stood by, neighboring countries entered the fray, driven by diverse motives. As members of ECOWAS, Nigeria, Ghana, Guinea, Sierra Leone, and Gambia were united in their desire for regional stability. Specific national interests were also at stake. A regional powerhouse with enormous oil wealth, Nigeria was under pressure from neighboring states with large Muslim populations to protect Liberian Muslims. As the linchpin of the West African economic community, Nigeria demonstrated its dominance by leading the ECOWAS intervention, while Ghana intensified its involvement to counter Nigerian influence. Guinea was worried about the fate of Liberian Muslims, many of whom had Guinean family and business ties. Sierra Leone and Gambia were troubled by Taylor's recruitment and training of their own dissidents, whom he had incorporated into his rebel forces. In August 1990, ECOWAS sent troops to Monrovia to effect a ceasefire. Operating under the name Economic Community of West African States Monitoring Group (ECOMOG), the 4,000-man force—which grew to 16,000 three years later—was led by Nigeria and included important contributions from Ghana, Guinea, and, to a lesser extent, Sierra Leone and Gambia. Contributing nations shouldered some of the expenses, with Nigeria paying the lion's share. The United States also supported the ECOMOG intervention with significant financial and diplomatic resources.

The prominent roles played by the United States and English-speaking African countries contributed to a new set of problems. France considered the ECOMOG operation further proof of anglophone attempts to encroach on its proclaimed sphere of influence in West Africa. French protégés in the region were hostile to US influence in Liberia and felt threatened by Nigeria's growing power. Burkina Faso and Côte d'Ivoire countered anglophone dominance by supporting Taylor's rebel movement.[5] Burkina Faso's President Compaoré, whose 1987 coup had been supported by Côte d'Ivoire—and allegedly, by the French secret services—helped equip Taylor's NPFL and allowed it to traverse his country when transiting between Liberia and Libya. He also sent Burkinabe soldiers to fight alongside Taylor's men. Côte d'Ivoire's President Houphouët-Boigny allowed NPFL forces to use his country as a rear base and transfer point for weapons sent from Burkina Faso. Meanwhile, Ivoirian nationals joined the NPFL, and Ivoirian businessmen and government officials made enormous profits by supplying Taylor with weapons and facilitating the

Photo 8.1. An ECOMOG soldier from Nigeria provides security for ECOMOG personnel from Mali as they disembark a US military aircraft at Roberts Field, Monrovia, February 20, 1997. Photo by SSgt. Paul R. Caron/US Air Force.

illicit export of diamonds, gold, iron ore, timber, and rubber to finance his war effort.

Although presented as a stabilizing force, ECOMOG quickly became part of the problem. Rather than keeping the peace, ECOMOG soldiers sucked the country dry, absconding with railway cars, mining equipment, trucks, and natural resources—anything they could sell abroad. With wry gallows humor, Monrovians quipped that ECOMOG stood for "Every Car or Moving Object Gone."[6] Unable to beat Taylor outright, the international force encouraged the formation of new rebel groups to oppose the NPFL and provided them with arms in exchange for booty. Since they profited from prolongation of the war, ECOWAS members could not be counted on to end it. On September 9, 1990, the forces of Prince Johnson, who had broken from the NPFL, captured, tortured, and killed Samuel Doe. By the end of the month, Taylor was fighting Johnson's troops north of Monrovia and ECOMOG soldiers in the eastern suburbs.

In March 1991, as the peacekeeping operation foundered, Taylor further internationalized the war by opening a second front in Sierra Leone, where Joseph Momoh's government threatened his supply route. To undermine Momoh, Taylor helped organize, train, and equip the Sierra Leonean rebel organization, the Revolutionary United Front. Led by Taylor's Libyan-trained ally and protégé, Corporal Foday Sankoh, the RUF modeled its strategy and tactics on those of the NPFL. Sankoh's rebels press-ganged boys and girls into RUF forces, where they were used as soldiers, porters, miners, cooks, and sex slaves. Brutalized RUF recruits were taught to abduct, rape, amputate, and kill, terrorizing the rural populace. They especially targeted chiefs, elders, traders, and agricultural development workers—anyone who was prosperous or associated with the Sierra Leonean government. Taylor's subversion in Sierra Leone led to Momoh's meddling in Liberia, where the Sierra Leonean government joined ECOMOG in financing and training a number of anti-Taylor rebel groups. The most important of these was the United Liberation Movement of Liberia for Democracy (ULIMO), which was founded by exiled Doe officials, soldiers, and supporters. By 1994 ULIMO had splintered, with Krahns and Mandingos gravitating toward different organizations. ULIMO-K (primarily Mandingo) was led by Alhaji Kromah, and ULIMO-J (primarily Krahn) was led by Roosevelt Johnson. Both leaders had held offices in the Doe regime.

By the early 1990s, the Liberian war had become a free-for-all between warlords, their personal followers, and their external backers, with plunder as its primary goal. Although ethnic rivalries were often cited as motivations for the conflict, the real competition was for natural resources, land, and power. Ethnicity was manipulated to achieve these ends. For the remainder of the decade, Liberia was run by warlords and criminal gangs who controlled the country's vast deposits of diamonds, gold, and iron ore, as well as its timber and rubber supplies, and who extracted its wealth through brutal regimes of forced labor. Presiding over an extensive criminal network with ties to foreign firms, Taylor amassed a fortune worth nearly half a billion dollars. He spent most of it on his effort to establish a powerful state that would expand its reach to the diamond-rich regions of Guinea and Sierra Leone.

Other countries and private interests also joined the resource rush. To thwart Taylor's state-building plan, Guinea backed ULIMO-K, which seized diamond mines on both sides of the Liberia-Guinea border. Guinean government officials enriched themselves through diamond and arms trafficking, profiting from strong ties between Guinean and Liberian Mandingo traders who smuggled Liberian diamonds and foreign weapons across the porous frontier.[7] Various Nigerian interests supported ULIMO-J, which took control of diamond mines northwest of the capital, while former Doe officials appropriated the state-owned rubber plantation outside the port city of Buchanan. European, American, and Japanese businesses bribed Taylor for the right to exploit resources in his domain. French firms were especially active, their interests advanced by Jean-Christophe Mitterrand, son of French President François Mitterrand and head of the government's Africa Cell from 1986 to 1992.[8] In 1991, NPFL-controlled areas served as France's third-largest source of tropical timber. Taylor also allowed a French company to run the world's largest iron mine, which was located along the Liberia-Guinea border.

Although Taylor's forces dominated much of the Liberian hinterland by the early 1990s, Nigerian-led ECOMOG presided over the capital city. Concluding that he could not rule Liberia without Nigerian support, Taylor agreed to participate in peace talks in Abuja and signed an accord in August 1995. The agreement provided for executive leadership by a Council of State composed of the former warring factions and a transitional period followed by elections. As the strongest of the rebel leaders, Taylor became Liberia's de facto ruler. When presidential elections were held in July 1997, the majority of voters cast their ballots for Taylor—many fearing that his defeat would result in a return to war. Taylor used his new position to establish a neopatrimonial state that continued to plunder Liberian and Sierra Leonean resources.

Just as the elections did not establish democracy, the Taylor presidency did not bring peace. By the late 1990s, at least seven rebel factions were operating in Liberia. All had external backers. Some foreign patrons were ECOWAS members that were simultaneously providing soldiers to the ECOMOG peacekeeping forces. All parties were violating a UN arms embargo imposed in November 1992. Guinea supported Liberians United for Reconciliation and Democracy (LURD) in response to attacks on its territory by NPFL forces and Guinean insurgents. The Krahn-dominated Movement for Democracy in Liberia (MODEL) received arms and militia fighters from Côte d'Ivoire after President Laurent Gbagbo, who assumed power in 2000, ended that country's decade-long support for Charles Taylor.[9] Other rebel factions were led by former NPFL commanders who had broken from the parent organization, primarily for political and financial gain. All of the factions mimicked the NPFL in both methods and objectives, abusing civilian populations as they plundered the country's riches.

Photo 8.2. Unidentified rebel fighters during the Liberian civil war, ca. 2003. Photo courtesy of James G. Antal and R. John Vanden Berghe/US Marine Corps.

Having delegated to ECOWAS the maintenance of peace and security in the subregion, the UN Security Council responded only incrementally to the threats posed by instability in Liberia and Taylor's aggression against Sierra Leone. The Security Council banned arms sales to Liberia in 1992, the purchase of Liberian diamonds in 2001, and the acquisition of Liberian timber in May 2003. These actions inhibited, but did not halt, Taylor's ability to procure weapons and did nothing to stem the flow of arms to rebel forces.

By April 2003, foreign-backed rebels had seized control of 60 percent of Liberia's territory, including most of the diamond mining areas. In June, LURD's onslaught reached the capital. During the siege of Monrovia in July and August, hundreds of civilians were killed and more than 2,000 were injured. The international community, including UN officials, African heads of state, and European diplomats, urged the United States, as the de facto but unofficial former imperial power, to take the lead in ending the crisis. The George W. Bush administration resisted, arguing that no direct American interests were at stake and that US forces were already spread thin by wars in Afghanistan and Iraq. Sweeping aside the history of US support for a succession of Liberian regimes, the White House embraced the post-Somalia prescription of "African solutions for African problems," maintaining that responsibility for resolving the conflict lay with Liberia, its neighbors, and the UN—not the United States.[10] As the battle for Liberia wound down, Washington remained largely on the sidelines, although it did help facilitate Taylor's resignation on August 11 and his subsequent exile to Nigeria.

On August 18, LURD, MODEL, the remnants of Taylor's government, and Liberian political parties and civil society organizations signed an ECOWAS-mediated peace accord in Accra, Ghana. The agreement provided for an interim government, elections, and a new national army that would incorporate both rebel and government soldiers. ECOWAS was authorized to establish a 3,500-person multinational peacekeeping force—once again led by Nigeria—to secure a ceasefire, keep the factions separate, and enable the safe delivery of humanitarian assistance. The ceasefire would be supervised and monitored by a Joint Monitoring Committee comprising representatives from ECOWAS, the UN, the AU, other members of the International Contact Group on Liberia, and signatories to the peace accord.[11] On September 19, the Security Council authorized the United Nations Mission in Liberia (UNMIL), which would incorporate the ECOWAS force and include up to 15,000 peacekeepers to help maintain law and order and prepare for elections.

The Liberian war was over, but the cost had been enormous. In violence that had consumed the country since the NPFL invasion in December 1989, an estimated 200,000 people had died, another 1.5 million had been displaced, and tens of thousands of women and girls had been raped. The country's infrastructure and economy had been devastated, and food insecurity was rampant. Liberia's $3.7 billion debt, much of it incurred by the Doe and Taylor regimes, was worth almost eight times the value of the country's annual gross domestic product. With poverty and underdevelopment rooted in nearly two hundred years authoritarian rule by a small elite, recovery would be difficult.

As the second postwar decade began, it was clear that some progress had been made. Presidential and legislative elections held in 2005 and 2011 were deemed by international observers to have been largely free and fair. They brought to power President Ellen Johnson Sirleaf, who had been a government finance minister and an official of the World Bank and United Nations Development Programme (UNDP). Africa's first democratically elected female head of state, Sirleaf received the Nobel Peace Prize in 2011 for her work on behalf of women's rights. As president, she mandated free and compulsory primary education and launched a Truth and Reconciliation Commission to investigate crimes committed during the civil war. Based on testimony from Liberians of all backgrounds, the commission concluded that the main causes of the war included poverty, corruption, unemployment, disputes over land and identity, and political, economic, and social inequalities. Sirleaf initiated a national dialogue on peace and reconciliation to address these underlying problems. Presidential elections in December 2017 peacefully transferred power to George Weah, who ran on a populist platform and took office in January 2018.

These hopeful signs masked a dire picture on the ground. Critics charged that the truth and reconciliation process sacrificed justice for peace, allowing war criminals to escape punishment, and that the Sirleaf government contributed to endemic corruption and nepotism rather than eradicating it. In 2017, Liberia continued to rely on foreign aid to stay afloat and on UNMIL to maintain security. Economic growth was stymied by a steep decline in iron ore and rubber prices, along with currency devaluation, inflation, and budget cuts. Liberia ranked 177 of 188 countries on the

UNDP Human Development Index for 2016. Life expectancy hovered at sixty-one years, and 84 percent of the population earned less than $1.25 per day. Nine in ten Liberian households lacked running water, and almost half had no toilet facilities. Few Liberians had access to electricity: the power grid served only the capital city, and just 10 percent of the city's population was connected to it. The thirteen-year civil war had prevented a generation of young people from acquiring basic education, and most had little hope of gainful employment. Moreover, the war's long-term consequences continued to emerge. The country's feeble rural health care infrastructure had been destroyed both by the war and by IMF structural adjustment programs that had reduced governmental spending and imposed user fees. More than a decade after the war ended, Liberia lacked clean water and sanitation facilities, rural clinics and hospitals, medicines, and medical supplies and equipment, and the imposition of fees made basic health services unaffordable for most Liberians. These conditions left the country extremely vulnerable. When the Ebola virus swept the country in 2014–15, it infected at least 10,600 people and killed more than 4,800.

In Liberia, as elsewhere, foreign military intervention had helped end a brutal war but failed to address the fundamental problems that had caused it. Governmental corruption and disputes over land and resources continued to undermine the country's stability, which in turn posed an ongoing threat to regional peace and security. A similar pattern was evident in neighboring Sierra Leone.

Setting the Stage in Sierra Leone: British Territory and the Neopatrimonial State (1808–1990)

The conflict in Liberia led to a proxy war in Sierra Leone, where instability provoked intervention by the UN, ECOWAS, neighboring countries, foreign mercenaries, and the UK. Outside forces ignited the conflagration, but it was fueled by local grievances embedded in the political, economic, and social inequalities of the colonial and postcolonial past. Like Liberia, Sierra Leone was established in the early nineteenth century as a colony for freed slaves. The UK administered the coastal settlement of Freetown as a crown colony from 1808, while the hinterland was added as a protectorate in 1896. The freed slaves and their descendants, known as Creoles, constituted a small, prosperous elite. Like their Americo-Liberian counterparts, they benefited disproportionately from the country's resources and from Western education provided by Christian missionaries.

After independence in 1961, Sierra Leone was ruled by corrupt dictators who presided over neopatrimonial regimes that undermined the official bureaucracy and treated the country's rich diamond deposits as their own. High-level government officials, military officers, and their foreign collaborators ran shadow states based on illicit economies that generated enormous wealth for the few. Meanwhile, the majority of the population was mired in poverty, especially in the rural areas, where economic development was virtually nonexistent. When Major-General Joseph Momoh, commander of the Sierra Leonean armed forces, assumed the presidency in 1985, the country's economy was in deep distress. Popular discontent was exacerbated by IMF and World Bank austerity programs that removed subsidies and price controls from essential consumer goods, forced massive layoffs of public employees, and imposed debt repayment programs that siphoned resources from public services. The external mandates also strengthened the position of regime loyalists, who benefited from privatization programs that rendered public assets into private hands.

The Sierra Leone Proxy War (1991–2002)

Sierra Leone's war began in March 1991, when the Revolutionary United Front launched an attack from Liberia. Although funded, trained, and equipped by Charles Taylor as an adjunct to the Liberian war, and reinforced by mercenaries and weapons from Burkina Faso, the RUF claimed to be championing the rights of rural people who were dominated by a venal urban elite. While corruption, tyranny, and poverty were real issues, the RUF made no attempt to win hearts and minds during its eleven-year war. Instead, it conducted a reign of terror against the rural population. Recruited from among alienated, unemployed youths and press-ganged children, RUF rebels hacked off limbs, raped women, destroyed the rural infrastructure, and killed civilians at will. Thousands of children were abducted during the war—the girls turned into cooks and sex slaves and the boys into brutal killers on the model of Charles Taylor's Small Boy Units.

Although the war did not begin over diamonds, control of Sierra Leone's enormous diamond wealth quickly became the main objective of

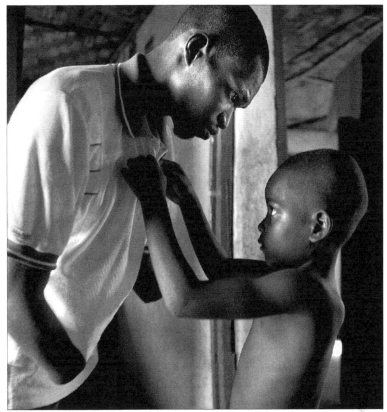

Photo 8.3. RUF victim Abu Bakarr Kargbo, assisted by his son Abu, Freetown, November 13, 2005. Photo by Yannis Kontos/Polaris.

RUF leaders, Charles Taylor, and diverse foreign interests. International smuggling operations that specialized in money laundering and trafficking in diamonds, guns, and drugs took control of the Sierra Leonean mines. Enormous quantities of diamonds were spirited across the Liberian border and sold to willing buyers in Belgium, Israel, Libya, Pakistan, Russia, and the United States. British and South African mercenaries and militant organizations like Hezbollah and al-Qaeda purchased diamonds as a means of laundering illicit wealth. Taylor received a large percentage from every diamond sale and used the proceeds to finance both the Liberian and Sierra Leonean wars.

The Momoh government responded to the NPFL-RUF invasion by assembling a counter force from among the 250,000 Liberian refugees and former Doe officials, soldiers, and supporters resident in Sierra Leone. Forming the core of what would become ULIMO, the Liberian recruits fought alongside the Sierra Leonean army from March 1991 and launched their first attack into Liberia in September. Like the RUF, the Momoh regime press-ganged children into the army and recruited unemployed youths in the border region, some of whom sought revenge for their families' deaths at the hands of RUF and NPFL rebels. The government forces were assisted by some 1,500 ECOMOG soldiers from Guinea and Nigeria, whose mission was to protect the peacekeeping force in Liberia from NPFL attacks originating in Sierra Leone. Corruption was rampant in this arena as well. ECOMOG officers and soldiers in the diamond regions were deeply engaged in illicit mining, sometimes working in close proximity to RUF prospectors.

In April 1992, a group of young Sierra Leonean army officers, disenchanted with wartime conditions and abysmal pay, toppled the Momoh regime and installed Captain Valentine Strasser as head of state. Although Strasser promised to end the war, improve the economy, and institute multiparty democracy, little changed. Strasser's entourage, like Momoh's, engaged in illicit diamond mining and other corrupt practices and recruited alienated youths and political thugs, who raped, pillaged, and killed throughout the war zone. To many rural dwellers, the army and the RUF were indistinguishable; they dubbed the new predators "sobels"—shorthand for "soldier-rebels." As the well-financed RUF gained the upper hand, the Sierra Leonean government mobilized Mende civilian defense forces along the Liberian border. Commonly referred to as the Kamajors (hunters), the militias were made up of local hunters and youths who were far more knowledgeable about the local terrain than RUF recruits and far more effective than the national army. The RUF retaliated with a campaign of terror against the civilian population, amputating arms, legs, hands, ears, noses, and genitals.

Foreign intervention assumed a new form in May 1995, when Executive Outcomes (EO) arrived to assist the Sierra Leonean government. Established in South Africa in 1989, EO was among the first of the private military companies that emerged at the end of the Cold War to supplement the work of national armies and police forces. Although they eschewed the label "mercenary," private military companies were, to many Africans, simply a new embodiment of an old phenomenon—white men with guns who were hired to do dirty jobs on the African continent.[12]

Most EO recruits were former South African Defence Force (SADF) operatives who lost their jobs when the South African wars in Namibia and Angola ended in the late 1980s and apartheid crumbled in 1994. Willing to work for anyone who would pay, EO helped Angola's Marxist government fight UNITA rebels in the 1990s, even though EO personnel, as SADF members, had waged an earlier campaign with UNITA to overthrow the same government. In Sierra Leone, EO trained the national army in counterinsurgency tactics, provided helicopter air support, transported troops and equipment, and helped locate RUF camps.

Strasser's military regime eventually returned the country to civilian rule, but even with EO support, it failed to end the war. Presidential elections were held in February and March 1996, and Strasser handed over power to the winner, Ahmad Tejan Kabbah, a civil servant who had held various posts in Sierra Leone but who had spent most of the preceding two decades working for the UNDP abroad. The RUF, which had not participated in the elections, did not recognize the new regime. Although the war continued, the RUF agreed to talk.

Mediation by the UN, the OAU, ECOWAS, the Commonwealth, and Côte d'Ivoire led to the Abidjan Accord, signed in November 1996.[13] The agreement required EO to withdraw from Sierra Leone, leaving state security in the hands of the national army and the Kamajor militias. The RUF, in turn, was to disarm in exchange for amnesty and reintegration into Sierra Leonean society. While EO did depart, the rebels fractured, and some continued to fight. Those who profited most from the war, including RUF leader Foday Sankoh, refused to lay down arms. In March 1997, Sankoh was arrested in Nigeria and RUF members who supported the peace process announced his ouster. In Sierra Leone, an RUF field commander and Taylor protégé, Colonel Sam Bockarie, took charge of the faction that wanted war. Kabbah's government was toppled in May by mutinous soldiers who feared that the peace accords would result in demobilization and a halt to their illicit mining activities. Recognizing their common interests, the coup leaders invited the RUF to join them in a coalition government led by Major Johnny Paul Koroma. RUF combatants entered the capital, plundering, raping, and killing, and launched a campaign of pillage and terror in the countryside dubbed "Operation Pay Yourself."

President Kabbah sought refuge in neighboring Guinea, from which he mobilized international support for a return to power and appealed to the UN and ECOWAS to intervene. In October 1997, the Security Council imposed an oil and weapons embargo on Sierra Leone and authorized ECOWAS to enforce implementation with ECOMOG troops.[14] In March 1998, a Nigerian-led ECOMOG force, assisted by the Kamajors, ousted the Koroma junta and reinstated the Kabbah government. The Security Council then established the United Nations Observer Mission in Sierra Leone (UNOMSIL), which authorized unarmed UN military observers, protected by ECOMOG troops, to monitor Sierra Leone's security situation, the disarmament and demobilization of armed groups, and respect for international humanitarian law. Although the RUF and the renegade soldiers had been expelled from Freetown, the capital, they dominated eastern Sierra Leone and its rich diamond fields. By December, rebel forces, strengthened by new recruits, controlled more than half the country. They were bolstered by South African mercenaries, whose SADF tactics and training overwhelmed the capabilities of the ECOMOG force.

In January 1999, rebel forces composed primarily of former Sierra Leonean army soldiers again overran Freetown. As they approached, the UN observers were evacuated. In an offensive dubbed "Operation No Living Thing," rebels rampaged through the capital, raping, mutilating, and slaughtering thousands. Hundreds of children were abducted, and 100,000 people were driven from their homes. Nigerian ECOMOG troops counterattacked, targeting rebels in densely populated areas with heavy artillery and bombs. By the time ECOMOG regained the capital three weeks later, some 3,500 civilians had died at the hands of either rebel or ECOMOG forces.

Western governments, led by the United States, pressured Kabbah to enter into yet another negotiated settlement with the RUF, endorsing a plan that was staunchly opposed by international human rights groups and by civil society organizations in Sierra Leone. Assured that the UN would send a peacekeeping mission once there was a peace to keep, Kabbah reluctantly agreed. In July 1999, the Sierra Leonean government and the RUF signed the Lomé Accord, which called for an end to hostilities, disarmament and demobilization of rebel combatants, and the formation of a government of national unity in which the RUF would assume senior positions. The RUF would be granted amnesty for crimes committed during the war, including the mass atrocities carried out in Freetown in January. The UN refused to endorse the amnesty clause, leaving open the possibility that international bodies might prosecute alleged perpetrators of genocide, war crimes, and crimes against humanity, as well as other violations of international humanitarian law.

Foisted on Sierra Leone from outside and without input from significant parties, the Lomé Accord was deeply flawed. Representatives of the mutinous former soldiers did not sign the agreement. Foday Sankoh, who had been convicted of high treason in October 1998, was released from prison, installed as vice president, and placed in charge of Sierra Leone's gold and diamond mines as well as other strategic minerals. Illicit mining, controlled by Sankoh's Black Guards, increased dramatically. Sankoh signed sales agreements with US, Belgian, and South African merchants that brought him enormous personal gain, while Nigerian peacekeepers also profited from the illegal diamond trade.

In October 1999, the Security Council authorized the establishment of the United Nations Mission in Sierra Leone (UNAMSIL), a 6,000-member peacekeeping force that would replace the ECOMOG troops. Including personnel from Guinea, India, Kenya, Nigeria, and Zambia, UNAMSIL was authorized to monitor the peace agreement, to oversee the disarmament and demobilization of rebel and militia forces, and to ensure compliance with international human rights law. It was a complex mission for which the peacekeepers were ill prepared. UNAMSIL's authority was immediately challenged. RUF leader Sam Bockarie, who opposed the peace agreement, broke with Sankoh and returned to the bush to fight. In May 2000, RUF rebels who objected to UN deployment in the diamond region renounced the ceasefire, took more than 500 UN peacekeepers hostage, and absconded with UN weapons and vehicles. The peace accord collapsed, and the UK, as the former colonial power, took charge. Elite British troops, including paratroopers and Royal Marines, assumed protection of Freetown, taking control of the port and airport and evacuating foreign nationals.

The UNAMSIL force was augmented after the May fiasco with a well-trained Pakistani contingent of more than 4,000 soldiers.[15] British troop strength was also expanded, reaching 1,000 in September. However, the RUF remained a serious threat. From September 2000 through April 2001, RUF rebels backed by Charles Taylor conducted a series of cross-border raids into Guinea to gain control of diamond mines and to harass Sierra Leonean refugees near the border. Hundreds of Guinean and Sierra Leonean civilians were wounded or killed. The incursions provoked a new wave of external involvement. Guinea's armed forces, enhanced by French and US weapons and British intelligence, helped train a thousand Kamajor fighters. Joint Guinean-Kamajor operations against the RUF in the diamond regions killed scores of Sierra Leonean civilians and destroyed numerous villages.

With UNAMSIL's backing, the Lomé Accord was slowly implemented. More than 75,000 rebels, militia members, and child soldiers were demobilized, and in January 2002, President Kabbah announced the war's end. Over the course of the eleven-year war, some 50,000 people had been killed and one-third of the population had been displaced. Thousands of women and girls had been raped, and an estimated 10,000 children had been conscripted as soldiers, porters, cooks, and sex slaves. As in Liberia, the war had devastated the country's social and economic infrastructure. Most of Sierra Leone's schools and health facilities had been destroyed. When the war ended, Sierra Leoneans earned on average only thirty-eight cents a day; a decade later, 57 percent of the population still subsisted on a daily allowance of less than one dollar. As in Liberia, recovery would be arduous. In both cases, the nation's problems were rooted not only in a decade-long war, but in two hundred years of authoritarian rule by a small elite.

Like Liberia, Sierra Leone took promising early steps. Presidential elections held in May 2002 resulted in another electoral victory for President Kabbah. In 2007 Kabbah was defeated by parliamentary opposition leader Ernest Bai Koroma in elections deemed free and fair by international observers. Koroma was reelected in 2012. President Koroma introduced free health care for children under the age of five and for pregnant and nursing women—although the absence of funds and trained health workers hampered the programs' effectiveness. He attempted to tackle corruption by granting greater investigative and prosecutorial powers to the official anticorruption commission and by firing a number of government ministers implicated in unethical practices. Sierra Leone also made a significant effort to expose abuses perpetrated during the war. A government-sponsored Truth and Reconciliation Commission collected testimony throughout the country that documented wartime violations of human rights and international humanitarian law. A UN-backed Special Court for Sierra Leone was established to prosecute those "who bear the greatest responsibility" for war crimes, crimes against humanity, and other serious violations of international humanitarian law committed after the signing of the 1996 Abidjan Accord.[16] In 2013, Sierra

Leone launched an effort to revise the 1991 constitution with a view to strengthening multiparty democracy and governmental transparency. The process was still ongoing in 2017.

As in Liberia, hopeful signs obscured a more problematic situation on the ground. A decade and a half after the war's end, Sierra Leone remained vulnerable on multiple fronts. Like Liberia, Sierra Leone relied heavily on foreign aid to sustain basic government services, and in 2016 the country faced bankruptcy. The collapse of iron ore prices had diminished the value of its second most important export. The plummeting value of its currency, high inflation, and severe youth unemployment imposed further burdens on a population that depended on foreign imports for many basic foods. Official corruption and the large-scale theft of natural resources exacerbated the economic crisis and contributed to citizens' loss of confidence in government. In 2016 Sierra Leone ranked 179 of 188 countries on the UNDP Human Development Index, and both rural and urban populations experienced widespread poverty. Life expectancy averaged only fifty-one years. Health care services, especially in the rural areas, were few and far between, and those that existed were inadequately financed, staffed, and equipped—the consequence of both war and IMF/World Bank structural adjustment programs. As a result, when the Ebola virus arrived in 2014, it quickly reached epidemic proportions, infecting at least 13,000 people and killing nearly 4,000 in less than two years.

In Sierra Leone as in Liberia, external military intervention helped end a vicious war. However, the underlying causes continued to fester. Governmental corruption and lack of accountability, deep political, economic, and social inequalities, and a neocolonial economic system that benefited only the few continued to threaten the country's stability and, by extension, that of the wider region.

Conclusion

The conflicts in Liberia and Sierra Leone, and international response to them, underscore the difficulties of weighing the pros and cons of foreign intervention and generalizing about the motivations and impact of external actors. Foreign intervention in response to instability or to protect civilian lives often masks mixed motives and conflicting interests. Neighboring states may intervene on legitimate grounds of self-defense, but they may also engage to protect more parochial public and private interests. Similarly, subregional multilateral organizations may intercede to restore stability in conflicts that impinge on their members' security. However, member states may work at cross purposes as they simultaneously pursue their own agendas. Global powers and the organizations they dominate tend to engage selectively, responding to instability and the threat to civilian lives in some regions but not in others, depending on the strength of their interests in those regions. Individuals and interest groups at all levels may profit from the chaos and thus have a stake in ensuring its perpetuation. Finally, motivations and roles may change over the course of a conflict, making it difficult to categorize actors and their interests.

These complexities also characterized other struggles in the Mano River region. When the wars in Liberia and Sierra ended, thousands of former rebels roamed the region seeking new battles, which would lead to further violence and destabilization. Many turned to Côte d'Ivoire, a pivotal sponsor of regional turmoil and a country where social discrimination and political and economic inequality provided fodder for new conflicts. Once again, neighboring countries, multilateral state-based organizations, and the former colonial power entered the fray—with mixed motivations and conflicting interests. The war in Côte d'Ivoire is the subject of chapter 9.

Suggested Reading

Several recommended books offer historical background on the Liberian crisis. Tom W. Shick, *Behold the Promised Land: A History of Afro-American Settlers in Nineteenth-Century Liberia* (Baltimore: Johns Hopkins University Press, 1980), examines the founding of Liberia by African American settlers, but does not investigate the impact on indigenous populations. Emily S. Rosenberg, *Spreading the American Dream: American Economic and Cultural Expansion, 1890–1945* (New York: Hill and Wang, 1982), illuminates the role of Firestone Tire and Rubber and the US government in twentieth-century Liberia. Reed Kramer, "Liberia: A Casualty of the Cold War's End," Africa News Service, July 1, 1995, provides a concise historical overview of the US relationship with Liberia from its founding in the nineteenth century until 1995.

The Liberian civil war is the subject of a number of works. Stephen Ellis, *The Mask of Anarchy: The Destruction of Liberia and the Religious*

Dimension of an African Civil War, 2nd ed. (New York: New York University Press, 2006), is especially recommended. It explains the origins and evolution of the war, focusing on corruption, the collapse of the state bureaucracy and neopatrimonial political system, the manipulation of ethnicity by politicians and warlords, and the role of indigenous religious belief systems. William Reno, *Warlord Politics and African States* (Boulder, CO: Lynne Rienner, 1998), described in the Suggested Reading for chapter 2, includes an insightful chapter on Liberian warlord politics. Bill Berkeley, *The Graves Are Not Yet Full: Race, Tribe and Power in the Heart of Africa* (New York: Basic Books, 2001), is a clearly written journalistic account that explores the ways in which Samuel Doe and Charles Taylor manipulated ethnicity to gain access to power and resources. Berkeley pays special attention to the role of the United States in the Liberian crisis. Mark Huband, *The Liberian Civil War* (Portland, OR: Frank Cass, 1998), is a personal memoir of the early years of the Liberian civil war by a journalist who was captured by Taylor's forces. Danny Hoffman, *The War Machines: Young Men and Violence in Sierra Leone and Liberia* (Durham, NC: Duke University Press, 2011), investigates the ways in which young men who were recruited into violent labor on rubber plantations and in diamond mines, community defense organizations, and other militias in the mid-1990s became a reservoir of mercenary labor for violent work elsewhere after the Sierra Leonean and Liberian wars ended.

Two recommended books examine the role of ECOMOG and the interests of neighboring countries in the Liberian civil war. See Adekeye Adebajo, *Liberia's Civil War: Nigeria, ECOMOG, and Regional Security in West Africa* (Boulder, CO: Lynne Rienner, 2002); and Karl P. Magyar and Earl Conteh-Morgan, eds., *Peacekeeping in Africa: ECOMOG in Liberia* (New York: St. Martin's, 1998). The regional implications of the Liberian war are considered in Global Witness, *The Usual Suspects: Liberia's Weapons and Mercenaries in Côte d'Ivoire and Sierra Leone* (London: Global Witness, 2003).

Several books provide insight into the origins of the Sierra Leonean crisis and the dynamics of the war. William Reno, *Corruption and State Politics in Sierra Leone* (New York: Cambridge University Press, 1995), examines the ways in which politicians and warlords collaborated with foreign business interests to generate wealth and patronage that undermined the bureaucratic state. Reno, *Warlord Politics and African States* (mentioned previously), includes an important chapter on warlord politics in Sierra Leone. David Keen, *Conflict and Collusion in Sierra Leone* (New York: Palgrave Macmillan, 2005), investigates the crisis of the patronage-based political and economic system and the response of those without political, economic, and social prospects. In *A Dirty War in West Africa: The RUF and the Destruction of Sierra Leone* (Bloomington: Indiana University Press, 2005), Sierra Leonean journalist and historian Lansana Gberie offers insights into the disintegration of the state, the nature of the RUF, the role of Liberia, and the impact of UN and UK intervention. In *Sierra Leone: Diamonds and the Struggle for Democracy* (Boulder, CO: Lynne Rienner, 2001), John Hirsch, US ambassador to Sierra Leone from 1995 to 1998, examines the decades leading up to the war, the social, economic, and historical context of the conflict, and the impact of regional and extracontinental powers. Ibrahim Abdullah, *Between Democracy and Terror: The Sierra Leone Civil War* (Dakar: CODESRIA, 2004), explores the origin of the conflict, the roles of internal and external actors, and the various efforts to end the war. Ian Smillie, Lansana Gberie, and Ralph Hazleton, *The Heart of the Matter: Sierra Leone, Diamonds, and Human Security* (Ottawa: Partnership Africa Canada, 2000), investigates the role of resources in the Sierra Leonean war.

Several works examine the crisis of Sierra Leonean youth and the experiences of child soldiers. Paul Richards, *Fighting for the Rain Forest: War, Youth and Resources in Sierra Leone* (Portsmouth, NH: Heinemann, 1996), and Krijn Peters, *War and the Crisis of Youth in Sierra Leone* (New York: Cambridge University Press, 2011), investigate corruption in the colonial and postcolonial states, the breakdown of rural societies, and the alienation of youth that led them to the RUF. Myriam Denov, *Child Soldiers: Sierra Leone's Revolutionary United Front* (New York: Cambridge University Press, 2010), explores the ways in which children were initiated into RUF violence and the challenges they faced in the postwar period. Hoffman, *The War Machines* (mentioned previously), focuses on young Sierra Leonean men who were recruited into violent labor by diverse groups and explores the regional implications after the war's end. Ishmael Beah, *A Long Way Gone: Memoirs of a Boy Soldier* (New York: Farrar, Straus and Giroux, 2007), is a powerful memoir of a child soldier press-ganged into the Sierra Leonean national army.

The role of outside powers in the Sierra Leonean conflict is the subject of several books. The impact of Liberian involvement is described in the general works on the Sierra Leonean war mentioned previously.

Two books focus on the UK. Andrew M. Dorman, *Blair's Successful War: British Military Intervention in Sierra Leone* (Burlington, VT: Ashgate, 2009), examines the UK's engagement in humanitarian intervention and its impact on Sierra Leone. Phil Ashby, *Against All Odds: Escape from Sierra Leone* (New York: St. Martin's, 2003), provides a firsthand account by a British major and UN military observer who was held hostage by the RUF. Funmi Olonisakin, *Peacekeeping in Sierra Leone: The Story of UNAMSIL* (Boulder, CO: Lynne Rienner, 2008), examines the successes and failures of the UN peacekeeping operation.

Map 9.1. Côte d'Ivoire, 2018. (Map by Philip Schwartzberg, Meridian Mapping, Minneapolis.)

9

Côte d'Ivoire

Civil War and Regime Change (2002–11)

AS THE WARS in Liberia and Sierra Leone wound down, another conflagration began in neighboring Côte d'Ivoire. Stemming from structural
inequalities in the political economy, and from regional instability generated by the conflicts in Liberia and Sierra Leone, the Ivoirian civil war
lasted from 2002 through 2011 and consumed as many as 13,000 lives.
External actors again intervened to shape the outcome. Multilateral entities, neighboring countries, and the former colonial power claimed
that they acted to restore regional stability and protect civilian lives.
However, in Côte d'Ivoire as elsewhere, they also promoted their own
political and economic agendas. Some mediated between the warring
factions but also fanned the flames. Members of ECOWAS, which sponsored a peacekeeping force, were far from neutral: Liberia and Burkina
Faso supported rebel factions, while other members backed the government. Roving bands of alienated, impoverished youths, no longer at war
in Liberia and Sierra Leone, sold their services to whoever would pay,
wreaking havoc and committing serious human rights abuses against the
civilian population.

The multilateral actors that intervened in Côte d'Ivoire included
bodies that were global (the UN), regional (the AU), and subregional
(ECOWAS). Their actions—or failure to act—were deeply influenced by
the particular interests of their members. ECOWAS dispatched a peacekeeping force that became a party to the conflict, while AU mediators
sent mixed messages that reflected the lack of internal consensus. France,
the former imperial power, played a dominant role in multilateral interventions in Côte d'Ivoire and also intervened bilaterally. It deployed a
large body of troops and staged significant military operations inside the

country, siding first with one side, then the other—as both sides accused Paris of blocking their victories. The UN established a peacekeeping mission once the conflict was officially over and joined French troops in military operations after the peace accord collapsed. Deemed by many Ivoirians to be representing French interests, the UN, like France, was tarred with the brush of neocolonialism.

This chapter examines foreign intervention in Côte d'Ivoire from 2002 to 2011. It begins with a discussion of inequalities that originated in the colonial and independence periods, which set the stage for the twenty-first-century conflict. External intervention was justified on the basis of the response to instability/responsibility to protect paradigm and was influenced by increasing international concern for honoring elections deemed free and fair by neutral observers. Although the conflict coincided with the post–September 2001 war on terror, terrorism was not a motivating factor in this case. As in Liberia and Sierra Leone, foreign actors interceded in Côte d'Ivoire with a variety of motives, and their undertakings had both positive and negative results. Although the conflict was eventually quelled, external intervention aggravated tensions over identity, citizenship rights, and access to resources, and conflicting interests within multilateral entities weakened their mandates and undermined peace agreements. The externally backed accords had only weak support from warring parties and had received little input from civil society organizations. Underlying grievances lingered, and only the losing side was held accountable for abuses perpetrated during the war.

Setting the Stage:
The Colonial and Postcolonial Context (1893–2002)

Claimed as a French colony in 1893, Côte d'Ivoire gained political independence in 1960 but retained close political, economic, and military ties to its former ruler. The new country was considered a model for developing African nations. The first two decades after independence were characterized by economic stability and prosperity for the country as a whole, although the benefits were unevenly distributed. The so-called "Ivoirian miracle" masked sharp divisions between haves and have-nots, which were marked by cleavages with regional and religious dimensions. The rich cocoa- and coffee-producing south was populated primarily by Christians and adherents of indigenous religions, while the less developed, predominantly Muslim north was forced to export laborers to work on the southern plantations. During the colonial period, residents of neighboring territories, notably Upper Volta (now Burkina Faso) and to a lesser extent Mali and Guinea, were brought to Côte d'Ivoire to work on cocoa and coffee plantations in the southeastern and central regions. After independence, many migrants remained, and their descendants contributed to growing ethnic and religious diversity in those regions.

President Félix Houphouët-Boigny, who ruled the country from 1960 to 1993, had exceptionally close ties to France and had served as a minister in the French government before independence. A Western-educated Christian, Baule chief, and prosperous planter, Houphouët-Boigny was among the African elites who had advanced under colonialism. During his three decades in power, he continued the economic policies of his colonial predecessors. He recruited migrants from other parts of Côte d'Ivoire, and from the neighboring countries of Burkina Faso, Mali, and Guinea, to work in the plantation economy, particularly on newly opened farms in the southwest. Baule farmers, who had originally inhabited the central region, were among the greatest beneficiaries of the southwestern expansion. The president generated strong political support by granting newcomers land rights in exchange for their labor. As a result, immigrants from neighboring countries and their descendants often outnumbered the original inhabitants, who frequently constituted less than one-third of the local population. Houphouët-Boigny's Democratic Party of Côte d'Ivoire (PDCI) also granted voting rights to immigrants, thus giving "strangers" control over local politics and bolstering the president's political base.

When times were good, these policies benefited the south but neglected the north in terms of resources, power, and services. When the cash crop economy failed, fallout from the Houphouët-Boigny program ignited regional and ethnic conflicts. The turning point came in the mid-1980s, when Côte d'Ivoire was struck by a severe economic crisis, triggered by worldwide oil price increases and plummeting international commodity prices. Cocoa and coffee, the country's primary exports and main sources of revenue, were especially hard hit, and Côte d'Ivoire began to accumulate enormous international debts. IMF-mandated austerity measures contributed to the crisis. In early 1990, IMF prescriptions led to massive pay cuts and layoffs for public employees, which in turn sparked protests by students, soldiers, and civil servants. Educated young men who were no longer able to find work in the urban areas began to return to their rural homes. Resentful of their diminished status, they made scapegoats of immigrant farmers, some of whom had grown wealthy while indigenous families had grown poorer. Alienated youths, whose numbers surged as the population grew, encouraged their communities to reclaim their patrimonial lands.[1]

Meanwhile, Ivoirian prodemocracy activists demanded an end to Houphouët-Boigny's autocratic rule, and France applied pressure from outside. In June 1990, burdened by commitments to failing economies and worried by popular unrest in Côte d'Ivoire, Zaire, and other francophone countries, Paris adopted a new approach to foreign aid. President François Mitterrand, a member of the French Socialist Party, informed French clients that there could be no development without democracy; henceforth, economic assistance would be tied to democratic reforms and human rights practices. Longtime dictators embarked on superficial reforms to establish a veneer of multiparty democracy that would protect their special relationships with France.

In October 1990, Côte d'Ivoire held its first multiparty elections since independence. Benefiting from the votes of immigrants, Houphouët-Boigny overwhelmed his rival, Laurent Gbagbo. A history professor with a doctorate from the Sorbonne, Gbagbo was a Christian and a member of the Bété ethnic group, which was indigenous to Côte d'Ivoire's southwestern region. He led the socialist Ivoirian Popular Front (FPI) and was especially popular among students and intellectuals. Although Houphouët-Boigny won the presidential elections, he was forced to allow others into his inner circle. To shore up his base, he appointed as prime minister Alassane Dramane Ouattara, a Muslim northerner and member of the Jula ethnic group whose professional qualifications included a PhD in economics from the University of Pennsylvania, a long career at the IMF, and a term as governor of the Central Bank of West African States.

Following Houphouët-Boigny's death in December 1993, Henri Konan Bédié, president of the National Assembly and Houphouët-Boigny's protégé in the PDCI, assumed the reins of power. Like his predecessor, Bédié was a Christian and a member of the Baule ethnic group. The new president's primary rivals included Prime Minister Ouattara—a fellow member of the PDCI who had acted as president during the last nine months of Houphouët-Boigny's life and who had hoped to succeed him— as well as opposition leader Laurent Gbagbo. Continuing economic decline exacerbated the political tensions. In 1994, France unilaterally devalued the African Financial Community (CFA) franc by 50 percent, effectively doubling the cost of Ivoirian imports.[2] Household income and living standards declined precipitously. Bédié boosted his following by stirring up ethnic and religious hatred. Blaming the country's economic plight on immigrant farmers and laborers and on northerners who shared the immigrants' ethnic and religious affiliations, he promoted the notion of *ivoirité*, developed by PDCI intellectuals, to distinguish people of "authentic" origin (southern) from others (northern and foreign). Reviving the ethnic alliances that had brought Houphouët-Boigny to power three decades earlier, Bédié recruited followers from among the Akan-speaking Baule and Agni peoples. Like the Baule, the Agni were predominantly Christian and had been early producers of cocoa and coffee. Historically, they had lived in the country's southeast. Within months of Houphouët-Boigny's death, the PDCI split. The Baule and Agni largely remained with Bédié, while northerners and immigrants tended to follow Ouattara into the new Rally of Republicans (RDR).

Rather than attempt to win the northern and immigrant vote, Bédié sought to obliterate it. Under his regime, northern candidates were disqualified and large segments of the population were disenfranchised. Members of particular ethnic groups were excluded from the definition of authentic Ivoirians and thus denied the right to vote. Shortly before the October 1995 presidential elections, a hastily passed electoral law prohibited the candidacy of individuals whose parents had been born outside Côte d'Ivoire. The law was intended to target Alassane Ouattara, who had a strong following among northerners and immigrants and whose father was believed to have been born in Burkina Faso. When Ouattara was barred from running, the RDR boycotted the elections. Gbagbo's FPI also staged a stay-at-home to defy Bédié's blatant power grab, and Bédié easily won reelection.

The RDR continued to challenge the dominance of southern Christians in the political arena. The next major opportunity came with presidential elections scheduled for October 2000. In August 1999, Ouattara, who claimed to have documentation that proved his Ivoirian origins, was chosen by the RDR as its candidate. Bédié charged that the documents were forged and launched an investigation. When Ivoirian courts ruled against Ouattara and nullified his nationality certificate, the government issued a warrant for his arrest. Outside the country at the time, Ouattara declined to return. On December 23, 1999, Ivoirian soldiers, angered by unpaid wages and poor living conditions, mutinied. The next day, middle-ranking officers ousted the Bédié regime. General Robert Guéï, a Christian and a member of the Dan ethnic group from the western region, formed the National Committee of Public Salvation. He promised to end corruption and return the country to civilian rule in nine months. French President Jacques Chirac, part of the Gaullist old guard that had favored Houphouët-Boigny's PDCI, advocated military intervention to restore Bédié to power. However, France's socialist prime minister, Lionel Jospin, who favored Gbagbo's socialist party, opposed intervention. With the government divided, France remained on the sidelines for the time being.

In July 2000, a new constitution designed to strengthen Guéï's hold on power was adopted by a popular referendum in which many northerners were not allowed to vote. Article 35 stipulated that candidates for the presidency and their parents all be of Ivoirian birth. On October 6, the Supreme Court, appointed by President Guéï, barred both Ouattara and Bédié from participating in the elections. Ouattara was excluded due to continuing questions about his nationality and Bédié for failing to submit an acceptable medical certificate. President Guéï and Laurent Gbagbo were left as the main contenders. The October 22 elections were boycotted by the two largest parties, whose candidates had been prohibited from running. Most of the disgruntled electorate stayed home, resulting in a voter turnout of only 37 percent. Although preliminary results favored Gbagbo, Guéï declared himself the winner. Protests by hundreds of thousands of Gbagbo supporters forced Guéï to flee the country, and Gbagbo claimed the presidency.[3] Bédié and Ouattara decried the elections as illegitimate and demanded new elections in which they would be permitted to run. The UN, OAU, EU, United States, and South Africa joined their call, while France, under the influence of Prime Minister Jospin and his Socialist Party allies, recognized Gbagbo as the new president.[4]

Gbagbo's ties to French political elites were decades in the making. Targeted by the Houphouët-Boigny regime for his trade union and political activities, Gbagbo had spent much of the 1980s in France, mingling with French intellectuals and members of the ruling Socialist Party. After returning to Côte d'Ivoire in 1988, he condemned French control over the Ivoirian economy and used rhetoric decrying neocolonialism to mobilize unemployed youths, students, and the poor. He was an important figure in the prodemocracy movement, which produced new political parties, civil society organizations, and opposition newspapers. Among these was the Student Federation of Côte d'Ivoire (FESCI), established in April 1990 to promote students' interests and advance the cause of multiparty democracy. When FESCI and the teachers' union mobilized secondary school and university students against the Houphouët-Boigny regime, members of both organizations were subjected to brutal repression and lengthy periods in detention. By 1998, FESCI was dominated by a pro-Gbagbo faction that met violence with violence, targeting not only the government but also members of rival organizations and political parties. Although they employed the rhetoric of human rights, FESCI militants increasingly resembled the criminal gangs and poorly paid soldiers who stole from the working poor to "pay themselves" what they believed they deserved.[5]

Like his student followers, Gbagbo began with appeals for people's rights. In the end, however, he attempted to ride to power by manipulating the fear and resentment of the lower classes, particularly the demographically overwhelmed and politically disenfranchised original inhabitants of the southwest. Over time, his anticolonial, anti-imperialist rhetoric was replaced by the language of nativism and xenophobia commonly employed by his rival, the former president Bédié. Having declared himself president in October 2000, Gbagbo turned his supporters against Ouattara's RDR—and by extension, against all northern and immigrant populations. In his native southwestern region, home to a large immigrant population, Gbagbo expanded his base by stirring up acrimony among the original inhabitants. Challenging them to reclaim the land of their forefathers, he directed their anger against the Jula and Malinke populations, who had roots in Côte d'Ivoire's northern savanna and far west and in Burkina Faso, Mali, and Guinea, and also against the Christian Baule from the central region, who had settled on choice cocoa and coffee lands in the southwest. He mobilized students and unemployed urban youths to pillage and destroy Jula shops and dwellings and attack purported foreigners and regime opponents. Using names, religious affiliations, and ethnic scarifications to determine who was "Ivoirian" and who was not, FESCI along with its militia spinoff, the Young Patriots, and Gbagbo's security forces assaulted, raped, and killed hundreds of civilians with impunity.[6]

In January 2002, Gbagbo announced security sector reforms that would result in the dissolution of a number of ethnically based paramilitary units and the replacement of northern military command-ers by southerners. On September 19, as the plan took shape, hundreds of disgruntled soldiers who were scheduled for demobilization attempted to overthrow the Gbagbo regime. The uprising was put down in Abidjan, the country's largest city and economic capital, but dissident soldiers took control in Bouaké, the country's second-largest city, and in Kor-hogo, the main city in the north. French troops arrived on September 22 to evacuate French nationals and other foreigners, while US Special Operations Forces came to evacuate Americans.

Foreign Intervention in Côte d'Ivoire (2002–3)

Foreign involvement in the conflict began almost immediately. Over the course of the next year, France sent soldiers to protect French citizens, in-vestments, and the government in power. Burkina Faso's President Blaise Compaoré, worried about the impact of a massive return of Burkinabe and their descendants, backed rebel forces that endorsed immigrants' claims to property and citizenship. Liberia, ruled by Charles Taylor, re-taliated for Côte d'Ivoire's support of Liberian rebels by backing Ivoirian rebel movements. Taylor and his associates also used the conflict as a means to continue their plunder of regional resources. ECOWAS and the UN contributed peacekeeping forces that were unable to keep the peace because the parties to the conflict had little interest in ending the war.

On September 28, 2002, President Gbagbo appealed for French intervention on his regime's behalf, claiming that the insurgents were backed by Burkina Faso and Liberia and that Côte d'Ivoire was the vic-tim of foreign aggression. Although Paris characterized the war as an internal affair, France had a significant stake in the outcome. More than 20,000 French citizens lived in Côte d'Ivoire, and French interests held 60 percent of the country's private investments. France responded with its largest intervention in Africa in nearly two decades. Numbering 2,500 troops at the outset, Operation Licorne ultimately included 5,300 soldiers from the French Foreign Legion, special forces, and army. Officially, Paris maintained that it had not interceded on behalf of the Gbagbo gov-ernment; rather, it had sent troops to help keep the peace and to serve as a buffer between the opposing sides. In fact, Paris provided logistical support to Gbagbo's forces, and French troops prevented the dissident soldiers from advancing on Abidjan—thus favoring the Gbagbo regime.

By October, the insurgent soldiers had gained the support of young intellectuals of northern origin. Among them was former student leader Guillaume Soro, a Christian Senufo who had been secretary-general of FESCI from 1995 to 1998, before the pro-Gbagbo faction dominated the organization. Under Soro's leadership, the breakaway troops formed the Patriotic Movement of Côte d'Ivoire (MPCI). Soro also mobilized 1,000 Jula hunter-warriors (*dozos*), about half of whom came from Mali, as well as anti-Gbagbo FESCI members. MPCI rebels and their allies quickly gained control of much of northern Côte d'Ivoire and some of the largest cities in the center. While the dissident soldiers had initially demanded financial compensation and reintegration into the Ivoirian armed forces, MPCI called for the establishment of a new political order that would result in Gbagbo's resignation, free and fair elections, and the end of regional and ethnic discrimination. Meanwhile, the Gbagbo regime mobilized thousands of southern civilians into ethnic militias, and FESCI and other pro-Gbagbo student organizations recruited some 6,000 southern youths into the Young Patriots, igniting a reign of terror in Abidjan.

To protect their own interests and to secure advantage, neighboring countries supported various Ivoirian rebel movements. Hoping to thwart a large return of Burkinabe to an already impoverished nation, Burkina Faso gave significant assistance to the MPCI. Liberian President Charles Taylor played a major role in establishing the Ivoirian Patriotic Movement of the Far West (MPIGO) and the much smaller Movement for Justice and Peace (MJP), both of which operated along the Liberian border and engaged in serious human rights abuses reminiscent of those committed during the Liberian and Sierra Leonean wars.[7] Beyond training, arming, and financing these movements, Taylor sent Sierra Leonean warlord Sam Bockarie and the RUF into western Côte d'Ivoire to fight alongside the Ivoirian rebels. The RUF joined Liberian renegades in a massive looting and killing spree. Gbagbo, in turn, employed European mercenaries and other hired soldiers from Liberia, Sierra Leone, South Africa, and Angola, who sought new wars as their own wound down.

Even as ECOWAS members threw their support to various factions, the West African subregional organization worked with the AU to mediate a resolution to the crisis. These efforts led to a ceasefire agreement in October 2002 between MPCI and the Gbagbo regime and another in January 2003 that included MJP and MPIGO. French troops who had

Photo 9.1. Rebel soldiers on patrol near the Liberian and Guinean borders in western Côte d'Ivoire, May 17, 2003. Photo by Luc Gnago/Reuters.

been part of the Operation Licorne deployment were authorized to monitor the ceasefire. In early January 2003, the French contingent was joined by 1,200 West African soldiers in the ECOWAS Mission in Côte d'Ivoire (ECOMICI), which was funded primarily by France.

In mid-January, French President Jacques Chirac sponsored a new round of peace negotiations in the towns of Linas and Marcoussis near Paris. Participating in the talks were the Gbagbo government, several Ivoirian political organizations, and the three rebel groups, which had united as the New Forces of Côte d'Ivoire (or Forces Nouvelles) under the leadership of Guillaume Soro. On January 24, these groups signed the Linas-Marcoussis Agreement, which was intended to resolve questions of citizenship, land ownership, and eligibility for electoral office. It also provided for the disarmament and demobilization of rebel forces and integration of the diverse fighting forces into a reformed security sector. The signatories agreed to respect the country's territorial integrity and to establish a Government of National Reconciliation that would include representatives of all parties to the agreement. While Gbagbo would remain as the interim president, his dominance would be checked by a consensus prime minister who would wield substantial powers, and the important defense and interior ministries would be led by members of the opposition. The interim government would organize free and fair elections, originally scheduled for October 2005. Article 35 of the constitution would be abrogated and the policy of *ivoirité* disavowed. Despite these measures, deep problems remained. The legal requirements for Ivoirian citizenship continued to discriminate against northern ethnic groups, and the onerous specifications for documentation precluded many from asserting their birthright.

Having mediated the ceasefire and peace negotiations, the international community also monitored the ensuing accord. On January 26, 2003, France and neighboring African states endorsed the Linas-Marcoussis Agreement. The UN Security Council followed suit and on February 4 gave ex post facto approval to the French and ECOWAS military interventions and strengthened their mandate to include the protection of civilians and humanitarian organizations in their operating zones. ECOWAS agreed to contribute 2,000 more troops to its mission. The Security Council deepened its involvement on May 13, when it established the United Nations Mission in Côte d'Ivoire (MINUCI), a peacekeeping mission with both civilian and military components, which was authorized to assist French and ECOWAS troops in monitoring and enforcing the Linas-Marcoussis Agreement. In May and June, the international forces established a confidence zone where armed Ivoirian groups were prohibited and which served as a buffer between the north and south.

Precarious Peace and Postponed Elections (2003–10)

Endorsed by warring parties at the highest levels and monitored by ECOWAS, the AU, and the UN, the Linas-Marcoussis accord failed to bring peace. Treating deeply rooted political, economic, and social problems as technical ones, the mediators presumed that all parties had a stake in abiding by the agreement and established no penalties for noncompliance. However, actors on both sides had reasons to perpetuate the violence. Pressured by France to sign, President Gbagbo complained that the accord was the product of French neocolonial meddling and charged that it undermined the legitimate Ivoirian government. Cognizant that implementation could result in his electoral defeat, he incited ethnic militias to continue their attacks in government-controlled territory and played on divisions within New Forces ranks. Other powerful individuals also profited from the absence of peace. Government officials, loyalist businessmen, and militia leaders enriched themselves from state resources—particularly coffee, cocoa, and oil revenues—as well as from illegal gold mining, rubber tapping, and timber cutting, the alienation of land from "foreigners," and money-laundering networks linked to drug and weapons trafficking. New Forces leaders trafficked guns and diamonds, controlled important cotton and cocoa resources, and levied taxes on trade and transport. Soldiers, militia members, and rebels used their powers of coercion to shake down civilians. None of these parties was anxious to see the return of law and order.

Opposed to a peace that might put an end to their plunder, Gbagbo and his associates encouraged Young Patriots and allied militias to wage bloody street battles, attacking northerners, foreigners, opposition party members, and others whom they blamed for the country's problems. Death squads made up of soldiers, police, and armed civilians conducted targeted assassinations for the Gbagbo regime. Although a peace accord had been signed, massacres of civilians continued, especially in the far west along the Guinean and Liberian frontiers, where government troops, progovernment militias and mercenaries, and rebels carried on the fight. In September 2003, New Forces charged that Gbagbo had retained all real power in his hands and those of his associates; New Forces members had not received their share of ministerial positions, and they had been sidelined from the government. Distrusting Gbagbo's commitment to the accord, rebels refused to disarm, and New Forces ministers withdrew from the government.

In April 2004, as the Linas-Marcoussis Agreement broke down, the UN Security Council transferred the ceasefire monitoring and enforcement powers of ECOWAS and MINUCI to the United Nations Operation in Côte d'Ivoire (UNOCI), a peacekeeping force with a Chapter VII mandate. UNOCI was designed to deploy as many as 6,240 military personnel to observe and monitor the ceasefire and implementation of the agreement and to investigate perceived violations. The new UN force would also assist the Ivoirian government in disarming, demobilizing, and reintegrating combatants, monitoring territorial borders, and organizing elections. While ECOWAS was expected to cede authority to the new UN force, Paris was not. As a result, France remained deeply involved in Côte d'Ivoire on its own terms. The French-run Operation Licorne provided the new UN mission with a rapid reaction force and more than two dozen French officers. Paris also retained its own contingent of some 4,000 troops under French command—and continued to protect French citizens, property, and national interests as it saw fit, just as it had in Rwanda. Seen by many Ivoirians as an occupying force that supported the rebellion, the French troops fueled considerable anti-French sentiment.

In early November 2004, the Gbagbo regime openly defied the Linas-Marcoussis Agreement by launching Operation Dignity, a military venture aimed at reconquering the north. Three days into the campaign, Ivoirian bombs hit a French military base in Bouaké, killing nine French soldiers and wounding thirty-seven. French planes destroyed most of the Ivoirian air force in retaliation. Decrying what he described as French neocolonialism, Gbagbo rallied the Young Patriots and other supporters in Abidjan. When pro-Gbagbo mobs attacked French citizens and property, some 8,000 French citizens and other foreigners left the country. As South African President Thabo Mbeki attempted to mediate under AU auspices, French troops fired on pro-Gbagbo demonstrators, killing dozens. On November 15, the UN Security Council imposed an arms embargo on Côte d'Ivoire, with exceptions made for UN and French troops. It also imposed sanctions on individuals deemed responsible for human rights abuses, war crimes, and obstructing the peace process. Gbagbo supporters charged that the UN, France, and the AU were not neutral parties, but rather, had sided with the former rebels and with Burkina Faso, which had been the rebels' primary backer.

International pressure led to some positive developments—although these measures failed to compensate for other failings. Shortly after the imposition of UN sanctions, the Ivoirian legislature passed bills aimed at resolving citizenship and land ownership issues. In April 2005, Gbagbo issued a presidential decree that suspended Article 35 of the constitution, as mandated by the Linas-Marcoussis Agreement, permitting Ouattara to run for president in elections scheduled for October 2005. However, the elections were postponed at the eleventh hour. Neither Gbagbo's militias nor the New Forces rebels had disarmed. The rebels refused to disarm before Gbagbo left power, and they demanded his departure as a precondition for elections. Gbagbo refused to hold elections before the rebels disarmed, and he declared that he would remain in office until elections took place. The UN and the AU supported Gbagbo's position and extended his term until the end of 2006. However, little progress was made in 2006, the presidential elections scheduled for October were postponed for yet another year, and the UN, AU, and ECOWAS again agreed to let Gbagbo remain in power in the interim.

As the Linas-Marcoussis Agreement foundered, African leaders initiated new rounds of discussions. When the South African–led AU mediation failed to resolve the crisis, Burkina Faso's President Compaoré, the acting president of ECOWAS, stepped in despite his questionable neutrality. In March 2007, following talks held in Burkina Faso's capital, Gbagbo and Soros signed the Ouagadougou Political Agreement (OPA), which was substantially similar to the Linas-Marcoussis accord and did not resolve the longstanding issues that had precipitated the conflict, including the contentious definition of Ivoirian citizenship. However, provisions were made to facilitate *proof* of citizenship for those who met the existing criteria but lacked the requisite documentation.

In contrast to previous agreements, the Ouagadougou process was led by the key Ivoirian players, who had concluded that neither side could win on the battlefield. Although a long-term solution remained elusive, participants in the talks hoped to stop the violence in the short term. The OPA included immediate benefits for the leaders of the warring parties—with the balance tipped in Gbagbo's favor. Gbagbo's presidential powers were guaranteed until such time as elections were held. Soro was made prime minister but was prohibited from running for president. The FPI continued to dominate the government, but New Forces members were appointed to the transitional cabinet. FPI ministers retained the powerful interior and defense portfolios, while New Forces appointees were awarded justice, tourism, and communications. Some leaders from other political parties were assigned to the cabinet, but once again civil society members were left largely on the sidelines. Once more, hopeful signs were overshadowed by harsh realities. Presidential elections, postponed again in 2007, were rescheduled for early 2008. However, those elections were put off until November 2009, and then until March 2010, as a result of continued delays in disarmament and ongoing disputes over citizenship and voter registration. In February 2010, Gbagbo dissolved both the government and the Independent Electoral Commission and delayed the elections one more time.

Contested Elections and Foreign Intervention (2010–11)

The long-delayed presidential elections, which had been postponed six times, finally took place in October and November 2010. By that time, Gbagbo had remained in office for five years beyond his original term— with the sanction of the international community. The incumbent led in the October polling, receiving 38.3 percent of the vote in elections that were viewed by outside observers as flawed, but for the most part free and fair. Ouattara received 32.1 percent of the vote, followed by Bédié, who won 25.2 percent. Because no candidate received a majority, a runoff election was required. Gbagbo's support was primarily in the south and among urban youth, while Ouattara's stronghold was in the north. Bédié, a former head of state with control over the powerful PDCI political machine that had run the country for four decades after independence, found followers in the southern and central regions. Both Ouattara and Bédié had significant backing in the rural areas, where half the voting population lived. Determined to defeat Gbagbo, Ouattara and Bédié had agreed to rally behind the stronger candidate in the event of a runoff. As a result, Bédié, the PDCI, and a number of smaller parties threw their support to Ouattara in the second round of elections, held in November 2010.

In December, the reconstituted Independent Electoral Commission determined that Ouattara had won 54 percent of the vote, while Gbagbo had won 46 percent. The UN representative in Côte d'Ivoire confirmed the results. On Gbagbo's instructions, Côte d'Ivoire's Constitutional Council overruled the electoral commission's findings and annulled the results in nine northern precincts, which had yielded hundreds of thousands of votes. The revised tally granted 51 percent to Gbagbo and 49 percent to Ouattara. Gbagbo refused to relinquish the presidency, and both candidates had themselves sworn in to office. The UN, EU, AU, ECOWAS, France, and the United States recognized Ouattara's victory and urged Gbagbo to step down. However, official positions masked dissention within the ranks. In the UN Security Council, Russia and China, which routinely distanced themselves from Western members on matters of foreign intervention and human rights, criticized the UN's Ouattara endorsement. In the AU, member states that supported Gbagbo's continued claim to the presidency included Gambia, Libya, Mauritania, and Zimbabwe, whose incumbent presidents had come to power through military coups or fraudulent elections. South Africa, which had played a significant role in mediating earlier agreements, suggested a power-sharing arrangement that would allow Gbagbo to retain some control, a position also endorsed by Angola. Other AU members recognized Ouattara's victory or remained neutral. In France, Gbagbo found support among those who opposed President Nicolas Sarkozy and his center-right Union for a Popular Movement, which resulted in the paradox of the left-leaning Socialist Party and the right-wing National Front promoting the same side.

Although most international power holders acknowledged Ouattara as the new president, Gbagbo controlled the state media and an army of 9,000 men. On Gbagbo's orders, Ivoirian borders were sealed, transmissions from international radio and television stations were blocked, and opposition newspapers were banned. The state-run media broadcast xenophobic messages and incited ethnically based violence—reminiscent of Rwanda during the 1994 genocide. In neighborhoods that had supported Ouattara, people were beaten and killed by Ivoirian security forces, and women who had mobilized voters were gang-raped by Gbagbo's soldiers and militias. Ouattara sought refuge in the Hotel du Golf, where he was guarded by 800 UN peacekeepers. On December 18, following attacks on UN peacekeepers by Ivoirian security forces and Young Patriots, Gbagbo ordered all UN and French troops to leave the country. Although the UN refused to decamp, its 9,000 peacekeepers failed to protect civilians against Gbagbo's forces. In the months that followed, at least 3,000 people were killed and as many as 1 million people were displaced as the country spiraled back into war. More than 100,000 Ivoirians fled into Liberia, and thousands of migrant laborers returned to Burkina Faso, Mali, and Guinea.

By March 2011, the most significant African and extracontinental bodies had rallied to Ouattara's side. The AU affirmed its binding recognition of Ouattara as the duly elected president, and ECOWAS called on the UN Security Council to strengthen its mandate in Côte d'Ivoire. The consensus of key African organizations was critical to the passage of a tough Security Council resolution on March 30 that allowed French and UN forces to protect Ivoirian civilians from sophisticated weapons in Gbagbo's arsenal. When the international forces destroyed the heavy weapons that protected Gbagbo's residence, they tipped the balance in favor of his opponents. New Forces combatants, reconstituted as the pro-Ouattara Republican Forces of Côte d'Ivoire (FRCI), arrived in

Photo 9.2. Anti-Gbagbo protester carries a sign that reads, "Gbagbo—too much blood was spilled because of you." Abobo neighborhood, Abidjan, March 3, 2011. Photo by Luc Gnago/Reuters.

Abidjan on March 31, 2011, and some 50,000 members of Gbagbo's military and security forces defected to join them.

With its focus on Gbagbo and his supporters, the Security Council resolution failed to protect civilians from Ouattara's forces. Human Rights Watch charged that in their campaign to take power, Ouattara followers collectively punished populations regarded as Gbagbo proponents—raping, pillaging, and executing some 1,000 civilians in the far west, then destroying their villages and food supplies. Victims were targeted on the basis of ethnicity, place of residence, or age. The pro-Ouattara forces quickly took control of most of the country, and when they reached Abidjan, members of ethnic groups perceived to be aligned with Gbagbo were again targeted. Although Gbagbo remained in the presidential palace, Ouattara gained command of the state-run television station. French troops and UN peacekeepers took Abidjan's airport, allowing airplanes to land and foreigners to be evacuated. On April 4, following attacks on the UN compound by pro-Gbagbo partisans, French and UN forces conducted military strikes on Gbagbo's home, offices, and military bases and engaged in ground operations in Abidjan. Paris claimed that its objective was to neutralize weapons that had been used against civilians, which was covered by its UN mandate, rather than regime change, which was not.

If regime change was not the stated objective of the French-UN mission, it was the underlying goal. On April 5, when Gbagbo's generals ordered their soldiers to cease fighting and to surrender their weapons to UN forces, France demanded that Gbagbo officially recognize Ouattara as the country's legitimate president. When Gbagbo refused, French and UN forces continued their assault on the presidential residence. On April 11, Ouattara's forces arrested Gbagbo and his wife Simone, as French helicopters hovered overhead. The unofficial objective had been achieved.

President Alassane Ouattara took office on May 21, 2011, and was elected to a second term in 2015. During his tenure, Côte d'Ivoire, like its neighbors, took important steps toward establishing a new order. Transparent multiparty elections were instituted. Presidential and legislative elections, held in 2015 and 2016, were deemed free and fair by international observers. A new constitution, which removed the controversial Article 35 nationality clause, was adopted by popular referendum, and the National Commission for Reconciliation and Compensation for Victims identified 316,000 victims of political violence since 1990 who might be eligible for reparations.

However, once again, significant grievances were not addressed and serious problems remained. Local conflicts over land and identity continued to fester, provoking new cycles of violence. Those with power continued to act with impunity. While former president Laurent Gbagbo, Young Patriots leader Charles Blé Goudé, and other high-level associates were prosecuted for war crimes and human rights abuses, President Ouattara refused to hold his own loyalists accountable. By the end of 2017, no pro-Ouattara leaders had been charged for abuses committed during the 2002–3 civil war. Although national courts had indicted some pro-Ouattara military commanders for crimes committed in 2010–11, none had been brought to trial, and several retained important positions in the armed forces. Little progress had been made in security sector reform. Although the heads of the army, police, and paramilitary gendarmes had been replaced, high-level commanders and the rank and file continued to abuse their powers. The security forces trafficked in cocoa, diamonds, and other natural resources and extorted money from civilians at illegal checkpoints and through unofficial "taxation." Gender violence remained widespread and unprosecuted. Despite these ominous signs, in 2017 UNOCI closed up shop and returned home, concluding that its mission had been accomplished.

Conclusion

In Côte d'Ivoire, as in Liberia and Sierra Leone, outsiders intervened with mixed motives, and their ventures had mixed results. Most external actors justified their involvement as a response to instability. Some were inspired by the responsibility to protect civilians and the sanctity of free and fair elections; others were driven by the desire for resources and power. In some instances, foreign intervention exacerbated tensions over identity, citizenship rights, and access to resources. This was especially true in the case of bilateral intervention, when the interests of external powers came to the fore. In other instances, foreign intervention served to lessen the conflict, which was more often the case when multilateral peacekeeping forces were involved. However, the effectiveness of peacekeeping missions was undermined by conflicting interests among constituent members, which resulted in inadequate mandates and continued support for warring parties that sabotaged peace agreements.

Peace accords were the product of struggle that reflected the interests of outside powers as much as those of internal entities. In Côte d'Ivoire, as elsewhere, civil society organizations were sidelined from the peace process. The final agreements were often signed under duress by parties that had no interest in implementing them. From 2003 to 2010, France, ECOWAS, and the UN failed to convince warring sides to implement the accords they had signed. For many contestants, the continuation of war meant a license to plunder, while peace imposed limits on access to power and wealth. With regional peace and security in jeopardy, France and the UN facilitated regime change in 2011, helping President-elect Ouattara remove his recalcitrant predecessor, Laurent Gbagbo, from power.

As Côte d'Ivoire struggled to build peace and democracy, other prodemocracy forces were gathering force north of the Sahara, and a number of conflicts ensued. Foreign intervention in North Africa during the Arab Spring uprisings and their aftermath (2011–17) shaped the outcomes in important ways. Chapter 10 focuses on external involvement in Tunisia, Egypt, and Libya during this period.

Suggested Reading

Two recommended books provide historical background that sheds light on the origins of the Ivoirian civil war. Aristide Zolberg, *One-Party Government in the Ivory Coast*, rev. ed. (Princeton, NJ: Princeton University Press, 1969), examines the political history of Côte d'Ivoire from the colonial period through the first decade of independence, focusing specifically on the ways in which Houphouët-Boigny's PDCI monopolized power, bought allies, co-opted opponents, and promoted ethnic divisions. Mike McGovern, *Making War in Côte d'Ivoire* (Chicago: University of Chicago Press, 2011), investigates the political, economic, social, and cultural foundations of the war, exploring tensions over identity-based rights and access to land, power, and resources.

Several articles explore the mobilization of ethnic groups as a method of gaining access to power and resources. See especially Jeanne Maddox Toungara, "Ethnicity and Political Crisis in Côte d'Ivoire," *Journal of Democracy* 12, no. 3 (July 2001): 63–72; Ruth Marshall-Fratani, "The War of 'Who Is Who': Autochthony, Nationalism, and Citizenship in the Ivoirian Crisis," *African Studies Review* 49, no. 2 (2006): 9–43; Richard Banégas, "Côte d'Ivoire: Patriotism, Ethnonationalism and Other African Modes of Self-Writing," *African Affairs* 105, no. 421 (2006): 535–52; Richard Banégas and Ruth Marshall-Fratani, "Côte d'Ivoire: Negotiating Identity and Citizenship," in *African Guerrillas: Raging Against the Machine*, ed. Morten Bøås and Kevin C. Dunn (Boulder, CO: Lynne Rienner, 2007), 81–111; and Bronwen Manby, *Struggles for Citizenship in Africa* (London: Zed Books, 2009).

The mobilization of youth and their violent tactics are investigated in Human Rights Watch, *"The Best School": Student Violence, Impunity, and the Crisis in Côte d'Ivoire* (New York: Human Rights Watch, 2008).

Two recommended sources examine the objectives and dynamics of the New Forces rebel movement and its allied hunter-warriors: Daniel Balint-Kurti, *Côte d'Ivoire's Forces Nouvelles*, Africa Programme Armed Non-State Actors Series (London: Chatham House, 2007); and Thomas J. Bassett, "Dangerous Pursuits: Hunter Associations (*Donzo Ton*) and National Politics in Côte d'Ivoire," *Africa* 73, no. 1 (2003): 1–30.

The regional components of the crisis, including the legacy of the Liberian and Sierra Leonean wars, are illuminated in Human Rights Watch, *Youth, Poverty and Blood: The Lethal Legacy of West Africa's*

Regional Warriors (New York: Human Rights Watch, 2005); and Global Witness, *The Usual Suspects: Liberia's Weapons and Mercenaries in Côte d'Ivoire and Sierra Leone* (London: Global Witness, 2003).

The role of resources in fueling the conflict is examined in Global Witness, *Hot Chocolate: How Cocoa Fuelled the Conflict in Côte d'Ivoire* (Washington, DC: Global Witness Publishing, 2007).

Several works consider the history, motivations, and impact of French intervention. Elizabeth Schmidt, *Foreign Intervention in Africa: From the Cold War to the War on Terror* (New York: Cambridge University Press, 2013), chap. 7, provides an overview of French political, economic, and military interventions in postcolonial Africa. Bruno Charbonneau, *France and the New Imperialism: Security Policy in Sub-Saharan Africa* (Burlington, VT: Ashgate, 2008), examines the French security and development policies in Africa that caused instability and furthered subordination and dependency. The Ivoirian case study illustrates how France embraced new norms of multilateralism and Africanization while continuing to promote its national interests in ways that caused and perpetuated conflict. Contributors to Bruno Charbonneau and Tony Chafer, eds., *Peace Operations in the Francophone World: Global Governance Meets Post-Colonialism* (New York: Routledge, 2014), analyze French involvement in peacekeeping, humanitarian interventions, and peace-building operations in francophone countries, including Côte d'Ivoire. Their book is one of the few comprehensive studies on this topic in English. Three works focus on France's hybrid conflict resolution strategy, which combined multilateral with unilateral actions and provided France with international legitimacy while allowing it to promote its own strategic and economic interests. See Maja Bovcon, "France's Conflict Resolution Strategy in Côte d'Ivoire and Its Ethical Implications," *African Studies Quarterly* 11, no. 1 (Fall 2009); Marco Wyss, "The Gendarme Stays in Africa: France's Military Role in Côte d'Ivoire," *African Conflict and Peacebuilding Review* 3, no. 1 (Spring 2013): 81–111; and Marco Wyss, "*Primus Inter Pares?* France and Multi-Actor Peacekeeping in Côte d'Ivoire," in *Peacekeeping in Africa: The Evolving Security Architecture,* ed. Thierry Tardy and Marco Wyss (New York: Routledge, 2014), 132–48. Finally, Bruno Charbonneau, "War and Peace in Côte d'Ivoire: Violence, Agency, and the Local/International Line," in *The Politics of International Intervention: The Tyranny of Peace,* ed. Mandy Turner and Florian P. Kühn (New York:

Routledge, 2016), 179–96, argues that French and UN military actions undermined Gbagbo and facilitated the victory of Ouattara's forces in what was essentially an externally imposed regime change. The influence of the international community beyond France is considered in two recommended works. Alex J. Bellamy and Paul D. Williams, "The New Politics of Protection? Côte d'Ivoire, Libya and the Responsibility to Protect," *International Affairs* 87, no. 4 (July 2011): 825–50, explores the impact of the international norm emphasizing the responsibility to protect civilian lives. Thomas J. Bassett and Scott Straus, "Defending Democracy in Côte d'Ivoire," *Foreign Affairs*, June 16, 2011, assesses the role of the AU and ECOWAS in resolving the Ivoirian crisis.

A number of reports explore the failed peace plans and the reasons for and implications of their failure. See especially several reports by the Brussels-based International Crisis Group: *Côte d'Ivoire: "The War Is Not Yet Over,"* Africa Report 72 (2003); *Côte d'Ivoire: No Peace in Sight,* Africa Report 82 (2004); *Côte d'Ivoire: Can the Ouagadougou Agreement Bring Peace?,* Africa Report 127 (2007); and *Côte d'Ivoire: Is War the Only Option?,* Africa Report 171 (2011). Abu Bakarr Bah, "Democracy and Civil War: Citizenship and Peacemaking in Côte d'Ivoire," *African Affairs* 109, no. 437 (October 2010): 597–615, argues that the peace accords formulated by external powers failed because they did not attend to the underlying causes of the conflict. Agreements developed by Ivoirians, Bah contends, have been more successful because they have addressed fundamental issues like citizenship and have allowed Ivoirians to take ownership of the process.

Three recommended journal articles provide overviews of the crisis that followed the 2010 elections, including the dynamics of pro- and anti-Gbagbo mobilization and the role of external forces. See Richard Banégas, "Briefing: Post-Election Crisis in Côte d'Ivoire: The Gbonhi War," *African Affairs* 110, no. 440 (July 2011): 457–68; Vasco Martins, "The Côte d'Ivoire Crisis in Retrospect," *Portuguese Journal of International Affairs,* no. 5 (Spring/Summer 2011): 72–84; and Giulia Piccolino, "David against Goliath in Côte d'Ivoire? Laurent Gbagbo's War against Global Governance," *African Affairs* 111, no. 442 (January 2012): 1–23. See also Charbonneau, "War and Peace in Côte d'Ivoire" (mentioned previously).

Three reports examine the aftermath of the postelection violence, including the culture of impunity that allowed serious human rights abuses to go unpunished and the failure to resolve underlying political and economic grievances in the far west. See two reports by Human Rights Watch, *"They Killed Them Like It Was Nothing": The Need for Justice for Côte d'Ivoire's Post-Election Crimes* (New York: Human Rights Watch, 2011), and *Afraid and Forgotten: Lawlessness, Rape, and Impunity in Western Côte d'Ivoire* (New York: Human Rights Watch, 2010). See also International Crisis Group, *Côte d'Ivoire's Great West: Key to Reconciliation*, Africa Report 212 (Brussels: International Crisis Group, 2014).

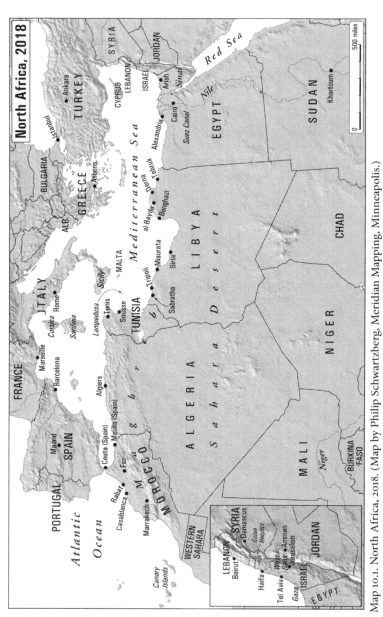

Map 10.1. North Africa, 2018. (Map by Philip Schwartzberg, Meridian Mapping, Minneapolis.)

10

The Arab Spring in North Africa

Popular Resistance, Backlash, and the Struggle for the Future (2011–17)

AS CÔTE D'IVOIRE moved haltingly toward national reconstruction and democracy, popular anger against entrenched dictatorships erupted in the Arab world. In January 2011, civil discontent led to mass uprisings across North Africa and the Middle East. Spearheaded by disenchanted students and other youth, who were joined by labor, professional, and women's organizations, the protests also attracted Islamist groups that had been victims of governmental repression.[1] First in Tunisia, then in Egypt, the protests toppled longstanding regimes in a matter of weeks. The Libyan insurgency, assisted by external military intervention, brought down the dictatorship within several months. Inspired by these successes, protests spread across the region in an awakening that became known as the Arab Spring.[2]

Among the Arab regimes in North Africa, only those in Morocco and Algeria were able to contain the protests. In Morocco, tens of thousands of citizens joined the demonstrations. However, King Mohammed VI offered superficial political reforms that divided the opposition and thwarted a major uprising. In Algeria, where prodemocracy protests had erupted in the late 1980s, fear of the consequences of instability and the inevitable government crackdown led many to keep their distance. The Algerian Awakening of 1988–90 had culminated in massive governmental repression and a bloody civil war (1991–2002), which deeply influenced popular and official responses to the 2011 movement.

Although the dictators in Tunisia, Egypt, and Libya were quickly overthrown, the implementation of fundamental political, economic, and social change in those countries was a more difficult matter.

Transformations of society from the bottom up are protracted processes that require years, if not generations, of struggle. In the interim, societies undergoing transformation are often wracked by instability and violence, and the inevitable backlash from remnants of the old regime and their external supporters serves as a check on progress. Eclectic opposition coalitions, no longer bound by their common struggle, often fracture, with some factions turning against others. In Tunisia, Egypt, and Libya, for instance, Islamist organizations that had been banned under the old regimes assumed powerful roles after their fall. In all three countries, secular liberals and leftists who had allied with the Islamists now opposed them, sometimes joining forces with the old order to counter the Islamists' burgeoning power. The growing presence of Islamist organizations—and, even more so, their violent spinoffs—was an important justification for external intervention during this period.

This chapter focuses on the Arab Spring (2011–13) and its aftermath (2013–17) in North Africa. The cases of Tunisia, Egypt, and Libya are highlighted, but the discussion also touches on Algeria and Morocco, where the protests dissipated quickly and did not instigate significant change. Foreign governments and entities intervened politically in Tunisia and Egypt and militarily in Libya in response to instability and, in the case of Libya, to protect civilian lives. Although never officially acknowledged, regime change was also an objective in Libya. As the conflicts deepened and international terrorist networks joined the fray, the war on terror served to justify further foreign engagement. France, the United States, NATO, the EU, Saudi Arabia, Qatar, and the United Arab Emirates were the most significant external actors. Whereas Western powers generally embraced the status quo during the Arab Spring and only reluctantly supported the democratic opposition, Qatar provided substantial resources to Islamist rivals of the old regimes. Saudi Arabia and the United Arab Emirates backed the dictators in Tunisia and Egypt and allied with the West in supporting regime change in Libya. In Tunisia and Egypt, France and the United States were reluctant to abandon the autocrats who protected their economic and strategic interests. When the Tunisian dictatorship fell, France, joined by the EU, attempted to influence the new order in its former colonial protectorate. The United States focused its attention on Egypt, which together with Israel was the linchpin of its Middle East policy. In both cases, Western powers attempted to minimize the influence of Islamist parties that had come to power through democratic elections, and they supported efforts to oust them. In the case of Libya, an exception to the norm, France rallied NATO to instigate UN-sanctioned airstrikes to protect civilian lives. The United States played a critical role in the air campaign, which ultimately resulted in regime change. When the government fell, secular liberals and moderate Islamists were pushed aside as old regime loyalists, local militias, and jihadis competed to fill the power vacuum.

In all three countries, the prospects for universally respected civil and human rights dissipated as old regime holdovers and secular liberals united in their opposition to Muslim fundamentalists—targeting moderate Islamists who were willing to work within the system as well as violent extremists. Some Western powers and their Middle Eastern allies supported the anti-Islamist actions in word and deed, while other powers supported the Islamist opposition. In Tunisia, the democratically elected Islamist-led coalition government was pressured to step aside to avoid further bloodshed. In Egypt, the military, backed by secular liberals, overthrew the democratically elected Islamist regime and instigated the bloody repression of all forms of opposition. Meanwhile, Libya descended into civil war as disparate forces fought to establish a new order that would promote their values and interests. In each case, outside powers intervened in the local conflicts in an attempt to shape their outcome. In Egypt and Libya, especially, foreign intervention after the Arab Spring intensified the violence and instability. The ouster of democratically elected Islamist governments and the repression of moderates strengthened the appeal of violent extremists; al-Qaeda and Islamic State forces soon flourished where none had been before.

Setting the Stage: Foreign Interests in North Africa (1960–2017)

In the decades preceding the Arab Spring uprisings, North Africa and the Middle East were dominated by neopatrimonial states. Power was concentrated in the hands of autocrats who distributed positions and resources to family members and associates and treated state assets as their own. Some states were ruled by monarchs, while others were run by secular presidential regimes—the so-called Arab republics—that had overthrown monarchies and embraced Arab nationalism during the periods of decolonization and the Cold War. Like the monarchies they had cast aside, the Arab republics had become bastions of personal rule characterized by nepotism, corruption, and political repression.[3] Fraudulent elections and the banning or repression of the political opposition belied their claims to republican status. Most regimes of both types had strong ties to the West, which offered political, economic, and military benefits in exchange for oil, natural gas, and participation in Western-led counterterrorism efforts.

In North Africa, as in the sub-Saharan region, France developed close relationships with leaders who assumed power after political independence, signing partnership agreements that protected French economic, strategic, and security interests. After Algeria's independence in 1962, French Arab policy supported secular nationalism in North Africa and the Middle East. The perceived anglophone menace loomed large in these regions, as it did in sub-Saharan Africa. France hoped to displace British dominance in its historical spheres of operation and to forestall the growth of US influence. During the 1990s, however, French relations with the Arab world deteriorated. France had joined the US-led coalition against Iraq in the First Gulf War (1990–91), and during the Algerian Civil War (1991–2002) France had maintained close ties to President Liamine Zéroual, a former general whose army brutally suppressed the Islamist opposition and was responsible for tens of thousands of civilian deaths. A series of bombings in France in 1995 by the Algerian-based Armed Islamic Group, followed by al-Qaeda's attacks on the United States in September 2001, prompted France to join the US war on terror, which deepened French ties to dictatorships that repressed Islamists.

As French influence in North Africa weakened, France sought support from other EU countries that shared its interest in promoting stable, pro-Western governments in the Mediterranean basin. In 2008, Paris spearheaded the establishment of the Union for the Mediterranean, which eventually included all EU member states, other European countries, and the North African nations of Algeria, Egypt, Mauritania, Morocco, and Tunisia. Although the Union embraced a broader mission, the goals of ensuring European access to North African natural gas, combatting terrorism, and stanching the flow of African migrants to Europe were among the European members' primary considerations.

Concerns about terrorism and energy resources also shaped US policies toward North Africa. During the periods of decolonization and the Cold War, the United States had supported corrupt dictators in North Africa and the Middle East who safeguarded US oil interests but whose policies led to widespread poverty, unemployment, and injustice in their countries. To maintain their hold on power, US-backed strongmen employed harsh security measures and manipulated regional, ethnic, and clan differences. They co-opted or destroyed institutions and organizations that might serve as alternative power bases; many were especially ruthless toward Islamists. Equally hostile to Islamist movements, the US government ignored its allies' human rights abuses and provided them with weapons and funding. Just as some US officials had confounded radical nationalists with communists during the Cold War, many in its aftermath failed to distinguish between organizations that promoted Islamic values in government and the minority that employed terrorism to accomplish their goals. The September 11, 2001, terrorist attacks on the United States and the ensuing war on terror exacerbated this tendency.

For many in the Muslim world, the US war on terror appeared to be a war against Islam. The words and actions of President George W. Bush seemed to confirm their suspicions. Five days after the 2001 attacks, the US president evoked images of Christian knights battling Saracens in the Holy Land when he cautioned, "This crusade, this war on terrorism is going to take a while."[4] A few days later, he warned, "Every nation in every region now has a decision to make: Either you are with us or you are with the terrorists."[5] Under the auspices of the war on terror, the Bush administration launched wars in Afghanistan in 2001 and Iraq in 2003, which had devastating consequences for citizens of those countries and for their neighbors. These wars also led to the expansion of al-Qaeda into new territories and to the emergence of the Islamic State.

Critics hoped that US policies toward the Muslim world would change under the leadership of Barack Obama, the first US president of African descent and one whose family members included Muslims. Four months after taking office, President Obama traveled to Egypt, where he acknowledged that the conflict between the Muslim and Western worlds had been "fed by colonialism that denied rights and opportunities to many Muslims, and a Cold War in which Muslim-majority countries were too often treated as proxies without regard to their own aspirations."[6] However, the Obama administration was soon consumed by its own war on terror. Although the administration withdrew US forces from Iraq in 2011, it oversaw a major troop surge in Afghanistan in 2009–12, devastating drone strikes in Pakistan and Yemen, and the introduction of Special Operations Forces into many predominantly Muslim countries. Moreover, the Obama administration continued the longstanding US practice of promoting the interests of Israel over the UN-sanctioned right of Palestinians to an independent state. All of these factors continued to degrade the reputation of the United States in largely Muslim countries.

When the Arab Spring erupted in 2011, the Obama administration struggled to balance US strategic and economic interests with rhetorical support for democracy. Its response to the uprisings was cautious and inconsistent. The administration gave verbal encouragement to the Tunisian protesters only after they had driven the long-reigning dictator from power, and it was slow to embrace the prodemocracy movement in Egypt. The United States eventually supported military action against the Qaddafi regime in Libya, but it continued to back autocratic rulers in Bahrain, Saudi Arabia, and Yemen, and it kept the disparate Syrian opposition movement at arm's length.

The United States and other Western powers thus faced a conundrum that pitted their democratic values against their antipathy toward the people's choice. This tension was especially evident in North Africa. In the Arab Spring's aftermath, Islamist parties dominated popular elections in Tunisia and Egypt, and their members assumed powerful roles in Libya. The Islamist parties were opposed by secular forces, which had joined them in confronting the old regimes, and by remnants of the previous orders. The ability of Islamists to win elections after years of banning and repression by Western-backed governments seemed to belie the common view that adherents of political Islam could not attain power by working within the system. However, a series of events—the ouster of the Islamist government in Egypt by a military coup (2013), the pressures placed on the Islamist-led government in Tunisia that resulted in its abdication (2014), and the disintegration of Libya into warring factions that set Islamists against Qaddafi loyalists and other secular forces—reinforced the earlier consensus. Renewed repression and marginalization of Islamists after the Arab Spring, and the tacit or open support of these measures by Western powers, resulted in new cycles of radicalization, violence, and anti-Western sentiment.

Western concerns conformed with those of the majority of Arab Gulf states, which tended to view the Arab Spring uprisings as a challenge to their authority. The monarchies of Saudi Arabia and the United Arab Emirates had long supported fundamentalist Islamic movements to counter Arab nationalism and other opponents of the ruling regimes.[7] In the 1950s and 1960s, the two countries had opened their doors to Egyptian

Muslim Brotherhood members who fled repression under Gamal Abdel Nasser's Arab nationalist government. Educated and upwardly mobile, many of these Egyptians achieved important positions in Saudi and Emirati educational, judicial, and private sectors, where a large number grew extremely wealthy. As economic inequality deepened in both countries, however, and Muslim Brothers harnessed that discontent, the two monarchies began to view the organization as a threat on par with violent extremists. During the Arab Spring, when Brotherhood-affiliated parties dominated popular elections in several North African countries, Saudi Arabia and the United Arab Emirates supported old regime remnants against moderate Islamists with significant popular followings. Both states provided substantial resources to anti-Islamist forces in Egypt and Libya, which became battlegrounds for intra-Gulf rivalries that opposed Saudi Arabia and the United Arab Emirates against Qatar.

An exception among the Gulf states, Qatar provided substantial support to participants in the Arab Spring revolts, particularly to moderate Islamists associated with the Muslim Brotherhood. Like Saudi Arabia and the United Arab Emirates, Qatar had offered refuge to Egyptian Muslim Brotherhood members in the 1950s and 1960s. In subsequent years, it had offered safe haven to a variety of Islamists and dissidents from many parts of the Muslim world, and in the 1990s it replaced Saudi Arabia as the Muslim Brotherhood's primary sponsor.

A small emirate, rich in oil and liquefied natural gas, Qatar had leveraged its wealth and strategic location into significant regional influence from the early 1990s onward. Having supported the US-led coalition during the First Gulf War (1990–91), Qatar joined in US counterterrorism efforts after September 2001, and in 2003 it replaced Saudi Arabia as the forward headquarters of the US military's Central Command (CENTCOM). The same year, a new constitution placed international mediation at the center of Qatar's foreign policy priorities. In the three years that preceded the Arab Spring, Qatar mediated talks concerning conflicts in Yemen, Lebanon, and Darfur, as well as disputes between Sudan and Chad and between Djibouti and Eritrea. In 2011–12, Qatar assumed the presidency of the Arab League. Having established itself as a regional leader with an increasingly global reach, Qatar viewed the 2011 uprisings as an opportunity to further augment its influence. In Tunisia and Egypt, the emirate used its vast financial resources and powerful Al Jazeera media network to support Islamist opposition movements. In Libya, Qatar allied with the West and mobilized Arab support for the NATO-led ouster of the Qaddafi regime. During the civil war that ensued, Qatar supported Islamist rebels that opposed remnants of the old regime that had joined the coalition backed by Saudi Arabia, the United Arab Emirates, and the West.

Tunisia, Part 1:
Popular Uprising and the End of a Dictatorship (2011–13)

The Arab Spring began in Tunisia, where a popular revolt overthrew a dictatorship backed by Western powers and established a democratically elected coalition government dominated by a once-banned Islamist party. In December 2010, urban workers, small business owners, professionals, and human rights activists—led by trade union, student, professional, and women's organizations—instigated massive street protests and general strikes against the regime of President Zine el-Abidine Ben Ali, a French-trained army officer who had seized power in 1987. Enraged by the country's endemic poverty, unemployment, and governmental corruption, and a regime that engaged in torture, rape, and murder, thousands of protesters took to the streets. On January 14, 2011, after twenty-nine days of demonstrations, Ben Ali ceded power and sought refuge in Saudi Arabia. The United States and France, which had regarded the Ben Ali regime as a bulwark against radical Islam and the guarantor of their economic interests, withheld even verbal support for the demonstrators until after Ben Ali's ouster.

In October 2011, Tunisian citizens elected a National Constituent Assembly that was charged with drafting a new constitution and appointing a transitional government. With more than 90 percent of Tunisia's registered voters participating, Ennahda, an Islamist party influenced by Egypt's Muslim Brotherhood, won a plurality of seats nationwide and in nearly every district. In response to its banning and repression under Ben Ali, Ennahda embraced human rights, democratic pluralism, and an inclusive, tolerant form of Islamism. Although Islamists had not played a significant role in the uprising, after Ben Ali's ouster Ennahda established a solid organizational base throughout the country, finding support among professionals, office workers, and small entrepreneurs, and building alliances with secular prodemocracy parties, trade unionists, and civil society activists. Its efforts were bolstered by financial support from Qatar and media access through Qatar's Al Jazeera network. The October elections resulted in the formation of an Ennahda-led coalition government that included two secular center-left parties.

10.1. Tunisians protest the Ben Ali regime, Kasbah Square, Tunis, January 28, 2011. Photo by Leomaros.

In the two years following the fall of the old regime, Tunisian civil society was vibrant, but unemployment continued to rise, with youth unemployment reaching 30 percent. Regional inequalities remained, and the security situation was fragile. Under pressure from diverse constituencies, the National Constituent Assembly deadlocked and constitution writing stalled. Dissatisfied with the pace of change, many Tunisians decried the lack of justice for victims of the Ben Ali regime and the government's failure to hold the perpetrators accountable. Taking advantage of the paralysis, Ansar al-Shari'a (Followers of Islamic Law) in Tunisia, a local insurgency group associated with al-Qaeda, and other extremist groups engaged in a number of violent actions. In September 2012, hundreds of protesters attacked the US Embassy in Tunis to assail a US-made video that denigrated the Prophet Muhammad. Ansar al-Shari'a endorsed the attack, while the Ennahda government condemned it. In 2013, Ansar al-Shari'a was linked to the assassination of two leftist opposition leaders. Although the assassins had no connection to Ennahda, secular parties accused Ennahda of being soft on violent Muslim extremists.

Tunisia, Part 2: Internal Unrest,
Foreign Pressure, and Political Compromise (2013–17)

By mid-2013, Tunisia's transitional government established after the October 2011 elections had begun to crumble. In July, sixty-five opposition members withdrew from the National Constituent Assembly, which led to the suspension of Tunisia's only elected body. Civil society organizations representing labor, employers, lawyers, and human rights groups moved into the breach. The so-called National Dialogue Quartet mediated months of discussions that resulted in Ennahda's agreement to step aside in January 2014 in favor of an unelected caretaker government dominated by secular parties that would lead the country through parliamentary and presidential elections in October through December of that year.[8] The move was hailed by secular organizations at home and abroad as a peaceful solution formulated by indigenous civil society organizations, in contrast to a violent dispensation imposed by external intervention or a military coup. However, Islamists and other critics decried the forced resignation of an elected Islamist-led government and charged that it was further evidence that Islamists stood little chance of winning and retaining power through peaceful means. Some of the marginalized concluded that violent extremism was the only remaining option.

Before relinquishing power, the Ennahda government signed into law a compromise constitution drafted and approved by the National Constituent Assembly. The product of two years of struggle and debate, the constitution laid the foundations for a secular state featuring separation of powers, an independent judiciary, and respect for universal rights and freedoms, including the rights of women. While freedom of belief, conscience, and expression were guaranteed, Tunisia's Arab identity was acknowledged, and Islam was accepted as the state religion. Under pressure from Western powers and Tunisia's secular civil society organizations, Ennahda had made broad concessions and eliminated reference to the establishment of an Islamic state under shari'a law. Having witnessed the overthrow of Egypt's elected president in July 2013, after his Islamist-dominated government pushed through a constitution that was widely opposed by secular forces, Ennahda was determined to find common ground that would forestall a return to dictatorship or descent into civil war. Although the overwhelming majority of legislators approved the constitution, Ennahda's compromises exacerbated divisions within the party and among Islamists more broadly.

During this period of internal turmoil, elements of the old regime resurfaced, hoping to manipulate popular discontent and fear of terrorism to facilitate a return to power. Under the new caretaker government, most Ben Ali government officials imprisoned after the Arab Spring were released—including the interior minister, who had been in charge of the police, and also the head of the presidential security service. Meanwhile, military tribunals reduced the sentences of police and soldiers who had been found guilty of killing and wounding protesters during the uprising. Several political parties were established by former Ben Ali officials to field candidates in the 2014 parliamentary and presidential elections. Critics warned that prodemocracy and human rights activists were being shunted aside as partisans of the former dictator and violent Muslim extremists struggled for dominance.

These concerns were not allayed by the election results, which promoted the forces of law and order and highlighted the country's regional and class divisions. Nidaa Tounes, a secular party founded in June 2012 to oppose Ennahda, brought together diverse constituents who shared a common opposition to Islamism. It rallied former members of Ben Ali's ruling party as well as secular liberals. Its supporters included the Tunisian General Labor Union—the liberal trade union federation that had spearheaded the Arab Spring uprising—and the Tunisian Confederation of Industry, Trade and Handicrafts, the most important employers' association. Both organizations had played key roles in the National Dialogue Quartet, which undercut the Islamists' power, and neither favored policies that would result in fundamental political, economic, and social change. Instead, they sought greater economic benefits for members of their own groups.

Nidaa Tounes won heavily among the secular middle classes, especially in the northern coastal cities, while Ennahda was favored by poorer marginalized populations, especially in the largely rural south near the Algerian and Libyan borders. Nidaa Tounes won a plurality of votes in the parliamentary elections, with Ennahda taking second place and smaller parties collecting the rest. More than half the new parliamentarians had been members of Ben Ali's party. In the presidential runoff elections, Nidaa Tounes founder Beji Caid Essebsi, who had served in the Ben Ali government and as interim prime minister after the Arab Spring, beat human rights activist and physician Moncef Marzouki, who had held the position of interim president since December 2011. A founder of the center-left secular party Congress for the Republic, Marzouki drew support from poorer marginalized populations, especially in the south. Habib Essid, a US-trained agricultural economist who had served both in the Ben Ali regime and in the Ennahda-led coalition government, was selected by parliament to serve as prime minister. His initial attempt to form a government that excluded Ennahda failed in a no-confidence vote. A second attempt resulted in a government that included Nidaa Tounes, Ennahda, and three smaller parties. Although it was the second-largest parliamentary party, Ennahda was awarded only one of the twenty-four ministerial positions. In January 2016, Ennahda again became the largest parliamentary party following mass resignations from Nidaa Tounes to protest President Essebsi's tightening grip on power and the appointment of his son as party head. Nonetheless, the Nidaa Tounes–led ruling coalition remained at the helm.

Poverty, repression, and marginalization led to the rise of violent Muslim extremism in Tunisia, as it did elsewhere. The Ben Ali regime had tortured and imprisoned large numbers of Islamists and forced many more into exile. Prison and exile provided fertile breeding grounds for extremist ideologies. Hundreds of Tunisians fought against the Soviet occupation of Afghanistan, and thousands joined the jihadi insurgency after Soviet withdrawal. Many rose through the ranks of al-Qaeda. After Ben Ali's ouster, significant numbers of Islamists and Muslim extremists were released from prison and returned from abroad. Many extremists gravitated toward the southern border regions near Algeria and Libya, where gun runners, drug traffickers, and jihadi cells were often interlinked. Local insurgents made contact with al-Qaeda in the Islamic Maghreb in the mountainous region along the Algerian border and also with Libyan jihadis who, by 2014 and 2015, had pledged allegiance to the leader of the Islamic State.

Veterans of the Soviet-Afghan War played a key role in the Tunisian jihadi insurgency, just as they had in Somalia and Sudan. Among the most prominent was Seifallah Ben Hussein (alias, Abu Iyadh al-Tunisi), who had risen through the ranks of al-Qaeda and who founded Ansar al-Shari'a in Tunisia in April 2011. Although the local insurgency group established links with al-Qaeda, some members later pledged allegiance to the leader of the Islamic State. The new Arab Spring freedoms permitted Ansar al-Shari'a extremists to preach and recruit among alienated, unemployed youths of all socioeconomic classes. By 2012, some 30,000 to 40,000 young people had joined the organization. In 2013, in the wake of the US Embassy attack and the assassination of Tunisian political leaders, the Ennahda-led government banned Ansar al-Shari'a in Tunisia and declared it a terrorist organization. Thousands of members left the country to avoid arrest. Some 1,500 Ansar al-Shari'a exiles joined extremist groups in Libya. Others moved on to Mali and Yemen, and an estimated 4,000 joined the insurgency in Syria, where most pledged allegiance to the leader of the Islamic State.

In Tunisia, Ansar al-Shari'a continued to operate underground, while new organizations emerged from its remnants. Intent on undermining the secular state, these organizations sought to destroy the tourism industry—a critical component of the national economy and the primary source of foreign currency. Attacks on Tunisian politicians persisted, but foreign nationals also became targets. In March 2015, gunmen attacked the Bardo National Museum in Tunis, killing twenty-one British, French, and Italian tourists and a Tunisian policeman. Jund al-Khilafah (Soldiers of the Caliphate) in Tunisia, which had trained in Libya and pledged allegiance to the leader of the Islamic State, claimed responsibility. In June, a Tunisian student fired on European tourists at a beach resort in Sousse, killing thirty-eight people and wounding dozens more. That shooter was also reputed to have links to Jund al-Khilafah.

The escalation of terrorist attacks following the installation of the Nidaa Tounes–led government exposed deep differences over methods for combatting violent Muslim extremism. Secularists in the government, many of whom had ties to the Ben Ali dictatorship, advocated strict control of mosques and preachers. Ennahda appointees to the Ministry of Religious Affairs were removed from their positions, even though they had condemned the terrorist attacks and the organizations that sponsored them. The ministry's monitoring commission was abandoned, and its previous responsibility for overseeing mosques was transferred to the police. Mainstream Muslims warned that such actions would make it more difficult for moderates to counter extremist views.

Civil liberties, the fruit of the Arab Spring, were quickly eroded. In early July 2015, the government declared a state of emergency, which permitted suspension of the freedom of assembly and the right to strike. Eighty mosques were shut down and investigated for links to extremists, and two preachers were banned—although neither the preachers nor the closed mosques had connections to the gunmen involved in the recent attacks. Parts of the border with Algeria were sealed off as military zones, and the government announced plans to construct a 100-mile-long wall along the border with Libya, where those implicated in the attacks had trained. On July 25, parliament passed a counterterrorism bill over the protests of Tunisian civil society organizations, including human rights groups, the bar association, and the journalists' union. The new law gave police enhanced monitoring and surveillance powers; it permitted suspects to be held without charge or legal assistance for fifteen days, and it provided for closed hearings in which witnesses could remain anonymous. Individuals who damaged property or caused disorder during demonstrations could be charged with terrorism, and freedom of speech was curtailed by clauses that defined public praise for terrorism as a criminal offense that could incur up to five years' imprisonment. Within months of the law's enactment, Amnesty International warned of growing evidence of arbitrary arrests, torture, sexual violence, and deaths in detention, reminiscent of the Ben Ali regime.

The toppling of Tunisia's Western-backed dictator had opened the door to violent extremist as well as democratic forces. Extremist activity, in turn, paved the way for further foreign intervention. European countries worried about the growing influence of Libyan-based Islamic State groups in Tunisia and cautioned that Tunisia could become a beachhead for future assaults on Europe. Following the 2015 museum and beach attacks, the EU expanded assistance to a Tunisian counterterrorism and security sector reform program and promised increased trade, along with social and economic development aid, in the hope of countering extremist recruitment. The United Kingdom, which lost thirty citizens in the beach attack, provided the Tunisian army with fifty Special Forces trainers, while France and Germany sent military advisors. The United States, which had already sent Special Operations troops to train Tunisian soldiers in counterterrorism tactics, launched surveillance drones from Tunisian bases to monitor Islamic State activity in Libya and included Tunisia's government in its eleven-country Trans-Sahara Counterterrorism Partnership (TSCTP).[9]

Egypt, Part 1: Popular Uprising, Military Intervention, and the Struggle for a New Order (2011–13)

Inspired by prodemocracy demonstrators in Tunisia and seven years of strike actions in their own country, Egyptians also took to the streets to protest a deepening economic crisis, governmental corruption, and political repression that resulted from decades of authoritarian rule. The target of their anger was President Hosni Mubarak, a former air force commander who took office in 1981 and presided over a police state with a widely feared security and intelligence apparatus. During Mubarak's tenure, the military amassed political and economic privileges while the civilian population suffered from rising unemployment, economic hardship, and political maltreatment. Fraudulent elections in November and December 2010 had returned the ruling party to power and decimated the opposition, including the Muslim Brotherhood, which lost eighty-seven of the eighty-eight seats it previously had held. On January 25, 2011, eleven days after Ben Ali's ouster in Tunisia, tens of thousands of Egyptian protesters took to the streets, demanding an end to Mubarak's three-decade reign. Their ranks quickly reached hundreds of thousands, including many striking workers. Riot police cracked down, attacking the demonstrators with water cannons, rubber bullets, tear gas, and concussion grenades.

In Egypt as in Tunisia, foreign powers had sustained the dictatorship. For more than three decades, the United States had served as the country's primary source of military aid and a major source of development assistance. Egypt had been the linchpin of US Middle East policy since 1979, when President Anwar al-Sadat (1970–81) signed a US-brokered peace treaty with Israel that ended more than thirty years of strife between the two countries—but left unresolved the claims of other Arab nations and the Palestinian people, who had not been included in the negotiations.[10] The Egyptian military played a key role in sustaining the treaty, and the United States considered the Mubarak regime (1981–2011) to be critical to the containment of Iran, to the war against al-Qaeda, and to promoting the regional stability that would ensure the security of Israel. Egypt also protected broader strategic and economic interests. The US Air Force routinely flew through Egyptian airspace. Egypt controlled the vital Suez Canal transit route; US Navy vessels passed through the canal as they journeyed to and from the Mediterranean Sea, Persian Gulf, and Indian Ocean, and 8 percent of the world's maritime shipping traversed the canal annually. Because of this special relationship, the United States had provided Egypt with $1.3 billion in military aid each year since 1987, monies that were used to purchase US-made weapons systems, to pay for US training of the Egyptian officer corps, and to hire the services of US defense contractors. It was an army trained and equipped by the United States that ultimately forced Mubarak to relinquish power.

Photo 10.2. A woman protesting the Mubarak government carries a sign that reads, "Mubarak is the worst one in Egypt. Get out Mubarak." Cairo, January 30, 2011. Photo by Floris Van Cauwelaert.

On February 11, 2011, following eighteen days of protests in which some 840 Egyptians were killed, Mubarak stepped down—his hand forced by his own military. While riot police and loyalist militias battled the demonstrators, the army refused to attack them. Determined to protect its status, privileges, and business interests, the army pressured the increasingly isolated president to surrender his authority to the Supreme Council of the Armed Forces. Outside Egypt, many of Mubarak's allies withheld support for the prodemocracy forces until it was certain that the president would not survive—at which point they celebrated his departure. Among those with an eleventh-hour change of heart was US President Barack Obama. Rejecting the counsel of his vice president, national security advisor, and secretaries of state and defense, all of whom cautioned that Mubarak's Egypt was the mainstay of regional stability, Obama urged the strongman to step aside. On February 11, Obama welcomed the resignation of America's longtime ally, proclaiming, "Egyptians have made it clear that nothing less than genuine democracy will carry the day."[11]

Egyptian Islamists did not lead the popular uprising, but like their counterparts in Tunisia, they benefited from the freedoms that resulted. The Muslim Brotherhood played a cautious but supporting role in the protests, concerned that failure could result in repression against the movement. Founded in 1928 and banned in 1954, the Brotherhood had been ruthlessly suppressed by President Gamal Abdel Nasser (1956–70), who viewed Islamists as a threat to his power. Under his authority, thousands of Brotherhood members were arrested and subjected to torture and long prison terms or execution. After Nasser's death, President Sadat released Brotherhood members from prison and allowed them to function openly—although the organization technically remained illegal. Using the Brotherhood to counter the liberal-leftist opposition as well as jihadi extremists, Mubarak permitted Brotherhood members to run for parliament as independents. Dominating Egyptian professional and student associations and using wealth earned in exile to provide social services no longer furnished by the state, the Brotherhood built a strong base of popular support. By 2005, Brotherhood members constituted the largest parliamentary opposition bloc; the regime responded to the new threat with renewed repression. After Mubarak's fall, the Brotherhood's political machine, solidly grounded in both urban and rural areas, far surpassed that of its rivals. Like Ennahda in Tunisia, Egypt's Muslim

Photo 10.3. An Egyptian protester mounts a bronze lion at the entrance to Qasr al-Nil Bridge, Cairo, February 1, 2011. Photo by Zeinab Mohamed.

Brotherhood also benefited from Qatar's financial support and from access to Al Jazeera media. The combination of these factors meant that Islamists were poised to influence, if not dominate, any new political order.

The Supreme Council of the Armed Forces, which had ridden to power on the back of the prodemocracy movement, announced that it would remain in place until presidential elections could be held. In the interim, the council would appoint a prime minister and cabinet, oversee a subordinate parliament, and influence the making of a new constitution. The military's incremental approach to democracy was endorsed by the United States and by many Egyptian liberals and secularists, who worried that early elections would be swept by the Muslim Brotherhood's newly established Freedom and Justice Party. Indeed, a coalition led by that party won a plurality of seats in the November 2011 parliamentary elections and dominated the parliament-appointed constituent assembly charged with writing the constitution.

Egypt's judiciary, which was staffed with Mubarak appointees, and Egypt's privileged military were determined to keep the Islamists at bay. In April 2012, an administrative court suspended the constituent assembly on the grounds that it had been improperly formed. On June 13, martial law, which had been in effect from 1981 through May 31, 2012, was effectively reinstituted as security forces were granted the power to arrest civilians and try them in military courts. The next day, the Supreme Constitutional Court ruled that one-third of the lower house of parliament had been illegally elected, and it ordered that body's dissolution—effectively nullifying elections in which 30 million Egyptians had voted. The military council appointed a new handpicked constituent assembly and issued a constitutional declaration on June 17 that reduced the president to a figurehead, arrogating to itself the final determination on the formation and dissolution of governments and the enactment of legislation.

The military's effective seizure of power on June 17, 2012, coincided with the election of Dr. Mohamed Morsi, a US-trained engineer and leader of the Muslim Brotherhood, to the Egyptian presidency with 51.7 percent of the vote. On June 30, Morsi was sworn in as Egypt's first democratically elected president. In July he struggled with Mubarak holdovers in the state bureaucracy and failed in his attempt to reconvene parliament. On August 12, Morsi reclaimed the power seized by the military by voiding the constitutional declaration that had gutted presidential authority. He also forced his defense minister, army chief of staff, and other generals to resign. Many Egyptians, from Islamists to liberal secularists, applauded his move. Returning the military to the barracks, however incomplete, was widely considered an important achievement for the Morsi presidency.

Challenges to Morsi's authority characterized the months that followed. The second constituent assembly quickly deadlocked, with the liberal and leftist minority opposing the positions taken by the Muslim Brotherhood and Salafi majority. As the secular opposition threatened to boycott the proceedings, demonstrators again took to the streets, this time protesting a growing economic crisis and the lack of movement toward a new political, economic, and social order. The courts, still replete with Mubarak-era judges, obstructed the constitution-writing process and did little to hold accountable Mubarak, his police, and his associates for corruption and human rights abuses. Frustrated by the courts' obstructionism, Morsi issued a decree temporarily exempting himself from judicial oversight in cases of presidential "acts of sovereignty" and matters relating to the protection of the constituent assembly and other elected bodies.[12] Unable to assert control over the military, police, intelligence services, judiciary, state bureaucracy, and political party that had wielded power for more than three decades, Morsi claimed that these measures were needed to guarantee the transition to constitutional democracy. He promised that the presidential powers would be returned to the status quo ante once a new constitution was in place and a new parliament elected. Fearing an Islamist coup, liberal and leftist secularists joined members of the old regime in organizing mass demonstrations that demanded Morsi's resignation.

At the end of November, the constituent assembly approved a draft constitution, authored primarily by Muslim Brotherhood and Salafi representatives and opposed by secular parties and the Coptic Christian Church. The proposed constitution did not grant religion a greater legal role than it had held under Mubarak. Nonetheless, some critics objected to the growing Islamist influence, while others were concerned that individual rights were not protected from future erosion and that the military retained its exemption from legal and parliamentary oversight. The opposition called for a boycott of the constitutional referendum held in December 2012, and only 30 percent of the electorate participated. Of those who cast their ballots, 64 percent approved the constitution: in other words, the constitution was favored by less than 20 percent of eligible voters. The opposition decried the constitution as illegitimate and urged the populace to prevent its implementation. During the first half of 2013, popular discontent intensified. Demonstrations demanding political reforms and strikes over poor wages and working conditions became increasingly frequent.

On June 30, 2013, the first anniversary of President Morsi's inauguration, millions of demonstrators took to the streets to protest the country's continuing political and economic crisis and to call for the president's removal. Egyptian police—holdovers from the Mubarak era who resented being governed by the Muslim Brotherhood members they once had imprisoned—refused to protect Brotherhood offices and supporters. Some even joined the anti-Morsi demonstrations. On July 1, the Supreme Council of the Armed Forces demanded that Morsi meet the public's demands or face military intervention. Two days later, the army ousted the president in a coup d'état and took him into custody. The Supreme Council arrested dozens of senior Brotherhood leaders, suspended the constitution, and installed an interim government led by Adly Mansour, chief justice of the Supreme Constitutional Court and a Mubarak appointee. The Brotherhood's media were shut down, and Morsi was held incommunicado in an undisclosed location. Prominent liberals, Muslim and Christian clerics, and even the Salafist al-Nour Party, which felt sidelined by the Morsi government, endorsed the military takeover.

In the end, the faceoff was one between "democrats who are not liberals and liberals who are not democrats."[13] The Muslim Brotherhood supported the democratic electoral process that had brought it to power, but not democratic pluralism or the protection of minority rights. Liberals and leftists, in contrast, defended minority rights, personal freedoms, and civil liberties, but not the elections that had brought Islamists to power. Rather than mobilizing the population to defeat Morsi in the next election, they called on the army to topple a democratically elected president. In the process, the old regime was restored and strengthened, and repression grew even more brutal than it had been in the Mubarak era.

Egypt, Part 2: Counterrevolution and the Return to Military Rule (2013–17)

Western powers, which had supported the Mubarak regime, stood by as remnants of the Mubarak military reasserted control. The Obama administration had advance notice of the coup. After President Morsi rejected an American plea that he accept a new prime minister and cabinet chosen by someone else, National Security Advisor Susan Rice warned his foreign policy advisor that the military takeover was about to begin. After the army seized power, President Obama called on the Egyptian armed forces "to return full authority back to a democratically elected civilian government as soon as possible through an inclusive and transparent process."[14] However, he pointedly did not demand the reinstatement of the democratically elected Morsi government. Nor did he characterize the military action as a coup, a label that would have prevented the annual transfer of $1.3 billion in US military aid.[15] The EU also remained on the sidelines. Catherine Ashton, the EU's foreign affairs and security policy chief, expressed sentiments similar to those of the US president. Her views were echoed by the UK, France, and Germany. After the coup, a dozen EU member states continued their role as Egypt's primary suppliers of military and police equipment.

With internal and external forces lined up against them, tens of thousands of Morsi supporters took to the streets, demanding the president's return to office. In the month that followed, nearly 300 Morsi proponents were killed by soldiers, police, and political opponents. Hundreds of Brotherhood members were arrested for sedition or for inciting violence, while Morsi adversaries acted with impunity. As the clampdown intensified, US officials continued to work with Mubarak holdovers and urged Morsi supporters to accept regime change as a fait accompli.

A new cabinet without Muslim Brotherhood representation was sworn in to office on July 16, 2013. Coup leader General Abdel Fattah el-Sisi, who had spent a year at the US Army War College and served as commander in chief of the Egyptian armed forces and defense minister in the Morsi government, remained the power behind the civilian government. Hundreds of thousands of Egyptians responded to Sisi's appeal to combat the Muslim Brotherhood's "terrorism" and took to the streets in support of the military government. On August 14, Egyptian security forces launched a twelve-hour assault on two Islamist encampments in Cairo, where tens of thousands of Morsi supporters continued to demand his reinstatement. More than 600 people were killed in Cairo and elsewhere as pro-Morsi protests swept the country. Within days, the death toll had reached more than 1,000. As the violence escalated, the government declared a state of emergency, suspended the right to trial or due process, and imposed measures tantamount to martial law. In September, the Muslim Brotherhood was banned and its assets confiscated. In December it was designated a terrorist organization, a classification that would lead to the closure of more than 1,000 Brotherhood-linked charities and NGOs that provided health care and other services to millions of low-income Egyptians.

External response to the repression ranged from mildly critical to openly supportive. The Obama administration signaled its disapproval of the regime's tactics by canceling joint military exercises scheduled for September 2013, and in October it placed a hold on some weapons and equipment sales. However, it continued to fund programs that advanced Egyptian counterterrorism initiatives, trained Egyptian military officers in the United States, and provided spare weapons parts. The EU halted arms sales but continued its security assistance programs, which were part of a €5 billion aid package. Neighboring autocracies with close ties to Europe and the United States stepped into the breach. Saudi Arabia publicly backed the military actions and vowed to compensate Egypt for any aid reduction. The United Arab Emirates and Israel also pledged their support and lobbied the West on the regime's behalf. Fearing the rise to power of both Islamists and secular liberals, three Arab Gulf states offered a combined total of $12 billion in assistance. Saudi Arabia, which had cut off aid to the Morsi government, promised $5 billion, Kuwait pledged $4 billion, and the United Arab Emirates provided a $1 billion grant and a $2 billion interest-free loan. By 2016, Gulf states had committed some $30 billion to Egypt in aid and investments, with Saudi Arabia contributing more than $25 billion. Only Qatar continued to support the deposed Morsi government and its Islamist backers.

Assistance from wealthy Gulf states that had withheld aid from the Morsi government, along with the end of obstruction by Mubarak holdovers in the bureaucracy, strengthened the position of the Sisi regime. The economic crisis and energy shortages that had sparked massive anti-Morsi protests began to dissipate. There were no more lines for gasoline and no more electricity outages. The police, who had been absent from the streets during the Morsi presidency, were again directing traffic and fighting crime—as well as attacking pro-Morsi demonstrators.

The suppression of government opponents continued into the new year. In January 2014, a new constitution that increased military and police powers—written in secret after the military coup—was approved by a popular referendum in which only 38 percent of the electorate participated. Massive preemptive arrests of government critics, including Islamist lawyers and parliamentarians, secular liberals, and leftists, had preceded the vote. The courts, still dominated by Mubarak appointees, handed down harsh sentences in mass trials that lacked due process.[16] In May, Sisi won presidential elections with 97 percent of the vote in a process that EU and US observers claimed was neither free nor fair. By 2015 more than 40,000 regime opponents had been detained, and a new counterterrorism law granted the state even more sweeping powers. Individuals who were deemed to "disturb public order and social peace," disrupt "national unity," or harm the economy could be investigated for terrorism and tried by special courts relying on questionable evidence.[17] Critics warned that the squelching of moderates and the closing of peaceful channels of dissent would inevitably increase support for violent extremists.

In its efforts to quash Islamism, the Sisi regime purposefully conflated moderates in the Muslim Brotherhood with violent Muslim extremists in the Sinai Peninsula. Like many twenty-first-century conflict zones, Sinai was a marginalized region where life was hard and opportunities few. Although it shared a border with Israel, was strategically located near the Suez Canal, and included the city of El Arish—a terminus of the El Arish–Ashkelon natural gas pipeline—Sinai was impoverished and underdeveloped. Lacking other options, the largely Bedouin population often resorted to smuggling, which had become the cornerstone of the local economy.

After Mubarak's ouster in 2011, residents of northern Sinai expelled the Egyptian security forces, and grassroots insurgency groups filled the power vacuum. The most visible was Ansar Beit al-Maqdis (Supporters of the Holy House), a Muslim extremist group that opposed the Muslim Brotherhood's nonviolent tactics as ineffective. A local organization with a domestic focus, Ansar Beit did not initially espouse global jihad. Ayman Zawahiri, the Egyptian physician who succeeded Osama bin Laden as al-Qaeda's leader, had offered his organization's support, but the local insurgency group's links to al-Qaeda remained informal. Ansar Beit's activities intensified in the wake of the 2013 military coup and stifling of Islamists. Focusing their efforts in northern Sinai, with forays into Cairo and the Nile Valley, Ansar Beit militants launched hundreds of attacks, targeting military and police forces, government officials, and foreign tourists. They also bombed the El Arish–Ashkelon pipeline, which provided Israel with 40 percent of its natural gas. Despite Ansar Beit's rejection of moderate Islamism, the Sisi regime charged that the Muslim Brotherhood was behind the Sinai insurgency, and the government used the violence to justify its anti-Islamist campaign. In Sinai, where the Egyptian military engaged in summary execution and wholesale destruction of homes and villages, antigovernment sentiment grew stronger.

As the counterinsurgency campaign in Sinai intensified, Ansar Beit's orientation began to shift and its membership splintered. In November 2014, Ansar Beit militants in Sinai pledged allegiance to the leader of the Islamic State and changed the organization's name to Islamic State–Sinai Province, while members in the Nile Valley retained ties to al-Qaeda. Having provoked the emergence of the Islamic State in Sinai, Sisi appealed to his allies for assistance. In February 2015, France announced that it would sell Cairo $6 billion worth of military equipment, including Rafale fighter jets and a naval frigate. In March, the Obama administration lifted its hold on arms and equipment sales to Egypt, opening the door to the delivery of F-16 fighter planes, Apache helicopters, Harpoon missiles, and shells and parts for M1A1 Abrams tanks. When it suspended the sales eighteen months earlier, the State Department had warned that Egypt would need to make "credible progress toward an inclusive, democratically elected civilian government through free and fair elections" before the deal could proceed.[18] Upon resuming sales, the administration cited US national security interests as the rationale.[19] In July 2015, the Egyptian military used F-16 war planes and Apache helicopters to create a buffer zone that would stanch the flow of weapons from Israeli-occupied Gaza into Sinai. Thousands of civilians were displaced, and more than 1,000 homes were destroyed in the process. The same year, Israel, which shared the Sisi regime's antipathy toward both the Muslim Brotherhood and the Islamic State, began a covert air campaign against militants in Sinai, with the tacit approval of Cairo. By the end of 2017, Israel had carried out more than 100 airstrikes inside Egypt, severely weakening the militants' ranks. As they lost territory and scattered, the insurgents turned their attention to civilian targets, homing in on Christians and Sufis, whom they killed by the hundreds.

From 2015 on, the war on terror was increasingly cited as the justification for US collaboration with the Sisi regime. A critical partner in regional counterterror actions, Egypt conducted airstrikes against Islamic State forces in Libya in 2015, following the murder of twenty-one Egyptian Christians in Libya, and it joined the United States in supporting the Saudi-led campaign against Iranian-backed Houthi rebels in Yemen. In August, Secretary of State John Kerry announced that the United States hoped to resume joint military exercises with Egypt, which had been suspended in 2013, and to expand the training of Egyptian police who would safeguard the border with Libya. In 2017 President Sisi visited the White House, where the new US president, Donald Trump, welcomed him with praise for his role in the war on terror and promised Washington's full support.

By then, the hopes inspired by Egypt's Arab Spring had been dashed. The Mubarak regime had been replaced by one that was even more repressive. Sisi's brutal suppression of Islamists helped radicalize thousands of young men who rejected their elders' appeals to refrain from violence, and imprisoned Muslim Brotherhood leaders retained limited influence. The United States, the EU, Israel, and regional Arab autocracies supported the Sisi regime, which they viewed as an ally in the struggle against Muslim extremists. Many analysts warned that the message to Islamists was clear: the democratic process is rigged against them. If Islamists are elected, they will be denied the right to govern—as evidenced in Algeria (1991), the Palestinian territories (2006), and Egypt (2013). Liberals and secularists will support democracy only if Islamists are excluded from power (Egypt, 2013 and Tunisia, 2014). Lacking a mass base, liberals and secularists rely on the army and police to suppress their opponents. Western powers express distaste for their methods but, sharing their hostility toward Islamists, continue to finance them. This message, conveyed by authoritarian regimes and their external allies, contributed to the radicalization of the region.

Libya, Part 1: Popular Uprising, Foreign Intervention, and State Collapse (2011)

Foreign intervention in Libya also contributed to regional radicalization. Days after Mubarak was forced to step down in Egypt, the Arab Spring arrived in Libya. Once again, popular protests against an authoritarian regime set off a chain of events. The target of Libyan demonstrations was the regime of Muammar al-Qaddafi, who had come to power in a 1969 military coup. Dominating a neopatrimonial state for more than four decades, Qaddafi, along with his family and his associates, controlled enormous wealth generated by Libya's rich oil and natural gas deposits. Much of the revenue was squandered on showcase projects at home and adventurism abroad, while domestic infrastructure deteriorated and health and education suffered.[20]

Governing through family, clan, and tribal ties, rather than through a professional bureaucracy, Qaddafi promoted social cleavages to keep potential rivals weak. Libya's Arab population was generally favored, while members of the Berber and Tubu ethnic groups were among the most repressed.[21] Qaddafi rewarded and punished individuals and groups based on loyalty to his regime and destroyed any institution that might challenge him. As a result, during Qaddafi's tenure, Libya had no parliament, trade unions, political parties, or nongovernmental organizations—in short, no organized civil society. Islamists were especially targeted. In both government and military, loyalties were divided by tribe and region. Distrustful of his own army, Qaddafi protected himself with a 3,000-member revolutionary guard that was supplemented by security forces and militia units run by his sons and by some 2,500 mercenaries from the impoverished Sahelian countries of Mali, Niger, Chad, and Sudan.

It was in this context that Libya's Arab Spring began. On February 16, 2011, inspired by the demonstrations in Tunisia and Egypt, protesters instigated a "day of rage" in the eastern city of Benghazi, a longtime center of anti-Qaddafi opposition. The security forces came down hard, killing more than 200 protesters and wounding 800 in three days' time. The protests quickly spread to other coastal cities, reaching the capital city of Tripoli and extending into western Libya. What began as a day of rage was rapidly transformed into an all-out rebellion against the Qaddafi regime. Military officers and high-level government officials defected. Local army units, police, and other state security forces, motivated in part by tribal and regional loyalties, joined the protesters, absconding with weapons from military stockpiles while arms flowed in from other countries. On February 23, as the western city of Misurata fell to rebel forces, Qaddafi called on thousands of African mercenaries and security force irregulars to defend the capital. Four days later, regime opponents established the National Transitional Council in Benghazi as their provisional government. The Arab League suspended Libya's membership and initiated contact with the rebels.

Photo 10.4. Rebels who have taken control of al-Bayda celebrate on abandoned Libyan army tanks, al-Bayda, Libya, February 25, 2011. Photo by ليبي صح.

Like his counterparts in Tunisia and Egypt, Qaddafi had cultivated international allies that protected his regime, but he also made enemies that worked toward its downfall. These alliances and oppositions came into play during the Arab Spring. When Qaddafi seized power in 1969, his plans were grandiose; he harbored both pan-Arab and pan-African ambitions. He aspired to succeed Egyptian president Gamal Abdel Nasser as leader of the pan-Arab movement, but his relationship with other Arab League members was often strained. Conservative Arab regimes allied with the West perceived Qaddafi as a threat to their power. They objected to his interference in the internal affairs of other countries, including Chad, Egypt, and Sudan on the African continent, and Lebanon, Palestine, Saudi Arabia, and Yemen in the Middle East. Snubbed by Arab states, Qaddafi turned his attention to sub-Saharan Africa, where he won supporters in the 1970s by attacking colonialism and neocolonialism and by providing weapons, money, and training to national liberation movements. In the 1970s and 1980s, Qaddafi recruited thousands of Bedouins and sub-Saharan Africans into his Islamic Pan-African Legion. Hoping to establish a grand Islamic empire in the Sahel, he sent his soldiers into battle in numerous countries in wars that consumed thousands of lives and displaced hundreds of thousands more. Libya's well-armed, war-hardened soldiers became a fearsome force of instability throughout the region.

Qaddafi's relationship with African governments, as with those in the Arab world, was volatile and changing. During the 1970s, the OAU embraced Qaddafi and his anticolonial message. However, during the 1980s and 1990s, Libyan military intervention in Chad and support for antigovernment forces in Liberia, Sierra Leone, and elsewhere led to the regime's increasing isolation. In another reversal, Qaddafi was welcomed back into the fold during the first decade of the twenty-first century. Using Libya's immense oil wealth to garner influence, Qaddafi and his associates invested some $5 billion in mines, mosques, hotels, mobile phone companies, and infrastructure across the African continent. Tripoli had a strong voice in the African Development Bank, where Libya's status as one of Africa's largest contributors gave it substantial voting power. Qaddafi played a major role in the establishment of the AU in 2002. His regime contributed 15 percent of the organization's budget and paid the membership dues of poorer countries. Two years before internal unrest and NATO airstrikes toppled his regime, Qaddafi was elected AU chair.

Qaddafi's relationship with the West was also fraught with contradictions and changed over time. During the Cold War, Qaddafi's anti-imperialist rhetoric, socialist policies, and nationalization of Western-owned oil operations raised serious concerns in the United States. The presence of Soviet military advisors and weaponry convinced Washington that Libya was a Soviet proxy, despite the regime's internal repression of communists. After the US Embassy in Tripoli was burned by protestors in 1979—in response to a rumor that the United States had led an attack on the Grand Mosque in Mecca—Washington severed diplomatic relations and added Libya to the State Department's list of state sponsors of terrorism, a designation that carried a number of economic restrictions. Further US sanctions were imposed between 1981 and 2001. In April 1986, following a deadly attack on a German discotheque patronized by US soldiers, the United States charged Libya with supporting international terrorism and bombed Tripoli and Benghazi in retaliation. The Libyan government was subsequently implicated in the 1988 bombing of a US civilian aircraft that resulted in 270 deaths and in the 1989 bombing of a

French airliner in which 171 people died. Further allegations led to UN and EU sanctions in 1992 and 1993.

After the Cold War, Libya and the United States reevaluated their relationship, finding common cause in their mutual hostility toward extremist organizations that embraced violent jihad. In 1995, the Libyan Islamic Fighting Group, organized by Libyan veterans of the Soviet-Afghan War, killed dozens of government soldiers in the eastern cities of Derna and Benghazi. Qaddafi's forces crushed the incipient insurgency and imprisoned large numbers of LIFG members.[22] Regarding al-Qaeda's influence as a threat to his own aspirations, Qaddafi was the first Arab leader to denounce the September 2001 attacks on the United States. Determined to end Libya's pariah status and to benefit from renewed foreign investment in the oil industry, Qaddafi began to cooperate with the United States on counterterrorism issues. He gave tacit approval to the US invasion of Afghanistan in October 2001 and shared intelligence that enabled Washington to hunt down al-Qaeda operatives. The 2003 war in Iraq, an indication that the government of President George W. Bush would follow through on his preemptive strike doctrine, may have influenced Qaddafi's subsequent decision to renounce terrorism, to destroy biological, chemical, and nuclear weapons stockpiles, and to abandon Libya's programs to develop weapons of mass destruction. The United States established a small diplomatic presence in Libya in 2004 and rescinded the travel ban that had prevented Americans from visiting that country. In 2006 Washington removed Libya from its list of state sponsors of terrorism, lifted economic sanctions—a special request of oil industry lobbyists—and restored full diplomatic relations. Intensifying their collaboration in the war on terror, the two countries shared intelligence, and the CIA sent terrorism suspects to Libya for interrogation and detention as part of its secret rendition program. Many of these suspects were LIFG members.

Other countries also welcomed Libya back into the fold. In 2003 and 2004, the UN and EU lifted their arms embargoes and other sanctions. French, British, German, Italian, and US interests began to invest heavily in Libyan oil and natural gas exploration and production. Before sanctions were imposed, Libya had been an important customer for French military aircraft and missiles. After sanctions were lifted, Italy, the UK, France, Germany, Russia, and Ukraine supplied Libya with weapons, military aircraft, spare parts, border security and surveillance equipment, and air defense and communications systems. British and Libyan intelligence collaborated in tracking down Libyan dissidents in the UK—particularly LIFG members—who were returned to Libya for interrogation and detention. Qaddafi also helped European countries stanch the flow of illegal migrants from sub-Saharan Africa to Europe. In exchange for billions of dollars in European trade, investment, and weapons, Qaddafi agreed to halt African migrants on Libyan shores, where they were herded into detention camps and employed in low-wage jobs.

Even as Libya renounced terror and normalized relations internationally, arbitrary arrests and imprisonment, torture, and disappearances continued on the domestic front. When the popular uprisings began in early 2011, Qaddafi's Western allies were quick to abandon him. On February 26, in a resolution promoted by France, Germany, the UK, and the United States, the UN Security Council voted unanimously to impose an arms embargo on Libya and sanctions against Qaddafi and his inner circle. The resolution also called on the ICC to investigate Libyan government attacks on civilians for evidence of crimes against humanity. France, the UK, and the United States closed their embassies in Tripoli. European governments and banks blocked Libyan accounts, and the Obama administration froze $30 billion in assets held by Qaddafi and his associates in the United States. President Obama called on Qaddafi to resign and ended cooperation between the US and Libyan armed forces.

As Qaddafi turned the full force of his military apparatus against civilian and rebel strongholds, the National Transitional Council appealed to the international community to impose a no-fly zone that would ground the Libyan air force and prevent it from attacking civilians. Libyan air-defense radars and missile batteries would have to be destroyed before foreign planes could patrol the skies. The international community was divided in its response. Some members charged that a no-fly zone would violate Libyan sovereignty. Others argued that it would demonstrate the UN's commitment to its responsibility to protect civilians from war crimes and crimes against humanity. Still others claimed that such a measure would be ineffective; because Qaddafi's forces were engaged in a ground assault, a no-fly zone would do little to protect civilian lives.

Russia, China, Germany, and the AU opposed the establishment of a no-fly zone.[23] The AU proposed mediation and dialogue that would include the Qaddafi regime and opposition forces, while Germany questioned the effectiveness of a no-fly zone unaccompanied by more invasive measures, which it resisted. France, the UK, the Arab League, and the six states of the Gulf Cooperation Council supported the no-fly zone option.[24] Within the Obama administration, the vice president, secretary of defense, chairman of the joint chiefs of staff, national security advisor, chief counterterrorism advisor, director of national intelligence, and a number of high-level military officials opposed military intervention, warning of the dangers of supporting rebels with possible al-Qaeda connections and of an anti-American backlash if the United States embroiled itself in another war against a Muslim nation. Moreover, Qaddafi was a bulwark against al-Qaeda in North Africa. If he were toppled and chaos ensued, extremists might fill the power vacuum. Other top officials, including UN Ambassador Susan Rice, senior National Security Council aide Samantha Power, and Secretary of State Hillary Rodham Clinton, who were deeply influenced by the US failure to thwart genocide in Rwanda and the Balkans in the 1990s, urged the president to support forceful military action.[25] Pressed by France, Italy, and the UK, which had promised to take the lead in a UN-sanctioned military operation, and confident that Arab League support would prevent a Muslim backlash, pro-intervention forces in the Obama administration gained ground.

On March 17, 2011, the UN Security Council imposed a no-fly zone over Libya and authorized designated member states to enforce it and to "take all necessary measures" to protect civilians, short of "a foreign occupation force."[26] Approved ten to zero with five abstentions, the resolution received support from France, the UK, and the United States, the three African members of the Security Council, and four other nonpermanent members. Russia, China, Germany, Brazil, and India abstained. South Africa and Nigeria had initially adhered to the AU position opposing the no-fly zone, but under pressure from the United States, they broke ranks to support the resolution.[27] To weaken the perception that Western nations were attacking a Muslim state to protect their oil interests, France, the UK, and the United States were adamant that Arab League forces must participate in financing the operation and enforcing the no-fly zone.

On March 19, US and European forces under French and British leadership initiated airstrikes against Libya. The United States played a critical role, destroying Libya's air defense systems and its missile, radar, and communications centers, while France and the UK attacked Libyan military convoys. By the end of the month, command and control of the air campaign was transferred to NATO—despite earlier concerns that a NATO operation might be perceived as a Western attack on Islam. Qatar, which held the Arab League presidency in 2011–12, convinced the organization to support the no-fly zone and to suspend Libya's membership, allaying some of the West's discomfort. However, most of the league's twenty-two member nations kept their distance, and only Qatar and the United Arab Emirates contributed aircraft to the no-fly zone patrol.

Although the stated purpose of the air campaign was to protect civilians from Qaddafi's forces, the Western-led coalition conducted a major assault on Libyan troops to persuade the army to turn against Qaddafi. Critics, including Russia, Turkey, and the Arab League, charged that the targeting of Libyan troops to provoke defections exceeded the limits of the UN mandate and that the coalition's ultimate objective was regime change, which had not been sanctioned by the UN.[28] Indeed, France, the UK, the United Arab Emirates, and other members of the coalition hoped to secure lucrative trade and investment opportunities in a post-Qaddafi Libya—including military sales and energy and infrastructure development.

Although the Security Council resolution called for dialogue leading to political reforms, NATO made no attempt to engage Libya in negotiations for a ceasefire and diplomatic settlement. Libyan offers to negotiate were rebuffed, and AU discussions with Qaddafi, which the organization had hoped would lead to a ceasefire and transition to democracy, were sidelined by the NATO bombings. On April 14, 2011, NATO foreign ministers released a communiqué indicating that Qaddafi's ouster was, in fact, their ultimate objective. By May the NATO bombing campaign had destroyed half of Libya's military capacity. High-level Libyan officials traveled to the United States and France with proposals for a transition to democracy that would include Qaddafi's departure. In July the AU proposed negotiations, to be mediated by the AU and the UN, which would lead to a ceasefire monitored by a UN peacekeeping force and the establishment of an inclusive interim government. Ultimately, a democratic constitution would be written and elections held. Bolstered by training and weapons from France, the UK, the United States, Qatar, and the United Arab Emirates, the rebels rejected the AU proposals and determined to fight to the finish. As they closed in on Qaddafi strongholds, the rebels targeted civilians whose tribal groupings were associated with

Qaddafi. The UN took no punitive action and made no effort to protect those civilians' lives. In August 2011, the rebels took the capital, and Qaddafi fled.

By September, powerful forces in the international community were openly backing an alternative Libyan regime. France, the UK, the United States, Qatar, the EU, the Arab League, the UN General Assembly, and even the internally divided AU had recognized the National Transitional Council as Libya's legitimate government. On October 20, a US Predator drone and a French warplane fired on Qaddafi's convoy, allowing Libyan rebels to capture, brutalize, and execute the former ruler. The NATO airstrikes had provided local insurgents the air cover they needed to foment regime change.

By the time the NATO military operation ended on October 31, the Libyan conflict had devolved into a violent struggle between allies and opponents of the Qaddafi regime and between factions of these camps. Revolutionary youths challenged their elders who had been technocrats and military officials under the old regime. Rival towns pitted their militias against one another for control of Libya's enormous oil, natural gas, and gold reserves as well as the country's energy infrastructure, strategic towns and airports, and central bank. Moderate Islamists vied with secularists, and both groups opposed violent Muslim extremists, including hundreds of LIFG members who had been freed from Qaddafi's prisons and foreign fighters who had answered al-Qaeda's call to join the rebellion. Elections in July 2012 established the General National Congress, the parliamentary body tasked with writing a permanent constitution. Although the new parliament was friendly to the West, it had little internal support.

Without governmental or civil society institutions to fill the power vacuum, regime change prompted the collapse of much of the social order. Qaddafi's departure unleashed violent retribution and score settling by groups set against one another during his rule. Hundreds of militias with as many as 250,000 members had formed along neighborhood, town, and tribal lines. Distrustful of militias from other regions, they refused to disarm or to recognize the authority of the central government. In Libya as elsewhere, moderate Islamists were confounded with violent Muslim extremists, and internal and external forces took harsh measures against both groups. In the eastern cities of Benghazi and Derna, Islamist militias that advocated participation in the democratic process were ousted by clan-based militias and former members of Qaddafi's security forces. The suppression of the moderates opened the door to violent Muslim extremists who targeted officials of the Muslim Brotherhood's Justice and Development Party, whom they criticized for working within the system. Criminal networks and jihadi organizations also entered the fray, and Libya became a magnet for violent actors of many sorts. Former CIA Deputy Director John E. McLaughlin charged that with new developments in Libya, "terrorists now have the largest area of safe haven and operational training that they've had in 10 years."[29] Thousands of civilians were caught in the crossfire.

Members of the UN Security Council who had pushed for military intervention were not keen to commit troops or treasure to support peacekeeping or nation building. Although the Security Council authorized a mission to restore public services and to assist in promoting a national dialogue, democratic elections, and a new inclusive constitution, it did not establish a peacekeeping operation to help integrate militias and former government troops into a disciplined national military. The limited UN mission failed to protect civilians from further violence or to secure Libyan arsenals. Sophisticated weapons from Qaddafi's stockpiles and flooded into neighboring countries, and foreign fighters from his vast security forces returned home.[30] Together they would contribute to the destabilization of the entire region. The lessons of Afghanistan in 1989, Somalia in 1993, and Iraq in 2003 had not been learned. The ill-conceived Libyan operation, where regime change led to a power vacuum without a viable plan to fill it, exposed once again the pitfalls of a military intervention that paid no regard to history or context.

Libya, Part 2: Muslim Extremism, Civil War, and Foreign Influence (2012–17)

The toppling of Qaddafi and the chaos that ensued offered new opportunities to violent Muslim extremists of both domestic and foreign origin, to regional militias that fought for a share of the spoils, and to old regime remnants that sought a return to power. By 2014, Libya was in the throes of civil war.

Bitterly opposed to Qaddafi, who had collaborated with the West in arresting its operatives, al-Qaeda had called on loyalists to support the anti-Qaddafi rebellion. Foreign fighters who answered the appeal included veterans of the anti-American insurgency in Iraq and former members of Saddam Hussein's military forces. Domestic fighters included LIFG members, many of whom had worked with al-Qaeda in Sudan and Afghanistan, and insurgents associated with new organizations like Ansar al-Shari'a, which established three separate entities in Libya, in the cities of Benghazi, Derna, and Sirte. The Ansar organizations focused on local issues, and initially none was connected to international terrorist networks. However, as the conflict intensified, all three established links to al-Qaeda, and some members of the Sirte contingent pledged allegiance to the leader of the Islamic State.[31]

In May 2014, General Khalifa Haftar, a former commander in Qaddafi's army and onetime CIA asset, assembled a new army and declared war on Islamist and jihadi forces—and on anyone else who opposed him. In a campaign dubbed Operation Dignity, Haftar's army made no distinction between Islamists who participated in the democratic process and Muslim extremists who assassinated establishment figures. Following an attack on the parliament building in Tripoli, General Haftar dissolved the General National Congress, where the Libyan Muslim Brotherhood's Justice and Development Party held the second-largest number of seats. New parliamentary elections, deemed deeply flawed by international observers, were held in June in the midst of violence, electoral boycotts, and shuttered polling stations. Voter turnout was estimated at 18 percent. Many seats were left unfilled, and others were abandoned by protesting parliamentarians. Nonetheless, a new parliamentary body called the House of Representatives was established on the basis of the election results. Western governments, which shared Haftar's anti-Islamist sentiments, recognized the House of Representatives as Libya's official parliament.

By August 2014, the conflict spiraled into a civil war. Two different governments contended for power. Haftar's supporters, including former members of Qaddafi's military, relocated the House of Representatives to the eastern city of Tobruk and established a governmental executive in al-Bayda, some 160 miles away. Haftar assumed the position of commander in chief of that government's armed forces. Haftar's opponents rallied to Libya Dawn, a coalition that controlled Tripoli and was dominant in the western and central regions. It continued to recognize the Tripoli-based General National Congress that Haftar had dissolved. Libya Dawn brought together an eclectic group of moderate Islamists, militias from Tripoli, Misurata, and other western cities, ethnic Berbers, extremist organizations such as Ansar al-Shari'a in Benghazi, and much of the formerly exiled opposition to Qaddafi. Among the Islamists were militias that had been deputized by the 2012 government to provide security in the absence of a functioning national army and police force. Islamist and jihadi groups that had been deeply fractured—and sometimes had targeted one another—found common cause in their opposition to Haftar and the old regime. By late 2015, fighting between the two factions had killed thousands of people and shut down or destroyed much of the country's oil and energy infrastructure.

The Libyan civil war opened the door to a new wave of foreign intervention, as external powers struggled to reshape the region in their own interests. Neighboring countries, regional and global powers, and multinational bodies lined up behind opposing sides. The Tripoli government was recognized by Turkey, Qatar, and Sudan, which were sympathetic to the Islamist factions. The Tobruk/al-Bayda government was recognized by the most powerful international entities, including the UN, the EU, the Arab League, the United States, Russia, Saudi Arabia, the United Arab Emirates, and Egypt. Sisi's Egypt supported the anti-Islamist campaign by launching airstrikes against Haftar's rivals in Benghazi and Derna and by allowing the United Arab Emirates to use Egyptian bases to attack Libya Dawn positions in Tripoli. Western powers gave diplomatic support to the Tobruk/al-Bayda government but hesitated to provide it with the military and counterterrorism assistance it requested, fearing that it might further radicalize the opposition.

The campaign against moderate Islamists was one of several factors that led to increased radicalization in Libya. The wars in Iraq and Syria also played a role. After Qaddafi's fall, Libyan militants had proceeded to Iraq, where they joined the anti-American insurgency, and to Syria, where they fought the Assad regime. Many had pledged allegiance to the Islamic State leader. When the Libyan civil war broke out, they returned home to organize. As US, French, and Russian airstrikes exerted pressure in Syria and Iraq, high-level Islamic State leaders also moved to Libya. By 2015, the Islamic State had established three Libyan provinces: Cyrenaica Province in the east, Tripolitania Province in the west, and Fezzan Province in the southern desert region. By early 2016, the Islamic State's fighting force in Libya was estimated at 5,000 to 6,500 men, including volunteers from Algeria, Egypt, Iraq, Saudi Arabia, Sudan, Syria, Tunisia, and Yemen, and also from sub-Saharan African countries. Islamic State forces gained control of the western city of Sirte, with its airport, military base, port, and waterworks, along with some 150 miles of the surrounding coastal region—which included rich oil and gas fields—and large sections of Derna in the east. They were also active in Tripoli, Libya's largest city and official capital, and in Misurata, the third-largest city, which contained an important port. By mid-2016, Libya had become the Islamic State's most important training ground for fighters bound for Syria and Iraq. Western counterterrorism experts warned that the Libyan affiliates were the region's most significant threat: they could readily extend their influence throughout North Africa, the Western Sahel, and into Europe.[32]

Using the war on terror as its justification, the United States targeted Islamic State, al-Qaeda, and unaffiliated operatives on Libyan soil. In October 2013, US Special Operations Forces raided Tripoli to capture Abu Anas al-Liby—a Libyan veteran of the Soviet-Afghan war, LIFG member, and al-Qaeda leader who allegedly helped plan the 1998 bombings of the US Embassies in Kenya and Tanzania. In June 2014, Special Operations Forces abducted Ahmed Abu Khattala, an unaffiliated operative who was believed to be a key figure in the September 2012 attack on the US consulate in Benghazi. Both men were rendered to the United States for prosecution.[33] In November 2015, a US airstrike in Derna killed Abu Nabil al-Anbari, leader of the Islamic State in Libya, who previously had headed al-Qaeda operations in Western Iraq. US airstrikes on the Islamic State's western Libyan headquarters near Sabratha killed some four dozen militants in February 2016. Noureddine Chouchane, the primary target and high-level Islamic State operative from Tunisia, was believed to be an organizer of the 2015 Tunisian museum and beach attacks and central to the funneling of African Islamic State recruits to Libya.[34]

During the final months of 2015, it was clear that a larger, Western-led military operation against the Islamic State in Libya was in the offing. French and US reconnaissance flights flew regularly over Islamic State bases in Sirte, Benghazi, and Derna, while US, British, French, and Italian special operations teams collected intelligence on the ground. However, foreign military intervention against the Islamic State would require the consent and cooperation of a Libyan government that was recognized as legitimate by the international community. As Western powers pressed for the establishment of a unity government that would collaborate with their counterterrorism agenda, critics warned that foreign military intervention could trigger a popular backlash, undermining any government that endorsed it.

In December 2015, following year-long negotiations sponsored by the UN, EU, AU, and Arab League, representatives of Libya's rival parliaments agreed to form a unity Government of National Accord, which would be led by the Presidential Council. Controversy dogged the agreement from the outset. Critics charged that it was prompted primarily by European security concerns and Western countries' desire to halt the influx of migrants from Libya rather than by the needs and aspirations of the Libyan people.[35] Influential preachers argued that a government appointed by non-Muslims could not be legitimate, a claim that resonated among many Libyan Muslims. Significant elements of both parliaments along with powerful factions on the ground, whose attempts to forge an alternative agreement had been dismissed by the international community, continued to oppose the deal. The new government did not control the capital city, Central Bank, National Oil Corporation, or Libyan Investment Authority—and did not have the means to do so.

Undeterred by these deficiencies, the UN Security Council endorsed the Government of National Accord and its Presidential Council as Libya's sole legitimate authority. Important regional militias, trained by British and US special operations forces, pledged loyalty to the new government. The existing Tripoli government agreed to step down in order to avoid further bloodshed—a move that split its parliament. Despite these developments, the accord remained on shaky ground as powerful actors continued to rebuff it. The House of Representatives in Tobruk, although recognized in the 2015 agreement as Libya's official legislature, refused to ratify it. The presidents of the rival Tobruk and Tripoli parliaments and the prime ministers of their respective governments rejected the new government's authority, and the EU and the United States imposed sanctions in retaliation. Egypt, Saudi Arabia, and the United Arab Emirates broke with their Western allies to join Russia in backing the House of Representatives. General Haftar, commander in chief of the Tobruk/al-Bayda government's armed forces, also repudiated the new regime. By 2017, Haftar's forces controlled most of eastern Libya, from Tobruk to Benghazi, and nearly all the country's oil ports. Egypt, the United Arab Emirates, and Russia provided the general with military support, and France insisted that Haftar, a key counterterrorism ally, be included in any political solution. As a result, in 2017, Libya had three rival governments rather than two.

Although they lacked authorization from an effective government, the United States and the UK moved to oust the Islamic State from Libya. In June 2016, Misurata militias loosely aligned with the Government of National Accord, reinforced by US and British intelligence, attacked the Islamic State stronghold in Sirte. Within weeks, they had taken control of a nearby airfield, military bases, and nearly all of the coastline previously under Islamic State control. In August, the United States supported the militias with airstrikes, citing as legal justification the Authorization for Use of Military Force granted by Congress to the president after the September 2001 terrorist attacks.[36] By December, the Misurata militias, assisted by 495 US airstrikes, had expelled the Islamic State from Sirte, dispersing militants across the eastern, western, and southern regions, where they established new cells. Others moved into Mali, Niger, and Nigeria, where they joined ongoing insurgencies and instigated new ones.

Foreign intervention was not universally welcomed. In Libya, critics charged that the disputed unity government, which had approved the action, did not have the authority to do so. Some claimed that the government was simply a proxy for Western interests. The militias from Misurata were generally not well received in Sirte, due to a longstanding rivalry between the two cities. Moreover, Misurata fighters, like those aligned with the Islamic State, were accused of committing atrocities against civilians, and their largely Islamist fighting forces were opposed by Haftar's army. In the United States, detractors warned that the Authorization for Use of Military Force, which sanctioned the targeting of nations, organizations, or individuals implicated in the 9/11 attacks, had no jurisdiction over Islamic State activities in Libya.

General Haftar, his allies in the Tobruk/al-Bayda government, and his rivals in Tripoli were not the only Libyan actors who stood to lose from the externally imposed unity agreement. In the post-Qaddafi era, Libya's long Mediterranean coastline, less than 300 miles from Europe, had become a launching pad for drug trafficking and human smuggling. The Libyan coast served as a key point of departure for hundreds of thousands of undocumented migrants, primarily from sub-Saharan Africa, who sought safety and sustenance in Europe. Human smuggling, especially, had become a lucrative enterprise in an otherwise dysfunctional economy. The collapse of the neopatrimonial state, the disruption of the formal economy, and the breakdown of law and order only partially explain the upsurge in human trafficking after Qaddafi's fall. Since 2008, European countries had paid the Libyan government tens of millions of dollars to halt the flow of migrants from African shores. After Qaddafi's ouster, the payments stopped, and migrants were herded onto vessels to attempt the treacherous, often deadly Mediterranean crossing. Profits from this illicit commerce, and from a growing Europe-bound drug trade, financed the activities of criminal gangs, regional militias, and the Libyan branch of the Islamic State. Because all of these groups benefited from the country's lawlessness, all had more interest in promoting war than peace. In 2017, a deal between Italy and Libyan militias, endorsed by EU interior ministers, returned thousands of migrants to Libya, where they were housed in detention camps, beaten, fed starvation diets, and forced to work without pay. Many were sold on auction blocks as modern-day slaves.[37]

Algeria and Morocco (2011–17)

Two North African countries stand in marked contrast to Libya and Egypt, where the aftermath of the Arab Spring brought even greater turmoil, and Tunisia, where those struggling for a new order continued to face serious obstacles. Algeria and Morocco were also swept up in the fervor of the moment, but the governments of both countries responded to mass demonstrations with limited concessions, the protests dissipated quickly, and the movements did not result in significant change. Algeria played a minor role in the Arab Spring. However, it was significant as the birthplace of extremist organizations whose influence spread in the uprisings' aftermath. Morocco exemplified a conservative government's successful co-optation, intimidation, and appeasement of opposition forces, a strategy that ultimately split the protest movement. The events in Algeria and Morocco and their impact on the region are encapsulated below.

In Algeria, as elsewhere, anger over poor living conditions and the lack of civil liberties sparked antigovernment demonstrations. In December 2010 and January 2011, protests targeted the high cost of staple foods and the scarcity of jobs, housing, utilities, infrastructure, and social services. Opposition parties, trade unions, and human rights organizations joined ordinary citizens to rally for increased political freedom and democracy. The demonstrations were initially met with a massive show of force. However, the government quickly turned to appeasement, using its enormous oil and natural gas wealth to offer temporary tax relief and to increase subsidies on basic foodstuffs. It promised new jobs programs and more affordable housing, and offered low-interest loans for new businesses. Finally, it lifted the state of emergency that had been in effect for two decades and announced an agenda of political reforms that would result in new electoral laws, media regulations, and an amended constitution. In tandem with concessions and promised reforms, the government waged a propaganda campaign that warned of the dangers of political instability, which, it claimed, would result in widespread death and destruction and provide an opening for terrorism and foreign intervention.

By the end of March 2011, most of the demonstrations had abated. The uprising in Algeria did not result in regime change, but instead produced limited accommodations and promises of more change to come. Multiparty parliamentary elections held in May 2012 were marked by low voter turnout; those who voted, however, returned the ruling party to power with an overwhelming majority. Domestic opposition groups cried foul, while EU, US, and Arab League observers endorsed the results. Meanwhile, the British policy institute Chatham House questioned the validity of the government's tally but noted that, in any event, the powerless parliament could do no more than rubber-stamp decisions taken by the president and his associates.

What had caused Algerian citizens to draw back, when so many others across the region surged forward? Experts pointed to the traumatic after-effects of the brutal civil war that had occurred two decades previously, and the fear, induced in part by government propaganda, that such events could happen again. The civil war had followed the Algerian Awakening, which began in October 1988 when thousands of Algerians instigated protests against corruption, inflation, the elimination of subsidies and social services, and repressive single-party rule by the National Liberation Front (FLN), which had led the country to independence in 1962. The government had responded first with violence and then with reform. Multiparty democracy was introduced, and elections for local assemblies were held in 1990. An Islamist party, the Islamic Salvation Front (FIS), won the majority of local assembly seats and control of some 800 municipalities. FIS also won a strong plurality in the first round of parliamentary elections held in December 1991; a second round was scheduled for January 1992. Fearing that the Islamist party would obtain more than two-thirds of the parliamentary seats, enabling it to alter the constitution, the Algerian armed forces staged a coup d'état on January 11 and cancelled the runoff elections. The new regime declared a state of emergency, banned all religious parties, and arrested thousands of FIS members.

The cancellation of the elections and repression of Islamists led to a brutal decade-long civil war, which claimed as many as 200,000 lives. Armed insurgents, loyal to disparate and sometimes warring organizations, took to the streets and mountains. The insurgents included groups loyal to FIS, which hoped to revive the political process that had resulted in its electoral victories, and emergent jihadi groups that sought to overthrow the secular state. Among the latter was the Armed Islamic Group (GIA), which was founded by Algerian veterans of the Soviet-Afghan War after the 1992 military coup. Rejecting FIS's moderate tactics, GIA targeted supporters of FIS, the Algerian government, and the civilian population.

In 1998, the Salafist Group for Preaching and Combat (GSPC) broke from GIA, condemning its massacres of Muslim civilians. Linked by their common service in the Soviet-Afghan War, GSPC attracted the attention of al-Qaeda, which provided financial and logistical support. On the fifth anniversary of the September 11, 2001, attacks, al-Qaeda selected GSPC as its North African representative, and in 2007 GSPC changed its name to Al-Qaeda in the Islamic Maghreb. AQIM was led by Soviet-Afghan War veteran Abdelmalek Droukdel, who had taken charge of GSPC in 2004. With the establishment of AQIM, the ripple effects of the Algerian crisis spread to other parts of North Africa. The Arab Spring and its aftermath strengthened AQIM's foothold in North Africa and introduced the group to the Western Sahel. Meanwhile, in Algeria, the generals who staged the 1992 coup remained the power behind Algeria's autocratic civilian regime, and the state security service, which had dominated the state since independence, kept close tabs on opposition activists. Unable to unite a fearful and divided citizenry in an enduring coalition, Algerian activists were overshadowed by militants in other countries during the 2011–13 Arab Spring.

Citizens of Morocco were motivated by the same concerns that inspired others in 2011. On February 20, thousands of protesters led by middle-class youths surged into the streets of Rabat and other towns and cities across the country. Rallying against political repression, corruption, economic inequality, unemployment, and inadequate social services, they called for constitutional changes that would reduce monarchical powers in favor of an elected parliament and recognize the Amazigh (Berber) language as an official one. The February 20 Movement was embraced by dozens of civil society and political organizations, ranging from leftists to Islamists. In early March, King Mohammed VI, an important ally of both France and the United States, released Islamists and other dissidents from prison and promised to appoint a committee to draft constitutional reforms that would establish an independent judiciary, more effective rule of law, and an elected government endowed with enhanced powers. However, significant limitations on the government's prerogatives ensured that real power would remain in the monarch's hands. The reforms were approved by a popular referendum in July, and parliamentary elections were held in November 2011. The moderate Muslim Brotherhood–affiliated Justice and Development Party, which had opposed the February 20 Movement, won a plurality of the vote. Its electoral victory permitted the party to hold the position of prime minister, lead a coalition government that included two secular parties, and claim eleven of thirty-one ministries, including higher education, justice, and foreign affairs.

Having pursued a dual strategy of co-optation and repression of Islamist organizations since the late 1970s, the Moroccan monarchy successfully used the Justice and Development Party to undermine support for the more radical and illegal Justice and Charity Party, which promoted social justice, a more equitable distribution of resources, and an accountable government based on Islamic law.[38] In contrast to its counterparts in Tunisia and Egypt, the Moroccan Muslim Brotherhood party retained control of the post–Arab Spring government, but it was unable to effect fundamental political, economic, or social change. The repression of political activists and independent journalists continued, and the February 20 Movement fractured, strained by conflicting views on monarchy, religion, and women's rights, and divided by region, generation, and socioeconomic class. Meanwhile, the two-decade-old Moroccan Islamic Combatant Group, founded by Moroccan veterans of the Soviet-Afghan War, was superseded by new jihadi groups with links to AQIM, and some 1,500 Moroccan fighters joined Islamic State forces fighting in Iraq and Syria.

Conclusion

In North Africa, as in Africa south of the Sahara, foreign intervention during the periods of decolonization and the Cold War installed and sustained dictators whose rule was characterized by economic inequality and political repression. During the Arab Spring, secular liberals, leftists, and Islamists in Tunisia, Egypt, and Libya were among those who mobilized successfully to oust the old regimes. Similar movements in Algeria and Morocco led to superficial reforms that curbed the uprisings and stymied more significant change. In the three countries where new orders were established, civil rights and liberties continued to be applied selectively, and hopes for economic transformation were not fulfilled. Remnants of the old regimes remained compelling forces and, in Tunisia and Egypt, they succeeded in regaining power.

Once again, foreign political and military intervention influenced the outcomes. In Tunisia, Egypt, and Libya, external interests acted in response to instability, and in the case of Libya, to protect civilian lives. Regime change was an additional but unstated objective in Libya. In all three countries, some Western, Middle Eastern, and regional powers and multilateral organizations joined local secularists to dampen the influence of moderate Islamists or even to repress them. Other external forces supported Islamist politicians and, in the case of Libya, Islamist militias. As legal means for expressing dissent or gaining power shut down, a growing number of alienated young men joined extremist camps. Al-Qaeda and the Islamic State emerged as powerful forces in places where they had had little or no previous presence. In Egypt and Libya, especially, external involvement heightened the violence and instability. International efforts to bring peace and stability foundered, as they tended to focus on external rather than internal interests and to exclude influential parties that outsiders opposed.

The Arab Spring and its aftermath had widespread political, economic, and social ramifications. As weapons, fighters, and refugees from the regional hotspots flooded into neighboring states, vast regions in North Africa and the West African Sahel were destabilized. Two countries that experienced the ripple effects were Mali and Nigeria. Instability and foreign intervention in those countries is the subject of chapter 11.

Suggested Reading

Several works on Islam and Islamism in contemporary Africa and the Middle East are especially recommended. A useful overview can be found in Benjamin F. Soares and René Otayek, eds., *Islam and Muslim Politics in Africa* (New York: Palgrave Macmillan, 2007), which investigates the impact of political liberalization, economic reform, state weakness, and globalization on the practice of Islam. Case studies focus on Muslim youth activists, Muslim NGOs, Islamic law, and secularism and minority rights. International Crisis Group, *Islamism in North Africa I: The Legacies of History*, Middle East/North Africa Briefing 12 (Cairo/Brussels: International Crisis Group, 2004), provides a concise historical contextualization of Islamism in North Africa. Contributors to Samer S. Shehata, ed., *Islamist Politics in the Middle East: Movements and Change* (New York: Routledge, 2012), examine the character of diverse Islamist movements in North Africa and the Middle East and their roles in domestic and international affairs. See also the Suggested Reading for chapter 2.

The Arab Spring is the subject of a number of useful studies. Roger Owen, *The Rise and Fall of Arab Presidents for Life* (Cambridge, MA: Harvard University Press, 2012), explores the origins and dynamics of the presidential regimes that dominated Middle Eastern and North African politics during the second half of the twentieth century and explains why they were challenged during the Arab Spring. Several works provide helpful analyses that investigate the causes, significance, and consequences of the uprisings in North Africa and the Middle East: Tariq Ramadan, *Islam and the Arab Awakening* (New York: Oxford University Press, 2012); James L. Gelvin, *The Arab Uprisings: What Everyone Needs to Know* (New York: Oxford University Press, 2012); and Paul McCaffrey, ed., *The Arab Spring* (Ipswich, MA: H. W. Wilson, 2012). Gilbert Achcar, *The People Want: A Radical Exploration of the Arab Uprising*, trans. G. M. Goshgarian (Berkeley: University of California Press, 2013), explores the political, economic, and social roots of the Arab uprising, focusing on youth unemployment, governmental repression, corruption, and the impact of US policies. It also includes a valuable assessment of the significance of Qatar and its Al Jazeera television network in shaping events.

Two recommended works focus on the role of youth in fomenting the Arab Spring. Juan Cole, *The New Arabs: How the Millennial Generation Is Changing the Middle East,* 2nd ed. (New York: Simon and Schuster, 2014), investigates youth movements in Tunisia, Egypt, and Libya, exploring their grievances, aspirations, and use of technology and social media to mobilize against the presidential regimes. Journalist Robin Wright, in *Rock the Casbah: Rage and Rebellion across the Islamic World* (New York: Simon and Schuster, 2012), highlights the voices of young men and women who hoped to promote fundamental cultural change and to reclaim Islam from extremist minorities.

Several important studies examine the aftermath of the Arab Spring, focusing on conflicts between secularists and Islamists, the repression of prodemocracy forces, and the reemergence of authoritarian regimes. See especially Mark Lynch, *The Arab Uprising: The Unfinished Revolutions of the New Middle East* (New York: Public Affairs, 2012); Lin Noueihed and Alex Warren, *The Battle for the Arab Spring: Revolution, Counter-Revolution and the Making of a New Era* (New Haven, CT: Yale University Press, 2012); Robert F. Worth, *A Rage for Order: The Middle East in Turmoil, From Tahrir Square to ISIS* (New York: Farrar, Straus and Giroux, 2016); Gilbert Achcar, *Morbid Symptoms: Relapse in the Arab Uprising* (Stanford, CA: Stanford University Press, 2016); and I. William Zartman, ed., *Arab Spring: Negotiating in the Shadow of the Intifadat* (Athens: University of Georgia Press, 2015).

Other works examine the impact of foreign intervention during the Arab Spring. Especially useful are two studies by Kristian Coates Ulrichsen that explore the prominent role of Qatar, which, unlike other Gulf states, viewed the revolts not as a challenge to its authority but as an opportunity to strengthen its regional and global influence. Kristian Coates Ulrichsen, *Qatar and the Arab Spring* (London: Hurst, 2014), and *Qatar and the Arab Spring: Policy Drivers and Regional Implications* (Washington, DC: Carnegie Endowment for International Peace, 2014), investigate Qatar's involvement in mediation, financial support, and media coverage during the Arab revolts. See also Achcar, *The People Want* (mentioned previously).

For Tunisia, important historical context is provided in Kenneth J. Perkins, *A History of Modern Tunisia*, 2nd ed. (New York: Cambridge University Press, 2014), which examines the country's political, economic, and social dynamics from the mid-nineteenth century to the aftermath of the Arab Spring. Pia Christina Wood investigates French support for the Ben Ali dictatorship in the years before the Tunisian uprising in "French Foreign Policy and Tunisia: Do Human Rights Matter?" *Middle East Policy* 9, no. 2 (Summer 2002). Alcinda Honwana, *Youth and Revolution in Tunisia* (London: Zed Books, 2013), focuses on the role of youth, especially cyber activists, in the Tunisian revolt. Michael J. Willis, *Politics and Power in the Maghreb: Algeria, Tunisia and Morocco from Independence to the Arab Spring* (New York: Columbia University Press, 2012), investigates political, Islamist, and Berber identity movements in the Maghreb, with special reference to Tunisia. Veteran journalist David B. Ottaway, *The Arab World Upended: Revolution and Its Aftermath in Tunisia and Egypt* (Boulder, CO: Lynne Rienner, 2017), examines the causes of the revolutions and the nature of the states formed in its aftermath.

A number of works explore conflicts between secularists, Islamists, and violent extremists in Tunisia in the years after the Arab Spring. See especially Anne Wolf, *Can Secular Parties Lead the New Tunisia?* (Washington, DC: Carnegie Endowment for International Peace, 2014); Kasper Ly Netterstrøm, "The Islamists' Compromise in Tunisia," *Journal of Democracy* 26, no. 4 (October 2015): 110–24; Monica L. Marks, *Convince, Coerce, or Compromise? Ennahda's Approach to Tunisia's Constitution*, Brookings Doha Center Analysis Paper 10 (Washington, DC: Brookings Institution, 2014); and Monica Marks, *Tunisia's Ennahda: Rethinking Islamism in the Context of ISIS and the Egyptian Coup*, Rethinking Political Islam Working Paper (Washington, DC: Brookings Institution, 2015).

Several important studies provide a historical framework for the uprising and its aftermath in Egypt. Afaf Lutfi Al-Sayyid Marsot, *A History of Egypt: From the Arab Conquest to the Present*, 2nd ed. (New York: Cambridge University Press, 2007), provides a useful overview. Malcolm Kerr, *The Arab Cold War: Gamal 'Abd Al-Nasir and His Rivals, 1958–1970*, 3rd ed. (New York: Oxford University Press, 1971), explores the turbulent relations between Nasser's Arab nationalist regime and the conservative monarchies in neighboring Arab states. Steven Cook,

The Struggle for Egypt: From Nasser to Tahrir Square (New York: Oxford University Press, 2011), traces Egypt's transformation from leader of the Arab world under Nasser, through the corrupt regimes that sustained US Middle East policy, to the rise of the Muslim Brotherhood and the prodemocracy forces that overthrew the Mubarak regime. Ottaway, *The Arab World Upended* (mentioned previously), examines the causes of the uprising in Egypt and explores the reasons for the revolution's failure. Achcar, *Morbid Symptoms*, investigates the aftermath of the Arab Spring in Egypt, where progressive forces competed with remnants of the old regime and with Islamic fundamentalist movements to shape the future. Jason Brownlee, *Democracy Prevention: The Politics of the U.S.-Egyptian Alliance* (New York: Cambridge University Press, 2012), explores the collaboration between the United States and successive Egyptian regimes, Washington's delayed support for the prodemocracy movement, its hopes for a successor government run by a Mubarak associate, and its continued support for authoritarian rule. David D. Kirkpatrick, *Into the Hands of the Soldiers: Freedom and Chaos in Egypt and the Middle East* (New York: Viking Penguin, 2018), examines the relationship through 2017. Egyptian journalist Mohannad Sabry, *Sinai: Egypt's Linchpin, Gaza's Lifeline, Israel's Nightmare* (Cairo: American University in Cairo Press, 2015), explores the Sinai insurgency and the social, economic, and political issues at its root.

A number of recommended works provide historical background to the uprising and subsequent conflict in Libya. J. Millard Burr and Robert O. Collins, *Africa's Thirty Years' War: Libya, Chad, and the Sudan, 1963–1993* (Boulder, CO: Westview Press, 1999), examines the long-term consequences of three decades of war that implicated Libya, Chad, and Sudan, as well as France, the United States, the OAU, and the UN. Yehudit Ronen, *Qaddafi's Libya in World Politics* (Boulder, CO: Lynne Rienner, 2008), investigates the four decades of Qaddafi's rule, exploring Libya's shift from the Arab Middle East and the Soviet Union to Africa and the West. Geoff Simons, *Libya and the West: From Independence to Lockerbie* (Oxford, UK: Centre for Libyan Studies, 2003), examines regional conflicts, human rights abuses, and state terrorism under Qaddafi, along with Western involvement in Libyan affairs since independence. Ethan Chorin, *Exit the Colonel: The Hidden History of the Libyan Revolution* (New York: PublicAffairs, 2012), written by a former US foreign service officer in Libya (2004–6), examines human rights abuses and regional disparities under Qaddafi and the events that led to the uprising.

Chorin's assessment of relations between Qaddafi and the West from 2003 to 2011 is particularly insightful.

The dynamics of the Libyan revolt and its aftermath are investigated in several important studies. Lindsey Hilsum, *Sandstorm: Libya in the Time of Revolution* (New York: Penguin, 2012), written by a British journalist stationed in Libya during the Arab Spring, chronicles the Libyan uprising at the grassroots. Contributors to Jason Pack, ed., *The 2011 Libyan Uprisings and the Struggle for the Post-Qadhafi Future* (New York: Palgrave Macmillan, 2013), examine the role of economics, ethnicity, region, religion, and external actors in the uprising and its aftermath. Other significant works examine ethnic, clan, regional, and religious rivalries in post-Qaddafi Libya. Peter Cole and Brian McQuinn, eds., *The Libyan Revolution and Its Aftermath* (New York: Oxford University Press, 2015), provides historical context that explains Libya's inability to form a unified state in the Arab Spring's aftermath. Other destabilizing factors in post-Qaddafi Libya are explored in Frederic Wehrey, "What's Behind Libya's Spiraling Violence?" *Washington Post*, July 28, 2014, and Frederic Wehrey and Ala' Alrababa'h, "Rising Out of Chaos: The Islamic State in Libya," *Diwan: Middle East Insights from Carnegie*, March 5, 2015. Nicholas Pelham, "Libya in the Shadow of Iraq: The 'Old Guard' versus the *Thuwwar* in the Battle for Stability," in *The Politics of International Intervention: The Tyranny of Peace*, ed. Mandy Turner and Florian P. Kühn (New York: Routledge, 2016), 218–28, attributes some of the instability to the inaction of Western powers that intervened to oust Qaddafi and subsequently disengaged. Frederic Wehrey, *The Burning Shores: Inside the Battle for the New Libya* (New York: Farrar, Straus and Giroux, 2018), provides a nuanced assessment of the country's breakdown after Qaddafi's fall, including insights gleaned from interviews conducted across the country.

Several works examine the impact of foreign intervention during the Libyan uprising and its aftermath. Alex J. Bellamy and Paul D. Williams, "The New Politics of Protection? Côte d'Ivoire, Libya and the Responsibility to Protect," *International Affairs* 87, no. 4 (July 2011): 825–50, explores the history, application, and challenges of the UN's "politics of protection," with special reference to Libya. Stephen R. Weissman, "In Syria, Unlearned Lessons from Libya," *In These Times*, April 19, 2013, considers the ways in which NATO powers undermined AU initiatives for a negotiated transition to democracy and chose instead to intervene militarily to remove Qaddafi from power. Aidan Hehir and Robert Murray, eds., *Libya: The Responsibility to Protect and the Future of Humanitarian Intervention* (New York: Palgrave Macmillan, 2013), contests the dominant narrative, which deems intervention in Libya to have been an effective and positive action motivated by the responsibility to protect. Contributors to the volume argue that the authorization, conduct, and justification of that intervention will have negative consequences for future humanitarian interventions and for international peace and security. Two recommended articles focus on the role of foreign intervention in Libya's post–Arab Spring civil war: Frederic Wehrey and Wolfram Lacher, "Libya's Legitimacy Crisis: The Danger of Picking Sides in the Post-Qaddafi Chaos," *Foreign Affairs,* October 6, 2014; and Frederic Wehrey, "Is Libya a Proxy War?" *Washington Post,* October 24, 2014.

A number of studies explore political transformations in Algeria, which did not experience regime change during the Arab Spring, but where brutal repression of Islamists in the 1990s influenced the 2011 uprising and its aftermath. Several works focus on the Algerian independence war. See especially Alistair Horne, *A Savage War of Peace: Algeria, 1954–1962* (New York: New York Review Books, 2006); and Frantz Fanon's classic work, *The Wretched of the Earth,* trans. Richard Philcox (New York: Grove Press, 2004), which examines the psychological impact of colonialism and liberation. Matthew Connelly, *A Diplomatic Revolution: Algeria's Fight for Independence and the Origins of the Post–Cold War Era* (New York: Oxford University Press, 2002), investigates Algerian decolonization in the context of the Cold War and examines the ways in which Algerian nationalists played on divisions between the French colonial power and its allies. Robert Malley, *The Call from Algeria: Third Worldism, Revolution, and the Turn to Islam* (Berkeley: University of California Press, 1996), traces Algeria's transformation from a symbol of revolutionary socialism to a battleground between secular and religious forces that culminated in a brutal civil war. James D. Le Sueur, *Algeria Since 1989: Between Democracy and Terror* (London: Zed Books, 2010), examines how Algeria's attempts to move from authoritarianism to democratic pluralism were thwarted by a military coup intended to block the rise to power of an elected Islamist government. Willis, *Politics and Power in the Maghreb* (mentioned previously), explores Algerian political, Islamist, and Berber identity movements, as well as the role of the military in Algerian politics and society. J. N. C. Hill, *Identity in Algerian Politics: The Legacy of Colonial Rule* (Boulder, CO: Lynne Rienner, 2009), investigates the political, economic, and social upheaval of the 1990s, when Algerian national identity was contested, Islamism and Berberism emerged as powerful forces, and foreign interests intervened. Bruce Maddy-Weitzman, *The Berber Identity Movement and the Challenge to North African States* (Austin: University of Texas Press, 2011), also illuminates the role of the Berber identity movement, focusing on both Algeria and Morocco.

Morocco, like Algeria, experienced political reforms but did not undergo regime change during the Arab Spring. Several studies shed light on the relative stability of the Moroccan monarchy. Susan Gilson Miller, *A History of Modern Morocco* (New York: Cambridge University Press, 2013), assesses the government's strong ties with the West, episodes of political repression and reform, détente with Islamists, involvement with the war on terror, and reaction to the Arab Spring. Willis, *Politics and Power in the Maghreb* (mentioned previously), investigates political, Islamist, and Berber identity movements in the Maghreb, with special reference to Morocco. Bruce Maddy-Weitzman and Daniel Zisenwine, eds., *Contemporary Morocco: State, Politics and Society Under Mohammed VI* (New York: Routledge, 2011), examines the establishment of political parties, the evolving relationship between the monarchy and Islamists, the growing impact of civil society, and the role of the Amazigh (Berber) renaissance. Maddy-Weitzman, *The Berber Identity Movement and the Challenge to North African States* (mentioned previously), also illuminates the role of the Berber identity movement in Morocco. James N. Sater, *Morocco: Challenges to Tradition and Modernity* (New York: Routledge, 2010), examines the politics of inclusion and exclusion in contemporary Morocco, the country's economic conditions, and its role in the region.

Islamism in Morocco is the subject of several recommended works. See especially Marvine Howe, *Morocco: The Islamist Awakening and Other Challenges* (New York: Oxford University Press, 2005); Mohamed Daadaoui, *Moroccan Monarchy and the Islamist Challenge: Maintaining Makhzen Power* (New York: Palgrave Macmillan, 2011); Malika Zeghal, *Islamism in Morocco: Religion, Authoritarianism, and Electoral Politics*, trans. George Holoch (Princeton, NJ: Markus Wiener, 2008); and Eva Wegner, *Islamist Opposition in Authoritarian Regimes: The Party of Justice and Development in Morocco* (Syracuse, NY: Syracuse University Press, 2011). Avi Max Spiegel, *Young Islam: The New Politics of Religion in Morocco and the Arab World* (Princeton, NJ: Princeton University Press, 2015), highlights the role of youth in Morocco's religious politics, where they have played a major role in shaping and contesting competing visions of Islam and Islamism.

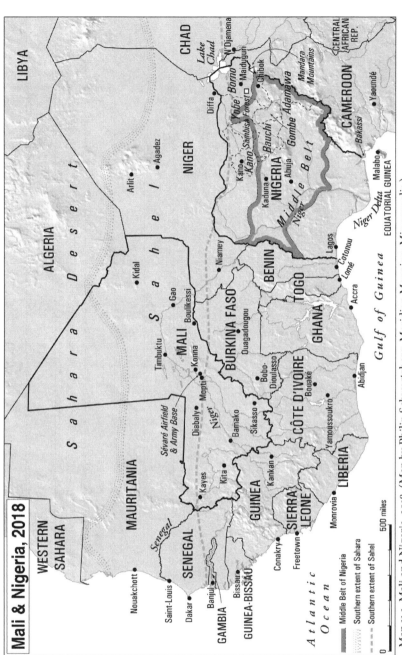

Map 11.1. Mali and Nigeria, 2018. (Map by Philip Schwartzberg, Meridian Mapping, Minneapolis.)

11

Mali and Nigeria

Military Intervention and
Unforeseen Consequences (2009–17)

FALLOUT FROM THE Arab Spring in North Africa had widespread ramifications elsewhere. The chain of events unleashed by Qaddafi's ouster was felt throughout the region as sophisticated armaments from Libyan arsenals fell into the hands of criminals and insurgents in North Africa and the Western Sahel. Guns, guerrillas, and refugees swept into neighboring states and destabilized weak regimes.

In Mali, Qaddafi's demise fueled a separatist movement, a jihadist insurgency backed by al-Qaeda affiliates, a military coup, and foreign military intervention. Neighboring states, Western countries, and multilateral bodies justified their intervention both as a response to regional instability and as an effort to combat international terrorism. External players included ECOWAS, the AU, the UN, the EU, France, and the United States, as well as foreign jihadis from the al-Qaeda network.

In Nigeria, a conflict in the northeast that was focused on local grievances established links to al-Qaeda when Nigerian insurgents, who had trained in Mali's al-Qaeda camps, returned home with weapons acquired from Libyan stockpiles. As the Nigerian conflict expanded into Cameroon, Chad, and Niger, it attracted fighters from Mali, Mauritania, and Algeria—as well as support from the Islamic State. Neighboring countries, attacked by Nigerian insurrectionists and threatened by the influx of refugees, joined forces with the Nigerian military to respond both to regional instability and to the threat from international terrorist movements. In some cases, they operated under AU auspices; in others, they functioned as ad hoc collectives. The subregional bodies, ECOWAS and the Economic Community of Central African States (ECCAS), assisted in mediation efforts. Justifying their intervention according to both paradigms, Western nations—led by the United States, France, the UK, and various EU member states—provided military training, technical, and financial support.

In both Mali and Nigeria, the foreign military operations decimated insurgent forces in some areas but dispersed them to others, where the rebels targeted unprotected civilian populations. Ordinary citizens were caught in the crossfire, victimized by both insurrectionary and governmental forces. The abuse of civilians by state security personnel, and the failure of the international forces to protect them, undermined broader counterterrorism objectives. In both Mali and Nigeria, foreign intervention resulted in some short-term gains. However, long-term solutions remained elusive. The governments in Bamako and Abuja failed to address the deeply rooted grievances that had precipitated the insurgencies in marginalized areas. They did not redistribute state resources to provide badly needed infrastructure and governmental and social services to the neglected northern regions. Once the military forces withdrew, extremist groups in both countries reestablished themselves in remote areas where they operated with renewed vigor.

This chapter examines the mix of factors that led to the conflicts in Mali and Nigeria, which by late 2017 had not been resolved. It begins with regime change in Libya, which had significant regional consequences, particularly for Mali but also for Nigeria. Foreign intervention in Libya, purportedly to restore stability and protect civilian lives, led to widespread regional destabilization and the deaths of thousands of civilians in other countries. Both case studies expose the intervening powers' flawed understanding of the social and political dynamics in the contested areas.

Setting the Stage: Mali and Its Saharan Neighbors (2011–17)

The spillover effects of the Libyan turmoil had serious consequences in sub-Saharan Africa. For Mali, the impact was especially devastating. When the anti-Qaddafi insurgency began, some 1.5 million sub-Saharan Africans were living in Libya, the vast majority recruited by the government to work in low-wage jobs. Thousands were migrants whose onward travel to Europe had been thwarted by the Libyan government in exchange for billions of dollars in European trade, investment, and weapons. As the rebellion intensified, Qaddafi bolstered his security forces with some 2,500 mercenaries from impoverished sub-Saharan countries. His military personnel also included well-trained fighters from the Tuareg ethnic group, a nomadic Berber people with significant populations in Algeria, Mali, and Niger, and smaller concentrations in Burkina Faso, Libya, and Nigeria. Thousands of Tuaregs in the Libyan security forces responded to his appeal for help, and countless others crossed the borders from Mali and Niger to join his cause.

Although critical to Libya's economic development, sub-Saharan Africans constituted an impoverished underclass that was regularly subjected to racism, xenophobia, and scapegoating for the country's social and economic ills. The presence of sub-Saharan African mercenaries among Qaddafi's fighting forces exacerbated popular hostility during the uprising, when militants singled out sub-Saharan Africans for retaliation, and untold numbers were robbed, beaten, raped, and lynched. Violence, instability, and the targeting of foreign nationals led to a mass exodus of civilians during the insurgency, while Qaddafi's ouster led to an outflow of foreign fighters armed with sophisticated weapons.

The scattering of the Tuareg fighters had immediate consequences in Mali, where Tuareg nationalists, who had long struggled for greater autonomy, instigated an armed struggle for independence. Like many African countries, Mali included a mix of ethnic groups that had been ruled as a unit by an external colonial power. The population comprised Tuaregs and Arabs, primarily in the north, and sub-Saharan African ethnic groups, primarily in the south, where the seat of government was located. Northern Tuaregs, who historically were nomadic pastoralists, had conducted a sustained resistance to French conquest in the late nineteenth century. During the colonial and postindependence periods, they were marginalized politically, economically, and socially. Resisting the rules and regulations of nation-states, they disregarded national boundaries imposed by outsiders and moved freely throughout the region, seeking food and water for their herds—and later, wage employment or illicit economic opportunities. Devastating droughts in 1968–74 and 1980–85 and the damaging effects of desertification destroyed the livelihoods of many pastoralists and pushed large numbers of young Tuareg men into Libya, where they worked in the oil industry or joined the Islamic Pan-African Legion and fought for Libya in Chad and Sudan. Although thousands remained in Libya after the immediate crises ended, others returned home to lead a succession of rebellions against the Bamako government.

The 2011–13 Tuareg insurgency in Mali that followed Qaddafi's fall was the most recent of many that had plagued the government since independence in 1960. The rebellions grew from grievances stemming from the country's deep structural inequalities that deprived northern Tuaregs of educational, developmental, and political opportunities. Since independence, Tuaregs had struggled for greater control over their land—including the rich uranium deposits beneath the soil—along with greater regional autonomy and a halt to pollution by foreign mining companies. The rebellions had been brutally repressed, and successive peace agreements had led to unfulfilled promises and renewed fighting. A 1992 accord resulted in the integration of more than 3,000 Tuareg fighters into the Malian military, police, and civil service. However, other grievances continued to fester. Tuareg populations lacked adequate drinking water, electricity, roads, clinics, and schools. Large numbers of men were unemployed, and many turned to smuggling and other criminal activities. New insurgencies erupted during 2007–9. When those conflicts ended, legions of Tuareg fighters again left for Libya, where they joined Qaddafi's security forces and elite desert military units.

While Tuareg nationalists turned to Libya, the Malian government found a ready benefactor in the United States, which approached the conflict in northern Mali as one emanating from international terrorism. The Bamako-Washington alliance would exacerbate tensions between the Malian government and the Tuareg populations. Bamako became a key player in US counterterrorism initiatives in the Western Sahel. It joined the US-led Pan-Sahel Initiative (PSI), established in 2002, and its successor organizations, the Trans-Sahara Counterterrorism Initiative (TSCTI) and the Trans-Sahara Counterterrorism Partnership (TSCTP). These programs provided Bamako with military equipment, logistical support, and border control training and offered the services of US Special Operations Forces, who trained Malian military personnel in counterterrorism and combat techniques. The initiatives brought the Bamako government into conflict with Tuareg populations in two ways. First, they required Mali to establish a military presence in the Sahara, which violated internal peace agreements that had reduced the army's numbers in Tuareg-inhabited areas. Second, when the 2007–9 insurgency began, US Army Special Forces helped the Bamako government combat it.

Although the United States justified its intervention as a strike against terror, the 2007–9 rebellion was not the work of international terrorist organizations. Rather, it was embedded in the deep political, economic, and social inequalities of the Malian system, which had been compounded by ecological devastation resulting from drought and desertification, especially in the northern region. The government's historical neglect of the north—and the consequent absence of economic development, employment, and governing institutions there—provided fertile ground for illicit activities and extremist ideologies that crossed international boundaries. The lawless region had attracted smugglers and bandits who offered economic opportunities, and later, jihadis who promoted visions of an alternative society. With few alternatives, many northerners participated in the illicit activities and embraced the new ideologies. However, neither crime nor religion caused the 2007–9 rebellion.

The Malian conflict also stimulated involvement by neighboring states and by France, the region's dominant external power. These countries justified their interventions as a response to instability and to what they described as a terrorist threat. In March 2009, the governments of Algeria, Libya, Mali, and Niger agreed to cooperate in securing their borders against smugglers, bandits, and AQIM militants.[1] The United States provided substantial support for the regional efforts, some of which resulted in abuses of civilian populations. Meanwhile, some of the same countries operated at cross purposes. France, Algeria, and Mauritania assisted the Tuareg rebellions in Mali in the hope that the secular insurgencies would help drive AQIM from the region. However, Tuareg rebels were doing business with the AQIM militants and criminal networks that these countries sought to undermine. Malian government officials also colluded with the outlaws, reaping a share of their smuggling and hostage-taking proceeds in exchange for turning a blind eye.

It is in this context that the fallout from the 2011 Libyan uprising should be viewed. When the Libyan protests began, Malian Tuaregs were already prominent among Qaddafi's crack desert troops. After Qaddafi's death, some 3,000 Malian Tuaregs returned home with all-terrain vehicles, shoulder-launched antiaircraft guns, rocket-propelled grenades, and other sophisticated weapons looted from Libyan arsenals. In November 2011, the National Movement for the Liberation of Azawad (MNLA) emerged from several smaller Tuareg organizations and declared its intent to establish an independent state in northern Mali.[2] The MNLA leader, Mohammed Ag Najim, had served as a colonel in Qaddafi's army and commanded an elite desert unit. The Libyan veterans were joined

Photo 11.1. An MNLA fighter stands guard in Boulikessi, Mali, near the border with Burkina Faso, June 2012. Photo by Ferhat Bouda/Redux Pictures.

by elite Tuareg units from the Malian army who had been trained by US Army Special Forces as part of the US counterterrorism initiative. Responding to Ag Najim's appeal, they defected from the national army with their weapons and vehicles. In addition, 1,600 Tuareg soldiers who had been incorporated into the Malian security forces under the terms of the 1992 peace agreement aligned with the secessionists, as did some Tuareg members of parliament. The MNLA conquest began on January 17, 2012, with attacks on the Malian army in half a dozen northern towns. The cities of Gao, Timbuktu, and Kidal fell quickly to the MNLA as the Malian armed forces collapsed and fled.

The impact of Qaddafi's downfall was compounded by the effects of US counterterrorism initiatives. On March 22, 2012, Mali's elected president, Amadou Toumani Touré, was overthrown in a military coup led by a US-trained army captain, Amadou Haya Sanogo, who had participated in the US State Department's International Military Education and Training program.[3] Claiming that they had deposed the president because of his ineffective response to the Tuareg insurgency and his role in perpetuating a corrupt and repressive governing system, the coup leaders suspended the constitution and established a military junta. Although Mali had been touted in the West as a model of African democracy, the country had suffered from serious electoral irregularities, a rubber-stamp parliament, political repression, and endemic corruption among ruling elites. Foreign powers quickly condemned the coup. The Obama administration called for the return of democratic rule and, as mandated by US law, withheld military, security, and development aid, discontinued the counterterrorism program, and withdrew US Army Special Forces from Mali.[4] The EU halted all nonhumanitarian aid, ECOWAS imposed economic sanctions, and ECOWAS and the AU suspended Mali's membership.

Rather than bringing order and stability, the coup set the stage for the dissolution of the Malian state. On April 6, 2012, having gained control of more than two-thirds of the country, the MNLA announced the formation of a secessionist state called the Islamic State of Azawad. By late May, however, the MNLA was financially broke. Hoping to enhance its resource base and secure its foothold, the secular secessionist movement formed an alliance of convenience with Ansar Dine (Defenders of the Faith), a newly formed Salafi jihadist group led by Iyad Ag Ghali, a leader of an earlier Malian insurgency. Ag Ghali had been exposed to fundamentalist teachings by Pakistani missionaries in northern Mali in the 1990s and in Saudi Arabia, where he had held a diplomatic post from 2007 to 2010. Closely associated with AQIM, Ansar Dine had considerable resources at its disposal. The weakened MNLA accommodated Salafi demands and conceded that the Tuareg state would be an Islamic one, governed by Islamic law. By June, the MNLA, Ansar Dine, and various AQIM factions controlled separate spheres in Mali's north. Well endowed with money and weapons, Ansar Dine and AQIM rapidly outmaneuvered the MNLA. Within months, an AQIM splinter organization, the Movement for Unity and Jihad in West Africa (MUJWA), had emerged as a new force in northern Mali. While the MNLA and Ansar Dine were indigenous organizations, AQIM and MUJWA were dominated by foreign fighters.

Although initially divided on the question of foreign military intervention, Mali's postcoup government eventually requested UN assistance. The international community was equally divided in its response. In October 2012, France and ECOWAS took the lead in pushing for UN intervention under a Chapter VII mandate. Voicing concerns about the spread of terrorism, France called for immediate action to expel Muslim extremists from Mali's north and to reunite the country. Although it was

Photo 11.2. An Ansar Dine fighter in Timbuktu, Mali, 2012. Photo by Magharebia.

silent about its economic interests, France was deeply dependent on nuclear energy and was aware of untapped uranium deposits beneath the deserts controlled by the Tuareg insurgents.[5] Moreover, Mali possessed significant oil reserves. The United States supported the notion of military intervention but argued that such action should be delayed until after Mali had elected a new civilian government, which would allow Washington to resume military and economic aid.[6] Moreover, in Washington's view, the political problems that had led to the crisis needed to be addressed, and the Malian army, which should play a leading role in any military effort, had to be properly trained. A number of other nations and NGOs urged restraint. The International Crisis Group warned that "turning northern Mali into a new front in the 'war on terror'" could obscure the legitimate grievances of the northern populations, increase human rights abuses and interethnic conflict, and stimulate AQIM reprisals in other countries.[7]

Meanwhile, Washington and Paris looked for surrogates to carry out their agenda and lobbied African countries to contribute to a military intervention force. Beyond the ECOWAS alliance, three countries were especially important: Chad, which had significant experience with desert fighting, and Mauritania and Algeria, which shared long borders with Mali and were major sources of AQIM fighters. All three countries had participated in Western counterterrorism initiatives. However, Algeria, which possessed the strongest military force in North Africa, opposed foreign intervention in Mali, particularly if France were involved. Algiers worried that such an operation, especially if it were spearheaded by AQIM's primary Western nemesis, might push AQIM militants back into Algerian territory and stimulate unrest among Algerian Tuaregs. Given its horrific experiences in the 1990s, Algeria was wary of associating itself with a French-led campaign to eradicate Muslim extremists from a neighboring country and warned that regional destabilization could ensue.

While France and the United States pressured non-ECOWAS countries, ECOWAS proposed its own intervention plan. On November 11, the organization agreed to provide 3,300 troops from member states, who would train and equip Malian soldiers to retake the north. The ECOWAS soldiers would not be peacekeepers, but instead would constitute an intervention force similar to the AU force in Somalia. The AU endorsed the plan, with the expectation that Western countries would provide most of the financial and logistical support. The UN secretary-general recommended that the Security Council approve the proposal, but he noted that political reconciliation, which required addressing the north's longstanding grievances, was essential for reunification and that military action should remain a last resort. International human rights organizations urged extreme caution, raising concerns about the Malian military's long record of human rights abuses and suggesting that populations with legitimate grievances would be treated as terrorists. Many warned of the humanitarian catastrophe that would result from airstrikes and ground attacks.

On December 20, 2012, the UN Security Council voted unanimously to endorse the ECOWAS/AU plan and authorized the establishment of the African-led International Support Mission in Mali (AFISMA). Limiting the involvement of Western troops in order to minimize the possibility of backlash, AFISMA was slated to be an all-African intervention force made up of troops from ECOWAS and other AU countries. The EU agreed to send 400 officers, led by a French commander, to train Malian troops. The United States, which was legally barred from directly assisting the Malian regime, offered to help train, equip, and transport the

ECOWAS and AU contingents. Funding for the operation was provided by the EU, supplemented with bilateral support from Australia, India, Japan, and Norway.

Provoked by the threat of foreign military intervention, Ansar Dine, AQIM, and MUJWA launched a southward advance, taking the central Mali town of Konna on January 10, 2013. Konna was less than 40 miles from the Sévaré airfield and army base, which the government needed to conduct military operations in the north, and less than 400 miles from Bamako. Fearing that the jihadi insurgents would move unimpeded into the capital, the Malian government appealed to France.

Casting aside the international plan that had been months in the making and that would have limited Western military involvement on the ground, France embarked on a unilateral military action it dubbed Operation Serval. By January 11, hundreds of French troops had arrived in Sévaré to reinforce the struggling Malian army. Within days, French warplanes were attacking jihadi training camps, weapons depots, and other positions throughout the north.[8] French President François Hollande declared that Paris would stop the jihadi advance to the south, retake the north, restore Mali's territorial integrity and the authority of the central government, and eradicate terrorist bases. Foreign powers that initially had supported the carefully crafted multilateral proposal switched their allegiance to the French operation. Chad provided 2,000 troops, which were placed under French command. The United States supplied drone and satellite surveillance, cell phone monitoring, and tanker aircraft that allowed French warplanes to refuel in flight. Washington also offered logistics support, troop transport, and payment for a large portion of the operation's expenses.

Even as France engaged in intensive air attacks, a second column of mostly AQIM fighters moved west along the Mauritanian border, taking the military outpost of Diabaly, less than 300 miles north of Bamako. With two-thirds of the country under their control, the jihadi insurgents were closer to the capital than they had been before the French intervention. The Malian army was unable to mount an effective counterattack, even with French air support. Paris announced that it would increase its troop strength from 800 to 2,500. President Hollande promised that French forces would remain in Mali until they had halted the jihadi offensive, extremist fighters were captured, killed, or forced out of the country, and the capital was secured. By the end of January, French and Chadian troops, belatedly supplemented by 1,400 AFISMA personnel, had retaken

Photo 11.3. Chadian army soldiers participate in Operation Serval and AFISMA, near Kidal, Mali, April 3, 2013. Photo by Patrick Robert/Corbis via Getty Images.

several important northern cities and towns. The insurgents retreated to the mountains near the Algerian border, where they used the relative security of their remote hideaways to prepare for attacks elsewhere.

As the jihadi forces gained ground, the Western response grew more vociferous. British Prime Minister David Cameron referred to their activities as "a global threat" that required "a global response," one that could last decades.[9] US officials defined the insurgency as an al-Qaeda operation. The September 2001 Authorization for Use of Military Force permitted the US president to use military force only "against those nations, organizations, or persons he determines planned, authorized, committed, or aided the terrorist attacks that occurred on September 11, 2001, or harbored such organizations or persons."[10] Therefore, in order to legally justify the use of lethal force in Mali, the United States had to assert—if not prove—that the fight in northern Mali was against al-Qaeda. Because the insurgents had links to AQIM, an al-Qaeda affiliate, the United States claimed the right to intervene.[11] US Defense Secretary Leon Panetta warned, "We have a responsibility to go after al-Qaeda wherever they are. We're going after them in Yemen and Somalia, and we have a responsibility to make sure that al-Qaeda does not establish a base for operations in North Africa, in Mali."[12]

Critics of the Western-led operation cautioned that ill-conceived actions could have unforeseen consequences; Europe and the United States were again fighting forces they had trained, armed, and funded to combat other foes. Dissenters worried that the precipitous military intervention in Mali, with no clear endgame, could result in a Vietnam- or Afghanistan-like quagmire and engender even deeper hostility toward the West. Large numbers of civilian casualties could rally Muslim extremists worldwide and transform Mali into a launching pad for terrorist attacks throughout the region. Human Rights Watch reported that Malian security forces and civilians of other ethnic groups were abusing Tuareg and Arab civilians, and that these attacks had intensified after the French intervention.

Indeed, the extremist backlash began almost immediately. Jihadis had warned that they would attack countries supporting the Mali intervention. Algeria, which had allowed French planes to fly through its airspace, was the first target. A major producer of oil and natural gas for Western Europe and the United States, Algeria depended on these resources for 97 percent of its export earnings and 60 percent of its governmental revenues. On January 16, 2013, jihadi militants from several countries seized an internationally managed natural gas field near the Algeria-Libya border and took dozens of foreign workers hostage. The attack was led by al-Mulathameen (Masked Brigade), an al-Qaeda faction founded by Mokhtar Belmokhtar, an Algerian veteran of the Soviet-Afghan War and the Algerian civil war and a former AQIM leader.[13] A reluctant participant in the Mali operation, Algeria had been subjected to enormous pressure from France and the United States to accommodate their needs. Hardened by its own civil war, Algeria refused to pay ransoms or negotiate with terrorists and generally responded forcefully to terrorist attacks. Accordingly, the Algerian military launched assaults on the natural gas complex on January 17 and 19. At least thirty-eight hostages and twenty-nine militants were killed. Niger, which had contributed troops to the Mali intervention force and allowed France and the United States to use its territory as a base, was targeted on May 23, when suicide bombers attacked two strategic sites in the Tuareg-Berber region of central Niger: a Nigerien military compound in Agadez and a French-owned uranium mine near Arlit, about 135 miles from the Algerian border. More than twenty people were killed, and the mine was badly damaged. Al-Mulathameen and MUJWA claimed responsibility.

French military intervention in Mali, like French involvement in Rwanda and Côte d'Ivoire, preempted or hijacked multilateral initiatives under African or UN auspices. In each instance, the UN Security Council either ignored the breach or authorized French actions after the fact. After the Mali intervention, a UN Security Council resolution passed on April 25 retroactively endorsed the French military operation. The same resolution vested the United Nations Multidimensional Integrated Stabilization Mission in Mali (MINUSMA) with the power to protect Malian civilians and UN personnel and to help Mali's unelected governing authorities establish state administration and stability throughout the country.[14] The UN forces were permitted to operate in collaboration with Malian security forces, which remained under the authority of the unelected postcoup government and had not yet been retrained to comply with internationally accepted human rights practices. The UN mission was authorized to include up to 12,640 military and police personnel, who would assume the functions of AFISMA, the rushed African-led operation that had been overshadowed by the French intervention. Finally, the Security Council resolution empowered French forces to intervene in support of MINUSMA if requested by the UN secretary-general.

Despite the large French and UN presence, the northern insurgencies continued. In July 2013, France increased its troop numbers to 3,500. In August, the Algerian al-Qaeda group, al-Mulathameen, merged with MUJWA to form al-Mourabitoun (The Sentinels). The strengthened organization continued to challenge government and international forces. Tuareg nationalists also kept up the pressure, regularly defeating the Malian army. By May 2014, the MNLA had regained control of much of northern Mali. Once again, France responded militarily. In August, Paris initiated Operation Barkhane, a counterterrorism program modeled on the US TSCTP, which was intended to counter Muslim extremists from Mauritania to Chad. Headquartered in Chad, Operation Barkhane included a permanent deployment of more than 3,000 French soldiers—a number that had increased to 4,000 in 2017—as well as contingents from Burkina Faso, Chad, Mali, Mauritania, and Niger. Regular French troops were stationed in Chad and Niger, and French special operations forces were based in Burkina Faso. Chad served as the center of French air power, which included Mirage fighter jets, while reconnaissance drones were based in Niger and the logistics hub was located in Côte d'Ivoire. Like its US counterpart, the French initiative was weakened by its disproportionate focus on Western and regional security interests rather than on the political and economic grievances underlying the rebellions.

Expecting France to take the lead in its former colonies, the United States played a critical supporting role. After assisting the French intervention in Mali in January 2013, the United States flew daily drone surveillance missions from an air base outside of Niamey, Niger. Tracking the movements of insurgents who had retreated to the extensive, lightly populated desert and mountain regions, US Air Force personnel gathered intelligence that helped the French military determine targets for its airstrikes. In September 2014 Washington announced that it would establish a second drone base in Niger, this one located in Agadez, close to the site of large uranium deposits and 150 miles from the French mines near Arlit. Within surveillance range of several countries, the Agadez base would allow the United States to monitor Muslim extremists in Niger, Mali, Nigeria, Chad, and southern Libya, which, since Qaddafi's ouster, had become a key transit corridor for al-Qaeda and Islamic State–linked fighters, weapons traffickers, and drug smugglers.

While France and the United States focused on counterterrorism, Algeria brokered a peace accord under UN auspices. Although it had warily supported the military operation in Mali, Algeria believed that a political solution that emphasized inclusion and compromise was more likely to diminish the threat along its eastern and southern borders. Between May and October 2015, rival Tuareg insurgent groups—the Coordination of the Movements of Azawad (CMA) and a group known as the Platform—signed various agreements with the Bamako government. However, the insurgents violated the ceasefires, the government failed to implement promised reforms, and fighting resumed. The International Crisis Group charged that the accords, written primarily by international mediators, had been imposed from outside and emphasized foreign security agendas rather than local interests. External powers had prioritized the reestablishment of law, order, and stability and focused on ending the Tuareg rebellion so that the Malian military and international forces could turn their attention to the jihadist

Photo 11.4. French Operation Barkhane personnel speak with an elder in Mali's southern region, March 17, 2016. Photo: TM1972/Wikimedia Commons.

insurgency. Local groups, in contrast, were concerned about the militarized political and economic system and the lack of social services, employment, justice, and political autonomy in the north. Although these structural issues were at the source of the conflict, the 2015 agreements did not adequately address them.

A further weakness of the 2015 accords was their failure to include all parties to the conflict, including newer jihadi organizations. Ansar Dine and the allied Macina Liberation Front, which originated among Fulanis in central Mali, had been excluded from the talks.[15] Local entrepreneurs, who engaged in illicit trafficking and whose private armies were implicated in human rights abuses, were not brought into line. Corrupt government officials and antigovernment insurgents—including CMA and Platform members—benefited from these illicit activities and opposed any efforts to hamper them.

Meanwhile, jihadi organizations were transformed rather than defeated. As foreign armies ousted jihadi fighters from northern Mali's cities and towns and shut them out of peace agreements, militants shifted their focus to civilian populations in unprotected rural villages and to high-profile targets that captured world attention. Central Mali, which had been ignored in the peace accords, and border regions near Niger, Burkina Faso, and Senegal were particularly vulnerable, and citizens of former French colonies that participated in the French-led military operations were singled out for retaliation. The November 2015 terror attack on the Radisson Blu hotel in Bamako was emblematic of this change. In that assault, militants from al-Mourabitoun, AQIM, and the Macina Liberation Front seized 170 hostages, targeting especially non-Muslim Malians and foreigners. Twenty-two hostages were killed when Malian, French, and US security forces stormed the hotel.

In December, al-Mourabitoun formally affiliated with AQIM, and the invigorated organization continued its southward movement. In 2016 it extended its operations to Burkina Faso, which had contributed a large contingent to the UN mission in Mali and where France maintained a military base; to Niger, which had also assisted the mission; and to Côte d'Ivoire, the logistics hub for French military operations. On January 15, al-Mourabitoun and AQIM militants attacked a luxury hotel and nearby café in the Burkinabe capital of Ouagadougou that killed at least thirty people, including nationals of several Western countries.[16] Similarly, in March, AQIM struck a beach resort in Côte d'Ivoire, killing more than a dozen citizens of Côte d'Ivoire, Burkina Faso, Cameroon, Mali, France, and Germany—countries that were central to the region's counterterrorism operations. By the end of the year, jihadis had gained control of large swaths of territory in Mali's rural areas, from which they launched assaults on provincial towns. In early 2017, the jihadis' new strategy met with some success: Burkina Faso announced that it would withdraw from peacekeeping missions in Mali and Sudan to focus on the growing threat at home.

As al-Qaeda adapted to new circumstances in Mali, the Islamic State also found an opening. In 2015 a minority of al-Mourabitoun members left the organization to form the Islamic State in Mali, subsequently renamed the Islamic State in the Greater Sahara. In late 2016, the organization claimed responsibility for attacks against military outposts in northern Burkina Faso near the Mali border, and against a prison in Niger's capital, Niamey. In the Mali-Niger border region, where herders and farmers of various ethnic groups competed for scarce resources, the Islamic State group found support among Fulanis who had been victims of intercommunal violence. Al-Qaeda regained the initiative in March 2017, when Ansar Dine, al-Mourabitoun, and the Macina Liberation Front merged to form Jama'at Nusrat al-Islam wal-Muslimin (Group for the Support of Islam and Muslims). With each constituent dominating a particular geographic region, the new al-Qaeda-linked organization promised greater coordination and a wider regional reach.

As 2017 drew to a close, Mali remained in turmoil. Much of the north continued to be deprived of a functioning government and basic social services. Jihadi organizations profited, and even gained legitimacy, by providing security and conflict resolution assistance. New sources of violence had also emerged. In northern Mali, the CMA splintered, and insurgent organizations based on local ethnic alliances proliferated. As nonsignatories to the accords, the community-based groups fought to obtain recognition and benefits. In central Mali, conflicts over land and other resources spawned bandits, community defense forces, and new groups of jihadis. Foreign military intervention in Mali—without consideration for the grievances and desires of affected populations—was bound to fail. Because it led to intensified extremist violence in Mali and its expansion to neighboring countries, and because in many instances it exposed vulnerable populations to retaliatory attacks, foreign intervention arguably did more harm than good.

Setting the Stage in Nigeria: Inequality and Insurgency in the Northeast (2009–17)

Not far from the turmoil in Libya and Mali was Nigeria, the continent's most populous nation, largest economy, and greatest producer of oil. As a regional powerhouse, Nigeria maintained a high profile in international peacekeeping, playing a significant diplomatic and military role on the continent as well as in the West African subregion. At the same time, Nigeria suffered from numerous internal conflicts, some with serious subregional ramifications. A vast and complex country, comprising more than 250 ethnic groups, diverse geographic regions, and many religions, Nigeria was marked by huge disparities in wealth and living standards, both within regions and between them. After the Cold War, inequalities in the distribution of wealth, power, and resources provoked a number of local and regional conflicts in Nigeria. Although these struggles predated the strife in Libya and Mali, instability in those countries contributed to an insurgency in Nigeria's northeast that in turn led to foreign military intervention. The northeastern insurgency and its ramifications are the focus of this case study.

To be properly understood, the northeastern insurrection must be considered in context. During the early twenty-first century, the region was one of several conflict zones in Nigeria. In each zone, civil strife had specific local catalysts as well as overarching causes that grew from Nigeria's political, economic, and social structures. Simplistic analyses often reduce complex multicausal processes to single-issue rivalries rooted in religious, ethnic, or regional differences. In the case of Nigeria, it is common to paint a scenario that pits a predominantly Muslim north against a mostly Christian south. There is some truth to this portrayal. In Nigeria, as in Sudan, Côte d'Ivoire, and Mali, disparities between north and south do exist, and they were sharpened during the colonial and postindependence eras.

During the colonial period, northern Muslim elites were incorporated into the British system of indirect rule, which provided them with political recognition and material benefits in exchange for their role in implementing colonial policies. Sensitive to the interests of the Muslim rulers, British authorities curtailed the activities of Christian missionaries in the north, which limited the number of Western schools and health care facilities in that region. As the colonial seat and the center of missionary focus, the south received an incommensurate share of schools, clinics, and job opportunities. After independence, the disparities continued. In the north, modern schools and clinics remained scarce, and northerners suffered disproportionately from high levels of poverty and unemployment. Growing rates of joblessness were worsened by the imposition of an IMF structural adjustment program in 1986 and other free market reforms throughout the 1990s, which decimated northern industries that were unable to compete with cheap foreign goods. The collapse of the northern textile industry had ripple effects that drove cotton producers out of business. Mismanagement of land and water resources and climate change by-products such as drought, desertification, and devastating floods exacerbated the situation, destroying livelihoods based on herding, farming, and fishing.

Although the disparities favor the southern region, the model based on a north-south dichotomy offers an overly optimistic assessment of the south and masks deep divisions within that region. Poverty, inequality, and underdevelopment in the south are perhaps most evident in the

Niger Delta. Most of Nigeria's oil is produced in the Delta region, where pollution by Western-owned oil companies has destroyed the fishing and agricultural industries and the majority of the population lives in extreme poverty. Oil wealth accounts for the bulk of state revenues and greases a vast patronage system of corrupt government and military officials that transcends regional and ethnic boundaries. Very little of this wealth has been used to benefit Delta communities.[17] The unequal distribution of oil wealth and the environmental and economic destruction caused by oil industry negligence have sparked significant popular protests, ranging from nonviolent civil disobedience in the early 1990s to violent actions by armed groups in the early twenty-first century that included sabotaging oil and natural gas facilities and kidnapping foreign oil workers. Until the onset of the insurgency in the northeast, the Niger Delta was the site of Nigeria's most serious unrest.

The north-south binary also ignores Nigeria's Middle Belt—the borderlands where north and south overlap and where people of diverse ethnic and religious backgrounds have interacted in both peaceable and violent ways. In the middle region, Fulani herders, who are predominantly Muslim, and farmers of diverse ethnicities, who are largely Christian, have a long history of relatively peaceful coexistence. However, since the turn of the twenty-first century, drought and desert encroachment, intensified by climate change, have led to violent clashes over land and water. As in the Darfur region of Sudan, where particular modes of production are also associated with specific demographic sectors, disputes between herders and farmers over scarce resources have spiraled into religious and ethnic conflicts in which thousands of people have been killed.

Finally, the north-south paradigm glosses over differences within the vast northern region. Residents of Nigeria's northeast suffer some of the lowest human development indicators in the world. In 2010, 71.5 percent of the population lived in absolute poverty, more than 50 percent were malnourished, and 31 percent did not have access to safe water. Prospects for the future were bleak: 40 percent of the children did not attend school, and 40 percent of the adults were unemployed; youth were even more likely to be jobless. In the border region linking Nigeria with Cameroon, Chad, and Niger, more than 30 million people depended on the waters of Lake Chad. However, the lake was drying up—destroying the fishing, farming, and herding sectors in the process. With a rapidly growing population and little industry or modern education available, deepening poverty resulted in large out-migrations of people in search of resources. These factors, together with a profoundly corrupt government and abusive security forces that operated with impunity, generated feelings of hopelessness that provided fertile ground for extremist ideologies.

Although Nigeria is divided by ethnicity, region, and religion, the country's most fundamental cleavages are along class lines. Nigerian elites, like elites elsewhere, have more in common with one another than with less privileged members of their own ethnic, regional, or religious group. However, fissures within the ruling oligarchy are deep, and internal divisions are often marked by these demographic differences. During much of the period of northeastern neglect, Nigeria was ruled by northern Muslim elites, many of whom had military backgrounds.[18] A large number of these officials were members of the Fulani ethnic group, which in the nineteenth century had established the powerful Sokoto Caliphate in the northwest. The caliphate's Sufi rulers had been incorporated into the British system of indirect rule, and their sons were among the few northerners who had access to Western education. The descendants of these Fulani emirs, chiefs, and judges and their Hausa or Fulani wives assumed positions of power after Nigeria's independence.[19] In contrast, insurgents in the northeast were generally members of the small Kanuri ethnic group. Their antecedents had resisted absorption into the Sokoto Caliphate and had been a source of slaves for Fulani elites.

Boko Haram and Ansaru

It was in this context that the northeastern insurgency began to take shape. The insurgency was led by two groups: Jama'atu Ahlis-Sunna Lidda'awati Wal-Jihad (People Committed to the Propagation of the Prophet's Teachings and Jihad), commonly known as Boko Haram, and Jama'atu Ansarul Muslimina Fi Biladis-Sudan (Vanguards for the Protection of Muslims in Black Africa), commonly known as Ansaru.[20] Boko Haram, established first, was the more important of the two groups. Ansaru was a splinter organization formed by disaffected Boko Haram members.

Boko Haram was founded in 2002 in Maiduguri, capital of the northeastern state of Borno, which borders Cameroon, Chad, and Niger. Led by the cleric Mohammed Yusuf, Boko Haram was initially a nonviolent

Salafist group, influenced by Saudi thinkers, which rejected Sufi teachings and focused on the moral deterioration of Nigerian society under Western influence. Viewing Western education as the entrée for an elite few into a corrupt system, Boko Haram responded to social problems with solutions emerging from fundamentalist religious beliefs and advocated building a society based on Islamic law. Although it criticized Western cultural influences, Boko Haram did not oppose Western technology or technical education. Aspiring to diminish poverty and to promote economic development in the marginalized region, the organization financed microcredit schemes and provided food and shelter to jobless youths, widows, and children. It appealed to uneducated young men whose traditional livelihoods had been undermined, and to the educated but unemployed. Many without prospects were attracted to the organization's critique of corruption, message of equality, and call for a more meaningful life through adherence to fundamental religious values.

Boko Haram's earliest adherents were primarily clerics, students, and unemployed Western-educated professionals. Most members were Kanuri, a function of the organization's origins in Kanuri-dominated Maiduguri. Initially, they attempted to lead lives apart from what they perceived as a corrupt and decadent society. Over time, however, their objectives changed, prompted by police actions against northeastern residents, escalating clashes between Muslims and Christians in other regions, and Western support for corrupt, repressive Nigerian regimes. As Boko Haram's objectives changed, so did its tactics and targets. The organization turned first to violence against the state, then to terror against civilian populations, expanding its focus from what it deemed impious Muslims and their illegitimate government to Nigerian Christians and foreigners. Eventually, Boko Haram's sporadic violence developed into a full-blown insurgency that aspired to overthrow the Nigerian state and establish a new one based on Islamic law.

Boko Haram's shift to violence began in 2009, triggered by the police shooting of seventeen of the group's members at a funeral. After militants responded by attacking a police station, security forces killed more than 800 people, including Boko Haram leader Mohammed Yusuf, who was executed extrajudicially while in police custody. Under its new leader, Abubakar Shekau, Boko Haram retaliated by targeting police, soldiers, government officials, and Muslim clerics who collaborated with the Nigerian state. As the insurgency spread through Borno, Yobe, Bauchi, and

Kano States, the organization turned its focus to other Muslims it deemed impure—traditional leaders, teachers, students, and health workers involved in polio vaccination campaigns, who were accused of dispensing antifertility drugs to reduce the Muslim population. Attacks on infrastructure were expanded from government offices and police stations to include schools, mosques, and beer halls. Although Boko Haram's early membership was primarily Kanuri, ethnicity was not the organization's focus. Recruited from among alienated urban youth, the first insurgents targeted traditional leadership and rural populations, whose pre-Islamic practices they deemed impure, irrespective of ethnicity. Many of its victims were Kanuri.

Until 2011, Boko Haram concentrated its attention on Nigeria's northern region. That year, however, it moved into the Middle Belt, staging attacks in the capital city of Abuja, where it claimed responsibility for assaults on both the national police and UN headquarters. Boko Haram also began to target Christians, attacking several churches on Christmas Day. By 2015, Boko Haram militants controlled most of Borno State and were responsible for violent assaults across 20 percent of Nigeria, as well as in Cameroon, Chad, and Niger. The toll on the civilian population was enormous. Boko Haram incursions killed an estimated 20,000 people between 2009 and 2017 and forced another 2.8 million from their homes in Nigeria and neighboring countries. Young men and boys were press-ganged as fighters, and women and girls were forced into sexual slavery as the "wives" of fighters who, because of their poverty, had minimal prospects for marriage—and thus, for social adulthood. The insurgency disrupted farming, fishing, and trade, resulting in acute food shortages and increased malnutrition.

Like its grievances, Boko Haram's focus and finances were both local and regional. Although the organization made contact with al-Qaeda in the early stages of its insurgency, it was not an al-Qaeda affiliate, and it did not rely on the international terrorist network for funding or direction. Boko Haram's activities were largely supported by bank robberies, extortion, kidnapping for ransom, and other criminal activities. Al-Qaeda's most significant contributions to the Nigerian organization were training and weaponry. According to UN, EU, and Western government sources, some Boko Haram members were trained by AQIM, al-Shabaab, and al-Qaeda in the Arabian Peninsula (AQAP). In 2012–13, Boko Haram fighters reportedly fought alongside AQIM and MUJWA cadres in northern Mali, and many returned home with weapons from Qaddafi's stockpiles. Some sources claim that foreign jihadis joined Boko Haram, bolstering the ranks of external fighters who had been recruited or press-ganged from Cameroon, Chad, and Niger.[21] In sum, the involvement of international terrorist networks was limited. Boko Haram's focus remained close to home, and its targets were the "near enemy" rather than the "far enemy."

Although Boko Haram retained its local orientation, its organization, philosophy, and tactics transformed over time. In January 2012, following an attack on the northwestern city of Kano that killed as many as 300 people, the organization split, giving rise to a new group that opposed the indiscriminate killing of Muslims. Jama'atu Ansarul Muslimina Fi Biladis-Sudan, or Ansaru, was established by Boko Haram members who had left Nigeria after the 2009 crackdown. Many early members were Western-educated Hausa-Fulanis from Nigeria's northwest who aspired to renew the glory of the old Sokoto Caliphate and who advocated attacks against Nigerian Christians and the government, rather than against local Muslims. The organization's leader, Khalid al-Barnawi (alias, Abu Usamatal Ansari), had been a close associate of Mohammed Yusuf. Some early members had trained with al-Shabaab in Somalia and AQIM in Mali and Algeria. They tended to possess more skills than the Boko Haram cadres who had remained in Nigeria, and they were more deeply influenced by al-Qaeda's global jihadist focus. Ansaru concentrated on Nigerian security forces and high-profile figures instead of carrying out indiscriminate attacks that would disproportionately affect civilian populations. Unlike Boko Haram, Ansaru also targeted Westerners, particularly engineers and construction workers employed in the north, whom they kidnapped for ransom.

Although domestic concerns remained at its core, the conflict in northeastern Nigeria was affected by the insurgencies in Somalia, Libya, and Mali in three important ways. First, those upheavals strengthened al-Qaeda's presence on the continent, giving the network access to Nigerian militants, who in turn benefited from its sophisticated weapons, military training, and broader jihadist perspective. Second, actions taken by UN forces in northern Mali, as well as pressure from Nigerian and AU troops in Nigeria, compelled Boko Haram to collaborate with Ansaru, which extended the reach of al-Qaeda's "far enemy" orientation. When UN troops in Mali disrupted its AQIM supply line in 2013, Boko Haram kidnapped Westerners for ransom for the first time, and by late

2016 it was also attacking Western and military targets. (The impact of internal and external military intervention is considered in the sections that follow.) Third, the Libyan insurgency opened the door to the Islamic State, which took a keen interest in northeastern Nigeria. Although Boko Haram embraced some aspects of al-Qaeda's ideology and accepted the network's assistance, it established formal ties with the Islamic State.

Fundamental disagreements between al-Qaeda and the Islamic State were mirrored by those between Ansaru and Boko Haram. Ansaru adopted the "Guidelines for Jihad," written by al-Qaeda leader Ayman al-Zawahiri, which instructed jihadis to minimize Muslim civilian casualties. Al-Qaeda had publicly criticized the Islamic State, which had emerged from al-Qaeda's Iraqi affiliate and its associates, for its harsh treatment and indiscriminate killing of Muslim civilians in Syria, charging that such actions were contrary to Islamic teachings. In February 2014, al-Qaeda severed ties with the Islamic State. Similarly, in February 2015, Ansaru condemned Boko Haram's killing of innocent Muslims and the organization's attacks on mosques and markets, where Muslims were likely to be victims.

As Ansaru confirmed its loyalty to al-Qaeda, Boko Haram showed increasing preference for the Islamic State. Boko Haram declared its support for the Islamic State leader in 2014 and officially pledged allegiance in March 2015. Although the Nigerian organization maintained its local focus, its new connections gave it greater access to financial, material, and technical support. The Islamic State linkage also raised Boko Haram's global profile, allowing it to attract a growing number of foreign fighters. In April 2015, the Islamic State began to refer to Boko Haram as the Islamic State in West Africa—its first province in sub-Saharan Africa.[22]

The Nigerian Government Response

The Nigerian government responded to the northeastern insurgency with a heavy-handed crackdown that terrorized the civilian population. Declaring a state of emergency in Borno, Yobe, and Adamawa States, the government of President Goodluck Jonathan (2010–15) granted the military extraordinary powers to arrest suspects and seize property. Security forces engaged in a scorched earth campaign that burned thousands of homes and killed as many as 8,000 civilians between 2009 and 2015. More than 1,000 people were executed extrajudicially, and an estimated 7,000 died in military custody—beaten, starved, suffocated, tortured, or shot to death. During the same period, tens of thousands of civilians were arbitrarily arrested, and countless others "disappeared" or were held in detention incommunicado. Government-backed vigilantes—the so-called Civilian Joint Task Force—which was composed primarily of youths armed with knives, machetes, and bows and arrows, rounded up and abused men whom they accused of being Boko Haram members and turned them over to the Nigerian security forces. Within the civilian population, these tactics generated deep-seated fear of the Nigerian military and their associates and, in many cases, increased support for Boko Haram. As the violence intensified, fissures emerged in the Boko Haram organization. Moderates, who wished to negotiate a peace agreement, proved easy targets for the government, and most were removed through death or detention. In consequence, the hardline faction under the leadership of Abubakar Shekau consolidated its power.

Although the Nigerian military showed few qualms about attacking civilians, it was reluctant to confront Boko Haram. Poorly equipped soldiers, whose pay was routinely stolen by higher-ups, had little incentive to fight. When challenged by Boko Haram, Nigerian soldiers often withdrew, leaving weapons and equipment in their wake. As a result, by May 2014 Boko Haram controlled much of the country's northeast. Saddled with a dysfunctional army weakened by deep-seated corruption, the Nigerian government hired some 300 South African private military contractors in 2014–15 to train an elite Nigerian strike force to counter the threat. Most of the contractors were former South African Defence Force members, some of whom had fought with Koevoet, an apartheid-era counterinsurgency unit charged with widespread human rights abuses in Namibia and southern Angola.[23]

Pledging to defeat Boko Haram, General Muhammadu Buhari, a member of the Hausa-Fulani elite in Nigeria's northwest and a favorite of the Nigerian prodemocracy movement, was elected president in March 2015.[24] Buhari fired the high-level military officials who coordinated the government's counterinsurgency strategy and who had been widely criticized for human rights abuses, incompetence, and corruption. He implemented rapid improvements in logistics, equipment, and air support and in the timely payment of soldiers' wages. He instigated a far-reaching anticorruption investigation aimed at the public, private, and military sectors and promised to hold accountable those responsible for human rights violations. Finally, he appealed to the international community for assistance. Buhari made good on some of these promises, indicting more than 300 people and businesses for theft and misappropriation of military funds. However, in 2017, human rights organizations found that ongoing corruption in the military continued to obstruct successful counterinsurgency measures and that Nigeria's international partners, who provided arms and aid to the government, were complicit.

The International Response

UNITED STATES

A powerful anglophone country in a largely francophone region dominated by French interests, Nigeria was of special concern to the United States. The United States was the country's largest foreign investor, with significant investments in Nigeria's petroleum, mining, and wholesale trading sectors. Nigeria, in turn, was an important supplier of crude oil to the United States, as well as its primary counterterrorism partner in northwest Africa, where it played a central role in the TSCTP.

Despite their close collaboration and common interests, Nigeria and the United States experienced periodic strains in their relationship. The Abuja government resented the criticisms leveled by US officials, particularly during the Obama administration. Terence McCulley, the US ambassador to Nigeria from 2010 to 2013, stated publicly that military actions against Boko Haram were insufficient to root out violent extremism; the Nigerian government must also address endemic corruption, political repression, human rights abuses, poverty, and the general lack of accountability. Secretary of State John Kerry subsequently echoed these concerns. The Leahy provision in the US Foreign Assistance Act was another source of tension. Although the United States provided Nigeria with millions of dollars annually in military aid, that support came with restrictions. The Leahy language, which prohibits US assistance to foreign military or police units that have engaged in gross human rights violations without penalty, proved to be a significant obstacle to US support for Nigerian military operations.[25] The Nigerian military had a long history of corruption. Commanders routinely stole soldiers' pay and siphoned off funds intended for critical ammunition and equipment. The result was low morale among the rank and file, refusal to engage with the enemy, and widespread desertion. Because human rights abuses were so common, US personnel were hard pressed to find Nigerian military units with which they could work, and evidence that Boko Haram had infiltrated the Nigerian intelligence and security services made them reluctant to share information with their Nigerian counterparts.

Anxious to halt the spread of al-Qaeda and Islamic State influence in West Africa, the United States sought alternative ways to assist the Nigerian military. The establishment of the Nigerian Army Special Operations Command (NASOC) in January 2014 opened the way to renewed US-Nigerian military cooperation. Because NASOC included newly organized military units that had no record of human rights abuses, US personnel were permitted to train them. As a result, during 2014, more than 200 US Special Operations troops prepared Nigerian forces to challenge Boko Haram in the north and other militants in the Niger Delta. Although US counterterrorism instruction stressed the need to respect human rights, protect civilians, address underlying grievances, and hold security forces accountable, US impact in these areas remained weak.

The intensification of US support in 2014 was motivated in part by Boko Haram's kidnapping of 276 schoolgirls from the town of Chibok in April. Although Boko Haram militants had killed nearly 20,000 civilians and abducted thousands of boys, girls, and women since 2009, it was the seizure of the schoolgirls that caused an international outcry. Pushed by media and popular attention, the United States sent eighty Special Operations Forces troops and dozens of experts from the State Department, Pentagon, and FBI to assist in finding and aiding the victims. Deploying reconnaissance aircraft and unmanned surveillance drones, US military personnel flew hundreds of missions over 37,000 square miles in the heavily forested northeast. However, they found little that might help locate the girls, and the Nigerian military failed to act on the scant information provided.

Frustrated by the corruption and incompetence of the Nigerian security forces, US trainers and specialists increasingly focused on the armed forces of neighboring Cameroon, Chad, and Niger, which they hoped would boost Washington's efforts in Nigeria. In March 2015, US instructors in Chad were joined by experts from other Western countries and 1,200 African troops for a three-week counterterrorism training exercise. Boko Haram's declaration of allegiance to the leader of the Islamic State coincided with the conclusion of that event.

The election of General Buhari as Nigeria's new president in March 2015 initially did little to assuage tensions between Washington and Abuja. Like his predecessor, President Buhari publicly dismissed claims of human rights abuses by the Nigerian military and charged that Washington's refusal to provide his country with strategic weapons had "aided and abetted" the terrorists.[26] He nonetheless removed a number of high-level military officials, including the heads of the army, navy, and air force, and initiated anticorruption and security sector reforms. By 2016 the United States was again working closely with the Nigerian military, despite the ongoing concerns of human rights organizations and some members of Congress. The Trump administration, which took office in January 2017, made clear that the common goal of fighting terrorism would take precedence over other concerns.[27]

Subregional Response

The conflict in Nigeria, like those in other subregions, had spillover effects in neighboring countries that threatened to destabilize a wide geographic area. Anxious to contain the insurgency before it could undermine their own societies, Nigeria's neighbors were motivated by both the response to instability and war on terror paradigms. However, dealing with Nigeria required finesse. As a regional powerhouse possessing Africa's largest economy and one of its strongest militaries, Nigeria was among the most important contributors to UN, AU, and ECOWAS peacekeeping missions in Africa. It had spearheaded military and diplomatic efforts to end conflicts far beyond the West African subregion and was widely regarded as a continental leader. Given Nigeria's stature and influence, neither the AU nor ECOWAS was willing to exert pressure on Abuja to address local grievances, political corruption, and security force abuses. Unwilling to admit its inability to resolve its own problems, the Jonathan government had resisted the notion of a UN intervention force and only reluctantly engaged its neighbors in an alternative counterinsurgency scenario.

Under intense international scrutiny following the Chibok kidnappings, President Jonathan asked France to organize a meeting to focus on subregional security concerns. The May 2014 gathering included Nigeria and four neighboring francophone states: Benin, Cameroon, Chad, and

Niger. Diplomats from the United States, France, the UK, and various EU member states were also present. At the May meeting, Nigeria and its neighbors agreed to share and coordinate intelligence, to engage in joint border surveillance, and to increase military cooperation to counter the growing threat to subregional stability. At a follow-up meeting in October, the five West and Central African states agreed to establish a multinational military force to combat Boko Haram that would be modeled on the AU force fighting the al-Shabaab insurgency in Somalia. Representatives from the UN, AU, and the five neighboring countries then met in February 2015 to iron out the details, again with the participation of the major Western powers. In March, the AU approved the Multinational Joint Task Force (MNJTF), slated to include as many as 10,000 troops from the five West African countries, and asked the UN to endorse and finance the endeavor. A Security Council statement in July commended the efforts of the AU, ECOWAS, and ECCAS to develop a comprehensive strategy, but it did not provide the political and financial commitment the AU had sought. Other extracontinental entities provided some assistance. The EU and the United States each pledged approximately $45 million. Washington also announced that it would establish a new drone base in Cameroon and send 300 US troops to provide intelligence, surveillance, and reconnaissance assistance, while France offered military training and equipment.

Meanwhile, joint task force members began their offensive. In January and February 2015, some 5,000 Chadian troops forced Boko Haram militants from a number of northeastern Nigerian towns while Chadian planes bombed insurgent outposts along the Nigeria-Cameroon border. Boko Haram launched retaliatory attacks into Cameroon, Chad, and Niger, targeting villagers near the frontier and striking into the heart of Chad's capital, N'Djamena. By October, members of the African coalition had assigned 8,700 troops to the multinational task force and were using their national armies to fight Boko Haram within their own borders.

Given the historical rivalry between Nigeria and France and its protégés for subregional domination, the establishment of the multinational coalition was both notable and problematic. Nigeria and Cameroon harbored deeply rooted and enduring tensions. A decades-long border dispute over the oil-rich Bakassi region had been resolved in favor of Cameroon in 2002, but Nigeria only conceded the territory in 2012. Like the anglophone powerhouse, all four francophone countries were marked by poverty, corruption, and security forces that had engaged in human rights abuses. US-trained troops in Niger had been accused of committing atrocities against Tuareg civilians in 2007–8. Chadian troops who participated in an AU peacekeeping mission in the Central African Republic had been implicated in attacks on civilians in 2013–14, and Chadian, Cameroonian, and French soldiers in the Central African Republic had been accused of sexually abusing children during the same conflict. Finally, Nigeria chafed at the prospect of being rescued by its poor francophone neighbors and the increased French influence that would likely ensue.

Despite the internal tensions, the African regional task force proved more effective than the Nigerian armed forces, and by early 2016 it had regained much of the territory once held by the insurgents. However, Boko Haram insurrectionists, like those in Somalia and Mali, were not

Photo 11.5. Nigerien soldiers fighting Boko Haram in Diffa, Niger, near the border with Borno State, Nigeria, March 2015. Photo by Voice of America.

defeated. No longer in control of vast expanses of territory, they shifted their tactics, increasing the number of high-visibility suicide bombings in crowded marketplaces, mosques, and unprotected villages. Military pressure in Nigeria forced militants across international borders, and they established new operational bases in Cameroon, Chad, and Niger. By 2017, some 8.5 million people in the Lake Chad basin suffered from extreme food insecurity as a result of both climate change and the regional conflict. Experts continued to warn that the threat could not be suppressed by sheer military might, but instead required increased support for social, economic, and infrastructural development, substantive participation by local citizens, responsive and accountable government, and the establishment of trust between local communities and the state.

The Nigerian government and its external backers responded to the insurgency with enormous military force, but they did little to begin the fundamental political, economic, and social transformation necessary for a lasting peace. Increased counterterrorism spending was a boon to the corrupt Nigerian military bureaucracy, which siphoned off billions of dollars to finance personal luxury and political patronage. Illegal financial flows from Nigeria tripled between 2001 and 2017. With much to gain from a war economy, Nigeria's military elite had little incentive to seek political, economic, and social transformation or to work for an enduring peace. Foreign military support strengthened this corrupt system.

Conclusion

Regime change in Libya, fomented by internal rebellion and foreign intervention, had ramifications that penetrated into the Western Sahel. In Mali and Nigeria, an influx of weapons, fighters, funding, and training fueled existing grievances and incipient insurgencies. Foreign powers and entities also intervened in these countries, justifying their actions according to the response to instability/responsibility to protect and war on terror paradigms.

In Mali, weapons and fighters unleashed by Qaddafi's fall bolstered a simmering separatist insurgency and gave birth to a jihadi one. These insurrections in turn sparked an internal coup and external military intervention. The involvement of foreign powers and entities completed the circle by attracting fighters from the international al-Qaeda network. In northeastern Nigeria, local grievances emerging from regional inequalities and economic marginalization gave rise to a religious movement that proposed to remedy these ills through a return to the fundamentals of Islam. A ruthless government crackdown on the movement and the surrounding population provoked an insurgency that attracted Nigerian fighters who had trained with AQIM in Mali and returned home with Libyan weapons. Instability in northeastern Nigeria penetrated into Cameroon, Chad, and Niger and stimulated intervention by foreign powers and multinational organizations, as well as by jihadis linked to al-Qaeda and the Islamic State. In both Mali and Nigeria, insurgents scattered by foreign militaries regrouped in new areas and transformed their tactics. They escalated attacks on soft targets, which placed civilians at even greater risk.

In both cases, foreign military intervention brought short-term gains but failed to produce long-term solutions that would resolve underlying grievances. Although feared for their brutal tactics, insurgents in both countries generated some support by providing services and a means to redress local grievances, however limited. Yet neither Bamako nor Abuja embarked on serious efforts to reestablish governmental and social services in the areas from which the insurgents had been expelled. Instead, they continued to concentrate power and resources in the urban centers inhabited by the majority of voters and political elites. In 2017, Mali actually intensified its military-heavy, law-and-order focus. Together with Burkina Faso, Chad, Mauritania, and Niger, Mali helped institute a new G5 Sahel Joint Force with a broader mandate and geographic reach than MINUSMA or MNJTF. Comprising as many as 5,000 military, police, and civilian personnel, the multinational force was established to fight terrorism, organized crime, and illegal migration and to help to restore state authority across the Sahel. The AU approved the plan, the EU offered financial support, and France convinced the UN Security Council to authorize and fund the enterprise.

At the end of 2017, prospects for the success of the G5 Sahel Joint Force were dim. The Trump administration, which hoped to reduce Washington's UN peacekeeping contributions, succeeded in weakening the force's mandate and blocked its funding from the UN peacekeeping budget, although it promised some bilateral US support. If sufficient funding is found, the new entity will still face many of the obstacles that confronted its predecessors. Local populations, historically neglected by corrupt governments and abused by police, customs officials, and security forces, will have little reason to support another externally driven law-and-order initiative that will likely expose them to retaliation and threaten the underground economy that enables them to survive.

In West Africa, both internal and external forces have promoted military responses to political, economic, and social problems. In the cases of Mali and Nigeria, multinational bodies, neighboring states, and France played significant roles in promoting the military-driven agendas. In those instances, the United States had a relatively minor impact. However, in other African conflicts, the influence of Washington's pro-military orientation was strong and its imprint on the war on terror paradigm especially critical. The continuities and changes in US Africa policy after the Cold War and their increasing militarization are the subject of chapter 12.

Suggested Reading

For an overview of conditions in the Western Sahel that provoked recent conflicts, see Frederic Wehrey and Anouar Boukhars, eds., *Perilous Desert: Insecurity in the Sahara* (Washington, DC: Carnegie Endowment for International Peace, 2013). Contributors consider the interplay of political, economic, and social inequalities, climate change, transnational criminal networks, and extremist ideologies.

The Mali crisis and its causes are the subject of several recommended works. Susanna D. Wing, "Mali: Politics of a Crisis," *African Affairs* 112, no. 448 (July 2013): 476–85, explores the background to the crisis by examining the strengths and weaknesses of the Malian government from the 1990s through 2013. Jean Sebastian Lecocq, *Disputed Desert: Decolonisation, Competing Nationalisms and Tuareg Rebellions in Northern Mali* (Boston: Brill, 2010), investigates longstanding grievances in northern Mali and the source of the 2011–13 Tuareg insurgency. Lawrence E. Cline, "Nomads, Islamists, and Soldiers: The Struggles for Northern Mali," *Studies in Conflict and Terrorism* 36, no. 8 (August 2013): 617–34, explores the origins of the Tuareg insurgency, the diverse groups competing for power in 2013, and the impact of counterterrorism policies. Stephen Kinzer, "Libya and the Limits of Intervention," *Current History* 111, no. 748 (November 2012): 305–9, argues that the secessionist movement and jihadi takeover in northern Mali were a consequence of foreign intervention in Libya. Raising issues relevant to Mali, Benedetta Rossi, *From Slavery to Aid: Politics, Labour, and Ecology in the Nigerien Sahel, 1800–2000* (New York: Cambridge University Press, 2015), explores hierarchical relationships that existed historically between Hausa and Tuareg peoples in Niger and the ways in which postindependence governments undermined local livelihoods.

The controversy over foreign intervention in Mali is the subject of several works. Gregory Mann, "Africanistan? Not Exactly: The Dangers of International Intervention in Mali," *Foreign Policy,* July 24, 2012, warns of the perils of external intervention in a complex, volatile situation. Gregory Mann and Bruce Whitehouse, "Mali: Listening without Drones," *African Arguments,* March 13, 2013, warns that the US policy of privileging counterterrorism over good governance has done more harm than good in Mali and argues that a lasting peace must be grounded in an inclusive political process. Lori-Anne Théroux-Bénoni, "The Long Path to MINUSMA: Assessing the International Response to the Crisis in Mali," in *Peacekeeping in Africa: The Evolving Security Architecture,* ed. Thierry Tardy and Marco Wyss (New York: Routledge, 2014), 171–89, examines the evolution of ECOWAS, AU, French, and UN intervention in Mali. Bruno Charbonneau and Jonathan Sears, "Defending Neoliberal Mali: French Military Intervention and the Management of Contested Political Narratives," in *The Politics of International Intervention: The Tyranny of Peace,* ed. Mandy Turner and Florian P. Kühn (New York: Routledge, 2016), 229–50, investigates the political interests behind French and UN intervention and peace building and the ways in which external and internal interests and priorities diverged.

Useful overviews of the crisis in northeastern Nigeria include International Crisis Group, *Curbing Violence in Nigeria (II): The Boko Haram Insurgency,* Africa Report 216 (Brussels: International Crisis Group, 2014); and Amnesty International, *Nigeria: More than 1,500 Killed in Armed Conflict in North-Eastern Nigeria in Early 2014* (London: Amnesty International, 2014). For a journalist's account based largely on interviews with Nigerian civilians, see Mike Smith, *Boko Haram: Inside Nigeria's Unholy War* (London: I. B. Tauris, 2015).

A number of recommended works focus on the political, economic, and social causes of the Boko Haram insurgency in Nigeria. Paul Lovejoy, *Jihad in West Africa during the Age of Revolutions* (Athens: Ohio

University Press, 2016), examines the eighteenth- and nineteenth-century jihads that led to the expansion of slavery in West Africa—notably in the Sokoto Caliphate—and provides important historical context for the current crisis in northeastern Nigeria. Leena Koni Hoffmann, *Who Speaks for the North? Politics and Influence in Northern Nigeria*, Africa Programme Research Paper (London: Chatham House, 2014), focuses on regional dynamics in Nigeria, with special attention to the northeast. It rejects the prevailing north-south paradigm as simplistic because it fails to consider diversity and inequalities within each of these regions or to acknowledge other regional divisions. Moses E. Ochonu, *Colonialism by Proxy: Hausa Imperial Agents and Middle Belt Consciousness in Nigeria* (Bloomington: Indiana University Press, 2014), considers the role of rulers from the Hausa-Fulani caliphate, who served as proxies for British colonial authority in the largely non-Muslim Middle Belt, and links their exploitative domination to the violence that affects that region today. Brandon Kendhammer, *Muslims Talking Politics: Framing Islam, Democracy, and Law in Northern Nigeria* (Chicago: University of Chicago Press, 2016), investigates democracy, Islamic law, and terrorism in the Nigeria's north, emphasizing working-class perspectives.

Several important studies examine climate change and demographics as factors in the northern crisis. Michael J. Watts, *Silent Violence: Food, Famine, and Peasantry in Northern Nigeria* (Athens: University of Georgia Press, 2013), investigates the links between climate, political economy, and famine in northern Nigeria. Aaron Sayne, *Climate Change Adaptation and Conflict in Nigeria*, Special Report 274 (Washington, DC: United States Institute of Peace, 2011), and Erika Eichelberger, "How Environmental Disaster Is Making Boko Haram Violence Worse," *Mother Jones*, June 10, 2014, examine the ways in which drought, desertification, and the drying up of Lake Chad have intensified regional conflicts over land and water. Paul Lubeck, "Explaining the Boko Haram Insurgency: Globalization, Demography, and Elite Fragmentation," presentation at the Ali Vural AK Center for Global Islamic Studies, George Mason University, October 30, 2014, explores the roles of population growth, climate change, globalization, poverty, regional and ethnic inequalities, corruption, and governmental oppression in the emergence and transformation of Boko Haram (https://vimeo.com/114587770). David Michel and Ricky Passarelli, "The Climate Wars Are Already Here," *Foreign Policy*, December 17, 2014, focuses on population and climate change–induced water shortages in the Niger River Basin, which have led to resource conflicts and the emergence of extremist groups in Nigeria, Niger, and Mali.

Other recommended works examine Boko Haram in the context of politico-religious movements in Nigeria more generally. Virginia Comolli, *Boko Haram: Nigeria's Islamist Insurgency* (London: Hurst, 2015), explores precolonial Islamic movements in northern Nigeria, the role of the northern Muslim aristocracy in the colonial system, and the emergence of radical groups in the northeast that opposed these politico-religious power holders. N. D. Danjibo, *Islamic Fundamentalism and Sectarian Violence: The "Maitatsine" and "Boko Haram" Crises in Northern Nigeria* (Ibadan: Peace and Conflict Studies Programme, Institute of African Studies, University of Ibadan, 2009), considers a recurrent pattern of religiously linked violence in Nigeria that has been associated with poverty, massive youth unemployment, and the failure of good governance. The author argues that modernity has been viewed as the cause of these social ills and that religion has been used as tool to mobilize against them. Abimbola Adesoji, "The Boko Haram Uprising and Islamic Revivalism in Nigeria," *Africa Spectrum* 45, no. 2 (2010): 95–108, investigates the emergence of radical religious sects in Nigeria in the context of economic dislocation, the emergence of party politics, and the growth of Islamic fundamentalism worldwide. Marc-Antoine Pérouse de Montclos, ed., *Boko Haram: Islamism, Politics, Security and the State in Nigeria*, West African Politics and Society Series, vol. 2 (Leiden: African Studies Centre, 2014), examines Boko Haram both as a struggle between Muslims and as contention between a fundamentalist sect and secular society over the role of Western values and Islamic law. The collection includes the assessments of several Nigerian scholars. Alexander Thurston, *Boko Haram: The History of an African Jihadist Movement* (Princeton, NJ: Princeton University Press, 2017), draws on Hausa and Arabic documents, videos, and interviews to explore the organization's evolving political and religious presence in the Lake Chad region.

Two studies investigate Boko Haram's appeal and recruitment strategies, as well as the impact of governmental repression. Marc-Antoine Pérouse de Montclos, *Nigeria's Interminable Insurgency? Addressing the Boko Haram Crisis*, Africa Programme Research Paper (London: Chatham House, 2014), considers the origins and evolution of Boko Haram in the context of deep-seated local grievances, corruption and military rule, the openings offered by the democratic transition, and elite struggles to maintain power and privilege through the mobilization of a base. Anneli Botha and Mahdi Abdile, *Getting Behind the Profiles of Boko Haram Members: A Summary* (Finn Church Aid, International Dialogue Centre/KAICIID, Network of Religious and Traditional Peacemakers, and Citizen Research Centre, October 2016), explores motivations for radicalization and the Boko Haram recruitment process, based on interviews with former Boko Haram members and individuals who resisted radicalization.

John Campbell, US ambassador to Nigeria from 2004 to 2007, offers an American foreign policy perspective on the crisis. John Campbell, *U.S. Policy to Counter Nigeria's Boko Haram*, Council Special Report 70 (Washington, DC: Council on Foreign Relations, 2014), examines the origins of the conflict, the Nigerian government response, and the role of and prospects for US policy. See also John Campbell, "Meet the Ruthless New Islamist Group Terrorizing Nigeria," *The Atlantic*, March 11, 2013, which assesses the impact of Ansaru.

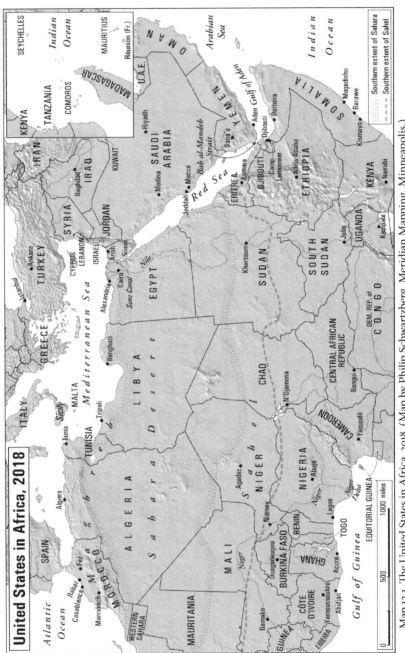

Map 12.1. The United States in Africa, 2018. (Map by Philip Schwartzberg, Meridian Mapping, Minneapolis.)

12

US Africa Policy after the Cold War
(1991–2017)

THE EIGHT PRECEDING chapters present cases of foreign intervention in Africa that were justified by the two dominant post–Cold War paradigms: response to instability/responsibility to protect and the war on terror. The United States was a major player in many of these cases, but it was not the only one. France and the United Kingdom sent troops to the continent through bilateral and multilateral arrangements, and global, regional, and subregional organizations sponsored multinational intervention and peacekeeping forces. African countries also intervened in their neighbors' affairs. Often, the United States was not the most significant external actor. Yet as the last remaining superpower, it played an outsized role. Although Africa was relatively marginal to US interests during this period—subordinate to US concerns in Europe, East Asia, and the Middle East—Washington's decision to intervene, its refusal to engage, or even a delay in its response often shaped the end result. As a permanent member of the UN Security Council and primary funder of UN operations, the United States wielded enormous power and was not hesitant to use it to advance its interests. For this reason, US Africa policy merits a chapter of its own and provides a vantage point from which to assess the policies and actions of other major actors.

Although the United States exerted undue influence, it could not always impose outcomes that were optimal for its national interests. Despite its political, economic, and military clout, Washington relied on allies to take the lead in countries that were peripheral to US concerns. Allies and adversaries at all levels set limits. Sometimes the interests of less powerful actors held sway and precluded Washington's preferred results. When the United States did intervene, it justified its involvement according to the dominant paradigms—as a response to instability and the responsibility to protect civilian lives, or as a component of the war on terror. After the September 2001 attacks on the United States, the war on terror was referenced more frequently, and the US counterterrorism agenda assumed greater prominence in US Africa policy. Washington provided money, training, hardware, and equipment to dozens of strategically located countries that were considered vulnerable to terrorist activity; it also provided air support in conventional military actions and engaged in a growing number of covert military operations. The increasing securitization of US Africa policy after September 2001 shifted attention and resources away from some countries and toward others, and privileged military security over broader forms of human security that focused on poverty, disease, climate change, and governance.

Setting the Stage:
From the War on Communism to the War on Terror

To understand US Africa policy after the Cold War, one must place it in historical context. US policies toward the continent underwent several transformations during the periods of decolonization, the Cold War, and their aftermath. Although there were distinctions between the policies of different presidential administrations, continuities were pronounced. During the Cold War, Washington's chief concern was combatting communism. US policymakers tended to view conflicts in incipient African nations through an East-West lens. As a result, they commonly ignored local circumstances, undermined radical nationalist movements and states, and backed pro-Western governments that were repressive and undemocratic. When the Cold War ended, the United States severed ties to many of its erstwhile allies. Once they were no longer useful as regional policemen, their human rights abuses and corrupt practices increasingly appeared as impediments to US interests. Bilateral US aid to African countries declined in the early 1990s, even as political and economic pressures peaked, and dictatorships once propped up were allowed to fall. Former client states like Somalia, Zaire, and Liberia descended into chaos. Where civil society institutions and prodemocracy movements were weak, warlords and insurgents moved into the power vacuums.

As regional instability grew in the mid-1990s, Washington responded with renewed attention to Africa. Focusing on the economic distress that had provoked much of the political crisis, Presidents Bill Clinton and George W. Bush promoted free market reforms, trade in lieu of aid, and debt relief for the poorest African countries. Both administrations addressed the role of the HIV/AIDS epidemic in Africa's social and economic decline and allocated increased funding to health initiatives. Before the September 2001 attacks on the United States, the war on terror played a marginal role in US Africa policy. The US military intervention in Somalia, for instance, was triggered by the threat of regional instability and a growing concern with the protection of civilian lives. Although the United States provided significant financial and material support to UN peacekeeping operations during the 1990s, after the Somalia debacle it was reluctant to participate in multinational ventures that might entail American boots on the ground, and it actively blocked UN intervention to stop the Rwanda genocide.

After 9/11, US Africa policy was again reevaluated, with three important consequences. First, Washington paid closer attention to economic deprivation and political chaos. Impoverished nations with weak state apparatuses were viewed as potential breeding grounds for political extremism—which now took the form of terrorism rather than communism. As a result, Washington sought to bolster economies, strengthen military alliances, provide financial assistance and training, and open military bases in dozens of African countries. Second, the Pentagon assumed responsibility for a number of revamped humanitarian and development assistance programs that previously were under civilian authority, and the human security/human rights agenda of USAID was eclipsed by the counterterrorism program of the Defense Department and the CIA. The military structures established in response to terrorism were often ill suited to the peacekeeping and peace-building tasks they were expected to accomplish. Third, target countries were chosen according to new criteria. As war and instability engulfed the Middle East, the United States' access to its customary sources of foreign oil was threatened and the terrorist menace assumed a growing importance on the US foreign policy agenda. US Africa policy focused increasingly on countries that were either rich in oil and natural gas or strategic to the war on terror or both.

After September 2001, the George W. Bush administration's war on terror became the new anticommunism.[1] Just as domestic insurgencies arising from local grievances were mistaken for communist aggression during the Cold War, the vague rubric of international terrorism was used to explain a range of civil disturbances in the early twenty-first century. African dictators who had appealed to the West by playing up the communist menace were replaced by a new generation of strongmen who won support by cooperating in the fight against terrorism. Aided by US military and economic largess, they cracked down on domestic dissent. By the end of the Barack Obama administration, the United States was focused on four organizations in Africa that were deemed a threat both to that continent and to Europe: al-Shabaab in Somalia, al-Qaeda in the Islamic Maghreb, the Islamic State provinces in Libya, and Boko Haram in Nigeria.

Concerns about terrorism converged with US strategic and economic concerns. The protection and expansion of US economic interests were critical during the Clinton, Bush, and Obama administrations, although the relative weight of these elements varied. While the war on terror paradigm emerged during the Clinton administration, it is largely identified with the George W. Bush presidency, and it played a significant role in the Africa policies of Barack Obama. During all three administrations, perceived national interests were key factors in determining where the United States chose to intervene or not to intervene, and the responsibility to protect paradigm increasingly served as a rationale for intervention when other interests were also at stake. Because Africa was in most cases deemed tangential to US concerns, all three presidents generally preferred that other countries (the former colonial powers) or multilateral entities (the UN, EU, AU, or subregional organizations) assume the lead in resolving African crises. Only when these actors failed did the United States take military action, and then only if the crises threatened US interests. The varying emphases of US Africa policy during three post–Cold War presidential administrations, those of Clinton (1993–2001), Bush (2001–9), and Obama (2009–17), are assessed below, while the first year of the Trump administration (2017–) is surveyed in chapter 13. The present chapter concludes with an examination of the US war on terror in Africa after 9/11.

The Clinton Administration (1993–2001)

President Bill Clinton took office one year after the collapse of the Soviet Union. During his administration, US Africa policy was characterized by initial disengagement, followed by renewed interest and increased involvement. American triumphalism, rooted in the belief that the United States had won the Cold War, diminished Washington's concern for Africa as a strategic asset.[2] Conflicts in what once were Cold War battlegrounds fell from Washington's radar screen, even as abandoned strongmen, disintegrating patronage networks, and leftover weapons fueled new contests for wealth and power. Humiliated by the debacle in Somalia and no longer challenged by Soviet competition, the United States had little desire to engage and began instead to promote the notion of "African solutions for African problems."[3] During his first term, President Clinton rejected the responsibility to protect paradigm that had underpinned President George H. W. Bush's intervention in Somalia, and the Clinton administration thwarted effective UN action to stop the genocide in Rwanda.[4] A presidential directive in May 1994, one month after the genocide began, set limits on US participation in UN peacekeeping operations. The United States would not commit troops unless the president determined that the mission promoted US interests and that there was an imminent threat to international peace and security. The United States would reduce its contributions to peacekeeping costs from more than 30 percent to 25 percent, requiring other nations and state-based multilateral organizations to shoulder a greater share of the burden and African countries to assume greater responsibility for resolving what were deemed African problems. In most cases, US troops would serve only under US commanders.

The Clinton administration shied away from direct military engagement in Africa until August 1998, when it ordered a cruise missile attack against alleged al-Qaeda targets in Sudan—using the emergent war on terror paradigm as justification. In the interim, President Clinton launched the African Crisis Response Initiative (ACRI), which stressed African responsibility for peacekeeping on the continent, with the United States and its Western allies in a supporting role. African partners that were judged to be committed to democratic governance and civilian rule were offered training and equipment that would enhance their capacities to respond to instability or humanitarian crises and to engage in multilateral peacekeeping operations. In this way, African rather than US troops would assume the risks and provide the manpower that served both African and US interests. The Clinton program was later tarnished by evidence that partner governments were using US training and equipment to quash internal dissent and interfere in neighboring countries.

Simultaneous with the pullback from military involvement, the Clinton administration and Congress scaled back diplomatic engagement and pared down economic aid. The staff of the State Department's Africa Bureau was significantly reduced, and nine USAID missions in Africa were shut down. US economic aid to sub-Saharan Africa declined by 27 percent from 1992 to 1996.

During his second term in office, President Clinton embarked on a strategy of low-profile reengagement with Africa. Economic and political crises on the continent had led to widespread instability that threatened international peace and security, and Clinton was compelled to respond. Stymied by a Republican-dominated Congress that opposed his funding initiatives, the president emphasized trade over aid. The revamped Africa policy was launched with a presidential tour of six African nations in early 1998, where Clinton promoted the notion of mutually beneficial partnerships based on trade and investment that would replace the aid and dependency of the past. To encourage African partners to engage in significant economic reforms, the Clinton administration promoted debt relief for countries that adopted IMF/World Bank structural adjustment programs.

The Clinton administration also embraced a new generation of African leaders who came to power as the Cold War waned. Most were military men who had led successful insurgencies against corrupt and repressive regimes.[5] The new leaders were expected to usher in a new era of efficient and responsible government and free market economics. Although the Clinton administration proclaimed its support for the expansion of democracy, promoting multiparty elections, good governance, and strong civil society institutions, the new leaders adopted Western norms only selectively. Reminiscent of their Cold War predecessors, they imposed the neoliberal economic reforms mandated by international financial institutions and Washington, but eschewed multiparty democracy and repressed the political opposition. Valuing stability more than democratization, the Clinton administration, like previous administrations, turned a blind eye to its allies' abuses.

The cornerstone of the Clinton administration's new Africa policy and the culmination of its market-oriented approach was the African Growth and Opportunity Act of 2000 (AGOA), a bipartisan congressional initiative that expanded trade between the United States and sub-Saharan Africa.[6] Designed to enhance US access to African commodities and to create new markets for US goods, AGOA was the product of a half decade of negotiations between the Clinton administration, Congress, and US corporate interests. AGOA's primary beneficiaries were Americans. While many African political leaders supported the bill, African civil society organizations, including trade unions and human rights groups, had no voice in shaping it, and many opposed its central features.[7]

One of several free trade laws and agreements enacted during the Clinton administration, AGOA expanded the access of sub-Saharan African countries to US markets if they met certain eligibility requirements. Like the IMF/World Bank structural adjustment programs that preceded them, many of these stipulations undermined African sovereignty. Conditions imposed on AGOA partners included adherence to the neoliberal principles of the Washington Consensus that had crippled African societies in the 1980s. To qualify for AGOA trade preferences, African countries were required to demonstrate their embrace of market-based economies that would protect private property and limit government involvement (no price controls, subsidies, or state ownership). They also had to enact measures to facilitate US trade and investment: this meant no tariffs on US goods, even if such imports undermined local industries or promoted unemployment, and no preference to locally owned businesses over US corporations. Partner governments could not take actions counter to US national security or foreign policy interests. They could not support acts of international terrorism—as defined by the United States—and they were obliged to cooperate in international efforts to eliminate terrorist activities. Beyond protecting US political and economic interests, eligible governments were expected to adhere to Western norms concerning good governance and civil and human rights. They were required to promote the rule of law, political pluralism, civil liberties, and worker protection, and to reduce poverty, corruption, and bribery; finally, they could not engage in gross human rights violations.[8] The United States was empowered to determine each year whether countries met the requirements, and the US president could eliminate countries from the list of beneficiaries without the possibility of appeal.[9] This provision, in particular, deterred potential investors from backing African enterprises.

Although US trade with sub-Saharan Africa increased significantly after AGOA's passage—primarily after President Clinton left office—the law did not help African countries diversify their economies, promote good governance, or eliminate corruption. In fact, AGOA undermined African potential for sustainable economic development and weakened African political institutions. In the economic sphere, extractive enterprises remained dominant, and oil and strategic minerals continued to be the mainstay of African exports to the United States. African agricultural commodities were disadvantaged by the law's provisions that barred sugar, tobacco, peanuts, and beef from the duty-free list—all products for which African countries might have a competitive advantage.[10] In consequence, AGOA benefits accrued primarily to US businesses and to a small number of African elites in a limited number of countries. In the political sphere, the law strengthened governments that were beholden to foreign interests and eroded the social contract between the government and the governed. Regimes in resource-rich countries often ranked among the lowest in terms of government accountability.[11] Although some countries were suspended from AGOA as a result of human rights violations, undemocratic political transitions, or concerns about terrorism, many countries flouted the good governance, economic transparency, and human rights provisions and remained AGOA beneficiaries. Countries that were rich in oil and strategic minerals were most likely to receive special treatment.

The George W. Bush Administration (2001–9)

President George W. Bush continued and elaborated on many aspects of Clinton's Africa policy. In the economic realm, he, too, emphasized trade and market-oriented economic growth according to neoliberal norms prescribed by the US government. Although the Clinton administration laid the groundwork for AGOA, its impact was more notable during the Bush administration, when Congress extended its lifespan and strengthened its provisions. The president and his congressional allies also expanded economic assistance programs, arguing that poverty was a recipe for instability.

Bush initiatives led Congress to allocate more than $5 billion annually to humanitarian aid in Africa, primarily to combat HIV/AIDS and malaria—a sum that exceeded any previous appropriation. The President's Malaria Initiative was credited with saving the lives of nearly 2 million African children between 2006 and 2014. The President's Emergency Plan for AIDS Relief (PEPFAR) represented the largest commitment by any country to combat a single disease beyond its borders. Although HIV/AIDS activists generally agreed that PEPFAR played a central role in stemming the AIDS tide in Africa and elsewhere, many charged that pressure from the Christian right and other conservative interest groups—which resulted in the favoring of premarital abstinence and fidelity programs, severe limitations on condom distribution and services for sex workers, and a prohibition on needle exchanges—imposed foreign values and greatly reduced the program's effectiveness. Moreover, PEPFAR disproportionately benefited large US pharmaceutical manufacturers and pushed up costs in developing countries by imposing a near-total ban on the use of generic drugs. Finally, the Bush administration's unilateral effort under US control diverted significant potential support from the Global Fund to Fight AIDS, Tuberculosis and Malaria, a collaborative multinational endeavor promoted by a range of governments, NGOs, private businesses, civil society organizations, and affected communities.

To further the economic development and good governance agenda, the Bush administration established the Millennium Challenge Corporation (MCC), a congressionally funded government entity that was independent of the State and Defense Departments and of USAID. The MCC rewarded countries that adopted free market reforms, anticorruption and good governance practices, and poverty reduction programs, and that encouraged political participation by civil society organizations. Recipient countries, including a number from Africa, were selected by a board of directors composed of US government and corporate officials according to criteria that were intended to separate the process from US strategic and economic interests.[12] In 2006, only eleven of thirty-seven African countries on the AGOA-eligible list were also deemed worthy of MCC funding. However, measures taken to depoliticize foreign aid were weak, and they were undermined by other MCC principles. The free market reforms at the core of the MCC program were mandatory— and these formulations for economic restructuring were central to the US global mission.

In the political and military arenas, the Bush administration renewed US engagement where Clinton had been reluctant. The response to instability/responsibility to protect paradigm was still influential and guided US diplomatic initiatives in Sudan as well as US support for military operations against Joseph Kony and the Lord's Resistance Army in

Uganda. However, the decision to intervene or not intervene remained linked to America's perceived national interests—particularly in the realm of economics and security. Conflict mediation and humanitarian intervention were often undertaken with an eye to protecting or expanding US access to strategic resources or strengthening US counterterrorism partners. The heightened prominence of the war on terror paradigm became evident over the course of the eight-year Bush presidency, although Africa continued to rank low on the list of US foreign policy priorities. During the Bush years, the United States participated in several multilateral ventures on the continent. However, those in charge preferred to operate independently and refused to subordinate US interests, policies, and troops to other authorities.

Although the Bush administration's foreign policy maintained some continuities with that of its predecessor, it also manifested fundamental differences. The Bush worldview was deeply influenced by neoconservative thinkers who had emerged in the 1960s to challenge the domestic and foreign policy agendas of the New Left, a political movement that promoted government-run social programs at home and opposed military adventurism abroad. Neoconservatives held prominent positions in the Bush State and Defense Departments, on the National Security Council, and in the Washington think tank world—most notably in the Project for the New American Century (PNAC). A number of high-ranking administration officials had signed PNAC's 1997 statement of principles, which proclaimed that the United States had won the Cold War and thus had earned the right "to shape a new century favorable to American principles and interests." The statement contended that to accomplish its mission, the United States needed a strong military that it was ready to use, a bold foreign policy that promoted American ideals, and leaders who embraced America's "global responsibilities." If the United States failed in its duty, it would "invite challenges to [its] fundamental interests." Hence, it must take preemptive action to "shape circumstances before crises emerge, and to meet threats before they become dire."[13] PNAC's views were reflected in the Bush administration's 2002 national security strategy, which asserted that the global strength and influence of the United States were without equal and brought with them "unparalleled responsibilities, obligations, and opportunity" to promote freedom worldwide.[14]

The Bush doctrine of preemptive war, outlined in the 2002 national security strategy, was also a product of the neoconservative vision.

Formulated after the September 2001 terrorist attacks, the doctrine justified unilateral military operations to protect American security and embraced the strategy of preemptive strikes to ward off future threats. The doctrine was to be applied in countries that harbored or assisted organizations deemed by the US State Department to be foreign terrorist organizations that threatened American security—whether or not the host country was at war with the United States.[15] Although US military actions against terrorist targets predated the Bush administration, it was President George W. Bush who coined the phrase "war on terror" shortly after 9/11.[16] The new orientation would have serious implications for US Africa policy during the Bush and Obama administrations.

The war on terror transformed a number of longstanding American practices, some of which impinged on US Africa policy. Among the first casualties was a decades-old ban on foreign political assassinations. In 1976, the US Senate Select Committee to Study Governmental Operations with Respect to Intelligence Activities, known as the Church Committee, published an in-depth investigation of US involvement in the assassinations of foreign leaders.[17] The previous year, neoconservative stalwart Dick Cheney, then deputy chief of staff to President Gerald Ford, had led the executive branch campaign to stymie the congressional inquiry into the CIA's targeted killings.[18] In response to the public outcry that followed the Church Committee's revelations, President Ford issued an executive order in 1976 that forbade US government participation in political assassinations abroad. For more than twenty-five years, this directive remained US policy—at least officially. The protocol began to erode shortly after 9/11, when Congress granted President Bush the power to authorize the use of military force "against those nations, organizations, or persons he determines planned, authorized, committed, or aided the terrorist attacks that occurred on September 11, 2001, or harbored such organizations or persons."[19] These war powers laid the groundwork for a subsequent presidential finding that authorized the CIA to capture or kill al-Qaeda militants worldwide, whether or not they had been involved in the September attacks.

The 2001 Authorization for Use of Military Force had ripple effects in Africa. In 2004, President Bush empowered the US Special Operations Command to conduct covert military operations to capture or kill suspected members of the al-Qaeda network anywhere in the world—even in countries that were not at war with the United States and without those countries' consent. The Pentagon subsequently dispatched Special Operations troops to African and Asian nations to collect intelligence and to capture or kill alleged terrorists—a practice that intensified under the Obama administration.

The military components of US Africa policy were strengthened under the Bush administration. Clinton's ACRI was reformulated as the Africa Contingency Operations Training and Assistance program (ACOTA). The revamped initiative emphasized instruction for peace enforcement as well as peacekeeping and replaced the direct training of foreign troops with projects that focused on training the trainer; US military personnel imparted skills to African partners, who then trained their own countries' troops. Although this innovation reduced the number of American boots on the ground, it also offered participants an opportunity to disregard externally imposed human rights and good governance practices. In 2005, ACOTA was incorporated into the Bush administration's Global Peace Operations Initiative (GPOI), which represented the US contribution to the Group of Eight industrialized nations' "G8 Action Plan on Expanding Global Capability for Peace Support Operations."[20] Focusing on Africa especially, GPOI's goal was to assist partner nations in training and equipping troops that would be used in UN, regional, and subregional peacekeeping missions.

During the Bush administration, repressive African regimes routinely played up the international terrorist threat as a means of obtaining US funds and military assistance—just as their predecessors had exaggerated the communist menace during the Cold War. In many instances, security forces that had been trained and financed by the United States were used to crack down on internal opposition and fight regional wars, rather than to counter actual terrorist threats. Governmental repression and US support for those responsible resulted in backlashes that heightened hostility toward the United States. As a result, instead of winning hearts and minds, US intervention tended to alienate local populations, rendering them more susceptible to the appeals of international terrorist organizations and undermining America's long-term security interests.

The Obama Administration (2009–17)

Despite an anticipated break from tradition, the Obama administration built on the Africa policies of previous administrations. The new team extended AGOA's lifespan, expanded PEPFAR and the President's Malaria Initiative, and increased the quantity of military and security assistance granted to African allies. Like his predecessors, President Obama promoted greater trade and investment opportunities in Africa and emphasized the benefits to US businesses. Amplifying PEPFAR's scope, he launched the Global Health Initiative (GHI) to develop a comprehensive strategy to improve health worldwide, with significant implications for Africa. President Obama also continued to prosecute the war on terror. However, he rejected the neoconservative remake-the-world agenda of the Bush administration and was wary of committing US troops to another unwinnable war. Spurning the unilateralism favored by his predecessor, Obama looked to multinational institutions to spearhead military actions and expected US allies to take the lead in their historic spheres of influence. He tended to oppose direct US military intervention when there was no immediate threat to American national security, but his administration contributed US money, materiel, and even Special Operations Forces to actions led by others.

Like his predecessors, President Obama built strategic partnerships with oppressive regimes that were expected to safeguard US interests. Some counterterrorism partners employed US training and equipment against domestic opponents and civilian populations at home and in neighboring countries. Ethiopia and Kenya used US resources to crack down on political opponents and restrict Muslim rights. Security forces in Kenya, Nigeria, and Uganda perpetrated rape, torture, and extrajudicial killings. Rwanda and Uganda supported a rebel insurgency in the Democratic Republic of Congo, and US-trained and -financed troops in South Sudan and the DRC committed mass rape and other atrocities.

During President Obama's tenure, the resort to force was rationalized by both the response to instability/responsibility to protect and the war on terror paradigms. Although Obama rejected some Bush administration conventions, such as the use of torture and secret "black site" prisons abroad, he continued the practice of extraordinary rendition—that is, delivering terror suspects to third countries where they were likely to be tortured.[21] He intensified the use of US Special Operations Forces on covert missions to kidnap and kill, and expanded the program of targeted assassinations by airstrikes and unmanned drones. On President Obama's watch, covert actions under the auspices of US intelligence agencies were favored as low-cost, politically palatable alternatives to large-scale military engagements under Pentagon authority. Covert operations and the targeted killing of terrorism suspects became the primary counterterrorism tools of the Obama administration.

The Trump Administration (2017–)

Donald Trump's upset victory in the presidential elections of November 2016 moved US Africa policy into unknown territory. As a candidate, Trump had little to say about the world's second most populous continent, and the silence continued after he took office. However, Trump's statements and actions in other arenas suggested the nature of his thinking and the potential course of future policies. The Trump administration will likely favor military solutions to regional problems and downplay the importance of economic development, good governance, and human rights. Like his predecessors, President Trump will almost certainly strengthen US-African military alliances and reinforce African counterterrorism capabilities, targeting countries that are rich in oil and natural gas or focal points in the war on terror. He will probably continue to minimize the number of American boots on the ground, using military technologies and African personnel to implement policies deemed to be in the US interest. Such policies will strengthen corrupt, authoritarian regimes, intensify local grievances, and increase regional instability. They are likely to accelerate the movement toward radicalization and violence, undermining rather than accomplishing America's official goals.

The War on Terror in Africa (2001–17)

Since the September 11, 2001, terrorist attacks on the United States, concern about the spread of violent extremism associated with a small Muslim minority has strongly influenced the direction of US Africa policy. Approximately 40 percent of Africa's population is at least nominally Muslim. Most adherents live in North Africa, West Africa, and along the East African coast, although Muslim communities can also be found in Central and Southern Africa. Some members of these communities have harbored hostility toward the United States. They have been angered by the presence of US troops in Saudi Arabia, site of the holy cities of Mecca and Medina; by the wars in Afghanistan, Iraq, Syria, Somalia, and Libya, which have caused the deaths of hundreds of thousands of Muslims; and by the decades-long plight of Palestinians in Israeli-occupied territories. Some African Muslims, like members of other groups, have resented US exploitation of the continent's oil and US support for repressive regimes that have abused local populations. However, very little of this rancor has led to acts of terrorism, and only a small minority of Muslims worldwide have embraced violence as a means of achieving their goals. As a result, when President George W. Bush referred to the 2001 war on terror as a "crusade," he reinforced the belief of many that the United States was waging a war not against terrorism but against Islam.[22] This determination intensified Muslim distrust of US motives and actions in Africa.

Muslim extremist organizations have emerged in some parts of Africa, but they have few, if any, connections to the events of September 2001. Supported by only a tiny minority of African Muslims, some have roots in US Cold War policies that sustained repressive African regimes. Several US allies, particularly in North Africa, banned Islamist parties, imprisoned thousands of their members and sympathizers, and barred them from participating in the electoral process. Although most of these partisans continued to eschew violence, some turned to armed struggle. Their homegrown organizations embraced diverse movements and individuals; their origins and grievances were local, and their focus was on the "near enemy." Although some groups eventually received support from international jihadi networks, even they retained their own agendas. Other extremist bodies had both distant and local origins. Many were founded by veterans of the Soviet-Afghan War, who had been recruited by the United States and its allies to fight the Soviet occupation of Afghanistan. After Moscow's withdrawal, they had returned home to organize local jihadist organizations that focused on purportedly impious, but nominally Muslim, governments in their own countries.

Despite a plethora of evidence to the contrary, the dominant actors in the US security establishment tended to view African extremist organizations as part of a broad-based global movement that threatened American lives and security. As a result, the US State Department classified many of them as "foreign terrorist organizations." Because US residents are barred from providing "material support or resources" to such organizations, the designation had serious implications for the organizations' associated schools, hospitals, charities, and money transfer companies that were heavily reliant on foreign remittances, especially from African diasporic communities.[23] Rather than winning hearts and minds, these punitive actions generated further animosity toward the United States.

After September 2001, US Africa policies prioritized aid to African counterterrorism partners who were expected to maintain stability in their own countries and regions. Security assistance programs in the State and Treasury Departments and in USAID were strengthened, and civilian personnel performed a growing number of security- and defense-related functions. In the State Department, the Antiterrorism Assistance Program provided training, equipment, and technology to security and police officials in partner nations, and the Foreign Military Financing program built counterterrorism capabilities in friendly countries, enhanced border and maritime controls, and improved security sector capacities. The African Coastal and Border Security program provided patrol vessels and communications equipment to help African countries police their borders, shorelines, and coastal waters. Billed as a vehicle to combat smuggling, piracy, and terrorist operations and to protect fishing, oil production, and the coastal environment, the program was controversial in contested regions like the Niger Delta, where local claims to economic and political rights conflicted with activities of the Nigerian government and international oil interests. Finally, the State Department's International Military Education and Training program brought African military officers to US military institutions for instruction. Although the curriculum included such topics as democratization, rule of law, and human rights protection, the program's primary objective was to create viable African partners in the war on terror. As the previous case studies demonstrate, the human rights and good governance provisions of US aid agreements were waived or ignored if US national security interests were deemed to warrant it.

In addition to the State Department programs, the Defense Department provided military training and logistical support in exchange for access to African bases, ports, and other facilities. Agreements with Algeria, Gabon, Kenya, Mali, Morocco, Namibia, São Tomé and Príncipe, Senegal, Tunisia, Uganda, and Zambia guaranteed the United States use of military facilities in those countries for refueling, transit, combat, surveillance, and other functions. In 2017, the United States maintained forty-six military bases, outposts, and staging areas in at least twenty-four African countries.

East Africa and the Horn became the first African front in the US war on terror. US concern about the region began before the 2001 attacks, but escalated in their aftermath. From 1991 to 1996, al-Qaeda's world headquarters were in Sudan. When Khartoum expelled the organization in May 1996, as a result of pressure from the United States, Saudi Arabia, and the UN Security Council, al-Qaeda moved its headquarters to Afghanistan and transferred its East African operations to its Nairobi cell. The State Department's Antiterrorism Assistance Program helped establish Kenya's Anti-Terrorism Police Unit in 1998, the same year that al-Qaeda's Nairobi cell orchestrated deadly attacks on the US Embassies in Kenya and Tanzania. In 2002, al-Qaeda claimed responsibility for assaults on an Israeli-owned hotel and civilian airliner in Kenya. The United States believed that the perpetrators had trained in Somalia and used that country as a transit route for weapons and operatives. Southern Somalia replaced Nairobi as al-Qaeda's regional nerve center in that same year.

Central to US counterterrorism efforts in East Africa was Camp Lemonnier, located in Djibouti, a country strategically situated on the narrow Bab al-Mandeb Strait at the juncture of the Red Sea and the Gulf of Aden.[24] Established in 2002, Camp Lemonnier was the first US military base opened in Africa since the Cold War. The camp was home to the new Combined Joint Task Force–Horn of Africa (CJTF-HOA), which included some 1,800 military and civilian personnel. CJTF-HOA's mission was to discover and destroy international terrorist networks in the Horn, East Africa, and Yemen, and on the adjacent Indian Ocean islands.[25] It conducted patrols of the Red Sea, Gulf of Aden, and Indian Ocean, engaged in military actions, and assisted in training the military forces of its partner states. During the 2006 Ethiopian invasion of Somalia, CJTF-HOA provided the Ethiopian army with satellite photos and other intelligence to help it locate insurgents, and Camp Lemonnier served as a base for US air attacks against alleged al-Qaeda operatives. To counter the appeal of extremist ideologies, CJTF-HOA instigated a strategy that integrated defense, diplomacy, and development efforts in the region. US military personnel built schools, clinics, and hospitals; they dug wells and provided medical and veterinary services. However, these public relations initiatives sometimes backfired. Local Muslim leaders warned that a US "humanitarian intervention" reminiscent of the one in Somalia a decade before could attract foreign fighters to local struggles, resulting in even greater insecurity for the civilian population.

In 2003, the United States launched the East Africa Counterterrorism Initiative (EACTI), a $100 million multi-department program to combat terrorist activities in Djibouti, Eritrea, Ethiopia, Kenya, Tanzania, and Uganda.[26] Personnel from these countries were trained in border, coastal, and aviation security, and in general police work. EACTI also established programs to thwart money laundering and terrorist financing, along with education programs to undermine the appeal of extremist ideologies. Just as the Cold War had produced many unsavory partnerships, the war on terror resulted in assistance to governments that were engaged in human rights abuses. EACTI partners included Ethiopia, which was described by USAID as "the linchpin to stability in the Horn of Africa and the Global War on Terrorism."[27] Yet the Ethiopian government detained and killed political opponents, perpetrated electoral fraud, and suppressed dissent. Kenya, another EACTI partner, engaged in systematic harassment of Muslim citizens, who constituted approximately 11 percent of the population, and in 2007 the Mwai Kibaki regime engaged in electoral fraud that unleashed a wave of ethnically targeted killings that left more than 1,000 civilians dead. Political and community leaders were implicated in planning the attacks, and human rights organizations charged that the police were responsible for nearly 40 percent of the deaths. The same year, the EACTI-funded Anti-Terrorism Police Unit in Kenya arrested civilians who were alleged to be al-Qaeda operatives and transferred them to Ethiopia, where they were brutally interrogated in the presence of FBI and CIA operatives. In EACTI's most recent reconfiguration, Partnership for Regional East Africa Counterterrorism (PREACT), member countries Burundi, Rwanda, South Sudan, and Sudan have engaged in serious human rights abuses against large segments of their populations and have manipulated ethnicity to perpetuate the regimes in power.

The Maghreb and the Sahel

The Maghreb and the Sahel constituted the second African front in the US war on terror. Bounded by the Mediterranean Sea to the north, the Sahara Desert to the south, and the Atlantic Ocean to the west, the Maghreb embraces Libya, Tunisia, Algeria, Morocco, the disputed territory of Western Sahara, and Mauritania. Mauritania serves as a bridge to the Sahel, the Sahara's southern borderlands, which stretch more than 3,000 miles from Senegal in the west to Eritrea in the east. Portions of Senegal, Mauritania, Mali, Burkina Faso, Niger, and Nigeria form the Western Sahel; parts of Cameroon, Chad, and the Central African Republic constitute the central region; while sections of Sudan, South Sudan, and Eritrea make up the east. After the Cold War, the Maghreb's large, sparsely populated, loosely governed spaces hosted a wide range of criminal, insurgent, and jihadist organizations whose networks extended into the Western Sahel and aroused the concerns of Europe and the United States.

In 2002, the US government launched the Pan-Sahel Initiative (PSI), which included Chad, Mauritania, Mali, and Niger, countries that suffered from acute poverty, political instability, environmental degradation, and a regular cycle of devastating droughts.[28] Together these countries were home to more than 44 million Muslims. The PSI's mission was to enhance border control to impede the movement of terrorists and traffickers in guns and drugs, who crossed porous national boundaries with ease. In 2005 the PSI program was extended and transformed into the five-year, $500 million interagency Trans-Sahara Counterterrorism Initiative (TSCTI). Like its counterpart in East Africa, TSCTI's mission was to strengthen regional counterterrorism capabilities and to thwart the spread of extremist ideologies. TSCTI's military program, Operation Enduring Freedom–Trans Sahara (OEF-TS), provided equipment, logistical support, and border control training, as well as US Special Operations Forces who trained regional partners in counterterrorism and combat techniques. TSCTI's civil component included USAID programs to promote education and good governance, State Department programs to enhance airport security, Treasury Department aid to curb money laundering, and FBI assistance in tracking down illegal operatives. TSCTI members also joined the United States and other Western countries in annual military exercises dubbed Flintlock, which were organized by the US Special Operations Command Africa (SOCAFRICA).[29] In 2017, the renamed Trans-Sahara Counterterrorism Partnership (TSCTP) included eight Sahelian countries (Burkina Faso, Cameroon, Chad, Mali, Mauritania, Niger, Nigeria, and Senegal) and three Maghrebian partners (Algeria, Morocco, and Tunisia).[30]

US counterterrorism partners in North, West, and Central Africa, as in East Africa and the Horn, included corrupt governments that engaged in serious human rights abuses. Burkina Faso was ruled for twenty-seven years by Blaise Compaoré, a military strongman whose regime engaged in violence against civilians, arbitrary arrests and detentions, and support for brutal insurgencies in neighboring countries. Chad was run by Idriss Déby, another military despot, who seized power in 1990 and whose corrupt regime was responsible for widespread arbitrary arrests, torture, rape, and murder. Opponents viewed Déby's counterterrorism partnership with the West as an attempt to bolster a regime without internal legitimacy. A succession of Nigerian governments were also deeply corrupt and engaged in major human rights abuses against civilian populations, especially in the oil-rich Niger Delta and the volatile northeast.[31]

Critics of US policies in the Sahel argued that most of the conflicts were local in origin. The dire political and economic conditions of the Sahelian countries made them ripe for insurgency, and the insurrectionists generally had little if any connection to international terrorist organizations. Many of the targeted groups were more criminal than jihadist, blending religious extremism with drug and weapons trafficking, which funded their operations and provided livelihoods to people with few alternatives. Rather than addressing the deprivation and inequality at the root of the conflicts, Washington's counterterrorism partners played up the terrorist threat to obtain US military assistance. The policies backfired when US-trained security forces cracked down on internal opposition and intervened in neighboring countries. Such actions fueled extremism and rendered local populations more susceptible to international terrorist appeals.

AFRICOM

The establishment of the United States Africa Command (AFRICOM) during the George W. Bush administration signaled the growing importance of Africa to US security concerns. In February 2007, President Bush announced plans to create a unified military command that would oversee US Army, Navy, Air Force, and Marine activities in Africa. This development was significant. During the Cold War and its aftermath, responsibility for US military activities on the continent had been divided between the European, Central, and Pacific Commands, attesting to Africa's adjunct status in the geopolitical arena. The European Command (EUCOM) had jurisdiction over forty-three African countries, most of which were in sub-Saharan Africa and all of which had been European colonies, Liberia excepted. The Central Command (CENTCOM) had jurisdiction over Egypt and the Greater Horn—including Djibouti, Eritrea, Ethiopia, Kenya, Somalia, and Sudan—as well as the Middle East and Central Asia. The Pacific Command (PACOM) covered the Asia-Pacific region, from the west coast of the United States to Madagascar, Seychelles, and the other Indian Ocean islands. Seen through lens of US-European relations or the Cold War, Africa as a self-contained entity was not high on the US priority list. The establishment of AFRICOM was concrete evidence that Africa had migrated from the periphery to the core of US security interests.

AFRICOM became fully functional in October 2008. Its headquarters were originally intended to be located in Africa. However, hosting the US military entity was politically unpalatable for most African countries, and few were willing to risk becoming terrorist targets. Therefore, AFRICOM established its base in Stuttgart, Germany, where EUCOM was headquartered. Employing the human security/human development discourse that characterized the Bush administration's economic assistance policy, AFRICOM documents argued that poverty, corruption, and dysfunctional states breed discontent and provide fertile ground for terrorism. To counter the threat effectively, the United States must engage in "armed social work," linking strategic and humanitarian interests by implementing free market–led economic development, diplomacy, and defense measures.[32] AFRICOM's civil-military mission included staff members from the State Department, USAID, and other governmental departments and agencies. However, the Defense Department was by far the strongest partner in terms of resources, personnel, and authority, and the security and counterterrorism initiatives of the defense and intelligence communities dominated AFRICOM's agenda.

From the outset, AFRICOM and its mission faced heavy criticism. As was the case during the Cold War, the State and Defense Departments chose partner countries on the basis of strategic and economic considerations; the countries' records on good governance and respect for democracy and human rights were of secondary concern. AFRICOM's top priorities were to counter regional instability and to fight international terrorism in areas of strategic interest to the United States. As a result, the organization focused on countries that were rich in oil, natural gas, and uranium, were near important transportation and communications routes, or were the site of extremist activities. AFRICOM's detractors warned that if military priorities dominated the agenda, humanitarian initiatives would be suspect, and the long-term objective of winning hearts and minds would be undermined by short-term military operations. They charged that AFRICOM militarized diplomatic, development, and police functions that were more effectively performed by civilians.

As the Pentagon took over initiatives previously under the jurisdiction of USAID, soldiers engaged in activities for which they were not trained—and trained experts were shunted aside. Threats to human security, such as poverty, disease, climate change, corruption, and political oppression, were considered problematic only insofar as they led to chaos and instability that opened the door to extremist recruitment. The counterterrorism lens distorted the US response. US-led training programs emphasized elite counterterrorism forces and underplayed the importance of civil policing and humane responses to epidemics and climate-related disasters. As a result, African partners often engaged in abuses against civilian populations and were implicated in military coups, strengthening the insurgencies they were expected to combat.

Finally, AFRICOM personnel often continued past trends of conflating local grievances with international terrorism and strengthening the military capacity of armed forces that attacked civilians. Increased US military presence sometimes sparked popular backlashes, exacerbating rather than abating regional insecurity. Although AFRICOM was billed as promoting "African solutions to African problems," its programs were not developed in consultation with African civil societies, and US rather than African security concerns dominated its agenda.[33] As a result, AFRICOM and its constituent programs frequently intensified rather than reduced international terrorist threats.

The War on Terror under the Obama Administration (2009–17)

The enactment of policies justified by the war on terror paradigm intensified during the Barack Obama administration. Many people, at home and abroad, had hoped that the first US president of African descent would have a deeper understanding of African realities and would implement policies that embraced political, economic, and social rights. President Obama spoke to these aspirations in June 2009 when he addressed the global Muslim community from Cairo, Egypt. "I've come here to Cairo to seek a new beginning between the United States and Muslims around the world," the president announced. "One based on mutual interest and mutual respect, and one based upon the truth that America and Islam are not exclusive and need not be in competition." He affirmed that the United States and Islam "share common principles—principles of justice and progress; tolerance and the dignity of all human beings." He reiterated earlier assertions that "America is not—and never will be—at war with Islam."[34] President Obama revisited some of these themes the following month in Accra, Ghana, where he spoke of a US-Africa partnership "grounded in mutual responsibility and mutual respect" and emphasized US support for "strong and sustainable democratic governments."[35]

Obama's Cairo speech highlighted ambitious goals, but it also included words of caution. In tandem with his affirmation of friendship, the American president warned that the United States would "relentlessly confront violent extremists who pose a grave threat to our security."[36] It was the definition of "threat to our security" that became the greatest obstacle to a new, mutually beneficial US Africa policy. It was soon evident that in this domain, the Obama and Bush administrations were more alike than different. Less than a month after President Obama took office, the International Commission of Jurists (ICJ) repudiated the Bush administration's counterterrorism policies. An ICJ investigative panel, which included eight senior lawyers and judges from around the world, condemned as "legally and conceptually flawed" the Bush administration's "conflation of acts of terrorism with acts of war" and concluded that "the use of the war paradigm has given a spurious justification to a range of serious human rights and humanitarian law violations."[37] The Obama administration substituted the phrase "overseas contingency operation" for the Bush administration's "war on terror," but it abandoned the war on terror in name only. In Africa, the United States expanded on the policies that had guided US military activities during the previous decade. The Obama government continued to use African proxies to implement US policies and strengthened ties to corrupt, repressive regimes that used US funds, training, and equipment to suppress dissent and maintain control over natural resources. President Obama also broadened his predecessor's program of targeted assassinations and intensified the use of US Special Operations Forces and remotely controlled drones to track down and kill terror suspects.

The administration failed to forge the relationship of "mutual interest and mutual respect" that President Obama promoted in Cairo.

Such relations were thwarted not only by the wars in Afghanistan, Iraq, and Syria, which many Muslims viewed as campaigns against Islam, but also by drone strikes, targeted assassinations, and commando operations outside the war zones. During the Obama presidency, covert operations in Africa multiplied, resulting in civilian casualties that sometimes provoked an upsurge in terrorist activity. The number of US military and Defense Department personnel working in Africa fluctuated from 5,000 to 8,000. This number included some 1,000 US Special Operations Forces and private military contractors who worked from dozens of outposts, airstrips, and military bases in East Africa, the Horn, and across the Sahel. From these far-flung locales, they ran surveillance and reconnaissance missions conducted by turboprop planes and remotely piloted drones, launched air and drone attacks, and staged commando actions by Special Operations Forces.[38]

SPECIAL OPERATIONS FORCES

Worn down by the long wars in Afghanistan and Iraq in the early twenty-first century, Americans were reluctant to sacrifice more lives and treasure in faraway places that had little apparent impact on their lives. Sensitive to the domestic political climate, the Obama administration was also anxious to minimize local resentments against foreign troops. It refrained from sending large numbers of US combat soldiers to fight African wars. Instead, it sent smaller contingents of military personnel to gather intelligence, provide logistical support, train and advise African security forces, and accompany African trainees on missions. The US-trained troops served as US proxies on the continent. Elite commando units called Special Operations Forces were the Obama administration's military instrument of choice. These forces gathered intelligence and engaged in reconnaissance, counterterrorism, and unconventional warfare operations. Although characterized as trainers and advisors, they often played significant, if rarely acknowledged, combat roles. Functioning largely under the radar, they carried out activities not subject to public scrutiny, and the domestic political costs of their endeavors were relatively low. Working under the authority of the United States Special Operations Command (SOCOM), which coordinated special operations in all branches of the US armed forces, these specialized units included the US Army's Delta Force, Army Special Forces (Green Berets), Army Rangers, Navy SEALs, Marine Raiders, and others.[39] Within these publicly acknowledged entities, a subgroup of "black units" controlled by the Pentagon's highly secretive Joint Special Operations Command (JSOC) engaged exclusively in covert operations.[40] Established in 1980 after the failed attempt to rescue American hostages from the US Embassy in Iran, JSOC answered only to the US president or secretary of defense. Neither official was required to request permission from Congress to approve an operation or to report to Congress in its aftermath.

During the Obama presidency, JSOC and the CIA competed with one another to control the US war on terror. Boundaries between the military and intelligence sectors grew increasingly blurred, and distinctions between their missions, capabilities, and leadership dissolved. In September 2009, General David H. Petraeus, then commander of CENTCOM, signed the "Joint Unconventional Warfare Task Force Execute Order," a secret directive that authorized the deployment of US Special Operations Forces to nations in the Middle East, Central Asia, and the Horn of Africa to gather intelligence and establish liaisons with local military forces. The directive extended the Bush administration practice of engaging in covert military activities in countries with which the United States was not at war. It also expanded on the Bush policy by making such activities routine—permitting the creation of networks to penetrate and destroy militant groups in those countries, allowing joint operations with local counterterrorism forces, and laying the groundwork for future US attacks. While covert actions by the CIA required reports to congressional intelligence committees, actions undertaken under the new directive—by US military rather than intelligence agencies—did not.[41]

By the end of President Obama's first term, JSOC was clearly the dominant player in the war on terror. Special Operations Forces, endowed with much larger budgets than the CIA, engaged in both intelligence gathering and counterterrorism. The CIA, in turn, had become far more militarized. From September 2011 to November 2012, the intelligence agency was led by a military man, the same General Petraeus who had intensified US military involvement in covert activities outside official war zones.[42] A large portion of the CIA budget was designated for paramilitary activities, and CIA paramilitary bodies worked closely with JSOC forces.

Under President Obama's leadership, US Special Operations Forces in Africa tracked and killed suspected terrorists and trained and equipped local security forces to carry out missions in America's interests. US Special Operations Forces provided support for multiple interventions in Somalia aimed at destroying the al-Shabaab network; they trained AMISOM soldiers from Burundi, Kenya, and Uganda in counterinsurgency tactics; and they engaged in targeted assassinations. In Central Africa, US Special Operations Forces coordinated the African armies searching for Joseph Kony, leader of the Lord's Resistance Army, which had long terrorized parts of Uganda, the Central African Republic, the DRC, and South Sudan. The armies from these countries, trained by the US military, also engaged in extensive human rights abuses in their own countries.

DRONES

The blurring of lines between military and intelligence activities—and competition between the Pentagon and the CIA—was also evident in drone warfare. Armed drone programs in the Afghan war zone were run by the Defense Department, while purportedly covert programs in Pakistan were controlled by the CIA. In Yemen, the Pentagon's JSOC and the CIA ran separate programs, while JSOC was in charge of drone operations in Somalia, which were launched from Camp Lemonnier in Djibouti. The use of armed drones outside official war zones increased dramatically during the Obama presidency and expanded into new arenas in Yemen and Somalia. The CIA and JSOC deployed drones to kill high-level al-Qaeda officials, but also low-level operatives and their associates, who were not direct threats to the United States. Targets were selected on the basis of secret evidence, which, in the absence of trials, was never revealed. Because attacks required no American boots on the ground, drone usage meant fewer US casualties. Moreover, it was easier to kill terror suspects than to capture and try them, and their extrajudicial elimination circumvented the problem of determining where to house them after the CIA's secret overseas prisons were closed.

Just as the use of torture and secret prisons had generated debate when President Obama took office, the CIA's foray into paramilitary activities and the Pentagon's involvement in intelligence gathering provoked contention at the beginning of his second term. Some administration officials argued that the CIA should return to its traditional work of recruiting spies and gathering and analyzing intelligence, leaving lethal operations to the military, while the Pentagon should refrain from intelligence gathering and focus on military operations. This position was in keeping with the 9/11 Commission's 2004 recommendation that "lead responsibility for directing and executing paramilitary operations, whether clandestine or covert, should shift to the Defense Department."[43] Critics of existing practices argued that the move would provide greater public scrutiny of American killings abroad. The US military is required to adhere to international laws of war, while the CIA often does not. The Pentagon's operations are based on publicly available policies, while the CIA's covert operations are not officially acknowledged—reports to congressional intelligence committees notwithstanding. History has demonstrated time and again that secrecy impedes accountability and transparency promotes it.

In the face of mounting criticism, the Obama administration began to reevaluate the lethal drone programs. Drone strikes and their "collateral damage"—including women, children, the elderly, and men who were killed simply because of their age, location, or association—had generated enormous hostility toward the United States. Indeed, the killing of innocents had become a focal point of international criticism and a recruiting tool for al-Qaeda and its affiliates. None of Washington's Western allies supported drone or other targeted killing programs. In a May 2013 speech at the National Defense University, President Obama announced the imminent end to the use of "signature strikes" outside the Afghan war zone and Pakistani tribal areas. These highly controversial strikes permitted the targeting of individuals or groups based solely on their location (proximity to terror suspects) or on their conduct (suspicious behavior that might link them to al-Qaeda and its allies). In practice, any military-age man who happened to be in an area where terrorist activity was suspected was considered fair game. In the future, the president announced, drones would be launched outside war zones only if the targets posed a "continuing and imminent threat to the American people" and could not be thwarted in any other way, and only if there were a "near-certainty that no civilians will be killed or injured" by the drone strike. The related Presidential Policy Guidance also mandated high-level interagency approval of the proposed actions, removing such authority from commanders on the ground.[44]

Despite the president's pronouncement, US drone policy was slow to transform. In August 2013, US forces launched nine drone strikes in Yemen that killed more than three dozen people, including insurgents fighting the Yemeni government and young men who the US feared might become insurgent leaders of the future. In 2015, US drone strikes in Somalia killed al-Shabaab leader Adan Garar, who was alleged to have planned the 2013 Kenyan mall attack, and two other senior commanders. It was not clear that any of the targets posed a "continuing and imminent threat to the American people" and could not be stopped by other means. A turf war between the House and Senate Armed Services Committees, which supported the transfer of authority for armed drones from the CIA to the Pentagon, and the House and Senate Intelligence Committees, which upheld the CIA's jurisdiction, also obstructed significant policy change.

TARGETED ASSASSINATIONS

With commandos, drones, and missiles at its disposal, the Obama administration permitted the Pentagon and the CIA to ignore the long-standing US ban on political assassinations abroad. Although the ban had been eroded by his predecessors, President Obama embraced targeted killings on an unprecedented scale and authorized JSOC and the CIA to draw up kill lists. He personally approved each name, as well as every strike carried out in Yemen and Somalia and the riskiest ones in Pakistan. In Somalia, al-Qaeda officials were the first targets. In September 2009, President Obama authorized Navy SEALs to kill Kenyan national Saleh Ali Saleh Nabhan, head of the al-Qaeda East Africa cell that orchestrated the 1998 US Embassy bombings and the 2002 attacks on an Israeli-owned hotel and airliner. Nabhan and several associates were killed in southern Somalia when Navy SEALs strafed their convoy. In January 2012, Bilaal al-Barjawi, the former head of al-Qaeda intelligence in Kenya, who was also implicated in the embassy bombings, was killed by a US drone strike near Mogadishu. Other US missile attacks homed in on high-level al-Shabaab operatives, including al-Shabaab's top leader, Ahmed Abdi Godane, who was killed in a targeted airstrike in September 2014—more than a year after President Obama's May 2013 speech. US forces made no attempt to capture and try these suspects before a court of law.

The Obama administration's targeted killing program caused an outcry at home and abroad. Critics charged that US actions violated international law. Philip Alston, the UN special rapporteur on extrajudicial, summary, or arbitrary executions from 2004 to 2010, questioned the US government's presumed right to target and kill individuals anywhere in the world. He claimed that "this strongly asserted but ill-defined license to kill without accountability [will do] grave damage to the rules designed to protect the right to life and prevent extrajudicial executions."[45] Other critics argued that the targeted killings violated domestic as well as international law. The legal justification for US military activities in Somalia was the Authorization for Use of Military Force, granted by Congress to the president after the September 2001 attacks on the United States. The 2001 law permitted the president to target nations, organizations, and individuals implicated in those attacks. The connection to Somalia, however, was tenuous. Al-Qaeda targets in Somalia had had nothing to do with the 9/11 attacks. Al-Shabaab had begun to associate with al-Qaeda only in 2007, and it did not formally affiliate until 2012. Nonetheless, both the Bush and Obama administrations used the authorization to justify their fight against al-Qaeda and its associates worldwide, and under President Obama targeted killings were extended to include the Islamic State, which emerged from al-Qaeda's Iraqi affiliate and its associates in 2006.

President Obama tacitly acknowledged the discrepancy between the targets authorized by Congress in 2001 and many of those selected by his administration. In his May 2013 speech, he noted that al-Qaeda's primary leadership had been destroyed and that the United States could not justify its current policies on the basis of the 2001 congressional resolution. Observing that not every group that "labels themselves al-Qaeda will pose a credible threat to the United States," he remarked that many are "collections of local militias or extremists interested in seizing territory. . . . most are focused on operating in the countries and regions where they are based." He concluded that the 2001 mandate needed to be refined and eventually repealed so that the United States did not find itself in a perpetual war, with presidents wielding "unbound powers" and democratic practices falling by the wayside.[46]

Although Obama adopted regulations that limited drone strikes and other counterterrorism measures outside of war zones, he reverted to past practices when he considered them necessary for self-defense. During the summer of 2016, the president exempted parts of Libya from the 2013 regulations, and between August and December 2016, AF-RICOM forces conducted 495 airstrikes against the Islamic State stronghold in Sirte. As the United States intensified military action in Somalia, increasing the exposure of US and allied personnel, Obama invoked the self-defense exclusion and broadened its definition to include the AU and Somali troops whom US soldiers were training, advising, and assisting. In November 2016, the United States began to treat al-Shabaab as an "associated force" of al-Qaeda. This designation allowed the administration to broaden its targets from al-Shabaab leaders with established al-Qaeda links to rank-and-file members whose ties were less certain.[47]

Conclusion

Although US Africa policy went through several transformations after the Cold War, the approaches of the Clinton, Bush, and Obama administrations exhibited more commonalities than differences. All three presidents expected other states or multilateral organizations to assume the premier role in resolving African crises. All three touted the notion of African solutions for African problems, but in fact used African soldiers to implement American solutions to protect American interests. If US partners and proxies failed, Washington engaged more directly. During all three administrations, political or military intervention as a response to instability or humanitarian crises was more likely in areas of strategic or economic concern or in those menaced by international terrorism.

The United States largely ignored African crises during the first post–Cold War decade. However, the continent returned to the US radar screen after the September 2001 terrorist attacks, and the war on terror became a focal point of US Africa policy. During the second post–Cold War decade, US policymakers increasingly viewed impoverished African nations with dysfunctional states as potential breeding grounds for violent extremism. Drawing on American Cold War strategies, they strengthened US-African military alliances and reinforced African security enforcement capabilities. In choosing its partners, Washington focused primarily on countries that were endowed with energy resources or critical to the war on terror, even though these countries were often governed by corrupt, oppressive political and military elites. Despite rhetoric that promoted human rights, democracy, and accountable and responsive governance, US assistance frequently strengthened authoritarian, kleptocratic regimes. The failure of the counterterrorism approach was evident when US-trained security forces targeted political opponents and civilians and staged coups against democratically elected governments. Blowback resulting from governmental abuse and foreign support for unjust regimes sometimes strengthened local insurgencies. After September 2001, the increasing securitization of US relief and development assistance blurred the lines between humanitarian and military endeavors, putting at risk the credibility—and sometimes the lives—of foreign aid personnel.

The expansion of extremist influence and the intensification of extremist activities in countries targeted by the United States and Western-led coalitions underscored the flawed premises of US Africa policy after the Cold War. As the Obama presidency drew to a close in 2016, the hope for a transformative Africa policy that stressed education, economic development and opportunity, government accountability, and respect for human rights was undermined by deepening US involvement in local conflicts in partnership with abusive governments. The election of the Donald Trump as president in November 2016 rendered the prospects for a constructive policy even less likely. A preliminary assessment of US Africa policy during the Trump administration's first year is the subject of chapter 13.

Suggested Reading

A number of recommended works examine US policy toward Africa after the Cold War. Donald S. Rothchild, "The U.S. Foreign Policy Trajectory on Africa," *SAIS Review* 21, no. 1 (Winter/Spring 2001): 179–211, explores continuities in US Africa policy from John F. Kennedy to George W. Bush, with special emphasis on the Bill Clinton administration. Rothschild argues that the United States kept a low profile and limited its involvement under both Democratic and Republican administrations. Brian J. Hesse, "Celebrate or Hold Suspect? Bill Clinton and George W. Bush in Africa," *Journal of Contemporary African Studies* 23, no. 3 (September 2005): 327–44, makes a similar case and focuses on the Clinton and George W. Bush administrations. Stephen J. Morrison and Jennifer G. Cooke, eds., *Africa Policy in the Clinton Years: Critical Choices for the Bush Administration* (Washington, DC: CSIS Press, 2001), investigates a range of issues that drove US policy in Africa during the Clinton-Bush years, including economic distress, the HIV/AIDS crisis, political instability, genocide and war crimes, international terrorism, and access to energy resources. Letitia Lawson, "U.S. Africa Policy since the Cold War," *Strategic Insights* 6, no. 1 (January 2007), assesses George

H. W. Bush's attempt to forge a New World Order in the aftermath of the Cold War, a vision that was premised on multilateralism and political reform, and examines the Clinton administration's retreat from Africa after the Somalia debacle. The reluctance to get involved—the so-called Somalia Syndrome—resulted in the push for African solutions for African problems that marked subsequent presidential administrations.

Works that focus specifically on the Clinton administration include James D. Boys, *Clinton's Grand Strategy: US Foreign Policy in a Post–Cold War World* (New York: Bloomsbury Academic, 2015). Boys argues that after George H. W. Bush's failed attempt to build a New World Order, Bill Clinton replaced the Cold War policy of containment with one of "engagement and enlargement" that was premised on the notion that US national security required market-based prosperity and democracy abroad. Peter Rosenblum, "Irrational Exuberance: The Clinton Administration in Africa," *Current History* 101, no. 655 (May 2002): 195–202, and Frank Smyth, "A New Game: The Clinton Administration on Africa," *World Policy Journal* 15, no. 2 (Summer 1998): 82–92, assess the Clinton administration's Africa policy experts and the new African leaders they cultivated.

US Africa policy during the George W. Bush administration is considered in Raymond W. Copson, *The United States in Africa: Bush Policy and Beyond* (New York: Palgrave Macmillan, 2007), which offers a critical assessment of the younger Bush's aid, trade, development, democracy, peacekeeping, and security projects.

One recommended work considers Africa policy during the Obama administration, while another provides the historical framework that influenced the humanitarian interventionists on the Obama team. Mark Landler, *Alter Egos: Hillary Clinton, Barack Obama, and the Twilight Struggle Over American Power* (New York: Random House, 2016), examines Obama's Africa policy and explores Secretary of State Hillary Clinton's role in making it. While both leaders were proponents of US intervention, Obama emphasized multilateralism and avoidance of conventional bilateral military engagement and preferred covert operations over direct military action. Clinton, in contrast, advocated more active military engagement and favored military intervention along traditional lines. Samantha Power, *A Problem from Hell: America and the Age of Genocide* (New York: Basic Books, 2002), analyzes six twentieth-century genocides and the US government's failure to stop them. Power became a prominent member of the Obama foreign policy team, first as a senior National Security Council aide and then as UN ambassador, where she was among the leading advocates of humanitarian intervention in Qaddafi's Libya.

Three recommended studies consider the impact of US Africa trade policies after the Cold War, and one investigates US development assistance during the same period. The trade policies and their premises are outlined in Witney Schneidman and Zenia A. Lewis, *The African Growth and Opportunity Act: Looking Back, Looking Forward* (Washington, DC: Brookings Institution, 2012). Strong, Africa-centered critiques of the trade policies are provided in Carol B. Thompson, "US Trade with Africa: African Growth & Opportunity?" *Review of African Political Economy* 31, no. 101 (September 2004): 457–74; and T. A. Mushita, "An African Response to AGOA," *Southern African Economist* 14, no. 6 (2001), 17–19. Shai A. Divon and Bill Derman, *United States Assistance Policy in Africa: Exceptional Power* (New York: Routledge, 2017), shows how the United States promoted its geopolitical and economic interests in Africa through the strategic deployment of development aid.

Several works examine the militarization of US Africa policy and the war on terror's impact on African countries. Andrew J. Bacevich, *Washington Rules: America's Path to Permanent War* (New York: Metropolitan Books, 2010), which includes a broader geographic focus, challenges the view that American security necessitates a permanent US military presence worldwide and argues that growing US militarism is both unaffordable and dangerous. Kelechi A. Kalu and George Klay Kieh, eds., *United States–Africa Security Relations: Terrorism, Regional Security and National Interests* (New York: Routledge, 2013), explores transformations in US-Africa security relations from the Cold War through the war on terror. Gordon Adams and Shoon Murray, eds., *Mission Creep: The Militarization of US Foreign Policy?* (Washington, DC: Georgetown University Press, 2014), examines the growing role of the Pentagon in determining and implementing US policies abroad. Contributors to Malinda S. Smith, ed., *Securing Africa: Post-9/11 Discourses on Terrorism* (Burlington, VT: Ashgate, 2010), investigate the impact of the war on terror on a number of African societies. Especially recommended is Smith's chapter, "The Emperor's New Clothes? Terrorism Thinking from George Bush to Barack Obama" (193–222), which considers continuities and changes in antiterrorism policies from the George W. Bush to the Barack Obama administrations. John Davis, *Africa and the War on Terrorism* (Burlington, VT: Ashgate, 2007), examines the effects of the war on terror in Africa and considers the roles of US Special Operations Forces and the African Union. Daniel Volman and William Minter, "Making Peace or Fueling War in Africa," *Foreign Policy in Focus*, March 13, 2009, critiques Washington's reduction of resources for the UN and other multilateral institutions, its strengthening of bilateral military ties, and its focus on counterterrorism and access to natural resources, rather than humanitarian concerns. Danny Hoffman, "Military Humanitarianism and Africa's Troubling 'Forces for Good,'" *Items: Insights from the Social Sciences* (Social Science Research Council), May 2017, explores the consequences of US-Africa training programs that have militarized responses to poverty, disease, climate change, and corruption.

Three works that focus on AFRICOM are especially recommended. Daniel Volman, "AFRICOM: What Is It and What Will It Do?" *ACAS Bulletin* (Association of Concerned Africa Scholars), no. 78 (Winter 2007): 2–14, provides a concise overview of the history, features, and ramifications of AFRICOM. Terry F. Buss, Joseph Adjaye, Donald Goldstein, and Louis Picard, eds., *African Security and the African Command: Viewpoints on the US Role in Africa* (Sterling, VA: Kumarian Press, 2011), presents a range of views on AFRICOM and its objectives, activities, and impact, including commentary from African sources. Robert G. Berschinski, *AFRICOM'S Dilemma: The "Global War on Terrorism," "Capacity Building," Humanitarianism, and the Future of U.S. Security Policy in Africa* (Carlisle, PA: Strategic Studies Institute, US Army War College, November 2007), critiques the post-9/11 model of military engagement in Africa, military involvement in humanitarian and development operations, and Washington's misunderstanding of various antigovernment movements.

Other works examine the war on terror during particular presidential administrations. Gilles Kepel, *Beyond Terror and Martyrdom: The Future of the Middle East,* trans. Pascale Ghazaleh (Cambridge, MA: Harvard University Press, 2008), critiques the George W. Bush administration's war on terror as a cover for a broader political agenda in Middle East: guaranteeing access to Iraqi oil, safeguarding the state of Israel, imposing Western forms of government, and implementing regime change in Iran. Dana Priest and William M. Arkin, *Top Secret America: The Rise of the New American Security State* (New York: Little, Brown, 2011), examines the secret security apparatuses that emerged after the September 2001 terrorist attacks and includes a chapter on the Joint Special Operations Command. Jeremy Scahill, *Dirty Wars: The World Is a Battlefield* (New York: Nation Books, 2013), investigates US covert operations during the George W. Bush and Barack Obama administrations, focusing on the activities of US Special Operations Forces outside established war zones, where they engaged in kidnappings and targeted killings. Mark Mazzetti, *The Way of the Knife: The CIA, a Secret Army, and a War at the Ends of the Earth* (New York: Penguin, 2013), examines US Special Operations Forces in Yemen, East Africa, and Pakistan and explores the transformation of the CIA from spy agency to paramilitary force. Daniel Klaidman, *Kill or Capture: The War on Terror and the Soul of the Obama Presidency* (Boston: Houghton Mifflin Harcourt, 2012), considers internal debates within the Obama administration as it escalated the use of targeted killings and covert operations. Nick Turse, *Tomorrow's Battlefield: U.S. Proxy Wars and Secret Ops in Africa* (Chicago: Haymarket Books, 2015), focuses on America's secret wars in Africa during the Obama administration, while Nick Turse, "The U.S. Military Moves Deeper into Africa," TomDispatch.com, April 27, 2017, investigates the expansion of US military bases and secret operations on the continent.

Several works focus on the intensification of drone warfare during the Obama administration and include some reference to Africa. See especially Hugh Gusterson, *Drone: Remote Control Warfare* (Cambridge, MA: MIT Press, 2016); Jeremy Scahill and *The Intercept* staff, *The Assassination Complex: Inside the Government's Secret Drone Warfare Program* (New York: Simon and Schuster, 2016); David Cortright, Rachel Fairhurst, and Kristen Wall, eds., *Drones and the Future of Armed Conflict: Ethical, Legal, and Strategic Implications* (Chicago: University of Chicago Press, 2014); and Peter L. Bergen and Daniel Rothenberg, eds., *Drone Wars: Transforming Conflict, Law, and Policy* (New York: Cambridge University Press, 2014).

A number of works explore the broader issues of globalization, insecurity, and the US war on terror. David Kilcullen, *The Accidental Guerrilla: Fighting Small Wars in the Midst of a Big One* (New York: Oxford University Press, 2009), provides an overview of the interactions of local insurgencies, international movements, and the war on terror. James Mittelman, *Hyperconflict: Globalization and Insecurity* (Stanford, CA: Stanford University Press, 2010), examines the impact of globalization on security and world order, the growing involvement of nonstate actors in regional conflicts, and the implications of the overriding political, economic, and military power of the United States.

Several works examine the impact of the war on terror on specific African subregions. For the Horn of Africa, see the Suggested Reading for chapter 4, especially Robert I. Rotberg, ed., *Battling Terrorism in the Horn of Africa*, and Peter Woodward, *US Foreign Policy and the Horn of Africa*. For West Africa, see George Klay Kieh and Kelechi Kalu, eds., *West Africa and the U.S. War on Terror* (New York: Routledge, 2012), which investigates the societal crises underlying the rise of terrorism in West Africa and examines US counterterrorism policies. Jeremy Keenan, *The Dark Sahara: America's War on Terror in Africa* (New York: Pluto Press, 2009), questions the extent of al-Qaeda activity in the Western Sahel and posits that the United States has used terrorism as an excuse to expand military activities in that region in pursuit of other objectives.

Three works explore the complex web of terrorist financing through African money transfer companies, Muslim charities, and commodities. See Douglas Farah, *Blood from Stones: The Secret Financial Network of Terror* (New York: Broadway Books, 2004); Ibrahim Warde, *The Price of Fear: The Truth behind the Financial War on Terror* (Berkeley: University of California Press, 2008); and Global Witness, *For a Few Dollars More: How al Qaeda Moved into the Diamond Trade* (London: Global Witness, 2003).

For scholarship that explores the relationship between Islamic fundamentalism, Islamism, and violent extremism, see the Suggested Reading for chapter 2. For an examination of these issues in the Horn of Africa, see the Suggested Reading for chapters 4 and 5, especially Alex de Waal, ed., *Islamism and Its Enemies in the Horn of Africa*; Gregory A. Pirio, *African Jihad: Bin Laden's Quest for the Horn of Africa*; Ken Menkhaus, *Somalia: State Collapse and the Threat of Terrorism*; and Donald Petterson, *Inside Sudan: Political Islam, Conflict and Catastrophe*. For West Africa, see the Suggested Reading for chapter 11, especially Virginia Comolli, *Boko Haram: Nigeria's Islamist Insurgency*; N. D. Danjibo, *Islamic Fundamentalism and Sectarian Violence: The "Maitatsine" and "Boko Haram" Crises in Northern Nigeria*; Abimbola Adesoji, "The Boko Haram Uprising and Islamic Revivalism in Nigeria"; Marc-Antoine Pérouse de Montclos, ed., *Boko Haram: Islamism, Politics, Security and the State in Nigeria*; and Alexander Thurston, *Boko Haram: The History of an African Jihadist*

Movement. See also William F. S. Miles, ed., *Political Islam in West Africa: State-Society Relations Transformed* (Boulder, CO: Lynne Rienner, 2007), which examines the evolving relationships between religion and state in several West African countries and considers the impact of the September 2001 terrorist attacks on domestic politics and foreign policies.

13

Epilogue

Trump and Africa (2017–)

AS THE OBAMA presidency entered its final days in 2016, pundits widely anticipated that Hillary Rodham Clinton, the former US senator and secretary of state, would replace him. US Africa policy would continue much as before, but with the potential of becoming even more militarized.[1] However, in a stunning upset, Donald Trump carried the electoral college on November 8, and on January 20, 2017, a man without political or military experience took command of the world's most powerful nation. His victory pushed US Africa policy into uncharted terrain. Trump had said little about Africa on the campaign trail, and the silence continued during his first months in office. However, his statements and actions concerning Islam, terrorism, immigration, climate change, military intervention, human rights, and foreign aid offer insights into his thinking and suggest the direction of future policies.

Like his predecessors, President Trump will likely strengthen US-African military alliances and reinforce African security enforcement capabilities, concentrating on countries that are rich in energy resources or central to the war on terror. He will probably persist in using African soldiers as proxies to implement US solutions to African problems. Such policies would signal continued US support for authoritarian, kleptocratic regimes that contribute to local grievances and would intensify the movement toward radicalization and violence. The enactment of a transformative US Africa policy that emphasizes education, economic development and opportunity, government accountability, and respect for human rights is less likely in the current political climate than ever before.

This chapter assesses the potential impact on Africa of Trump's attitudes and actions in regard to Islam and terrorism; Muslim immigration;

climate change; military intervention versus development, diplomacy, and human rights; and foreign aid.

Misconceptions about Islam and Terrorism

President Trump holds a distorted view of Islam that will influence his policy toward Africa, home to approximately one-third of the world's 1.8 billion Muslims. He harbors a deep suspicion of the religion and tends to conflate diverse Muslim groups, confusing terrorist networks like al-Qaeda and the Islamic State with organizations that work within established political systems, such as the nonviolent Muslim Brotherhood. These views evoke the "clash of civilizations" thesis promoted by American political scientist Samuel P. Huntington, which regards Islam as fundamentally incompatible with the Judeo-Christian values that are the foundation of Western civilization.[2] Warning that "Islam hates us," Trump has vowed to "defeat Radical Islamic Terrorism."[3] These extremist views have been refuted by most reputable scholars of religion and rejected by Trump's two immediate predecessors, Presidents George W. Bush and Barack Obama. However, they have remained popular in right-wing circles and among Trump's closest advisors. As a result, they gained momentum during the 2016 presidential campaign and in its aftermath.

Trump's inner circle includes a number of right-wing ideologues who promote fallacious views of Islam. In his administration, the most prominent have been his first national security advisor, Lt. Gen. Michael T. Flynn, and his attorney general, Jeff Sessions, as well as former chief political strategist Stephen K. Bannon, senior policy advisor Stephen Miller, and former deputy national security assistant Sebastian Gorka. His first secretary of state, Rex W. Tillerson, although generally not deemed a right-wing ideologue, has referred to both the Muslim Brotherhood and al-Qaeda as "agents of Radical Islam."[4] Although General Flynn was forced to resign within weeks of taking office, his claims that radical Muslims are waging war against the United States and that extreme measures are needed to defeat them had already taken root. Bannon and Gorka also left the White House during the first year but continued, especially in the case of Bannon, to influence the president's thinking. Subsequent events offered proof that the Trump administration would collaborate with any regime willing to combat "radical Islam," regardless of the regime's human rights record. President Trump's high praise and special treatment of Russia's Vladimir Putin, Saudi Arabia's King Salman, Turkey's Recep Tayyip Erdogan, the Philippines' Rodrigo Duterte, and Egypt's Abdel Fattah el-Sisi are clear examples of this trend.

If Trump's early actions are revealing, his words are also important, as judicial rulings and firestorms over his tweets have demonstrated. President Trump's refusal to abandon reference to "radical Islamic terrorism" is further indication of his misunderstanding of Islam and his erroneous conflation of religion and violent extremism. President Obama had publicly repudiated the notion of "radical Islamic terrorism," because it wrongly associated the world's 1.8 billion Muslims with the actions of a fringe element whose actions were deemed un-Islamic by established religious scholars and by most Muslims. Instead, Obama described al-Qaeda and Islamic State militants as "violent extremists" who were peddling "warped ideologies . . . [in] their attempt to use Islam to justify their violence." He concluded, "All of us have a responsibility to refute the notion that groups like [the Islamic State] somehow represent Islam, because that is a falsehood that embraces the terrorist narrative."[5]

President Trump's second national security advisor, Lt. Gen. H. R. McMaster, agreed with President Obama's assessment. A career army officer with a mainstream view of foreign policy, McMaster also rejected "radical Islamic terrorism" as inappropriate terminology, arguing that terrorists behave in ways that are "un-Islamic" and warning that the United States needed to retain Muslim allies in the war on terror.[6] McMaster's views have wide support among career officials in the State and Defense Departments and other agencies that work with the National Security Council. However, Trump persisted in his use of the inflammatory terminology, despite warnings by seasoned professionals that such language bolsters extremists' claims that the United States is at war with Islam and legitimizes their pretense to represent the Muslim faith.

President Trump's mischaracterization of extremist violence is rooted in his misunderstanding of its causes, which has prevented him from developing an appropriate and effective response. Addressing Muslim world leaders in May 2017, Trump urged harsh treatment of extremists: "Drive them out of your places of worship. Drive them out of your communities. Drive them out of your holy land. And drive them out of this earth."[7] In prescribing force alone to counter terrorism, the president exhibits a failure to comprehend the political, economic, and social grievances that engender extremism and the importance of education, employment, and representative, transparent governance in combatting it.

President Trump's erroneous conceptions of Islam have led him to confound nonviolent and violent organizations. A case in point is the Muslim Brotherhood, one of the most important Islamist organizations in North Africa and the Middle East, which boasts millions of members and supporters and engages in educational and charity work, as well as religious and political activities. Although some adherents engaged in violent protest after World War II, the organization renounced violence in the 1970s. This shift led to the departure of dissenters, who established other organizations. Following their repudiation of armed struggle, Brotherhood members engaged in politics and participated in elections—when ruling regimes permitted. In the aftermath of the Arab Spring, Brotherhood parties, with their powerful organizational networks, won national elections in Egypt, Morocco, and Tunisia.

Despite the Muslim Brotherhood's decades-old renunciation of violence, the Trump administration has considered designating the group a foreign terrorist organization. Such a move was rejected by the Obama administration and the UK, but has been promoted by US allies Egypt, Saudi Arabia, and the United Arab Emirates. Many autocratic rulers in the Muslim world consider the Muslim Brotherhood to pose a threat on par with that of violent extremists. Although the organization is not violent, it is embedded in a strong popular base and grassroots political structures, and it has the potential to challenge repressive, unrepresentative governments. Some of Trump's closest advisors are proponents of the Muslim Brotherhood/terrorist equation. Before assuming the role of White House political strategist, Stephen Bannon cast the Muslim Brotherhood as "the foundation of modern Terrorism."[8] As secretary of state designate, Rex Tillerson equated the Muslim Brotherhood with al-Qaeda, and he considered the defeat of both organizations to be of equal importance.[9] However, many career officials in the State Department, National Security Council, and CIA contest this assessment. A terrorist designation would shut down Brotherhood charities, mosques, and other entities in the United States, freeze the organization's US assets, outlaw financial interactions with US interests, and end the issuance of US visas to Brotherhood members. The career officials warn that a terrorist designation could alienate allies, increase polarization, and encourage radicalism in countries where the Brotherhood has strong support. Moreover, it would close communication channels with moderate Islamists, who are important collaborators in the fight against violent extremism. Finally, designating the Muslim Brotherhood a terrorist organization could reinforce extremists' claims that the United States is at war with Islam and that nonviolent opposition and accommodation with Muslim moderates and the West are futile. This outcome would have serious ramifications for US-African relations.

The Muslim Travel Ban

President Trump's distorted and hostile view of Islam is also evident in his attempt to impose a US travel ban on citizens from several predominantly Muslim countries, including three countries in Africa. As a candidate, Trump had advocated "a total and complete shutdown of Muslims entering the United States" while the country established an ideological screening process that would allow the government to admit only "those who share our values." He had called for "extreme vetting" that would exclude not only terrorists and their sympathizers, but also "any who have hostile attitudes towards our country or its principles." Candidate Trump had promoted the temporary suspension of immigration from regions that had "a history of exporting terrorism" while such procedures were being implemented. Finally, he had proclaimed that as president, he would "establish a Commission on Radical Islam . . . to identify and explain . . . the core convictions and beliefs of Radical Islam, to identify the warning signs of radicalization, and to expose the networks in our society that support radicalization."[10]

On January 27, 2017, one week after his inauguration, President Trump issued an executive order that temporarily suspended entry into the United States of people from seven predominantly Muslim countries: Iran, Iraq, Libya, Somalia, Sudan, Syria, and Yemen. After a 90-day pause, Christians and adherents of other minority religions from these countries would be given priority entry over Muslims. The admission of all refugees would be suspended for 120 days, after which all applicants would be subjected to a special screening—beyond the 18-month process already required for security clearance—to keep out "radical Islamic terrorists." Refugees from Syria would be barred indefinitely, and the number of refugees accepted for resettlement in the United States would be reduced from a limit of 110,000 in 2017 to 50,000.

Condemnation of Trump's action was immediate and widespread. US allies, human rights organizations, and citizens in Muslim-majority countries decried the order as another signal that the United States opposed Islam, rather than violent extremism. They warned that the measure would alienate friends, hinder efforts to win hearts and minds, and play into the hands of extremists. US citizens and residents protested at airports, in Washington, DC, and in towns and cities across the country. Within days, more than 1,000 State Department employees signed a memo opposing the travel ban, and dozens of lawsuits were filed by states, NGOs, and individual plaintiffs. On February 3, a federal judge in Washington state blocked enforcement of the order nationwide, and six days later the federal appeals court in California upheld the ruling on the grounds that the executive order denied due process to permanent residents, individuals holding visas, and refugees—all of whom are protected by the US Constitution. In response, President Trump issued a revised order on March 6 that removed Iraq from the list of countries covered by the travel ban, eliminated the indefinite ban on Syrian refugees, exempted from exclusion permanent residents and individuals currently holding visas, and omitted language giving preference to persecuted religious minorities in the predominantly Muslim states.

Criticism continued unabated. On March 10, 134 career diplomats, national security officials, and foreign policy experts from both Republican and Democratic administrations sent an open letter to the president charging that the revised ban would damage US national security and America's position as a world leader, promote the view that the United States opposed Islam, and fuel radicalization. Former CIA director John Brennan called the revised order "simplistic and misguided," because it wrongly assumed that nationality was "responsible for a potential terrorist act." He claimed that it would alienate potential allies, who would see the ban as "profiling specific nationalities."[11]

The attorneys general of Hawaii, Maryland, Massachusetts, Minnesota, New York, Oregon, and Washington sued to block the revised order, charging that it was unconstitutional. On March 15, a federal judge in Hawaii blocked the revised travel ban nationwide, invoking candidate Trump's call for "a total and complete shutdown of Muslims entering the United States" as "significant and unrebutted evidence of religious animus driving the promulgation of the Executive Order and its related predecessor." As a result, the ruling held, the order violated the constitutional proscription against religious discrimination. Moreover, the order's "focus on nationality," rather than on acts of the individuals barred, undermined its stated purpose of protecting Americans from terrorist attacks.[12] Hours later, a federal judge in Maryland issued a separate ruling, noting that the purpose of the order seemed to be "the effectuation of the proposed Muslim ban" that Trump had advocated during his presidential campaign.[13] The Trump administration immediately appealed both rulings.

On May 25, 2017, the federal appeals court in Virginia upheld the Maryland ruling, noting that the revised travel ban "drips with religious intolerance, animus and discrimination" and contravened the First Amendment prohibition against government establishment of religion. Furthermore, it appeared that the executive order's "stated national security interest was provided in bad faith, as a pretext for its religious purpose."[14] On June 12, the federal appeals court in California upheld the Hawaii determination that the revised travel ban violated federal law in suspending entrance to the United States of whole classes of people with discriminatory intent and without adequate justification. The Trump administration appealed the lower court rulings to the Supreme Court, which initially agreed to hear the cases. However, in October 2017 the Supreme Court dismissed the appeals of both decisions on the grounds that the temporary travel ban had expired and the cases were now moot. The high court also vacated the federal appeals court decisions, which precluded their use as precedent.

Meanwhile, on September 24, 2017, hours before the expiration of the second travel ban, President Trump issued a third iteration of the policy. Rather than imposing a temporary prohibition on entry, the new ban bars indefinitely nearly all travel to the United States by citizens of Chad, Iran, Libya, North Korea, Somalia, Syria, and Yemen. In addition, some citizens of Iraq and Venezuela will be subjected to increased restrictions or vetting. Citizens of the listed countries who have permanent legal residency or who seek refugee status in the United States will not be affected, and those with temporary visas will be permitted to stay until their visas expire. To deflect the charge that the measures specifically targeted Muslims, two non-Muslim-majority countries (North Korea and Venezuela) were added to the original lists, and the restrictions were tailored to each country according to its security capabilities as assessed by the Trump administration.

On October 17, the day before the third ban was to take effect, federal district courts in Hawaii and Maryland blocked the wholesale exclusion of citizens from Chad, Iran, Libya, Somalia, Syria, and Yemen, which would affect some 150 million people. Like the first two bans, the courts determined, the new proclamation discriminated on the basis of nationality and religion. Moreover, the administration failed to substantiate claims that the admission of citizens from these countries would harm US interests. The federal appeals courts in California and Virginia also ruled against the administration's blanket prohibitions. However, the Supreme Court allowed the Trump administration to fully implement the ban while legal challenges proceeded. In early 2018, Trump lifted travel restrictions on citizens of Chad, a key US counterterrorism partner. However, in June 2018, the Supreme Court upheld the travel ban in its entirety, rejecting lower court arguments concerning religious and national discrimination.

The Trump administration also took action to restrict the number of refugees entering the United States, particularly from Muslim-majority countries. In September 2017, President Trump announced that refugee resettlement in the United States would be capped at 45,000 during fiscal year 2018, a 59 percent reduction from the ceiling of 110,000 instituted during the Obama administration's last year in office. On October 24, 2017, following a months-long hiatus in new refugee admissions, President Trump ended the suspension but issued an executive order that subjected individuals from eleven unidentified countries to an additional 90-day security screening. The countries in question were reported to be Egypt, Iran, Iraq, Libya, Mali, North Korea, Somalia, South Sudan, Sudan, Syria, and Yemen. Nine of the eleven are Muslim-majority countries, and together they account for more than 40 percent of the refugees resettled in the United States in recent years. The administration also ended the ability of resettled refugees to bring to the United States spouses and children who remained outside the country.

The Trump administration's reluctance to admit Muslim refugees fleeing conflict and oppression strained US relations with European, as well as African and Asian, allies. At the G7 summit of industrialized countries in May 2017, the United States rejected an Italian draft report on human mobility that framed mass migration as a humanitarian crisis that required a sensitive global response. The Italian document recognized migrants' rights, acknowledged their positive contributions to host countries, and noted the dire factors that drive people to become refugees. Trump officials offered instead a brief statement that asserted "the sovereign rights of states to control their own borders and set clear limits on net migration levels as key elements of their national security."[15] As the most powerful of the G7 countries, the United States prevailed, and Italy's communiqué was jettisoned. In December 2017, the Trump administration exacerbated tensions when it withdrew from discussions concerning the UN-sponsored Global Compact on Migration, which promotes the resettlement, education, and employment of refugees and migrants. Matters were brought to a head in January 2018, when President Trump referred to some Africa nations as "shithole countries" and suggested that citizens from these countries are not desirable immigrants. His comments provoked outrage in African, European, and US diplomatic circles, where his remarks were widely condemned.[16]

Climate Change

If violent conflict is a major impetus for human migration, the calamitous effects of climate change—devastating droughts and floods, destructive storms, rising sea levels, and severe food and water shortages—are at the source of numerous contemporary conflicts, including many in Africa. Although industrialized countries in the northern hemisphere historically have produced most of the greenhouse gases that promote climate change, poorer countries in the Global South have suffered most of the consequences.

The Paris Agreement of 2015 was an unprecedented attempt by the world community to address the growing climate crisis and to assist those that were most affected. A legally binding document that was nearly a decade in the making, the Paris Agreement was signed by 195 countries. Signatory states developed their own targets for greenhouse gas reduction, pledged to do their best to meet them, and agreed to provide mandatory updates on their progress. Historically the world's largest polluter, the United States promised that by 2025 it would cut greenhouse emissions by 26 to 28 percent below its 2005 levels.

Donald Trump campaigned against President Obama's climate policies, which he claimed were destroying the US coal industry and killing jobs. He pledged that if elected, he would revoke his predecessor's greenhouse gas regulations and withdraw from the Paris climate accord.

President Trump quickly made good on his promises. On May 28, 2017, he signed an executive order that rescinded the regulations intended to reduce greenhouse gases. His 2018 budget proposal eliminated funding for Obama's Global Climate Change Initiative, which promoted low-carbon economic growth in developing countries, and ended US support for UN climate change programs. On June 1, Trump announced that the United States would withdraw from the Paris Agreement. Moreover, it would not pay the $2 billion balance of a $3 billion US commitment to help poor countries cope with the effects of climate change. The Trump administration's climate polices, like those pertaining to Muslim countries and peoples, will have significant implications for Africa.

Dominance of Military Action over Development, Diplomacy, and Human Rights

The Trump administration's actions in the foreign policy arena will also have major consequences for Africa. In what he has billed as an "America First" foreign policy, President Trump has promised to champion "American interests and American national security" over all other considerations.[17] The problem lies less in the ultimate objective than in the president's narrow understanding of national interests and security. When considering interests, President Trump defines "national" in ways that exclude many groups residing within US borders; the well-being of these populations is ignored. Where security is concerned, the president adopts a limited law-and-order interpretation that emphasizes the defense of international borders from foreign military threats, rather than the more expansive concept of "human security" favored by the UN, which focuses on people rather than territory. The broader definition embraces health, education, employment, environment, and respect for human rights and civil liberties as factors critical to human well-being.[18] The safeguarding of both national interests and national security requires a multidimensional approach that addresses the prime causes of the problems that plague the world today. Career officials in the military and diplomatic arenas warn that President Trump's embrace of simplistic understandings and his impulse to respond with military might are misguided, ineffective, and dangerous.[19]

To a greater degree than any of his predecessors, President Trump has surrendered foreign and national security policy to the military. His high-level appointments—both in the Cabinet and among senior White House staff—reveal a heavy reliance on military commanders, who, by training, will be inclined to offer military over social, economic, and political solutions. The National Security Council, an interagency body that advises the president on foreign policy and national security matters, is administered from the White House, rather than the Pentagon, to ensure that the military does not dominate US foreign policy decisions.[20] It is chaired by the president's national security advisor, who typically has been a civilian.[21] However, President Trump's first two national security advisors were US Army generals—one retired (Michael Flynn) and one active duty (H. R. McMaster). Nearly half of the senior policy and leadership jobs on the Trump National Security Council are held by active or retired military officers, even though historically most of these positions have been filled by career civil servants and other civilian experts from outside the government. The new military dominance is also evident in President Trump's Cabinet-level appointments. His defense secretary (Jim Mattis) and his first homeland security secretary and second chief of staff (John Kelly) are retired US Marine Corps generals, while his interior secretary (Ryan Zinke) is a former US Navy SEAL commander. His first CIA director and second secretary of state (Mike Pompeo) is a former army captain.

The Trump administration's proposed budget for fiscal year 2018 and related policy prescriptions underscored the president's preference for military action over development, diplomacy, and human rights. The budget blueprint called for a 10 percent increase in military spending and a reduction of State Department and USAID funding by up to 37 percent. Meanwhile, the first secretary of state, Rex Tillerson, pushed for the elimination of as many as 2,300 State Department jobs—an estimated 9 percent of the agency's global workforce. Challenged in Congress from both left and right, the bill that was signed into law in March 2018 retained the military increases but reinstated many of the diplomacy and foreign aid cuts the White House had requested. The original proposal, however, offers insight into the administration's objectives and priorities.[22]

President Trump's inclination toward military action has also been evident on the ground. During his first months in office, the president intensified US military activities in Yemen, Syria, Iraq, Afghanistan, and Somalia, and made threats against North Korea. He promised that aggressive military action to defeat the Islamic State would be a centerpiece of his foreign policy. However, conflicting statements and mixed signals have muddied the waters, and the actual trajectory of his policies remains unclear. As both candidate and president, Trump asserted that his "America First" policy meant that the United States would no longer serve as the world's peacekeeper, and his proposed budget for fiscal year 2018 would reduce US contributions to UN peacekeeping efforts by 50 percent. In Africa, this may mean that the Trump administration will continue the Bush and Obama strategies of strengthening African security forces in their counterterrorism efforts in order to minimize the number of American boots and casualties on the ground—although there are other indications that the number of US military personnel in Africa will increase. At the same time, the United States is likely to diminish its involvement in postconflict reconstruction and development; Trump promised on the campaign trail to "end the era of nation-building" and to focus instead on destroying "Radical Islamic terrorism."[23] Such an approach, characterized by Daniel Benjamin as the "hyper-militarization of the fight against terror," fails to address the poverty, unemployment, insecurity, and absence of accountable governance that lie at the root of violent extremism.[24] It likely to intensify regional instability and increase the potential for radicalization and violence.

In Africa, the military's increased influence quickly surfaced in Somalia. Only days after the president's inauguration, Defense Secretary Jim Mattis proposed that military commanders be granted more authority in conducting strikes and raids against suspected al-Shabaab targets without the burden of interagency review in Washington. The Obama administration had deferred such authority to high-level civilian and military officials from several government agencies, who considered the wider implications of such actions, including risks to civilians and to US military personnel and ramifications for broader US national security interests. High-ranking career officials in the national security establishment opposed the proposed change of policy; more than three dozen signed a letter to Mattis that warned against the relaxation of counterterrorism standards outside of war zones. "Even small numbers of unintentional civilian deaths or injuries . . . can cause significant strategic setbacks," they wrote. Such events could increase the reluctance of allies to collaborate and could boost extremist recruitment and violence.[25] Other critics claimed that the easing of constraints could serve to intensify past practices that had proven to be ineffective or even counterproductive.

US strikes against al-Shabaab leaders had frequently resulted in civilian deaths that generated considerable anti-American sentiment. The targeted killings did not significantly weaken the organization, and the dead leaders were often replaced by others who were even more extreme. Despite these protests, President Trump signed a directive on March 29 that designated much of Somalia an "area of active hostilities," permitting war zone regulations to apply for 180 days or more.[26] This classification obviated the need for high-level interagency approval of raids against al-Shabaab targets, accepted greater potential for civilian casualties, and allowed individuals to be targeted simply because they were suspected to be members of al-Shabaab, not because they were a direct threat to the lives of Americans or American partners.[27]

During Trump's first year in office, the number of US airstrikes and drone attacks in Somalia escalated dramatically, killing dozens of civilians as well as hundreds of alleged al-Shabaab militants. The insurgent organization responded by intensifying its focus on soft targets; in October 2017 alone, al-Shabaab truck bombs killed more than 500 people in Mogadishu. The following month, the United States expanded the war on terror to Puntland, where it conducted its first airstrikes against the Islamic State's Somali affiliate. Meanwhile, the number of US Special Operations troops in Somalia approached 500, double the 2016 tally.

The new policy in Somalia foreshadowed intensified military activity elsewhere on the continent. The Trump administration extended the relaxed regulations on drone strikes and commando raids to other African regions where the United States perceived a threat, and it increased the number of Special Operations troops in Africa to some 2,000. In October 2017, four US Army Special Forces soldiers were killed in Niger, where 800 US Special Operations troops were stationed, and in November the Nigerien government granted Washington permission to fly armed attack drones, as well as unarmed surveillance drones, from a base near the capital city. The armed drone program, aimed at militants in Mali and Niger, will require hundreds of additional US military personnel. Finally, in March 2018, the US broadened its drone operations in Libya from Islamic State targets in the north to include AQIM militants in the south. All of these actions signaled an expansion of America's war on terror in North Africa and the Sahel.

US Africa policy would also be affected by other counterterrorism measures under review by the Trump White House. In January 2017, draft executive orders circulating within the National Security Council revealed the administration's interest in resurrecting the CIA's secret "black site" prisons, where terror suspects were detained and tortured, and in reinstating the agency's aggressive interrogation tactics, which most international legal experts had deemed torture. During the George W. Bush administration, secret CIA prisons in Africa—later closed by President Obama—were located in Egypt, Ethiopia, Djibouti, Libya, and Morocco. Disagreement within the Trump Cabinet and among Republicans in Congress put both the secret prison and harsh interrogation orders on hold.[28]

The president's misunderstanding of the causes of violent extremism and his preference for force over development and diplomacy had significant consequences for US Africa policy. However, his prescriptions also faced serious opposition from high-level career officials in both the military and foreign policy establishments. In February 2017, 121 retired generals and admirals wrote to Congress to protest the proposed aid and diplomacy cuts in the 2018 budget. "The State Department, USAID, Millennium Challenge Corporation, Peace Corps and other development agencies are critical to preventing conflict and reducing the need to put our men and women in uniform in harm's way," they wrote. "The military will lead the fight against terrorism on the battlefield, but it needs strong civilian partners in the battle against the drivers of extremism—lack of opportunity, insecurity, injustice, and hopelessness."[29] Retired General Colin Powell, who served as secretary of state in the George W. Bush administration, called the State Department and foreign aid cuts a narrow, misguided understanding of putting "America first" that would undermine US economic interests and security.[30] In sum, the Trump budget proposal bucked the military and diplomatic consensus that US counterterrorism measures must tackle the underlying causes of instability and extremism, providing solutions that embrace health, economic development, and accountable governance. Military action alone would only exacerbate tensions and play into the hands of violent extremists.

Other powerful stakeholders also opposed reductions in foreign aid. The US Chamber of Commerce, arguably the most powerful lobby in the United States, has historically supported "a robust international affairs budget," which it describes as "a critical tool . . . to ensure America's national security" and central to the promotion of US economic interests.[31] In Congress, Democrats and Republicans alike understood the importance of diplomacy and the key role played by foreign aid in building international alliances and strengthening the US economy. American businesses and members of Congress were well aware that foreign assistance programs include "buy American" clauses that subsidize US agricultural, manufacturing, defense, and shipping sectors, and that greater prosperity in Africa expands future markets for US goods and services. They knew that foreign aid programs, which constitute approximately 1 percent of the federal budget, create thousands of American jobs, and that a healthier, more stable world enhances US security. As a result, the much-contested spending bill signed by President Trump in March 2018 included a relatively small reduction in the State Department and USAID budgets, rather than the 37 percent the administration had requested.

Beyond budget and staffing cuts, the Trump White House has diminished the role of diplomacy in other ways. The first secretary of state, Rex Tillerson, a former chairman and chief executive officer of the transnational oil and gas company ExxonMobil, had no previous government experience. Under his leadership, the State Department was sidelined. Foreign policy decisions traditionally made with input from high-ranking State Department officials were made instead by political advisors in Trump's inner circle, often without expert advice or consultation. An unprecedented number of career officials in the State Department resigned or were dismissed as the Trump administration took office, and high-level resignations continued throughout the first year. Months into the Trump presidency, nearly 200 senior staff positions that require Senate confirmation had not been filled, and there were no recommendations in the pipeline. Secretary Tillerson's knowledge of Africa was limited, and at the close of 2017, there was no permanent assistant secretary of state for African affairs and no US ambassadors in strategically important countries such as the Democratic Republic of Congo, Egypt, Somalia, South Africa, and Sudan.

Marginalized by Trump's inner circle and lacking in diplomatic experience and expert guidance, Tillerson nonetheless signaled a new emphasis for the State Department under his leadership. Human rights as an element of US foreign policy would be minimized. As head of ExxonMobil, Tillerson had had regular dealings with corrupt and repressive governments worldwide. In Africa, his corporation worked closely with kleptocratic, authoritarian regimes in the oil-rich countries of Angola, Equatorial Guinea, Nigeria, and Chad. At his Senate confirmation hearings in January 2017, Tillerson was reluctant to call out human rights violators—despite the fact that an important State Department task is the annual publication of human rights reports for countries that maintain political and economic relations with the United States.[32] In March, he failed to appear at the event marking the official release of the department's 2016 human rights report, even though for the past four decades the release has featured a press briefing and remarks by the secretary of state. In May, Tillerson lectured State Department diplomats and staff on the distinction between values and policy, noting, "Our values around freedom, human dignity, the way people are treated—those are our values. Those are not our policies." He concluded that if the United States expects other countries to adopt American values, it will create "obstacles to our ability to advance on our national security interests, our economic interests."[33] When asked by a senior State Department official to provide more specific policy direction for diplomats, Tillerson responded, "It's very simple. End terrorism. End radicalization. Deal with China."[34] This approach had significant ramifications for US Africa policy.

The increased marginalization of good governance and human rights in US foreign policy has been accompanied by a closer embrace of autocrats and human rights abusers. During his first months in office, President Trump praised Vladimir Putin of Russia, King Salman of Saudi Arabia, Recep Tayyip Erdogan of Turkey, and Rodrigo Duterte of the Philippines. He extended this pattern to Africa, where he honored Egyptian dictator Abdel Fattah el-Sisi, whose regime was waging a brutal campaign against Islamist and secular opponents, and Nigerian President Muhammadu Buhari, who had failed to hold accountable security forces that perpetrated human rights abuses against the civilian population. "We are very much behind President el-Sisi," Trump affirmed during the Egyptian president's White House visit. "He's done a fantastic job in a very difficult situation."[35] Meanwhile, Nigeria was slated to purchase a dozen Super Tucano attack planes, a sale that had been halted by the Obama administration because of the Nigerian military's abysmal human rights record. Egypt and Nigeria are the linchpins of US counterterrorism initiatives in their respective regions. This partnership remains Trump's overriding, if not his sole, concern.

Aid to Africa under Fire

As President Trump's first year in office made clear, the continent of Africa does not interest Donald Trump—unless it poses a threat or provides a benefit to the United States. As a candidate, Trump made few explicit references to Africa. After the election, his transition team submitted to the State and Defense Departments a list of Africa-related questions that stressed counterterrorism and economic concerns over humanitarian and development goals. Questioning the value and effectiveness of US humanitarian assistance, his staffers asked, "With so much corruption in Africa, how much of our funding is stolen?"[36] Yet only a few weeks into his presidency, Trump signed a law that revoked the Cardin-Lugar anticorruption/transparency regulation, which required US businesses dealing with corrupt governments in oil-, gas-, and mineral-rich countries to reveal the details of their transactions. Several African countries were affected by this regulation, which was intended to stem bribery and corruption and help citizens of resource-rich countries hold their governments accountable. Greater government accountability would facilitate escape from the poverty-amid-affluence syndrome often associated with the "resource curse." Supporters of Cardin-Lugar argued that corruption intensifies poverty and conflict and that human rights, good governance, and financial transparency are fundamental to US economic and national security. The Trump administration responded that publicizing the nature of their business arrangements would make US companies less competitive. During Tillerson's tenure at the helm of ExxonMobil, the oil giant had lobbied hard against Cardin-Lugar, which exposed the corporation's dealings with corrupt regimes in Angola, Equatorial Guinea, Nigeria, Chad, and elsewhere.

Downplaying the importance of transparency and good governance, President Trump has demonstrated a similar disinterest in African health—except insofar as diseases found in Africa might affect the United States. During the 2014–16 Ebola epidemic, which killed more than 11,000 people in Guinea, Liberia, and Sierra Leone, candidate Trump decried the airlifting of US health workers, who had been infected while caring for African victims, to a treatment facility in Atlanta, Georgia. He tweeted, "Stop the EBOLA patients from entering the U.S. Treat them, at the highest level, over there. THE UNITED STATES HAS ENOUGH PROBLEMS!"[37] The American patients were treated in a special isolation unit at Emory University Hospital, a joint enterprise of Emory and the US Centers for Disease Control and Prevention. The unit is one of the few facilities worldwide that can care for such highly infectious patients while simultaneously protecting those who are attending them. There are no such facilities in Africa. Although no Americans died in the epidemic, the only Ebola-related question posed by the Trump transition team was "How do we prevent the next Ebola outbreak from hitting the U.S.?"[38]

Even PEPFAR, George W. Bush's signature anti-AIDS initiative, was questioned. By 2016, the Bush program, which focuses primarily on Africa, had helped treat more than 11.5 million people worldwide with life-saving medications. It had trained some 220,000 health workers and enabled more than 74.3 million people to receive HIV testing and counseling. In sub-Saharan Africa, PEPFAR projects have promoted increased social stability and economic development. Yet the Trump transition team queried, "Is PEPFAR worth the massive investment when there are so many security concerns in Africa? Is PEPFAR becoming a massive, international entitlement program?"[39] The failure to understand the HIV/AIDS epidemic as a security concern, not to mention a global humanitarian crisis, is indicative of the Trump administration's weak grasp of the underlying causes of human insecurity.

The proposed 2018 budget offered further proof of the administration's disregard for African health. Historically, the United States has been the world's largest contributor to global health funding, providing billions of dollars each year to combat HIV/AIDS, tuberculosis, malaria, and other preventable diseases and to provide childhood vaccinations, family planning, and maternal care services. Most of this funding is allocated to programs in some thirty African countries, where US contributions for malaria prevention saved the lives of nearly 2 million children between 2006 and 2014. The Trump administration's proposed budget would have downsized State Department/USAID global health allocations by 26 percent. These cuts would have resulted in a 20 percent reduction in US spending on antiretroviral drugs, a 17 percent decline in funds for PEPFAR, and 11 percent less for anti-malaria programs. Public health researchers and advocates asserted that if the proposed cuts to AIDS treatment programs were enacted, at least 1 million more people would die, primarily in sub-Saharan Africa, and more than 300,000 children would be orphaned. Core constituencies rallied, and the spending bill pushed through Congress in March 2018 retained HIV/AIDS funding at the 2017 level.

Beyond reductions on the HIV/AIDS front, the proposed 2018 budget would have virtually eliminated aid to overseas family planning programs, which provide birth control and reproductive health care to women across the Global South. These cuts would have led to a greater number of unwanted pregnancies and maternal deaths and, in consequence, to intensifying cycles of poverty. However, congressional bargaining retained international family planning and reproductive health at their 2017 levels. Left in place was the Mexico City Policy, commonly referred to as the "global gag rule." Introduced by the Reagan administration in 1984, the policy prohibits the provision of US government family planning assistance to foreign NGOs that discuss abortion as a method of family planning—even if those organizations do not promote or offer abortion services. Since 1973, the Helms amendment to the US Foreign Assistance Act has precluded the use of foreign aid funds for abortions. However, until the Mexico City Policy took effect, US family planning assistance could be given to organizations that tapped other sources for abortion-related purposes.

Since its inception, the Mexico City Policy has been routinely rescinded by Democratic administrations and reinstated by their Republican successors. Shortly after taking office, President Trump restored the gag rule that Obama had revoked—and went one step further. The new administration expanded the policy from family planning assistance to include global health assistance of any kind, affecting some $9.5 billion provided through the Departments of State and Defense, USAID, and other government agencies. In many of the affected countries, foreign NGOs sponsor local clinics that offer all health services available in the area: testing and treatment for HIV/AIDS, malaria, and tuberculosis; women's and children's health care, including screenings, immunizations, and nutrition; family planning counseling and contraceptives; prenatal and maternal health care—and sometimes abortion services or counseling. If abortion is mentioned in a clinic, or if an international NGO sponsoring the clinic provides abortion counseling or services anywhere in the world, none of its programs may receive US government funds. Experts warn that the new rules will devastate African health care services, increase infant and maternal mortality, and have a severe impact on surviving family members.

The proposed budget would have threatened African well-being in other ways. Trump's budget request included significant cuts in US food aid at a time when nearly 20 million people in Nigeria, Somalia, and South Sudan were facing dire food insecurity. It recommended a 43 percent decrease in funds for international disaster relief, while climate change–induced droughts and floods were threatening many African populations. It called for the elimination of the United States African Development Foundation, which supports local projects focusing on the most vulnerable populations in thirty African countries. Reflecting the administration's "America First" emphasis, the 2018 budget also proposed a 44 percent decrease in US allocations to international organizations, with the notation that "funding for organizations that work against US foreign policy interests could be terminated."[40]

Portions of the Trump budget proposal, rejected by Congress, would have jeopardized numerous UN programs that address poverty, health, security, development, climate change, and humanitarian assistance—with major implications for Africa. As the UN's largest single donor, the United States provides 22 percent of the institution's $5.4 billion annual operating budget and 28.5 percent of its $7.9 billion annual peacekeeping budget. Projected reductions in US support—including a 50 percent cut in peacekeeping payments—would have imperiled many of the UN's basic programs. The cost-cutting actions would have placed the United States in violation of the UN Charter, which authorizes the General Assembly to apportion budgetary responsibilities to member nations. Those allocations are determined primarily on the basis of the countries' wealth. Washington's failure to make its obligatory contributions for two or more years should, in theory, lead to its loss of voting rights in the General Assembly. Given America's position as a world power, it is unlikely that this sanction would be applied. However, default on its commitments would severely damage US standing in the global arena.

Conclusion

When Donald Trump assumed the US presidency in January 2017, US Africa policy entered a period of profound uncertainty. At the helm of the world's most powerful country was a man without political experience who surrounded himself with advisors who were similarly lacking in diplomatic involvement and expertise. Without vision or plan, and failing to fill an unprecedented number of important diplomatic positions, President Trump has maintained some of his predecessors' policies through inertia. Like Presidents George W. Bush and Barack Obama, Trump has emphasized regional counterterrorism initiatives, military alliances, and training programs, along with joint exercises and operations.

He is likely to intensify the trend toward minimizing US support for economic development, good governance, and human rights—a course indicated both by official statements and by actions that have rewarded corrupt or brutal regimes. During his first year in office, President Trump escalated US military involvement in the Horn of Africa, North Africa, and the Sahel, loosening rules of engagement intended to guard against mission creep and civilian deaths.

In other areas, Trump's statements and actions suggest significant departures. Unlike his predecessors, President Trump has demonized a religion practiced by hundreds of millions of Africans, identifying Islam with the violent actions of a small minority whose claims to legitimacy are rejected by the vast majority. He has taken actions that have deeply offended Muslims, including important US allies. The administration's proposed budget for fiscal year 2018 would have significantly increased military spending while dramatically reducing funds for diplomacy and foreign aid. Although Congress did not sustain the deep cuts to aid, given the importance of foreign assistance to US diplomacy and the US economy, the Trump initiative provides further evidence of his shift in goals and priorities. The undoing of Obama's climate policies will also have significant ramifications for Africa. If the Trump administration continues on this course, it will further undermine African people's health and well-being, strengthen corrupt, authoritarian regimes, intensify local grievances, and increase regional instability. Such developments are likely to accelerate the movement toward radicalization and violence, undermining rather than accomplishing America's stated goals.

Conclusion

Assessing the Impact of Foreign Intervention

IN THE DECADES following the Cold War, numerous African countries were the subject of foreign political and military intervention. Neighboring states and subregional, regional, and global organizations and networks interceded in their affairs, supporting both war-making and peace-building processes. The Cold War paradigm as justification for intervention was replaced by two new ones: a response to instability, with the corollary of the responsibility to protect civilian lives, and the war on terror. During the post–Cold War period, the majority of externally driven actions were legitimized as responses to instability. The war on terror justification, which predated the 9/11 attacks, was used with increasing frequency in its aftermath. This book investigates the impact of those interventions through the lens of case studies from East, Central, West, and North Africa. Its findings support four central propositions.

First, regardless of the rationale, external powers tended to intervene only where their own political, economic, and strategic interests were at stake. In many instances, the promotion of their own interests was the underlying motivation. The failure to intervene when interests were not at risk also had critical consequences. Although foreign intervention sometimes benefited civilian populations, many actions had harmful results, both immediately and in the long run.

Second, the war on terror, like its Cold War antecedent, augmented foreign military presence in Africa and increased outside support for repressive regimes. The US case is especially notable. In both Republican and Democratic administrations, the counterterrorism agenda took precedence over concerns for basic human rights and broader forms of human security. Programs enhancing military security were privileged over those that approached human security more holistically. Safeguarding access to energy resources and strategic minerals and strengthening allies in the war on terror often overrode other considerations. Rather than promoting peace and stability, US military intervention often exacerbated local conflicts and undermined prospects for regional peace.

Third, the securitization of US Africa policy had enormous implications, transferring attention and resources from destitute populations in some countries to those in regions of greater strategic importance. However, the United States was not the only external actor in Africa after the Cold War. The United Nations, the African Union, the European Union, and numerous African subregional organizations played important diplomatic and peacekeeping roles, and in some cases engaged in multilateral military enforcement actions. France, a former colonial power, never relinquished its sense of imperial entitlement; it retained a strong military presence in Africa and demonstrated a will to use it on many occasions. Paris, like Washington, harnessed its influence in the UN and NATO to further its African agenda. After the Cold War, emerging powers in Africa, Asia, and Latin America wielded new diplomatic and economic clout. They leveraged their authority both to promote their own interests in Africa and to advance peace and security initiatives. The success of externally backed accords depended on the degree to which all parties to the conflicts and representative civil society organizations were engaged. Agreements that were imposed from above or outside were least likely to succeed.

Public pressure for intervention in response to humanitarian crises in Africa also contributed to foreign involvement. Activists in Western countries, in particular, pushed governments and international bodies to protect civilians' lives. However, well-meaning advocates frequently viewed complex situations as straightforward battles between good guys and bad guys—with Western countries playing the part of savior. Too often they perceived their allies as faultless and sought to isolate their opponents through sanctions or prosecution, undermining prospects for negotiations between parties essential to resolving the conflicts. They often failed to consult those affected by the conflicts and to promote the solutions offered by local populations.[1] Seeking quick resolutions to entrenched problems, Western human rights advocates sometimes proposed military solutions that historically have undermined the goals they support.

Fourth, foreign intervention in response to the war on terror tended to intensify rather than diminish conflicts, and external involvement in response to instability often rendered local conflicts more lethal. Even humanitarian missions, which were established to protect civilian lives, sometimes had deadly consequences. Like more militaristic initiatives, they were frequently undermined by weak mandates, insufficient funds, and the competing interests of the parties involved. The seduction of quick military fixes undermined long-term prospects for enduring peace because underlying political, economic, and social grievances were ignored.

As these case studies demonstrate, foreign military intervention has sometimes resulted in short-term gains, but military actions have generally failed to produce enduring solutions. Those in charge have rarely addressed the deeply rooted local problems and grievances that provoked the conflicts. Frequently they have failed to distinguish between oppositional forces with different objectives, and they have refused to negotiate with parties they find objectionable.[2] Counterterrorism operations have been especially damaging. Government actions against civilian populations in insurgent areas have been notoriously brutal, and externally directed drone and missile strikes have killed countless unarmed civilians. Such encounters have sometimes increased local support for antigovernment insurgencies. Foreign-led victories over guerrilla fighters have generally been short-lived. Scattered by powerful military forces, insurgents have tended to regroup in new areas and transform their tactics to focus on soft targets, placing civilians at even greater risk.

History has shown that there will be no peace if underlying grievances are not addressed, domestic and foreign militaries continue to victimize local populations, and dysfunctional states fail to provide basic social and security services.[3] Since the early 1990s, African prodemocracy movements have demanded better education, employment, health care, clean water, sanitation, electricity, and roads, along with programs to rehabilitate rank-and-file fighters and counter future radicalization. They have demanded responsive democratic governments that respect the rule of law, eliminate corruption, and address such contentious issues as climate change, pollution, and the inequitable distribution of resources. They have called for an end to harsh counterinsurgency campaigns and to the impunity of military and police personnel who have engaged in human rights abuses.

These concerns are longstanding, and there are no easy fixes or short-term solutions. Fundamental political, economic, and social transformations will take decades. In the interim, peace agreements will be negotiated. Those that are imposed from above or outside, with little buy-in from relevant groups on the ground, have the least chance of success. Those most likely to succeed are those that give voice to men, women, elders, youth, and other civil society members, and that integrate these constituencies into the discussions from start to finish. Important parties must not be silenced or sidelined. Islamists who are willing to work within the democratic process must be allowed to do so. If they are not permitted to participate, to take office after winning elections, or to govern without special constraints, many will reject the systems that are rigged against them. Some will seek rectification in violent extremism. Citizens who are abused or neglected by their governments or who seek a semblance of order and security where none exists may respond to extremists' appeals. There will be no end to conflicts if insurgent groups are barred from the discussions; a refusal to negotiate with those defined as terrorists will doom any deals that might result. The adoption of popularly supported accords is a crucial first step. However, such agreements can be effectively implemented only if governments are responsive to the people's will and held accountable. Foreign support for repressive governments that act with impunity and represent only a privileged elite, military strikes that kill civilians, and commercial engagement with corrupt governments and enterprising warlords will perpetuate violence and instability on the continent.

At the close of 2017, many of the conflicts discussed in this book were unresolved. Debates about the merits and demerits of foreign intervention remain contentious, and experts disagree. Critical constituencies have been noticeably absent from mediation efforts. The voices of African civil societies have not been central to the discussions, nor have the concerns of affected populations been foremost on the agenda. Peace initiatives are doomed to fail if these groups are not their top priority. This book does not claim to offer solutions. Rather, its goal is to question faulty assumptions, to expose superficial understandings and simplistic analyses, and to offer deeper knowledge to those hoping to glean lessons from the past that will enhance future prospects for positive social change.

Notes

Foreword

1. Full disclosure: I served as a consultant on both books, reviewing drafts, discussing the topics, and raising difficult-to-answer questions with the author.

2. For early assessments of the options for US Africa policy, see "USA/ Africa: No Policy? Bad Policy? Or Both?," *AfricaFocus Bulletin,* http://www .africafocus.org/docs17/usa1708.php.

3. The full text of Mandela's speech in Trafalgar Square, London, on February 3, 2005, is available on the BBC News website, http://news.bbc .co.uk/1/hi/uk_politics/4232603.stm.

Chapter 1: Outsiders and Africa

1. Emblematic of this perspective is Robert D. Kaplan's "The Coming Anarchy: How Scarcity, Crime, Overpopulation, Tribalism, and Disease Are Rapidly Destroying the Social Fabric of Our Planet," *Atlantic Monthly* 273, no. 2 (February 1994): 44–77.

2. Commonly referred to as the United Kingdom (UK), the country is officially the United Kingdom of Great Britain and Northern Ireland.

3. This study uses United Nations (UN) terminology, which describes Africa as a world "region" and North, West, Central, East, and Southern Africa as "subregions." Regional organizations are those that embrace the African continent, whereas subregional organizations include members from specific geographic areas within it. The term "global" describes entities with members from multiple continents. However, common usage requires some flexibility. Discussions of regional interests, conflicts, or stability, for instance, do not refer to continentwide phenomena, but rather to those confined to a smaller geographic area within Africa.

4. The German sociologist Max Weber describes patrimonialism as a system of political domination in which all power emanates from the ruler and the state apparatus has no independent power base. The Israeli

sociologist Shmuel Noah Eisenstadt describes neopatrimonialism as a system of political domination that includes a veneer of codified laws, a state bureaucracy, and a legal distinction between the public and private spheres. However, the ruler continues to use state resources for his own benefit and to buy the allegiance of clients inside and outside the official bureaucracy. These clients operate on behalf of their patron rather than the state or the citizenry.

5. Neoliberal economic models promoted by the International Monetary Fund, the World Bank, and the US government require the privatization of state-owned enterprises and limited state involvement in the economy, eliminating subsidies, price controls, and protective tariffs.

6. Warlords are leaders of armed antigovernment movements who act outside the state apparatus. They seek political and military power in order to establish control over resources for their own benefit and that of their family members and close associates. Many are disgruntled former officials of neopatrimonial states whose patrons no longer have the means to purchase their allegiance.

7. The African Union was founded in 2002 to integrate the continent politically and economically and to promote peace, security, stability, and sustainable development. It superseded the Organization of African Unity (OAU), which was established in 1963 by thirty-two independent African states to promote African unity and emancipation.

8. UN General Assembly, "2005 World Summit Outcome," paras. 138–39, adopted September 15, 2005.

9. For further elaboration on Islamist beliefs and identity, see chapter 2.

10. The Gulf states include the seven Arab states that border the Persian Gulf: Bahrain, Iraq, Kuwait, Oman, Qatar, Saudi Arabia, and United Arab Emirates.

11. Quoted in Adam Hochschild, *King Leopold's Ghost: A Story of Greed, Terror, and Heroism in Colonial Africa* (New York: Houghton Mifflin, 1998), 58.

12. Kwame Nkrumah, *Neo-Colonialism: The Last Stage of Imperialism* (New York: International, 1966), ix.

13. The African continent ranks either first or second in world reserves of bauxite, chromite, cobalt, industrial diamonds, manganese, phosphate rock, and platinum-group metals. In 2014, the African percentage of world mineral reserves included chromite (85 percent), manganese (82 percent), columbo-tantalite or "coltan" (80 percent), phosphate rock (80 percent), cobalt (50 percent), bauxite (32 percent), uranium (21 percent), gold (15 percent), and petroleum (8 percent). Africa also produces 65 percent of the world's diamonds.

14. According to World Resources Institute data for 2012, the top ten greenhouse gas producers are China, the United States, the European Union, India, Russia, Japan, Brazil, Germany, Indonesia, and Mexico. This group includes Western countries that have intensified greenhouse gas emissions since the Industrial Revolution, as well as several members of the influential BRICS group of countries with rapidly expanding economies, which includes Brazil, Russia, India, China, and South Africa.

15. A 2014 report by the United Nations Convention to Combat Desertification forecast that by 2020, 60 million people may be fleeing the expanding desert regions of sub-Saharan Africa for North Africa and Europe. By 2050, the number permanently displaced by desertification could reach 200 million. See United Nations Convention to Combat Desertification, *Desertification: The Invisible Frontline* (Bonn: UNCCD, 2014), 9. For a US military assessment of the role of climate change in violent conflict, ideological extremism, and authoritarianism in Africa, see three reports by the CNA Corporation: *National Security and the Threat of Climate Change* (Alexandria, VA: CNA, 2007), *National Security and the Accelerating Risks of Climate Change* (Alexandria, VA: CNA, 2014), and *The Role of Water Stress in Instability and Conflict* (Alexandria, VA: CNA, 2017).

16. When discussing ethnicity in Africa, four factors should be considered. First, ethnic groups are social rather than biological constructions, and they change over time. Second, in many parts of Africa, ethnic identification is a relatively recent phenomenon. Ethnic belonging was often determined by outsiders and was rooted or solidified in colonial policies. Third, ethnic groups may be marked by flexible boundaries that allow people to move between them—albeit over a considerable period of time. Fourth, during times of crisis, ethnicity can be manipulated by powerful social actors to rally supporters in an in-group against others in an out-group—largely to the benefit of social, economic, and political elites.

17. The 21st Century Maritime Silk Road project and the Silk Road Economic Belt together constitute China's One Belt, One Road initiative. The Silk Road Economic Belt is a production and trading network that extends from China to Europe, embracing the historical Silk Road land route as well as other countries in South and Southeast Asia.

18. One notable exception to this generalization was South Africa's military intervention in Lesotho in 1998. Pretoria justified the intervention on humanitarian grounds—although critics claimed the regional powerhouse was simply pursuing its own strategic and economic interests. See Siyabonga Patrick Hadebe, "South Africa's Military Intervention

in Lesotho in 1998: A Critical Overview," http://www.academia.edu/1330315/South_African_military_intervention_in_Lesotho.

19. Zaire was renamed the Democratic Republic of Congo in 1997.

20. The Sahel (derived from the Arabic word for "shore") refers to the Sahara Desert's southern borderlands, which stretch more than 3,000 miles from Senegal in the west to Eritrea in the east.

Chapter 2: The Post–Cold War Context

1. UN General Assembly, "2005 World Summit Outcome," adopted September 15, 2005, paras. 138–39. R2P is common shorthand for the responsibility to protect.

2. See United Nations Charter, Chapter VI, "Pacific Settlement of Disputes"; Chapter VII, "Action with Respect to Threats to the Peace, Breaches of the Peace, and Acts of Aggression"; and Chapter VIII, "Regional Arrangements." The UN Charter was adopted in San Francisco on June 26, 1945, and is available on the United Nations Treaty Collection website.

3. Genocide was defined as "acts committed with intent to destroy, in whole or in part, a national, ethnical, racial or religious group." See UN General Assembly, Resolution 260, "Prevention and Punishment of the Crime of Genocide," December 9, 1948, 174, available on the United Nations Treaty Collection website.

4. Preamble to the United Nations Charter (see note 2 above).

5. "Vienna Declaration and Programme of Action," June 25, 1993.

6. United Nations Charter, Chapter I (see note 2 above).

7. UN General Assembly, "2005 World Summit Outcome," paras. 138–39 (see note 1 above).

8. Islam's two main branches, the Sunni and the Shi'a, are the product of a schism that occurred after the prophet Muhammad's death in 632 CE. The Shi'a argued that Muhammad's successor should be a blood relation ordained by Allah, while the Sunni claimed that the successor should be chosen by a council of religious elders based solely on his qualifications. Although both groups agree on the fundamental tenets of Islam, they disagree about the basis of religious and political authority, which has resulted in different interpretations of Islamic law.

9. After the war, the mujahideen sold the weapons on the black market, where they fell into the hands of Iran's Revolutionary Guard, Central Asian drug smugglers, and insurgent forces in Iraq and the Soviet-controlled territories of Armenia, Azerbaijan, Chechnya, Georgia, and Tajikistan.

10. The concept of jihad is discussed below.

11. The glossary includes definitions of these and other terms associated with Islam.

1. In 2017, NATO's twenty-eight member states included Albania, Belgium, Bulgaria, Canada, Croatia, Czech Republic, Denmark, Estonia, France, Germany, Greece, Hungary, Iceland, Italy, Latvia, Lithuania, Luxembourg, the Netherlands, Norway, Poland, Portugal, Romania, Slovakia, Slovenia, Spain, Turkey, the United Kingdom, and the United States.

2. The Nordic countries include Denmark, Finland, Iceland, Norway, and Sweden, and their autonomous regions (Åland Islands, Faroe Islands, and Greenland).

3. Of the seven Arab states bordering the Persian Gulf, Saudi Arabia, the United Arab Emirates, and Qatar played notable roles. The other Arab Gulf states are Bahrain, Iraq, Kuwait, and Oman.

4. Warlords, who led armed movements outside the state apparatus and often included former government officials, played key roles in post–Cold War conflicts in Somalia, Liberia, Sierra Leone, Côte d'Ivoire, and the Democratic Republic of Congo. In their new positions, they continued to use the patronage networks of the old regime to plunder and distribute resources and to buy loyalty. They also established personal militias, composed of alienated, unemployed young men, to loot resources and eliminate rivals. Their political and economic partners included foreign businesses and criminal networks, which served as conduits for the clandestine exportation of natural resources and the importation of weapons, both of which fueled the conflicts.

5. The Horn of Africa includes Djibouti, Eritrea, Ethiopia, and Somalia, while the Greater Horn includes these countries and adds Burundi, Kenya, Rwanda, South Sudan, Sudan, Tanzania, and Uganda.

6. In 2013–15, the United States, EU member states, Japan, Canada, and Australia provided 81 percent of the UN peacekeeping budget; the United States alone contributed 28.4 percent.

7. "Constitutive Act of the African Union," Lomé, Togo, July 11, 2000, and "Protocol on Amendments to the Constitutive Act of the African Union," Addis Ababa, Ethiopia, February 3, 2003.

8. EU member states in 2017 included Austria, Belgium, Bulgaria, Croatia, Czech Republic, Denmark, Estonia, Finland, France, Germany, Greece, Hungary, Ireland, Italy, Latvia, Lithuania, Luxembourg, Malta, the Netherlands, Poland, Portugal, Republic of Cyprus, Romania, Slovakia, Slovenia, Spain, Sweden, and the United Kingdom, which in 2016 voted to leave.

9. During the 2011 Arab Spring uprisings, for instance, Qatar was exceptional among the Gulf monarchies for its support for moderate Islamist forces, which Saudi Arabia, Bahrain, and the United Arab

Emirates considered as much a threat to their power as the prodemocracy movements.

10. Arab League member states in 2017 included Algeria, Bahrain, Comoros, Djibouti, Egypt, Iraq, Jordan, Kuwait, Lebanon, Libya, Mauritania, Morocco, Oman, Palestine, Qatar, Saudi Arabia, Somalia, Sudan, Syria, Tunisia, United Arab Emirates, and Yemen. Brazil, Eritrea, India, and Venezuela had observer status.

11. ECOWAS member states in 2017 included Benin, Burkina Faso, Cape Verde, Côte d'Ivoire, Gambia, Ghana, Guinea, Guinea-Bissau, Liberia, Mali, Niger, Nigeria, Senegal, Sierra Leone, and Togo. (Mauritania withdrew from the organization in December 2000.)

12. ECCAS member states in 2017 included Angola, Burundi, Cameroon, Central African Republic, Chad, Democratic Republic of Congo, Equatorial Guinea, Gabon, Republic of Congo, Rwanda, and São Tomé and Príncipe.

13. ICGLR member states in 2017 included Angola, Burundi, Central African Republic, Democratic Republic of Congo, Kenya, Republic of Congo, Rwanda, South Sudan, Sudan, Tanzania, Uganda, and Zambia. (South Sudan joined in 2012.)

14. IGAD member states in 2017 included Djibouti, Eritrea, Ethiopia, Kenya, Somalia, South Sudan, Sudan, and Uganda. (Eritrea joined in 1993, and South Sudan joined in 2011.)

15. SADC member states in 2017 included Angola, Botswana, Democratic Republic of Congo, Lesotho, Madagascar, Malawi, Mauritius, Mozambique, Namibia, Seychelles, South Africa, Swaziland, Tanzania, Zambia, and Zimbabwe.

16. G7 members in 2017 included Canada, France, Germany, Italy, Japan, the United Kingdom, and the United States. Until 2014, when Russia was suspended following its annexation of Crimea, the organization was known as the Group of Eight (G8).

17. G20 members in 2017 included Argentina, Australia, Brazil, Canada, China, France, Germany, India, Indonesia, Italy, Japan, Mexico, Republic of Korea (South Korea), Russia, Saudi Arabia, South Africa, Turkey, the United Kingdom, the United States, and the European Union.

18. Salafism is a movement within Sunni Islam that originated in Saudi Arabia. Its adherents advocate a return to the righteous practices of the Prophet Muhammad and the early fathers of the faith (Salaf) and promote a strict, literal interpretation of Islamic teachings. (See the glossary for further detail.)

19. Originally an Algerian insurgency group called the Salafist Group for Preaching and Combat (GSPC), the organization assumed the name al-Qaeda in the Islamic Maghreb after joining the international terrorist

network in 2007. GSPC had splintered from the Armed Islamic Group (GIA), itself an offshoot of the Islamic Salvation Front (FIS), which had won a plurality in Algeria's 1991 parliamentary elections. Fearing that FIS would dominate parliament and rewrite the constitution, the Algerian military staged a coup and cancelled runoff elections, which sparked the beginning of a decade-long civil war (see chapter 10).

20. Ansar (Followers or Supporters) is a core name that has been adopted by numerous, often unrelated, organizations. In this book, the full name is included when the organization is first introduced, followed by an abbreviated version on subsequent mention. Further identifying information is provided if required for clarity.

21. The Levant is a region on the eastern Mediterranean Sea that stretches from Greece to the ancient province of Cyrenaica in eastern Libya and includes Cyprus, Egypt, Iraq, Israel, Jordan, Lebanon, Palestine, Syria, and Turkey.

22. According to the "Guidelines for Jihad" released by al-Qaeda leader Ayman al-Zawahiri in 2013, jihadis should minimize Muslim civilian casualties. Al-Qaeda publicly charged that the Islamic State's ruthless practices were contrary to Islamic teachings.

Chapter 4: Somalia

1. Turkey and the United Arab Emirates have military bases in Somalia, and Turkey trains thousands of Somali soldiers.

2. Uganda and Kenya, the mainstays of an AU peacekeeping force, were among the most notable targets. Al-Shabaab operations in those countries that killed scores of civilians include the July 2010 bombings in Uganda that killed 76 people who were watching a broadcast of the World Cup soccer finals; the September 2013 attack on a shopping mall in Kenya that killed 67 people; and the April 2015 attack on a university in eastern Kenya that killed 147 students.

3. British Somaliland stretched from east to west along the Gulf of Aden, while Italian Somaliland extended southward from the Gulf of Aden along the Indian Ocean coast.

4. The perception of Somali clans as rigid categories with deep historical roots was widely disseminated in the classic study by I. M. Lewis, *A Pastoral Democracy: A Study of Pastoralism and Politics among the Northern Somali of the Horn of Africa* (New York: Oxford University Press, 1961). Lewis posits that Somalia has six clan-based families, which are further divided into clans, subclans, patrilineages, and smaller segments. Abdi Samatar's critique of this perspective is discussed in the Suggested Reading section at the end of this chapter.

5. All dollar amounts in this book are US dollars unless otherwise indicated.

6. Within the Darod clan family, some segments were especially privileged. These included the Marehan (Siad Barre's father's clan), Ogaden (his mother's clan), and Dhulbahante (the clan of his son-in-law, who was also head of the feared National Security Service).

7. Aidid was a member of the Habar Gidir clan and Ali Mahdi belonged to the Abgaal clan, both part of the Hawiye clan family.

8. Clan cleansing, or massive clan-based violence against civilians, is examined in depth in Lidwien Kapteijns, *Clan Cleansing in Somalia: The Ruinous Legacy of 1991* (Philadelphia: University of Pennsylvania Press, 2013).

9. The northwest (Somaliland) and northeast (Puntland) were less affected by the famine and ensuing devastation, which resulted in different political trajectories in those regions.

10. Quoted in John G. Sommer, *Hope Restored? Humanitarian Aid in Somalia, 1990–1994* (Geneva: Refugee Policy Group, 1994), 22.

11. Quoted in Sommer, *Hope Restored*, 16. Natsios served as director of USAID's Office of US Foreign Disaster Assistance (OFDA) from 1989 to 1991 and as assistant administrator of USAID's Bureau for Food and Humanitarian Assistance, which included the OFDA, from 1991 to 1993.

12. CENTCOM had jurisdiction over US military activities in Egypt and the Horn of Africa, as well as in the Middle East and Central Asia.

13. Numerous Western intelligence sources allege that Mohammed Atef, al-Qaeda's military chief and an Egyptian veteran of the Soviet-Afghan War, led the al-Qaeda contingent that trained the Somali forces. In November 1998, Osama bin Laden and Mohammed Atef were indicted in a US federal court for conspiring to kill Americans outside the United States, including in Mogadishu in October 1993. See "US Grand Jury Indictment Against Usama bin Laden," United States District Court, Southern District of New York, November 6, 1998.

14. The 2004 report of the National Commission on Terrorist Attacks Upon the United States (the 9/11 Commission) determined that the charges against al-Barakat were baseless; there was no evidence that the organization had funded either al-Itihaad or al-Qaeda.

15. The UN Security Council Al-Qaida Sanctions Committee removed al-Barakat from its sanctions list in February 2012.

16. US Agency for International Development, *Bureau for Africa: Program, Activity, and Reference Information*, vol. 1, *Angola–Namibia* FY 2006 (Washington, DC: USAID, 2006), 74.

17. Because they oppose religious innovations and new interpretations, Salafis reject the mystical spiritual practices and tradition of tolerance associated with Sufism, which incorporates pre-Islamic beliefs and practices.

18. Quoted in Chris Tomlinson, "Somalia's Islamic Militia Rebuffs U.N.," *Washington Post,* July 25, 2006.

19. UN Security Council, Resolution 1725 (2006), December 6, 2006.

20. Quoted in Ken Menkhaus, "The Crisis in Somalia: Tragedy in Five Acts," *African Affairs* 106, no. 424 (July 2007): 378.

21. The legal justification for US military activities in Somalia was the Authorization for Use of Military Force, granted by Congress to the president after the September 2001 terrorist attacks on the United States. Because actions were authorized only against nations, organizations, or individuals implicated in those attacks, the use of this law against those not involved in 9/11 has been hotly contested. See Public Law 107-40, Joint Resolution to Authorize the Use of United States Armed Forces against Those Responsible for the Recent Attacks Launched against the United States (Authorization for Use of Military Force), September 18, 2001.

22. The criteria for and consequences of the designation "foreign terrorist organization" can be found on the US State Department website.

Chapter 5: Sudan and South Sudan

1. Sudanese Arabs are people of diverse African ethnic makeup who speak Arabic, have embraced some aspects of Arab culture, and are predominantly Muslim.

2. Following a coup attempt in 1971, Nimeiri severed ties to the Sudanese Communist Party and executed many of its leaders.

3. A descendant of Bedouin Arabs and Arabized Berbers, Qaddafi assumed power in Libya after a 1969 military coup. Embracing the pan-Arabism of Egyptian President Gamal Abdel Nasser, Qaddafi hoped to establish a vast Arab Islamic state in North Africa. He also articulated a pan-African vision and extended Libyan influence south of the Sahara, where his diplomatic overtures were supplemented by development projects financed by Libyan oil revenues.

4. John Garang, commander in chief of the SPLA from 1983 to 2005, advocated a democratic, secular, and united Sudan, in which all populations would share in the country's power and resources. His death in a helicopter crash in July 2005, weeks after joining a north-south coalition government, led to new leadership that supported southern secession.

5. Sadiq al-Mahdi was a great-grandson of Muhammad Ahmad ibn Abd Allah, who had expelled the Ottomans and British from Khartoum

in 1885. His grandfather, Sayyid Abd al-Rahman al-Mahdi, a Sufi imam, founded the Umma Party in 1945.

6. The criteria for and consequences of the designation "state sponsor of terrorism" can be found on the US State Department website.

7. The files in question included information about al-Qaeda operatives who would play key roles in the 1998 US Embassy bombings in Kenya and Tanzania.

8. The United States, the United Kingdom, and Norway, known as the Troika, would continue to play significant mediation roles in Sudan after 2005 and in South Sudan after 2011.

9. Among the Darfur rebel organizations that joined the SRF were the Justice and Equality Movement (JEM), the Sudan Liberation Army–Abdel Wahid (SLA-AW), and the Sudan Liberation Army–Minni Minawi (SLA-MM), discussed below.

10. IGAD-Plus included the members of IGAD as well as representatives from the UN, the AU, and the EU; the Troika of the United States, the UK, and Norway; China, a key economic partner and permanent member of the UN Security Council; and South Africa, Nigeria, Algeria, Chad, and Rwanda, representing the continent's five regions.

11. The Janjaweed phenomenon first emerged during the civil war in Chad, where the crisis in the nomadic way of life was even more pronounced than in Darfur. The term was also used to describe the ethnic militias involved in the Arab-Fur War.

12. Founded in 1909, the National Association for the Advancement of Colored People is now commonly known by its acronym, NAACP.

13. *Report of the International Commission of Inquiry on Darfur to the United Nations Secretary-General*, Geneva, January 25, 2005, 4.

14. UN General Assembly, "2005 World Summit Outcome," adopted September 15, 2005, paras. 138–39.

15. Quoted in Joel Brinkley, "Security Council Agrees to Send Troops to Darfur," *New York Times*, February 4, 2006.

16. Whereas the original SLA had included both Fur and Zaghawa members, the splinter groups were more starkly organized along ethnic lines. SLA-AW attracted mostly Fur adherents, while the SLA-MM was composed primarily of Zaghawa members.

17. Quoted in Johan Brosché and Daniel Rothbart, *Violent Conflict and Peacebuilding: The Continuing Crisis in Darfur* (New York: Routledge, 2012), 68.

18. Mike Pflanz, "Bin Laden Calls for Jihad on Darfur Force," *Telegraph* (UK), October 25, 2007.

19. A second arrest warrant, on charges of genocide, was issued in July 2010. In December 2014, the ICC suspended its case against Bashir, noting that ICC member countries continued to allow Sudan's president to come and go unimpeded and that the UN Security Council had ignored numerous appeals for assistance in facilitating his arrest. China, Russia, and the United States were among the Security Council members that failed to act. Apart from their political and economic considerations, none of these countries had ratified the ICC treaty.

20. Quoted in Colum Lynch, "Sudan's 'Coordinated' Genocide in Darfur Is Over, U.S. Envoy Says," *Washington Post*, June 18, 2009.

21. Quoted in Brian Knowlton, "White House Unveils Sudan Strategy," *New York Times*, October 20, 2009. The Obama administration suspended a number of sanctions in January 2017, and the Trump administration revoked them permanently in October of that year. However, Sudan was not awarded debt relief and retained its designation as a state sponsor of terrorism.

22. Although Tijani al-Sisi, a Fur intellectual, chaired the LJM, critics claimed that he was not representative of the Fur population. Having spent decades in exile, he was out of touch with local issues, and he had not participated in the armed struggle.

23. A referendum in April 2016 offered the choice of five ethnically based states or a single regional state—each to be led by a Khartoum-appointed governor. Proponents of unification argued that a united Darfur could more effectively counter the central government's power. The conditions surrounding the vote were widely criticized. Most of the 2.6 million Darfuris who were displaced could not vote, and balloting occurred amid violence and insecurity. The opposition boycotted the referendum, voter turnout was low, and the results were contested. While Khartoum claimed that nearly 98 percent of the voters favored the five-state option, the US State Department asserted that the referendum results were not "a credible expression of the will of the people." Quoted in Zeinab Mohammed Salih and Jeffrey Gettleman, "Light Turnout for Vote in Darfur on Region's Future," *New York Times*, April 11, 2016.

Chapter 6: Rwanda

1. The former Belgian Congo was known successively as Congo-Léopoldville (1960), Congo-Kinshasa (1966), Zaire (1971), and, finally, Democratic Republic of Congo (1997).

2. French political, economic, and military pacts with autocratic African leaders led to numerous French military interventions during the

postcolonial period. The neocolonial relationship was referred to by its detractors as Françafrique.

3. Concerned by the influence on exiled Tutsi activists of radical nationalists like Congolese leader Patrice Lumumba, colonial officials claimed to be saving Hutu peasants from both Tutsi feudalism and Tutsi communism.

4. The United States, which was expected to pay for one-third of the mission's costs, had advocated a force of only 500.

5. A 400-page report released by a French judicial commission in January 2012 corroborated the Belgian-US claim. New evidence has again shifted suspicion to the RPF, which stood to benefit from the leadership struggle that followed Habyarimana's death. See Alex de Waal, "Writing Human Rights and Getting It Wrong," *Boston Review*, June 6, 2016.

6. Susan Rice, director for international organizations and peacekeeping on the US National Security Council in 1994, was among those who opposed use of the term genocide. During an interagency teleconference in late April, she remarked, "If we use the word 'genocide' and are seen as doing nothing, what will be the effect on the November [congressional] election?" Quoted in Samantha Power, "Bystanders to Genocide," *Atlantic*, September 2001.

7. UN Security Council, Resolution 912 (1994), April 21, 1994. See also "Special Report of the Secretary-General on the United Nations Assistance Mission for Rwanda," S/1994/470, April 20, 1994, paras. 15–18. Although the initial plan was to leave behind only 270 UN troops, that number was later raised to 450.

8. Quoted in Department of Public Information, United Nations, "Rwanda—UNAMIR: United Nations Assistance Mission for Rwanda," September 1996.

9. The UN suppressed the report—a decision that was supported by the United States—to avoid tarnishing the new RPF-dominated government as well as the UN mission. See "The Gersony Mission" in Alison Des Forges, *"Leave None to Tell the Story": Genocide in Rwanda* (New York: Human Rights Watch, 1999).

Chapter 7: The Democratic Republic of Congo

1. The former Belgian Congo was known successively as Congo-Léopoldville (1960), Congo-Kinshasa (1966), Zaire (1971), and, finally, Democratic Republic of Congo (1997). For the sake of clarity, this chapter uses "Zaire" for the period 1960–96, "DRC" for the period 1997–2017, and "Zaire/DRC" when both are applicable.

2. See, especially, Gérard Prunier, *Africa's World War: Congo, the Rwandan Genocide, and the Making of a Continental Catastrophe* (New York: Oxford University Press, 2009).

3. Mobutu collaborated with Congolese secessionists, Belgium, and the CIA to assassinate the Congo's first prime minister, Patrice Lumumba, in 1961.

4. For elaboration on this argument, see Michael G. Schatzberg, *Mobutu or Chaos: The United States and Zaire, 1960–1990* (Lanham, MD: University Press of America, 1991).

5. Originally the United Nations International Children's Emergency Fund, and currently the United Nations Children's Fund, UNICEF is generally referred to by its acronym.

6. Several parties to the conflict were also members of subregional organizations that were charged with mediating peace agreements. ICGLR members that participated in the violence included Angola, Burundi, Chad, DRC, Rwanda, Sudan, Uganda, and Zambia. SADC members included Angola, DRC, Namibia, Zambia, and Zimbabwe.

7. Known as Katanga from the colonial period until 1971 and as Shaba from 1971 to 1997, the region reverted to its earlier name after Mobutu's ouster.

8. The name Mai-Mai derives from the Swahili word *maji* (water). It refers to the ritual water that, along with magical potions and charms, was used by local defense force members to protect themselves from enemy bullets.

9. In May 2008, Bemba was arrested in Belgium and turned over to the ICC to face charges of war crimes and crimes against humanity in connection with actions committed by his forces in the Central African Republic in 2002–3, when MLC mercenaries quashed an internal rebellion on behalf of the ruling regime. Bemba was convicted of those crimes in March 2016. However, the conviction was overturned in June 2018 on the grounds that as a "remote commander" he could not be held responsible for his soldiers' crimes.

10. An ICC arrest warrant in August 2006 charged Ntaganda with war crimes. A second ICC arrest warrant, issued in July 2012, accused him of having committed crimes against humanity.

11. Following dissent within the rebel ranks, Ntaganda sought refuge in Rwanda in March 2013, where the Kagame regime was either unwilling or unable to protect him. Ntaganda then surrendered to the US Embassy and asked to be transferred to the ICC, perhaps concluding that confinement in The Hague was the only way to save his life. His trial, which began in September 2015, was ongoing in 2017.

12. As the National Security Council's director for international organizations and peacekeeping in 1994, Rice was among those who opposed US intervention to stop the Rwandan genocide. Subsequent remorse and frustrations with Mobutu and Laurent Kabila pushed her toward Rwanda.

As assistant secretary of state for African affairs during the Second Congo War, Rice developed a close relationship with RPF leader Paul Kagame, who served as Rwanda's vice president and minister of defense after the genocide and became president in 2000. As US ambassador to the UN (2009–13) and national security advisor (2013–17), Rice consistently refused to criticize Rwanda's abuses in the DRC.

Chapter 8: Liberia and Sierra Leone

1. Named for the river that originates in the highlands of Guinea and forms a border between Sierra Leone and Liberia, the Mano River region has long been understood to embrace those three countries. Sometimes Côte d'Ivoire is included because of the four countries' interlocking conflicts and their regional ramifications.

2. Between 1805 and 1820, a number of countries, including the United States, passed laws that outlawed the trans-Atlantic slave trade. The British law of 1807 was perhaps the most significant. It prohibited the slave trade throughout the British Empire, and the UK embarked on a naval campaign to compel other countries to comply with its ban on the trade across the Atlantic.

3. Most of Doe's associates were of the Krahn ethnic group, one of the smallest, poorest, and least educated populations in Liberia.

4. Speakers of closely related Manding languages are known in different West African countries by various names, including Mandingo, Malinke, Mandinka, and Jula (also spelled Juula, Dyula, Dioula), which means "trader," a profession historically associated with Manding speakers. They are often viewed as one ethnic group with regional variations.

5. Some of the motivations were personal as well as political. Houphouët-Boigny's goddaughter, Désirée Delafosse, was the widow of President William Tolbert's son, Adolphus, who had been killed by Doe's forces after the 1980 coup. After her husband's death, Delafosse settled in Burkina Faso, where she became close to Blaise Compaoré, who was also a Houphouët-Boigny protégé.

6. Quoted in Joshua Hammer, "Into Anarchy," *Newsweek* 127, no. 18 (April 29, 1996): 39, 41.

7. In Guinea, Mandingos are more commonly called Malinkes.

8. From 1960 to 2007, French-African affairs were largely directed from the Africa Cell, a secretive body that worked under the personal direction of the French president to safeguard French interests in Africa. Although officially disbanded under President Nicolas Sarkozy (2007–12), its work continued under other auspices.

9. Gbagbo's support base included Ivoirian Krahns, who are called the Guéré or Wè in Côte d'Ivoire.

10. See Ann Mezzell, "US Policy Shifts on Sub-Saharan Africa: An Assessment of Contending Predictions," *Africa & Francophonie: Air & Space Power Journal* 1, no. 4 (Winter 2010): 79–96.

11. The International Contact Group on Liberia included representatives from the UN, the AU, ECOWAS, Nigeria, Ghana, the United States, the UK, Germany, Spain, Sweden, and the World Bank.

12. Private military companies are not included in the definition of mercenary used in the UN Mercenary Convention because, in theory, their members do not engage in combat—evidence to the contrary notwithstanding. See UN General Assembly, Resolution A/RES/44/34, "International Convention against the Recruitment, Use, Financing and Training of Mercenaries," December 4, 1989.

13. The Commonwealth (officially, the Commonwealth of Nations) includes fifty-three member states. Most were previously part of the British Empire. Its mission is to promote the development of free and democratic societies, peace and prosperity, and improvement in the lives of its members' citizens.

14. The number of ECOMOG troops in Sierra Leone would ultimately reach 13,000, of whom 12,000 were Nigerian.

15. The number of UNAMSIL personnel eventually rose to 23,000.

16. The Special Court was established in 2002 by the United Nations and Sierra Leone pursuant to Security Council Resolution 1315 of August 14, 2000. See "Statute of the Special Court for Sierra Leone."

Chapter 9: Côte d'Ivoire

1. According to the World Bank, 37.9 percent of Côte d'Ivoire's adult population was between the ages of fifteen and twenty-four in 2000.

2. Côte d'Ivoire, like most former French colonies on the continent, was a member of the African Financial Community, a monetary union whose participants shared a common currency, the value of which was linked to the French franc. Monetary and financial regulations were determined in Paris, and France was permitted to devalue the CFA currency without consulting African governments.

3. Guéï was assassinated in September 2002 by pro-Gbagbo security forces following the coup attempt that sparked the Ivoirian civil war.

4. The OAU was succeeded by the AU in July 2002.

5. Similar terminology and justifications were used by the RUF during its 1997 "Operation Pay Yourself" campaign in Sierra Leone.

6. Charles Blé Goudé, who served as FESCI secretary-general from 1998 to 2001, founded the Young Patriots in 2001.

7. MPIGO recruited heavily among the Dan/Yacouba people, who in Liberia are called the Gio. Taylor had garnered support from Gio populations along the Ivoirian border during the Liberian civil war.

Chapter 10: The Arab Spring in North Africa

1. Islamist involvement in the uprisings was particularly notable in Egypt, Jordan, Saudi Arabia, Syria, Tunisia, and Yemen.

2. Some analysts prefer the terms Arab Uprising or Arab Awakening in reference to the popular upheavals in North Africa and the Middle East during 2011–13. They note that the events were characterized by social and economic as well as political concerns, which distinguished them from European movements for political freedom and democracy such as the Prague Spring of 1968, the Croatian Spring of 1971, and the popular movements that led to state breakdown and regime change in Eastern Europe in 1989–91.

3. The monarchies included Bahrain, Jordan, Kuwait, Morocco, Oman, Qatar, Saudi Arabia, and the United Arab Emirates. The Arab republics included Algeria, Egypt, Iraq, Lebanon, Libya, Syria, Tunisia, and Yemen.

4. "Remarks by the President upon Arrival, the South Lawn," September 16, 2001, http://georgewbush-whitehouse.archives.gov/news/releases /2001/09/print/20010916-2.html.

5. Transcript of President Bush's address to a joint session of Congress on Thursday night, September 20, 2001, http://edition.cnn.com/2001 /US/09/20/gen.bush.transcript/.

6. "President Obama's Speech in Cairo: A New Beginning," Cairo University, Egypt, June 4, 2009, https://2009-2017.state.gov/p/nea/rls/rm /2009/124342.htm.

7. Wahhabism, an ascetic religious reform movement within Salafism, has a strong, officially sanctioned presence in both Saudi Arabia and the United Arab Emirates. Wahhabi teachings, like many other Salafist strains, stress law and order and obedience to authority.

8. In October 2015, the National Dialogue Quartet, comprising the Tunisian General Labor Union, the Tunisian Confederation of Industry, Trade and Handicrafts, the Tunisian Order of Lawyers, and the Tunisian Human Rights League, was awarded the Nobel Peace Prize for its role in moving the country toward a pluralistic democracy based on human rights and rooted in civil society. The Norwegian Nobel Committee did not mention that one of the Quartet's goals was to sideline moderate Islamists.

9. In 2017, TSCTP members included Algeria, Burkina Faso, Cameroon, Chad, Mali, Mauritania, Morocco, Niger, Nigeria, Senegal, and Tunisia.

10. In signing a separate peace with Israel, Egypt broke ranks with the rest of the Arab world, where the special deal negotiated outside the UN framework was widely perceived as treachery. Egypt was suspended from the Arab League for a decade. The 1979 treaty returned to Egypt the Sinai Peninsula, seized by Israel during the 1967 war, but left the other occupied territories in Israel's hands. Israel retained control of the Gaza Strip (Egypt), the Golan Heights (Syria), East Jerusalem (Jordan), and the West Bank of the Jordan River (Jordan). The accords also left unsettled the fate of the Palestinian people, who had lost their homes during Israel's war of independence (1947–49) and in the Arab-Israeli wars of 1967 and 1973. Although the UN had recognized Palestinians' right of return to their homeland and to an independent state defined by borders established in 1949, Palestinians had little hope of realizing those rights without Egypt's support.

11. "Obama's Remarks on the Resignation of Mubarak," *New York Times*, February 11, 2011.

12. David Kirkpatrick and Mayy El Sheikh, "Seeming Retreat by Egypt Leader on New Powers," *New York Times*, November 26, 2012.

13. Samer S. Shehata, "In Egypt, Democrats vs. Liberals," *New York Times*, July 2, 2013.

14. "Statement by President Barack Obama on Egypt," July 3, 2013, http://www.whitehouse.gov/the-press-office/2013/07/03/statement-president-barack-obama-egypt.

15. The Consolidated Appropriations Act of 2012 prohibits US aid "to the government of any country whose duly elected head of government is deposed by military coup d'état or decree." This prohibition remains in effect until "a democratically elected government has taken office" (https://www.gpo.gov/fdsys/pkg/PLAW-112publ74/pdf/PLAW-112publ74.pdf).

16. In one case, 529 Brotherhood supporters received death sentences for killing a single police officer during demonstrations that followed the coup. In another, more than 680 Brotherhood members were sentenced to death for an attack on a police station in which no one was killed.

17. Quoted in "With Washington's Complicity, Egypt Cracks Down on Critics," editorial, *New York Times*, July 16, 2015.

18. State Department spokeswoman Jen Psaki, quoted in Spencer Ackerman and Ian Black, "US Trims Aid to Egypt as Part of Diplomatic 'Recalibration,'" *Guardian*, October 9, 2013.

19. Critics charged that support for Egyptian security forces contravened the Leahy provision in the US Foreign Assistance Act, which

prohibits aid to foreign military or police units if there is credible evidence that they have "committed a gross violation of human rights" and have not been held accountable. See Section 620M of the US Foreign Assistance Act of 1961, as amended, https://legcounsel.house.gov/Comps/Foreign%20 Assistance%20Act%20Of%201961.pdf.

20. After taking power, Qaddafi had instituted free health care and education for all Libyans, dramatically improving the quality of life in these areas. However, in April 1973, revolutionary committees took charge of hospitals and universities, and during the ensuing cultural revolution health and education standards declined and infrastructure crumbled.

21. Ethnic groups tended to be clustered regionally: Berbers in the central region, Tubus in the south (also in Chad and Niger), and Tuaregs in the west (also in Algeria, Burkina Faso, Mali, and Niger).

22. During the Arab Spring uprising, rebels released hundreds of LIFG militants from prison, and many joined the revolt that overthrew the Qaddafi regime.

23. The African Union Ad Hoc High-Level Committee on Libya, established by the AU Peace and Security Council, released a statement on March 20, 2011, that opposed foreign military intervention. The committee, comprising five African heads of state, proposed exile for Qaddafi and his replacement by an interim government.

24. The Gulf Cooperation Council is a political and economic alliance that includes the monarchies of Bahrain, Kuwait, Oman, Qatar, Saudi Arabia, and the United Arab Emirates. Iraq, which also borders the Persian Gulf, is the only Arab Gulf state that is not a member.

25. These officials, and others who promote war as means of accomplishing humanitarian ends, are sometimes called "liberal interventionists," "humanitarian interventionists," or "humanitarian hawks."

26. UN Security Council, Resolution 1973 (2011), March 17, 2011.

27. The nonpermanent members that supported the resolution included Bosnia and Herzegovina, Colombia, Gabon, Lebanon, Nigeria, Portugal, and South Africa. South Africa, Nigeria, and Gabon were AU member states, and South Africa had served on the AU Ad Hoc High-Level Committee on Libya.

28. On April 4, 2011, while the Libyan operation was still in process, French and UN forces conducted military strikes and ground operations in Côte d'Ivoire. In Côte d'Ivoire, as in Libya, the official objective was the destruction of weapons that had been used against civilians. In both cases, the unstated goal and end result was regime change.

29. Quoted in Eric Schmitt, "Embassies Open, but Yemen Stays on Terror Watch," *New York Times*, August 11, 2013.

30. Weapons from Qaddafi's stockpiles made their way to Algeria, Chad, Egypt, Gaza, Mali, Niger, Nigeria, Somalia, Sudan, Syria, and Tunisia, where they armed secular insurgents, religious extremists, and criminals.

31. The Benghazi organization attracted world attention on September 11, 2012, when it attacked the US consulate in that city, killing four Americans, including the US ambassador to Libya. Although the assault occurred on the eleventh anniversary of the al-Qaeda attacks on the United States, it was prompted by a US-made video that had provoked hundreds of protesters to attack the US Embassy in Tunisia and had inspired anti-American demonstrations in Egypt, Morocco, nine sub-Saharan African countries, and elsewhere in the Muslim world. In 2014, the US State Department included the Ansar organizations in Benghazi and Derna on its official list of foreign terrorist organizations, and the UN Security Council, at the urging of France, the UK, and the United States, designated both as associates of al-Qaeda.

32. Suffering significant territorial losses in Iraq and Syria in 2015 and 2016, the Islamic State began to shift its focus from building a local caliphate—an Islamic state equipped with governmental and social services—to attacking the "far enemy." The retaliatory bombing of a Russian airliner over Egypt in October 2015 and attacks on a concert hall, sports stadium, restaurants, and bars in Paris in November 2015 were indicators of this transformation. Threatened by the Islamic State's growing popularity, al-Qaeda affiliates responded in kind. In early 2016, al-Qaeda operatives assaulted soft targets in Mali, Burkina Faso, and Côte d'Ivoire that were favored by Western civilian and military personnel.

33. Abu Anas al-Liby died from liver disease in January 2015, days before his scheduled trial. In November 2017, Ahmed Abu Khattala was convicted of supporting terrorism.

34. By late 2017, Chouchane's death had not been confirmed.

35. The UN conference that brokered the deal was co-chaired by Italy and the United States. It brought together fifteen Libyan delegates, representatives from Libya's neighbors (Algeria, Chad, Egypt, Niger, Sudan, and Tunisia), and the P5+5 group—that is, the five permanent members of the UN Security Council (France, the United Kingdom, the United States, Russia, and China) plus Germany, Italy, Spain, the EU, and the UN. Germany, Italy, and Spain were among the EU's largest receiving countries for African and Middle Eastern migrants.

36. Public Law 107-40, Joint Resolution to Authorize the Use of United States Armed Forces against Those Responsible for the Recent Attacks Launched against the United States (Authorization for Use of Military Force), September 18, 2001.

37. See video included in Nima Elbagir, Raja Razek, Alex Platt, and Bryony Jones, "People for Sale: Where Lives Are Auctioned for $400," CNN, November 14, 2017.

38. The Justice and Charity Party had initially joined the February 20 Movement, but later withdrew its support.

Chapter 11: Mali and Nigeria

1. A legacy of the Algerian civil war, AQIM was one of wealthiest al-Qaeda franchises worldwide, largely as a result of the millions of dollars it reaped from trafficking in drugs, weapons, fuel, tobacco, and other goods, as well as from kidnapping for ransom. AQIM frequently collaborated with ethnic groups, clans, and criminal networks whose goals differed from those of al-Qaeda but who had grievances against the same authorities.

2. Azawad, derived from the Tuareg term for savanna, is the historical name for a region that includes northeastern Mali, western Niger, and southern Algeria.

3. Sanogo had received military training in the United States on several occasions, including basic officer training at Fort Benning, Georgia; intelligence training at Fort Huachuca, Arizona; English-language training at Lackland Air Force Base, Texas; and further training at the US Marine Corps base in Quantico, Virginia.

4. As noted previously, the Consolidated Appropriations Act of 2012 prohibits US aid "to the government of any country whose duly elected head of government is deposed by military coup d'état or decree." This prohibition remains in effect until "a democratically elected government has taken office."

5. In 2013, Niger was the world's fourth-largest uranium producer, and it provided approximately one-fifth of the uranium used in French nuclear reactors. Mali's uranium deposits were much less extensive. However, France was concerned by the transnational nature of the Tuareg insurgency, which historically had affected Niger, and by the potential for severe regional destabilization.

6. Presidential elections held in July and August 2013 resulted in victory for former prime minister Ibrahim Boubacar Keïta. When he took office in September, the way was cleared for a resumption of direct US assistance to the Bamako government.

7. International Crisis Group, *Mali: Avoiding Escalation*, Africa Report 189 (Brussels: International Crisis Group, 2012).

8. As the former colonial power in more than a dozen West and Central African countries, France continued to maintain troops and stage military interventions throughout the region. In 2015, some 3,500 French

troops were stationed in Burkina Faso, Chad, Mali, Mauritania, and Niger. French weapons, vehicles, fighter aircraft, transport planes, and helicopter gunships were housed in several countries, and they were frequently activated to protect French interests.

9. Quoted in Anthony Faiola and Michael Birnbaum, "Algerian Forces Search Facility after Deadly Standoff Ends," *Washington Post*, January 20, 2013.

10. Public Law 107-40, Joint Resolution to Authorize the Use of United States Armed Forces against Those Responsible for the Recent Attacks Launched against the United States (Authorization for Use of Military Force), September 18, 2001.

11. AQIM, then called the Salafist Group for Preaching and Combat, became al-Qaeda's North African representative five years after the 9/11 attacks.

12. Quoted in Edward Cody and Craig Whitlock, "French Warplanes Hit Central Mali in Fierce Fighting Between Soldiers, Islamist Guerrillas," *Washington Post*, January 14, 2013.

13. Belmokhtar had been a member of the Algerian organization GIA and its spinoff, GSPC, which became AQIM. Al-Mulathameen splintered from AQIM in December 2012 to report directly to the al-Qaeda leadership. The organization had acquired large quantities of Libyan weapons after Qaddafi's fall and benefited financially from Belmokhtar's position as head of a cigarette-smuggling monopoly in the Sahel and his lucrative trafficking in weapons, drugs, and hostages.

14. UN Security Council, Resolution 2100 (2013), April 25, 2013.

15. Although the people refer to themselves as Fulbe or Peul, the Hausa referent, Fulani, is more widely used by outsiders. The Macina Liberation Front aspired to reestablish a Fulani empire that had existed in Mali in the nineteenth century.

16. Other attacks in Burkina Faso were carried by Ansarul Islam, a new organization alleged to be a branch of Ansar Dine. The organization's founder, a Burkinabe Fulani cleric, Malam Ibrahim Dicko, had fought with MUJWA in Mali, where he was influenced by the Macina Liberation Front. Like his Macina associates, Dicko aspired to reestablish a Fulani kingdom that existed prior to French conquest.

17. According to the World Bank, 1 percent of the Nigerian population controlled 80 percent of the nation's wealth in 2013. Most of that wealth was derived from oil.

18. Civilian governments administered Nigeria during the periods 1960–66, 1979–83, and 1999–present. Military governments ruled in 1966–79 and 1983–99. Military rule during the latter period was punctuated by

a two-and-a-half-month interlude of civilian rule, followed by a military coup, in 1993.

19. Fulani elites intermarried with local Hausas and many elites adopted the Hausa language. Today, the ethnic group is often referred to as the Hausa-Fulani. Forming Nigeria's largest ethnic group, Hausa-Fulanis have been the dominant political force in Nigeria since independence.

20. Boko Haram (Western Education Is Forbidden) refers to the contempt adherents felt for Western-educated elites and their corrupt patronage system. It is sometimes translated as "The Sham of Western Education Is Forbidden."

21. Nigerian government sources assert that militants from Algeria, Mali, and Mauritania joined Boko Haram. These claims have been disputed by some experts and have not been verified by independent sources.

22. Boko Haram's new title has also been translated as the Islamic State's West Africa Province.

23. The private military contractors—mercenaries, to their critics—were employed by Specialized Tasks, Training, Equipment and Protection International, a company chaired by Eeben Barlow. Barlow was a former SADF officer and the founder of Executive Outcomes, the private military company that was hired in the 1990s to fight UNITA insurgents in Angola and RUF insurgents in Sierra Leone.

24. Buhari's father was Fulani and his mother of Hausa and Kanuri descent. His maternal grandfather, a Kanuri, was born in what is now Borno State, an area at the heart of the northeastern insurgency. After earning a master's degree from the US Army War College in 1980, Buhari first came to power in 1983 following a military coup that overthrew a democratically elected government. He was ousted by another coup two years later.

25. See Section 620M of the US Foreign Assistance Act of 1961, as amended, https://legcounsel.house.gov/Comps/Foreign%20Assistance%20Act%20Of%201961.pdf.

26. Quoted in "Nigeria's Buhari Presses for Military Aid, Pledges 'Zero Tolerance' for Corruption," United States Institute of Peace, July 22, 2015.

27. Days before leaving office, President Obama blocked the sale of twelve Super Tucano attack planes to the Nigerian air force after it bombed a displaced persons camp, killing hundreds of civilians and aid workers. In April 2017 President Trump asked Congress to authorize the sale, noting Nigeria's importance as a counterterrorism partner.

Chapter 12: US Africa Policy after the Cold War (1991–2017)

1. For the origins of the Bush administration policy, see George W. Bush, "Address to a Joint Session of Congress and the American People,"

September 20, 2001, and US State Department, "The Global War on Terrorism: The First 100 Days."

2. Admirers of President Ronald Reagan (1981–89) claimed that his policies had defeated America's Cold War rival. Reagan himself shared the credit with his close ally, British Prime Minister Margaret Thatcher, and with Soviet reformer Mikhail Gorbachev, general secretary of the Central Committee of the Communist Party of the Soviet Union and de facto leader of that country.

3. See Ann Mezzell, "US Policy Shifts on Sub-Saharan Africa: An Assessment of Contending Predictions," *Africa & Francophonie: Air & Space Power Journal* 1, no. 4 (Winter 2010): 79–96.

4. The responsibility to protect paradigm was crystalized in a 2005 UN General Assembly resolution. However, the philosophy and justification for intervention predated the resolution (see chapter 2).

5. The new leaders most favored by the Clinton administration included Yoweri Museveni of Uganda, Meles Zenawi of Ethiopia, Isaias Afwerki of Eritrea, and Paul Kagame of Rwanda.

6. The African Growth and Opportunity Act was signed into law as Title I of the Trade and Development Act of 2000 (Public Law 106-200).

7. T. Andrew Mushita, a Zimbabwean NGO leader, dubbed the law the "*American* Growth and Opportunity Act." See T. A. Mushita, "An African Response to AGOA," *Southern African Economist* 14, no. 6 (2001): 17.

8. AGOA eligibility requirements are described in Section 104 of PL 106-200 (see note 6 above).

9. African countries that attempted to protect domestic industries have been targeted for expulsion. In 2015, South Africa was threatened over plans to ban US chicken imports, and in 2017, Kenya, Rwanda, Tanzania, and Uganda were pressured when they moved to bar imports of used American clothing and shoes. South Africa, Kenya, Tanzania, and Uganda backed down, but Rwanda was suspended from the AGOA beneficiaries list.

10. These exceptions were included at the behest of US agricultural interests, which also lobbied successfully to retain US sugar and tobacco subsidies in the US Farm Bill.

11. See Transparency International's 2017 Corruption Perceptions Index for country rankings.

12. For 2017 MCC funding criteria, see "Guide to the MCC Indicators for Fiscal Year 2017."

13. Project for the New American Century, "Statement of Principles," June 3, 1997. See also Project for the New American Century, *Rebuilding America's Defenses: Strategy, Forces and Resources for a New Century* (Washington, DC: PNAC, 2000).

14. The White House, *The National Security Strategy of the United States of America,* September 2002, 1.

15. The criteria for and consequences of the designation "foreign terrorist organization" can be found on the US State Department website.

16. President Bush proclaimed, "Our war on terror begins with al Qaeda, but it does not end there. It will not end until every terrorist group of global reach has been found, stopped and defeated." "Address to a Joint Session of Congress and the American People," September 20, 2001 (see note 1 above).

17. United States Senate, *Alleged Assassination Plots Involving Foreign Leaders: An Interim Report of the Select Committee to Study Governmental Operations with Respect to Intelligence Activities* (Washington, DC: US Government Printing Office, 1976).

18. See declassified documents on the website of the National Security Archive: *White House Efforts to Blunt 1975 Church Committee Investigation into CIA Abuses Foreshadowed Executive-Congressional Battles after 9/11,* Electronic Briefing Book 522, July 20, 2015, and *Gerald Ford White House Altered Rockefeller Commission Report in 1975; Removed Section on CIA Assassination Plots,* Electronic Briefing Book 543, February 29, 2016. As secretary of defense in the George H. W. Bush administration (1989–93), Cheney helped direct US involvement in the First Gulf War (1990–91), which included the invasion of Iraq. Over the protests of many neoconservatives, the first President Bush stopped short of overthrowing Saddam Hussein. The second President Bush, deeply influenced by then Vice President Cheney and other neoconservatives, finished the job in the Second Gulf War (2003–11).

19. Public Law 107-40, Joint Resolution to Authorize the Use of United States Armed Forces against Those Responsible for the Recent Attacks Launched against the United States (Authorization for Use of Military Force), September 18, 2001.

20. G8 members included Canada, France, Germany, Italy, Japan, Russia, the United Kingdom, and the United States. Russia was suspended in 2014 following its annexation of Crimea. The organization was then called the Group of Seven (G7).

21. The United States is not a signatory to the UN's International Convention for the Protection of All Persons from Enforced Disappearance (adopted December 20, 2006, and entered into force December 23, 2010), available on the United Nations Treaty Collection website.

22. Shortly after 9/11, President Bush told reporters, "This crusade, this war on terrorism is going to take a while." "Remarks by the President Upon Arrival," September 16, 2001, http://georgewbush-whitehouse.archives.gov/news/releases/2001/09/20010916-2.html.

23. For the legal ramifications of the designation "foreign terrorist organization," see note 15 above.

24. Each year, 40 percent of global maritime trade, including 4 percent of the world's oil traffic, passes through the narrow 20-mile passageway that separates Yemen on the Arabian Peninsula from Djibouti and Eritrea on the Horn of Africa. Counterterrorism operations against jihadi insurgencies in Yemen and Somalia have heightened Djibouti's strategic value. In 2017, Camp Lemonnier was home to more than 4,000 US military and civilian personnel, including members of the Combined Joint Task Force–Horn of Africa (CJTF-HOA) and the Joint Special Operations Command (JSOC). Djibouti also hosted French, Japanese, Italian, and Chinese military bases, and Saudi Arabia announced plans to construct one. NATO, the EU, Germany, Spain, and the UK also staged military operations from Djibouti.

25. In 2017, the CJTF-HOA area of operations encompassed Burundi, Djibouti, Eritrea, Ethiopia, Kenya, Rwanda, Seychelles, Somalia, Tanzania, and Uganda. Its broader area of interest included the Central African Republic, Chad, Comoros, Democratic Republic of Congo, Egypt, Madagascar, Mauritius, Mozambique, South Sudan, Sudan, and Yemen.

26. In 2009, EACTI was replaced by the East Africa Regional Strategic Initiative (EARSI), which expanded to include Comoros, Djibouti, Eritrea, Ethiopia, Kenya, Mauritius, Seychelles, Somalia, Sudan, Tanzania, and Uganda. EARSI was transformed into the Partnership for Regional East Africa Counterterrorism (PREACT), which included Burundi, Comoros, Djibouti, Ethiopia, Kenya, Rwanda, Seychelles, Somalia, South Sudan, Sudan, Tanzania, and Uganda.

27. US Agency for International Development, *Bureau for Africa: Program, Activity, and Reference Information*, vol. 1, *Angola–Namibia* FY 2006 (Washington, DC: USAID, 2006), 74.

28. In 2016, Niger was near the bottom of the global UNDP Human Development Index, ranking 187 out of 188. Chad ranked 186, Mali 175, and Mauritania 157.

29. Flintlock 2017 included more than 2,000 troops and commando trainers from twenty-four African and Western partner nations. Participating African states were Algeria, Burkina Faso, Cameroon, Cape Verde, Chad, Mauritania, Morocco, Niger, Nigeria, Senegal, and Tunisia. Western states that provided military trainers were Australia, Austria, Belgium, Canada, Denmark, France, Germany, Italy, the Netherlands, Norway, Spain, the United Kingdom, and the United States.

30. Although technically part of both the Maghreb and the Sahel, Mauritania is typically associated with the Sahelian countries.

31. Chad's public sector was deemed to be among the world's most corrupt in 2017. Transparency International ranked it 165 out of the 180 countries evaluated for the 2017 Corruption Perceptions Index. Nigeria ranked 148.

32. US Department of the Army, *Counterinsurgency,* Field Manual 3-24 (Washington, DC: Government Printing Office, 2006), 193. The manual is authored by US Army Lt. General David H. Petraeus and US Marine Corps Lt. General James F. Amos. See also David Kilcullen, "Twenty-Eight Articles: Fundamentals of Company-Level Counterinsurgency," *IO Sphere,* Summer 2006.

33. William E. "Kip" Ward (AFRICOM commander), "General Ward Discusses Goals for AFRICOM," transcript of news conference at Foreign Press Center, Washington, DC, October 3, 2007.

34. "Remarks by the President on a New Beginning," Cairo University, June 4, 2009, https://obamawhitehouse.archives.gov/the-press-office/remarks-president-cairo-university-6-04-09.

35. "Remarks by the President to the Ghanaian Parliament," Accra, July 11, 2009, https://obamawhitehouse.archives.gov/the-press-office/remarks-president-ghanaian-parliament.

36. "Remarks by the President on a New Beginning" (see note 34 above).

37. *Assessing Damage, Urging Action: Report of the Eminent Jurists Panel on Terrorism, Counter-terrorism and Human Rights* (Geneva: International Commission of Jurists, 2009), 49.

38. Along with the permanent base at Camp Lemonnier in Djibouti, US Special Operations Forces and private contractors used facilities in Botswana, Burkina Faso, Burundi, Cameroon, the Central African Republic, Chad, Ethiopia, Gabon, Ghana, Kenya, Liberia, Libya, Mali, Mauritania, Niger, Senegal, Seychelles, Somalia, South Sudan, Tunisia, and Uganda.

39. Navy SEALs are the US Navy's special Sea, Air, and Land teams.

40. Core JSOC units include the Army's Delta Force, 160th Special Operations Aviation Regiment, and 75th Ranger Regiment; the Navy's SEAL Team 6; and the Air Force's 24th Special Tactics Squadron.

41. Following the exposure of CIA involvement in the assassination of foreign leaders and other illegal activities during the Cold War, the CIA was required to subject its covert activities to congressional oversight, reporting to the Senate Select Committee on Intelligence and the House Permanent Select Committee on Intelligence, established in 1976 and 1977, respectively. These committees control the CIA's budget, and they must be informed before the CIA embarks on covert operations. However, committee members are not permitted to share secret information with other members of Congress or with the public.

42. General David H. Petraeus was commander of the Multi-National Force in Iraq (2007–8), CENTCOM (2008–10), and the NATO-led international forces in Afghanistan (2010–11) before becoming CIA director (2011–12).

43. *The 9/11 Commission Report: Final Report of the National Commission on Terrorist Attacks Upon the United States,* July 22, 2004, 415.

44. "Remarks by the President at the National Defense University," Fort McNair, Washington, DC, May 23, 2013, https://obamawhitehouse .archives.gov/the-press-office/2013/05/23/remarks-president-national -defense-university. See also the declassified Presidential Policy Guidance, "Procedures for Approving Direct Action Against Terrorist Targets Located Outside the United States and Areas of Active Hostilities," May 22, 2013, https://www.justice.gov/oip/foia-library/procedures_for _approving_direct_action_against_terrorist_targets/download.

45. Quoted in Charlie Savage, "U.N. Report Highly Critical of U.S. Drone Attacks," *New York Times,* June 2, 2010.

46. "Remarks by the President at the National Defense University" (see note 44 above).

47. Quoted in Charlie Savage, Eric Schmitt, and Mark Mazzetti, "Obama Expands War with al-Qaeda to Include Shabab in Somalia," *New York Times,* November 27, 2016.

Chapter 13: Epilogue

1. See, for instance, *New York Times* journalist Mark Landler's *Alter Egos: Hillary Clinton, Barack Obama, and the Twilight Struggle over American Power* (New York: Random House, 2016), which includes an examination of Obama's Africa policy and speculates on prospects for continuity and change in a future Hillary Clinton administration. Landler argues that while both leaders were proponents of US intervention, Obama avoided direct military engagement, preferring covert operations, while Clinton favored military intervention along traditional lines.

2. See Samuel P. Huntington, "The Clash of Civilizations?," *Foreign Affairs* 72, no. 3 (Summer 1993): 22–49.

3. Trump interview with Anderson Cooper, CNN, March 9, 2016, http://www.cnn.com/videos/politics/2016/03/10/donald-trump-islam-intv -ac-cooper-sot.cnn; "Donald Trump's Speech on Fighting Terrorism," Youngstown, Ohio, August 15, 2016, http://www.politico.com/story/2016 /08/donald-trump-terrorism-speech-227025.

4. Secretary of State Designate Rex Tillerson, Senate Confirmation Hearing Opening Statement, January 11, 2017, 5, https://www.foreign .senate.gov/imo/media/doc/011117_Tillerson_Opening_Statement.pdf.

President Trump fired Secretary of State Tillerson in March 2018 and named CIA director Mike Pompeo as his new choice for the top diplomatic position. As a member of Congress, Pompeo co-sponsored a bill that would have designated the Muslim Brotherhood a terrorist organization.

5. "Remarks by the President at the Summit on Countering Violent Extremism," Washington, DC, February 19, 2015, https://obamawhitehouse .archives.gov/the-press-office/2015/02/19/remarks-president-summit -countering-violent-extremism-february-19-2015. See also "Obama: Why I Won't Say 'Islamic Terrorism,'" CNN Presidential Town Hall, September 28, 2016, http://www.cnn.com/videos/politics/2016/09/29/president-obama-town -hall-radical-islam-sot.cnn.

6. Quoted in Mark Landler and Eric Schmitt, "H. R. McMaster Breaks with Administration on Views of Islam," *New York Times*, February 24, 2017. In March 2018, President Trump fired General McMaster and named John R. Bolton, a staunch advocate for the use of US military might, as his third national security advisor. Bolton has advocated designating the Muslim Brotherhood a foreign terrorist organization.

7. Quoted in Peter Baker and Michael D. Shear, "Trump Softens Tone on Islam but Calls for Purge of 'Foot Soldiers of Evil,'" *New York Times*, May 21, 2017. A transcript of Trump's speech in Saudi Arabia, May 21, 2017, is available at http://www.cnn.com/2017/05/21/politics/trump-saudi -speech-transcript/.

8. Quoted in Peter Baker, "White House Weighs Terrorist Designation for Muslim Brotherhood," *New York Times*, February 7, 2017.

9. Secretary of State Designate Rex Tillerson, Senate Confirmation Hearing Opening Statement, 5 (see note 4 above). See also International Crisis Group, *Counter-terrorism Pitfalls: What the U.S. Fight against ISIS and al-Qaeda Should Avoid*, Special Report 3 (Brussels: International Crisis Group, 2017), 15.

10. "Donald J. Trump Statement on Preventing Muslim Immigration," news release, Donald J. Trump for President, Inc., December 7, 2015 (removed from the campaign website after the November 2016 elections); and "Donald Trump's Speech on Fighting Terrorism," Youngstown, Ohio, August 15, 2016 (see note 3 above).

11. "John Brennan: Donald Trump's Travel Ban 'Simplistic and Misguided,'" video, BBC Newsnight, April 3, 2017, https://www.youtube.com/watch?v =ERgIFF9S8Qs. See also Julian Borger, "Donald Trump Travel Ban 'Simplistic and Wrongheaded,' Says Former CIA Chief," *Guardian*, April 4, 2017.

12. Quoted in "Highlights from Court Ruling Halting Trump's Revised Travel Ban," *New York Times*, March 15, 2017.

13. Quoted in Alexander Burns, "2 Federal Judges Rule Against Trump's Latest Travel Ban," *New York Times,* March 15, 2017.

14. Quoted in Adam Liptak, "Appeals Court Will Not Reinstate Trump's Revised Travel Ban," *New York Times,* May 25, 2017.

15. Quoted in Patrick Wintour, "Hopes for Refugee Crisis Plan Fall into Chasm Between G7 and Trump," *Guardian,* May 26, 2017.

16. Nicole Gaouette and David McKenzie, "African Union, African UN Envoys Demand Trump Apology," CNN, January 13, 2018. In September 2017, citizens of Sudan were removed from the list of those with Temporary Protected Status in the United States, and in March 2018, Liberians lost their right to Deferred Enforced Departure. Both programs had allowed citizens from these conflict zones to live and work in the United States on a legal basis.

17. "America First Foreign Policy," posted by the US Embassy and Consulates in Saudi Arabia, January 23, 2017, https://sa.usembassy.gov /america-first-foreign-policy/.

18. See United Nations Development Programme, *Human Development Report 1994* (New York: Oxford University Press, 1994), 2–3.

19. See, for instances, notes 24, 25, 29, and 30 below.

20. The principal agencies represented on the National Security Council are the Departments of State, Treasury, Defense, Justice, Energy, and Homeland Security, and the CIA. Other key participants include the White House chief of staff, director of national intelligence, chairman of the Joint Chiefs of Staff, and US ambassador to the United Nations.

21. From the National Security Council's establishment in 1947 until the Trump administration, only three national security advisors have been military officers: Brent Scowcroft (Ford and George H. W. Bush administrations) and John Poindexter and Colin Powell (Reagan administration). Scowcroft resigned from active duty on assuming the position, while Poindexter and Powell did not.

22. Trump's budget proposal for fiscal year 2019, released in February 2018, requested a 26.9 percent cut in State Department funding from the 2017 level, as well as decreased amounts for foreign aid. In his first State of the Union address, President Trump urged Congress to ensure that US foreign assistance dollars "only go to America's friends." See "President Donald J. Trump's State of the Union Address," January 30, 2018, https://www.whitehouse.gov/briefings-statements/president -donald-j-trumps-state-union-address/.

23. Donald Trump's remarks in Charlotte, North Carolina, August 18, 2016, http://www.politico.com/story/2016/08/donald-trump-never-lie-227183.

See also Trump's inaugural address, January 20, 2017, https://www.whitehouse.gov/inaugural-address.

24. Daniel Benjamin, "Is Trump Fighting Terrorism? Or Is He Just Tweeting about It, While Making It Worse?" *Politico,* June 4, 2017. Ambassador Benjamin was the State Department's coordinator for counterterrorism during the Obama administration.

25. US officials' letter to Defense Secretary James Mattis, "Principles to Guide U.S. Counterterrorism Use of Force Policies," March 10, 2017, https://assets.documentcloud.org/documents/3515908/Use-of-Force-Principles-FINAL.pdf. See also Charlie Savage and Eric Schmitt, "Trump Administration Is Said to Be Working to Loosen Counterterrorism Rules," *New York Times,* March 12, 2017; and International Crisis Group, *Counterterrorism Pitfalls* (see note 9 above).

26. Quoted in Charlie Savage and Eric Schmitt, "Trump Said to Ease Combat Rules in Somalia Intended to Protect Civilians," *New York Times,* March 30, 2017.

27. See Presidential Policy Guidance, "Procedures for Approving Direct Action Against Terrorist Targets Located Outside the United States and Areas of Active Hostilities," May 22, 2013, https://www.justice.gov/oip/foia-library/procedures_for_approving_direct_action_against_terrorist_targets/download. In 2016, the Obama administration broadened the definition of self-defense—and thus the grounds for permissible use of force in Somalia—to include actions by the AU and Somali troops whom US soldiers were training, advising, and assisting.

28. President Trump's support for secret prisons and harsh interrogation methods was underscored by his appointment of Gina Haspel as his second CIA director. After the 9/11 attacks, Haspel ran a CIA "black site" prison in Thailand where terrorism suspects were tortured.

29. Letter from retired generals and admirals to Congress on fiscal year 2018 budget, February 27, 2017, http://www.usglc.org/downloads/2017/02/FY18_International_Affairs_Budget_House_Senate.pdf. See also International Crisis Group, *Counter-terrorism Pitfalls* (see note 9 above).

30. Colin Powell, "Colin Powell: American Leadership—We Can't Do It for Free," *New York Times,* May 24, 2017.

31. US Chamber of Commerce, "Foster Development through Trade and Aid," September 13, 2016, https://www.uschamber.com/issue-brief/foster-development-through-trade-and-aid.

32. See, for instance, the exchange between secretary designate Rex Tillerson and Senator Marco Rubio at Tillerson's Senate confirmation hearings, January 11, 2017, https://www.youtube.com/watch?v=6X38kocND64.

33. Julian Borger, "Rex Tillerson: 'America First' Means Divorcing Our Policy from Our Values," *Guardian*, May 3, 2017. See also US Secretary of State Tillerson's remarks to US Department of State employees, May 3, 2017, https://www.state.gov/secretary/20172018tillerson/remarks/2017/05/270620.htm.

34. Quoted in Roger Cohen, "The Desperation of Our Diplomats," *New York Times*, July 28, 2017.

35. Quoted in Peter Baker and Declan Walsh, "Trump Shifts Course on Egypt, Praising Its Authoritarian Leader," *New York Times*, April 3, 2017.

36. Quoted in Helene Cooper, "Trump Team's Queries about Africa Point to Skepticism about Aid," *New York Times*, January 13, 2017.

37. Cooper, "Trump Team's Queries."

38. Cooper, "Trump Team's Queries."

39. Cooper, "Trump Team's Queries."

40. Executive Office of the President, Office of Management and Budget, *Major Savings and Reforms: Budget of the U.S. Government, Fiscal Year 2018*, 71, https://www.whitehouse.gov/sites/whitehouse.gov/files/omb/budget/fy2018/msar.pdf.

Conclusion: Assessing the Impact of Foreign Intervention

1. For insightful analysis and examples, see Alex de Waal, "Writing Human Rights and Getting It Wrong," *Boston Review*, June 6, 2016.

2. For an incisive analysis of these issues, see International Crisis Group, *Exploiting Disorder: Al-Qaeda and the Islamic State*, Special Report 1 (Brussels: International Crisis Group, 2016).

3. See International Crisis Group, *Counter-terrorism Pitfalls: What the U.S. Fight against ISIS and al-Qaeda Should Avoid*, Special Report 3 (Brussels: International Crisis Group, 2017).

Glossary

Allah: God.

Ansar: Helper, follower, partisan, supporter of Muhammad; originally, it referred to citizens of Medina who assisted Muhammad after he fled from Mecca.

barakat: Blessing.

caliph (or *khalif*): Successor to Muhammad as the political and spiritual leader of the Islamic state.

caliphate: The political-religious state of the Muslim people and the lands ruled by the caliph.

dar: Homeland.

emir (or *amir*): Political or military leader; commander of the faithful.

Hadith: Traditions concerning the teachings, deeds, and sayings of the Prophet Muhammad.

hajj: Pilgrimage to Mecca, a duty for all adult Muslims who are physically and financially able.

Islam: A religion whose name derives from the Arabic word *salema,* which means peace, purity, submission, and obedience. The name of the religion implies submission to Allah's will and obedience to his law. The two main branches of Islam, Sunni and Shi'a, agree on its five pillars: (1) faith in a monotheistic deity, Allah, whose messenger is Muhammad; (2) engaging in prayers five times daily; (3) giving alms to the poor; (4) fasting during the holy month of Ramadan; and (5) making a pilgrimage to Mecca (*hajj*) at least once, if physically and financially able. The Qur'an is the central religious text of Islam, which was revealed by Allah to his prophet, Muhammad.

Islamic fundamentalism: A strand of Islam that rejects religious
  innovation or adaptation in response to new circumstances.
  Practitioners of religious fundamentalism, more generally,
  advocate a return to basic religious principles and the strict
  application of religious law. Fundamentalism often emerges
  as a reaction to liberalizing trends within a religion or to
  secularization in the broader society. It represents a struggle
  between tendencies within a given religion, rather than a clash
  between religions. The descriptor *religious fundamentalism*
  was first associated with late nineteenth-century Protestant
  Christians in the United States who embraced a literal
  interpretation of the Bible. Like their Christian counterparts,
  Islamic fundamentalists promote strict observance of their
  religion's basic tenets and laws. Their movements have gained
  strength in the face of the religious innovation, Westernization,
  and secularization that followed the establishment of European
  colonialism in the twentieth century and globalization in the
  twenty-first. The vast majority of Islamic fundamentalists are
  law-abiding and oppose violent jihad, focusing instead on
  the ethical, moral, and personal aspects of jihad (see below).
  They believe that an Islamic state will emerge from a Muslim
  community (*umma*) that has been purified from within through
  preaching and proselytizing and that such a state cannot be
  established through political or armed struggle.

Islamic terrorism: Commonly used but misleading term that associates
  religious doctrine with terrorist activity. *Islamic fundamentalism,*
  radical Islamism, and *political Islam,* which also appear in this
  glossary, are not equivalent to Islamic terrorism. Muslims
  who engage in terrorism and claim religious justification for
  these activities constitute a minuscule minority of Muslims
  worldwide, and their actions are strongly condemned by the
  majority. Although violent extremists deploy the language
  and symbols of religion to justify their actions, their turn to
  terrorism was often inspired by social, political, and economic
  grievances rather than by religious beliefs. This study rejects
  the use of the term Islamic terrorism as both inaccurate and
  dangerous.

Islamism: A social, political, and religious ideology and movement that
  emerged in response to European colonialism and the social
  instability wrought by encounters with the West. Its adherents

hold that Islamic principles should serve as the basis of the social, political, and legal order and guide the personal lives of individual Muslims. Often led by intellectuals rather than clergy members, Islamist movements focus on social and political change rather than on religious doctrine. Moderate Islamists work within established institutions and political processes to pursue social and political reforms that, they hope, will result in states that are premised on Islamic law and built from the bottom up. Radical Islamists strive to monopolize political power so that they can construct Islamic states from the top down. Islamists do not reject all aspects of Western culture, and they may even embrace Western education and technology as useful tools for the construction of Islamic states. Islamists, in contrast to jihadis (defined below), reject the use of violence to achieve their objectives.

Janjaweed: "Devils on horseback," an insulting Arabic term for bandits who roam the desert in Chad and the Darfur region of Sudan, robbing inhabitants. More recently, the term has been used to describe Arab militias in the Arab-Fur War (1987–89) and in the Darfur conflict (2003–).

jihad: Effort or struggle. A person who engages in jihad is a *mujahid* (plural, *mujahideen*). Jihad has three interrelated meanings: first, the inner spiritual struggle to live righteously, as a good Muslim; second, the struggle to build and purify the Muslim community; and third, the struggle to defend the Islamic faith from outsiders, with force if necessary. The first meaning, which refers to a personal spiritual struggle, constitutes the greater jihad. The second and third meanings, which focus on the outside world, make up the lesser jihad. Historically, jihad has been understood first and foremost as an inner struggle that begins with the self and extends outward to the broader society. Those who undertake such struggles believe that social and political reforms are best achieved through preaching, proselytizing, and mobilizing the masses to effect change from the bottom up. Engaging in the lesser jihad is held to be a collective duty of the Muslim community, as determined situationally by established religious and legal authorities, rather than a permanent personal duty as determined by individuals or self-appointed preachers. Since the onset of the war on terror, Western observers have frequently collapsed all forms of jihad into one, erroneously defined as a "holy war" against nonbelievers. The concept of holy war originated among Christians in medieval Europe to justify crusades against Muslims; it has no direct counterpart in mainstream Islamic thought. Jihad is not one of the five pillars of Islam and thus is not a practice that is essential to Muslim identity.

jihadi (adjective, *jihadist*): A militant Muslim activist who opposes the secular sociopolitical order at home, and Westernization and globalization more broadly, and who engages in armed struggle to establish an Islamic state. The term is not synonymous with *mujahid*, which refers to a person engaged in any of the three forms of jihad outlined above. The term *jihadi* was coined in the early twenty-first century by militants who self-identified as such. Jihadis who focus on local struggles against purportedly impious Muslim or secular regimes constitute the majority of this minority faction, while those who focus on distant or non-Muslim regimes—the so-called global jihadis—are a tiny minority of the minority movement.

jihadism: A minority insurgent movement that broke from Islamism and employs violence in the name of religion. Jihadism emerged in the context of severe social, political, and economic inequalities, and in many cases, political persecution. The movement has primarily attracted young men who feel alienated from mainstream society. Its adherents reject the traditional interpretation of the lesser jihad as a collective struggle of the Muslim community, determined by officially recognized religious and legal authorities, and define it instead as a personal one, to be determined by each individual as he or she sees fit or by self-described clerics. From the early 1970s until the mid-1990s, jihadis generally targeted local secular and Muslim regimes that they deemed impure (the "near enemy"), with the goal of overthrowing them and Islamizing state and society from the top down. However, from the mid-1990s, a small minority began to focus on distant impious or non-Muslim regimes (the "far enemy"), heralding the emergence of global jihad. This minority within the jihadi movement tends to conflate defensive and offensive actions, claiming that violence against apostate regimes and their foreign backers is a defense of Islam. Western commentators often overlook these distinctions, failing to differentiate between jihadist factions and frequently merging

Islamism and jihadism under the misleading rubric of "Islamic terrorism." Some erroneously deem both movements a threat to Western societies and argue that both must be opposed in an open-ended war on terror and an effort to restructure the Muslim world. Policies based on this misunderstanding have tended to result in increased hostility and an even greater threat to the West.

Koran: See *Qur'an.*

Mahdi: Messiah.

Muhammad: Founder of the Islamic faith and believed by Muslims to be Allah's last prophet (c. 570–632 CE).

mujahid (plural, *mujahideen*): See *jihad.*

neocolonialism: The political and economic domination of nominally independent countries by former imperial powers, by private foreign interests in the independent countries, or by any other external capitalist entity or power.

neoconservatism: A movement that emerged in the 1960s to challenge the domestic and foreign policy agendas of the New Left, which promoted government-run social programs at home and opposed military adventurism abroad. In the 1990s, neoconservatives claimed that the United States had won the Cold War and therefore had the right to reshape the world according to American values and interests. They argued that this task required a bold foreign policy and a strong military that the United States was prepared to use to promote American ideals and interests. Neoconservatives advocated preemptive action to tackle perceived threats and to forestall crises before they occurred. During the George W. Bush administration, neoconservatives held high-level positions in the State and Defense Departments, on the National Security Council, and in the Washington think tank world. Their views were reflected in the 2002 national security strategy, which outlined the Bush doctrine of preemptive war.

neoliberalism: An economic philosophy popularized in the 1980s that advocated limited government involvement in the economy and called for an end to government subsidies, price controls, and protective tariffs. Neoliberal structural adjustment programs mandated by the International Monetary Fund, the World Bank, and the US government as a condition for loans required the privatization of state-owned enterprises, the promotion of free trade, economic deregulation, and currency devaluation, and the reduction of government spending.

neopatrimonialism: The German sociologist Max Weber (1864–1920) defined *patrimonialism* as a form of autocratic government in which all power emanates from the leader and in which civilian and military personnel are loyal to that leader, rather than to the state or its citizenry. The Israeli sociologist Shmuel Noah Eisenstadt (1923–2010) coined the term *neopatrimonialism* to describe a form of government that includes a veneer of codified laws, a state bureaucracy, and a legal distinction between the public and private spheres, but in which the ruler still uses state resources for his own benefit and to buy the allegiance of clients inside and outside the official bureaucracy. Because access to power and resources is at the personal discretion of the leader, the patron-client system often undercuts the official state bureaucracy.

political Islam: Sometimes used as a synonym for *Islamism,* although it constitutes only one aspect of a social, political, and religious ideology and movement. Although political Islam employs the language of religion, it represents a political rather than a religious response to Westernization. Its adherents do not reject modernity, but they repudiate a particular brand of modernity. They refute the claim that the Western definition of modernity is a universal one and embrace an Islamist variant in its place.

Qur'an (or *Koran*): The central religious text of Islam, which was revealed by Allah to his prophet, Muhammad.

Sahel: "Shore" of the Sahara Desert, referring to the desert's southern borderlands that stretch more than 3,000 miles from Senegal in the west to Eritrea in the east. The Western Sahel comprises portions of Senegal, Mauritania, Mali, Burkina Faso, Niger, and Nigeria. Parts of Cameroon, Chad, and the Central African Republic constitute the central region, while sections of Sudan, South Sudan, and Eritrea make up the east.

Salaf: Pious ancestors or predecessors; denotes the first three generations of Muslims, including Muhammad's companions and followers.

Salafism: A strict, literal interpretation of Sunni Islam that advocates a return to the righteous practices of the Prophet Muhammad and the early fathers of the faith (the pious ancestors or *Salaf*). The Salafist reform movement emerged in the late nineteenth century in response to Western cultural intrusion during the periods of conquest and colonialization. Because they oppose religious innovations and new interpretations, Salafis reject modern Islamic schools and brotherhoods. They also renounce the mystical spiritual practices and tradition of tolerance associated with Sufism, which incorporates pre-Islamic beliefs and practices.

Contemporary Salafist movements not only seek modernization on their own terms, but they also aspire to purge Muslim societies of both pre-Islamic and Western cultural influences. Contemporary Salafis can be divided into three groups: (1) those who focus on the personal and reject political engagement (quietist Salafis); (2) those who strive to establish political, legal, and religious systems according to Islamic precepts (Islamist Salafis); and (3) those who embrace violent jihad as a permanent, personal religious duty (jihadist Salafis). Most Salafis are quietists. Of the minority that engage politically, only a small percentage embrace violent jihad. Al-Qaeda and the Islamic State are Salafi jihadist organizations.

Shari'a: Islamic law, which regulates most aspects of life, including the personal, social, religious, and political.

sheikh: Man of great power; Bedouin tribal leader; a religious honorific to denote a learned person; a term used for the royal families in the Middle East.

Shi'a (adjective, *Shi'ite*): One of two main branches of Islam, and a person who adheres to Shi'a beliefs. Disagreement over the line of succession led to a schism in Islam after Muhammad's death in 632 CE. Shi'as claim that only blood relations of the prophet, ordained by Allah, can succeed Muhammad. They believe that Ali, Muhammad's cousin and son-in-law, was his first legitimate successor. Shi'as differ from Sunnis concerning the basis of religious and political authority and in their interpretation of Islamic law.

Shura: Consultative council in Muslim communities.

Sufism: Mystical spiritual traditions associated with Sunni Islam that focus on believers' personal experience with the divine, rather than on the following of religious laws. Sufis have a tradition of tolerance toward other religious practices and often incorporate pre-Islamic beliefs and practices.

sultan: Ruler of a Muslim state, especially within the Ottoman Empire.

sultanate: The territory ruled by a sultan.

sunnah: Prescribed Muslim way of life based on the sayings and teachings of the Prophet Muhammad.

Sunni: One of two main branches of Islam, and a person who adheres to Sunni beliefs. Sunnis, who constitute the majority of the world's Muslims, argue that Muhammad's successors should be chosen by councils of religious elders based on qualifications rather than bloodline. They claim that Abu Bakr, Muhammad's father-in-law and companion, was his first legitimate successor. Sunnis differ from Shi'as concerning the basis of religious and political authority and in their interpretation of Islamic law.

talib: Seeker of the truth; student.

umma: Community of Muslims.

Wahhabism: An ascetic religious reform movement within Salafism that was influenced by the writings of Muhammad ibn Abd al-Wahhab (1703–92), a preacher and scholar from central Arabia. The official creed of Saudi Arabia, Wahhabism stresses the importance of law and order and obedience to established authority. The movement rejects religious innovation as heretical and advocates a return to the Qur'an and the Hadith for religious truth.

Wahhabi influences gained strength in North Africa in the wake of the Middle Eastern oil boom of the 1970s. Many North Africans who sought work in Saudi Arabia and other Gulf states embraced Wahhabi beliefs and practices while there and proselytized when they returned home. At the same time, Saudi-based charities distributed their new riches across the Muslim world, spreading Wahhabi teachings through their mosques, schools, and clinics. Disenchanted by the failed promises of secular movements such as Arab nationalism, liberalism, and socialism, which had united Arabs in the struggle against colonialism, alienated young men, in particular, rejected Western forms of modernism and looked to religion for responses to poverty, corruption, and growing social and economic inequality.

Wahhabi influence in Africa south of the Sahara is a more recent phenomenon. Historically, most Muslims in West Africa and the Horn have practiced tolerant strains of Sunni Islam that incorporated pre-Islamic beliefs and practices. However, after the Cold War, Saudi-based Wahhabi charities, schools, and clinics were welcomed into communities that had few social services or alternative sources of funding. Good works performed by these charities, openings provided by the Arab Spring, and hostility to Western-backed oppressive regimes resulted in increased Wahhabi influence in Mali, Mauritania, Niger, Nigeria, Somalia, and Sudan and other countries in the Sahel and the Greater Horn.

warlord: A leader of an armed antigovernment movement who acts outside the state apparatus and who makes no attempt to mobilize subject populations around an ideology, to administer the territory he controls, or to reform corrupt and dysfunctional governing systems. Many men who became warlords had held political or military positions in previous neopatrimonial regimes, and they utilized those patronage networks after those regimes fell. They seek power in order to gain control of resources, which they then distribute to benefit family members and associates and to buy loyalty and protection. Operating outside formal governmental institutions and the rule of law, they establish political and economic partnerships that include criminal networks and foreign businesses, which serve as conduits for the clandestine exportation of natural resources and importation of weapons. They are inclined to perpetuate rather than to resolve conflicts, which present them with opportunities to gain power and wealth.

Index

Ahlu Sunnah Wal Jama'a, 91
Aidid, Hussein Mohammed, 83
Aidid, Mohammed Farah, 76–83, 86, 400n7
AIDS. *See* HIV/AIDS
Akan, 219
Akazu, 144–45, 147. *See also* Rwanda
Åland Islands, 397n2
Albania, 397n1
Albright, Madeleine, 108
Algeria: Arab Spring, 239–40, 279–83, 289;
  border region, 249–51, 300–301, 303–4,
  306, 412n2; civil war, 60, 239, 242, 280–81,
  289, 304, 412n1, 399n19, 412n1; corruption
  and repression, 242, 279–81, 289; counterterrorism, 297, 300–301, 304, 346, 349,
  409n9, 417n29; criminal networks, 250,
  297, 411n30, 412n1, 413n13; diplomacy and
  intervention, 49, 77, 242, 297, 301, 304,
  306, 398n10, 402n10, 411n35; economy,
  279–80, 304; elections, 280–81, 399n19;
  ethnicity, 289–90, 295, 301, 410n21;
  France, 242, 289, 301, 304; independence
  war, xx, 242, 280, 289; Islamic State, 63,
  250, 275; Islamism, xx, 44, 242, 264, 281,
  289–90; jihadism, xxi, 21, 33, 60–61, 242,
  279, 281, 293, 399n19, 411n30, 413n13,
  414n21; military coup, 281, 289, 399n19;
  oil and natural gas, 280, 304; prodemocracy movement, 239, 279–80, 289; al-Qaeda, 60–61, 250, 281, 297, 300–301, 304–5,
  315, 398–99n19, 412n1, 413n13; reforms,
  280–81, 283; secularism, 289, 297, 408n3;
  terrorist attacks, 281, 304; United States,
  305–6, 346, 348–49, 409n9, 417n29
Algerian Awakening, 239, 280
Algerian Civil War (1991–2002). *See* Algeria
Ali Mahdi, Mohamed, 76, 78, 400n7
Al Jazeera, 245–46, 257, 285
Allah, 35, 396n8, 425, 429, 430, 431
Alliance for the Re-liberation of Somalia
  (ARS), xix, 90–91
Alliance for the Restoration of Peace and
  Counter-Terrorism (ARPCT), xix, 84–85
Alliance of Democratic Forces for the
  Liberation of Congo-Zaire (AFDL), xix,
  165–69, 174
Alston, Philip, 358–59
Amazigh (Berber language), 282, 290
America First, xiv, 22, 377, 378–79, 381, 387,
  421n17, 423n33. *See also* Trump, Donald
America Mineral Fields, 166–67
American Colonization Society, 189. *See also*
  Liberia
Americo-Liberian, 188–92, 201–2
al-Anbari, Abu Nabil, 276

Anglo American Corporation, 166–67
Anglo-Egyptian Condominium, 103, 117, 131
Angola, 223, 230, 317, 398nn12–13, 398n15; di-
  amonds, 14, 170; DRC, 48, 56–58, 162, 166,
  168, 170–71, 405n6; Executive Outcomes,
  205, 414n23; oil, 170, 382, 414n23; UNITA,
  xxiv, 162, 166, 170–71, 191, 205, 414n23
Ansar, 104–5, 399n20, 425
Ansar al-Islam, 61
Ansar al-Shari'a: in Benghazi, 61, 274–75,
  411n31; in Derna, 61, 274, 411n31; in Sirte,
  61, 64, 274; in Tunisia, 62, 64, 247, 250–51
Ansar Beit al-Maqdis, 61, 63–64, 262–63
Ansar Dine, x, 61–62, 299–300, 302, 307,
  308–9, 413n16
Ansari, Abu Usamatal. *See* al-Barnawi,
  Khalid
Ansaru, 62, 312, 315–16, 329
Ansarul Islam, 413n16
Anyidoho, Henry Kwami, 157
apartheid, xv, 58, 205, 317; antiapartheid
  movement, 122
Arab Awakening, 408n2. *See also* Arab Spring
Arab-Fur War, 119, 402n11, 427
Arab Gathering, 118, 121
Arabian Peninsula, xix, 33–34, 88, 314, 417n24
Arabic language, 104, 113, 116–17, 328, 401n1
Arab Islamic State, 118, 401n3
Arab-Israeli wars and peace accords, 409n10
Arab League, 48, 49, 83–84, 127, 280, 409n10;
  Libya, 54, 265–66, 270–72, 275, 277; mem-
  bers, 54, 245, 265–66, 271, 398n10, 409n10;
  mission, 53–54
Arab monarchies, 107, 241–42, 244–45, 282,
  286, 290, 397–98n9, 408n3, 410n24
Arab nationalism, 6–7, 33, 53, 104, 118, 241–42,
  244, 432–33
Arab people, 48, 54, 102–4, 106, 116–21, 123,
  125–26, 128–29, 401n1
Arab republics, 33, 241–42, 408n3
Arab Spring, 5, 20–21, 239–40; Arab League,
  265, 270–72, 275, 277, 280; AU, 269–72,
  277, 288–89, 410n23, 410n27; causes, 239,
  241–42, 246, 252–53, 265–66, 279–80,
  282–83; EU, 240, 242, 252, 260–62, 264,
  272, 275, 277, 279–80; foreign intervention, 5, 15, 20–21, 48, 54, 233, 239–46, 248,
  252, 259–61, 263–64, 269–79, 283; France,
  240–42, 246, 252, 260, 263, 268–72, 278;
  Islamic State, 241, 250–52, 263–64, 274–76,
  278–79, 283, 288, 411n32; Islamism,
  239–46, 248–50, 255, 257–65, 272, 274–75,
  278, 281–86, 289–91, 345, 408n1; media,
  245–46, 257, 259, 280, 285; NATO, 240–41,
  245–46, 267, 271–72, 288–89; al-Qaeda,

conflict diamonds. *See* trade, illicit

Congo, Belgian. *See* Congo, Democratic Republic of (DRC)

Congo, Democratic Republic of (DRC), vi, ix, x, ix, xx–xxiii, 41, 49, 68–69, 153, 160–63, 181–82, 187–88, 396n19, 403n1, 404n1; Angola, 48, 56–58, 162, 166, 168, 170–71, 405n6; AU, 161, 175, 178–80; Belgium, 162–63, 182–83; Burundi, 48, 56–58, 168, 170–71, 405n6; child soldiers and laborers, 164–65, 174–75, 177; ECCAS, 56, 398n12; economic crisis, 162–64; elections, 168, 172–73, 177, 180; EU, 175, 177–78; foreign intervention, 48, 56–58, 153, 161, 163, 164–71, 177–79, 184, 405n6; France, 19, 141, 150–52, 162–63, 166–67, 170, 172, 179; human rights abuses, repression, and corruption, 162–63, 168–69, 176–78, 180, 183; Hutu, 145, 151, 153, 158, 161–68, 174–75, 178, 180, 184–85; ICGLR, 56–58, 161, 178–79, 398n13, 405n6; military, 162–64, 166–69, 171–80; militias, 170, 173, 175, 177, 180, 397n4; natural resources, 13–14, 159, 161–62, 165–67, 170–72, 174, 176, 178–80, 397n4; OAU, 171; peace accords, 162, 165, 171–72, 174–76, 178–79; prodemocracy movement and civil society, 163, 168, 171–72, 218; rebels, 163–76, 178–79; Rwanda, 19–20, 48, 57, 135–36, 138, 141, 145, 150–53, 155, 158–59, 161–76, 178–81, 183–85, 343, 405n6; SADC, 58, 161, 170, 178–79, 398n15, 405n6; sexual violence, 164, 166, 170, 175, 177–78; Tutsis, 138, 145, 164–66, 169, 174, 178; Uganda, 48, 57, 164–72, 174, 178–79, 184, 343, 405n6; UN, 51, 153, 161, 164–68, 171–72, 176–80; United States, 162–64, 166–68, 175–76, 178, 182–83, 191, 332, 343, 356, 382, 405–6n12, 417n25. *See also* Congo War, First; Congo War, Second

Congo, Republic of, 13, 398nn12–13, 398n15

Congo-Kinshasa. *See* Congo, Democratic Republic of

Congo-Léopoldville. *See* Congo, Democratic Republic of

Congolese Rally for Democracy (RCD), xxiii, 169, 172, 174

Congo War, First, 161, 164–68

Congo War, Second, 161, 164–65, 168–174, 183, 405–6n12

Congress for the Republic, 249–50

Congressional Black Caucus, 122

Convention on the Prevention and Punishment of the Crime of Genocide, 27, 122, 149, 396n3

Coordination of the Movements of Azawad (CMA), xx, 306–7, 309

Coptic Christian Church. *See* Christianity

corruption, 1, 3–4, 10–11, 14, 16, 24, 28, 33, 47, 52, 241–42, 321–22, 432–33. *See also specific countries*

Côte d'Ivoire, vi, ix, xxiii, 214–37, 411n32; AU, 20, 215, 223, 225, 227–30, 236; Burkina Faso, 49, 194, 215, 217, 219, 221–23, 227–28, 230; cash crops, 14, 216–17, 219, 221, 226, 232, 235; Christians, 216–21, 223; citizenship and identity, 216, 219, 221–22, 224–28, 232–34, 236; civil unrest, 217–18, 220, 221–22, 225, 230–34, 236–37; civil war, x, xxi, xxii, xxiii, 14, 187, 215, 221–32; constitution, 220, 225, 227, 232; economy, 216–20, 407n2; ECOWAS, xx, 56, 215, 222–30, 233, 236–37, 398n11; elections, 216, 218–20, 223–33, 236; ethnicity, 217–23, 225–26, 230–31, 234; foreign intervention, 20, 42, 187–88, 210, 215–27, 229–33, 236; France, 10, 187, 215–20, 222–27, 229–33, 235–36, 305–6, 308, 407n2; Guinea, x, 217, 221, 224, 226, 230, 406n1; human rights abuses, repression, and corruption, 215–16, 218, 220–21, 223, 226–27, 231–32, 236–37; illicit activities, 226, 232, 235, 397n4; immigrants and migrant labor, 217–19, 221–22, 230; inequality, 210, 215–18, 220–21, 225, 234, 237, 310; land, 217–18, 221, 224, 226–27, 232, 234; Liberia, x, 48–49, 191, 193–94, 198, 205, 210–11, 215–16, 222–24, 226, 230, 234–35, 406n1, 406n5, 407n9, 408n7; Mali, 217, 221, 223, 230, 308; mercenaries, 210, 215, 223, 226, 235–36; military, 217–18, 220–24, 226–27, 230–32, 407n3; Muslims, 216–18; natural resources, 226, 232; peace accords, 41, 216, 224–28, 233, 236; prodemocracy movement and civil society, 216, 218, 220–21, 228, 233; rebels, 215, 222–24, 226–31, 234, 408n7; regime change, 231–33, 236, 410n28; SADC, 58; sexual violence, 221, 230–33, 237; Sierra Leone, 210, 215–16, 223, 233–34, 406n1; South Africa, 58, 68–69, 220, 223, 227–30; students, xx, 217–18, 220–23, 234, 408n6; terrorist attacks, 308, 411n32; UN, xxi, xxiv, 20, 51, 215–16, 220, 222, 225–33, 235–36; United States, 220, 222, 229; youth, 215, 217–18, 220–21, 223, 226–27, 229–30, 232, 234–35, 407n1, 408n6

counterterrorism. *See* US Africa policy; war on terror

coups, military. *See specific countries*

Creole, 201

Guéï, Robert, 220, 407n3
Guéré/Wè, 407n9
Guinea, Republic of, x, 13, 48, 187, 194, 197–98, 204–8, 217, 221, 224, 226, 230, 384, 398n11, 406n1, 406n7
Guinea-Bissau, 398n11
Gulf Cooperation Council, 269–70, 410n24
Gulf of Aden, 17, 73, 347, 399n3
Gulf of Guinea, 13
Gulf states, 8, 48, 244–45, 261, 285, 394n10, 397n3, 432
Gulf War, First, 33–34, 107, 242, 245, 416n18
Gulf War, Second, 63, 416n18

Habré, Hissène, 192
Habyarimana, Agathe Kanziga, 144
Habyarimana, Juvénal, 139, 141–44, 146, 148, 150–51, 157, 163, 165, 404n5
Hadith, 425, 432
Haftar, Khalifa, 274–75, 277–78
Hague, The, 123, 405n11
hajj, 425
Hamitic Myth, 137–38
Hargeisa, 75
Hausa and Hausa-Fulani, 311–12, 315, 317, 326–28, 413n15, 414n19, 414n24
Hawaii, 373–75
Helms amendment. See US Foreign Assistance Act
herders. See agriculture, African
heroin. See trade, illicit
Hezbollah, 203
Hirsch, John L., 97, 212
HIV/AIDS, 24, 333, 338–39, 361, 385–86
Hizbul Islam, 91
Hollande, François, 302
Holocaust Museum. See US Holocaust Memorial Museum
holy lands, 7, 33–34, 82, 243, 344, 370
holy war. See Christianity; jihad
Horn of Africa, ix, xx, 13, 34, 48–49, 60, 70, 83, 88, 95–96, 98, 105, 107–8, 117, 347–51, 354–55, 366, 388, 397n5, 400n12, 417n24, 433
Hotel du Golf, 230
Houphouët-Boigny, Félix, 193–94, 217–21, 234, 406n5
Houthi rebels, 264
Howe, Jonathan, ix, 81
humanitarian crises, xiv, 9, 55–56, 65, 71, 77, 94, 97, 149–50, 166, 301, 335, 360, 375, 385, 390
humanitarian hawks, 410n25
humanitarian intervention, 8, 25–26, 30, 41–43, 55, 66, 80, 97, 150–51, 156–57, 166–67, 213, 235, 289, 340, 347–48, 361–64, 391, 395–96n18, 410n25

humanitarian law, 129, 206–8, 353
humanitarian lobbies, 25, 27, 42
humanitarian relief, xi, 2, 25–26, 50, 78–79, 89–90, 97, 108, 110, 123–24, 126–27, 149–50, 163–64, 199, 225, 299, 333, 338, 351–52, 364, 384, 387
human rights, xiii–xv, 4–5, 15–16, 22, 25–31, 41–43, 47, 52–53, 55–57, 76–77, 86, 89–91, 97, 127, 129, 132, 139, 144–47, 152, 158–59, 162–64, 168, 176–78, 181, 184, 191, 206–208, 215, 218, 221, 223, 227, 229, 231–32, 236–37, 241, 243, 246, 248–49, 252, 258, 280, 286–87, 300–301, 304–5, 307, 317–22, 332–33, 337–38, 342, 344, 346, 348–51, 353, 356, 360–61, 368–69, 373, 377–78, 382–84, 388–91, 404n5, 404n9, 408n8, 409–10n19, 418n37. See also civil liberties; humanitarian relief; specific countries
Human Rights Watch, 164, 231, 304
human security, 332–33, 351–52, 377, 385, 389–90
human trafficking, 5, 278–79. See also children; kidnapping for ransom; slavery
Hungary, 397n1, 397n8
Huntington, Samuel P., 369
Hutu: Burundi, 145, 168; DRC, x, 158, 161–68, 174–76, 178–80, 184–85; Rwanda, ix, x, xxiii, 135–59, 161–68, 174–76, 178–80, 184–85, 404n3
Hutu Front for Democracy in Burundi, 145

Ibrahim, Khalil, 106, 119–20, 126
Iceland, 397n1, 397n2
Idi Amin, 140
imperial powers, European, xii, 2–3, 9–10, 13, 46, 181, 187, 334, 429. See also Belgium; colonialism; France; Portugal; United Kingdom (UK)
Impuzamugambi, 145
India, xix, 8, 13–14, 58, 65, 67–68, 207, 270, 302, 395n14, 398n10, 398n17, 399n3
Indian Ocean, 13, 32, 73, 253, 347, 351
indirect rule, 137, 310, 312
Indonesia, 395n14, 398n17
Industrial Revolution, 9, 395n14
Interahamwe, 145, 147
Inter-Congolese Dialogue, 171
Intergovernmental Authority on Development (IGAD), xxi, 49, 55, 57, 72, 83–84, 87, 102, 110–12, 114–15, 398n14, 402n10
Intergovernmental Authority on Drought and Development, 57
Interim Emergency Multinational Force, 172
International Bill of Human Rights, 27
International Commission of Jurists (ICJ), xxi, 353

Italy, 10, 47, 85, 111, 148, 268–70, 279, 376,
397n1, 397n8, 398n16, 398n17, 411n35,
416n20, 417n29
al-Itihaad al-Islamiya, 75–76, 81–84, 86,
400n14
Ivoirian miracle, 216–17
Ivoirian Patriotic Movement of the Far West
(MPIGO), xxii, 223–24, 408n7
Ivoirian Popular Front (FPI), xxi, 218–19, 228
ivoirité, 219, 225
Ivory Coast. *See* Côte d'Ivoire

Jahba East Africa. *See* Islamic State in Soma-
lia, Kenya, Tanzania, and Uganda
Jabhat al-Nusra, 63
Jama'at al-Tawhid wa'al-Jihad, 64
Jama'at Nusrat al-Islam wal-Muslimin, 62,
308–9
Jama'atu Ahlis-Sunna Lidda'awati Wal-Jihad.
See Boko Haram
Jama'atu Ansarul Muslimina Fi Biladis-Sudan. *See* Ansaru
Janjaweed, 121, 123, 125, 402n11, 427
Japan, 47, 65–66, 197, 301–2, 395n14, 397n6,
398nn16–17, 416n20, 417n24
Jerusalem, East, 409n10
jihad, 19, 49; Afghanistan, 6, 31–34, 43–45,
60–62, 73, 75–76, 81, 88, 90, 107–8, 250, 268,
276, 281, 283, 304, 345, 400n13; Algeria, 250,
281, 304, 315; apostate regimes, 5–7, 32–33,
37–38, 313, 345, 428; definitions, 34–38,
316, 399n22, 426–29, 431; Egypt, 255, 262;
global, 37–38, 44–45, 262, 315, 428; greater
and lesser, 36–37, 427–28; history, 31–34,
344–45, 349–50; Libya, 241, 250–51, 268,
273–76, 315–16, 325–26; Mali, 251, 293, 297,
299, 302–4, 306–9, 315, 323, 325–26; near
and far enemies, 37, 44, 315, 345, 411n32,
428; Nigeria, 312, 315–16, 324, 326–27,
366–67; organizations, xix, xxi, xxii, 59–64;
recruits, 6, 31–33, 37–38, 43–45, 60, 63, 73,
98–99, 250, 252, 276, 283, 313–15, 328–29,
345, 352, 357, 379, 428; Somalia, 71–72, 75,
82, 86–88, 98–99, 250, 315, 366, 400n13;
Sudan, 107–8, 126, 133, 250, 366; Tunisia,
250–51. *See also specific organizations*
jihadist organizations. *See* al-Qaeda; Islamic
State; *specific organizations*
Johnson, Prince, 193, 196
Johnson, Roosevelt, xxiv, 196
Joint Special Operations Command (JSOC),
xxi, 355–56, 358, 365, 417n24, 418n40
Joint Unconventional Warfare Task Force
Execute Order, 355
Jonathan, Goodluck, 316, 320

Jonglei State, 114
Jordan, 53, 63, 398n10, 399n21, 408n1, 408n3,
409n10
Jordan River, 409n10
Jospin, Lionel, 220
Juba, 111
Jubba River, 73
Judaism, 27, 369
Judeo-Christian values, 369
Jula (also spelled Juula, Dyula, Dioula), 218,
221, 223, 406n4. *See also* Mandingo
Jund al-Islam, 61
Jund al-Khilafah in Algeria, 63
Jund al-Khilafah in Tunisia, 64, 251
Justice and Charity Party, 282, 412n38
Justice and Development Party: Libya,
273–74; Morocco, 282
Justice and Equality Movement (JEM), ix,
xxi, 106, 114, 119–20, 123, 125–29, 402n9

Kabarebe, James, 165, 168–69, 171–72
Kabbah, Ahmad Tejan, 205–6, 208
Kabila, Joseph, 172–73, 175, 177–78, 180
Kabila, Laurent-Désiré, 165–72, 405–6n12
Kagame, Paul, 152, 156, 175, 405–6nn11–12,
415n5
Kamajors, 204–6, 208
Kampala, 92
Kano (city), 315
Kano State, 313–14
Kanuri, 312–14, 414n24
Kargbo, Abu Bakarr, x, 203
Kasai Central Province, 180
Kasai Province, 180. *See also* East Kasai Province
Kashmir, 33
Katanga Province, 170, 405n7. *See also* Shaba
Province
Kayibanda, Grégoire, 139
Keïta, Ibrahim Boubacar, 412n6
Kennedy, John F., 361
Kenya, 33–34, 57, 59–60, 115, 207, 343, 397n5;
Islamic State, 64, 93–94; Somalia, 48, 60,
64, 72–74, 82–83, 85, 88, 92–95, 356, 358,
399n2; subregional organizations, 49,
398nn13–14; Sudan, 109–10; United States,
33–34, 74, 83, 85, 88, 109, 276, 343, 346–48,
351, 356, 358, 369–70, 402n7, 415n9,
417nn25–26, 418n38
Kenya Defence Forces, 93
Kerry, John, 122, 264, 318
Khartoum, 102–4, 109, 111, 113, 118–20, 124–25,
127–30, 133, 401–2n5, 403n23
Khattala, Ahmed Abu, 276, 411n33
Kibaki, Mwai, 348
Kidal, 298, 303

kidnapping for ransom, 14, 297, 304, 308, 314–16, 412n1, 413n13. *See also* human trafficking

Kigali, 136, 141, 144, 146, 149–51

Kiir, Salva, 112–15

Kimonyo, Jean-Paul, 156

Kinshasa, 167–69, 172, 403n1, 404n1

Kisangani, 166–67, 169, 182

Kismayo, 93

Kivu, North. *See* North Kivu Province

Kivu, South. *See* South Kivu Province

Koevoet, 317

Kolwezi, 167

Konna, 302

Kony, Joseph, 339–40, 356

Koran. *See* Qur'an

Korhogo, 222

Koroma, Ernest Bai, 208

Koroma, Johnny Paul, 205–6

Krahn, 190–91, 193, 196, 198, 406n3, 407n9

Kromah, Alhaji, xxiv, 196

Kuwait, 75, 82, 107, 261, 394n10, 397n3, 398n10, 408n3, 410n24

Lackland Air Force Base, 412n3

Latvia, 397n1, 397n8

law, international, 23, 26–27, 29, 41, 176, 357–59; humanitarian, 129, 206–8, 353; human rights, 26, 30–31, 129, 207–8, 353; war, 357–59. *See also specific laws, conventions, and treaties*

League of Arab States. *See* Arab League

League of Nations, 27, 137, 145

Leahy provision. *See* US Foreign Assistance Act

Lebanon, 53, 245, 266, 398n10, 399n21, 408n3, 410n27

Leopold II, King, 9–10

Léopoldville, 403n10, 404n1

Lesotho, 395–96n18, 398n15

Levant, xxi, 62, 399n21

Liberation and Justice Movement (LJM), xxi, 128

liberation movements, African, xii, xxiii, 15, 51–52, 62, 106, 111, 266, 297, 299

Liberia, vi, ix, 186, 350, 406n1; Americo-Liberians, 188–92, 210; AU, 20, 199, 407n11; Burkina Faso, 48, 192–94; Christians, 193; civil war, insurgencies, and civil unrest, x, xxi–xxii, xxiv, 48, 67, 181, 189–90, 192–94, 196–204, 208, 210–11, 215–16, 222, 397n4, 408n7, 421n16; Côte d'Ivoire, x, 48–49, 191, 193–94, 196, 198, 205, 210–11, 215–16, 222–24, 226, 230, 234–35, 406n1, 406n5, 407n9, 408n7; diamonds, 14, 196–97, 199, 202–3, 207, 2011; economy, 189–91;

200–201; ECOWAS, x, xx, 20, 56, 67, 194–99, 204, 211, 398n11, 407n11; ethnicity and ethnic conflict, 189–93, 196–97, 211, 406nn3–4, 408n7; foreign intervention, 20, 25, 181, 193–94, 197–98, 209, 210–11, 216, 233, 397n4, 407n11; France, 194, 197; government, 189–93, 196–201, 209, 211, 397n4; Guinea, x, 48, 194, 197–98, 207; human rights abuses, repression, and corruption, 188–93, 196–201, 211, 223, 397n4; illicit activities and resource theft, 13–14, 181, 189, 194, 196–99, 200–203, 207, 210–11, 222, 397n4; Joint Monitoring Committee, 199; Libya, 48, 191–94, 196, 203, 267; military, 190–91, 193; Muslims, 193–94; Nigeria, 192, 194–95, 197, 199, 204, 407n11; poverty and inequality, 188–90, 200–202, 397n4, 406n3; sanctions, 198–99; Sierra Leone, 20, 48–49, 192–94, 196–99, 201–5, 211–12, 234–35; slavery, 188–89, 201; UN, xxiv, 10, 51, 181, 198–200, 407n11; United States, 188–95, 199, 210, 332, 350–51, 384–85, 407n11, 418n38, 421n16; warlords, 192–94, 197, 211, 397n4; youth, 193, 202, 210–11, 215, 397n4

Liberians United for Reconciliation and Democracy (LURD), xxi, 198–99

al-Liby, Abu Anas, 276, 411n33

Libya, 249–50, 348, 399n21, 408n3, 410n27, 411n35; AU, 59, 229, 269–72, 277, 288–89, 410n23, 410n27; Arab Islamic state, 104–5, 118–20, 266–67, 295, 401n3; Arab League, 54, 265–66, 270–72, 275–77, 398n10; Arab Spring, x, 239–40, 264–72, 283, 285, 287–88; Chad, 104–5, 118, 131, 192, 265–67, 287, 295, 410n21, 411n30, 411n35; civil war, 241, 244, 272–79, 288; Egypt, 49, 264, 266, 275, 277–78, 401n3, 411n30, 411n35; EU and members, 20–21, 268–70, 272, 275, 277, 279, 411n35; foreign intervention, 20–21, 42, 233, 240–41, 264, 270–72, 275–78, 283, 287–89, 294, 325–26, 410n23; France, 20–21, 241, 268–72, 276–78, 287, 410n28, 411n31, 411n35; General National Congress, 272, 274; Government of National Accord, 277–78; House of Representatives, 274, 277; human rights abuses, repression, and corruption, 264–65, 269, 271–72, 278–79, 287, 295; Islamic State, 64, 241, 250–52, 274–76, 278–79, 283, 288, 334, 359, 380; Islamism, 240–41, 244–46, 265, 272–75, 278, 283; Italy, 268, 270, 276, 279, 411n35; Liberia and Sierra Leone, 48–49, 191–94, 196, 203, 267; Mali and Nigeria, 21, 265, 270, 278, 293–98, 304, 309–10, 314–16, 323–26, 410n27, 411n30; mercenaries, 265, 293–94;

Marxism-Leninism, 74
Maryland, 373–75
Marzouki, Moncef, 249–50
Masalit, 117, 128
Massachusetts, 192, 373
Mattis, Jim, 378–79
Mauritania, 21, 49, 229, 242, 293, 297, 300–302, 305, 324, 348–49, 398nn10–11, 409n9, 412–13n8, 414n21, 417nn28–30, 418n38, 430, 433
Mauritius, 398n15, 417nn25–26
Mbeki, Thabo, 227
Mbuji-Mayi, 166–67
McCulley, Terence, 318
McLaughlin, John E., 273
McMaster, H. R., 370, 378, 420n6
Mecca, 33, 35, 344 425; Grand Mosque, 267
Medina, 33, 344–45
Mediterranean Sea, 17, 242, 253, 278–79, 348, 399n21
Mende, 204
mercenaries, 20, 75, 166–68, 188, 201–5, 206, 211, 223, 226, 265, 294–95, 317, 405n9, 407n12, 414n23; International Convention against the Recruitment, Use, Financing and Training of Mercenaries, 407n12
Mexico, 386, 395n14, 398n17
Mexico City Policy, 386
Middle East, ix, xiii, xxvi, 5–6, 17, 20, 31–32, 46, 48, 73, 107–8, 122, 190, 239–43, 253, 266, 283–84, 287, 331, 333, 351, 355, 364, 371, 400n12, 408n2, 411n35, 431, 432
middle powers, 47
migration, 13, 53, 99, 107, 118, 217–19, 221–23, 230, 242, 269, 277–79, 294, 311–12, 324, 351, 368–69, 372, 375–76, 411n35. See also refugees
Millennium Challenge Corporation (MCC), xxi, 339, 381, 415n12
Miller, Stephen, 369
Minnesota, 373
Misurata, 265, 274–76, 278
Mitterrand, François, 139, 197, 218
Mitterrand, Jean-Christophe, 197
Mobutu, Joseph-Désiré. See Mobutu Sésé Seko
Mobutu Sésé Seko, 162–64, 166–70, 174, 182–84, 188, 405n3, 405n7, 405–6n12
Mogadishu, ix, 75–76, 78, 80–81, 84–92, 98–99, 143, 358, 380, 400n13
Mohammed. See Muhammad, Prophet
Mohammed VI, King, 239, 282, 290
Mohamud, Hassan Sheikh, 92
Momoh, Joseph, 192–93, 196, 202–4
money laundering, 203, 226, 323, 348–49
monotheism, 35, 63, 425

Monrovia, 193–96, 199
Moroccan Islamic Combatant Group, 283
Morocco, 13, 32–33, 54, 169, 239–40, 242, 279, 282–83, 290–91, 346, 348–49, 371, 381, 398n10, 408n3, 409n9, 411n31, 417n29
Morsi, Mohamed, 257–61
Moscow, xi
mosques, 45, 251, 267, 314, 316, 323, 371, 432
al-Mourabitoun, 61–62, 64, 305, 308
Movement for Democracy in Liberia (MODEL), xxii, 198–99
Movement for Justice and Peace (MJP), xxii, 223–24
Movement for the Liberation of Congo (MLC), xxii, 169, 172, 405n9
Movement for Unity and Jihad in West Africa (MUJWA), xxii, 61–62, 299, 302, 304–5, 314–15, 413n16
Mozambique, 398n15, 417n25
al-Mua'qi'oon Biddam. See al-Mulathameen
Mubarak, Hosni, x, 61, 108, 252–55, 257–62, 264, 287
Mugabe, Robert, 170
Muhammad, Prophet, 35, 53, 247, 396n8, 398n18, 425, 429–32
Muhammad Ahmad ibn Abd Allah, 103, 401–2n5
Muhammad ibn Abd al-Wahhab, 432
mujahid (plural, mujahideen), 32–33, 36–38, 61, 64, 396n9, 427–29
Mujahidin of Kairouan, 64
al-Mulathameen, 60–61, 304–5, 413n13
multilateral organizations. See specific organizations
Multi-National Force in Iraq, 419n42
Multinational Joint Task Force (MNJTF), xxii, 321, 324. See also Nigeria
Museveni, Yoweri, 140–41, 155, 415n5
Muslim banks, 33, 82–83, 108
Muslim Brotherhood, 45, 92, 104–5, 107, 244–46, 253, 255–64, 273–74, 282, 287, 369, 371–72, 409n16, 419–20n4, 420n6. See also specific countries
Muslim charities, 33, 82, 108, 261, 345–46, 366, 371, 432–33
Muslim courts, xxi, 62, 82, 84–92, 98
Muslim population, 344–45, 349, 369–70. See also Islam

NAACP, xxii, 122, 402n12
Nabhan, Saleh Ali Saleh, 358
Nairobi, 93, 99, 347
Namibia, 48, 58, 168, 170–71, 205, 317, 346, 398n15, 405n6
Nasser, Gamal Abdel, 244–45, 255, 266, 286–87, 401n3

northern and southern regions, 310–12, 327–28; oil and natural gas, 309, 311, 318, 346, 382, 413n17; poverty and inequality, 293–94, 309–14, 323–24, 327–28, 350, 386, 413n17; al-Qaeda, 21, 62, 293, 315–16, 319, 324; regional influence, 49, 55–56, 59, 67, 194, 197, 199, 206, 309, 318, 320–22, 402n10, 407n14; Sierra Leone, 204–7, 407n14; Somalia, 314–16, 321; South Africa, 53, 59, 317; terrorism, 294, 313–14, 316, 323–24; UK, 294, 310, 312, 321, 327–28; UN, 59, 62, 150, 270, 314–16, 320–21, 410n27; United States, 294, 306, 318–21, 325, 334, 343, 349, 382–84, 386, 409n9, 410n27, 414n27, 417n29

Nigerian Army Special Operations Command (NASOC), xxii, 319

Niger River, 327–28

Nile Valley, 61, 63–64, 103–4, 262–63

Nimba County, 191, 193

Nimeiri, Jaafar, 104–6, 401n2

9/11. *See* terrorist attacks

9/11 Commission. *See* National Commission on Terrorist Attacks Upon the United States

Nkrumah, Kwame, 10

Nkunda, Laurent, 174–75

Noah and Ham, 137

Nobel Peace Prize, 200, 408n8

nomads, 117–19, 295, 325, 402n11

Non-Aligned Movement, 58, 127

nongovernmental organization (NGO), xxii, 11, 29, 76, 78–79, 97, 126, 150, 158–59, 261, 265, 284, 300, 339, 373, 386

Nordic countries, 47, 397n2

North Africa, vi, ix, xiii, xxvi, 5, 17, 20, 46, 48–49, 54, 60, 107–8, 233, 238–42, 244–45, 270, 276, 279, 281, 283–84, 290, 293, 301, 303–4, 344–45, 371, 380, 388–89, 393n3, 395n15, 401n3, 408n2, 413n11, 432

North America, xii, 32, 60

North Atlantic Treaty Organization (NATO), xiii, xxii, 20–21, 47, 54, 240–41, 245–46, 267, 271–72, 288–89, 390, 397n1, 417n24, 419n42

North Eastern Province, 93

North Kivu Province, 171–72, 175

North Korea, 374–75, 378

Norway, 111, 301–2, 397n1, 397n2, 402n8, 402n10, 408n8, 417n29

al-Nour Party, 259

Ntaganda, Jean Bosco, 175–78, 405nn10–11

Ntaryamira, Cyprien, 146

Nuer, 113–14

al-Nur, Abdel Wahid, xxiii, 125, 128, 402n9

Nuremberg trials (1945–49), 27

Oakley, Robert B., 97

Obama, Barack, 375–77; Islam, 243–44, 352–54, 369–71; war on terror, 43, 127–28, 243, 334, 341–434, 352–365, 379, 381, 387, 419n1, 422n24, 422n27. *See also* Obama, Barack, Africa policy; *specific countries*

Obama, Barack, Africa policy, 18, 21–22, 342–44, 352–54, 362, 388; authoritarian regimes, 244, 255–56, 259–61, 263, 269, 299, 318, 343, 383, 403n21, 414n27; economic and development aid, 299; economic, energy, and strategic interests, 244, 255, 263, 343; health, 386, 342–43; military aid, 260–61, 263, 299, 318, 342–43, 354–56, 359–60, 379, 383, 414n27; military intervention, 270–71, 342–44, 353–62, 365, 379, 419n1, 422n27; responsibility to protect, 41, 127–28, 270, 343, 362–63; trade and investment, 342–43

Obote, Milton, 140

occupied territories, 344–45, 409n10

Oceania, 17

Ogaden, 400n6, 96

Ogaden War. *See* Somali-Ethiopian War

oil. *See* energy resources

Okba Ibn Nafaa Brigade, 62, 64

Oman, 394n10, 397n3, 398n10, 408n3, 410n24

Omega navigation station, 190

One Belt, One Road Initiative, 397n17

Operation Amaryllis, 148

Operation Artemis, 172

Operation Barkhane, x, 305, 307

Operation Dignity: Côte d'Ivoire, 227; Libya, 274

Operation Enduring Freedom–Trans Sahara (OEF-TS), xxiii, 349

Operation Licorne, 222–24, 227

Operation Noroît, 141–44

Operation Pay Yourself, 205, 407n5

Operation Provide Relief, 78

Operation Restore Hope, 79, 97

Operation Serval, x, 302–3

Operation Turquoise, 150–51

opium. *See* trade, illicit

Oregon, 373

Organisation of the Islamic Conference, 127

Organization of African Unity (OAU), xxii, 25, 49, 51–52, 54, 74, 142, 150, 157, 171, 205, 220, 267, 287, 394n7, 407n4

Orientale Province, 171–72

Ottoman-Egyptian rule, 103–4, 132, 401–2n5

Ottoman Empire, 53, 103, 43

Ouagadougou, 308

Ouagadougou Political Agreement (OPA), xxiii, 228, 236

356–60, 366, 369–71, 400n13, 402n7, 411n31, 411n33. *See also names of affiliate organizations*
al-Qaeda in Iraq (AQI), xix, 63
al-Qaeda in the Arabian Peninsula (AQAP), xix, 314
al-Qaeda in the Islamic Maghreb (AQIM), xix, 60–64, 250, 281, 283, 297, 299–304, 308–9, 314–16, 324, 334, 380, 398–99n19, 412n1, 413n11, 413n13
Qatar, 13, 394n10, 410n24; Al Jazeera, 245–46, 257, 285; Arab League, 54, 245, 271, 398n10; Arab Spring, 20–21, 54, 240, 245–46, 257, 261, 271–72, 275, 285, 397n3, 397–98n9; constitution, 245; Egypt, 54, 245, 255, 257, 261; international mediation, 128, 245, 285; Islamism, 240, 245, 255, 257, 397–98n9; Libya, 54, 245–46, 271–72, 275; monarchy, 408n3, 410n24; Muslim Brotherhood, 245, 255, 257; oil and natural gas, 245; regional influence, 245, 285; Saudi Arabia, 245–46, 261, 275, 397–98n9; Tunisia, 245–46; United Arab Emirates, 245–46, 261, 275, 397–98n9; United States, 245
Qur'an, 44, 82, 425, 430, 432
Quiwonkpa, Thomas, 190–93

Rabat, 282
Radisson Blu Hotel, 308
Rally of Republicans (RDR), xxiii, 219, 221
Ramadan, 35, 425
Reagan, Ronald, 105, 191, 386, 415n2, 421n21
Red Sea, 17, 73, 347
refugees, x, 20, 26, 29, 53, 75, 96, 99, 118–19, 135, 138, 141, 143, 145–47, 149–50, 152–53, 158, 163–67, 184–85, 187, 203–4, 207, 283–84, 293, 372–76. *See also* migration
regional policeman, 3, 11, 139, 162, 189, 332
religion. *See* Christianity; Islam; Judaism
Republic of Congo. *See* Congo, Republic of
Republic of Korea. *See* South Korea
Republican Forces of Côte d'Ivoire (FRCI), xxi, 230–31
resource curse, 384
resources, illicit trade. *See* trade, illicit
resources, natural. *See* commodities; energy resources
response to instability/responsibility to protect (R2P), xxii–xxiii, 2, 5, 8, 18–23, 25–26, 29–31, 42, 65, 71, 94, 101–2, 107, 110–11, 116, 124, 127, 130, 136, 161, 187, 209, 216, 233, 236, 240, 269, 283, 288–89, 297, 320, 323, 331–32, 334–35, 339, 343, 360, 389, 391, 396n1, 415n4

Revolutionary United Front (RUF), x, xxiii, 193, 196, 202–8, 212–13, 223, 407n5, 414n23
Rhodesia, 75. *See also* Zimbabwe
Rice, Susan, 108, 127, 178, 260, 270, 404n6, 405–6n12
Roberts Field, 190–91, 193, 195
Robertson, Pat, 193
Romania, 397n1, 397n8
Rome, 99
Ruandi-Urundi, 137, 145
Ruberwa Manywa, Azarias, 172
al-Ruqai, Nazih Abdul-Hamed. *See* al-Liby, Abu Anas
Rusesabagina, Paul, 156
Russia, xiii–iv, xix, 30, 47–48, 50, 58, 65, 68, 114, 149, 203, 229, 268–71, 275, 277–78, 369–70, 383, 395n14, 398nn16–17, 403n19, 411n 32, 411n35, 416n20. *See also* Soviet Union
Rutherford, Kenneth R., 97
Rwanda, vi, ix, 34, 134, 397n5, 398nn12–13, 402n10; Belgium, 137–38, 142–43, 145, 147–48, 153, 157l Burundi, 135, 138, 145–48, 152, 154–55, 158; Catholic Church, 138, 147, 156; DRC, x, xx, 19–20, 48, 57, 135–36, 138, 141, 145, 150–53, 155, 158, 161–76, 178–81, 183–85, 343, 404n3, 405n6; 405n11, 405–6n12; drought and environmental degradation, 139–40, 155; economy, 139–41, 145, 155–56; ethnic and political violence and repression, 135–36, 138–39, 142, 144–50, 152–59, 164, 166, 184, 404n9; ethnicity, 135–39, 143, 145, 148, 154–56, 164; extremist ideology and actors, xix, xxiii, 135, 138–49, 151, 153–55, 157, 161–62, 164, 166, 168, 175–76, 178–80; foreign intervention, 19, 42, 122, 130, 135, 141, 144, 155; France, ix, 19, 135–36, 139, 141–43, 146, 148, 150–51, 153, 155, 157, 164, 166–68, 227, 305; genocide, 19–20, 25–26, 29, 48, 51, 122, 130, 135–36, 144–46, 148–59, 161–66, 171, 174-75, 181, 183–85, 230, 270, 333, 335, 361, 404n6, 405–6n12; government, xxii, 19, 135, 139, 141–58, 163–66, 404n9, 405–6n12; Hutu Power, 145, 147–49, 151, 153, 161, 166, 168; Hutu Revolution, 138; Hutus, ix, x, xxiii, 135–59, 161–68, 174–76, 178–80, 184–85, 404n3, 404n9; insurgency, xxiii, 19, 135–36, 140–53, 155–59, 163–68, 174, 184–85, 404n5, 404n9, 405–6n12; military, 141–47, 151, 153, 161. 163, 165–66, 168–70, 172, 174–75, 178, 184; militias, 141–42, 144–47, 151, 153, 155, 163, 166; OAU, 142, 150, 157; poverty and inequality, 138–43, 145, 155; refugees, x, 20, 135, 138,

Index | 459